GENETIC INROADS INTO THE ART OF JAMES JOYCE

Genetic Inroads into the Art of James Joyce

Hans Walter Gabler

https://www.openbookpublishers.com
©2024 Hans Walter Gabler

This work is licensed under an Attribution-NonCommercial 4.0 International (CC BY-NC 4.0). This license allows you to share, copy, distribute and transmit the text; to adapt the text for non-commercial purposes of the text providing attribution is made to the author (but not in any way that suggests that they endorse you or your use of the work). Attribution should include the following information:

Hans Walter Gabler, *Genetic Inroads into the Art of James Joyce*. Cambridge, UK: Open Book Publishers, 2024, https://doi.org/10.11647/OBP.0325

Copyright and permissions for the reuse of the images included in this publication may differ from the above. This information is provided in the captions and in the list of illustrations.

Further details about CC BY-NC licenses are available at
http://creativecommons.org/licenses/by-nc/4.0/

All external links were active at the time of publication unless otherwise stated and have been archived via the Internet Archive Wayback Machine at https://archive.org/web

Any digital material and resources associated with this volume will be available at
https://doi.org/10.11647/OBP.0325#resources

ISBN Paperback: 978-1-80064-884-5
ISBN Hardback: 978-1-80064-885-2
ISBN Digital (PDF): 978-1-80064-886-9
ISBN Digital ebook (EPUB): 978-1-80064-887-6
ISBN XML: 978-1-80064-889-0
ISBN HTML: 978-1-80064-890-6

DOI: 10.11647/OBP.0325

Cover image: Paul O'Mahony, *James Joyce* (2009), https://bit.ly/3ZKANwf
Cover design by Jeevanjot Kaur Nagpal

Contents

Introduction	1
Towards a Critical Text of James Joyce's *A Portrait of the Artist as a Young Man*	11
The Genesis of *A Portrait of the Artist as a Young Man*	71
James Joyce's *Dubliners* Critical Edition 1993	109
James Joyce's *A Portrait of the Artist as a Young Man* Critical Edition 1993	143
Forty Years of Steering an Edition Through Turbulences of Scholarship and Reception	161
James Joyce's Text in Progress	197
The Rocky Road to *Ulysses*	221
James Joyce's *Hamlet* Chapter	257
From Hamlet to Scylla & Charybdis: Experience into Art	271
Emergence of James Joyce's Dialogue Poetics	315
Structures of Memory and Orientation: Steering a Course Through Wandering Rocks	347
Composing *Penelope* Towards the Condition of Music	373
Ulysses 1922 and the Golden Mean: Shaping His Text Into Book	395
'Love, yes. Word known to all men.'	407
Ulysses 1984: To Edit and Read in Flow of Composition	417
Acknowledgments	435
Bibliography	437
Index	445

Introduction

This book collects essays from over half a century on the writing and art of James Joyce. My thinking and my writing in this vein began as a matter of chance and coincidence. Engaged as I was after my doctorate in pursuing the study of Elizabethan and Jacobean drama, I met with scepticism a request I received to contribute to an assessment of James Joyce's *A Portrait of the Artist as a Young Man*. My colleague, Wilhelm Füger, was planning a collection of essays discussing the novel and asked me to write a chapter about its text. Why he fixed on me to contribute on this subject was—yes because[1] I had just returned to Munich from twenty-one months' immersion in Anglo-American (in fact, altogether US-American) Textual Criticism and Bibliography under the tutelage of Fredson Bowers in Charlottesville, VA. Joyce's *A Portrait* had attracted me before, in my earliest days as an undergraduate studying English Literature in Frankfurt. I now explored the literature about it —and saw that at its core there lay distinct problems of a text-critical and potentially editorial nature. I attempted, though, to fend off Wilhelm Füger's request: 'But it's all been done. Just to summarise that and to write it up (again): that's boring.' 'But we want it in German', he responded. So I was hooked.[2]

Delving in depth into the problem, I soon realised that by no means had everything been done. Significant documentary sources stood to be (re-)discovered. The essay 'Towards a Critical Text of James Joyce's *A Portrait of the Artist as a Young Man*' eventually headed the 1974 volume of *Studies in Bibliography*. It now opens the present collection. Its strictly text-critical and potentially editorial mode was soon complemented in

---

[1] James Joyce, *Ulysses*, episode 18, line 1 (and re-sounded throughout the episode).
[2] The outcome was: Hans Walter Gabler, 'Zur Textgeschichte und Textkritik des *Portrait*', in *James Joyces "Portrait": Das Jugendbildnis im Lichte neuerer deutscher Forschung*, ed. by Wilhelm Füger (Munich: Goldmann, 1972), pp. 20-38.

1975/1976 by my first excursions into a genetically critical analysis of Joyce's composition and writing, and thus of the transmission of the novel-in-progress through material documents into publication. The essays this elicited became fused in 'The Genesis of *A Portrait of the Artist as a Young Man*' of 1998. At its core stands the recognition of the novel's structured complexity. Joyce carefully centred its five chapters on the middle chapter, Chapter 3, and sub-divided this in turn into three segments. The middle segment comprises Father Arnall's hell sermons. They form the novel's dead centre. Chapters 1 and 2 lead towards, and Chapters 4 and 5 lead away from that axis. Moving beyond it through Chapters 4 and 5 to end *A Portrait*, Joyce devised Chapter 5 in four segments and thereupon proceeded to mirror into Chapter 1 the four-segment structure attained for the closing chapter. This was achieved in revision by shifting the 'Christmas Dinner scene' from (originally) Chapter 2 to Chapter 1. Chapters 1 and 2 and Chapters 4 and 5 thus symmetrically bracket Chapter 3. Hugh Kenner appreciatively commented that although Joyce's chiastic design had been there to see all the time, it had taken sixty years to be discerned.

Beyond these beginnings, uncovering fresh ground for *A Portrait*, I received another nudge from Wilhelm Füger: ought I not now to tackle the follow-up? To take the road I felt increasingly beckoning anyhow? Some editing had already been attempted on Joyce's early prose. *Ulysses*, however, was text-critically and editorially still a completely open field. I embraced the encouragement. I felt confident in my dual professional background: my upbringing on Shakespeare and English drama from around 1600, and the foundations subsequently gained in scholarship and genetic criticism from Anglo-American Textual Criticism and Bibliography, from *Editionswissenschaft* in Germany, and indeed also from French *critique génétique*. From the mid-1970s onwards, I thus chose to steer my scholarly and critical course for near half a century on the waves of James Joyce's oeuvre.

The concept of editing James Joyce's *Ulysses* using a methodological fusion of textual criticism, scholarly editing, and genetic criticism matured during three preparatory years. On the basis of a substantial grant from the Deutsche Forschungsgemeinschaft, seven years of intense cooperative teamwork followed.³ This resulted in the edition in three volumes of James Joyce, *Ulysses. A Critical and Synoptic Edition*, which saw publication on 16 June (Bloomsday), 1984. The edition was justly, I believe, recognised as a fresh departure in scholarly editing, and indeed equally so, though for distinct sets of reasons, in both the Anglo-American and the European professional fields.

While my work on *A Portrait of the Artist as a Young Man* had been theoretical, written with the possibility that I might one day edit the novel, the preparations for, and labour on *Ulysses* demanded a practical realisation issuing in the full-scale critical and synoptic edition itself. Hence, no essay can be provided for the present collection that chimes with the earlier text-critical and text-genetic essays for *A Portrait*. The analytical and explicatory reflections on the *Ulysses* edition that were written closest in time to its publication are the Introductions to the critical editions of *A Portrait of the Artist as a Young Man* and of *Dubliners* of 1993 that followed *Ulysses*. Both Introductions are here reproduced from their re-allocation (slightly revised) to the respective Norton Critical Editions of 2007 and 2006. What each of these Introductions aims to assert, both practically and (as it were) theoretically, is that, given the state of transmission of the text to be edited, the Anglo-American mode of scholarly editing remains thoroughly valid. This clear positioning helps to sharpen further the contrasting editorial and genetically critical solutions found for editing *Ulysses*.

The high praise lavished on the *Ulysses* edition at its publication in 1984 began within less than a year to be overshadowed. The 'Joyce Wars', as they were declared at the time, found their moment in international scholarly debates; and indeed their echo reverberated into more general cultural awareness during the late twentieth century. The generations since have tended to perceive those 'wars', if at all, as past history. My essay of 2018 on steering the *Ulysses* edition through the turbulence of scholarship and reception, incorporated in the present collection, endeavours to formulate my double perspective of today on these events: that is, I believe I can both re-imagine the past moment as the

---

3   The team (fluctuating somewhat over seven years): Wolfhard Steppe, Claus Melchior, Charity Scott-Stokes, Harald Beck, Kinga Thomas, Walter Hettche, Danis Rose (for a few months), Mike Groden (during a productive though sadly grey and rainy July 1978).

editor working in the 1980s, and assess the facts and related issues from the outsider perspective of the (engaged) critic of the 2020s. In 'Seeing James Joyce's *Ulysses* into the Digital Age', I look back as editor and critic together on what the edition's erstwhile critics thought and saw—or overlooked or failed to see—as well as where and how their views and propositions remain valid.

Re-reading my essays—and sometimes retouching them, if only slightly—has demanded that I re-view and re-experience my shifting focus on, and awareness and perception of, Joyce's creativity and his conceptual progress from his epiphanies (1902-1903) to mid-*Ulysses* (1918). 'James Joyce's Text in Progress' begins a sequence of essays that critically explore Joyce's creativity and achievement from a genetic perspective. Proceeding from this essay of 1990 —and after a fourteen-year interim across the new millennium—follows the 'Rocky Road to *Ulysses*' analysis of 2004. It sets in motion a dynamic stumbling forward, rock by rock (as it were), and so gains and communicates both feeling for and understanding of *Ulysses* in progress. The dynamics of genetic writing in progress, in other words, crave a consonant dynamic approach in critical analysis and interpretation. Pursuing the paths of creation and composition requires, moreover, reading and re-reading over time. This is the fundamental attitude that admits a genetic focus on the full range of observation, thought, analysis, and explication.

The essays that accumulated in publication from 2020 to 2022 will, I hope, prove the point. Stimulated by Irina Rasmussen's take on Joyce's modernist poetics as manifested in Scylla & Charybdis of 1918,[4] I traced the episode's core Hamlet lecture back to its origins in Joyce's oeuvre. It seems to have been considered as a segment in Chapter V of *A Portrait of the Artist as a Young Man*. The *Portrait* fair copy has what might be seen as an entry and an exit marker where Stephen Dedalus would have gone into and, hours later, left the National Library. The Hamlet lecture was ultimately not written into *A Portrait*, however. It was replaced by a movement centred on the composition of a villanelle poem. The Hamlet version withheld in 1913, whatever it may have been like, was eventually turned into the second of the two chapters with which

---

4   Irina Rasmussen, 'Riffing on Shakespeare: James Joyce, Stephen Dedalus and the Avant-Garde Theory of Literary Creation', *Joyce Studies Annual 2019* (New York: Fordham University Press, 2019), pp. 33-73.

Joyce chose to begin composing the new novel *Ulysses*. The first *Ulysses* chapter was fully drafted 1914 to mid-1915 in Trieste. It was developed from the (Gogarty)/Buck Mulligan materials left over from *A Portrait* and became the Telemachus episode that opens *Ulysses*. The second composition for the novel, which followed on closely, was what Joyce called the 'Hamlet chapter'. It was the first full text written upon the Joyces taking up residence in Zurich in mid-1915—and thus, no doubt, it was also composed from *A Portrait* leftovers. Joyce offered the 'Hamlet chapter' for pre-publication to Ezra Pound, at Pound's request, in 1916, though in the event Pound did not take him up on the offer. From the 1916 version, since lost, derives in turn the earliest extant draft for Scylla & Charybdis from late 1918.

Joyce's engagement with Shakespeare and Hamlet is traceable specifically to the months of study he spent preparing for his *Amleto* lectures at the Triestine Scuola Populare in late 1912 to early 1913. Making this line out has defined for me not only the main trajectory of the creative transfiguration of the episode into original composition, from its first apparently intended—yet retracted—inclusion in *A Portrait* through to Scylla & Charybdis. It has also made discernible Joyce's self-aware progression of thought, poetological choice and decision-making in his art from its early beginnings. Even at the age of eighteen, he had already expressed aphoristically his understanding of William Shakespeare as one who stood apart from the contemporary playwrights of 1900: 'Shakespeare was before all else a literary artist; [...His] work [...] was literature in dialogue.'[5]

Over the years, the constellations shifted in which Joyce's creative transfiguration of his reading, as well as his self-reflection and artistry, found interpretable expression. This I endeavour to explore in a triad of essays. 'James Joyce's Hamlet Chapter' (2020) deepens the argument that Stephen Dedalus' Hamlet performance originated during the gestation of Chapter V of *A Portrait of the Artist as a Young Man*. This entails the observation that not integrating a Hamlet performance by Stephen Dedalus in *A Portrait* also meant sacrificing a progression through one day only for the novel's fifth chapter. A continuous morning-to-evening flow appears to have been pre-designed for it. In the event, however,

---

[5] 'Drama and Life', in *James Joyce: Occasional, Critical, and Political Writings*, ed. by Kevin Barry (Oxford and New York: Oxford University Press, 2000), p. 23.

Stephen's villanelle composition, unspecified in time, won out over his afternoon lecture to the librarians in the National Library. Yet the one-day design was only shelved, not forgotten. It was reasserted for the full eighteen episodes of *Ulysses* entire.

The second and third essays in the Shakespeare-Hamlet triad deepen in complexity. 'From Hamlet to Scylla & Charybdis: Experience into Art' (2021) endeavours to elucidate the poetics underlying the genetic progress from the (lost) Hamlet chapter of 1916 to the late 1918 draft that closely precedes the fair copy of New Year's Eve 1918. Auxiliary to the essay's lines of argument, I link to a basic text version I have constructed of Stephen's Hamlet performance from the 1918 draft.[6] This enables me to develop the genetic argument in stages. Not least, it allows me to focus on the transformation and transconfiguration of the author-character relationship. The *alter-ego* co-existence of James Joyce with Stephen Dedalus, as lived through *Stephen Hero*, *A Portrait*, and now through to the ninth episode of *Ulysses*, ends. James Joyce sets Stephen Dedalus free; and with him Buck Mulligan, too. Both live on through the second half of *Ulysses* solely as free characters both of and in the fiction.

'Emergence of James Joyce's Dialogue Poetics' (2022), third in the triad, re-illuminates as it re-encompasses the advance of Joyce's poetics that shaped his art. The progress from the epiphanies via *Stephen Hero* and *A Portrait* to the Scylla & Charybdis midpoint of *Ulysses*, shows how he emulated and achieved a mode of writing akin to Shakespeare's, which Joyce in 1900 singled out and defined as 'literature in dialogue'.

'Structures of Memory and Orientation: Steering a Course Through Wandering Rocks' (re-incorporated with revisions from its original Open Book Publishers presentation in 2018) and 'Composing Penelope Towards the Condition of Music' (2023, original to this volume) round off the sequence of essays devoted to individual episodes of *Ulysses*. The Wandering Rocks episode opens the novel's second half on fresh grounds of poetics. Penelope closes it by expanding *Ulysses* ultimately into dimensions of music. The nineteen segments of Wandering Rocks represent the obstructive ever-wandering rocks through which, in Greek myth, Jason and the Argonauts successfully navigate on their quest

---

6   To be found at: Hans Walter Gabler, *Basic-Hamlet Proposition* (2020), https://www.academia.edu/50815114/Basic_hamlet_proposition

for the Golden Fleece. The rocks' elusiveness in the myth is artfully re-configured in this episode by means of apparently stray text snippets properly contextualisable only in some other segment or segments, outside the one that houses them. This text patterning, erratic, or seemingly so, challenges the reader to grasp the connections and make sense of them. The episode plays this game with the reader, the text's Jason substitute, both within and across the chapter segments and even back into preceding episodes, particularly the eighth, Lestrygonians. In its content, the chapter is the novel's most Dublin-centred episode. Yet it does not tell Dublin in an orthodox narrative sense or mode. To paraphrase Samuel Beckett: 'It does not tell something'—that is, it does not tell Dublin, the city, or the life of its selected inhabitants: 'it is that something itself'.[7] It is Dublin itself. Over and above 'Dublin', in imaginative superimposition marking out the episode segments as a seascape of rocks, wander the text snippets as rock fragments, challenging us to focus on and make sense of them.

'Composing Penelope Towards the Condition of Music' establishes the novel's end beyond the closing of its Aristotelian teleologic beginning–middle–end sequence of seventeen episodes through to Ithaka. The eighteenth episode, by contrast, is devised to model an ever-presence in language. Close genetic analysis of the process of composing the draft manuscript shows how its text flow, ever enriched, integrates to create an illusion of subjectively timeless presence akin to the experience of playing or hearing music. Objectively real time recedes, to foreground a subjective experience of time in seemingly timeless presence. The episode with which *Ulysses* thus ends is—again—not about something. It creates the thing itself, the experience of a condition of music.

Three essays, also first published here, focus in conclusion on essential moments of James Joyce's encompassing command of his art and his determination to realise it. This book's methodology of editorial scholarship interwoven with criticism in genetically critical depth now provides a foothold for sampling three issues from *Ulysses* that have remained controversial, beyond the Critical and Synoptic Edition of *Ulysses*, throughout the past decades. The issues are: Did Joyce proportion the text body of the novel in its first edition? Is Stephen

---

7   Samuel Beckett, 'Dante... Bruno. Vico... Joyce', in *Our Exagmination Round his Factification for Incamination of Work in Progress* (London: Faber & Faber, 1929), p. 14.

Dedalus' silent assertion of 'Love, yes. Word known to all men.' a valid text element in *Ulysses*? How does a critical and synoptic edition enable us to experience the processes of composition in time through which language becomes transubstantiated into the art of literature?

'*Ulysses* 1922 and the Golden Mean: Shaping his Text into Book' details Joyce's proportioning the text body of *Ulysses* over a final four months in 1921 for the Darantiere printers, who were as busy in Dijon as Joyce was in Paris to ready the first edition for publication on 2 February 1922. Joyce made sure that, between Nausikaa and Oxen of the Sun, the body of the book divided into precisely equal stretches, and was thus halved into a day-time and a night-time sequence of 366 pages each (that is, two 'years' of pages; 1922 was a leap-year). Over and above that, Joyce ensured that the *Ulysses* text body extended in proportion by page count to the ratio of the Golden Mean, the *sectio aurea* or *sectio divina* of ancient tradition and significance. That he could possibly have striven for, let alone accomplished this feat has long been held in general doubt. Happily, looking back after four decades into the final appendix of our three-volume critical and synoptic *Ulysses* edition helped decisively to ascertain that he did.

How, in the Scylla & Charybdis episode, does Stephen Dedalus convey what to him are the essentials of Shakespeare's late plays to his audience of librarians in Dublin's National Library? And how does he reassure himself in silent self-dialogue that he knows what he is talking about? Joyce's autograph fair copy sets this out unambiguously and in full clarity. Yet the climax of his words to the librarians and his ensuing self-reflection, comprising two entire paragraphs, are no longer present in the published first-edition text. A rational assessment of their presence in the authorial fair copy, and their absence in the typescript serving as printer's copy for the book publication, builds strictly on bibliographical evidence. This establishes that the cause for the two-paragraph lacuna was an eye-skip, hence a human error in the pre-publication transmission. Embedded in the second of the two paragraphs affected is Stephen Dedalus' silent affirmation of 'Love, yes. Word known to all men.' Ascertaining a non-authorial error in the transmission reaffirms the two paragraphs in their entirety. The two paragraphs can only be restored comprehensively, as by dint of method they must, with Stephen Dedalus' silent line of thought incorporated.

Ulysses 1984: To Edit and Read in Flow of Composition' is my envoy to this book of essays from 1974 to 2024 that support the scholarly editing and explore the genetically critical dimension of James Joyce's writing and art from its beginnings to the accomplishment of *Ulysses*. Its rich and highly variant pre-publication materials in particular were new wine not to be poured into the old bottles of the orthodox practices of scholarly editing. Multiple states of his composition writing have survived. The progress they evidence render his art explorable and analysable in the processes antecedent to his work's publication as text to be read, enjoyed, and interpreted. Preparatory therefore to securing *Ulysses* as accomplished, I ascertained from all surviving pre-publication evidence the stages and states of composing the novel antecedent to the text product that eventually resulted. I edited the evidence for *Ulysses* as the novel emerged in genetic progress. The conceptual challenge was to edit the material documentation of the work's gestation and growth to sparkle in fusion with a genetically critical awareness of the progress in time of its processes of composition. In the 1980s, nothing but book print was available to render accessible and to present the process of creating and accomplishing *Ulysses* over time. Our edition therefore resorts to visualising in synopsis the successive stages of the novel's genetic progress. The methodology evolving from it was new and was seen as innovative. But conceptual understanding and appreciation of the potential of the genetically critical approach has as yet not widely translated into its further application and use. The essay that ends this book is an invitation to reflect, from Simon Dedalus' musical climax in the Sirens episode, on future realisations of the possibilities of *Ulysses. A Critical and Synoptic Edition*. The edition has become translatable into and genetically explorable in the digital environment that textual scholarship and genetic criticism together today command.

Munich, 30 September 2023

Towards a Critical Text of James Joyce's *A Portrait of the Artist as a Young Man*

A Portrait of the Artist as a Young Man, the book which James Joyce had been writing for ten years since embarking upon it in Dublin in 1904, was completed in manuscript in Trieste in 1914. Fifty years later, in 1964, the Viking Press published a 'definitive text, corrected from the Dublin holograph'.[1] Though not critical, and although presenting a text which even the scholar who prepared it does not consider truly definitive, this edition of the novel represents the first attempt ever made to relate its printed versions back to the authorial manuscript. For the first time also—though not published with the text—an account appeared of the textual history of *A Portrait of the Artist as a Young Man* from the manuscript of 1913/14 to the Jonathan Cape edition of 1924, the last in which the author himself had a hand.[2] Some problems of the text and of its transmission have there been recognised and solved. The presence of others has not been noticed and sometimes not even suspected. Nor has all available documentary material relating to the textual history of the novel as yet been recorded. In this chapter, therefore, I propose first to describe and interpret three documents from British libraries, all preserved by Harriet Shaw Weaver and in 1951 and 1952 given by

---

1   James Joyce, *A Portrait of the Artist as a Young Man*. The definitive text, corrected from the Dublin holograph by Chester G. Anderson, ed. by Richard Ellmann (New York: The Viking Press, 1964).

2   Chester G. Anderson, 'The Text of James Joyce's *A Portrait of the Artist as a Young Man*', *Neuphilologische Mitteilungen*, 65 (1964), 160-200. This is a but slightly revised version of the Introduction to Chester G. Anderson, 'A Portrait ... Critically Edited ...', unpubl. Ph.D. dissertation, Faculty of Philosophy (Columbia University, 1962).

her to the British Museum and to the Bodleian Library, Oxford, which clarify essential stages of the publishing history and the transmission of the text, and then to discuss the central issues of an overall textual hypothesis which could form the basis of an editorial approach to create a true critical edition of the novel.

The *Egoist* Tearsheets

The first printed text of *A Portrait of the Artist as a Young Man* was serialised in *The Egoist*, London, in 1914 and 1915. Tearsheets from *The Egoist* were circulated in 1915 and 1916 during the sustained, though long unsuccessful, efforts of literary agent James B. Pinker, Ezra Pound, and above all Harriet Shaw Weaver to find an English publisher—and later, when the firm of The Egoist Ltd. had been founded for the very purpose of publishing *A Portrait*, to find a printer in England willing to take on the novel in book form. The search[3] ended only when B. W. Huebsch of New York undertook both to publish *A Portrait* in the United States and to supply The Egoist Ltd. with the sheets for 750 copies,[4] which became the first edition of the book to be published in England.[5] Over time, successive lots of tearsheets of the serialised *Egoist*

---

3 It is described in much detail, which often corrects assumptions by Anderson, 'The Text ...', pp. 190 ff., in chapters 5 and 6 of Jane Lidderdale and Mary Nicholson, *Dear Miss Weaver. Harriet Shaw Weaver 1876-1961* (New York: The Viking Press, 1970).
4 The exact number delivered was 768. See Lidderdale, *Dear Miss Weaver*, p. 128.
5 Contrary to the nomenclature in John J. Slocum and Herbert Cahoon, *A Bibliography of James Joyce, 1882-1941* (New Haven: Yale University Press, 1953), it is bibliographically correct only to speak of one first edition, the first impression of which was published in two separate simultaneous issues variant merely in the two distinct states of the title page, and issued in two different bindings. The variant title pages are both conjugate in their sheets and were probably printed by stop-press alteration from separate plates for which the identical typesetting of author and title was used. There is distinct type-damage to four separate letters (the 'e' in 'the', the 'a' in 'a', the 'M' in 'Man' and the 'C' in 'JOYCE') which positively secures the identification. Owing to the absence of B. W. Huebsch's publisher's device from the title page of the London issue, its typographical layout differs in the wider spacing between the two lines each for author and title: the lines 'BY | JAMES JOYCE' have as a block been moved further down the page. Beyond that, the variance of the title pages is merely in the alternative imprints. This first edition was never corrected but for a few minor alterations in its plates and ran out in 1950 in its 44th impression, while a second American edition, editorially corrected by Harry Levin, began its run in 1947 and went into many impressions and several separate issues, American and English. The edition named by Slocum-Cahoon 'The First English Edition, English

printing were sent across the Atlantic, corrected and uncorrected, and in complete sets of the text as well as in units of two or three chapters. What has survived of these several dispatches to America now forms three separate complete sets of tearsheets in the Slocum Collection at Yale University.[6] One of them—EC–A—gains its integrity as a set from having served as the printer's copy for the Huebsch edition (H).

The library of the British Museum in London holds a fourth set of tearsheets. It came to the British Museum from Harriet Shaw Weaver in October 1951. Following Anderson's sigla I shall call it EC–W. This set does not enter the transmission of the text of *A Portrait* beyond the *Egoist* serialisation, but it clarifies some aspects of the transfer into print of the typescript, which itself is largely lost, by providing evidence that none of the censoring cuts which affect the *Egoist* text in its published form were made until the last moment before publication. In its substantive readings, Joyce's text was set up as unimpaired as the typescript transmitted it by the compositors of all three printers employed by *The Egoist* during the serialisation of the novel. The EC–W tearsheets prove that printing-house editors must be held responsible for the cuts.[7] EC–W contains as an insert the left column of a proof of page 289 (*The Egoist*, 1 August 1914) which begins Chapter III of the novel. It includes the entire five-paragraph passage in print which was subsequently removed from

---

sheets' (1918) is in truth the second edition of the novel, and it is the 'first English edition' only in so far as it is the fountainhead of the authorially corrected English line of the text. Of the fifth impression of the original American first edition, there was in 1921 once more a separate issue for The Egoist Ltd. in London. This is not the 'third edition' (nor, of course, the fifth). Bibliographically, the reset Jonathan Cape publication of 1924 is the true third edition. As it is reset from the London edition of 1918, it might under the special circumstances governing the textual transmission of this novel be termed the second English edition. It had numerous impressions until it was replaced in 1956 by the reset Jonathan Cape illustrated edition (the third in England).

6   These have been seen and described by Chester G. Anderson: see Anderson, 'The Text ...', pp. 186–190.
7   Lidderdale, *Dear Miss Weaver*, pp. 92, 99, and 103 gives vivid accounts of when and how Harriet Weaver was forced to give in to the demands for excision; with respect to the sentences omitted near the end of Chapter IV, Harriet Weaver herself wrote in the margin of Joyce's letter to her of 24 July 1915: '... the managers of the firm objected to certain expressions.... That was why the *Egoist* changed printers.' James Joyce, Letters II, pp. 355 fn. (Full reference to James Joyce's as yet published letters is: *Letters of James Joyce*, ed. by Stuart Gilbert, vol. I (New York: Viking Press, 1957, ²1966) [*Letters* I]; *Letters of James Joyce*, ed. by Richard Ellmann, vols. II and III (New York: Viking Press, 1966). [*Letters* II; *Letters* III]).

the published version of the full page. A short poem, spaced widely so that it corresponds in length to the excised *Portrait* passage, seems to have been inserted as a filler where the 1 August instalment ends at the bottom of the left-hand column on page 291. Similarly, after the published version of p. 128 of *The Egoist*, 2 August 1915, part of a galley proofsheet is inserted which corresponds to a large section of the text found on p. 128, second column, and p. 129, first column, and contains in print both the brief piece of dialogue censored in publication and the twice-repeated word 'ballocks' subsequently replaced by asterisks. Of particular interest in EC–W, moreover, is the fact that all of Chapter IV is in galley proof. Herein also the two sentences near the end of the chapter, which to Joyce's recorded dismay[8] had disappeared from the published text, are found in print. Their removal caused some respacing and resetting of lines and indeed introduced one new substantive error in the published *Egoist* text. Further collation shows that the galley proofs of Chapter IV are wholly uncorrected and that, while their correction before publication removed many printer's errors, it also introduced new errors into the text.

EC–W, Harriet Weaver's set of tear- and proofsheets of the *Egoist* serialisation of *A Portrait of the Artist as a Young Man*, is now bound in hard covers in a volume of sixty leaves, which, but for three exceptions—fols. 3–4, 5–6 and 30–31 being conjugate—are separately mounted. The binding was done after the set's accession to the British Museum, and there are signs that before binding it consisted of three, or rather four, individual parts. The text itself came in three separate bundles, with Chapters I and II each by itself, and Chapters III, IV, and V together in a brown paper folder. The British Museum shelf mark is pencilled on each first leaf of these three sections. Because of a bookbinder's decision, moreover, one leaf and two once-folded sheets of errata to Chapters III and IV (with one single erratum for Chapter V) in Joyce's own hand must now be regarded as the fourth section of the set. These manuscript errata lists, although never an integral part of the set of tear- and proofsheets, once accompanied the text in a green envelope, as is stated in a note in Harriet Weaver's hand on the brown paper folder

---

8   James Joyce to Harriet Weaver, 24 July 1915, *Letters* II, 355.

to Chapters III–V. After binding, the volume as a whole may now be described as follows:

On fol. iv the *Egoist* text begins as page 50 of *The Egoist* of 2 February 1914. This first tearsheet is backed by a pasted-on sheet of white paper, now smudged and grey, which serves as a title page. On it is written in green crayon between ruled lines: 'A Portrait of the Artist | as a Young Man'; the roman numeral I is centred in parentheses—also in green crayon—under the lower rule. The writing is probably Joyce's own. In the bottom left-hand corner are three notes in pencil in Harriet Weaver's hand: 'Prepared by Mr Joyce', 'No corrections here H.S.W.' and 'Nor have I a copy of those of first two chapters'. In the bottom right-hand corner is affixed a printed business card reading: 'It is requested that all communications respecting this M.S. be addressed to—James B. Pinker, Literary Agent, Talbot House, Arundel Street Strand, London [—] Folio'. The name and address 'James B. Pinker . . . London' have been struck out in pencil and replaced by the pencilled address in Harriet Weaver's hand: 'The Egoist Oakley House, Bloomsbury St. London W.C.'

Fols. 2–6 of the bound volume are the manuscript errata lists referred to above, evidently misplaced by the binder in being inserted here. Fol. 2 is a single leaf and is virtually blank but for the three lines written at the top of its recto: '*Errata* | "Egoist." 1/ix/914: p. 330, col. 2, par 8, l. 2: delete "of herrings" | "Egoist" 1/vi/915: p. 95, col. 2 par. 4, l. 14: for "immediate" read "mediate"'.[9] Fols. 3–6 are two once-folded ruled foolscap sheets with four pages each of manuscript corrections to Chapters III and IV. Fol. 3r is headed 'Chapter III'; fol. 5r is headed 'Chapter IV' in Joyce's hand. To the left and right of the heading 'Chapter III' are additional notes in pencil and probably in Harriet Weaver's hand (all of Joyce's writing being in ink): '[Pages are those of *The Egoist*]' and '*A Portrait of the Artist as a Young Man* Corrections to Egoist'. Vertical ruled lines in ink divide columns for 'Page | Paragraph | Line | Column | Incorrect | Correct' in the corrections to Chapter III and '. . . . [Column | Line | . . . .' in those to Chapter IV.

Fols. 7–16 are the *Egoist* tearsheets of Chapter I; fols. 18–26 those of Chapter II. In the upper outside corners of fols. 18–26 recto and verso

---

9   The latter correction refers to Chapter V. These were perhaps the two errata of which Harriet Weaver enclosed a slip in her letter to B. W. Huebsch of 24 July 1916. (*Letters* I, 92 f.)

the arabic numbers 1–18 have been written in pencil and have been partly cropped. The asterisked divisions between the subsections of both chapters have been underscored, or scored out, in green crayon. In both chapters also, all columns and part-columns of *Egoist* text not belonging to *A Portrait* have been pasted over with strips of white paper; whole pages have sometimes been pasted together and sometimes been backed with white paper for the same purpose of obliterating extraneous matter.

Fols. 17 and 27 are the front and back covers of Chapter II. 17v and 27r+v are blank. On 17r the inscription, in green crayon, 'Portrait of the Artist | as a Young Man | (II)' is in the same hand as that on the title-page for Chapter I. In pencil, at the bottom of the page, are again the following notes by Harriet Weaver: 'Prepared by Mr. Joyce'; 'No corrections here.—H.S.W.' and 'Nor have I copy of those of first two chapters—H.S.W'. These cover leaves deserve special attention, and I shall return to them below.

Fols. 28 and 60, again blank but for the inscription on fol. 28r, are of brown paper and were in all probability once conjugate as a folder holding the tear- and proofsheets of Chapters III–V and, in addition, the green envelope with the manuscript corrections to Chapters III and IV. Fol. 28r is inscribed in faded black ink: 'Portrait of the Artist | as a Young Man. | Chapters III,IV.V' in what looks like the same hand as that writing the pencilled notes over the manuscript corrections to Chapter III (fol. 3r) and was in all probability Harriet Weaver's. Added after the roman numeral V in black unfaded ink, and definitely by Harriet Weaver, is: 'from | The Egoist, see Mr. Joyce's corrections to | chapters III+IV in green envelope'.

Fol. 29r consists of the left column only of a page proof of the first page of the *Egoist* instalment for 1 August 1914, and contains in print, as described above, the five-paragraph passage from near the beginning of Chapter III which was cut from the published text. The passage, having once been crossed out in pencil, but with the pencil strokes erased, is boxed in orange crayon. Words from a pencilled marginal note only partly legible can be made out as 'Censored, . . . does not appear in . . . *Egoist* of Aug 1'. Another marginal note in ink between orange crayon lines reads, amusingly: 'This paragraph which was deleted by the prinsters [sic] is to be inserted as marked'. The marking referred to is made in the appropriate place in the margin of fol. 30r. Fol. 29v is blank. The *Egoist* text of Chapter III occupies fols. 30–36. All extraneous matter is here simply crossed out in pencil and/or orange crayon. An orange crayon note at the bottom of fol. 36v gives the direction: 'go to Chap. IV'. Fols. 37–42 contain Chapter IV in galley proof, in seven long columns which, except for fol. 42 with columns 'SIX' and 'SEVEN', are printed one to a galley. Each galley, about twice the length of an *Egoist* page, is folded over once and bound into the present volume for the length of its bottom half only. All versos of the galleys are of course blank. Fol. 42 contains in each of its columns one of the two sentences later censored. They are both underscored and marked in orange crayon. Written in orange crayon between the columns is the note 'deleted by printers [illegible name in parenthesis]'. The bracketed illegible name is crossed out in black ink, and beneath, with an arrow to 'printers', the name is given as 'Messrs Jas. Truscott + Son'.[10]

Fols. 43–59 are the *Egoist* tearsheets of Chapter V, with all extraneous matter crossed out in blue crayon. Interleaved as fol. 55 is the section of a galley proof containing in print the censored passages from Chapter V, as already described. This galley, moreover, also has proof corrections in thin black ink, objecting to the inking of spaces, to broken letters and to spacings between the regular punctuation and the dashes Joyce used instead of inverted commas to set off direct speech. The corrections have been made in the published *Egoist* text. Later than the proof corrections is the crossing out in blue crayon of most of the text in this galley, leaving only the censored lines circled in black ink, with the marginal note 'these lines were deleted by printers—to be inserted as in original text'. The corresponding note for the place of insertion is to be found in the right-hand margin of fol. 54v. Further down in the galley, the two instances of 'ballocks' are underscored in blue crayon, and blue crayon crosses are set against all three textual corrections to be made. Fol. 55v is blank, and in the left margin of fol. 56r the word 'ballocks' is again twice written in in black ink.

Seen as a whole, EC–W contains three further sets of markings which should be recorded. In Chapters I–IV, there are two partly concurrent

---

10   Partridge & Cooper Ltd., whose name appears in the *Egoist* colophon, were a subsidiary of James Truscott and Son. These were the managers with whom Harriet Weaver had to contend. Cf. above, note 7, and Lidderdale, *Dear Miss Weaver*, p. 91.

sets of line counts. One of them is in short marginal strokes in thin black ink marking every hundredth line of printed text. Starting afresh at the beginning of each chapter, it is almost faultlessly accurate; but it is also purely mechanical, as is shown by the count for Chapter III which begins in the column of the page proof and runs on into the first column of the published text without allowing for the repetition here of lines already counted. The other set, which is present in Chapters I, II and IV only, is in pencil. In Chapters II and IV it, too, marks off roughly every hundredth line, though it is less accurate and usually deviates by several lines from the line count in ink. In Chapter I, the corresponding divisions in pencil fluctuate between eighty-two and 151 lines in length. In each of the chapters where they appear, the pencilled divisions are serially numbered. In Chapter I and II, there are also a few accompanying additions of figures to be found in the margins. In Chapter V there are no line counts. The tearsheets for this last chapter, however, are the only ones to show a few traces of correction beyond the restoring of censored passages. On fol. 43v, a pencilled marginal note specifies 'dashes all through not inverted commas'; on fol. 46r the twice-repeated misprint 'Epitectus' is each time corrected to 'Epictetus', and in close to twenty instances spread over several pages 'aesthetic' is corrected to 'esthetic' in accordance with Joyce's orthography. Finally, there are throughout the text marginal markings in pencil and indelible pencil which draw attention to a series of apparently undesirable passages of text. None of the restitutions of *Egoist* censorings are so marked, but there is a clear connection between all the markings in pencil in that they note passages which have to do with urine and excrement—beginning, indeed, on the first page with the sentence 'When you wet the bed, first it is warm then it gets cold.'—or else might be considered to have a blasphemous ring to them.[11] The markings in indelible pencil, present towards the end of Chapter II and in Chapter III only, stand against two instances of Stephen's sexual fantasies.[12]

---

11   With reference keyed to the Viking [Anderson] text, the passages in question are: p. 7.13-14/I, 13-14; 43.11-18/I, 1261-1277 ; 44.32-35/I, 1325-1328; 137.24-30/III, 1260-1267; 138.6-9/III, 1279-1282; 151.5-9/IV, 138-142; 192.8-11/V, 639-642; 200.3-5/V, 920-922; 205.22-28/V, 1114-1119; 206.30-32/V, 1158-1160; 211.29-31/V, 1337-1339; 212.5-7/V, 1350-1352; 242.27-30/V, 2424-2427.
12   P. 98.35-99.10/II, 1363-1373 and p. 115.31-116.7/III, 488-499. The same (?) indelible pencil has bracketed a part-column on p. 71, 16 February 1914 (i.e. Viking [Anderson] p. 22.6-37/I, 526-556), but there is no link in contents between this passage and the other two.

Fols. 17 and 27, the front and back covers of Chapter II, give the initial clue to the interpretation of the evidence set out above. The tearsheets for the first two chapters, as was seen, are separately claimed to have been prepared, with the careful pastings and markings in green crayon described, by James Joyce himself. Corroborative evidence that Harriet Weaver's repeated statement to this effect means what it says comes from the nature of the covers. On closer inspection, they prove to be the two halves of a broadsheet-size piece of thin white cardboard, with printed text in Italian which has been pasted over with white paper.[13] Against the light, the entire text of the two halves put together, though cropped at the top, is clearly legible as four columns of print setting out the rights and duties of tenants of apartment houses: when to pay rent; the duty of heads of families to provide separate bedrooms for children of different sexes over the age of six; strictures on sub-letting, on keeping pets, etc., etc. The text ends in one line of type across the bottom of the four columns: 'Il presente Regolamento venne approvato dalla G[iu]nta municipale, nella seduta del 6 Febbraio 1912.' and is signed 'IL CONSIGLIO DIRETTIVO'. Being printed on one side only of a thin white cardboard sheet, it looks very much like the general regulations for tenants such as one often finds affixed somewhere near the main entrances of apartment houses in countries like Germany, Switzerland or Austria. In Italy, apparently, the imposition of such rules has never been, nor is to this day, customary. But Trieste in its authoritarian Austrian days may have had them.[14] Thus, from the handmade covers to the tearsheets of Chapter II, it would seem that it was indeed James Joyce himself who carefully pasted up the instalments of Chapters I and II of *A Portrait*, and that he did so in Trieste, shortly after 15 July 1914, when Chapter II ended in *The Egoist*. Thereafter, although Joyce did not leave Trieste until June 1915, he would not have been able to attend to the subsequent chapters in the same manner. For, as we learn from his

---

13   The full sheet either was cut from the beginning, serving as a divider between the chapters and a protective end cover, or else was used by Joyce as a folder for Chapter II, in which case the British Museum binder cut it apart and inadvertently turned fol. 27 upside down.

14   To Professor Giorgio Melchiori of Rome, who was most conveniently at hand in the British Museum reading room when I made this discovery, I am grateful for confirming my guess as to the nature of the document and for supplying the further information here given.

letter to Harriet Weaver of 24 July 1915 from Zurich (*Letters* II, 355), he received no copy of *The Egoist* in Trieste subsequent to the issue of 15 July 1914. The letter of 24 July 1915, itself an acknowledgement of the receipt of the copies to date of *The Egoist* for 1915, specifies that Joyce had 'not yet seen the numbers for 1 and 15 August, 1 and 15 September and 15 December [1914]'.[15]

The Joyce correspondence, besides allowing some inferences as to how EC-W as a whole came about in its present state, makes it possible to trace with some accuracy the history of the first two chapters therein, and incidentally explains the care with which they were prepared. They were the first part, submitted by Joyce himself, of the copy for Grant Richards who, on the basis of the contract for *Dubliners*, had first refusal of Joyce's books until 15 June 1919.[16] On 3 July 1914, Joyce wrote to Grant Richards: 'I shall of course, as agreed between us, give you the opportunity of publishing [*A Portrait of the Artist as a Young Man*] next year in book. If you cannot find the papers I could send you my copies.' (*Letters* II, 335 f.), and on 30 April 1915, to Harriet Weaver '... the first half of the book was forwarded to him by me last July'.[17] In an undated letter, probably late in January, 1915, Joyce further informed Richards: 'My friend Mr Ezra Pound will send you the fourth, fifth and third chapters of my novel so as to save time' (*Letters* II, 336). Richards had apparently undertaken 'to give a definite answer within three weeks after the completed MS was in his possession',[18] and Joyce was anxious to press his decision, as in the meantime James B. Pinker had made an offer to act as Joyce's literary agent. Ezra Pound was to negotiate an agreement with him on Joyce's behalf, and Joyce wrote to Pound on 17 March 1915: 'The rest of the *Portrait of the Artist* had better be sent on to Grant Richards as soon as it is ready. ... If he decides not to publish ... I am quite willing to entrust the disposal of the rights to Mr Pinker'.[19] On 24 March, Joyce wrote again to Richards (*Letters* II, 337) saying he presumed that the complete copy of the book was now in his possession, but the next day he wrote to Harriet Weaver:

---

15 *Sic*; should be: 1 and 15 August, 1 September and 1 and 15 December.
16 Cf. Anderson, 'The Text ...', p. 190.
17 *Letters* I, 80; 'the first half can refer only to Chapters I and II, as no more had yet been published in July 1914.
18 Letter to Ezra Pound of 17 March 1915, *Letters* III, p. 508.
19 Ibid.

Mr Grant Richards, publisher, has the right of refusal of [my novel]. I believe the greater part of the novel is now in his hands. If the last instalments (May to August) have been set up I should be very much obliged if you could have a proof of them pulled. I am sure that Mr Pound will send them on to Mr Grant Richards. My reason for troubling you is that, in view of Mr Pinker's offer, I think it is to my advantage to know as soon as possible Mr Grant Richards' decision (*Letters* II, 338).

Ballantyne, Hanson & Co., the printers of *The Egoist* since the February issue (in which Chapter V commenced) had not yet, however, set up type beyond the issue for 1 April. To oblige Joyce, and in order to enable Richards to reach a decision on the book publication, Harriet Weaver therefore, late in March, 1915, risked parting temporarily with the pages of the Chapter V typescript which had not yet been set up.[20] This was technically possible because for the May issue, which was a special Imagist number, the serialisation of *A Portrait* was to be interrupted. There was consequently a time lapse between instalments of two months. On 22 April, Harriet Weaver informed Joyce accordingly, specifying when she needed the typescript returned.[21] Joyce replied on 30 April, (*Letters* I, 79 f.), and on 7 May he wrote to Pinker: 'The fifth chapter of my novel must . . . be returned to *The Egoist* not later than the 20 May as it is needed for the June issue' (*Letters* II, 341). On 18 May Richards rejected the novel,[22] whereupon the disposal of the book rights went to Pinker. The copy which Richards had received piecemeal between July 1914 and April 1915 must also have gone to Pinker. Certainly the tearsheets Joyce

---

20 Late in March 1915 (*c.* 29 March) Ezra Pound wrote: 'Dear James Joyce: I took the final chapter of your novel to Grant Richards this a.m.' (*Pound/Joyce. The Letters of Ezra Pound to James Joyce, with Pound's Essays on Joyce*. Edited and with Commentary by Forrest Read (New York: New Directions, 1967), p. 33). In a letter of 22 April to Joyce, Harriet Weaver specifies that 'Mr. Pound sent Mr. Grant Richards . . . the part of the M.S. of your novel which has not yet been set up, together with a complete set of the numbers of 'The Egoist' in which it has appeared up to date. I asked for the M.S. to be returned by 20 May. This would give Mr. Richards two months in which to consider it'. For access to those of Harriet Weaver's letters to James Joyce which concern the publishing of *A Portrait*, in photostats of the holograph originals, I am grateful to Miss Jane Lidderdale [see further fn. 32]. While quotations from them here and below are according to my own transcription, reference should be made to the edition of John Firth, 'Harriet Weaver's Letters to James Joyce 1915-1920', *Studies in Bibliography*, 20 (1967), 151-188.
21 See quotation fn. 20.
22 Cf. Richard Ellmann, *James Joyce* (Oxford: Oxford University Press, 1982), p. 400.

had sent him from Trieste of Chapters I and II did, as is witnessed by the Pinker business card on the front leaf of Chapter I in EC-W.

How much of the rest of EC-W originally belonged to the Richards-Pinker copy is less easy to decide. Chapter V stands apart in the set because it alone has the deletions of extraneous matter in blue crayon and contains no line counts. Chapters I, II and IV are linked by the line counts in pencil, not present, as the ones in ink are, in Chapter III. Chapters III and IV in turn are linked by the orange crayon used for cancellations and marginal annotations, and, in addition, by the original title inscription in faded black ink on the brown paper folder: 'A Portrait of the Artist as a Young Man. Chapters III, IV', to which a dot in the centre of the line and the roman numeral 'V' seem to have been added later. (An even later addition on the brown paper folder are the words in permanent black ink: 'from *The Egoist*, see Mr Joyce's corrections to chapters III+IV in green envelope'.) As the handwriting is apparently Harriet Weaver's, the brown paper folder still extant may well have been the one in which she originally, in February/March 1915, gave Ezra Pound Chapters III and IV for Grant Richards' perusal, but whether both chapters in EC-W are still in the identical sheets in which Richards read them is another question. The absence of line counts in pencil in Chapter III suggests that only Chapters I, II and IV have survived in the present set from the earliest discernible moment of its previous history. There is a possibility that the line counts in pencil are traces of Grant Richards' deliberations over the novel. This would put the galley proofs of Chapter IV among the material gathered together for him by Ezra Pound. It would also mean that an earlier set of tearsheets of Chapter III was replaced by the present set (which has no pencilled line counts) some time after EC-W left Richards. On the other hand, Chapter III shares the line counts in ink with Chapters I, II and IV, but not with Chapter V. Logically one would therefore assume that Chapter III in its present state became part of EC-W before Chapter V in its present state did.

It was in July 1915 that Joyce's London friends and agents were most urgently pressed by the author to enter into negotiations about the book publication of the novel with nothing but a wholly unexpurgated text. On 24 July, Joyce read the end of Chapter IV in the January issue of *The Egoist* as forwarded to him in Zurich and discovered that whole sentences had been left out. He wrote immediately to Harriet Weaver to complain about the carelessness of the printers, adding: 'My MSS are in Trieste but I remember the text and am sending the correct version of [the] passages [in question] to my agent. The instalments printed by Ballantyne, Hanson and Co (February to July) are of course carefully done. I hope the other printers did not set up the numbers which I have not seen. . . .' (*Letters* II, 355). But they had done so; and when, a week later, Joyce had received and read the remaining issues for 1914 (1 August to 15 December), he wrote even more urgently to Pound:

> I find that deletions have been made in my novel: in the issues of 1 August and 1 January. Who has the typescript? Can you send me the pages corresponding to these instalments? If Mr Pinker has it you need not send it. If he has the published version I must have these deleted passages typed at once and sent to him as part of the novel which he is submitting to Martin Secker and Co for publication. (31 July; *Letters* II, 358).

Already, however, there was a reply to his letter of 24 July under way from Harriet Weaver, explaining the textual corruptions and reassuring him that the censored passages were not lost. Harriet Weaver wrote on 28 July:

> It was because of Messrs. Partridge+Coopers' stupid censoring of your novel that we left them—that is, they had objected once or twice to things in other parts of the paper, but their behaviour over your novel was the crowning offence. They struck out a passage on Aug. 1st of last year. I could not help it. The rest was set up correctly until they came to the latter part of chapter four where as you have seen some sentences were omitted. I then submitted the whole of chapter five to them. They declined to set it up as it stood + so we left them.
>
> I am sorry to say that Messrs. Ballantyne are now acting in the same way. . . .
>
> Mr Pinker has proofs containing all the deleted matter. I hope you will not have this annoyance when the novel comes to be printed in book form. . . .

The deletions of 1 January 1915 were in print in the Chapter IV galleys, and the Chapter III deletion of 1 August 1914 is contained in the column of the page proof prefixed to the Chapter III tearsheets in EC-W. From the absence of pencilled line counts in these tearsheets on the one hand, and the mechanically uniform application therein of the line counts in ink on the other, it seems probable, indeed, that Harriet Weaver, acting upon Joyce's letter of 24 July, supplied Pinker with a complete new set of Chapter III tearsheets plus the additional column of the page proof for the beginning of the chapter (rather than with this page proof only) for the actual purpose of his submitting the novel to Secker. At the time, however, she may hastily have entered therein pencil markings only, now partly erased or overruled in orange crayon. The orange crayon markings in their turn, which provide a firm link between the extant sheets of Chapters III and IV, would seem to be later than the pencilled deletions of extraneous matter in Chapter III. They were doubtless made by Harriet Weaver also, but at a time when both chapters as they survive were in her hands at once. As the main function of the orange crayon is to mark and draw attention to the censored passages, she may not have applied it to this end until EC-W eventually passed into her hands and was sent by her to various printers and at least one publisher.

After the return of the Chapter V typescript needed as copy for the forthcoming 1 June to 1 September instalments, the Richards-Pinker copy, then in the hands of Pinker, was incomplete. But the *Egoist* printers appear to have had the entire chapter in type by the end of July. Pinker was able to reassure Harriet Weaver, who feared otherwise after the renewed interference of Ballantyne's in the 1 August issue, that he had submitted to Secker not the expurgated but the complete text in galleys of the last two fifth-chapter instalments.[23] The proof markings in the galley slip still extant among the Chapter V tearsheets suggest that Pinker got the galleys from the printers at the end of July when, with the corrections made, the pages for the 1 August issue of *The Egoist* had been imposed. There would have been galleys for him, too, specially pulled, for the portion of the text to be published in September. The February-June instalments would have been in the complete issues of *The Egoist* for these months, as was the case with the copy submitted to Richards (see above, fn. 20), or else already in tearsheets, as in the present EC-W. The present Chapter V tearsheets, however, with their blue crayon cancellations of extraneous matter, were in all probability assembled in Pinker's office after the publication of the last instalment on 1 September, as the blue crayon markings therein are uniform throughout. At the same time, the absence of line counts in ink suggests that the tearsheets which now make up Chapter V in EC-W are not

---

23 Cf. Lidderdale, *Dear Miss Weaver*, pp. 104 f.

identical in any part with the state of the copy for Chapter V at the time when the inked line counts were made. It seems possible that the inked line counts were made by Martin Secker & Co. in August 1915. When they refused to publish and returned the novel to Pinker, the makeshift copy for Chapter V was replaced by the present uniform one, incorporating a galley slip for the censored passages only, which would thus be all that remains of the Chapter V copy as submitted to Secker.[24] But with Chapter V replaced, EC-W as it now survives was complete. It would thereafter have been *the* copy which Pinker circulated among the London publishers whom he hoped to interest in Joyce's novel. The set passed from Pinker to Harriet Weaver in April 1916, presumably, when Pinker finally consented to the proposed publication by The Egoist Ltd. and the agreement to that effect had been signed by author, agent and publisher. Harriet Weaver duly noted on the title pages of Chapters I and II that they had been 'prepared by Mr Joyce' and changed the return address from Pinker's to that of The Egoist Ltd.

Now may have begun the copy's round not of publishers, but of printers,[25] and it was for this purpose, as suggested, that Harriet Weaver emphasised the censored passages for restitution in Chapters III and IV and marked the exact positions of insertion in all three chapters affected by cuts. This seems to have been done in two distinct stages: the markings in orange crayon in Chapters III and IV are earlier, and some at least of the marginal notes and positionings in black ink are later, as witnessed by the black ink superinscription over orange crayon at the end of Chapter IV. Lastly, the manuscript errata lists in their green envelope were included in the set after 25 May and before 9 June 1916 (see *Letters* II, 378-379), and note taken of their presence in permanent black ink

---

24 A renewed scrutiny of the inserted galley slip reveals an ink stroke in the margin about halfway down the column which does not stand against a correction to be made. It looks like the line-count strokes of Chapters I-IV, but divides off line 2254 of Chapter V as printed. However, if it may be assumed that the cumulation of fifty-three lines of italicised verse in the preceding sections of the chapter was disregarded in the count, the marking would be seen to stand against line 2201 of the regular text, reflecting a next to faultless line-count in hundreds. The observation would help to argue for the correctness of our assumptions about the fates of EC-W.

25 Harriet Weaver had submitted the novel to printers before, while Pinker was still searching for a publisher (see Lidderdale, *Dear Miss Weaver*, chapter 6 *passim*); refusals from printers were coming in ever faster, so she may for some time have been circulating two copies of the text.

on the brown paper folder for Chapters III-V. The pencilled notes on Chapters I and II, finally—'No corrections here. H.S.W.' and 'Nor have I copy of those of first two chapters. [H.S.W.]'—were obviously also made in two stages, and while the latter would seem the counterparts to the note about 'Mr. Joyce's corrections to chapters III+IV in green envelope', the former may refer to corrections in the sense of reinsertions of censored text and thus correspond to the markings of omissions in Chapters III-V. Again, the latter notes also suggest that EC-W was out of Harriet Weaver's hands when the marked-up tearsheets of Chapters I and II arrived with a letter from Joyce of 9 June (else she might have transferred the authorial corrections to her copy). By this time the publication of *A Portrait* in New York (and first by John Marshall) was under consideration, to be printed from other copy than EC-W. This set was once more at hand when William Heinemann had been persuaded to read Joyce's novel for himself and Ezra Pound on 12 July urged Harriet Weaver to send him the complete text.[26] She mentions in one of her two letters of 7 September to Joyce that she had sent Heinemann her copy containing 'the deleted sentences' and that he had not yet given it back (although he had declined to publish by 19 August). When the set finally returned to her it could serve no further purpose, for the book publication of *A Portrait* was then firmly in the hands of B. W. Huebsch of New York. There is some reason, incidentally, to suspect that most of the observed markings of undesirable passages of text are William Heinemann's (presumably those in pencil, at least, if not those in indelible pencil), on the grounds that if they were the marks of an earlier reader they would not have been left standing in the margins to catch a later reader's attention. EC-W remained in Harriet Weaver's possession until she gave it to the British Museum in 1951.

As a document relating to the publishing history of *A Portrait of the Artist as a Young Man*, EC-W is thus of considerable interest. In terms of the textual history of the novel, its relevance, while specific, is yet narrowly circumscribed. Of greatest potential value and importance for the establishing of a critical text are its authorial errata lists. Their position must be assessed in relation to the documents central to the textual transmission, and in particular to EC-A, the printer's copy for H.

---

26 *The Selected Letters of Ezra Pound 1907-1941*, ed. by D. D. Paige (London: Faber & Faber, [1950] 1971), p. 85.

This entails a reconsideration of the nature and date of EC-A.[27] Anderson describes EC-A as fully and, except for some additional markings clearly made in the printing house, uniformly corrected in Joyce's own hand, and identifies it with a set of tearsheets dispatched by Harriet Weaver on 31 March 1916—and described by her in a letter of that date—to E. Byrne Hackett. Hackett in his turn sent it on to B. W. Huebsch in portions, beginning on 4 May 1916 (Lidderdale, *Dear Miss Weaver*, p. 122). By 2 June Huebsch thereupon felt able to make a provisional offer, and on 16 June he proposed firmly to publish the book (Lidderdale, *Dear Miss Weaver*, p. 123; Anderson, 'The Text ...', p. 189). But the copy in which he read the text cannot have been the one he eventually printed it from: EC-A cannot be identified as the Hackett copy. For it is a fact that Huebsch not only agreed to printing 'absolutely according to the author's wishes, without deletion' (*Letters* I, 91), but also made great efforts to obtain copy with Joyce's own corrections. Had he been in the possession of EC-A from the outset, the lengthy exchange of letters about the author's corrections between him, Harriet Weaver and James Joyce himself, extending over more than four months from 16 June to 24 October 1916, would have been pointless.[28]

In May 1916, it looked as if John Marshall of New York was going to publish *A Portrait*. For The Egoist Ltd. in London, Harriet Weaver was proposing an agreement along the same lines as the one which later came into effect with B. W. Huebsch, namely that sheets of the American printing be supplied for the English edition. James Joyce was interested in the details of correction and proofreading, and an exchange of letters between him and Harriet Weaver in late May and early June establishes what copy and what corrections were available, or were made available, for Marshall. To Joyce's enquiry of 25 May,

> I do not know where the proofs are to be read. . . . Would it help in any way if I read and checked the third, fourth and fifth chapters which I have in the instalments from 1 August 1914 to 1 September 1915? If the printers set from them this would weed out some of the errors but of

---

27 Miss Lidderdale's discussion of the dates and events leading up to Huebsch's publication of *A Portrait* (*Dear Miss Weaver*, chapter 6 *passim*) differs radically from Anderson's hypotheses (Anderson, 'The Text ...', pp. 190 ff.). Being much more fully based on documentary evidence, her account serves as my frame of reference.

28 Anderson, 'The Text ...', p. 188 f. is aware of the facts. Curiously, he does not recognise the bearing they have on determining the provenance of EC-A.

course not the new ones which they will put in . . . But it would be almost as much trouble to find the places in the new proofs as the paging will be different. (*Letters* II, 378)

Harriet Weaver replied on 31 May:

> I have still the typescript of Chapter V and I am sending this off today to Mr. Marshall asking him to let his printers set up from this exactly as it stands, without adding commas or capitals. As I was stupid enough to destroy the rest of the typescript it would be a help if you would kindly do what you suggest and weed out errors in chapters III and IV. If you will then send them to me . . . I will insert the passages deleted by our printers and forward them to Mr. Marshall. . . . I will despatch to you today cuttings containing chapters I+II and perhaps you will correct them also and let me have them back. I shall ask Mr. Marshall either to send me proofs or have them corrected according to the corrected text.

Before 9 June, when he returned the cuttings of Chapters I and II after taking less than twenty-four hours over correcting them, Joyce had already dispatched separately the corrections for Chapters III and IV (*Letters* II, 379). There can be no doubt that what Harriet Weaver received from him and acknowledged in a letter dated 12 June were the errata lists to Chapters III and IV as they survive in EC-W. As the letter of 25 May seems to suggest, Joyce had his copy of the *Egoist* text of the last three chapters already annotated when he wrote, or else did the annotation while awaiting Harriet Weaver's reply, and he certainly did not spend more than a day or two over tabulating the corrections when she asked for them. The authorial errata lists for Chapters III and IV (EC-W, fols. 3-6) can therefore be dated very narrowly to the first week of June, 1916. Moreover, yet another very definite fact emerges from the correspondence as quoted: at no time between the end of July 1914 and 8 June 1916 had James Joyce had in his possession a full set of tearsheets of *A Portrait*. The set which was sent to Hackett on 31 March 1916 and was passed on by him to Huebsch, if it contained any corrections at all apart from the insertions of the deleted passages as referred to in Harriet Weaver's covering letter (Anderson, 'The Text ...', p. 189), cannot have been corrected by Joyce. It cannot, therefore, have been EC-A.

The copy which was thus assembled for John Marshall to print from was described to B. W. Huebsch six weeks later: 'I have written to ask

Mr Marshall to send on to you his copy of the text which contains Mr Joyce's corrections. . . . Mr Joyce would like the book printed exactly according to this corrected text (the fifth chapter being the original typescript)'.[29] For a month Huebsch waited to hear from Marshall and to receive the corrected text from him and then, on 25 August, wrote to him in Quebec, while at the same time informing Harriet Weaver that no contact had as yet been established. Probably still confident, however, that the Marshall copy would soon be in his hands, he added that—subject to Pinker's cabled agreement to certain modifications of the publishing contract—'I shall proceed at once with the setting up of the book' (*Letters* I, 93). But Huebsch never obtained the corrected text from Marshall. In letters of 8 September and 20 September to Harriet Weaver he again specifically mentions this fact, and thereafter the matter is dropped because Harriet Weaver was supplying him with alternative copy.[30] By 8 September, still without copy to print from, Huebsch decided to accept an offer Harriet Weaver had made on 19 August (the day she had learnt that William Heinemann was definitely not willing to publish *A Portrait* in England): 'request that you send me the duplicate offered . . . as I presume it contains corrections not to be found in the copy I have'. Harriet Weaver had in fact anticipated this request immediately on receiving Huebsch's letter of 25 August in London on 6 September. Without a moment's delay, she had marked up new tearsheets of Chapters III and IV from the authorial errata lists in her possession and posted them that same evening. Tearsheets of Chapters I, II and V she annotated as far as she was able to from memory—that is, she entered in them the kinds of corrections she remembered Joyce had made in the copy for Marshall—and she mailed them with a covering letter to Huebsch the next day; and she cabled to New York that the Joyce corrections were on their way. But, as she emphasised to Huebsch, she was at the same time sending another set of cuttings of Chapters I, II and V to Joyce, asking him to enter his

---

29 Harriet Weaver to Huebsch on 24 July 1916, *Letters* I, 93.
30 The reference is here repeatedly to the unpublished Weaver-Huebsch correspondence. I gratefully acknowledge being given permission to use it. It seems safe to say that Huebsch indeed never received the Marshall copy. For had it passed into his hands, he would, even though not printing from it, have handed it over to John Quinn to whom Joyce in 1917 sold all material relating to the first book edition which Huebsch held, and it would now be found in the Slocum Collection at Yale.

authentic corrections and to post them straight to New York to avoid further delay.[31] Joyce duly corrected them but returned them to the *Egoist* office (*Letters* I, 95), whereupon Harriet Weaver forwarded them to New York on 23 September: 'I have this morning received from Mr Joyce his corrections of Chapters I, II+V of his novel, which I send you herewith [. . .] there seem to be a good many more corrections than I sent you.' The receipt of Chapters I-V as marked up and sent by Harriet Weaver on 6 and 7 September (with Chapters III and IV only containing authorised corrections from the authorial errata lists) was acknowledged by Huebsch on 20 September, though he refused to begin to print from them (he apparently even believed that he had not yet received the complete text of the novel): 'I have received your . . . letters . . . enclosing revised copy of Chapters I, II, III, IV and V. . . . I am afraid that it will scarcely be worth while going ahead until we have the complete copy because in the long run we will lose time by making many corrections in the chapters following those above named. I shall not go ahead until I get the rest of the book whether it be from Mr. Joyce or from Mr. Marshall, though the latter seems unlikely'. On 6 October, the authorially corrected tearsheets of Chapters I, II and V had arrived in New York, and on 17 October Huebsch was able to write: 'You will be glad to know that the book is in the hands of the printer and I hope to be able to get it out during the present season'.

---

31 See the account of the events in London on 6 and 7 September, 1916, in Lidderdale, *Dear Miss Weaver*, p. 125; and compare with the letter from Harriet Weaver to Huebsch of 7 September as quoted by Anderson, 'The Text ...', p. 190. This letter is now found attached to a complete set of tearsheets known as EC-B. Nowhere is there any documentary evidence, however, that 'EC-B' was an integral set of *Egoist* tearsheets from the outset. Rather, from the facts as they now begin to emerge, I would infer that the one and only copy which ever became an identifiable unit was the printer's copy. Not even this copy, however, secured integrity until the printers stamped its sheets with serial numbers. For example, it had not before and probably did not then contain the holograph insert (leaf no. 35). The other sets (EC-B and EC-C) had no natural integrity as physical objects until they became identifiable as catalogued units in the Slocum Collection. I suggest that, at various times, portions of the text (chapters and inserts, sections annotated and not annotated) were shuffled and reshuffled between them, the last time probably by Mr. Slocum himself. For the Quinn sale catalogue still speaks of three sets, *each* 'containing manuscript corrections by the author and Miss Weaver' (quoted by Anderson, 'The Text ...', p. 187). But EC-C now has no corrections.

From the documentary evidence of the Weaver-Huebsch correspondence, then,[32] it would seem that Huebsch's printer's copy in Chapters I, II and V consisted of *Egoist* tearsheets corrected by Joyce himself between 7 and 23 September, and in Chapters III and IV of tearsheets marked up by Harriet Weaver from the authorial errata lists in her possession on 6 September 1916. Yet Anderson (p. 188) asserts that EC-A, which was undoubtedly Huebsch's printer's copy, is uniformly corrected in Joyce's hand. For the purposes of this article I have not been able to inspect EC-A in the Slocum Collection to ascertain how exhaustive Anderson's description of it is. If Chapters III and IV in EC-A are without question corrected by Joyce himself, this fact would still need to be explained. But it is true that Anderson never considers the possibility of EC-A being a composite copy, while the preceding descriptions of EC-W and the lost Marshall copy argue that it would only follow precedence if it was, and only strengthen the belief that the conclusions drawn from the evidence of the Weaver-Huebsch correspondence are sound. Moreover, even if all non-printing-house annotation in all chapters of EC-A as described is 'in black ink by a pen with a very fine point', the possibility is not ruled out that the corrections were in fact made by two different pens. For it may be observed in the galley-proof insertion in Chapter V of EC-W that proof marking in London (by Harriet Weaver?) was also done with black ink in very fine strokes. In addition, there is at least one piece of internal evidence from variants in compound words which would further urge a re-examination of the agent or agents correcting EC-A. Joyce's intention was to alter a majority of the text's hyphenated words into one-word compounds. But, as Harriet Weaver explained to Huebsch in a letter of 2 May 1917, 'in most places where he had crossed [the hyphens] out, he meant the words to be joined together but the printers have misunderstood and, in many places, separated them' (*Letters* II, 393 fn.). Consequently, Joyce's corrections to the Huebsch edition (and Harriet Weaver's additions thereto) contain

---

32 Added footnote in 2022: Back in the early 1970s, exploring the genesis of *A Portrait of the Artist as a Young Man* as I then was, Richard Ellmann kindly brought me into contact with Jane Lidderdale. She had at the time just published her biography of her aunt, Harriet Shaw Weaver. Towards it, Richard Ellmann had lent her his cache of the Huebsch-Weaver correspondence, which therefore I was enabled to peruse in the London house of Jane Lidderdale. Quotes from the correspondence are my transcriptions, unless otherwise specified.

eighty-seven requests to join together separated compounds. Their distribution, however, is sixty-nine (all told) in Chapters I, II and V and only eighteen in Chapters III and IV, of which only nine are corrections to separations introduced in H. Harriet Weaver's instructions—if it was she who marked up Chapters III and IV in EC-A—appear to have been less subject to misinterpretation than Joyce's. What is beyond doubt, however, is that Huebsch's printer's copy was not the set of tearsheets dispatched from London on 31 March, reaching Huebsch via Hackett by 2 June 1916. Consequently, Joyce's manuscript errata lists to Chapters III and IV now surviving in EC-W, which were tabulated in the first week of June, are of an earlier date than is the marking of corrections for these chapters in EC-A. If Anderson's description were found to be valid and the corrections in Chapters III and IV of EC-A are in Joyce's own hand, their authority would confirm that of the errata lists or supersede it in cases of conflict. But if the marking of Chapters III and IV in EC-A was done simply by copying Joyce's manuscript corrections, these represent the only authoritative alterations to the *Egoist* text of Chapters III and IV in preparation of the first book edition.

The First and Second Editions (H and B): Joyce's Corrections and the Printer's Copy for B

With EC-W, Harriet Weaver in 1951 gave to the British Museum a list of corrections to the 1916 New York and London edition (H) of *A Portrait of the Artist as a Young Man*.[33] It is headed: 'CORRECTIONS. *A portrait of The Artist as a Young Man*. B. W. Huebsch: New York: 1916. The Egoist Ltd: London: 1916.', and bears the typewritten signature on its last page: 'JAMES JOYCE, Seefeldstrasse 73III Zurich VIII'. This is a carbon of a sixteen-page typewritten list with 364 typewritten entries for 365 separate corrections to be made. It is clear that it is yet another copy of Joyce's 'nearly 400' corrections to the first edition.[34] These are still

---

33 Incidentally, she also gave her own complete run of *The Egoist* which the British Museum library did not possess before. Cf. Lidderdale, *Dear Miss Weaver*, p. 425.
34 364 is the number of corrections counted by Cahoon in Joyce's manuscript list (Y). I count entries (364) and corrections to be made (365; two separate instances of 'public-house' > 'publichouse' are given one entry). These corrections sometimes involve more than one change. Anderson counts 373 changes (cf. footnote, p. 162).

extant in the original manuscript (Y). Joyce wrote them out in Zurich in April, 1917, and sent them to Pinker in London on 10 April, requesting: 'Kindly have them typed (with copy) and forwarded by two successive posts to my publishers in New York' (*Letters* II, 393). The corrections are also extant in a typescript ribbon-copy (YT). From the description given of YT (Anderson, 'The Text ...', p. 197) it would seem that the Harriet Weaver copy of corrections in the British Museum is its carbon copy; I shall call it YTW. A note across the top of page 1 of the list, unsigned and undated, yet doubtless in Harriet Weaver's hand, states:

> Copy of corrections made by Mr. Joyce to 1st edition. Sent to Mr. Huebsh [sic] August 16, 1917 but were not made before printing of sheets for 3rd English edition (1921). Were made in 2nd English edition, printed in Southport, 1917. Were made also before printing of Jonathan Cape edition of 1924[.]

But although YTW appears to be the carbon copy of YT as described by Anderson, it differs from YT in that seventeen further corrections are interlined in it in their appropriate positions, in pencil, and in Harriet Weaver's handwriting. Their number establishes a connection to the two handwritten pages with a total of seventy corrections in Harriet Weaver's hand (YW), now accompanying YT, and bearing a note: 'Sent by Miss Weaver May 2/17'. In April 1917, then, James Joyce and Harriet Weaver independently drew up lists of corrections to H.[35] Anderson states that of the seventy corrections in YW, seventeen—all of them departures from EC-A in H—are omitted from Y/YT. Harriet Weaver appears to have conflated Joyce's list and her own, adding in YTW the seventeen errors Joyce had missed. The total number of entries in YTW is thus 381, the total of corrections 382.

From Joyce's letter to Pinker of 10 April as quoted, from the fact that he informed Harriet Weaver on 7 July that Pinker had his corrections (*Letters* I, 107) and from Harriet Weaver's note on YTW,[36] one might be

---

Attempting to apply his criteria, I count at least 379 changes. Yet I believe we are all describing the same body of corrections.

35 Anderson has no real ground for assuming (footnote, p. 197) that YW was written *before* Y: Y was completed by 10 April, YW was compiled between 18 April and 2 May, arriving in New York on 15 May (see below).

36 The note, however, was written at some later date, after 1924; perhaps even as late as 1951.

led to infer that Pinker never forwarded the typescript and carbon he had been asked to prepare but kept them until Harriet Weaver had been alerted to their existence and took it upon herself to send the ribbon copy to Huebsch very belatedly on 16 August, while using the carbon in preparation of her own second edition. But the Weaver-Huebsch correspondence reveals that the facts were different. The corrections seem indeed to have been typed at Pinker's office, and both the ribbon and the carbon copy must have been sent to Huebsch in the manner ordered by Joyce. Huebsch then returned the carbon copy to London at Harriet Weaver's request. When she wrote her explanatory note on YTW she misremembered the exact details: what she mailed to Huebsch on 16 August 1917 was not the whole set of corrections, but only a handwritten list with 16 entries which contained fifteen of the seventeen additional corrections of YTW, plus one correction of a typist's error.[37] This one correction is the clinching piece of evidence: it would not make sense if YTW were not the carbon copy of YT, and its entry in Harriet Weaver's short supplementary list, as indeed this whole list itself, is meaningful only if never typescript and carbon together, but merely the carbon copy alone, was in her hands. The list, on one side of a single quarto-sized sheet of writing paper, is still extant among the unpublished Weaver-Huebsch correspondence.

From the letters, the facts can be filled in in greater detail.[38] In the latter half of April 1917, Harriet Weaver was beginning to consider bringing out a second edition of *A Portrait*. Ideally, she wanted another joint operation with New York, but as import restrictions forbade the further purchase of printed sheets, she requested to be allowed to buy moulds of the New York edition instead.[39] She was aware that the text of the first edition needed correction but did not want to ask Joyce to

---

37 The date they were mailed to Huebsch, which is authentic, is suggestive: on 16 August, the Brighton printers who at first were going to print the English edition retracted their offer. Thus, Harriet Weaver—despairing momentarily that the book would ever be printed in England—may have wished that all corrections were in the hands of the publisher who alone thus far had the text of *A Portrait* in print. In the event, of course, only the second Egoist Press edition and its descendants ever incorporated Joyce's 'nearly 400' corrections.

38 For the events which lead up to finding a printer in England for the second edition, Miss Lidderdale (*Dear Miss Weaver*, pp. 139 ff.) has drawn upon the Weaver-Huebsch correspondence and largely recorded the relevant details.

39 Harriet Weaver to B. W. Huebsch, 18 April 1917.

correct it as he was at the time suffering acutely from his disease of the eyes. Instead, she compiled her own list of corrections (YW) and sent it to Huebsch on 2 May. It arrived in New York on 15 May, the day after Huebsch, in reply to her request of 18 April, had written to Harriet Weaver:

> I have just received from Mr. Pinker a long list of corrections to be made in the plates, but unfortunately I have just printed a second edition from the first plates and unless there is a very large demand for the book, this edition is likely to last for a considerable time. I presume that you have received a duplicate list of the corrections. Under the circumstances, probably you would not want me to send you moulds.

But neither from Pinker nor from Joyce had Harriet Weaver received a copy of the corrections. So, with no hope now of getting the corrected text from New York in either sheets or moulds, she decided to publish independently in England, with a reset text. On 6 June, she asked Huebsch to send her the corrections and suggested he have a copy made for her so as not to endanger the original in wartime Atlantic transit. Huebsch was pleased to oblige:

> I take pleasure in enclosing a copy of the corrections. . . . I am keeping a copy of the corrections here for my own use. It will be available for you if disaster overtakes the copy that I am forwarding.[40]

It was not until 28 July (or thereabouts) that the carbon copy from Huebsch arrived in London. But meanwhile, Joyce had notified Harriet Weaver on 7 July that Pinker had his corrections. She replied on 18 July: 'I got your corrections from your agent and the printers now have the book in hand'.[41] The printers she refers to were the Pike's Fine Art Press of Brighton who on 16 August refused to print without deletion. Thus, the corrections as Harriet Weaver got them from Pinker before YTW arrived in London at the end of July did not enter the transmission of the text.

YTW was used to annotate the printer's copy for the second edition of *A Portrait of the Artist as a Young Man*, printed in Southport, England, in

---

40 B. W. Huebsch to Harriet Weaver, 9 July 1917.
41 Pinker must have kept the corrections on file in yet another typescript copy; for the manuscript original (Y) was sold to John Quinn sometime in June, 1917; by 10 July, Joyce had received Quinn's acknowledgement (*Letters* I, 104).

1917—by Robert Johnson & Co., the same printers who had been employed on *The Egoist* by Dorothy Marsden before Harriet Weaver became the editor (Lidderdale, *Dear Miss Weaver*, pp. 142-43)—and published by The Egoist Ltd. in London in 1918. This printer's copy has survived, and it was given by Harriet Weaver to the Bodleian Library, Oxford, between 10 and 19 March 1952. Yet it was not until 1967 that even the Bodleian Library, alerted by Harriet Weaver's biographers, became aware of the special nature of the volume which Weaver had most unobtrusively entrusted them with. She is said to have brought it along one day 'in her open-top bag' (Lidderdale, *Dear Miss Weaver*, p. 426). Its relevance to the publishing history and the textual transmission of *A Portrait* has not yet been recognised or recorded. The volume is bound in the original dark green cloth of the London first edition, but as the body of the book is broken completely loose in the spine, the original binding is now merely folded around it. The book has been given a dark green slipcase for protection. A note in ink by Harriet Weaver is tipped in to the front flyleaf:

> The pencilled corrections in this copy of the first English edition of *A Portrait of the Artist as a Young Man* were made by me from a list of corrections sent by Mr. Joyce for the second edition, printed in Southport and published by *The Egoist* in 1917. They do not appear in the third edition (1921) for which sheets were again imported from the U.S.A. but they do appear in Mr. Jonathan Cape's edition (reset) of 1924.
>
> Harriet Weaver
4 Rawlinson Road
Oxford
March 10th, 1952

On collation, the majority of the pencilled annotations in the Bodley copy (HB) is found to be a very faithful transcript of YTW.[42] Of the changes

---

42 HB is apparently not identical with the copy marked up and given before 16 August 1917, to the Pike's Fine Art Press in Brighton to print from. They returned a book with 'passages marked in blue pencil' to be 'modified or removed'. (Lidderdale, *Dear Miss Weaver*, p. 142). There are no traces of blue pencil markings in the Bodley volume. The discrepancy in the number of corrections between the handwritten list sent to Huebsch on August 16 (fifteen corrections plus removal of one typing error) and the additional entries in pencil in YTW (seventeen corrections plus removal of two obvious typing errors) may have its explanation here. The fifteen corrections in the handwritten list may have been the result of annotating the copy for Pike's; the two additional ones may have been added to YTW in preparation

called for in its 381 entries, Harriet Weaver fails to delete one comma, deletes another without warrant and fails to change a third into a colon. The identification of the volume as the printer's copy for B, immediately rendered likely by the pencilled alterations and additions in Harriet Weaver's hand to the copyright and printing notices on the verso of the title-page, rests mainly on a set of sparse but unmistakable printing-house markings. For long stretches of the book, there are little pencilled crosses at the bottom of verso pages, or the top of recto pages, at regular intervals of four pages. Sometimes these divide off a syllable or a word or two at the end of a page or the beginning of the next, and the first word or syllable of a recto page is occasionally pencilled in at the bottom of the preceding verso page. B is of course virtually a page-for-page reprint of H, despite its smaller typeface. But inevitably the text on any given page in B does not always coincide with the word or syllable of its counterpart in H. Yet in every case where the text is out by a syllable or a word or two on pages marked in HB as described, the new page beginnings correspond exactly to the marked divisions. Typical compositorial notes like 'Line short' or 'Two short', sometimes initialled by the person who wrote them, finally clinch the matter: the Bodley volume is the printer's copy for B, with the majority of its compositorial stints clearly marked. A further analysis, not yet undertaken, would probably make it possible to distinguish from the markings, from the typographical layout of the pages, and presumably from the treatment of punctuation and the like in the text itself, between two or more compositors.[43]

The observance of Harriet Weaver's annotations by the printers of B was very faithful. In less than half a dozen instances were her directions misunderstood and the corrections not made according to intention.

---

of the printer's copy for Johnson's of Southport. As Harriet Weaver then spotted another six misprints and hyphenation errors in the course of annotating HB which were never entered in YTW, it must remain an open question—until all relevant documents can be reexamined in preparation of a critical edition—whether it is merely a happy coincidence that YW and YTW concur in the number of seventeen corrections in excess of Joyce's authentic 365.

43 To complete the record, a set of pencilled notations on the back flyleaf (verso) should be observed: '26-41 234-246 280-292 for Sesame book 1942'. If taken as page references, '26-41' comprises the greater part of the Christmas dinner scene in Chapter I; '234-246' the conversation between Stephen, Davin and Lynch until just before the esthetic theory section in Chapter V; and '280-292' the final conversation with Cranly. I have not investigated the relevance of these jottings.

Only one marked correction was not carried out: p. 87.9 in B still reads 'reverie' (for: 'revery') in perpetuation of a typescript spelling which had passed via *Egoist* to H.[44] Thus all YTW corrections, but for these exceptions, duly entered the text of B. In addition, another six misprints and hyphenation errors, which had eluded both Joyce and Harriet Weaver before, were marked by her and corrected by the printers. Beyond that, Harriet Weaver took it upon her own authority to remove wholesale, from about the middle of Chapter III onwards, all intermediary and final dashes in direct speech, and to introduce alternative punctuation consequent upon their removal where necessary. This altered the entire system of Joyce's designation and punctuation of dialogue in so far as it had survived in print. In the manuscript, there are dashes in place of the 'perverted commas' which Joyce so abhorred not only at the beginning of every direct speech but also before and after interruptions (where in print one is accustomed to commas and inverted commas: i.e.—said Stephen—rather than . . . .,' said Stephen, '. . .), and at the end, where the dash in fact frequently stands without a further mark of punctuation. In the first printed text of *A Portrait* in *The Egoist*, this system of punctuation, so conspicuously idiosyncratic, has disappeared from the first two chapters and the first one and a half instalments of the third, and been replaced by initial dashes followed by regularised punctuation (though of course not inverted commas) in the middle and at the end of direct speeches. In these positions, Joyce's dashes—though not his dashes as combining the functions of all punctuation: especially at the ends of speeches periods have mostly been placed before dashes in print—break through only towards the end of the second instalment of Chapter III of 15 August 1914, which was the fourth instalment printed by Partridge & Cooper. These printers had set inverted commas in *A Portrait* (as elsewhere) when they began to print *The Egoist* on 1 July 1914. In their second instalment of 15 July, which was the end of Chapter II, and their

---

44 The corresponding section of the typescript which served as printer's copy for *The Egoist* happens to survive. Curiously, the typist first spelled 'revery' according to the manuscript, but the final 'y' was altered in ink to 'ie' by an undeterminable agent. Joyce himself did sporadically enter corrections in ink in the typescript, but the 'ie' does not appear to be in his hand. The spelling 'reverie' occurs several times in *The Egoist*. It was successfully eradicated by Joyce himself in all instances but the present one. It is highly probable that the failure to observe his Y instruction at B: 87.9 was spotted and amended by him when he proofread J.

third, the beginning of Chapter III, they adopted the styling observable uniformly before in the initial ten instalments printed by Johnson & Co. of Southport. They carried it over even into three full pages of their fourth instalment, the manuscript text of which contains the final dash in three individual instances. With two printing houses conforming to the same pattern of variation in such accidentals, one might be inclined to suspect that the eventual change reflects a change in their copy, i.e. that the typescript made from Joyce's manuscript reproduces the manuscript punctuation of dialogue only from the middle of Chapter III onwards. The fragments of typescript of Chapters I and II which survive—and which will be described in greater detail below—show that this was not so. They contain all dashes, plus (on the typist's own authority) additional punctuation at the ends of speeches, and sometimes most illogically even before speech interruptions, in Chapter I, and an exact reproduction of Joyce's own styling in Chapter II, on which a different typist worked. That it was the first and not the second typist's styling which was eventually adopted by both the Partridge & Cooper and the Ballantyne compositors might indicate that the identical typist typed all chapters except Chapter II (a possibility which, on broader evidence, will be discussed later). The move towards a more complete observance in *The Egoist* of the authorial punctuation of dialogue was, as such, quite possibly the result of editorial direction. The full system of dashes (though augmented by regularised final punctuation) manifests itself in print after Harriet Weaver's taking over as editor, albeit with a delay of three and a half instalments. But the delay is explicable: the first editorial concern was to get rid of the inverted commas. Reference to the typography of the Joyce text in the earlier *Egoist* issues would have been appropriate and sufficient to guide Partridge & Cooper's compositors in the treatment of their second instalment. Thereafter, dialogue is virtually absent from long stretches of the text in Chapter III. Harriet Weaver would only have become alerted to the styling of the typescript as more frequent dialogue resumed in the chapter's second half, whereupon she may have given directions that it be fully adopted in print. This of course is but speculative reasoning. Yet the resulting fact is that the punctuation of direct speech is inconsistent not only in the *Egoist* serialisation but also in the first book edition. It is the lack of uniformity in the typographical appearance of the book which Harriet

Weaver remedied in her preparation of the printer's copy for B in 1917. She then standardised the punctuation of dialogue according to the styling of the initial chapters. The overall appearance of the text in print was thereby improved in the 1918 edition, however unauthorised this second editorial intrusion. One hardly feels called upon, therefore, to argue with Harriet Weaver's restyling. It must at present be left open whether even a critical edition should revert to the punctuation of the manuscript, unless, following the manner of the typist of Chapter II, it were to reproduce all clashes strictly without any additional punctuation in the middle and at the end of speeches. Yet such a procedure would run the very real risk of ultimately obscuring rather than clarifying the text. Moreover, it should be observed that the dashes appear very much as a calligraphic feature of the manuscript; as a visual expression of the individuality of the author in his handwriting, it would take careful collaboration of editor and printer to recapture this satisfactorily on the printed page. To fulfil the author's objective of avoiding inverted commas, it would seem sufficient to maintain Harriet Weaver's styling by preserving merely the initial dash in a direct speech. Nevertheless, it is true that the interference of typist(s), editor(s) and compositors has often altered and obscured the original sentence divisions of the dialogue in the novel. These await full restoration in a critical text.

* * *

New data about the textual transmission of *A Portrait of the Artist as a Young Man* have thus emerged from the discussion of three documents from its publishing history. Their influence on editorial decision-making and procedure has been incidentally considered. It now remains to outline a comprehensive editorial hypothesis on the basis of which a critical edition could be envisaged.

The Text from Manuscript to Print

In its authoritative textual witnesses, *A Portrait of the Artist as a Young Man* presents an almost classic case of linear and uncontaminated textual transmission. The fair-copy holograph manuscript (D) is the only primary authoritative text of the novel. From it, five texts of secondary authority descend in linear succession: the typescript

(T), the first printed version in the *Egoist* serialisation (E), and the first (H), the second (B) and the third (J) book editions. None of these secondary stages of transmission of the text relates back to any earlier stage than the one immediately preceding it, nor is the text of D ever conflated or 'contaminated' with any of the secondary stages of authoritative transmission.[45] In establishing a critical text it should therefore be possible in principle to apply W. W. Greg's editorial rule, which postulates that a critical text should reproduce the earliest accessible authoritative text in spellings, punctuation and all other accidentals as well as in the body of its substantive readings, and that variants from the texts of secondary authority be admitted only when they are the result of correction and revision by the author and thus positively supersede the authority of the original reading.[46] The basic text of *A Portrait* is the author's manuscript. Authorial correction and revision intervened at each stage of transmission between D and J, thus conferring secondary authority on each of the textual witnesses T, H, B and J. It is the extent to which their variants are authoritative which must in each case be determined. For the text in H and B, the documents that contain the intervening authorial corrections and revisions survive. These are the errata lists to Chapters III and IV in EC-W, and EC-A, the printer's copy with Joyce's corrections to Chapters I, II and V, for H; and the 'nearly 400' authorial corrections (Y), plus the printer's copy, HB, for B. Thus the authority, or lack of authority, of the variants in the first and second book editions is demonstrable. The proofsheets of the two, or probably three rounds of correction which Joyce read for J have, however, not been preserved.[47] The authority of variant readings in J, therefore, can upon close and discriminating analysis of the total B-J variance be established by inference only. Lastly, and most seriously, the typescript made from D and used as printer's copy for E, that is to say one of the authoritative textual witnesses themselves, is almost entirely

---

45 The texts in the editions of Harry Levin (in *The Portable James Joyce* and elsewhere; cf. Anderson, 'The Text ...', p. 167) and of Anderson/Ellmann (1964) are both conflated texts. The latter in particular, which draws on the manuscript, albeit not in a readily controllable manner, which on analysis proves to be unsystematic, provides—in the true technical sense of the word—a contaminated text.
46 Cf. W. W. Greg, 'The Rationale of Copy-Text', *Studies in Bibliography*, 3 (1950-51), 19-36.
47 See the discussion of the Jonathan Cape edition below.

lost. There is consequently next to no documentary evidence available of possible authorial alterations before the text was typed, nor of typists' omissions or commissions, nor of authorial correction and revision of the typescript; nor can, other than by inference, printing-house changes in E be separated from the total body of D-E variance. Here lies the rub; for in view of the large and weighty discrepancy in the text between D and E, it is only by successful differentiation of all these separate stages of authoritative and non-authoritative interference which, hypothetically, the text passed through from D to E that a true critical text can emerge.

[The external facts with which to fill this hiatus in the textual transmission are these. The fair-copy manuscript—bearing the date 'M.S. 1913' on its holograph title-page—was (it is assumed) written out by Joyce between December 1913 and late October/early November 1914.[48] Chapters I-III were merely copied over from papers (now lost) which had contained them in a virtually final textual stage for several years. But Chapters IV and V were only conceived in their final form during these months and written (though doubtless preliminary material existed for them, too) before they were copied to complete the fair-copy manuscript. The typescript followed the manuscript in hot pursuit, chapter by chapter. As from 2 February 1914 onwards the *Egoist* serialisation, too, was progressing in fortnightly instalments, the inference is that each chapter of the typescript was prepared with considerable haste and received only superficial authorial attention before being dispatched to London. No proof of the *Egoist* text was read by Joyce.][49]

The internal evidence of the D-E variants should confirm or modify the assumed external facts. In the transmission of the text from D to E, the issues most critically at stake are the nature of the typescript,

---

48 It should be noted here that no scholar with bibliographic and paleographic expertise has yet investigated the Dublin holograph. Until it has been fully described and analysed, neither the above dates can be given with full assurance, nor is it possible to say whether or not our present conception of how the text of the novel evolved will need to be modified.

49 Note added 2022: This paragraph is left standing, bracketed, for the record of my lines of argument of 1974. It is however the present essay's one paragraph that only summarizes Anderson's findings. The critical edition of *A Portrait of the Artist as a Young Man* of 1993 eventually lays out my own analysis of the novel's composition process, 1907 to 1914. See below, 'James Joyce's *A Portrait of the Artist as a Young Man*, Critical Edition 1993. INTRODUCTION'.

the evidence (if any) of authorial correction and revision before the typescript left Trieste, and the nature and degree of printing-house interference with the text as it appears in print. Collation reveals most immediately the variation in accidentals. Close to 600 commas have been added in E and superimposed upon a system of commas, colons, semicolons and periods (with only the occasional exclamation or question mark) which has otherwise been left largely intact. As the workmen of three printing-houses in succession set the text for *A Portrait*, it can be asserted that, on the whole, the additional commas were put in by them. The three printers did very nearly equal thirds of the novel: of the total of 123.5 printed *Egoist* columns, Johnson & Co. set 41.5, Partridge & Cooper 41.5, and Ballantyne, Hanson & Co. 40.5 columns (approximately). But the distribution of added commas is such that Johnson & Co. in ten instalments added no more than sixty, or about three commas in each two columns of print, while Partridge & Cooper in eight instalments added 277 (seven per column), and Ballantyne & Hanson in seven instalments 229 commas (fewer than six per column).[50] There is, moreover, a considerable fluctuation in numbers from one instalment to the next—Partridge & Cooper added sixty-six commas on 1 July 1914, their first instalment, and only eight a fortnight later—and even from page to page and column to column. This quite clearly reflects the punctuation habits of different workmen. Moreover, the scarcity of added commas in the Johnson & Co. section of the text— itself undoubtedly the work of more than one compositor—reinforces the conclusion that the later inundation of the *Egoist* text with commas was a printing-house restyling of the text. It strongly suggests that the typescript did not essentially alter the manuscript punctuation.

The *Egoist* departure from the manuscript in other accidentals, such as capitalization, and hyphenation or two-word division of compounds, is far more restrained.[51] There is throughout the sections of the three printers a fairly even sprinkling of added hyphenations or

---

50 The figures for the *Egoist* variants here and below derive from double collation (D-E, D-J) which, though done with all possible care, has not been counter-checked. They should therefore be taken as approximations to indicate relations.

51 To assert that in E 'printinghouse stylesheets triumphed almost completely over the copy in punctuation, hyphening, capitalization, and other accidentals' (Anderson, 'The Text ...', p. 185) is much too sweeping a statement. As regards hyphenation and capitalization, it is not true.

compound divisions, and of added capitals. A distinction of typescript and printing-house characteristics does not clearly manifest itself. On the contrary, it seems likely that a good number of compounds were hyphenated in E because they happened to be divided from one line to the next in T, as a good number of others are evidently hyphenated in print because they were demonstrably so divided in D and thus, by inference, entered the text of T with hyphens. Other hyphenations, such as 'good-bye', or the inevitable printed forms 'to-day', 'to-morrow', etc., were undoubtedly made according to a style sheet by the printing-house compositors, and sometimes possibly by a typist before them. Typists' and compositors' habits likewise would seem to be the cause of added capitalization, such as the almost invariable spellings Protestant, Jesuit, Jews, Church, Mass, etc. for Joyce's protestant, jesuit, jews, church, mass. But it is very important to note that the added hyphenations and capitalizations, while of course unauthoritative in the *Egoist* text, are yet not inconsistent with the overall manuscript styling. A large majority of the hyphenated and capitalised nouns and adjectives which occur in the *Egoist* text preserve faithfully the manuscript readings. Hyphenations and two-word divisions of compounds as well as capitalizations were largely eliminated by Joyce himself when he corrected the text for H and B. But his new directions then amount to no less than a systematic restyling of the text in print with respect to these accidentals.

If the sometimes excessively liberal addition of commas in the *Egoist* text is regarded as a special case—and good reason for doing so lies in the fact that Joyce's original punctuation is both unorthodox and extremely light—the general treatment of accidentals in the printed text suggests, even more so than before,[52] that the workmen engaged on E were careful and competent. This creates a certain 'climate of opinion' for the consideration of the substantive variants. There is, for example, an astonishing number of omissions of single words, phrases and even whole sentences from the text in E.[53] Anderson infers, and I believe quite rightly, that in the majority of cases these are typist's errors. In particular, he persuasively demonstrates (pp. 171 ff.) how the style of Joyce's prose

---

52 Cf. Anderson, 'The Text ...', pp. 178 and 185.
53 I count at least 106 instances of such omission, equalling almost exactly one-third of the total of D-E substantive variance: nineteen instances in Chapter I, twenty-eight in II, twenty-two in III, nine in IV and twenty-eight in V.

by its repetitive rhetoric lends itself to the omission of phrases and sentences. His explanation of such errors by means of literary analysis can often be strengthened by taking note of the bibliographical evidence: where words and phrases are repeated in the text, their inscription on the manuscript page is frequently such that a typist's eye-skip in copying appears to be the most likely mechanical reason for the omission of phrases and sentences. By contrast, the omission of single words, which occurs with fair regularity throughout the text, is not strictly the same phenomenon, and not as clearly explicable by literary or bibliographical criteria. It should, however, by way of hypothesis, and as a calculated methodical expedient, be acceptable to group all omissions together and provisionally to designate all omission in the extant text of E as an area of typescript error. If an omission is thus taken to be an error by principle of method, the question becomes negligible whether in actual fact it was a typist's or a compositor's blunder. The important consequence within the editorial hypothesis is that all variants in question are regarded as not authorised and that the original manuscript readings would demand to be restored in their place. If, on the other hand, the general rule in individual instances appears inapplicable, very good reasons must be found for a textual omission in E to be accepted as an authorial cut and thus to be editorially respected.

Implied by such reasoning is the truth of the assumption that the typescript was only superficially read by the author before being dispatched to London. To infer thereupon from the variants themselves, i.e., from the accumulation of omissions in the extant text of E, that Joyce indeed missed a hundred or more such errors in the typescript would be an argument self-defeating in its circularity unless support for it be found outside the circle. This problem, in its turn, is secondary to the basic question—which yet remains to be tested—as to whether the author gave any attention at all to the text of the novel after completing the fair-copy manuscript (and before correcting E for H). The editorial difficulties presented by the missing typescript would of course be considerably diminished if it could be positively demonstrated that he did not. Answers to the open questions must be sought by scrutinizing those groups of D-E variance that have not previously been analysed, and by relating the omissions to them.

The substantive variants in E—317 in all by my count—are omissions, additions, and substituted readings. The additions are invariably confined to single words. They are few in number and make up a large part of what must be considered corrections of the manuscript text, of which there are twenty-nine in all throughout the novel. These corrections, even if they involve an additional word, are mostly obvious enough, as when 'shuffling along . . . in old pair of blue canvas shoes' becomes '. . . in an old pair . . .' (61.20/II, 48),[54] and they can often easily be accounted for as the unaided work of the typist. That the typist had leeway to correct without specific directions by the author—or that a compositor far from Trieste did so by force of circumstance, should an incomplete or erroneous reading, real or fancied, have survived into his copy—is rendered likely when a miscorrection occurs, or a pedantic observance of grammatical congruence in tense or number sounds conspicuous. Except when miscorrection or style-sheet rectification of grammar are obvious, an edited text will of course accept the complete rather than the incomplete readings, regardless of whether or not the authority of each single addition can be ascertained. In Chapter V at least, if not before, such editorial policy can be justified by observing three individual one-word additions, two of them corrections of incomplete manuscript readings and one a genuine textual revision, which cannot reasonably be explained as anything but authorial in origin. No typist or compositor would have known how to complete the sentences: 'What was their languid but the softness of chambering?' (:languid grace; 233.9/V, 2089), or '. . . a stasis called forth, prolonged and at last by what I call the rhythm of beauty.' (:dissolved by; 206.23/V, 1151. 'ended' would perhaps have been an unguided guess), nor can anyone but the author be thought to have changed Cranly's toothpick at 229.33/V, 1972 into a 'rude toothpick', thus weaving once more into the fabric of the text the main characterizing adjective for Cranly. On the strength of these variants alone, authorial attention to the text between D and E must be admitted and taken into account as a real possibility. Automatically, it

---

54 Page/line references are to the 1964 Viking printed text as used in its 1968 reprint in: *James Joyce, A Portrait of the Artist as a Young Man*. Text, Criticism, Notes, ed. by Chester G. Anderson (New York: The Viking Press, 1968). The quotations, however, give the manuscript readings unless otherwise indicated.

becomes a major concern of the editorial hypothesis to define its nature and extent.

Thus, the readings substituted in E for good manuscript readings become the focus of attention: they become suspect of being authorised changes. The total number of altered readings is large, but many of them are immediately recognizable as errors (as for example the numerous substitutions of singular forms for the plural, and *vice versa*), or at the very least as being 'indifferent' and thus not even cumulatively strong enough to prove their origin as authorial: definite articles alternate with indefinite articles, or articles with possessive pronouns; 'those' stands for 'these', alternative prepositions are introduced, or the relative pronouns 'which' and 'who' replace relative 'that' as it is frequently used by Joyce. Yet other variants, again clearly errors, are identifiable as simple misreadings of Joyce's handwriting: 'jacket' becomes 'pocket', 'cracked' becomes 'crooked', 'harsh' becomes 'hoarse', 'like' becomes 'little', 'Kenny' becomes 'Kenory', 'slap' becomes 'step', 'burned' becomes 'turned', 'diseased' becomes 'disclosed', 'hear' becomes 'bear', 'head' becomes 'lead', 'true' becomes 'fine', the nonce-word 'nicens' becomes the none-word 'niceus', and the sentence 'A rim of the young moon cleft the pale waste of sky like the rim of a silver hoop embedded in grey sand' is made to read, 'A rim of the young moon cleft the pale waste of sky line, the rim of a silver hoop embedded in grey sand'. Once all such variants are discounted, only very few readings remain which deserve closer attention. There should be no doubt, for example, that in the list of Stephen's classmates in Chapter II:

> Roderick Greets
> John Lawton
> Anthony MacSwiney
> Simon Mangan (70.25-28/II.373-376)

The names Greets and Mangan were altered to Kickham and Moonan by the author before they thus entered the printed text in E. There is precedence for the authorial change Mangan > Moonan in the manuscript (Anderson, 'The Text ...', p. 170). This renders authorial attention here all the more probable, though it just could mean that an observant typist of his own accord had altered the present reading to bring it into conformity with the others. That this was not the case is suggested by the number of instances in which the name Mangan still stands unaltered in E. Moreover, it would not do to seek different explanations for two changes at the same point in the text: and the alteration of Greets to Kickham can be authorial only. Similarly, the retitling of 'Father' Barrett as 'Mr' Barrett at 30.1/I, 801 in the Christmas dinner scene in Chapter I would seem to be a Joycean correction. Authorial correction and revision further manifests itself where identical changes are spaced out in the text. For example, the 'avenue of limes' which leads up to Clongowes—and it was apparently an avenue of limes—is an 'avenue of chestnuts' throughout the manuscript. In print, the change has been consistently made once each in Chapters I, II and III.[55]

These few variants taken together confirm that Chapters I to III received authorial attention at the typescript stage of transmission. Apart from 'chestnuts' > 'limes' (24.10/I, 601) and 'Father' > 'Mr' (30.1/I.801), however, there is in Chapter I only one more variant—'in the square' > 'there' (43.24/I, 1283)—for which, under the guidelines of the hypothesis here developed, authority can be claimed with some confidence. The remainder of the substituted readings in this chapter are either obviously erroneous, or misreadings of Joyce's handwriting, or else too indifferent in character to be made out as authorial in origin. The situation in Chapter II is similar. To Greets > Kickham, Mangan > Moonan, and 'chestnuts' > 'limes' (93.11/II, 1167), it would again seem safe to add only one or perhaps two more variants: 'turning back in irresoluteness' > ' turning in irresolution' (83.31/II, 839-840); and 'watching her as he undid her gown' > 'watching her as she undid her gown' (100.35/II, 1433-1434).[56] There is admittedly a group of three further variants which, occurring within a few pages of each other, might suggest an intermittently closer authorial attention to the

---

55   The revision is a fascinating instance of a redoubled recall of fact. I put on record here, in 2022, that when this essay in 1973 had already gone to press, a visit to Clongowes revealed to me the double lining of the avenue: one line of chestnuts, one of limes.

56   This is a fascinating variant. Stephen also notes 'the proud conscious movement of her perfumed head' which accompanies the undoing of the gown. Moreover, the next paragraph in the text makes it clear that Stephen and the young woman stand apart in her room: '. . . she came over to him and embraced him. . .' 'Watching her as he undid her gown', therefore, which very clearly is the manuscript reading, appears to be a genuine Freudian slip of the author. It need not, of course, have been corrected by him. A typist or compositor would have been capable of spotting the inconsistency.

typescript: 'arching their arms above their heads' > 'circling their arms above their heads' (74.6/II, 497), 'the old restless moodiness had again filled his heart' > '... had again filled his breast' (77.20/II, 618), and 'the patchwork of the footpath' > 'the patchwork of the pathway' (79.1/II, 670). However, careful scrutiny of the original readings as they look in Joyce's handwriting makes it virtually certain that 'circling' and 'breast' are really misreadings of 'arching' and 'heart'. The apparent cluster is thus reduced to a single variant. By noting further that 'footpath' in several other instances throughout the novel is Joyce's unvaried term for 'pavement', one is led to reject 'pathway' as a typist's or compositor's unauthorised substitution.

Thus, where variants in E are substituted for good manuscript readings, Chapter I appears to contain but three, and Chapter II a maximum of five authorial corrections. Of this total of eight, six (or five) show concern with factual accuracy ('Mr' Barrett, and 'limes' [twice]) or internal consistency of the text (Kickham, Moonan, 'limes' again, and 'he' > 'she', if this was an authorial correction). The two others seem concerned with a greater appropriateness ('there' as substituted for 'in the square') or fluency ('turning in irresolution') of expression. Under the criteria by which these eight variants were separated from a host of erroneous or indifferent readings, no variants at all—except the third instance of 'chestnuts' > 'limes' (108.34/III, 242) early in Chapter III—can be made out with assurance in Chapters III and IV. It is only in Chapter V that the correcting and revising hand of the author is again unmistakably present. The corrections here appear to have been made as reticently, or superficially, as in the first two chapters, but, where they occur, to have been made for similar reasons. Owing to the length of the chapter, their total number is slightly higher than before. Yet six of them, that is two-thirds of a total of nine, are clustered within twelve pages of the printed text. 'His toothpick' > 'his rude toothpick' (229.33), which represents both a stylistic improvement and a concern for greater precision, has already been referred to. Precision and factual accuracy is also the aim of 'Drumcondra' > 'Lower Drumcondra' (188.32/V, 519), 'unesthetic emotions' > 'not aesthetic emotions' (206.10/V, 1138) and 'northward' > 'southward' (238.23/V, 2278), while improvement of style and expression predominantly motivate the changes 'benevolent mirth' > 'benevolent malice' (210.27/V, 1299), 'ringless' > 'toneless'

(227.22/V, 1890),⁵⁷ 'old swans' > 'a game of swans' (228.20/V, 1923), and 'brief hiss' > 'soft hiss' (232.32/V, 2076). To this latter variant, the ninth and last in the list: 'brief hiss' > 'swift hiss' (226.27/V, 1860) is related, which however would seem to require emendation. At 232.27/V, 2071: '... and a soft hiss fell again from a window above', 'soft' is the original manuscript reading, while at lines 226.27/V, 1860 and 232.32/V, 2076 the manuscript still has 'brief hiss'. In revision, 232.32/V, 2076 follows 232.27/V, 2071 to read 'soft hiss'. But surely it is the sentence at 226.27/V, 1860, which in the manuscript reads 'A sudden brief hiss fell from the windows above him...' that both occurrences on p. 232/V, 2071, 2076 are meant to recall. The revision was presumably retroactive, the author going back to alter 'brief hiss' on p. 226/V, 1860 after having unified the readings on p. 232/V, 2071, 2076 to 'soft hiss'. I take it that 'swift hiss' at 226.27/V, 1860 is an error of the E compositor, who misread 'soft' as it was written by hand in the typescript, and would therefore emend to 'soft hiss' on the strength of the parallel revision at 232.32/V, 2076.

Thus, in the field of substitute readings, where initially all variants were suspected of being authorial in origin, the number of authoritative changes in the *Egoist* text has been narrowed down to a total of eighteen. All other variant readings substituted in E for good manuscript readings, that is something like half of the 317 D-E substantive variants, must consequently be classed as unauthoritative. This large group of variants, then, seems in view of a projected editorial hypothesis to be practically identical in nature with that of the omissions, and by our comprehensive analysis it is thereby suggested that all substantive variants in E, with the exception of a small number of narrowly definable and identifiable readings, are unauthorised. This is a result attractive in its consistency and, though essentially hypothetical, it gains in probability from the three-pronged approach to the evidence as divided into three distinct groups of variants. It should be recalled at this stage, however, that the entire large group of the omissions was approached above with the initial expectation of a total lack of authorial interference and has so far been only provisionally designated as an area of exclusively unauthorised variation. Before final conclusions are

---

57 This revision, to avoid a quibble on Dixon's signet ring, is comparable to the E->H authorial change of 'trunk' > 'body' at 201.15/V, 967 to avoid a pun on the preceding 'whinny of an elephant'.

asserted, the omissions should therefore be briefly surveyed once more with regard to the fact that a certain degree of authorial attention to the text has meanwhile been ascertained. The authorial correction of the text was, it is true, evidently reticent and probably superficial, and to have established it as a fact cannot therefore in principle change our conception of the group of the omissions taken as a whole. Critically assessed in aggregate, they indicate that they were largely typist's errors which went by unnoticed in the author's reading of the typescript. In the three chapters in particular that contain more than one authorial variant each, there is not a single omission which, by its nature, suggests that it, too, might be authorial in origin. It is only in the latter half of Chapter III that doubts arise whether all omissions observed should be blamed on the typist (or compositor). At the rhetorical climax of the last of the hell sermons there is a passage which in the printed text has three separate omissions in brief succession:

> O what a dreadful punishment! An eternity of endless agony, of endless bodily and spiritual torment, without one ray of hope, without one moment of cessation, of agony [limitless in extent,] limitless in intensity, of torment [infinitely lasting,] infinitely varied, of torture that sustains eternally that which it eternally devours, of anguish that everlastingly preys upon the spirit while it racks the flesh, an eternity, every instant of which is itself [an eternity, and that eternity] an eternity of woe. Such is the terrible punishment decreed for those who die in mortal sin by an almighty and a just God. (133.10-20/III, 1106-1115)

According to the rules established by Anderson for the treatment of omitted phrases,[58] which have in principle been accepted above, there is no alternative to regarding these omissions as three errors by the typist. But thus to regard them means to accept that he nodded three times separately in rapid succession, and yet in a curiously systematic way. On literary grounds, on the other hand—and therefore by reasoning that lies outside the area of textual analysis based on the transmitting documents—it is tempting to see the author at work here, pruning an excess of repetitive rhetoric for the sake of stylistic improvement, and a heightened rather than a lessened impact of the words. Under this aspect, the three separate errors of the typist would appear transformed

---

58 Anderson, 'The Text ...', p. 177, singles out this passage as one of his examples.

into a single tripartite authorial cut. Were this to prove the only example in the text where omission became suspected of being authorial in origin, an editorial decision to respect it as such would be very hard indeed to defend, however much one's instinctive literary feeling were averse to restoring the full manuscript wording. But, very tentatively, something like a case can be made out for a repeated incidence of authorial cuts in the second half of Chapter III, whereby these would become identifiable and separable as a group from the other omissions, and thus editorially acceptable as readings in the variant form of the printed text. Three such omissions occur a few pages after the passage quoted which could also conceivably be due to a desire to reduce a repetitiveness of expression (as indicated):

> Was that then he or an inhuman thing moved by a lower [soul than his] soul? His soul sickened at the thought. . . . (140.1-2/III, 1342-1343).

> Confess! He had to confess every sin. How could he utter in words to the priest what he had done? Must, must. Or how could he explain without dying of shame? Or how could he have done such things without shame? A [madman, a loathsome] madman! Confess! O he would indeed to be free and sinless again! Perhaps the priest would know. O dear God! (140.14-20/III, 1354-1359).

> He could still escape from the shame. [O what shame! His face was burning with shame.] Had it been any terrible crime but that one sin! Had it been murder! Little fiery flakes fell and touched him at all points, shameful thoughts, shameful words, shameful acts. Shame covered him wholly like fine glowing ashes falling continually. (142.24-30/III, 1434-1440).

As it happens, it is in close vicinity to these passages that a later intentional deletion is recorded. The first of the errata on EC-W, fol. 2, is 'delete "of herrings"' and refers to 'Frowsy girls sat along the curbstones before their baskets [of herrings]' (140.26/III, 1365). This may be pure coincidence, and it proves no more than that Joyce was in fact capable of making a cut in *A Portrait*—an attitude of authorial self-criticism not readily evident otherwise in this text. This deletion has no intrinsic similarity to the four examples of omission in E here considered, and it can hardly be taken to reinforce an assumption that they are of authorial origin. If it were true that they are all genuine cuts, then this would indicate that the latter half of Chapter III, portraying as it does Stephen's intensely painful self-torture, gave particular pains in the writing and was textually fluid for longer than any other section of the novel. However, in the absence of the Chapter III typescript, any argument of textual or of literary criticism in relation to the variant passages must remain highly speculative.

On the whole, then, the variant readings in E caused by the omission of words, phrases and sentences from the manuscript text can now confidently be declared unauthoritative, as can the large majority of those variants in E that are substitutes for good manuscript readings. Conversely: on the basis of the preceding analysis, we consider, out of a total of 317 substantive variants between D and E, only eighteen substitute readings, most of twenty-nine corrections of incomplete or obviously erroneous manuscript readings, and possibly six omissions (occurring in four passages in the second half of Chapter III) as authorised. With respect to the body of D-E variance, provisional rules for establishing a critical text of *A Portrait of the Artist as a Young Man* may be set out as follows:

Of the variants in E,

1. *Admit* all corrections of incomplete and erroneous D readings that are not obviously either miscorrections or style-sheet rectifications of grammar and syntax;
2. *admit* eighteen authorial corrections and revisions;
3. *do not admit* other substitutes for good D readings, whether or not they seem individually possible as variants;
4. *do not admit* readings in E that are the result of omission of single words, phrases, or sentences of the D text (with the possible exception of six such variants in the second half of Chapter III);
5. *do not admit* the E variation in accidentals.[59]

---

59 These are provisional rules, as the facts and inferences concerning the subsequent rounds of authorial correction by which they must be augmented and modified have not yet been discussed. Yet they are also the central rules for establishing a critical text, as the results of a comprehensive analysis of the body of D-E variance must form the basis for any editorial hypothesis and procedure. It may be appropriate therefore in their light to indicate statistically whether 'the definitive text, corrected from the Dublin holograph . . . published in 1964 by The Viking Press, Inc.' has a claim to being definitive. Of the total of substantive variants, that is 317 by our

The Typescript

The hypothesis developed in the preceding pages for the total of the substantive D-E variance, a hypothesis which in turn must serve as the basis for a comprehensive theory of the textual transmission capable of governing editorial decision in establishing a critical text of *A Portrait of the Artist as a Young Man*, has, it is true, a narrow foundation. It depends on an evaluation of those variant readings in E which are substitutes for good manuscript readings; and only if, by this evaluation, it is ultimately correct to accept no more than eighteen such variants as authoritative, is it valid editorially to reject the other *Egoist* readings which belong to this group and, furthermore, to conclude by analogy that a great majority, if not all, of the *Egoist* variants resulting from the omission of manuscript readings are also unauthoritative. It is most fortunate, therefore, that—contrary to previous assumptions—there is no need to trust exclusively in the soundness of a logical construct. Rather, it has in fact been possible to trace large fragments of Chapters I and II of the Trieste typescript against which our hypothetical assumptions can be tested.

The typewritten fragments of the text of *A Portrait* come from the possession of Dora Marsden, founder of *The Egoist*, and still its editor when the first ten instalments of Joyce's novel were published. They contain the text for most of these ten instalments. Of sixty-eight numbered typewritten pages of Chapter I, only pages 1-15, that is the

---

count, twenty-nine (by our count) are corrections in E of manuscript error. This leaves 288 instances on which editorial decision must operate. Giving the editors the benefit of the doubt in the case of the possible six authorial cuts in Chapter III, we find that in 158 out of the 288 instances the editorial decision follows the rules here postulated, while in 130 instances it goes against them. The ratio of (what we would regard as) correct to incorrect is thus 55%:45%. Taking into account that several 'correct' decisions were in fact anticipated by the author in the course of his repeated subsequent corrections of the text, this is tantamount to a flat 50:50 ratio of hit and miss. Corresponding figures for the treatment of accidentals—which by reason of Joyce's fairly systematic later restyling of hyphenations and capitalizations could in any case not be based on the D-E variation—have not been worked out. Nor has the treatment in the Viking text of substantive variance in the later editions (H, B, J) been systematically analysed. The impression that it, too, is somewhat haphazard—and particularly so with regard to the J variants on which hypothetical inference must again operate—stems from cursory observation only. It would seem that these facts and conditions are due to the lack of a comprehensive and logically consistent hypothesis of the transmission of the text of *A Portrait* from the Dublin holograph (1913/14) to the third book edition (Jonathan Cape, 1924). This lack prevents the 1964 Viking edition from fulfilling the standards of a definitive text.

entire first instalment plus three sentences of the second, and the single pages 53 and 59 are missing. Of Chapter II, for which the page numbering starts afresh, pages 1-9 and 17-27, plus six lines of p. 28, are extant, which correspond to the first, the third and part of the fourth *Egoist* instalments of that chapter. The last fragment breaks off in the middle of the last *Egoist* instalment of the novel published under Dora Marsden's editorship. There are seventy-one pages and six lines of typescript in all. Upon collation against both D and E, a great number of readings, variant and invariant, in the text of these typewritten pages immediately suggest that they are indeed part of the Trieste typescript. Yet wherever there is no significant variation between the text in the typescript and in E, the process of transmission could, of course, be thought of as reversed. Order and direction of transmission are determined by those readings or typographical characteristics only which are invariant between D and the pages of the typescript, but variant between these and E. It is thus above all the reproduction in full of Joyce's manuscript system of dashes in dialogue in the typewritten pages, as against the absence of intermediate and final dashes in all dialogue in Chapters I and II in E,[60] which places the text of these pages firmly between that in D and in E and identifies the fragments as part of the Trieste typescript (T). Consequently, such instances of variation between D and T as the apparent, or indeed obvious, misreadings of Joyce's handwriting also attain value as evidence to secure this identification. They demonstrate, furthermore, that T was copied directly from D. That the extant fragments of typescript in their turn were used as printer's copy for E is not merely rendered likely by the circumstances of their preservation, but is also demonstrable from errors of a typographical nature in the typescript,[61] and by a large number of marks (crosses, queries, and the like) which would seem to have been added in the printing house.[62]

---

60   See above, pp. 44-46.
61   In particular, the typewriter used seems to have had no key for underlining. The underlinings in T which copy underlinings in D to indicate italics in print were done by hand and are missing in all those places in T where E fails to italicize.
62   This discussion is based on xerox copies of the extant pages which were kindly put at my disposal by Mrs Elaine Bate who now owns the originals, and to whom I am grateful for permission to use the copies for the purposes of this article. Since the article went to press, I have had the opportunity of inspecting the fragments themselves. They are the ribbon-copy typescript originals, on white typewriting paper 22.5 x 28.4 cm., uniformly watermarked CROXLEY MANIFEST BANK

When so much has been established, both the D-T and the T-E variance which occurs within the stretches of text preserved can be more closely analysed. In accidentals, D-T and T-E variation is clearly distinguishable. In both chapters, additional commas are very rarely indeed introduced in T. The Chapter I pages add four commas, the Chapter II pages add three. The typical typescript error in punctuation is rather one of omission of commas. Thirteen manuscript commas are missing in Chapter I, of which some have been restored in print and some not, and nine commas are missing in Chapter II, only one of which has been restored in E. The adding of commas to the printed text, although comparatively restrained in Chapters I and II, is thus clearly a compositorial commission. The increase in capitalizations, on the other hand, is pretty evenly distributed between T and E, while the printers again are responsible for the greater part, though not all, of the additional hyphenation of compounds in E. By contrast, it is the rare substantive variant that originates in E. What earlier collation established as D-E variance in substantives is in fact seen to be variation between D and T. This is as it should be according to the basic assumptions of our hypothesis for the transmission from D to E of the entire novel, and it is gratifying to find it confirmed for the sections of T preserved. A grouping of the D-E substantive variants, undertaken hypothetically before for the sake of a coherent textual theory, can now be based on firmer evidence. Moreover, to determine the exact source and point of origin of a variant becomes a practical necessity for defining the nature and degree of authority of the recovered intermediary textual witness.

| LONDON under a rampant lion, facing left, which holds in its front paws a standard, unfolding over its head and bearing the inscription LION BRAND. The ribbon ink, originally of a blackish colour, has been affected by damp and has largely turned purple. Each of the chapters separately was once stapled together very close to the left paper edge. Every sheet shows holes in the upper right-hand corner which appear to be the marks of the compositor's copy-holder. The rust-marks of paper clips indicate that the fragmentation of the typescript is of an early date, in all probability resulting from the manuscript's handling in the printing house. The authorial corrections can without much difficulty be isolated from the several stages of annotation in evidence. Page II.17, which is the first leaf of the last of the extant fragments, bears the inscription in watery-blue ink 'Portrait of The Artist as a young Man | by | James Joyce'. The handwriting is Ezra Pound's. The Dublin holograph, which I have also meanwhile been able to inspect, shows a series of pencil marks throughout Chapter I which in ten instances divide off page-beginnings of the typescript, and in two instances specify an (authorial?) re-paragraphing of the text, carried out in the typescript.

The omission from the typed text of words, phrases and sentences presents once again the crucial textual problem. D does not indicate any omissions. On the evidence of the typescript, it is no more likely that they represent authorial, and thus authoritative, cuts at a lost stage of transmission between D and T. As T was demonstrably typed from D, such a lost stage could in any case not be thought of as yet another full transcript of the text intervening between D and T. At the most, the possibility of authorial direction in the form of oral or written instructions to the typist might be considered if the omissions were hypothetically posited as authorial cuts. But not a single variant outside the group of the omissions would help to strengthen any speculatively posited authorial attention to the text between D and T. Even the simple corrections evident in T of incomplete or obviously erroneous manuscript readings could have been made by a typist on his own initiative; it need not be assumed that the author was consulted for them. The correction of one incomplete manuscript reading, indeed, which was not caught by the typist, is entered in T in the author's hand ('wondering' [66.23/II, 228]), thus allowing the inference that the others of its kind were done by the typist and consequently, on the evidence of this group of variants, no authorial correction intervened between D and T.[63] All further circumstantial evidence considered above, moreover, which suggests that the variants due to omission of manuscript readings were errors in typing is in no way invalidated by any new evidence from the typescript. The responsibility for the considerable degree of deterioration from manuscript to print of the text of *A Portrait* is still largely on a typist. He had to take all blame *in absentia* before. Now the extent of his inattention to the text can be more firmly assessed. With respect to omissions, the typewritten pages reveal that errors of omission were corrected, the corrections always being typed in, in only a few instances when they were caught in the course of the typing. A systematic reading by the typist of the finished typescript against copy seems not to have taken place. Beyond that, there is only one instance in the entire seventy-one

---

63 If it could be assumed that the conditions under which the typescript came about remained fairly constant throughout the five chapters, one would expect to find those corrections of incomplete manuscript readings in Chapter V which appear to be clearly authorial similarly to have been written into the typescript. This would agree with the evidence from authorial correction/revision and definitely indicate one round of authorial attention to Chapter V only.

pages and six lines of typescript preserved where the author himself caught a typist's omission and corrected it. It is this instance alone which must take all burden of proof,[64] in so far as proof can be supplied by the typescript, that the omission of manuscript matter in print was due to typescript error and does not represent intentional authorial cuts. The manuscript sentence: 'Perhaps that was why they were in the square because it was a place where some fellows wrote things for cod' (43.24) is rendered in the typescript as: 'Perhaps that was why they were because it was a place. . . .'. The author adds 'there' above the typewritten line, indicating the place of insertion by a caret between 'were' and 'because'. Clearly, 'in the square' are words erroneously omitted by the typist. The error was caught by the author (as so many of its kind were not) and corrected without collation against the manuscript.[65]

The typescript thus bears marks which unmistakably show that it was read by James Joyce himself, though they indicate at the same time that his reading, too, did not take the form of a thorough collation against the manuscript. This goes some way towards explaining why, as errors, the many omissions of manuscript readings should have been so

---

64 Proof, that is, as distinct from 'first-degree' inference from facts such as the inscription of the words on the manuscript pages which were observed earlier, to render plausible the explanation that the omissions were typist's errors; or 'second-degree' inference to the same effect, taking the form of conclusions drawn by analogy from an analysis of a different group of variants which were inferentially also declared to be non-authorial.

65 As it happens, 'there' seems on literary grounds to be a definite improvement over 'in the square', referring as it does to both outdoor and indoor locations in that square. The evidence of T creates a paradoxical situation, even an editor's dilemma. 'there', it is true, is confirmed to be authorial, as was hypothetically assumed before the T fragments came to light. At the same time, it is revealed not as a revision undertaken in view of the original reading, but as a spontaneous correction of a typist's error. As an instance of alternative phrasing it was never intended to replace, but rather to restore the reading which had accidentally got lost. What on first sight appears to be an authorial second thought is really an attempt to recover the wording of a first thought. Editorially this means that the original reading 'in the square' should be given preference over the authorial correction 'there', contrary to the general rule by which authorial corrections should replace original readings in a critical text, and despite the subjective judgement that 'there' be preferable to 'in the square' in its context. The editorial decision to adhere to textual logic over literary judgement is inevitable because the situation is not unique in the course of the transmission of *A Portrait*: when reading the E text for H, and H for B, Joyce belatedly spotted several further typescript errors of omission which he corrected without recourse to his manuscript. The results of his correction always differ from the original readings, though never, except in the present case, for the better.

consistently overlooked. Moreover, few and far between as are the marks which signalize Joyce's presence, they are also proof that his reading (as hypothetically assumed) was perfunctory only, and probably hasty. In the extant fragments of typescript there are only three instances in all of substantive authorial correction. In addition to the insertion of the omitted 'wondering', and of 'there' for the omitted 'in the square', the third authorial correction is 'Father' > 'Mr' (30.1). The part of our hypothesis that posited a scarcity of authorial corrections among the *Egoist* readings that replace good manuscript readings would thus also seem to be confirmed by the typescript. As it has already been shown that the text appears to have been given no authorial attention between D and T, it follows that all variants of this kind, too, were introduced by a typist and are non-authoritative, and that authority belongs only to those variant readings that are seen to have been entered in the author's hand in T. On the narrow basis provided by the extant fragments of typescript, this is an argument mainly by negatives. None of the passages of text in Chapter II where authorial correction was assumed are preserved in T, so that it cannot be positively shown that those variants alone are authorial in origin which were hypothetically singled out as such, although it is apparent from as much text as is extant that no other variants replacing good manuscript readings are authorial of which this was not expected. The same is true for the much longer fragment of Chapter I. Of the three variants in this chapter hypothetically assumed to have been authorial, the assumption has been confirmed without reservation for one (Father > 'Mr'), and with some modification, not touching on the fact of its authorial origin, for a second ('in the square' > 'there'). The third member of the group, however, is still invariant in T: the manuscript 'avenue of chestnuts' leading up to Clongowes is still an 'avenue of chestnuts'. The reading must have been altered between T and E.

If it is to be maintained that 'limes' for 'chestnuts' is an authorised variant, an influx of authority in some form must be assumed at a stage of transmission after the typescript was authorially corrected to the extent observable in its extant fragments, and before the printed *Egoist* text as typeset and proofread was published. This assumption is strengthened by the observation that 'limes' for 'chestnuts' in Chapter I is not an isolated instance of significant T-E variation. (There is no corresponding variation in the Chapter II fragments.) For the extant text of Chapter I, there is a total of nine substantive T-E variants. In two instances, T copies the manuscript readings correctly and there are marks of the printer's pen or pencil set against them in T, which suggest that the subsequent E variants originated in the printing house and are therefore unauthorised. In the remaining seven instances, on the other hand, T also varies from D and it is the original manuscript reading which has in each case been restored in E.[66] In three of these seven cases, the T variant is an error to which the manuscript reading is the obvious alternative; a compositor or printing house proofreader could easily have made the correction. Yet, in the remaining four cases, the correction of the T error can have been made only from a knowledge of the manuscript reading as restored. There are thus five instances of substantive T-E variation—interestingly enough confined to the second and third *Egoist* instalments—which make it an inevitable conclusion that the text of Chapter I, or part of it, was referred to an authority in the course of transmission between extant T (as authorially corrected) and E. In other words, the *Egoist* text of Chapter I was to some extent authoritatively proofread before publication. One possible explanation of this fact would be that proofsheets of the chapter, or of the two instalments concerned, were sent to Joyce in Trieste. No further indication, it is true, derives from a collation of corrected T and E that this was the case, nor is any documentary evidence available from letters or the like to show that Joyce ever proofread any part of the *Egoist* text. Yet if the typescript used as the *Egoist* printer's copy was the only copy of T which ever existed, the variants observed would allow no other conclusion.[67] If, however, T was typed, say, with a carbon copy, and thus

---

66   These seven instances are: father > uncle > father (26.11/I, 673); he had got > got > he had got (28.8/I, 739); or > [*om.*] > or (32.5/I, 876); Let it > let us > let it (32.8/I, 879); opinions > opinion > opinions (34.14/I, 953); MacManus > MacManns > MacManus (38.27/I, 1107); about it > about > about it (53.1/I, 1616). The variant chestnuts > chestnuts > limes occurs at 24.10/I, 601.

67   If it were assumed that as much text as made up the first three *Egoist* instalments was set up at once by the printers on receiving Chapter I in manuscript, then it would be possible to imagine that proofs of instalments two and three were passed to and fro between England and Trieste in the last days of January/early days of February 1914, while the first *Egoist* instalment of 2 February was already appearing. The change chestnuts > limes is involved, which is identically repeated in Chapters II and III. To ascertain when, where, and by what agent it was introduced into the final *Egoist* text in its first instance would carry implications for the timing of the

existed in duplicate, one might assume that the copy of T which did not serve as printer's copy contained the additional corrections, entered by hand by the author and/or typist, and was used for proofreading by some agent other than the author. No immediate proof is available as to which of these explanations, if any, is correct. Nevertheless, authoritative proofreading assuredly took place between the corrected T and E. It did not broadly affect the text, and the few variants involved assert their authority mainly on their own strength.

The hypothetical concept of the transmission of the entire text of *A Portrait* from D to E, such as it was derived from a comprehensive collation and analysis of these two textual witnesses, is thus in no way invalidated by further investigation of the transmission processes as controllable in those sections of the intermediary textual witness, the typescript, which happen to have been preserved. For most of Chapter I and for substantial fragments of Chapter II, that is for those stretches of text which correspond to the extant pages of typescript, the postulates of our hypothesis have been fully confirmed, and a clear differentiation of the several stages of transmission of the text from manuscript to print is amply indicated. The question that remains to be answered is what further inferences may be drawn for the full text of the novel by extrapolation from the positive facts established about the transmission of the first two chapters. The most important fact not yet considered of the extant fragments of T is that each of the first two chapters was typed by a different typist. This is clear from a difference in spelling habits: in the Chapter II fragments of the typescript, the name of the novel's hero is consistently spelled 'Stephan'; it was probably the author himself who painstakingly changed the spelling back to 'Stephen' in almost every instance. Moreover, Joyce's system of dashes in dialogue is regularly complemented by additional punctuation at the end, and sometimes rather illogically also in the middle, of direct speech in Chapter I, whereas in Chapter II the manuscript punctuation of dialogue is copied faithfully without additional marks of punctuation. Statistics derived from the incidence of substantive variance further corroborate a differentiation of typists. There is an average of 2.3 substantive variants per printed column in the 27.5 columns of *Egoist* text for Chapter I, as against an

---

completion of both the authorial fair copy and of the typescript for all of Chapter II, and the beginning, at least, of Chapter III.

average of 3.9 per column for Chapter II. Leaving out of account the 3+5 variants in Chapters I and II, which are with some certainty authorial corrections and revisions, the figures are 2.2/3.7. These figures comprise substantive variants of typescript and printing-house origin. But since it can be positively established that the printing house compositors were responsible for only a minority of the substantive D-E variants— in the sections of the text preserved in typescript, the compositors in Chapter I introduced nine out of fifty-three, or roughly the sixth part of the substantive variants, and in Chapter II three out of twenty-nine, or approximately only one-tenth—the averages per column of printed text give a fair indication of the relative trustworthiness of the two typists. The Chapter II typist was significantly less faithful to copy in substantives (though more so in accidentals); his spelling 'Stephan' may even suggest that his native tongue was not English.

When statistical calculations are extended over the remaining chapters of the novel, it is remarkable that the higher incidence of variation and error per column of printed text is confined to Chapter II. The corresponding figures for Chapters III-V (with and without authorial variants, and giving the typist the benefit of the doubt by assuming that the omissions in the latter part of Chapter III are authorial) are 2.4:2.1/2.35:2.35/2.1:1.9. They are thus very close to the incidence of variation in Chapter I (2.3:2.2). Noting that when the printed text introduces Joyce's dashes in dialogue from halfway through Chapter III onwards, it does so not in the strictly faithful manner of the typescript of Chapter II, but rather according to the pattern of that of Chapter I, combining the dashes with additional punctuation, one is tentatively led to conclude that the identical typist was employed on Chapters I and III-V, while a second person typed Chapter II only. The general uniformity of the kind of variants introduced and errors committed would appear to support the conclusion. The uniformity, it is true, extends over all five chapters. The statistics alone would, in the absence of any part of the typescript, not be very reliable as an aid to differentiating typists, since their figures indicate a varying amount only, and not a difference in nature of variants and errors. But once a second typist for Chapter II has been identified by several aspects of his extant handiwork, it is of no great consequence that he happened to be prone to the same kind of failings towards the manuscript as was the typist for Chapter I.

What is important is inferentially to conclude that he was responsible for Chapter II only, and thereupon to recognise that both the statistical figures and the uniform nature of the variants—that is, quantitative and qualitative arguments together—go to indicate that Chapters I and III-V in the typescript were the work of one other person, and one only. If, then, this conclusion is correct, it should greatly aid an editor in his evaluation of the total body of the D-E variation in substantives and, in particular, increase the assurance with which he posits that only a small minority of the substantive variants in E are the result of authorial correction and revision of the typescript.

Finally, the facts and inferences can be played with to speculate about the relative timing involved in the completion of the several sections of the manuscript and the typescript. By two typists, Chapters I and II could have been typed simultaneously. At least, it is not impossible to conceive that they were begun at about the same time, or else that their typing overlapped for some days, or a week or two, if it was Joyce's intention to get as large a section of the novel as possible to London as quickly as possible after Ezra Pound's enquiry of 15 December 1913 about printable material. But Chapter II was certainly not completed in typescript when Chapter I was, or they would have been dispatched together. Actually, the same typewriter may have been used for both: there are no typed underlinings in either chapter, and parentheses have regularly been substituted by dashes. Thus it is equally possible that they were typed in short succession after each other. It is not known when Chapter II arrived in London. But Chapter III, although belonging to that part of the novel which is assumed to have existed in final form since 1908, did not get there until 21 July (Ellmann, *James Joyce*, p. 354). Perhaps a second typist was employed on Chapter II because the first one was unavailable between January and July—unless the completion of the typescript for Chapter III was delayed by an interruption in the writing out of the fair-copy manuscript between Chapters II and III, or in the course of Chapter III. Only a physical examination of the manuscript itself might throw light on the circumstances under which Chapter III was copied out and typed.

On 1 August the war broke out, cutting off almost completely all postal connections between England and Austria. On 1 September, Chapter III ran out in *The Egoist*, and on 11 November Joyce managed to dispatch the typescript of Chapters IV and V via Switzerland. Provided that the typescript was completed in the regular order of the chapters, I would tend to infer that the typing of Chapters III to V proceeded at a fairly even pace between July and October, and consequently that there was no last-minute rush in the writing of the novel itself. The hiatus in publication between 1 September and 1 December has been taken to indicate that *The Egoist* caught up with James Joyce too soon (Ellmann, *James Joyce*, p. 354; Anderson, 'The Text ...', pp. 182 ff.). But surely it was primarily due to the outbreak of the war. It was probably an editorial unwillingness to have to break off in the middle of a chapter in case *The Egoist* would not be able to continue publication at all which made the instalments of Chapter III on 1 August, 15 August and 1 September as long as they are. At the rate of publication of the previous chapters, Chapter III would probably have lasted until October. Chapter IV is short, and if it was begun to be typed soon after completion of Chapter III in late July, it ought to have been ready sometime in August and could, but for the war, have been dispatched to London to succeed Chapter III without gap in *The Egoist*. After Chapter IV, there was still Chapter V to be typed, which is by far the longest chapter, constituting almost one-third of the entire novel. It is the state of its text in E which indicates that it was probably completed in typescript under no special time pressure. It has the lowest incidence of substantive variation and error and, moreover, it was given greater authorial attention in the typescript than any of the previous chapters. By contrast, Chapter IV is perhaps the only chapter which appears not to have been authorially corrected at all. Had it, by November, been sitting about in typescript for so long that Joyce in the end forgot to read it? Or was Chapter IV perchance the last of the chapters to be written? It is perhaps significant that it is the only chapter of which several of the fair-copy manuscript pages still show signs of thorough stylistic revision. It is also the chapter which Joyce in July 1915 claims to remember so well as to be able to restore the censored sentences without the aid of his manuscript. A thorough analysis of the manuscript might throw light on the question, and also serve more generally as a test of whether the preceding speculative inferences about the successive completion of manuscript and typescript are tenable.

The Book Editions

Our final discussion of the stages of transmission of *A Portrait of the Artist as a Young Man* from the first printing in *The Egoist* to the 1924 Jonathan Cape edition must be brief. The publishing history has essentially been dealt with by Chester G. Anderson. He has also considered many of the editorially relevant facts and inferences to be derived from it in his discussion of the *Egoist* tearsheets which served as copy for H, and the Y corrections of H for B (see pp. 186 ff., 196 ff.). In so far as a modification of his views proved necessary, this has been given in the course of our analysis of EC-W, YTW and HB. Beyond that, it may suffice to summarize somewhat categorically to what extent the text of the novel as published in H and B may be accepted as authoritative. With respect to substantive readings, all those corrections and revisions represent a final authorial intention editorially to be respected that James Joyce himself carried out in full view of the text as transmitted invariant from the manuscript. There are no problems here in so far as the several rounds of authorial attention to the text are documented in EC-A and Y. The one question not previously considered is whether the Y corrections are the only stage at which the author modified the final text for B. There are at least two substantive variants in B which would seem to warrant a closer investigation. At 215.27/V, 1478, the text in B reads 'When they passed through the passage beside Kildare house . . .', as against '. . . beside the royal Irish academy . . .' in H, and at 96.11/II, 1273 'ineffectualness' (H) is altered to 'ineffectiveness' in B. Neither Y nor HB contain directions for these changes. But as late as 25 November 1917, more than two months after the Southport printers had begun setting up B, Harriet Weaver was writing to Joyce: 'All your corrections have been made, including those you asked for in your last letter'. A careful scrutiny of all H-B variants, still to be undertaken, must endeavour to ascertain which were the additional changes which Joyce had requested; there can be little doubt that at least the first of the two alterations quoted were among them.

With respect to accidentals, the situation created by the author's corrections prior to H and to B is somewhat more complex, and for an editor methodically quite intriguing. When faced with the close to 600 additional commas in the text of the *Egoist* serialisation, Joyce went about restoring the light punctuation of his manuscript with considerable determination. This process continued into Y. His paramount concern doubtless was for the rhythms of his text, the essential qualities of which—'to liberate from the personalised lumps of matter that which is their individuating rhythm'—had been early adumbrated in the very first paragraph of the narrative essay 'A Portrait of the Artist' of 1904. Yet for the flexible rhythms of his novel, its semicolons and its colons, placed and distinguished from each other with great subtlety in the manuscript, are as important as its commas. It is surely an indication of the author's increasing distance in time from a state of complete immersion in the work that, in the course of his corrections, he was much more permissive towards the printers' alterations of the original semicolons and colons. As for the commas, of course, many of those added by printing-house compositors were left standing in the text despite all authorial efforts to eradicate them. There can be no question for an editor but that he reproduce in a critical text as closely as possible the manuscript pattern of punctuation.

However, Joyce's attention to the accidentals of the text as printed in fact took two directions. As has been noted above, his reduction of next to all capitalization, and his preference in print for compounds written together as one word, are tantamount to a restyling of the text with respect to these accidentals. In so far as it can be positively ascertained that they were made by the author, the changes are part of the total authoritative correction and revision of E and H. As such, they invalidate, in part, the pattern of the manuscript inscription which cannot be editorially restored whenever positive authorial direction is given to depart from it. Neither, however, should a critical editor (as opposed perhaps to a publisher's editor) for the sake of a new typographical consistency, and in an attempt to finish what the author began, go beyond his alterations. Quite a number of original capitalizations and word divisions in fact survived Joyce's restyling. These cannot but be left untouched in a critical text, which will thus, in the treatment of accidentals, appear thoroughly inconsistent.[68]

---

68 It is well to emphasize, however, that it appears to have been James Joyce's own concern for a pleasing typographical appearance of his text in print which motivated his changes of such accidentals as capitalizations and word divisions. With this in mind, it may be recalled that the question was raised and left open above whether consistency in the treatment of accidentals should in fact be extended to the adoption of the manuscript system of dashes in direct speech. On pragmatic grounds, I would

Inconsistency of the kind just advocated, however, is really an expression of editorial consistency based on a systematic enquiry into the extent of authority in each substantive textual witness. With regard to Joyce's *Portrait*, such consistency should be firmly extended to the last of the substantive texts, that of the Jonathan Cape edition of 1924 (J). Because its proofsheets have not been preserved, it presents greater textual problems than H and B. What attention James Joyce gave to it can only be inferred from external facts and the internal evidence of textual variants. A complete collation of B and J to ascertain all internal evidence has not yet been undertaken. But more is to be known of the external circumstances pertaining to this last phase of authoritative publication of the novel than has hitherto been realised. As mentioned by Anderson, Joyce reported to Harriet Weaver from Saint-Malo on 16 August 1924 that he had been reading revises for Jonathan Cape for ten days and had dispatched the proofs that day.[69] The company ledgers show that the book went into print on 28 August.[70] Antedating the August letter is a letter to Harriet Weaver of 11 July 1924, also from Saint-Malo. It states: 'Then Mr Cape and his printers gave me trouble. They set the book with perverted commas and I insisted on their removal by the sergeant-at-arms. Then they underlined passages which they thought undesirable. But as you will see from the enclosed: They were and, behold, they are not' (*Letters* III, 99 f.). I take this to mean that Joyce had received two sets of proofs from Jonathan Cape before 11 July. The context of the letter ('I left Paris in the usual whirl of confusion . . .') suggests that the second set arrived in Paris after Joyce's eye operation of 11 June and before he left for Saint-Malo on 6 or 7 July. Probably this was the set which he showed to Sylvia Beach who records her 'amazement at the printer's queries in the margins'.[71] The author's refusal to cut at the request of

---

    defer a decision in this matter until, by way of a practical experiment, a few sample pages were set up in type so as to show whether both printers and readers could within reason be asked to cope in full with the Joycean unorthodoxy of punctuation in dialogue. Robert Scholes in 'Some Observations on the Text of *Dubliners*: "The Dead"', *Studies in Bibliography*, 15 (1962), pp. 200 f., discusses the matter of Joyce's dashes in *Dubliners* and the later works. He has reduced Joyce's usage to initial dashes only in his Viking edition of *Dubliners* (1969).

69 Anderson, 'The Text ...', p. 199, and *Letters* I, 220.
70 Information by courtesy of Messrs. Jonathan Cape, London.
71 See Sylvia Beach, *Shakespeare and Company* (London: Faber & Faber, 1960), p. 56; and cf. Anderson, 'The Text ...', p. 199.

the printers had apparently been accepted by 11 July. 'The enclosed' in the letter to Harriet Weaver would seem to have been some token of consent from Cape to publish the text entire. The question is whether Joyce voiced his refusal by letter only or in a note accompanying the return of the corrected second proofs. Should he indeed not have had the time or energy to read them in the 'whirl of confusion' before his departure from Paris, one might be left to wonder whether the proofs with the printers' underlinings were the revises which were finally not read until August. But Joyce was not only habitually prompt in matters regarding the publishing of his books, but, as the letter of 11 July also records, he was able after the eye operation to see to the proofing of the instalments of the French translation of *Ulysses* due to appear in the review *Commerce* (Ellmann, p. 562). It is therefore likely that the second proofs were returned before he left for Saint-Malo, however superficially they may have been read. If this was so, the revises which he corrected for ten days in August were the third round of proofs read on the Jonathan Cape text.

James Joyce, then, obviously took full advantage of the one and only opportunity he was ever given to see *A Portrait* through the press. Of course, this does not mean that the edition into which he poured his efforts ten years after the completion of the manuscript presents a text to override all previous texts. The inevitable deterioration of the text in ten years of transmission has not been remedied in the edition of 1924. Nor has the text been extensively revised. Even a cursory perusal of J will satisfy an editor that the authorial proofreading was not by any means on the scale of Joyce's reading and revising in proof of the text of *Ulysses*. The comparison with the later work indeed emphasizes the remarkable reticence against change and revision which Joyce showed towards the text of *A Portrait* at every stage of correction. By analogy to the earlier rounds of authorial correction of the text, it should be expected that the proofreading of J which did take place affected both accidentals and substantives. That Joyce paid attention to the accidentals is proved, for example, when J, restoring the manuscript punctuation, reads: 'What is this your name is?' (50.1/I, 1508) against the typescript error perpetuated through B: 'What is this? Your name is?' But it is an exceptional case when it can be proved on internal evidence that the author was responsible for a variant in accidentals. Generally, the lack of documentation prevents editorial acceptance of such variation. The substantive variants in J, on the other hand, are susceptible to evaluation by which it should be possible satisfactorily to identify the authorial corrections and revisions. For example, the manuscript sentence: 'The doomsday was at hand.' (113.11/III, 397) was transmitted invariant through H. B, by the authorial direction of Y, changed to 'Doomsday', yet J reverts to the manuscript wording 'The doomsday' in what must be considered as the author's final decision on this reading, overruling the revision of Y. Similarly, the typescript error 'fellows' at 43.19/I, 1278 was transmitted unnoticed through B. J restores the singular 'fellow' of the manuscript. Finally, a subtle revision at 77.35, 'moment' for 'movement', indicates the author's care in proofreading. With 'movement' the manuscript had picked up 'a movement of impatience' of 77.28/II, 625, which itself is a recollection of 74.28/II, 517 and is only incidentally woven into the description of the situation of tension in the conversation between Heron, Wallis and Stephen (76.27-78.18/II, 588-652). Only in the 1924 re-reading of the text did Joyce himself realise that the proper reference of line 77.35/II, 632 should be to 'a shaft of momentary anger' of 77.12/II, 610.

Three sets of ground rules for establishing a critical text for James Joyce's *A Portrait of the Artist as a Young Man* may thus be established:

1. Base a critical text of *A Portrait of the Artist as a Young Man* on the holograph manuscript (D) of 1913/14.

2. In accidentals, accept the manuscript system of punctuation. Follow authorial directions as contained in EC-A and Y to restyle the manuscript capitalizations and word divisions.

3. In substantives, accept all authorial correction and revision as documented in the fragments of T, in EC-A and Y, or as ascertained by inference from an evaluation of the total body of substantive variance between each of the authoritative editions. Except for the corrections of incomplete manuscript readings in E (in so far as they are not manifest miscorrections or stylesheet rectifications of grammar and syntax), reject all non-authoritative variation in substantives.

With our present knowledge of the publishing history and the nature of the textual transmission of the novel, a critical edition, and maybe even a definitive text, of *A Portrait of the Artist as a Young Man* is not impossible to attain.

The Genesis of *A Portrait of the Artist as a Young Man*

James Joyce wrote and rewrote the novel that was to become *A Portrait of the Artist as a Young Man* in several phases between 1903 and 1914. He began *Stephen Hero* sometime in early 1903 but, after some seven chapters, attempted a reorientation with the narrative essay 'A Portrait of the Artist'. This he submitted to the Dublin literary magazine *Dana* in January 1904.[1] Upon its rejection, he fell back with renewed energy on *Stephen Hero* and carried it forward through twenty-five (of a projected sixty-three) chapters. Broken off in the summer of 1905 in favour of an undivided attention to the writing of the stories for *Dubliners*, *Stephen Hero* remained a fragment.[2] In September 1907, when the plans for a

---

1   The narrative essay appears to have given the origin for the date-line at the end of *A Portrait of the Artist as a Young Man*: 'Dublin 1904/Trieste 1914.' A photo-reprint of 'A Portrait of the Artist' is available in [vol. 7] of *The James Joyce Archive [JJA]*, 63 vols., ed. by Michael Groden, *et al.*, (New York and London: Garland Publishing, Inc., 1978), pp. 70-94. The essay has been reprinted, with many oversights and errors, in *A Portrait of the Artist as a Young Man: Text, Criticism, and Notes*, ed. by Chester G. Anderson and A. Walton Litz (New York: Viking Press, 1968), pp. 257-68. In a more reliable text, it appears in *The Workshop of Daedalus: James Joyce and the Raw Materials for* A Portrait of The Artist as a Young Man, ed. by Robert Scholes and Richard M. Kain (Evanston: Northwestern University Press, 1965), pp. 60-68.

2   From freshly assessed evidence, I argue in the 'Introduction', pp. 1-2, to James Joyce, *A Portrait of the Artist as a Young Man*, ed. by Hans Walter Gabler with Walter Hettche (New York and London: Garland Publishing, Inc., 1993), that Joyce indeed began his autobiographical novel sometime in the first half of 1903, that is, almost a year earlier than has hitherto been assumed. That he probably wrote just the first seven of the projected nine times seven (=sixty-three) chapters before setting down the narrative essay in January 1904 is indicated by the fact that the notes on the blank leaves of the 'Portrait of the Artist' copy-book concern *Stephen Hero* from Chapter VIII onwards. If taken with these modifications, the 'Appendix' to Hans Walter Gabler, 'The Seven Lost Years of *A Portrait of the Artist as a Young Man*', in *Approaches to Joyce's* 'Portrait'. *Ten Essays*, ed. by Thomas F. Staley and Bernard Benstock (Pittsburgh: University of Pittsburgh Press, 1976), pp. 53-56, should

revision of the fragment had sufficiently matured in Joyce's mind, he began to write *A Portrait of the Artist as a Young Man* in five chapters. This reached the state of an intermediary manuscript during 1907 to 1911.³ In 1913-14, the novel was completed. It is represented in its final state by the fair-copy manuscript in Joyce's hand now in the possession of the National Library of Ireland in Dublin. Moreover, complete textual versions or fragments of text from each of the major stages of the novel's eleven-year progression are still extant and identifiable. But it is also true that by far the majority of the materials, the plans, sketches, or intermediate drafts which as a body would have borne witness of its emergence, must be assumed to be lost. Nevertheless, close survey and careful scrutiny of those which survive make it possible to indicate some of the essential aspects of the work's genesis.

I

The only surviving textually complete document of *A Portrait of the Artist as a Young Man* is the Dublin holograph manuscript. In it, several strata of composition may be distinguished. The manuscript comprises $600(-1)^4$ leaves in Joyce's hand. Several orders of page-count may be found in the manuscript. The pencil numbering of the pages in Chapters I-III, and perhaps part of that in Chapter V, may be that of Harriet Weaver, who donated the manuscript to the National Library of Ireland. Page totals for each chapter have also been jotted in ink on the back of protective endpapers to Chapters II, III, and IV. They give the page count in a manner similarly found in some of Joyce's later manuscripts, and may be his. Chapter IV has a page numbering in large arabic numerals, mostly in ink, on the verso of the leaves. This numbering runs on without interruption through the first thirteen leaves of Chapter V. The sequence

---

remain essentially valid. A subsequent in-depth study, however, is Claus Melchior, 'Stephen Hero. Textentstehung und Text. Eine Untersuchung der Kompositions- und Arbeitsweise des frühen James Joyce', PhD dissertation, München (Bamberg, 1988).

3   Richard Ellmann, *James Joyce* (New York: Oxford University Press, 1982), pp. 264, 314, subsequently cited *as JJ*.

4   The one missing leaf is the first of the 'Fragments from a Late *Portrait* Manuscript' (Scholes/Kain, *Workshop*, p. 107), now at the British Library. It has been incorporated in its proper place in the photo-reprint of the Dublin holograph (*JJA*, vols. [9] and [10]).

begins with '239' for the first text page in Chapter IV and runs to '313' for fol. 13 of Chapter V (*JJA* [10], 741-882).[5]

For a stratification of the manuscript by which to distinguish the order of inscription, and at times of the composition of the text, this page count is the decisive clue. It links all of Chapter IV with the beginning of Chapter V. It also indicates that, inscriptionally, pages '239' to '313' are the earliest section of the Dublin manuscript. The absence of corresponding page numbering for Chapters I to III suggests that these chapters were inscribed later, an assumption strengthened by the fact that not 238, but 362 manuscript pages precede Chapter IV in the Dublin holograph. Accordingly, it is easy to see that the continuous page count, a vestige apparently of a through numbering of some other manuscript, was abandoned as of no further consequence for the remainder of Chapter V. Inscriptionally, therefore, this would also seem to be later than pages '239' to '313', though why the pattern breaks where it does is not readily discernible. Nor, of course, is it a foregone conclusion that Chapters I to III in their entirety preceded all of the main body of Chapter V in a relative chronology of inscription of the manuscript.

The page numbers '239' to '313' accord with Joyce's numbering habits in the *Stephen Hero* manuscript. To this, however, the numbered pages in the Dublin holograph cannot have belonged, since they follow so clearly from the five-chapter plan of *A Portrait*. They were consequently written at some time after September 1907. Perhaps their text was not conceived before February 1909, though this depends on what precisely Ettore Schmitz (Italo Svevo) read of *A Portrait* in January-February 1909.[6] The actual pages '239' to '313' belonged, I suggest, to the *Portrait* manuscript that narrowly escaped destruction in 1911, the 'original' original which, when rescued, was sorted out and pieced together in preparation of the final manuscript,[7] and in which there were 'pages . . . I could never have re-written' (*JJ*, 314). Contrary to the view that the fourth and fifth chapters of the novel were not brought into shape until 1914, after Ezra

---

5   The actual numbers are 239-41, 243-313. But, with no lacuna in the text, this is apparently a simple error in the numbering, as Harriet Weaver noted when she checked the manuscript: 'evidently a mistake for 242. H.S.W.'

6   *Letters of James Joyce*, vol. II, ed. by Richard Ellmann (New York: Viking Press, 1966), pp. 226 f. [*Letters* II].

7   *Letters of James Joyce*, vol. I, ed. by Stuart Gilbert (New York: Viking Press, 1957, ²1966), p. 136. [*Letters* I].

Pound's enquiry about publishable material had rekindled Joyce's desire to complete the novel—supposedly while the early chapters were already getting into print[8]—the evidence of the Dublin manuscript indicates that, in 1911, when *A Portrait* was almost annihilated, Joyce had completed Chapter IV and begun Chapter V. Indeed, Chapter IV, the only section of the Dublin holograph which has come down inscriptionally intact from the earlier manuscript, appears also to be the only part of the final text which represents without significant and extensive changes the novel in the textual state of 1911.

As applied to the pre-1911 leaves actually preserved in the Dublin manuscript, Joyce's posthumously reported remark about pages he could never have rewritten would seem to mean merely pages which he saw no further need to reinscribe. It is surely significant that Chapter IV in the Dublin manuscript is the only chapter which to any marked extent shows traces of Joyce's revising hand. Consider the final heightening of the paragraph, steeped in the symbolism of Pentecost, which begins: 'On each of the seven days of the week he further prayed that one of the seven gifts of the Holy Ghost might descend upon his soul' (IV.51-53). In the manuscript, it originally ended: 'to whom, as God, the priests offered up mass once a year, robed in scarlet'. This is revised to read: 'robed in *the* scarlet *of the tongues of fire*' (*JJA* [10], 751). Or consider how much denser and richer, how much more both threatening and alluring, becomes the passage which in the manuscript originally read:

> No king or emperor on this earth has the power of the priest of God. No angel or archangel in heaven, no saint, not even the Blessed Virgin herself has the power of a priest of God, the power to bind and to loose from sin, the power, the authority, to make the great God of Heaven come down upon the altar and take the form of bread and wine. What an awful power, Stephen!—

By revisional amplification, this becomes:

---

8   On this point Anderson (Chester G. Anderson, 'The Text of James Joyce's *A Portrait of the Artist as a Young Man'*, *Neuphilologische Mitteilungen*, 65 (1964), 160-200 (pp. 182-84)) and Ellmann, *JJ*, 354, basically agree. I follow these authorities in 'Zur Textgeschichte und Textkritik des *Portrait'*, in *James Joyces "Portrait": Das Jugendbildnis im Lichte neuerer deutscher Forschung*, ed. by Wilhelm Füger (Munich: Goldmann, 1972), p. 22; and also—though with a cautionary footnote after first looking into the fair-copy manuscript—in 'Towards a Critical Text of James Joyce's *A Portrait of the Artist as a Young Man'*, *Studies in Bibliography*, 27 (1974), 1-53 (p. 28).

> No king or emperor on this earth has the power of the priest of God. No angel or archangel in heaven, no saint, not even the Blessed Virgin herself has the power of a priest of God: *the power of the keys,* the power to bind and to loose from sin, *the power of exorcism, the power to cast out from the creatures of God the evil spirits that have power over them,* the power, the authority, to make the great God of Heaven come down upon the altar and take the form of bread and wine. What an awful power, Stephen!— (IV.382-391; *JJA* [10], 793)[9]

Correspondingly, Stephen, in his imaginings of priesthood, as originally worded,

> longed for the office of deacon at high mass, to stand aloof from the altar, forgotten by the people, his shoulders covered with a humeral veil, and then, when the sacrifice had been accomplished, to stand once again in a dalmatic of cloth of gold on the step below the celebrant . . . . If ever he had seen himself celebrant it was as in the pictures of the mass in his child's massbook, in a church without worshippers, at a bare altar . . . and it was partly the absence of a rite which had always constrained him to inaction.

But in the text as interlinearly revised in the manuscript, his longings and reflections are enriched and particularised in much detail. Also, as in the preceding passage, the revision results in greater syntactical as well as rhythmical complexity:

> He longed for the *minor sacred* offices, *to be vested with the tunicle* of *sub*deacon at high mass . . . his shoulders covered with a humeral veil, *holding the paten within its folds,* and then, *or* when the sacrifice had been accomplished, to stand *as deacon* once again in a dalmatic of cloth of gold on the step below the celebrant . . . If ever he had seen himself celebrant it was . . . in a church without worshippers, *save for the angel of the sacrifice,* at a bare altar . . . and it was partly the absence of *an appointed* rite which had always constrained him to inaction . . . (IV.412-426; *JJA* [10], 795-97)

Anyone familiar with Joyce's revisional habits in shaping *Ulysses* and *Finnegans Wake* will here recognise in rudimentary form the patterns and procedures which reach such complexity in the processes of

---

9   All references (by chapter.line numbers) are to James Joyce, *A Portrait of the Artist as a Young Man*, ed. by Hans Walter Gabler with Walter Hettche (New York and London: Garland Publishing, Inc., 1993; and New York: Vintage International, Vintage Books, 1993). Italics indicating revisions are mine.

composition of the later works. Conversely, although the examples quoted are the only passages in which compositional revision clearly manifests itself in *A Portrait*, these examples, together with our general knowledge of Joyce's later working habits, make us more keenly aware of the likelihood of revision, perhaps even extensive revision, in the course of the emergence of *A Portrait* at lost stages of its textual development.

Pages '239' to '313', salvaged intact from the manuscript of 1911, will not have been the only pages which Joyce 'could never have re-written'. Such others as there were he apparently recopied, taking advantage in the process of the opportunity for revising and expanding his earlier text. Positive evidence derives from Ettore Schmitz's letter of 8 February 1909, that, for example, certain 'sermons' as part of the third chapter then existed. Consequently, they were also in the manuscript of 1911. In one form or another they would textually seem to go back even to February or March of 1904. The notes for *Stephen Hero* at the end of the 'Portrait' copybook testify to the plan for the inclusion in Chapter XI(?) of 'six lectures', in a sequence outlined as:

1)	Introductory, evening before	1st Day
2)	Death	
3)	Judgement	2nd Day
4)	Hell	
5)	Hell	3rd Day
6)	Heaven morning after	4th Day[10]

In *A Portrait*, by contrast, we have one introduction and three sermons on four consecutive evenings. Of the three sermons, the first, on death and judgment, is not given verbatim, but as reported speech, filtered through Stephen's mind. Only the second and third sermons are fully developed as insets of pulpit oratory. Hell is the subject of both; and despite the preacher's promise in his introduction to put before the boys 'some thoughts concerning the four last things...death, judgment, hell and heaven' (III.277-279), there is in *A Portrait* no sermon on heaven. In the late part of Chapter III, instead, heavenly mercy comes as an immediate and intensely personal experience to Stephen on the morning after the fourth day of the retreat: 'The ciborium had come to

---

10 *JJA* [7], p. 86; Scholes/Kain, *Workshop*, p. 69.

him' (III.1584). Revision, then, is indicated not merely between the two extreme stages of, on the one hand, the outline plan for Chapter XI of *Stephen Hero* and its unknown realisation, and, on the other, the final version of Chapter III of *A Portrait*, but also as a developmental process in the course of the emergence since 1907-08 of the third chapter of the five-chapter *Portrait*.

About the emergence not only of Chapter III, but of the entire pre-1911 portion of the novel, further inferences are possible from Ettore Schmitz's letter. The only third-chapter matter it expressly mentions are 'the sermons'. It gives no indication of the chapter's conclusion. By its initial reference to a fragmentary ending of the text it is even open, I suggest, to the interpretation that the third chapter was unresolved in the sections of the work in progress that Joyce allowed his pupil and critic to read. Schmitz feels unable to submit a rounded opinion about the work, partly for want of competence, but partly also because the text breaks off at a crucial moment: 'when you stopped writing you were facing a very important development of Stephen's mind'. At the same time, his letter appears to indicate that, in a discontinuous manner of composition, Joyce had by late 1908 or early 1909 already proceeded beyond Chapter III in his rewriting of *Stephen Hero* into the five-chapter *Portrait*. For Schmitz continues: 'I have already a sample of what may be a change of his mind described by your pen. Indeed the development of Stephen's childish religion to a strong religion felt strongly and vigorously or better lived in all its particulars (after his sin) was so important that no other can be more so'. (*Letters* II, 226)

This is an obscure comment if referring to Chapter III alone, and to nothing of *A Portrait* beyond it. It makes good sense, however, if considered as a reflection on the first section of Chapter IV which precisely describes 'a strong religion felt strongly and vigorously or better lived in all its particulars (after [Stephen's] sin)'. Without a knowledge of the subsequent offer and rejection of priesthood and the culminating scene on the beach, Schmitz would not have grasped the ironic implications of the fourth chapter's opening section; nor would he have realised that Stephen's way lay towards art, not religion. But he saw accurately enough that Joyce was 'facing a very important development of Stephen's mind'. The reference to having a sample of Stephen's altered mind described by Joyce's pen suggests that Schmitz had read a textual fragment drafted for the continuation of the novel beyond the point where Joyce had 'stopped writing'. Together with the subsequent explicit mention of the sermons, it suggests that, as Schmitz read it, the third chapter ended with the sermons and the dejection and contrition they caused in Stephen, and that Joyce in 1909 had not yet formulated the last transitional section, which, by way of Stephen's confession, absolution, and communion, is linked to the opening of Chapter IV.

With the hindsight of our reading experience, the thematic and narrative logic of that transition seems so clear that it is hard to conceive of any great problems encountered in the writing of it. However, several observations converge which may suggest that Joyce did not achieve it easily. The most important of these derives physically from the Dublin manuscript itself and indicates that the end of Chapter III as we now have it is a very late piece of writing. On fol. 100 of Chapter III in the Dublin holograph, the communal prayer which concludes the last of the hell sermons ends, with Joyce's characteristic three asterisks marking the sectional subdivision, halfway down the page. Below, the final section opens with a clear palaeographic break: the pen, the ink, the slope of the hand, and the typical letter formations which remain identical from here on for the last twenty-nine leaves of the chapter are all distinctly different from the style of inscription of the preceding one hundred pages, and particularly of that of the two hell sermons on fols. 40-100. As will be seen, there is a distinct palaeographic link between Chapter III, fols. 40-100 (*JJA* [10], 557-667), and Chapter V, fols. 112-120 (*JJA* [10], 1089-1105). If, as was argued earlier, the main body of Chapter III was itself re-transcribed after 1911 (and probably revised, and perhaps augmented, in the process), the evidence now shows that the final section was inscribed, and therefore added to the main transcription, at yet a later stage. It is conceivable that the end of Chapter III was among the latest sections to be inscribed in the Dublin holograph.

In a first draft, Chapters I to III of *A Portrait* were written between September 1907 and 7 April 1908 (*JJ*, 264, 270). They are the chapters that Ettore Schmitz comments on in his letter of 8 February 1909. He praises the second and third chapters, but he criticises the first: 'I think it deals with events devoid of importance and your rigid method of observation and description does not allow you to enrich a fact which is not rich by itself. You should write only about strong things' (*Letters*

II, 227). The physical evidence of the Dublin manuscript shows that, in consequence, not only were Chapters I to III written out anew after the near destruction, in 1911, of the earlier *Portrait* manuscript; by inference from the page numbering in the leaves which survive from it, the initial chapters were also augmented by a total of 124 manuscript pages. Beyond a recopying of salvaged text, this bespeaks thorough and probably extensive revision.[11]

We know from an entry in Stanislaus Joyce's diary that in September 1907, Joyce's plan for rewriting *Stephen Hero* was 'to omit all the first chapters and begin with Stephen . . . going to school' (*JJ*, 264). This was the way out of the difficulty over the first chapters of *Stephen Hero* which Joyce had commented on before to his brother (*Letters* II, 90). The new conception was realised. In the first school episode, the incomplete alteration of the name Mangan to Moonan in the early pages of the Dublin manuscript demonstrates positively a copying from earlier papers.[12] That would put at least this episode of Stephen's illness at Clongowes among the matter contained in the 1911 manuscript, and hence probably into Chapter I as read by Ettore Schmitz in 1909, and, consequently, as written between 8 September and 29 November 1907. No new chapters dealing with Stephen's childhood were written then or later to precede this beginning.

The first chapter of the novel as we now have it, however, opens with a brief section of great significance which, on the narrative level, relates Stephen's childhood. It represents the final expression of Joyce's original intention to encompass the earliest years in his hero's life. Its consummate artistry, resulting from a great concentration and condensation of thought, imagery, symbolism, and meaning, has often been admired and commented upon.[13] In the manifold attempts at elucidating the complexity of the opening of *A Portrait*, there seems to be an agreement that, to adopt Hugh Kenner's

---

11 Quantitatively, however, it is unlikely that the earlier text was augmented by a full fifty percent, as the addition of 124 pages to the original 238 might suggest. As compared to the inscription of Chapter IV, the columns of text in the freshly inscribed chapters are distinctly narrower, especially so throughout Chapter I. This factor alone would account for many more pages in the new manuscript portion.
12 As noted in Anderson, 'The Text', p. 170n.
13 See especially Hugh Kenner, *Dublin's Joyce* (London: Chatto and Windus, 1955), pp. 114-116.

musical terminology, it functions as an overture anticipating the main themes and developments of the novel. As such, it gives every impression of having been written in view not only of the whole as planned, but of the whole of the subsequent composition as executed, or largely executed, in the details of its narrative progression and symbolism. Though no positive textual proof for this is available, I venture to suggest that the opening section of Chapter I was written at a late stage of the textual genesis of the novel. It had found its shape and place by late 1913, of course, when from the Dublin holograph originated the novel's transmission into print via the typescript prepared from the manuscript. But the opening section with which we are familiar may have formed no part, and (though this is speculation only) may have had no textual equivalent or alternative in Chapter I as read by Ettore Schmitz in 1909 and as contained in the manuscript of 1911.

A general palaeographic impression gained from the Dublin holograph is that the final inscription of Chapter II preceded that of Chapter I. An assumption of this order of revision gains support from the observation that at some stage in the seven-year textual history of *A Portrait*, the Christmas dinner scene was moved from Chapter II to Chapter I. This was a revision of utmost significance, to which we shall return. Suffice it here to say that, by all available evidence, Chapter I acquired its final shape in stages, and that Joyce's awareness of its potential for meaning grew over an extended period of composition. Nor would the internal textual evidence of the chapter's growth seem inconsistent with an assumption that Ettore Schmitz's criticism added incentive to the revising of it. Schmitz could hardly have denied 'strength' to a Chapter I opening as the present one does, and including the Christmas dinner scene.

Therefore, the act of revision by which the Christmas episode was transferred from Chapter II to Chapter I appears to have been undertaken after February 1909. A still later dating is suggested by Joyce's 'Alphabetical notebook'. Among its materials, which in their majority are projections for Chapter V of *A Portrait,* and for *Ulysses*, there are just a few entries which indicate that both the Christmas dinner scene and the novel's second chapter were still on Joyce's mind in 1909-10. Under the heading

'Pappie', and after an entry which can be dated to Christmas 1909,[14] we find these further entries:

> He calls a prince of the church a tub of guts . . .
>
> He offers the pope's nose at table. . . .
>
> He calls Canon Kean frosty face and Cardinal Logue a tub of guts.
>
> Had they been laymen he would condone their rancid fat.[15]

At some time after Christmas 1909, then, the dialogue of the Christmas dinner scene must have been revised sufficiently to put these quotations from John Stanislaus Joyce into the mouth of Simon Dedalus. Three further entries in the notebook—one under 'Pappie', and two under 'Dedalus (Stephen)'—point to Chapter II. The names of Pappie's college friends[16] provide material for the Cork episode (II, 109-119); and I take the entries for Stephen Dedalus which read, 'The applause following the fall of the curtain fired his blood more than the scene on the stage' and 'He felt himself alone in the theatre', to refer, respectively, to the Whitsuntide play (II, 94 ff.), and to the scene in the anatomy theatre in Cork (II, 112 ff.). Taken together, this evidence suggests a late revision of Chapters I and II, possibly sometime in 1910, or, indeed, in the course of assembling the novel after its near destruction in 1911.

II

The last of Joyce's *Dubliners* stories, 'The Dead', has been widely interpreted as signalling a new departure in his art, leading to achievements such as the first chapter of *A Portrait*. The two have commonly been viewed in close temporal sequence, since it is known that *A Portrait* was begun in September 1907, immediately after the composition of 'The Dead' (*JJ*, 264). From the account here given of the state of the final manuscript and of the stages of composition and revision to be reckoned with in the novel's initial chapters, it follows, however, that only Chapter IV can be safely assumed to have existed

---

14 'He gave me money to wire to Nora on Christmas Eve.' *JJA* [7], p. 145, and Scholes/Kain, *Workshop*, p. 103.
15 *JJA* [7], pp. 145-6, and Scholes/Kain, *Workshop*, p. 104.
16 Ibid.

before 1911 as it survives in the completed novel. Chapters I to III, by contrast, attained their final shape only after that date, and are therefore, in the form in which we possess them, five or more years removed in time from *Dubliners*, and the consummation of its art in 'The Dead'. Paradoxically, it is Chapter V, although presumably the last to be written, which from the vantage point of the finished *Portrait*, and on the evidential basis of the textual documents still extant, reaches back furthest into the novel's textual history and Joyce's artistic development.

Materials from the textual history have been preserved more amply for the fifth chapter than for the earlier ones. They bear witness to the fact that the transformation of the extant *Stephen Hero* fragment (the chapters which Joyce himself called the 'University episode' of that novel) into Chapter V of *A Portrait* passed through several stages of experiment. Since the first thirteen pages of the chapter in its final form were contained in the *Portrait* manuscript of 1911, it appears that the earliest traceable attempts at rewriting preceded its attempted destruction. They seem to have been aimed at only a slight modification-by-condensation of the *Stephen Hero* materials which, one may assume, would have preserved their essentially additive narrative structure. At the end of Chapter XV and midway through Chapter XVIII in the *Stephen Hero* manuscript, we find the entries 'End of First Episode of V' and 'End of Second Episode of V' (*JJA* [8], 95 and 239). The final *Portrait* text does not realise the linear revisional plan that these entries point to. What materials have been salvaged from the *Stephen Hero* university episode—e.g., the fire-lighting incident with the dean of studies, the music-room scene with Emma Clery, the episode of the Stephen-Emma-Father Moran triangle, as well as numerous brief descriptive and characterising phrases earmarked for transfer in the *Stephen Hero* manuscript—now reappear out of their earlier order, changed and integrated into different settings and contexts.[17]

---

17 In his 1944 edition of *Stephen Hero* (*James Joyce, Stephen Hero.* Edited from the Manuscript in the Harvard College Library by Theodore Spencer. A New Edition, incorporating the Additional Manuscript Pages in the Yale University Library and the Cornell University Library, ed. by John J. Slocum and Herbert Cahoon (New York: New Directions, 1944; 1963)), Theodore Spencer judged Joyce's red and blue crayon markings in the manuscript to be cancellations. See his 'Editorial Note', p. 18. The evidence has meanwhile been thoroughly reconsidered by Claus Melchior (see above note 2).

Against the foil of the original *Stephen Hero* incidents and scenes, Joyce searched for a new novelistic technique and new forms of expression through language and style. Increasingly, the narrative was internalised. The hero's mind and consciousness became a prism through which the novel was refracted. Characters were functionalised as correlative to theme. A workshop fragment happens to have survived which paradigmatically reveals the inner logic of the process of artistic reorientation.

The document in question is one (and the only genuine one) of the two 'Fragments from a Late *Portrait* Manuscript'.[18] An external, purely orthographic indicator, though by its nature a significant one, of the fact that it distinctly postdates *Stephen Hero*, is the revised spelling 'Dedalus' (for earlier 'Daedalus') of Stephen's family name. It also postdates *Stephen Hero* by its introduction of Doherty, alias Oliver St. John Gogarty. The fictional name appears as early as the Pola notebook entries for *Stephen Hero* of 1904.[19] But when Joyce in the summer of 1905 discontinued the writing of *Stephen Hero*, he had not yet reached the point where he would have brought Gogarty into the narrative—although his friends in Dublin who were granted the privilege of reading the finished chapters were eagerly awaiting that moment (*Letters* II, 103). Doherty is not finally cast as a character in *A Portrait*, but reappears as Buck Mulligan in *Ulysses*. The Doherty fragment therefore has been viewed as an early vestige of *Ulysses*.[20] But by its situational context, it has a place more immediately within a *Portrait* ambience.

The Doherty episode of the preserved fragment constitutes a section of a kitchen scene between Stephen and his mother. On the manuscript leaf, it is preceded by the last half-sentence from a paragraph which, as A. Walton Litz has observed, appears to be the end of a new rendering of the episode that concluded Chapter XIX (in Joyce's numbering) of *Stephen Hero*.[21] The pencil addition to the end of Chapter XIX in the *Stephen Hero* manuscript, 'If I told them there is no water in the font to symbolise

---

18 *JJA* [10], pp. 1219-1222, and Scholes/Kain, *Workshop*, pp. 107-08.
19 Scholes/Kain, *Workshop*, p. 85.
20 A. Walton Litz, *The Art of James Joyce* (London: Oxford University Press, 1964), Appendix B, pp. 132-35.
21 Litz, *The Art*, p. 137.

that when Christ has washed us in blood we have no need of other aspersions', is reflected in the fragmentary phrase 'shed his blood for all men they have no need of other aspersion'. The kitchen scene to which the Doherty episode itself is genetically linked followed, after some pages, in Chapter XX (in Joyce's numbering) of *Stephen Hero*. Vestigially, therefore, the manuscript fragment gives evidence of an attempt at linear rewriting of *Stephen Hero* by a foreshortening of its episodic sequence.

Yet technically and stylistically, at the same time, the fragment exemplifies a breakthrough towards the narrative mode of the final *Portrait*. It begins in the middle of Stephen's mental reflection on his own mixed feelings towards Doherty's habits of mocking and blasphemous self-dramatisation, and it breaks off as mother and son, confronting one another over the dregs of a finished breakfast in the midst of general disorder in the kitchen, embark upon a dialogue which would appear to be heading towards a new version of the conversation, in *Stephen Hero*, about Stephen's neglect of his Easter duty. There, as they talk, Stephen is made to reveal his inner state at length, while his mother is only gradually brought to a realisation and awareness of the fact that he has lost his faith. After four wordy pages, the dialogue ends:

> Mrs Daedalus began to cry. Stephen, having eaten and drunk all within his province, rose and went towards the door:
>
> —It's all the fault of those books and the company you keep. Out at all hours of the night instead of in your home, the proper place for you. I'll burn every one of them. I won't have them in the house to corrupt anyone else.
>
> Stephen halted at the door and turned towards his mother who had now broken out into tears:
>
> —If you were a genuine Roman Catholic, mother, you would burn me as well as the books.
>
> —I knew no good would come of your going to that place. You are ruining yourself body and soul. Now your faith is gone!
>
> —Mother, said Stephen from the threshold, I don't see what you're crying for. I'm young, healthy, happy. What is the crying for? . . . It's too silly . . .[22]

---

22 Joyce, *Stephen Hero*, p. 135; *JJA* [8], pp. 441-43.

From this conclusion, Joyce in the fragment distils the new beginning of an exchange of words:

—It is all over those books you read. I knew you would lose your faith. I'll burn every one of them—

—If you had not lost [the] your faith—said Stephen—you would burn me along with the books—(*JJA* [10], 1221-2)

Within the fragment as it stands, however, this beginning (there is no telling where it would have led, since Joyce himself does not seem to have seen his way to following it up; the fragment ends at the top of its late manuscript page) is only the conclusion of a thoroughly internalised scene. It is primarily Doherty, and not his mother, who is Stephen's antagonist, and he is present not in person, but in Stephen's thoughts. It is in Stephen's mind that his coarse and boisterous blasphemies are called up, the 'troop of swinish images . . . which went trampling through his memory' (*JJA* [10], 1219). The particulars of Doherty's self-dramatisation 'on the steps of his house the night before', as remembered by Stephen, all function for Joyce as the artistically objective correlative of Stephen's rejection of church rituals and Christian beliefs. Together with the subsequent description of the dirt and disorder in the kitchen they serve to create the mood of Stephen's dejection and weariness—totally different from the defiant 'Mother . . . I'm young, healthy, happy. What is the crying for? . . . It's too silly' of *Stephen Hero*—out of which the dialogue grows, and then breaks off.

The technique in the act of rewriting is one of inversion in several respects. From being displayed in external dialogue, the theme of the episode is presented as a projection in narrative images (centred on the antagonist) of the protagonist's mind and memory. The facts and attitudes which emerged only gradually in the fully externalised scenic narration by dialogue, are now anticipated by the economy of poetic indirection. The fragment of conversation which remains begins on the note, and, in foreshortening, on the very word with which its model ended. Mood and atmosphere are enhanced and incidentally altered; the effect of condensation is great on all levels of thought, language, and character presentation. The overall gain in intensity is enormous. Constituting as it does a point of intersection between the earlier episodic pattern of *Stephen Hero* and the new evolving narrative principles and techniques, the 'late *Portrait* fragment' thus reveals the significance of Joyce's intermediary *Portrait* experiments.

What presumably remained problematic, however, was to adhere to the device of presenting as a scene at all the crucial moment in the process of Stephen's separation from home, fatherland, and religion. As a scene, it may have been felt to give still too much personal and emotional bias to an at the core intellectual conflict and decision. In the fragment, of course, it depends, additionally, on the introduction into the larger narrative context of the new and essentially insincere character Doherty. The experiment of using him as a correlative and a mocking projection of Stephen's serious rejection of Christian values was abandoned. This meant that the scene between Stephen and his mother could not take even the shape into which it was tentatively revised. In the final text of *A Portrait,* by further radical narrative condensation, the confrontation of mother and son over the question of the Easter duty was deleted altogether, entering the novel only by way of report in Stephen's final conversation with Cranly.

The elimination of the kitchen scene has broader implications, for it appears that the narrative progression of Chapter V as ultimately achieved is determined no longer by scenes, but by conversations and reflections. This seems to be the result of the later revisional experiments of which, now, the notation of the text in the pages of the Dublin fair-copy manuscript itself bears witness. The final chapter of the novel divides into four sections. They are no longer 'episodes' in the manner of the Christmas dinner scene, or the Cork episode, or Stephen's flight to the seashore at the end of Chapter IV. 'Movements' may perhaps be an apter term for them. The second and fourth movements, essentially static, are given to the composition of the villanelle and to Stephen's diary excerpts. It is only in the more dynamic first and third movements that, by a complex sequence of thematically interlocking conversations, the narrative is effectively carried forward.

As with the novel as a whole, so with Chapter V in particular, the Dublin manuscript helps to distinguish phases of inscription which permit inferences about the order of composition of its parts. Of fols. 112 ff., for example (beginning 'What birds were they?' (V.1768; *JJA* [10], 1089), Chester G. Anderson has suggested, from observations on variations in Joyce's handwriting, that they may have been among the first to reach the form they have in the Dublin holograph.[23] This is incorrect insofar as Chapter IV is inscriptionally clearly the earliest part of the fair-copy manuscript. Nevertheless, Anderson's guess conforms with an impression, gained from further comparison, that the particular variation in Joyce's handwriting observable in fols. 112-20 (through the entire passage that ends 'went up the staircase and passed in through the clicking turnstile' (V.1863-4; *JJA* [10], 1105) recurs also in fols. 39-100 of Chapter III, that is, throughout the two hell sermons (III.538-1170). At the bottom of fol. 39, the new hand sets in with the paragraph beginning 'The chapel was flooded by the dull scarlet light' (III.523; *JJA* [10], 555). The change of hand on the same page clearly puts the inscription of fols. 1-39 before that of fols. 39-100. Thereafter, the second obvious inscriptional discontinuity in Chapter III after fol. 100 (*JJA* [10], 677), together with the palaeographic likeness of the hell sermon section with fols. 112-20 of Chapter V, suggests—in addition to strengthening the earlier argument for a later inclusion of the final transitional section of Chapter III—that Joyce at this point proceeded directly from the third chapter to fair-copying the nine-page opening of the fifth chapter's third movement. This, as will be remembered, is a passage which richly orchestrates the novel's symbolism. In tone and imagery, it is particularly close to the latter half of Chapter IV. Since the hell sermons, to which it is palaeographically linked in the inscription of the Dublin holograph, represent text essentially salvaged from the *Portrait* manuscript of 1911, the text of fols. 112-20 in Chapter V, too, may be of pre-1911 origin.

The remainder of the third movement in Chapter V may then not only have been inscribed later, as the change in the style of the hand after 'and passed through the clicking turnstile' on fol. 120 indicates; it may also have been written appreciably later. When the textual continuation was ready to be fair-copied and Joyce returned to the middle of fol. 120 to join it on where he had left off writing, the beginning of the late preceding paragraph read: 'A sudden brief hiss was heard and he knew that the electric lamps had been switched on in the readers' room'. This was revised to 'A sudden brief hiss fell from the windows above him' (V.1860; *JJA* [10], 1105) to correspond to the parallel phrase which

---

23 Anderson, 'The Text', p. 179n.

occurs within the subsequent text on fol. 131: 'and a soft hiss fell again from a window above' (*JJA* [10], 1127). The manner of the revision, undertaken interlinearly on the manuscript page, is reminiscent of the similar revisions observed in Chapter IV and may well support a view that, here as there, Joyce was only after a passage of time returning to text earlier inscribed.

A manuscript section in Chapter V, clearly set off as an insert from its surroundings, is that of the villanelle movement. Its sixteen manuscript pages are (but for the last one) inscribed with a different ink and a different slope of the hand on different paper. The verso of fol. 95 (*JJA* [10], 1055), which ends the chapter's first section, is smudged and has yellowed. Similarly, fol. 112 (*JJA* [10], 1089), the first page of the third movement, shows traces of having been outer- and uppermost in a bundle. From this evidence it would appear that, for an appreciable time, sections one and three of the chapter existed separately and apart, and that the villanelle movement was later inserted between them. Further observation shows that the last of the sixteen manuscript pages of the villanelle movement is again on paper similar or identical to that used for the rest of the chapter (although this in fact is a mixed batch). Moreover, the leaf (fol. 111; *JJA* [10], 1087) is also heavily smudged on its verso and bears the mark of a huge paper clip. But for the two lines of running prose at the top, it contains only the complete text of the villanelle as concluding the movement. A closer inspection of the preceding leaf reveals that the words in its last two lines are spaced out uncommonly widely and are not brought out as far to the right edge of the paper as the text on the rest of the page. The article 'the' which is the first word on fol. 111 could easily have been accommodated at the bottom of fol. 110. Therefore, fol. 110 was inscribed after fol. 111, or, in other words, fol. 111 appears to be the last leaf of the villanelle section from an earlier inscriptional (and probably textual) state.

The section in its final state was inserted in its present position in the Dublin manuscript only after the preceding ninety-five pages of text as written were finally fair-copied—and appreciably later at that, as witnessed by the smudged appearance of fol. 95v. This is clear from the fact that it opens, with the palaeographic break described, in the lower third of fol. 95. That the final transcription of the villanelle movement also postdates the writing of fols. 112-20 is rendered similarly probable by the other physical evidence referred to: the different paper of the insert, and the smudging of fol. 112 itself. But whether the second movement in its original conception is later than the other parts of Chapter V is less easy to determine. On the contrary, considering the marks of wear and tear on fol. 111v, it is not even out of the question that the villanelle section in an earlier unrevised state also belonged to the pages of the rescued 1911 manuscript which Joyce 'could never have rewritten'. But this, from the evidence, cannot be demonstrated. What the inscriptional stratification in Chapter V of the Dublin manuscript shows, however, is that Joyce did what he later claimed to have done, assembling the chapter by piecing together sections of manuscript. The chapter was by no means inscribed in the fair-copy manuscript in the regular order of the final text (as the other four chapters apparently were in themselves, though they were not written out in the regular order of the chapters), nor was it probably composed in that order.

On the whole, the indication is that the final shape and structure of Chapter V of *A Portrait of the Artist as a Young Man* evolved gradually as Joyce was working on the diverse materials which in the end he succeeded in unifying in this final chapter of the novel. In it, the villanelle interlude on the one hand, and, on the other hand, the orchestration of the novel's imagery and symbolism in the opening pages of the chapter's third movement, are seen from the evidence of their inscription in the fair-copy manuscript to have early roots in the chapter's conceptual genesis. The narrative framework which structurally supports these poetically highly imaginative passages is anchored in the sequences of conversations in the first and third movements and their relation to one another. Their relationship, which, as indicated, appears to reflect Joyce's final experiments at shaping the chapter, may also be seen in terms of a history of the text.

It is movements one and three in Chapter V that reuse the largest quantity of *Stephen Hero* materials; and of the two, the first takes the greater share. This section is also that part of the chapter where greatest emphasis is placed on establishing and maintaining narrative progression in action and in time. That such narrative progression is structured by a sequence of conversations, and no longer by episodes, becomes clear precisely from the fact that *A Portrait* salvages (though often with significant modification) dialogue from *Stephen Hero*, while abandoning the loose episodic framework to which it was there tied. The altercation developing from the fire-lighting by the dean of studies, or the exposition of Stephen's aesthetic theories, are outstanding examples. The close adaptation of a dialogue in dog Latin from *Stephen Hero* to comment upon the issue of signing or not signing the declaration for universal peace in *A Portrait* points to the revisional principle. The corresponding dialogue in *Stephen Hero* counterpoints the reading and reception of Stephen's paper on 'Art and Life', an incident which does not recur in *A Portrait*. Significantly enough, this is the only instance where *Stephen Hero* materials have been reused in *A Portrait* totally divorced from their earlier context. The original unity of episode and dialogue has been dissociated.

It is the achievement of the opening movement of Chapter V to develop Stephen's attitudes to church, university, and Jesuits; to show how he scorns the emotional idealism which motivates alike the declaration for universal peace and the arguments for Irish nationalism; and to set forth his aesthetic theories all in a sequence of encounters with fellow youths he talks to in the course of half a day's wandering through Dublin, from half-past ten in the morning in his mother's kitchen to sometime in the mid-afternoon on the steps of the National Library. This wandering movement, at the same time, is a narrative representation of Stephen's leaving his home and family and finding the theoretical basis for his art. The first section of the chapter takes him halfway into exile.

The third movement, by contrast, while of course gravitating towards Stephen's final encounter and conversation with Cranly, reflects upon and heightens imaginatively and symbolically the attitudes and the positions he has secured in movements one and two. It will be noted that the third movement begins at a place and time where the first ended, on the steps of the National Library in the late hours of an afternoon. Its action consists simply of Stephen's seeking out Cranly and separating him from the group of fellow students in order to walk alone with him and talk to him. The device is so similar to Stephen's sequestering one by one the dean of studies, Cranly, Davin, and Lynch earlier in the chapter as to suggest that at some stage in the genesis of Chapter V there existed a provisional and experimental plan for tying all the conversations on the issues he faces, and his going away from home into exile, to the narrative sequence of Stephen's wanderings through Dublin in the course of one day. It would have been in embryo the plan realised in *Ulysses*.

But the renouncing of church and faith in the final conversation with Cranly could then not have been linked to Stephen's falling out with his mother over his refusal to fulfil his Easter duty. For that, Stephen would have had to be brought back home once more in the course of the day, which would have broken the chapter's continuous outward movement. Perhaps a sequence was temporarily considered which would have brought all conversations into one day without sacrificing this directional principle. The unfinished revision of the Easter duty conversation in the 'Fragment from a late *Portrait* Manuscript', by the reference to Doherty's 'standing on the steps of his house the night before',[24] would seem to be set in the morning. Perhaps it should be seen as a workshop alternative to the kitchen scene at the beginning of the chapter, which, by the evidence of the continuous authorial page numbering in Chapters IV-V, was in the 1911 manuscript and, therefore, possibly predates the fragment. It would, however, have very heavily weighted the opening of the chapter which, as it stands, begins so casually; and the different thematic order of the ensuing conversations it would have demanded may well have proved too difficult to bring into balance.

By retrospective inference from *Ulysses* we may catch a glimpse of yet another workshop alternative considered but rejected for Chapter V. The beginnings of *Ulysses*, we know, grew from overflow *Portrait* materials. Not only did the projected but abandoned Martello Tower ending for *Portrait* provide the opening for *Ulysses*. Notably early during the *Ulysses* years, too, Joyce also had a 'Hamlet' chapter in store (cf. *Letters* I, 101). This eventually became Scylla & Charybdis. Even as we possess it in the text of the fair copy as completed on New Year's Eve 1918, it is pivoted on Stephen Dedalus, centred on his aesthetics, and devised as a sequence of conversations. With these characteristics, it may in early conception date back to Joyce's experiments over the structure and text for the fifth *Portrait* chapter. Set as it is in the National Library, it would have fitted between the chapter's first movement ending on the library steps going in, and its third movement opening on those steps going out. It would indeed also have fulfilled the one-day time scheme for Chapter V that

---

24 *JJA* [10], p. 1220, and Scholes/Kain, *Workshop*, p. 107.

we have speculatively postulated. It would, however, have shown up the starkness of such a scheme. As an Easter duty conversation in the family kitchen would have unduly weighted the chapter opening, so a heady exchange about Hamlet, Shakespeare, and aesthetics would have overfreighted its middle. The chapter's progression, without the contrast in tone and mood of the villanelle movement, would have been utterly relentless.

Within the four-part composition of Chapter V as ultimately achieved, several structural principles are simultaneously at work, of which the organisation of the thematic and narrative progression in the first and third movements by means of a logical sequence of conversations is the dominant one. Each exchange requires an intellectual counter-position, and Stephen's dialogue partners are accordingly functionalised as Doherty is in the 'late *Portrait* fragment', though not as strenuously internalised. Of the inferred structural experiments, namely the attempt at confining the chapter's action to one day, and the sustaining of a continuous outward direction of Stephen's movements, neither was completely abandoned, or wholly sacrificed to the other. Although the villanelle movement stands between the first and third sections, thereby indeterminately lengthening the chapter's time span, the third movement still continues in time (late afternoon) and place (steps of the National Library) where the first ends. Simultaneously, by a subtle avoidance of definite place, the illusion at least is maintained of a continuous movement away from home and into exile. The narrative is so devised that once Stephen leaves his home by the kitchen door in the morning of the day on which the chapter opens, he is never visualised as returning there again. Care is taken not to localise his awakening to compose the villanelle in a bedroom of the family house. The Easter duty conversation, which—regardless of its place in the chapter—would have required a setting in Stephen's home, is eliminated from the narrative altogether. Nor is a specific home setting given for Stephen's discussion with his mother about the 'B.V.M.' in the diary entry of 24 March. Both physically and spiritually, in the end, his departure into exile is represented as an unbroken outward movement sweeping through the entire fifth chapter.

A few but quite specific textual observations finally help to establish the relative chronology of the chapter's four movements. The initial thirteen manuscript pages (of 1911) bring Stephen out of his mother's kitchen and start him on his wanderings across Dublin. The entire first section of the chapter draws copiously on *Stephen Hero*. Once the structural plan for a sequence of conversations had been decided upon, the remainder of the first movement would have followed materially and logically from the chapter's beginning. The third movement, in the integral shape of its final version, is distinctly later than the first, and as it stands in the Dublin holograph it may postdate the original conception of the villanelle movement. Significantly, it is only in the text of the third movement that Stephen is given his (*Ulysses*) attribute of an ashplant.[25] Also, the Gogarty figure who commonly goes by the name of Goggins is here once called Doherty (V.2534), indicating a relation of the third movement to the experiments of composition to which the 'Fragment from a Late *Portrait* Manuscript' directly, and perhaps the Scylla & Charybdis episode of *Ulysses* remotely, bear witness. There is no indication of when the finale of the chapter, the diary section, was planned or written. Though ending the manuscript, it may not have been last in composition. It was the villanelle movement, though perhaps drafted early, that in its final version was last inserted in its predetermined position in the holograph, to complete the fair-copy manuscript, and the entire novel.

III

In its four-part structure, the fifth chapter of *A Portrait of the Artist as a Young Man* is the exact symmetrical counterpart to the first. The childhood overture and two Clongowes episodes, separated by the Christmas dinner scene, are the mirror image of the two movements of Stephen's wanderings through Dublin, separated by the villanelle episode, and the diary finale. Genetically, the novel's beginning and its end appear closely interdependent.

It seems that it was a decision to abandon the sequential or cyclic narrative by episodes as used in *Stephen Hero* in favour of a chiastic centre design that broke the impasse in which Joyce found himself over *A Portrait* (and which may have contributed to the desperate action of

---

25 Four times, at V.1770, 1805, 2069 and 2233.

the attempted burning of the intermediary manuscript in 1911). The textual history of Chapter V documents this momentous change in the compositional concept, and there is much reason to believe that from the fifth chapter it retroactively affected the entire work. Discounting the overture and the finale, which functionally relate as much to the entire novel as they do to their respective chapters, the first and last chapters are each chiastically centred on the Christmas dinner scene and on the composition of the villanelle.

Of the three middle chapters, Chapters II and IV are in themselves still basically narrated in a linear sequence of episodes. So is Chapter III, although here the sequential progression is stayed by the unifying and centralising effect of a concentration on the single event of the religious retreat. But the chiastic disposition of the novel's beginning and end alters the functional relationships within the middle chapters. Chapters II and IV take on a centripetal and a centrifugal direction, and the religious retreat becomes, literally and structurally, the dead centre of the novel. If it has been correct to infer an earlier state of Chapter III where four, five, or even six sermons were given verbatim, and therefore of necessity in an overtly sequential manner, then the revision, which essentially left only the two hell sermons as rendered in the preacher's own words, was undertaken to emphasise the chapter's midpoint position in the chiastic structure of the book. Within Chapter III, divided by Joyce's familiar asterisks into three parts, the beginning in Nighttown and the close in Church Street chapel stand in obvious symmetrical contrast. From the close of Chapter II, the Nighttown opening leads naturally into the hell sermon centre. The long search for a satisfactory chapter conclusion to lead out of it, indicated by the late inclusion of the final twenty-nine manuscript pages, may reflect Joyce's awareness of how essential for the work's inner balance it was to give the narrative exactly the proper momentum at the onset of its centrifugal movement.

But Joyce's concern in the final shaping of *A Portrait of the Artist as a Young Man* was not structural only. It was also one of thematic and symbolic heightening. To this the reorganisation of Chapters I and II bears witness that can be inferred from close textual scrutiny.

In the novel's first chapter, three boyhood episodes follow the overture. The first and the third involve the reader intensely in Stephen Dedalus' sufferings away from home at Clongowes Wood College.

In between, the Christmas dinner scene stands out in contrast. At the same time, several devices of narrative design, poetic patterning, and thematic development serve to anchor this scene in its given position. Its opening sentence, 'A great fire, banked high and red, flamed in the grate' (I.716), appears as the reversal of the preceding fire-to-water modulation of 'The fire rose and fell on the wall. It was like waves. . . . He saw the sea of waves, long dark waves rising and falling, dark under the moonless night' (I.696, 700). The night, in Stephen's vision and dream, is that of Parnell's last return to Ireland. It is thus on Parnell that the first Clongowes episode mystically culminates. The motif is taken up and developed as a central theme of the Christmas dinner controversy. In its course, the anti-Parnellite incarnate among the characters is Dante. Consequently, the repeated instances where she and her symbolically green and maroon-coloured attributes (brushes first, then [I.713-14] dress and mantle) were introduced, also provide structural support and thematic preparation for the Christmas dinner scene.

By means of anticipations and projections of later developments, the episode equally points beyond itself in the novel. Stephen, unable to understand who is right and who is wrong in the dispute arising over the Christmas dinner, recalls by association that Dante 'did not like him to play with Eileen because Eileen was a protestant' (I.999-1000). Here, in repeating to himself the question—'How could a woman be a tower of ivory or a house of gold? Who was right then?' (I.1003-1005)—he provides himself with the words from which, in the second Clongowes episode, the epiphanous identification of Eileen with the Virgin will spring (I.1257-60). A similar connection is established in Stephen's thoughts between the Christmas turkey and Mr Barrett's pandybat: 'Why did Mr Barrett in Clongowes call his pandybat a turkey?' (I.801-2). Here the main motif of the chapter's concluding section is announced for the first time. Furthermore, the Christmas dinner scene, as it introduces the persons of the inner family circle into the action proper, characterises not only Dante, whose presence in the novel ends with this scene, and Mr Casey, who is here given his only appearance, but also Stephen's father and mother, to whom as characters in the novel our relationship is to a considerable extent determined by their roles in this scene. And it gives us a glimpse, at least, of uncle Charles. At the opening of Chapter

II, he will be seen to be of similar importance as friend and mentor to Stephen in his later, as Dante was in his earlier, childhood.

It is not certain that the reader would stop to wonder why uncle Charles should first, and somewhat flatly, be introduced directly into the action of the Christmas dinner scene without bringing with him the full stature of one of the early novel's important 'round' characters which he so vividly acquires later. Yet, surely, many details which we later learn about him—his serene and peace-loving nature, and his sincere piety—would help to explain (as they do in retrospect) his attempts to pacify Simon Dedalus and Mr Casey, as well as his own calm restraint during the heated argument. The reference to Mr Barrett at Clongowes and his pandybat, however, must give pause. It appears as a genuinely false lead, for within the fiction of *A Portrait*, it is not Mr Barrett but Father Dolan who wields the pandybat at Clongowes. While it is true that in the course of the second Clongowes episode 'old Barrett' (I.1293) is mentioned in passing as being somehow connected with the disciplinary system in force at Clongowes, there is here, it would seem, a contextual discrepancy sufficient to provide a clue to the discovery not only of successive revisions to the Christmas dinner scene, but also to its repositioning, in the final structuring of the novel, from a place it originally held in the second chapter, to its present location in the first chapter of *A Portrait*.

To trace the compositional process, it is necessary to go back to the planning notes for *Stephen Hero*. As entered on the blank leaves in the copybook containing the manuscript of the 1904 narrative essay 'A Portrait of the Artist', these provide for a 'Christmas party' in the eighth chapter, in a central position between 'Business complications', 'Aspects of the city' and 'Visits to friends', 'Belvedere decided on'.[26] In a letter of 7 February 1905, furthermore, James Joyce reminds his brother Stanislaus that 'Mrs Riordan who has left the house in Bray returns...to the Xmas dinner-table in Dublin' (*Letters* II, 79). If the wording 'Christmas party' in the notes may leave room for doubt,[27]

---

26 *JJA* [7], p. 92 and Scholes/Kain, *Workshop*, p. 73.
27 'Party' is an odd word to use for the family Christmas dinner; the reference just might be to the children's party of which Epiphany no. 3 (*JJA* [7], p. 54 and Scholes/Kain, *Workshop*, p. 13) gives the conclusion, subsequently slightly, if significantly, varied in II.322-49.

the letter is unequivocal in giving a Dublin setting to the Christmas dinner episode in *Stephen Hero*. It was doubtless assigned to the Christmas of 1892, a few months before Stephen (like James Joyce) entered Belvedere College. It is probably significant that Sullivan[28] identifies Mr Barrett of *A Portrait* as Patrick Barrett, S. J., a scholastic stationed at Belvedere College. The name would seem to point to the survival into *A Portrait* of textual vestiges from *Stephen Hero*.

In the *Portrait* paragraph immediately preceding Stephen's recollection of the name Mr Barrett had for his pandybat, the purchase of the Christmas turkey is related. Stephen's father 'had paid a guinea for it in Dunn's of D'Olier Street' (I.797), a poulterer and game dealer in Dublin's finest shopping district. But, as the family is still living in Bray at the time of the Christmas scene in *A Portrait*, one wonders— while not discounting Simon Dedalus', *alias* John Joyce's, predilection for living in style even in progressively adverse circumstances, which would presumably stretch to buying the Christmas turkey from only the choicest of poulterers—why the bird could not have been procured from somewhere nearer home. At least, Dunn's of D'Olier Street, a ten-minute walk at the most from 14 Fitzgibbon Street off Mountjoy Square, the first of the Joyce residences in Dublin (*JJ*, 35), would be a more natural place to buy it if the family were already living in the city, as the Daedalus family was at the time of the Christmas dinner episode in *Stephen Hero*. When the Christmas dinner scene was rewritten for *A Portrait*, therefore, materials from the *Stephen Hero* Christmas dinner episode appear to have been reused.

From the evidence of various textual details, it may be assumed that, as *Stephen Hero* was rewritten to become *A Portrait*, the scene initially retained the position it held in *Stephen Hero*. In fact, the very survival of the narrative detail about Dunn's of D'Olier Street is the more easily accounted for if the episode was originally cast in Dublin surroundings

---

28 Kevin Sullivan, *Joyce among the Jesuits* (New York: Columbia University Press, 1958), p. 92. Curiously, 'Mr' Barrett of *A Portrait* is titled 'Father' Barrett in the Dublin holograph, and even in the original inscription of the typescript copied from the manuscript. The change from 'Father' to 'Mr' is one of the very few alterations Joyce himself made in the typescript. The late revisional touch establishes particularly clearly that the character subsequently referred to in *A Portrait* as 'old Barrett' (I.1293) and 'Paddy Barrett' (I.1450) is thought of as 'a scholastic not yet admitted to the priesthood' (cf. Anderson/Litz, *A Portrait*, p. 494) and would seem to confirm Sullivan's identification of the historical character prototype.

not only in *Stephen Hero*, but in *A Portrait* also. Similarly, John Casey's opening of his story 'about a very famous spit' amuses by the unbashful expedient employed to relate the story to a new setting for the scene in the novel. 'It happened not long ago in the county Wicklow' is how John Casey might have begun in Dublin; 'It happened not long ago in the county Wicklow where we are now' (I.964-66) is how he begins in Bray. Also, that sentence about Mr Barrett, 'Why did Mr Barrett in Clongowes call his pandybat a turkey?' (I.801) would cause no disturbance at a point in the novel corresponding to the episode's position in *Stephen Hero*. One is struck by the specification 'Mr Barrett in Clongowes' and its reinforcement, as if in afterthought: 'But Clongowes was far away'. (I.803) This is just a little curious when Clongowes is the only school Stephen has so far experienced and from which he is away for a brief Christmas leave only. It would better fit the situation in Chapter II where he has left Clongowes never to return. At that point, too, Stephen's recollection of Mr Barrett's pandybat would not, as in the final text, have the signalising force of a first mention of the pandying motif. Rather, it would appear as but an incidental memory of the disciplinary atmosphere of Clongowes, introduced only when, as readers, we had already shared Stephen's gruesome experience of unjust punishment at Father Dolan's hands. At the same time, a passing reference to 'old Barrett' in the boys' conversation, establishing that Father Dolan was not the only punishing agent at Clongowes, would have prepared us for Mr Barrett. There would be no danger of reacting to him as to a false lead in the novel.

The strongest reason for assuming that the Christmas dinner scene was still set in a Chapter II context in an early *Portrait* draft is the way in which, even in its final form, it presents uncle Charles. He is essentially not characterised in the scene itself, and there is almost no previous indication that he belongs to the family circle. His proper introduction follows at the beginning of Chapter II. Here, in the summer after the Clongowes events, he energetically does all the shopping at Bray, and often covers ten or twelve miles of the road on a Sunday with Stephen and his father (cf. II.73-76). In the autumn, he moves with the family to Dublin, where he soon '[grows] so witless that he [can] no longer be sent out on errands'. (II.220-21) The uncle Charles of the Christmas dinner scene is this feeble old man, confined to the house, left behind when Simon Dedalus and John Casey go for their Christmas day constitutional. He sits 'far away in the shadow of the window' (I.723-24) and does not join in the other men's banter; nor is he given a thimbleful of whisky to whet his appetite. When all take their seats for dinner, he has to be roused gently: 'Now then, sir, there's a bird here waiting for you'. (I.784)

The novel's final text still shows the episode's initial place:

> He went once or twice with his mother to visit their relatives: and, though they passed a jovial array of shops lit up and adorned for Christmas, his mood of embittered silence did not leave him. . . . He was angry with himself for being young and the prey of restless foolish impulses, angry also with the change of fortune which was reshaping the world about him into a vision of squalor and insincerity. Yet his anger lent nothing to the vision. He chronicled with patience what he saw, detaching himself from it and tasting its mortifying flavour in secret. (II.243-52)

Here is the right time of year; and the violent quarrel between Dante, Mr Casey, and Simon Dedalus, all dear to Stephen in their several ways, may very well have served as the crowning epiphany to alter Stephen's view of the world about him. It is indeed Stephen's mood and state of mind at this point which provide the final clue that it was the first *Portrait* version of the Christmas dinner scene removed from Chapter II (and not its *Stephen Hero* prototype taken directly from that novel's eighth chapter) which was inserted, with careful, though not flawless adaptation, into the episode's final position in Chapter I. Stephen's detachment and his role of patient chronicler as here described explain admirably the style and point of view which make the scene stand in such striking contrast to the Clongowes episodes which now surround it.

In speculating (for there is not sufficient evidence to support safe inferences) about the shape of the novel's second chapter in detail before the Christmas dinner scene was removed from it, two alternatives, basically, may be considered. Either the present sequence of three disjunct epiphanies (II.253-356), exemplifying what Stephen saw and detachedly chronicled, was inserted to fill the gap; or else, the narrative units coexisted in a climactically additive structure, culminating in the disastrous Christmas dispute. The latter view gains support from a comparison with the notes for Chapter VIII of *Stephen Hero*. All materials which were there planned for narrative execution are contained in the second *Portrait* chapter in its final state, plus the Christmas dinner scene. This would imply that, in terms of its narrative structure, the initial draft of the second *Portrait* chapter was not radically distant from its *Stephen Hero* prototype. By retaining a markedly episodic pattern it would have held an intermediary position comparable to that of those lost stages of composition occurring in the process of remoulding Chapter V.

When, however, the Christmas dinner scene was repositioned, the shape of the new novel's second chapter changed, and despite the evidence suggesting that Chapter II was simply foreshortened by the length of an episode, we need not assume that in its final form it represents merely a torso of the narrative structure of the earlier version. At least one paragraph in the final text suggests revision after the Christmas dinner scene's removal which involved a reproportioning of the chapter, possibly extending to a substitution or addition of text. The paragraph in question concludes the present sequence of epiphanies and describes Stephen's attempt, unsuccessful for hours, to write a poem to E—— C—— the morning after their parting on the steps of the last tram the night before. As he doodles, he remembers himself similarly 'sitting at his table in Bray the morning after the discussion at the Christmas dinnertable, trying to write a poem about Parnell . . .' (II.367-69). He failed (as Joyce, in the corresponding autobiographical situation, reportedly did not). The presence of this reminiscence in the final text suggests that the Christmas dinner scene in at least one of its earlier forms, and so possibly in its first *Portrait* version, was followed by the description of a scene in which Stephen wrote a poem about Parnell. It is possible even that the paragraph in the present final version preserves in part the text of that description. The writing of the poem to E—— C—— would appear to be a substitution for the writing of the poem about Parnell. The event which occasions the poem to E—— C—— must be considered to hold the structural place of the Christmas dinner scene before its removal. That is, the epiphany about Stephen and Emma on the steps of the tram moved into this position by the same act of revision that removed the Christmas dinner scene.

Considering the Christmas dinner scene it its present revisional position, one may note several textual details still betraying that the episode was not original to Chapter I. From the portrayal of Dante in it, for example, references to her green and maroon-coloured attributes are conspicuously absent. The green and maroon mark young Stephen's way of grasping the opposition in Dante's shifting allegiance to Michael Davitt and Charles Stewart Parnell. Since the colours are otherwise so consistently associated with the Parnell motif in Chapter I, it is not easily conceivable that they should not in some manner have been woven in if the Christmas dinner scene from the beginning had been written to follow the first Clongowes section and had been evolved directly from it.

On the other hand, it appears that three passages, at least, were added wholly or in part to adapt the scene to its Chapter I setting. They are I.802-9, or possibly 802-16 (that is, all of the paragraph after 'But Clongowes was far away', and possibly much of the subsequent paragraph, too); I.990-1011, and I.1058-1073. These passages extend the point of view established as Stephen's and maintained throughout the remainder of the first chapter. They display the schoolboy's thought pattern, his stream of consciousness triggered by smells, warmth, the sensation of 'queerness', the sound of a voice, things nice or not nice, and his worry over the meaning of words, and over the rightness or wrongness of things. Without them, the episode is constructed almost wholly in dialogue, which, with the emotional reactions of all the characters to it (including Stephen's), is told by a narrator, verging on the omniscient, from the vantage point of an outside observer.

By inference, the dialogue structure, still predominant in the episode's final form, represents the shape of the scene before it was adapted to fulfil the functions of its Chapter I position. Yet the adaptation did not apparently leave the dialogue entirely untouched. Simon Dedalus' emphatic outburst, in response to John Casey's suggestion that the Irish priests 'hounded' Parnell into his grave: 'Sons of bitches! . . . When he was down they turned on him to betray him and rend him like rats in a sewer. Lowlived dogs!' (I.943-5) is imaginable in an earlier foreshortened form confined to canine imagery alone. The phrase 'and rend him like rats in a sewer' is a reference to the square ditch at Clongowes (cf. I.126-7 and 269-70; and see below) and would thus appear a late addition. Moreover, near this point in the dispute we find two further utterances of Simon Dedalus' which would seem to be late additions to the *Portrait* text because, from the evidence, they were made by John Joyce only at Christmas 1909 when James Joyce was at home in Dublin from Trieste. In his 'Alphabetical notebook', below an entry datable to Christmas 1909, Joyce reminded himself about several of his father's idiosyncrasies and characteristic remarks.[29] 'He offers the pope's nose at table', and 'He calls a prince of the church a tub of guts', 'He calls Canon Keon frosty face and Cardinal Logue a tub of guts' are the entries which refer to 'There's a tasty bit here we call the pope's nose' (I.903) and 'Respect! . . . Is it for Billy with the lip or for the tub of guts up in Armagh [i.e., Cardinal Logue, archbishop of Armagh]? Respect!' (I.923-4) Just how much altogether the earlier dialogue of the Christmas dinner scene was retouched or rewritten cannot be determined. From the instances that can be made out, however, it is clear that the episode was adapted with some care to its new position in Chapter I.

In James Joyce's childhood, the quarrel between John Joyce, John Kelly, and Hearn Conway which grew so noisy that it was heard by the Vances across the road, broke out over the Christmas dinner in 1891, when the Joyce family was still living in Bray (*JJ*, 34). It was by an act of 'poetic license', developing and responding to the narrative logic of *Stephen Hero* as it unfolded before him, that Joyce there gave the Christmas dinner scene a setting in 1892 and in Dublin, moulding it into the experience of an older Stephen who had, we may assume, an increased understanding of the events he witnessed. That is the direction the scene's exposition still points to: 'And Stephen smiled too for he knew now that it was not true that Mr Casey had a purse of silver in his throat'. (I.733-34) Exact autobiographical correspondence was not Joyce's primary concern. This circumstance should be borne in mind when, in *A Portrait,* the episode again takes place in 1891. 1891 was the year of Parnell's death. In the final *Portrait,* Chapter I is a chapter as much about Parnell and Ireland as about Stephen and Clongowes, and its strength derives from this thematic correspondence which establishes significant reference to areas its schoolboy world by itself does not reach.

It is Parnell's death and burial which provide the symbolic focus for the beginning of the novel. In order to make the historical event assume structural control over the fiction, the two and a half years, from September 1888 to April 1891, which James Joyce spent at Clongowes Wood College are condensed into Stephen's one year, autumn 1891 to spring 1892, at that school. James Joyce and Stephen Dedalus were

---

29 Cf. above, note 15.

at no time contemporaries at Clongowes. In Stephen's year there, the action proper of the novel opens on the day when he changes from '77' to '76' the number in his desk indicating the days which remain until he will rejoin his family. Christmas Eve is the day which the *Portrait* text, by means of Stephen's dream on the night when his fever develops, establishes as the date of reference for his calculation: 'Holly and ivy for him and for Christmas'. (I.476-77) According to the calendar, then, the novel opens on a day which falls exactly between the day of Parnell's death (6 October) and that of his burial (11 October). There can be no doubt about the significance; nor indeed of the fact that Joyce intentionally established the correspondence. For in the Dublin holograph of *A Portrait*, he erased the numerals which were first given as 'thir(ty?)-seven' and '(thirty?)six' and wrote in their stead 'seventy-seven' and 'seventy-six'. (I.101-2 and 282-3; *JJA* [9], 19, 45)

The seventy-sixth day before Christmas is 9 October. The next day Stephen is taken to the infirmary. He has a fever fantasy of his own death. They give him no medicine, but in the evening, as the fire rises and falls on the wall, he sinks into a recuperative sleep. In it, he has a dream or vision which synchronises his time and Parnell's. The scene which he sees under the dark moonless night is that of Parnell's return to Ireland's shore as the ship which carries his body approaches the pierhead. The harbour is Kingstown; the time is daybreak of 11 October 1891, the day when the Irish buried their dead hero. By extension of the sequential numbering, it is the morning of the seventy-fourth day before Christmas. Thus, at the end of the first *Portrait* episode Stephen does not die like Little; he recovers. There are for him no 'tall yellow candles on the altar and round the catafalque'. (I.598-99) In Stephen's sleep of convalescence, Parnell's death stands for his own: 'He is dead. We saw him lying upon the catafalque'. (I.709) Parnell dies so that Stephen may live. That is why, in the novel, Parnell's return across the waves of the Irish Sea to be mourned by his people and buried in Ireland's soil, and Stephen's return to life from a sickness-to-death (as he imagines it) are synchronised to take place during the same night and early morning hours of 11 October 1891.

From the vantage point of this moment of structural significance, one may discern patterns in the fictional web and their links with real events. It was the seventy-seventh day before Christmas, the first day specifically mentioned in the story (though the action proper does not set in until the next day), which saw the incident that caused Stephen's illness: 'Wells . . . had shouldered him into the square ditch the day before . . . It was a mean thing to do; all the fellows said it was'. (I.265-69) According to the calendar, this was 8 October. The narrative development of *A Portrait of the Artist as a Young Man*, then, proceeds from the meanness and injury Stephen suffered at the hands of a schoolfellow, and fellow Irishman, on the first post-Parnellite day in Irish history.[30] And it was on October 8th of another year, 1904, that a young Irish couple, James Joyce and Nora Barnacle, left Dublin's North Wall for a life of exile. With the superior touch of the artist in full control of his narrative, Joyce thus ensures that in a novel which leads into exile the beginning prefigures the end.

Here, to be sure, the allusion is indirect and thoroughly submerged. But the synchronisation of Stephen's and Parnell's time on the morning of 11 October is tangibly present in the narrative. It suggests further significant correspondences among the events from which it derives. It is true that, if the novel's succession of events is directly projected onto the historical calendar, they are not simultaneous. But it is worth observing that a day or date for Parnell's death is not given in *A Portrait*. If time may be thought to be condensed (silently, in the fiction) into the three days which in Christian countries are customarily observed between a death and a burial in remembrance of the three days of Christ's crucifixion, harrowing of hell, and resurrection, then time at the opening of *A Portrait* is seen to be moralised to link Parnell's betrayal and death with Stephen's fall, at the hands of Wells, into the square ditch at Clongowes. There, 'a fellow had once seen a big rat jump plop into the scum'. (I.126-7 and 269-70) In the Christmas dinner scene, as we have seen, Simon Dedalus is made to say of Parnell: 'When he was down they turned on him to betray him and rend him like rats in a sewer'. On Stephen's side of the equation, the assumed parallelism of significant action is strangely supported by the actual fact that, in 1891, 8 October, the day Stephen is shouldered into the square ditch, was a Thursday; 9 October, the day he falls ill and, in the evening, hurries to undress for bed saying his prayer quickly quickly 'before the gas was lowered so that he

---

30 Parnell died in England on 6 October, but the news only reached Ireland on the 7th (see, impressively, Scholes/Kain, *Workshop*, pp. 136-37). 8 October, therefore, can properly be said to be the first post-Parnellite day in Irish history.

might not go to hell when he died' (I.405-6) was a Friday;[31] 10 October, the day in the infirmary, a Saturday; and 11 October, when Stephen revives at the break of day, a Sunday. On Parnell's side, a similarly significant patterning of the events is prohibited by historical fact: Parnell died on 6 October and was buried on the sixth day thereafter. All the novel can do—and does—is not to relate such a fact when it does not tally with the symbolically charged patterns of the fiction. Only pure fiction would permit a narrative of pure significance. But by the patterned interaction of history and fiction as found at the opening of *A Portrait*, and throughout the novel, not only historical event and calendar time are moralised. The fiction, too, Stephen's early schoolboy experience (thoroughly insignificant by itself), acquires symbolic stature.

Significant structure, then, derives here not from an analogy of Joyce's autobiography and fiction, but from an interaction of history and fiction. The distinction needs stressing, since it has been through biographical bias that earlier criticism has failed to perceive clearly the meaningful and precise interrelationship of historical event, calendar time, and the narrative in Chapter I of *A Portrait*.[32] It remains most remarkable, of course, that the narrative detail by which everything falls into place, that is, the 'right' number of days which separate the events of the first Clongowes episode from Christmas, and thus also from the Christmas dinner, was not present in the text until introduced by revision in the fair-copy manuscript. Only then was the chapter's symbolic potential finally realised. James Joyce creatively responded to the disposition of the narrative and the juxtaposition of episodes that he had brought about. The observable act of revision in the final manuscript thus additionally contributes to proving that the Christmas dinner scene only found its present position in Chapter I late in the novel's textual history. Before it did, no particular significance would have attached to the numbers in Stephen's desk; any numbers would have served.

---

31 In bed, 'the yellow curtains'—yellow like the candles round the catafalque—'shut him off on all sides' (I.422-23). Stephen hears the prefect's shoes descending the staircase. They guide his feverish imagination to a black dog with eyes as big as carriage lamps, and the ghosts of inhabitants of the castle long deceased. The prefect comes back the next morning to take Stephen to the infirmary. Is he, by fleeting association, Stephen's guide, as in a *Divina Commedia*, in a descent to hell?

32 Arnold Goldman, 'Stephen Dedalus's Dream of Parnell', *James Joyce Quarterly*, 6 (Spring 1969), 262-64, anticipates important elements of the present argument, but remains puzzled by inconsistencies between Joyce's biography and the fiction.

IV

To sum up: from Stanislaus Joyce's testimony we know that James Joyce began to write *A Portrait of the Artist as a Young Man* in September 1907. By 7 April 1908, he had finished three chapters. These, we must assume, were first drafts of the novel's first half which do not as such survive. During the remainder of 1908, no more than partial drafts of Chapter IV appear to have been written. In February of 1909, Ettore Schmitz's praise and criticism of the three completed chapters, plus, apparently, an additional early stretch of narrative of Chapter IV, gave Joyce encouragement to continue with the novel. The only certain knowledge we have of his work between 1909 and sometime in 1911 is that he completed Chapter IV and entered upon the composition of Chapter V. All of Chapter IV and the first thirteen manuscript leaves of Chapter V survive intact in the Dublin holograph from the *Portrait* manuscript which was nearly destroyed in 1911.

Notes or draft materials for Chapters I-IV of *A Portrait* are generally absent, and all of Chapters I-XIV of the *Stephen Hero* manuscript, in particular, is lost. If an inference from these facts is possible, Chapters I-IV of *A Portrait* were, by 1911, or even perhaps as early as sometime in 1909, considered essentially completed. Joyce's 'Alphabetical notebook' contains materials used almost exclusively in Chapter V of *A Portrait*, and in *Ulysses*. Its inception appears to date from the months of Joyce's visit to Dublin in 1909,[33] where, while he was separated from his manuscript, his memory of persons and incidents would have been refreshed and enriched.

By Joyce's own dating in retrospect, the incident of the near destruction of the *Portrait* manuscript occurred in the latter half of 1911. This was a true moment of crisis in the prepublication history. The 'charred remains of the MS' (*Letters* I, 136) remained tied up in an old sheet for some months, and thus it was in 1912 that the writing of *A Portrait of the Artist as a Young Man* entered its culminating phase. According to the mark of division set by the manuscript pages that were transferred physically

---

33 The notebook gives the appearance of having been arranged, and begun with a run of its first entries through most of the alphabetical headings, at one time. Consequently, the datable entry under 'Pappie' (see above, note 14) takes on significance for the dating of the whole notebook.

into the Dublin holograph, Joyce's post-1911 labours were threefold. He composed all of Chapter V, or approximately the last third of the book, in its final form. From it, he devised an essentially new structural plan for the entire book. This involved a reorganisation of Chapters I and II, centred on repositioning and revising the Christmas dinner scene, that intensified symbolical historic and mythic correspondences in the text. Chapters I to III were recopied in their entirety. The operations were interrelated and interdependent, and the creative achievement, one may well believe, was on a scale that would have required the best part of two years' work.

In 1913, when the title page of the Dublin holograph was dated, the end appears to have been well in sight. On Easter Day 1913, Joyce himself envisaged finishing his novel by the end of the year (*Letters* I, 73). He may, however, as so often, have underestimated the time he would need to complete it. He signed the final manuscript page 'Dublin 1904 Trieste 1914', and the sections of text which apparently were last included in the manuscript, such as the end of Chapter III and the revised villanelle episode, may not have reached their final form much before they were required as copy for the Trieste typist in, presumably, the summer of 1914. But it is a conclusion from the preceding genetic critical approach that, in essence, the novel attained the shape and structure in which we now possess it during 1912 and 1913. Despite all the vicissitudes and misfortunes of his day-to-day life,[34] these were two years of concentrated creativity for James Joyce, as he was forging and welding together *A Portrait of the Artist as a Young Man*.

---

34   Ellmann, *JJ*, chapters 20 and 21 *passim*.

James Joyce's *Dubliners* Critical Edition 1993

Introduction

A True History, 1904-1914[1]

In the first days of July 1904, probably on the second or on the fourth of the month, the Irish mystic, poet and painter, and close friend of W. B. Yeats, George Russell (otherwise 'AE') wrote to James Joyce inviting him to submit a short story to *The Irish Homestead*—the weekly, self-styled 'Organ of Agricultural and Industrial Development in Ireland'. Russell asked for something 'simple, rural?, live-making?, pathos? ... not to shock the readers' (*Letters* II, 43).[2] The letter was timely. Despite his poverty, the twenty-two year old Joyce was in an expansive, confident mood. His burgeoning romance with Nora Barnacle was entering its fourth buoyant week, and he had begun to circulate among his friends and admirers the (incomplete) manuscript of his autobiographical novel *Stephen Hero*, on which he continued to work energetically.[3] Russell

---

1   This section, as based on fresh and original research in Dublin, was prepared in collaboration with John O'Hanlon and Danis Rose. Here, and throughout these present editions of *Dubliners* and *A Portrait of the Artist as a Young Man*, I am most grateful for their help and advice.
2   Though this letter is undated, from circumstantial evidence and from the chronology of subsequent events we can be reasonably certain that Russell must have written it on, or very shortly after, Saturday 2 July 1904.
3   His sister May lugged the bulky manuscript around to Constantine Curran (then living in Cumberland place, North Circular road, not too far from Joyce's father's house in Cabra) on 23 June. See *Letters of James Joyce*, ed. by Stuart Gilbert, vol. I (New York: Viking Press, 1957, ²1966) (*Letters* I, 55). After Curran had read and returned it, Joyce gave it to George Russell to read. According to Richard Ellmann,

included with his letter the current issue of the *Homestead* and advised: 'Look at the story in this paper.' That Joyce did so, and with important consequences for the development—then in embryo—of his *oeuvre*, has thus far slipped through the net of Joycean scholarship and biography.

That part of *The Irish Homestead* for which Russell solicited a contribution was a section entitled 'Our Weekly Story'. In the summer of 1904, however, there was a troubling dearth of copy. The issues of 21 May, 28 May, and 4 June contained no story at all, the section in the issues of 11, 18, and 25 June was taken up by a three-part novelette by Louise Kenny, and the issues of 9 and 16 July again had no story. It follows that the sole issue to which Russell could have been referring was that of 2 July, in which issue there was indeed a story: a short piece written by Berkeley Campbell entitled 'The Old Watchman'. It is a first-person narrative in which the narrator, a twelve-year old boy, recounts the circumstances of the death of an old man he had befriended who had fallen on hard times. If this sounds familiar, then it should; for it would appear that Joyce not only read the story: he rewrote it. Had he called his own story 'The Old Priest', which, but for its subtler complexities of meaning he might have done, then that would have advertised the fact. Even so, he put into 'The Sisters' clues to the source of his artifice. In Campbell's story—which of course had the date of the issue (2 July) just above the title—the old watchman (who it transpires is the son of a former Dean of St Patrick's Cathedral) is sixty-five years of age; in the *Homestead* version of 'The Sisters', the card fixed to the door of the house where the old priest died reads: 'July 2nd, 189—The Rev. James Flynn (formerly of St. Ita's Church), aged 65 years. R. I. P.'[4]

James Joyce (New York: Oxford University Press, ²1982), p. 163, and conventional wisdom, it was Russell's reading of *Stephen Hero* which inspired him to write to Joyce asking for a story for the *Homestead*. But it is surely much more likely—given the tight chronology and given the fact that on an earlier occasion Russell had responded unfavourably to the poems of *Chamber Music*—that Joyce lent him the manuscript only after Russell had approached him. Furthermore, as we shall see, Russell had a more practical reason for writing.

4   There are other, lesser echoes. Campbell's boy usually spoke to the old watchman (he had pleurisy) while he was huddled over his fire basket. Joyce's boy conversed with the old priest while, wrapped up in his greatcoat, he sat by his fireside. The old watchman is not named; though his replacement is: James. Reverberations may be felt, too, even beyond 'The Sisters'. The watchman spent his exile in Australia, which is also where the schoolfriend of Eveline's father went (see especially the *Irish Homestead* version of 4.32-35). The watchman's earlier Dublin prodigality in

By 15 July, Joyce had finished writing 'The Sisters' and, indeed, having already progressed beyond the idea of one story, had formulated an ambitious plan. In a letter to Constantine Curran he announced: 'I am writing a series of epiclets—ten—for a paper. I have written one. I call the series *Dubliners* to betray the soul of that hemiplegia or paralysis which many consider a city'.[5] H. F. Norman, the editor of *The Irish Homestead*, accepted 'The Sisters' for publication on 23 July, making one change only: 'I am changing the name of the Parish quoted in the obituary notice so as to make the details of the story more remote'.[6] He sent Joyce a sovereign in payment. By a curious, sad coincidence, the story appeared in the issue of 13 August 1904, the first anniversary of Joyce's mother's untimely death. In such humble circumstances did *Dubliners*, and, beyond that, James Joyce's prose masterpieces, see their beginning in print.

Joyce adopted a pseudonym for 'The Sisters' and signed the story 'Stephen Daedalus'. He continued this practice with the next four or, possibly, five stories, reverting to his own name only in the summer of 1905, well into his exile. Stephen Daedalus, of course, was the name he had given to the principal character in *Stephen Hero* and the name which he had recently begun to use in signing letters to his friends (see, for example, *Letters* I, 54-55). Apart from the first ('The Sisters') and the last ('The Dead') the *Dubliners* stories were not written in the order of

---

drinking and gambling, albeit clichéd, is not unlike Jimmy's in the finale of 'After the Race'. Lastly, the Electric Tramway Company's watchman at his fire basket would seem an avatar of Gumley, the corporation's watchman at his brazier in Eumaeus, the sixteenth episode of *Ulysses* (and this episode especially, one should recall, has its roots in the story 'Ulysses' originally contemplated for *Dubliners*).

5 See *Letters* I, 55, where 'epiclets' is given as 'epicleti'. This misreading—'Greeker than the Greeks' (*U* 9.614)—has over the years led to deep yet, alas, misguided critical exegesis (see, for example, Ellmann, *James Joyce*, p. 163). Skeptical at what seemed to him an oblique way of using Greek, Wolfhard Steppe, co-editor of James Joyce, *Ulysses. A Critical and Synoptic Edition*, prepared by Hans Walter Gabler with Wolfhard Steppe and Claus Melchior, 3 vols. (New York: Garland Publishing Inc., 1984, ²1986), privately surmised that the word might simply be 'epiclets' (i.e., 'little epics', an ordinary English diminutive). A reading of the original in University College, Dublin, has proved him right. The letter, incidentally, is rather ambiguously dated 'The Rain, Friday'. As there were showers on just about every Friday during that summer, the weather accounts are not terribly helpful. The cricket reports are more enlightening: uniquely, on the morning of Friday, 15 July, there was 'torrential rain' sufficient to put a stop to play.

6 Letter to James Joyce of 23 July 1904, now at Cornell.

their ultimate arrangement. The second, 'Eveline', appeared in *The Irish Homestead* on 10 September, and very likely was composed during the second half of July and/or the first weeks of August. At that time, Joyce had begun to think prospectively about his relationship with Nora, and these considerations certainly inspired, if obliquely, its theme. 'After the Race' was drafted while Joyce raced about Dublin touching friends and enemies alike for the wherewithal to get away from Ireland. The story was completed on 3 October 1904[7] and handed in to the *Homestead* office the following day, just four days prior to Joyce's departure with Nora from the North Wall docks.[8]

James Joyce always considered 8 October 1904 as the date of his 'first' marriage to Nora Barnacle (the 'second' being their civil wedding in London on 4 July 1931). The Joyces, after brief stays in Zurich and Trieste, settled down in Pola in Austria. It was while at Zurich, however, in late October that he began his fourth story. He called it 'Christmas Eve'. A month later, from Pola, he reported to Stanislaus that he had written 'about half' of it (*Letters* II, 71). By this he presumably meant the fragmentary fair copy of four pages which has been preserved.[9] Instead of finishing this story he recast it as, or replaced it by, 'Hallow Eve', which he sent to Dublin on 19 January 1905. 'Hallow Eve' was not accepted by *The Irish Homestead*, nor is it extant today in any manuscript version. (By the end of September 1905 Joyce had retitled it 'The Clay' and 'slightly rewritten it' [*Letters* II, 109]. Subsequently, this title was abbreviated to

---

[7] Joyce wrote from St Peter's terrace to Nora on this day: 'I am in such high good humour this morning that I insist on writing to you ... I got up early this morning to finish a story I was writing. When I had written a page I decided I would write a letter to you instead. Besides, I thought you disliked Monday and a letter from me might put you in better spirits', *Letters of James Joyce*, ed. by Richard Ellmann, vol. II and III (New York: Viking Press, 1966) (*Letters* II, 50). Ellmann has dated this letter 'About 1 September 1904'. This is certainly wrong. The possible contending Mondays are 30 August, 5, 12, 19 and 26 September, and 3 October. On the first date Joyce was still at 60 Shelbourne road; on the second at his uncle's in Fairview; on the third at the Tower; on the fourth back at his uncle's; and on the fifth had a bad cold and was feeling desolate (*Letters* II, 56). Which leaves 3 October. Furthermore, he signed the letter 'Jim', which he did only after his 'famous interview about the letters' with Nora on 9 September.

[8] Jim, it turned out, was no Eveline; nor, in their tryst, was Nora.

[9] All surviving manuscripts of *Dubliners* are reproduced in vol. [4] of *The James Joyce Archive*: James Joyce, *Dubliners. A Facsimile of Drafts and Manuscripts*, prefaced and arranged by Hans Walter Gabler, ed. by Michael Groden, *et al.*, 63 vols. (New York and London: Garland Publishing, Inc., 1978).

'Clay'.) For the next several months, while he waited in vain for good news from Dublin and during which time he decided to dedicate the collection to Stanislaus—he subsequently changed his mind about this—Joyce did not proceed with *Dubliners* but, instead, focused his energies on *Stephen Hero*. In early May, he wrote to Stanislaus promising he would write another story if he knew the result of 'Hallow Eve'. Eventually he began to think seriously about finding another publisher. On 3 June he asked Stanislaus to get permission from the *Homestead* to republish the first two stories. In the next six weeks he wrote the fifth and sixth stories—'The Boarding House' and 'Counterparts'—and sent them to Stanislaus in mid-July, quite possibly in the very manuscripts that still survive. The first of these, 'The Boarding House', is dated 1 July 1905 in the extant manuscript and is the last physically to carry the signature 'Stephen Daedalus'; yet the manuscripts of these two stories are, as documents, so clearly companion pieces that 'Counterparts' too may have borne the name Daedalus on its lost final leaf. Thereafter, Joyce relinquished the pseudonymous pose and signed all subsequent *Dubliners* stories in his own name.

The summer of 1905 was for James Joyce as difficult as it was eventful. His faith in himself and in the life he had created with Nora began to falter. He suspended work on the autobiographical novel *Stephen Hero*, abandoning it in effect as a fragment of twenty-five (out of a projected sixty-three) chapters. About *Dubliners*, however, he remained sanguine, believing (incorrectly as it turned out) that he could find a publisher to bring it out sooner rather than later and that it would bring in some much-needed money. The birth of his son Giorgio on 27 July spurred him on to greater efforts. The seventh story to be written was 'A Painful Case'. It exists both in a draft manuscript (originally entitled 'A Painful Incident'), which at least in part documents the process of composition, and in a fair copy signed and dated 'JAJ 15.8.05'. The eighth story, 'Ivy Day in the Committee Room', survives in two fair-copy manuscripts, of which the earlier is dated '29 August 1905', just two weeks later than the fair copy of 'A Painful Case'.[10] 'An Encounter' saw completion

---

10 For both of these stories, and for 'The Sisters' and 'After the Race', Joyce requested specific information in a letter to his brother of 24 September (*Letters* II, 109-112). Stanislaus authenticated details already present in them and in which, in the case of 'Ivy Day in the Committee Room', both manuscripts accord. The textual changes

about mid-September 1905 (within three weeks of 'Ivy Day') and was sent to Stanislaus on 18 September. 'A Mother', the tenth to be written, followed within a fortnight. Both of these stories are extant in fair-copy manuscripts.

Although Joyce's original plan (adumbrated in his letter to Constantine Curran of 15 July 1904 quoted above) of a suite of ten little epics was now complete, he had in the meantime changed his plans. Writing to William Heinemann on 23 September 1905, Joyce offered him *Dubliners*: 'a collection of twelve short stories.' On the following day he enumerated the sequence to Stanislaus: three stories of childhood, 'The Sisters', 'An Encounter', and another one (the as yet unwritten 'Araby'); three stories of adolescence, 'The Boarding House', 'After the Race', and 'Eveline'; three stories of mature life, 'The Clay', 'Counterparts', and 'A Painful Case'; and, completing the pattern, three stories of public life, 'Ivy Day in the Committee Room', 'A Mother', and the last story of the book (the as yet unwritten 'Grace'). (This arrangement, as we shall see, was subsequently altered at least twice.) By mid-October 1905 the eleventh story, 'Araby', was completed and the twelfth, 'Grace', begun. At the same time, as is indicated by the range of questions in the letter to Stanislaus of 24 September, Joyce was busy revising the existing texts. The opening story of the collection benefitted tangibly from his brother's investigations, as is evident from the few but important variants between the version represented by the *Irish Homestead* printing and the first of the two extant manuscripts for 'The Sisters'. The changes prove that this manuscript postdates *The Irish Homestead* and suggest late October 1905 as its date. It is significant that a first reconsideration of the opening of the book thus apparently coincided with the composition of the then concluding story, 'Grace'.

In the meantime, and apparently at the instigation of Stanislaus, Joyce wrote to Arthur Symons, who replied saying that he thought that Constable's might be interested in both *Chamber Music* and *Dubliners*. Joyce sent them the former but held back the latter, offering it instead to Grant Richards on 15 October, adding, foolishly perhaps, that he believed

---

one finds entered in the second fair copy of 'Ivy Day' (as opposed to those revealed by collation with the first fair copy) are not related to the period and occasion of its composition but to its later history. It was one of several stories over which, time after time, publication difficulties arose.

that 'people might be willing to pay for the special odour of corruption which, I hope, floats over my stories' (*Letters* II, 123). Richards asked to see the manuscript three days later.[11] Both 'Grace' and the revision of the earlier stories were completed by the end of November and he sent the manuscript to Richards on 3 December. He did not then know it, but the nine-year ordeal of getting his book *Dubliners* printed and published had begun.

During the following two months, while he waited for word, Joyce added a new story, 'Two Gallants'. Richards finally responded on 17 February 1906, making Joyce an offer which was accepted. The book was to be published in May or June or in September in a slim crown octavo volume priced at 5/—. A contract followed on 23 February. The previous day Joyce had sent Richards 'Two Gallants' with the instruction that it should be inserted between 'After the Race' and 'The Boarding House'. (This suggests that, perhaps when he sent the stories to Richards, Joyce had interchanged the positions of 'The Boarding House' and 'Eveline' from their order as cited in his letter to Stanislaus of 24 September.) Returning the contract signed on 28 February, Joyce wrote: 'I would like the printer to follow the manuscript accurately in punctuation and arrangement. Inverted commas, for instance, to enclose dialogue always seemed to me a great eyesore' (*Letters* II, 131). He added that he had written part of a fourteenth story ('A Little Cloud'). This was still unfinished on 13 March when he wrote to say that it was to be inserted between 'The Boarding House' and 'Counterparts'. It was finished on 22 April. Before it could be fair-copied and sent, however, the storm clouds began to gather. Richards passed the manuscript of *Dubliners* to his printer on 12 April and instructed him to prepare sample pages. By a stroke of the worst possible luck, it seems that when Joyce had sent him the thirteenth story, 'Two Gallants', Richards had not inserted it into its proper place in the sequence, but had merely placed it on top of the pile. To provide the sample pages, then, the printer chose the beginning of 'Two Gallants' and had at least two pages set up (these survive and are now at Harvard). When reading his compositor's handiwork the printer was horrified, scrawled 'We cannot print this' on the second proof, and sent it back to Richards. On 23 April Richards informed Joyce of the

---

11   For Grant Richards's side of the correspondence, see Robert Scholes, 'Grant Richards to James Joyce', *Studies in Bibliography*, 16 (1963), 139-60.

printer's refusal and added that he had strong objections to two passages in 'Counterparts'. He returned the manuscripts of the two stories and, further, asked for another word to replace 'bloody' in 'Grace'. Joyce replied three days later, refusing to compromise. A long and protracted correspondence ensued, in which Joyce made some concessions and Richards demanded more deletions (*Letters* I, 60-63, and II, 132-143). Finally, the parties appeared to reach agreement. On 19 June Richards sent back the entire manuscript to Joyce in order that he might make the necessary alterations. On its resubmission on 9 July Joyce stated that he had 're-arranged and renumbered the stories in the middle of the book' and that he had included 'A Little Cloud' in the position that he had earlier indicated. This sequence was to remain stable. He also said that he had rewritten 'The Sisters.' It may be assumed that Richards received the opening story at this time in its second extant fair copy. In 'Grace', by contrast, Joyce had removed only two instances of 'bloody'. These, however, exist undeleted in the extant fair copy, which also incorporates passages following from Joyce's research at the Biblioteca Vittorio Emanuele in Rome in November 1906 into the proceedings of the Vatican Council of 1870. Among the surviving manuscripts of the *Dubliners* stories, this fair copy of 'Grace' is thus identified as postdating the original negotiations for publication with Grant Richards. Incidentally, it bypasses Richards's censorial strictures.

At the end of July 1906, Joyce moved with his family to Rome. During August he contemplated rewriting 'After the Race' and he also asked Stanislaus to send him the manuscript of 'A Painful Case' as he wanted to revise it.[12] On 31 August he said that he had 'some loose sheets in my pocket about 5 pages' to add to 'A Painful Case', but that he did not have the energy to continue working. The heat and the inhospitability of Rome oppressed him and he began to feel homesick for the British Isles, 'rashers and eggs in the morning, the English variety of sunshine, a beefsteak with boiled potatoes and onions, a pier at night or a beach and cigarettes' (*Letters* II, 157). By 25 September his nostalgia had grown stronger. 'Sometimes thinking of Ireland it seems to me that I have been unnecessarily harsh. I have reproduced (in *Dubliners* at least) none of its ingenuous insularity and its hospitality' (*Letters* II, 166). It has often

---

12   *Letters* II, 148. This would seem to indicate that, in addition to the set sent to Richards, Joyce left a spare manuscript of *Dubliners* with Stanislaus in Trieste.

been said that in these words of Joyce lies the germ of the last story of *Dubliners*, 'The Dead'.[13] Yet the conception and execution of 'The Dead' lay still almost a year ahead. More immediately, Joyce added four days later: 'I have a new story for *Dubliners* in my head. It deals with Mr Hunter' (*Letters* II, 168). This story which—at least in this context—never got any further than its title, but which was centred upon a spontaneous act of hospitality, was to be called 'Ulysses'.

Out of the blue, Grant Richards wrote on 24 September 1906 breaking his contract and rejecting *Dubliners*. Joyce reacted by making new concessions, but to no avail. The manuscript was returned on 26 October. A barrister advised Joyce not to waste his money seeking legal redress. Wisely in this instance, he concurred. Summoning up a little energy and turning to his manuscript, he made some corrections: he added the name of the laundry where Maria worked—the 'Dublin by Lamplight Laundry'—to 'The Clay', revised 'Grace',[14] and re-introduced 'bloody' into 'Ivy Day in the Committee Room.' He also thought of another story, 'The Last Supper', about the son of his old landlady, but though he asked Stanislaus to supply details about the incident behind the idea for this story, and also (for the projected 'Ulysses') to send his reminiscences of Mr Hunter (a proto-model for Leopold Bloom), Joyce never wrote it. In early December he sent the partly revised manuscript of *Dubliners* to John Long, the publisher. For the next few months he did little else but read. He did, however, conceive of new 'titles' for stories: 'The Dead', 'The Street', 'Vengeance', and 'At Bay' (*Letters* II, 209)—to add to the already mentioned 'Ulysses' and 'The Last Supper'. In mid-January 1907, Long replied discouragingly and followed this up with a final rejection on 21 February.

In the meantime Joyce had had a bellyful of Rome. He felt it was time he made up his mind to become a writer. He handed in notice at the bank where he worked, packed his bags, and rearrived in Trieste (his palm out to Stanislaus) on or about 7 March. Nora was again pregnant. Joyce's first few months back in the city were spent striving to make ends

---

13   Though in this story surely the sentiment comes under heavy irony, and the general miasma of frustration and pathos that pervades *Dubliners*, far from being dispelled, is thickened.

14   It is probable that it was at this time that he wrote out the extant fair copy of this story.

meet until, in mid-summer, a few days before the birth on 26 July of his daughter Lucia, he was struck down with rheumatic fever. He spent a few weeks in hospital and another couple of months recovering. During this period of ill health he wrote the fifteenth, final story and capstone of *Dubliners*, 'The Dead'. It was finished on 20 September. Though only fragments of its beginning and end have survived from Joyce's seventy-seven-page holograph, the story's full text, (incompletely) corrected and amended by the author, is preserved in a scribal copy of eighteen typewritten pages and an allograph of thirty-eight pages in two hands, one of them Stanislaus Joyce's.[15] The composition of 'The Dead' marked the end of Joyce's creative engagement with *Dubliners*. He returned to his abandoned autobiographical novel, now entirely reconceived, reorganised and newly styled as *A Portrait of the Artist as a Young Man*.

Even now the saga of *Dubliners* was not over. On 24 September 1907 Joyce offered the book (now for the first time comprising all fifteen stories) to Elkin Mathews, the publisher of *Chamber Music*. Mathews asked to see the manuscript on 23 October, but laid it aside until after the Christmas season, and finally rejected it on 6 February 1908. When he turned it down, Mathews suggested sending the manuscript to Maunsel and Co. of Dublin,[16] but Joyce, preferring an English publisher, demurred and asked (on 9 February) for it to be returned to him. He next tried Hutchinson's (they refused to look at the manuscript), Alston Rivers (ditto), Sisleys (they wanted Joyce to pay), Greening and Co. (No!), Archibald Constable (No!), and Edward Arnold (No! yet again).

By the end of the year, Joyce began to come around to the idea of having the book published in Ireland and he conceived the idea of sending Stanislaus to Dublin to push the business on. On 13 February 1909 he wrote to Mathews and asked him to arrange for a communication with Hone (Joseph Maunsel Hone, the money behind Maunsel and Co., which George Roberts ran). This was done, and at the end of July Joyce himself (and not as originally planned Stanislaus) went to Dublin to meet Hone and Roberts. The negotiations went well and a contract

---

15 Only page 29, from the fifth word onwards, is in Stanislaus's hand. The 'family likeness' of the other hand suggests that it may be that of Joyce's sister Eileen.
16 In his letter (now at Cornell) Mathews wrote that he 'mentioned it to Mr. Hone (Maunsel and Co., Dublin) the other day, and he said "Oh, send the ms. on to us, as it might suit us"'.

was duly drawn up and signed on 19 August. *Dubliners* was to appear in March of the following year in dark grey binding with dark red lettering, at a price of 3/6 (*Letters* II, 230-38). Satisfied, and missing Nora considerably, Joyce returned to Trieste in early September.

Two months had not passed before he was back again in Dublin with a plan to set up the first cinema in Ireland. (The enterprise was not, for reasons not entered into here, a financial success.) According to his own account (*Letters* II, 292) it was while he was in Dublin in December that George Roberts first asked him to alter the narrative passage in 'Ivy Day in the Committee Room' dealing with Edward VII. He agreed, much against his will, and 'altered one or two phrases'.[17] He returned to Trieste at the beginning of January 1910.

On 23 March Roberts wrote promising the proofs in early April and publication in May. The proofs, however, did not turn up until June, during which month Joyce was 'very busy' correcting them. On 10 June Roberts wrote again and complained that he was still not happy with 'Ivy Day in the Committee Room' and asked that the entire passage referring to the late King be removed or entirely rewritten. Joyce corrected and returned both a set of galleys and a set of page proofs. Curiously, the proofs for 'Ivy Day' contained the original—and not the (presumed late 1909) autograph alternative—version of the disputed passage. Publication, scheduled for July, was nevertheless postponed once again. In December, Roberts set 20 January as the new publication date and he sent Joyce another set of the proofs of 'Ivy Day in the Committee Room.' He once again asked him to delete or radically to alter the passage concerning Edward VII. The evidence indicates that he sent Joyce a copy of the uncorrected early page proofs. (This point is of importance and we shall return to it later.) Joyce proposed either (a) deletion of the passage with a prefatory note of explanation added, or (b) arbitration as a solution of the matter (*Letters* II, 289). Roberts, infuriatingly, did not reply. On 10 June, at the end of his tether, Joyce wrote again repeating his proposal and threatening—if he failed to receive a reply forthwith—legal action. He further swore that he would communicate the whole affair to the press by way of a circular letter.

---

17 It is possible that it was on this occasion that he wrote in the 'alternative' passage on folio 16 of the extant (Cornell) manuscript.

For the second time the legal advice received was that it would not be worthwhile to sue. Redirecting himself, Joyce next determined—like Anna Livia in *Finnegans Wake*—to present the case to and to seek the opinion of the King (now George V, Edward VII's son), to whom on 1 August 1911 he accordingly sent the proofs of 'Ivy Day' with the disputed passage clearly marked.[18] Understandably declining to opine, the King ordered his private secretary to return the enclosures. Not entirely displeased with this partial success, Joyce immediately set about putting into effect the next phase of his campaign. First he carefully corrected and revised the moot passage[19] and had a number of slips of it printed (in an attractive art nouveau font, presumably locally in Trieste). He then wrote (on 17 August 1911) his famous 'Letter to the Editor' into which he pasted a copy of the reprinted fragment (*Letters* II, 291-93). Copies of the letter were sent to interested parties such as Grant Richards and to nearly all of the newspapers in Ireland. It appeared in the Belfast *Northern Whig* on 26 August with the passage from 'Ivy Day' omitted and—in full—in the Dublin-based *Sinn Féin* on 2 September. To a man, the major organs refused to publish it, and, in sum, it had no effect on Maunsel and Co.

Thoroughly depressed, and living in straitened circumstances, Joyce was at a complete loss as to what to do next. Around this time, also, he (temporarily) suspended work on *A Portrait of the Artist as a Young Man*.[20] The seasons passed. In 1912 he decided to send Nora—who was

---

18   This set of proofs—the sole surviving section of the early 1910 page proofs—is now at Yale. It is almost certainly the very set that Roberts had sent Joyce seven months earlier. The twin parallel lines in the margins of pages 193-194 marking the passage (see *James Joyce Archive*, vol. [5], pp. 79-80) might be Roberts's or they might be Joyce's. It is unlikely that when he sent it to the King the passage contained Joyce's autograph corrections and revisions (these would have confused His Majesty) or Joyce's smaller diagonal lines indicating the passage's beginning and end. These, as we shall argue, were added immediately *after* the King's return of the proofs to Joyce.

19   These improvements—which indicate an alteration of Mr Henchy's diction and a decision to remove some 'stage-Irish' spellings and punctuations—are of considerable textual importance in that, made just one year later when his memory was still relatively fresh, they probably correspond to those corrections and revisions made on the lost corrected copy of the early page proofs returned to Maunsel's.

20   Indeed, it may have been at this time that he threw the *Portrait* manuscript in the fire; see the 'Introduction' to the critical edition of *A Portrait of the Artist as a Young Man*, ed. by Hans Walter Gabler with Walter Hettche (New York and London: Garland Publishing Inc., 1993), p. 4.

anxious to see her family once more—with Lucia to Ireland. The new plan was for Nora to intercede at Maunsel's on her husband's behalf. She arrived in Dublin on 8 July and saw Roberts soon after, but to no avail. On another impulse, Joyce decided that he would himself travel at once to Ireland, bringing Giorgio with him. En route, while passing through London he called on Joseph Maunsel Hone. He, however, could do nothing. In Dublin he met Roberts who came up with a new proposal: Joyce could delete disputed passages in 'Ivy Day' and also in 'An Encounter' or, alternatively, he could buy out the book from him, printed and bound, and have it distributed by Simpkin Marshall of London. Joyce said he would think about it, and left for Galway to join Nora. Further negotiations ensued, with Roberts now suggesting that Joyce buy the sheets from him and offer them to Grant Richards. Joyce arranged for a solicitor, John G. Lidwell, to advise him and returned to Dublin. After much haggling and toing-and-froing, threats and counter-threats of legal action, the matter seemed to be settled between them: Joyce would publish the book himself; of the total costs for printing the book, named at £57, he would pay Roberts £30; £15 were due within fifteen days; on receipt, Roberts would let him have 104 copies of the sheets; and, on further receipt of a second £15 within a further fifteen days, he would hand over the remainder of the total of 1000 sheets (*Letters* II, 301-316). But this plan too came to grief in the end when the printer, John Falconer, refused to hand over even one set of the sheets. According to Joyce, Falconer said he was going to break up the type and burn the sheets. According to Roberts, the sheets were in fact guillotined (*Letters* II, 319n.). The following day, 11 September 1912, having managed to obtain from Roberts 'by a ruse' a complete set of proofs, James Joyce left Dublin in utter disgust, never again to return.

Such at any rate is the story that has come down to us. But is it true? There are several serious implausibilities in it. Take the question of the printer's hire: the £57 owed by Maunsel to Falconer for printing 1000 copies of *Dubliners*. This was by no means an inconsiderable sum in 1912. The printer's claim that he cared nothing for that money—or even just for the £30 that Joyce was to have been made to pay—is risible.[21] Hence, whether valued at £30 or £57, one wonders: was the

---

21 Joyce's later paranoid suspicion that his enemies in Dublin had paid the £57 is equally incredible.

merchandise available at all? Moreover, with 104 copies promised within two weeks, and a remaining 896 another two weeks ahead, the important question does not even begin to be answered of *when* and *why* 1000 copies, and copies of precisely *what* text, may be supposed to have been printed in the first place. While the events considered were those of the summer of 1912, *Dubliners* were set in galleys two years earlier. The surviving galley proofs of 'A Mother' are dated 8 June 1910 and those for 'The Dead' 19 June 1910. Assuming an even progress of work, this dates the galleys for 'Ivy Day in the Committee Room', specifically, to the early days of June, which would allow just enough time for Joyce to have corrected and returned them to inspire Roberts's letter to him of 10 June expressing dissatisfaction with the state of the passage on Edward VII. We know also that Joyce was still engaged in correcting proof on 24 June—by which time he must have been working on the early page proofs—and that he completed the task (*Letters* II, 287-88). Final page proofs—made from the corrected early page proofs—are extant for most of 'The Dead'; they extend from sheet R to sheet U and break off when it is clear that the rest of the story, and therefore the remainder of the book, does not stretch to fill another sheet. From the opening of the book, too, late page proofs—sheets A to K—exist up to and partly including 'A Painful Case'. This total of fifteen sheets of late page proofs extant was presumably pulled in June or July 1910. Six full sheets, however, are absent (i.e., sheets L-Q). So technically defined is this as a reservation of space that these sheets may in fact never have been printed. From June 1910, and yet more stubbornly from December 1910, George Roberts was not satisfied with the text as it stood. When, after his June letter, he wrote again in December, the final page proofs for 'Ivy Day' (and with them, by inference, those of the remainder of 'A Painful Case', and of all of 'A Mother' and 'Grace') seem not yet to have been prepared. Nothing happened in 1911 or in 1912 to make him change his mind about 'Ivy Day' or to induce him to give the order for the printing of 1000 copies of the whole of *Dubliners*. Such an order would have been tantamount to a decision to go ahead with publication. The conclusion to be drawn from these inferences and these facts is that the one thousand copies of the sheets of *Dubliners* never existed.[22]

While in London in transit to Trieste, Joyce tried without success to interest Ford Madox Hueffer's *English Review* in *Dubliners*. He also took it to Mills and Boon, to whom Padraic Colum had given him an introduction. On 13 September he handed over to Mr Boon the set of sheets he had wangled out of Roberts (*Letters* II, 320).[23] Ingenuous to the last, he included as a preface a copy (presumably a press cutting obtained in Dublin) of his letter to *Sinn Féin*. He considered that it would act as a 'selling point' for the book; whereas to the publisher it acted merely as a frightener. Boon had his letter of rejection in the post in less than a week.

In the year that followed, *Dubliners* once again did the rounds. In December, Joyce sent his set of Maunsel proofs to Martin Secker; in February 1913 he approached (for the second time) Elkin Mathews; in April John Long (ditto); and in July he tried Macmillan. There may well have been others. Finally, back at square one, on 23 November 1913 he wrote to Grant Richards and asked him to reconsider his 1906 rejection. Richards, who was a relatively decent chap for a publisher, had in the long interim experienced some twinges, if not pangs, of conscience over his earlier treatment of Joyce, and besides, Joyce did offer to cover part of the expenses of publication (*Letters* II, 324). Richards wrote back at once asking to see the book again. Joyce, still intent on the inclusion of his preface, quickly brought it up to date, entitled it 'A Curious History' (*Letters* II, 324-25) and submitted it, together with the set of Maunsel proofs. It is at this stage, finally, that these can be more specifically identified. As Robert Scholes has demonstrated in

---

22 Roberts's version, recounted to Richard Ellmann many years later, has the status of one of Hugh Kenner's 'Irish Facts'. Falconer's version, which we know only secondhand from Joyce's letters, must have been an embellishment of the truth made in the heat of the moment. Had Joyce realised such a state of affairs he would of course have lost the title of the broadside 'Gas from a Burner' which—energised with ire—he composed a few days later in the waiting room of a railway station at Flushing in Holland.

23 This fact is of importance as it confirms Joyce's statement that he obtained a 'complete set' of proofs from Roberts. Had it not been complete, he could not have offered it to a publisher while yet in transit; it would have had to be perfected with pages from the manuscript which we know Joyce had left behind him in Trieste.

his investigations of the text of *Dubliners*,[24] Richards's printer's copy was the Maunsel early page proofs. It was a set of these, therefore, that Joyce 'by a ruse' had obtained in Dublin in 1912.[25] With 'A Curious History' and the printer's copy, a title-page was also included (*Letters* II, 330).

While Joyce waited for news from Richards, a vortex of change entered his life in the person of Ezra Pound, brass band and bandwagon. At first drawn to and by the poetry, Pound soon became an important and influential advocate for *A Portrait of the Artist as a Young Man*. But he did not lack in engagement for *Dubliners*. Joyce sent him 'A Curious History' which Pound printed in his regular column in *The Egoist* on 15 January 1914. While the surviving correspondence is confusing and perhaps misleading on the subject,[26] it appears that he also sent him some stories. Writing as he did on 19 January that he was forwarding 'the' three stories (one of which was 'An Encounter') to the New York magazine *Smart Set*,[27] Pound must have had them in hand. Perhaps he was even temporarily in possession of the entire collection. That Joyce did assemble at some time after 1910, though more probably after 1912, a complete run of the *Dubliners* stories distinct (and textually different) from Richards's printer's copy is certain, as, apart from two pages of 'A Little Cloud', it has survived. It comprises: (a) the final proofs (pages [1]—160) of 'The Sisters' to 'A Painful Case'; (b) the manuscripts of 'A Painful Case' and 'Ivy Day in the Committee Room'; (c) the galley proofs of 'A Mother'; (d) the manuscript of 'Grace'; (e) the (incomplete)

---

24 Robert E. Scholes, 'Observations on the text of *Dubliners*' and 'Further Observations on the text of *Dubliners*', *Studies in Bibliography*, 15 (1962), 191-205, and 17 (1964), 107-22.

25 This reinforces the inference that the final page proofs for 'Ivy Day in the Committee Room'—and probably also those for 'A Mother' and 'Grace'—were never prepared, Roberts having told the printer to stop when he received back the (to him) inadequately revised early page proofs of 'Ivy Day'.

26 For Pound's letters to Joyce of the period, see *Pound/Joyce. The Letters of Ezra Pound to James Joyce, with Pound's Essays on Joyce*. Edited and with Commentary by Forrest Read (New York: New Directions Paperback, 1970), pp. 24-25.

27 On 14 February he sent on the magazine's reply (delicately described by Pound as a prime 'piece of bull shit'), which though lost was evidently a rejection. Read, *Pound/Joyce*, p. 24, assumes the other two were 'The Boarding House' and 'A Little Cloud' because, in May 1915, at the behest of B. W. Huebsch, *Smart Set* published these two stories. Read's argument is unsound, as the 1915 copy appears to have been provided by Huebsch.

final proofs (pages [257]-320) of 'The Dead'; and (f) the final pages of the manuscript of 'The Dead'.[28] It is thus possible that Joyce sent Pound the whole text in this exemplar.[29]

In the meantime, on 20 January 1914, Grant Richards replied requesting further information from Joyce. This was sent on 24 January (*Letters* II, 328-29). Joyce wrote: 'The book is in the form approved by me, i.e. with one or two slight changes already made'.[30] Richards finally agreed on 29 January to publish *Dubliners*, but shorn of the preface and with the dialogue dashes replaced by quotation marks. He sent a signed agreement on 23 March.[31] Setting from printed copy, Richards's printer bypassed galley-proof stage and in April sent page proofs to Joyce.[32] Joyce quickly corrected and returned these, expecting to see a revise. It

---

28 At the end of (b) is written 'Next Story of *Dubliners A Mother* in printed proofsheet'; at the end of (c) 'Next Story of *Dubliners Grace* in MS'; at the end of (d) 'Next Story of *Dubliners The Dead* part in book from page 160 to page 320 part in MS'; and at the beginning of (f) 'End of Story *The Dead*': all in the same markedly sprawling authorial hand. The late page proofs themselves (what Joyce calls the 'book', in which the unnumbered title page of 'The Dead' [257] follows page 160) are unmarked. In the *James Joyce Archive*, vol. [4], p. xxx, I essentially identified this mixed-copy assembly of the *Dubliners* text. But I was mistaken in suggesting that Richards's printer's copy was mixed.

29 But if he gave him only a selection, it is not impossible that he sent a typescript, as Read, *Pound/Joyce*, p. 1, holds. *Dubliners* as a whole, it is true, was never typed. But this was a time when Joyce, to prepare copy for the *Egoist* serialisation of *A Portrait of the Artist as a Young Man*, for the first time in his life employed a typist. In late March or early April (the letter is undated) Pound wrote again, saying that he had sent off 'Araby' to the US, of which again, therefore, he must have had a copy.

30 This would seem to indicate that the prize set of Maunsel early page proofs had meanwhile been lightly marked up. It also implies that Joyce had no distinct memory of the advanced textual state of the Maunsel late page proofs. On both points, see further below.

31 Richards added that his printer had mislaid pages 3-4 and 13-14 of 'The Sisters'. Three days later (on 26 March) Joyce sent off typed copies of the 'Sisters' pages in question (*Letters* II, 392-95). These would most easily have been prepared from the identically paginated 1910 late page proofs that constitute part of the mixed-copy set of the text.

32 In April 1914, the printer's copy was returned to Joyce along with two sets of the Richards page proofs (one of which, unmarked, still survives). The title page was sent back later (*Letters* II, 334). It is possible, also, that the missing pages 3-4 and 13-14 were found. The Maunsel early page proofs remained in Joyce's possession for many years. In May 1917 he described it to John Quinn as 'the only copy extant, so far as I know, of the burned first edition' (*Letters* II, 396). In 1927 he offered the set for sale to A. S. W. Rosenbach (*Letters* I, 252, and III, 161). Rosenbach, and after him other dealers, declined. It is not known when or how or if Joyce eventually disposed of them. Presently missing, they may resurface some day.

never came. Frustrated, he prepared a list of further corrections and sent them on to Richards on 14 May. The corrections were not made, nor has the list itself survived.

Dubliners, by James Joyce, in an edition of 1250 copies, was published by Grant Richards on 15 June 1914. In 1916, B. W. Huebsch of New York bought 504 sets of sheets from Richards and issued them as the first American edition.

The Document Relationships

Of each *Dubliners* story, there was first—after drafts that (save for that of 'A Painful Case') are all lost—an autograph fair copy. In fact, Joyce fair-copied the final draft text of most, if not all, stories more than once. The copies varied only slightly, as is witnessed by the two extant manuscripts of 'Ivy Day in the Committee Room'. Where only one exemplar survives, such differences as there were, are, as a rule, irrecoverable. Exceptions are 'The Boarding House', where the variants in the single extant fair copy indicate that behind the printed text was another, somewhat revised manuscript; and 'Eveline', which went into the book publication of *Dubliners* in a version—and therefore, doubtless, from a fair copy—significantly different from the text published in *The Irish Homestead*. For 'After the Race', by contrast, also first published in *The Irish Homestead*, the book text, although presumably not printed from the manuscript behind the *Homestead* but from another exemplar, shows very little revision. The opposite is true for 'The Sisters'. For this story, the *Homestead* and the book texts are radically different versions, each represented in one surviving fair copy. Of these, the first-version manuscript, as indicated, was prepared as the original copy of the story for the book as first submitted to Grant Richards in 1905, and thus postdates the *Irish Homestead* publication.

Joyce's original printer's copy for the *Dubliners* volume was a stable set of autograph fair copies which went to Grant Richards for the first time in November 1905, then a second time in June 1906, and finally to Maunsel and Co. of Dublin in 1909. The changes and substitutions in this set were few and specific. The first submission to Grant Richards in November 1905 consisted of the twelve stories originally planned, to which the thirteenth story —'Two Gallants'—followed in February 1906, while the negotiations over the publication were ongoing. The portfolio was returned in June 1906. In July, Joyce re-submitted it with the second version of 'The Sisters' in place of the first, a replacement leaf or two in 'Ivy Day in the Committee Room', and possibly in 'Counterparts', and the fourteenth story, 'A Little Cloud', inserted between 'The Boarding House' and 'Counterparts'. Thirteen of the fourteen manuscripts seen, and in the end declined, by Richards (and preliminarily even handled by his printers, as in the case of 'Two Gallants'), three years later became the copy for Maunsel in Dublin, with the addition now of 'The Dead', written in 1907. For 'Grace', as indicated, Maunsel received a fresh manuscript. The manuscript of the story submitted to Richards has not survived.

The Richards/Maunsel set of manuscripts is not entirely lost. The extant fair copies of 'The Sisters', 'An Encounter', 'A Painful Case', 'Ivy Day in the Committee Room' (the Cornell copy), 'A Mother', 'Grace' (being the post-1906 version) and 'The Dead' (with two large middle sections missing) belonged to it. The fair copies preserved of 'The Boarding House' and 'Counterparts', on the other hand,[33] as well as the other surviving fair copy of 'Ivy Day in the Committee Room' (the Yale copy), are manuscripts slightly pre-dating the assembly of the printer's copy in November 1905. While their pre-dating is suggested by minor, as-yet-unrevised readings, collation nevertheless confirms them as sufficiently satisfactory substitutes for their lost counterparts in the Richards/Maunsel set. With a view to the critical editing, this has implications for the choice of copy-text, a matter to which we shall return.

The Maunsel edition, though never published, went through three stages of proof in 1910: galleys, early page proofs and late page proofs. Each stage is documented by surviving fragments. Galleys exist for 'Counterparts', 'A Mother' and 'The Dead'. Of these, only those for 'A Mother'—the only surviving state of the 1910 typesetting for this story—comprise the complete text. For 'Counterparts', we have only a fragment of one galley slip, but the story is contained in full in the extant batch of late page proofs. 'The Dead' runs to fourteen galleys, with the end, to the length of probably one galley slip, missing. The early page

---

33 Their present location at Cornell, as part of the Stanislaus Joyce collection of Joyceana, would seem to identify them as vestiges of the set of *Dubliners* manuscripts held by Stanislaus (see above, fn. 12).

proof stage has been preserved for 'Ivy Day in the Committee Room' alone. For this story, in its turn, this is the only surviving state of the 1910 typesetting. The late page proofs only survive, finally, in a batch of two segments. The first contains the run of the projected book through its gathering K and breaks off four pages into 'A Painful Case'. The second segment, comprising gatherings R through U, sets in with the opening of 'The Dead' and ends a few pages short of the story's and the book's conclusion. The missing gatherings L-Q—which, as was argued above, were probably never printed—would have contained the major part of 'A Painful Case' and all of 'Ivy Day in the Committee Room', 'A Mother' and 'Grace'. With 'Ivy Day' and 'A Mother' in early page proof and galleys respectively, this means that only 'A Painful Case', except for a four-page opening, the entire 'Grace' and the conclusion of 'The Dead' are wholly unrepresented in any state of the 1910 typesetting. When Grant Richards rescinded his refusal of 1906 and offered to publish *Dubliners* in 1914, the Maunsel early page proofs became his printer's copy. The page proofs Joyce received, corrected and returned in April 1914 were the only proofs provided for the first edition. They survive in one unmarked set.[34]

The Transmission of the Text Through the Documents

Each *Dubliners* story reached its final stage of manuscript revision in the fair-copy exemplar incorporated in the Richards/Maunsel set of manuscripts. The galleys typeset from this set show conspicuous house styling, especially in the punctuation. In a first round of proof-reading, Joyce appears to have concentrated above all on removing hundreds of commas. He continued the process in proof-reading the early page proofs. At this stage, he also turned his attention to a restyling of compounds: the late page proofs show an extensive elimination of hyphens, and compounds now appear as either one-word or two-word formations. Exactly the same proof-reading labour was in 1915/16 exercised on *A Portrait of the Artist as a Young Man*. There, as can be demonstrated,

---

34 All surviving Maunsel and Richards proofs are reprinted in vols. [5] and [6] of *The James Joyce Archive*: James Joyce, *Dubliners. The 1910 Proofs and Dubliners. The 1914 Proofs*, prefaced and arranged by Michael Groden, ed. by Michael Groden, *et al.*, 63 vols. (New York and London: Garland Publishing, Inc., 1977).

Joyce's markings were often ambiguous, resulting in two-word divisions where he wished one-word formations. Without the corresponding documentary evidence for *Dubliners*, it cannot be determined which of the individual two-word compounds in the *Dubliners* late page proofs were meant by him as one word. Along with the restitution of Joyce's light punctuation in the galleys and early page proofs, and his restyling of compounds in the early page proofs, one may note a certain amount of lowering of capitals in a manner typical later for *Portrait* and *Ulysses*; and, of course, at both proof stages much necessary correction of typos was carried out. Most importantly, both the galleys and the early page proofs received an even spread of revisions. Though not numerous, they are significant throughout. The revisions made in the early page proofs are recoverable only in so far as the late page proofs survive, where, however, they stand out distinctly as authorial changes. In truth, all proof corrections, restylings and revisions that we claim as authorial must prove themselves by their kind and quality, since marked proofs have been preserved neither of the galley nor of the early page proof stage. Joyce's proof-reading on the Maunsel edition is traceable only by its results.

The circumstance that the early Maunsel page proofs served as printer's copy for Grant Richards helps to define with fair precision his proof changes to the Maunsel galleys. It is the textual state resulting from these, otherwise lost (except in the case of 'Ivy Day in the Committee Room'), which is represented in the 1914 typesetting, even though there is some indication—confirmed by inference from Joyce's letter to Richards of 24 January 1914 (*Letters* II, 328-29)—that the Richards printer's copy was touched up with additional corrections. On the other hand it is true that, derived as it is from the Maunsel early proofs, the first-edition text basically lacks the final round of Maunsel corrections and revisions. Marking the 1914 proofs meant repeating much of the work done once before on the Maunsel proofs. Again, a considerable accretion of commas was removed; compounds, which had re-acquired hyphens in large numbers, were again restyled without them, though not as consistently and radically as in the two rounds of Maunsel proofing. In so far as memory served, moreover, some of the final Maunsel revisions were once more introduced. Yet in all, Joyce did not gain control over the first edition to the extent he wished. He requested in vain that dialogue be styled not with 'perverted commas', but with the dialogue dash. Barred the opportunity, on which he had counted, of proofing revises, he drew up a list of corrections—a list which has not survived—only to find when the book was out that this, too, had been disregarded and that, furthermore, not all the changes marked in the proofs he read had in fact been carried out. After publication of the first edition, a further autograph list entitled 'Dubliners / Misprints' was assembled and still exists (see *James Joyce Archive*, vol. [4], pp. 51-63). It is not clear whether this is the list prepared by Joyce in 1915 for a putative second Grant Richards edition, or a revised version made in 1917 for B. W. Huebsch. The typed version of the list, however, was almost certainly made in 1917 (*Letters* II, 392-95). Beyond it, there is no evidence that Joyce attended to the text of *Dubliners* in his lifetime.

Hence, and in sum, it is not the Grant Richards first edition text of 1914, but the text of the Maunsel late page proofs of 1910, incomplete though these are, which represents *Dubliners* as most closely and consistently under Joyce's control in print.

The Choice of Copy Text

In the given situation of documents and textual transmission, Joyce's autograph is the obvious document to select as providing the base text for a critical edition. To edit from it could most easily be put into practice if, for each of the fifteen *Dubliners* stories, the autograph exemplar from the Richards/Maunsel set of manuscripts were still available. In fact, as indicated above, the Richards/Maunsel autograph does survive complete for six stories —'The Sisters', 'An Encounter', 'A Painful Case', 'Ivy Day in the Committee Room', 'A Mother' and 'Grace'—and fragmentarily for a seventh, 'The Dead'. For the remaining eight stories, the text of another document must stand in for the text of the lost Richards/Maunsel autograph. The text so vicariously eligible either precedes, or derives from, that in the lost autograph. In six cases, there is no real choice: it is the derivation, namely the 1910 typesetting in its only surviving state in the late page proofs, which provides the earliest extant documentation of the text for 'Araby', 'Two Gallants', 'A Little Cloud' and 'Clay', as well as— discounting the *Irish Homestead*'s heavily house-styled printings of the early story versions—for 'Eveline' and 'After the Race'. Yet in two cases—'The

Boarding House' and 'Counterparts' —an autograph manuscript and the 1910 typesetting hold out rival options. Favouring the 1910 setting would be the fact that the finally revised manuscript text stands behind it. Also, the state in which the 1910 setting survives, namely that of the late page proofs, incorporates the full range of Joyce's corrections and revisions. Yet, while these are definable and can be isolated (meaning that they may thus also, by way of emendation, be worked into another copy text), what remains undefinable is the incidence and extent of modification of the textual surface—in spellings, capitalisation, punctuation, word division and even perhaps wording—by compositors and in-house proofreaders. The autograph manuscript happily extant—even though it was not the actual copy for the typesetting—provides at the very least a welcome check on such potential modification. More positively, it gives a text fully authenticated in the author's hand, as against a text which, having passed through the hands and minds of scribes, typists, or in this case printer's compositors, must be assumed to have been infringed in its authenticity. Hence, given the option between an autograph shown by collation to be very close to the lost final autograph manuscript and a twice-worked-over typesetting from that lost autograph, it is the extant manuscript which, on balance, may be preferred to stand in for its lost near-descendant.

In the present edition, Joyce's autograph manuscripts therefore hold the copy-text wholly for eight stories, and partly for a ninth ('The Dead'), while the Maunsel typesetting, in the state of the late page proofs, provides the copy-text for six stories. 'The Dead', finally, offers a situation of somewhat greater complexity. The sections missing from its autograph manuscript survive in two immediate derivations: on the one hand in the 1910 galleys, and on the other hand in a transcript partly typed and partly written out in two hands (Eileen[?] and Stanislaus Joyce's). While the typist and the family amanuenses were clearly more faithful to Joyce's punctuation, their general accuracy is highly variable and their copying is, on the whole, a thoroughly amateur performance. Thus the option, arbitrary as it is, has been for the professional typesetting job. Choosing the 1910 galleys as copy text for the sections of 'The Dead' missing from the autograph manuscript serves also to bring the copy-text basis, in this instance too, most closely in line with the selection of the 1910 typesetting as copy text for those stories whose autograph manuscripts are wholly missing.

The Editing

The critical editing of *Dubliners* may be assessed by closely following the constant interaction of text and apparatus. The edited text forms the main section of the edition. It presents the copy text as critically modified by the acts of editing. These acts of editing are recorded in the apparatus. Setting them in relation to all textual material drawn upon in the editing, the apparatus is laid out in two main divisions: the notes and emendations, and the historical collation. The historical collation—to define the second apparatus division first—records the differences of the documents of transmission—the manuscripts, proofs and the published editions selected for collation—from the edition's text. The published texts singled out for collation in this edition are two only, the 1914 first edition and the Viking edition of 1967, prepared by Robert Scholes. This narrow selection is justified by the fact that—the autograph list of 'Dubliners / Misprints' apart—the author at no time had a hand in the numerous editions and re-issues of *Dubliners* after 1914, and in his lifetime. The historical collation, in thus situating the edition's text in relation to the selection of the work's text instantiations that it considers, ranks second in the apparatus division, a condition acknowledged by its placement as the second appended apparatus list at the end of the edition. Ranking first in the apparatus division are the notes and emendations which report and record how the edition's text was arrived at and established. Their prime function is emphasised by the further sub-division into the listing of the emendations of accidentals appended first, after the text section of the edition, and the record of verbal emendations—together with notes critically confirming the copy text, or otherwise briefly commenting on the edited text—arranged at the foot of the text pages.

The interaction of the edited text and the divisions and sub-divisions of the apparatus may be illustrated from 'The Dead'. Basically, the edited text reproduces the copy text, which, for the story's first section—defined as a section purely by the document situation—is provided by the fragment of the nineteen initial leaves still extant of Joyce's fair-copy autograph. (The paragraph beginning 'Lancers were arranged' (15.402) ends at the bottom of manuscript leaf 19 with the words: '...an Irish device and motto'.) The autograph text (MS) has been collated with the 1910 galleys (10G), the 1910 late page proofs (10), the 1914 proofs (14P), the 1914 first edition (14) and the 1967 Viking edition (67). Where all these collated witnesses agree, the fact is implied by the absence of any apparatus entry. If and when one or more of the witnesses offers a variant giving no cause to modify the reading of the (autograph) copy text, the textual difference is recorded in the historical collation, for example as: 15.23 Fullam,] Fullham, 14P; Fulham, 14, 67; or as: 15.70-71 out of doors] out-of-doors 14P-14, 67. The apparatus entry provides a reference by line number, according to the through-line numbering implemented in this edition for each of the fifteen *Dubliners* stories, and identifies the reading from the edited text by repeating it. The reading from the edited text may be the reading of the copy text upheld, as it is in these examples, or it may be an emendation replacing the copy-text reading. Reference and reading, or lemma, form an entry head marked off by a closing square bracket. Thereafter follow the collations, that is, the readings from the various documents and document states compared to the copy text, and as they compare to the reading of the edited text. This is the apparatus entry proper and should be read for its absences and presences. Absent from it is the mention of those collated readings which agree with the lemma. Present in the apparatus entry are only those document readings collated which differ from the copy-text reading upheld, or the emendation established, in the edited text. Thus, in the first example given above, the apparatus entry indicates that the spelling and punctuation 'Fullam', is the reading of the copy text, since in the entry no mention occurs of the manuscript, which here is the copy text, and that furthermore the Maunsel galleys and late page proofs, also not mentioned, share this form. Then it states that the first-edition proofs (14P) alter the spelling, while retaining the punctuation, to yield 'Fullham', and that the first edition (14), followed by the Viking edition (67), offer the second variant form 'Fulham,'. In the second example, the three words 'out of doors' are shown to have become hyphenated in the first-edition proofs, and retained as hyphenated through the first and Viking editions.

If and when, on the other hand, a collated witness offers a variant deemed to correct or revise the copy-text reading, this results in an emendation. The variant is introduced into the copy text to replace its original reading, thereby transforming the straight reproduction of the copy text properly into the presentation of the edited text. The emendation may be required because the copy text is faulty (this used formerly to be the only situation recognised in textual scholarship to call for emendation): a copy-text reading may be misspelled; or the punctuation may be wrong, or create ambiguous sense, by syntactic rules. Spellings and punctuation are the so-called accidentals of a text, and it has become customary to record the corrections and modifications of spelling and punctuation in a separate list of emendations of accidentals. The alternative to a given copy-text accidental will as a rule be found in a collated text, whence the editor will import it into the edited text; or the editor conjectures and introduces it on the strength of an original critical assessment.

The decision and the responsibility to emend are always the editor's. Always, and as a rule in each individual instance, an apparatus entry is provided. Certain types of silent emendation may however be specified and declared. Thus, the present edition does not record absent or present full stops after 'Mrs' and 'Mr', nor does it report accidentals marking the opening or closing of dialogue (dashes, inverted commas), unless in association with a collation record of other marks of punctuation. An apparatus entry of emendation will give, as the first item after the entry head, a source siglum for the emendation. Then, the entry's collation record regards the transmission from the copy text to the source point of the emendation only, leaving the variant history of the reading in question to be related in the historical collation. This emphasises the distinctive functions of the main divisions of the apparatus. The list of emendations analyses the transmission to justify the establishment of the edited text, while the historical collation renders the history of the text through all its documented readings. There is hence a regular and designed repetition of entries in the main divisions of the apparatus.

With accidentals, it is often at most a moot question whether a given variant in a collated document is of authorial or transmissional origin. The case is—or it may be—different with verbal variants, the so-called substantives of the text. While it is doubtless within the power of a typist or compositor versed in the language to rectify the obvious verbal slip, the quality of an authorial verbal correction by which to emend the copy text usually very soon becomes critically recognisable. With verbal changes, considered to be of most immediate concern to an edition's reader and user, convention has it that substantive emendations be subdivided from the emendations of accidentals. When an author correcting proof works over a transmissional record of his text, he will as often as not extend his labour to revising it. Hence, it has become editorial procedure in copy-text editing to consider authorial post-copy-text revisions as a type of correction by which (as in instances of correction of error) to emend the copy text. It is to highlight the emendation of the copy text by revisions in particular—constituting, as it does, the core of the method of copy-text editing—that the apparatus lists substantive emendations at the bottom of the text pages. This, too, is the place for notes, designed in analogy to the emendation entries, though lacking a siglum. On the one hand, these notes may be concerned with affirming the given copy-text reading (specifically against the attractiveness of the received reading which, if not added to the note, will be found in the historical collation). On the other hand, and more importantly, these notes open glimpses into the pre-copy-text history of the text, indicating acts of revision within the copy text when it is a Joycean autograph, or giving pre-revision readings from *The Irish Homestead* in the case of 'Eveline' and 'After the Race', or the galley-proof fragment in the case of 'Counterparts'.

For 'The Dead'—to return to our specific area of illustration—Joyce's autograph survives beyond leaf 19 in only two fragments —the single leaf 57, and leaves 74 to 77—to furnish the copy text for the edition. For the sections of the story missing in the autograph, the text in the galley proofs becomes the copy text. The galley proofs derive directly from the autograph, as does, collaterally, the typescript-and-amanuensis copy. The variants of the latter are reported in the apparatus, as a matter of course. Frequently, too, the typescript-and-amanuensis copy serves to emend the copy text. Indeed, as collateral to the copy text, it is highly likely that its text can correct the copy text. Not only, apparently, is it closer to the lost autograph in its pattern of punctuation than is the text of the galleys. In substantives, too, it stands about as good a chance as the text in the galleys to preserve an autograph reading. Thus, corrective emendation, which is always a significant aspect of the critical editing where a state of the 1910 typesetting furnishes the copy text, features, if anything, more strongly in the establishment of the text for 'The Dead' than for the remainder of the *Dubliners* stories. Revisional emendation, moreover, enters into its usual role. Here as throughout—and regardless of whether the copy text resides in the autograph or in a derived document—it requisitions for the critical text the variants deemed revisional changes in the late page proofs of 1910 and the 1914 first edition.

Thus, to specify by a few further examples from 'The Dead', the edited text allows Gabriel Conroy at 15.63-64 to reassure his aunts with the words 'Go on up. I'll follow', according to the text in print, though against the copy text, which lacks the two phrases. Similarly, it makes Gabriel anticipate his after-dinner speech as 'an utter failure' (15.136), not as 'a complete failure'; and it specifies that Gabriel's father was an employee of the 'Port and Docks' (15.150), not of the 'Post Office'. These are examples of emendation of the copy text as residing in the autograph. The collation pattern recorded in the apparatus shows that they answer to revisions performed in marking up the 1910 galleys and the 1914 proofs respectively. For the changes at 15.63-64 and 15.136, the 1910 late page proofs and the 1914 proofs, which derive from a set each of the 1910 early page proofs, agree in the revisions against the manuscript and the—unmarked—1910 galleys. Only if a parallel set of these galleys was marked with the revisions could they have become incorporated in the early-proof typesetting and thence transmitted both to the 1910 late proofs and the 1914 proofs. At 15.150, on the other hand, the revised first-edition text stands alone against the manuscript, the 1910 typesetting in both its surviving states (galleys and late proofs), and the extant unmarked 1914 proofs—in a parallel (and now lost) set of which, therefore, the change must have been marked.

Beyond 15.406, the breaking-off point of the initial autograph fragment, the copy-text to be confirmed, or else to be emended, is the galley-proof text. That it represents authentically the unrevised text of the lost autograph is best attested when the galleys and the typescript-and-amanuensis copy conform in a given reading; and conversely, it is against such agreement that the variants making their first appearance in later print—in the 1910 late page proofs and the 1914 proofs in conjunction, in the 1910 late page proofs alone, or in the first-edition text alone—are to be made out as revisions. Such is the case when Miss Ivors' brooch no longer bears 'an Irish device and motto', but only 'an Irish device' (15.406); or when Miss Ivors uses the racier term 'rag'

(15.421) for 'paper' to disparage the *Daily Express*. These revisions—both identifiable as revisions to the galleys, since the 1910 late page proofs and the 1914 proofs agree in them against the extant unmarked galleys and the typescript—become the edition's critical readings by emendation of the copy text. When the galley copy text and the typescript-and-amanuensis copy disagree, there may be a doubt as to which of them represents the lost autograph. In the case of a name, 'Clohissey's' at 15.432, which is the typescript reading, the galleys have 'O'Clohissey's'. Without further textual evidence, this, being the copy-text reading, would become the edition reading. But in fact, the form attested in the typescript re-appears in the 1910 late page proofs, no doubt as a deliberate correction. This suggests that the typescript reading in this instance derives authentically from the autograph and supports the decision to emend the copy text accordingly. In yet another type of situation, one is faced with an imperfectly achieved revision. At 15.523, 15.525 and 15.528 it is clear from the galley/typescript conformity that the authentic unrevised term is 'row' by which Gretta Conroy refers to the altercation between her husband and Miss Ivors; and Gabriel, in rejecting it, picks it up. In all three occurrences, the 1910 late page proofs change the term to 'words' (and alter the agreement in the verb). The fact that the 1914 proofs continue to read 'row' means that the change was a revision performed in (one set of) the 1910 intermediate page proofs. For the first edition, it is only for the third occurrence that the change was once more introduced in the course of marking up the 1914 proofs. Hence, by comparison to the 1910 late page proofs, the first edition offers an apparently hybrid text. This may be intentional or not; Joyce's final intention could at best be surmised. But a surmise is not strong enough to support a critical text. Not the author's intention, therefore, but only the documented history of the text can ultimately be claimed to constitute the objective foundation for a controlled subjective editorial decision. In the present case, that decision has privileged the treble revision documented in the 1910 late page proofs. The establishment of the critical text is fundamentally conditioned by the work's text itself and the critical assessment of its historical givens in transmission.

This is emphasised yet once more, and perhaps most strongly, by a passage characterizing Gabriel Conroy's mood during his final conversation with Gretta at night in the hotel room. It contains a sentence not heretofore present in the published text of *Dubliners*. The words, according to the double evidence of the galleys and the amanuensis copy, are: 'The irony of his mood changed into sarcasm.' Joyce's awareness of the presence of the sentence in the text at the time when he revised the early page proofs for the abortive 1910 edition is attested by the fact that he made an alteration in it. 'The irony of his mood soured into sarcasm' is the wording in the 1910 late page proofs. In the 1914 proofs, however, the entire sentence is missing, and we cannot know how and why it disappeared. That Joyce himself deleted it, is a possibility; but it is undemonstrable, and is also less than probable, since the 1914 proofs otherwise show no evidence of revision in that set (since lost) of the 1910 early page proofs which served as their copy. Even less is there evidence anywhere in *Dubliners*—except perhaps in 'Counterparts' and 'Ivy Day in the Committee Room', where, however, Joyce was contending with outside forces of censorship—that, from writing the text and affirming it by revision ('changed' to 'soured'), he would turn round and opt for an outright deletion.

The absence of the sentence from the 1914 text hence offers feeble grounds to infer an authorial intention on which to establish a critical text. Therefore, privileging once again the late 1910 state of the text over its 1914 state, the critical edition incorporates the sentence (15.1478). In justification, again, it refers to the history of the text, and quite specifically to the manifest history of the authorial writing culminating in the 1910 late page proofs. The reader and user of the edition, on his and her part, should however not fail to be aware of the conditionality and, in terms of the editorial rationale, the systemic contingency of the editorial decision. That is, the editorial choice should be recognised as the considered option it is.

It is, of course, the editorial apparatus which must guide such recognition. The apparatus is categorically not an adjunct to the text, but an integral element of the edition. The ways in which the editing shapes the edition into a critically established text are based on the discourse of the apparatus. Formalised in the meta-language of symbols and sigla according to received conventions, the apparatus situates the established text in relation both to the text's history and to editorial judgement and decisions. The text's history, specifically, is written into the edited text as well as into the apparatus. It may be comprehended and assessed, consequently, through entering into their dialogue. In a copy-text edition, the copy text may be thought of as providing the base line for the historical orientation. In the case of revisional emendations, it is the text's prospective history which is written into the edited text, since a change which occurred at a post-copy-text point in time is, as it were, anticipated by being incorporated in the edited text. Correspondingly, the text's retrospective history is written into the apparatus. The relationship is reversed for corrective emendations. For 'The Dead', when the galley-proof copy text is emended in accidentals according to the typescript-and-amanuensis copy, the governing objective is to 'backdate' the text by establishing the edited text to conform to the autograph state of syntactical and rhythmical articulation. The apparatus record consequently accommodates almost the entire prospective textual history.

Under such tenets for critical editing, editorial judgement and decision operate on the authorial writing in its document manifestations. It was a consequence of traditional author-centred copy-text editing to lock editorial activity in the finality of intention. The underlying theoretical concept was one of textual closure. Against it, the orientation towards the historicity of the writing process answers to the notion of an essential openness of the text. In editorial terms, textual openness is materially manifest in a text's progression through composition and revision, as well as through states and forms of transmission that are both authorially and 'socially' conditioned. Responding to the text's openness, editorial acts, judgements and decisions must equally be thought of as essentially open. They are informed, yet conditioned and relative, rulings on issues with which, in turn, one may take issue. Against the background of the recorded history of the text, the editor's and the reader's and user's assessments must necessarily interlock. The critical edition, formerly conceived as a scholarly demonstration of authorial and authoritative 'rights' and 'wrongs', is thus moved into a field of critical interchange where assessments of the degree and quality of the editorial solutions for given textual situations become significant categories of reception for the genre of scholarship termed the 'critical edition'.

The text of this edition, while offered as a reading text broadly within the standards and conventions of modern professional printing and publishing, endeavours yet to maintain the character of a scholarly edited text in preserving essential features of irregularity in the recoverable authorial writing. Word forms and word divisions, spellings, capitalisation and punctuation have been neither normalised nor modernised, nor have typographical matters such as abbreviations or ellipses been standardised. The emendations undertaken,[35] or the refusals to emend, are recorded in the apparatus, with a few specific exceptions. The absence or presence of full stops after 'Mr' and 'Mrs' is not noted, nor are quotation marks (inverted [or, as Joyce called them, 'perverted'] commas) surrounding dialogue speech reported, except when joined with emended punctuation. Full stops lacking in the copy text at the end of paragraphs have been supplied silently. At the end of dialogue speech they have been silently supplied only where the copy-text original is wholly unmarked, or marked by a dash only. Joyce's intermediate dialogue dashes have been explicitly emended. Taken together, this means that Joyce's manuscript habits of marking off the segments of dialogue speech by dashes have neither been followed, nor fully recorded. The patterns and effect of the manuscript mode of setting out dialogue is illustrated, and may be studied, in the draft and fair-copy texts from autographs included in the edition's section 'Manuscript Traces'. The convention adopted in this edition's main text, however, is that of opening dialogue dashes only, placed flush left. It is the typographical solution answering to Joyce's own strong views on the marking of dialogue which, in print, and at his forceful instigation, was realised in the third edition of *A Portrait of the Artist as a Young Man* (London: Jonathan Cape, 1924) and has now become the common feature of the critically edited texts of *Dubliners, A Portrait* and *Ulysses*.

The present edited text and that of Robert Scholes's Viking edition of 1967, while not concurring in every word, are close in their readings. Yet as a critical text established afresh from the earliest sources of the

---

35 It should be made quite clear that 'emendations' are to be understood as emendations of the copy text, and not in terms of changes in relation to the previous, unedited or edited, editions. Emendations, often drawing on the transmission, may in fact result precisely in agreement with the text in earlier print.

writing and transmission, our edition encompasses, beyond the words of the text, the totality of its presentation in print. Reading *Dubliners* in the critically established patterns of Joyce's punctuation and word forms gives a different feel, subtly altering the shadings of the sense, for this early Joycean text.

James Joyce's *A Portrait of the Artist as a Young Man* Critical Edition 1993

Introduction

The seminal invention for James Joyce's *A Portrait of the Artist as a Young Man* was the narrative essay 'A Portrait of the Artist'.[1] The essay survives in Joyce's fair hand (fair as originally written out, that is, before becoming much overlaid by revision and by extended deletions that indicate the text's reuse in later writing), in a copybook belonging to his sister Mabel, and bears the date 7/I/1904.[2] Submitted to the literary magazine *Dana* (as likely as not in the very copybook), it was rejected within less than a fortnight. According to Stanislaus Joyce in his *Dublin Diary*,[3] the rejection would seem to have spurred Joyce on to conceiving of an autobiographical novel, the opening chapters of which he wrote in the space of a couple of weeks. Stanislaus, moreover, claims that while sitting together in the kitchen on James Joyce's twenty-second birthday, 2 February 1904, as James was sharing his plans for the novel with him, it was he, Stanislaus, who suggested as title *Stephen Hero*. Accepting

---

1 'A Portrait of the Artist' is currently most conveniently available in: *James Joyce: Poems and Shorter Writings*, ed. by R. Ellmann, A. Walton Litz and John Whittier-Ferguson (London: Faber & Faber, 1991), pp. 211-18. The original is photographically reprinted in James Joyce, *A Portrait of the Artist as a Young Man. A Facsimile of Epiphanies, Notes, Manuscripts, and Typescripts*. Prefaced and Arranged by Hans Walter Gabler (New York and London: Garland Publishing, Inc., 1978) (= vol. [7] of *The James Joyce Archive*, 63 vols., ed. by Michael Groden, *et al.*), pp. 70-85.
2 i.e., January 7th, 1904.
3 Stanislaus Joyce, *The Complete Dublin Diary*, ed. by George H. Healey (Ithaca: Cornell UP, 1971), pp. 11-13.

this claim, Joyce scholarship has been led by Richard Ellmann's interpretation of Stanislaus's account[4] (see *JJ*, pp. 144-149) into taking it entire, and at face value. We have all persistently overlooked May Joyce's letter to James Joyce of 1 September 1916, in which she recalls her brother reading the early chapters to their mother when they lived in St. Peter's Terrace, and the younger siblings used to be all put out of the room. May used to hide under the sofa to listen until, relenting, James allowed her to stay.[5] This intimate personal memory puts the beginnings of Joyce's art in a different perspective. It suggests that he started his autobiographical novel almost a year earlier than has hitherto been assumed, probably some months at least before August 1903 when his mother died. The impulse thus seems to have sprung very immediately from his first experience of exile in Paris in 1902/03. 'A Portrait of the Artist' of January 1904 can appear no longer as seminal for *Stephen Hero*. Rather, defined as the conceptual outline for *A Portrait of the Artist as a Young Man* that it has always been felt to be, it stands out as Joyce's first attempt to break away from his initial mode of autobiographical fiction. Against Stanislaus Joyce's idealizing of his brother's triumphant heroism in defying *Dana*, we sense instead the stymying effect of that first public rejection. Digging his heels in, and continuing to write *Stephen Hero*, as in fact he did, was a retarding, even perhaps a retrogressive stage in Joyce's search for a sense of his art and a narrative idiom all his own. *Stephen Hero* was to falter by mid-1905, by which time it was through *Dubliners* that Joyce was freeing himself from its fetters.

In the course of 1904, Joyce wrote three stories for *The Irish Homestead*, 'The Sisters', 'Eveline' and 'After the Race'. They were the beginnings of *Dubliners*. With eleven chapters of *Stephen Hero* written, its immediate continuation preconceived, and ideas for further stories for *Irish Homestead* contribution in his head, Joyce left Dublin with Nora Barnacle on 8 October 1904 for Zurich, a destination that was to be changed en route for Trieste, and Pola. During Nora's pregnancy, Joyce carried *Stephen Hero* forward through its 'University episode'—the only fragment of

---

4   Richard Ellmann, *James Joyce* (New York: Oxford University Press, 1982), pp. 147-49, subsequently cited as *JJ*.
5   *Letters of James Joyce*, vols. II and III, ed. by Richard Ellmann (New York: Viking Press, 1966), pp. 382-83 [*Letters* II; *Letters* III]. Again, I wish to thank John O'Hanlon and Danis Rose for their help and advice in preparing these present editions of *Dubliners* and *A Portrait of the Artist as a Young Man*.

it which survives—and, closely coinciding with the birth of Giorgio Joyce, he suspended work on it in June 1905.[6] From mid-1905, Joyce turned wholly to the writing of Dubliners. The protracted endeavour, throughout 1906, to get the collection published ran insistently foul even as, in 1906/07, he capped the sequence with 'The Dead'.

The Emerging Novel

The time devoted to the writing of Dubliners, culminating in 'The Dead', was the gestation period of a fundamentally new conception for the autobiographical novel. Suspending it in 1905 had, as became apparent by 1907, been tantamount to aborting the sixty-three-chapter project of Stephen Hero in favour of beginning afresh the five-chapter novel A Portrait of the Artist as a Young Man. Chapter I was written between 8 September and 29 November 1907. Reworked from Stephen Hero, it omitted entirely the seven initial chapters of that novel—those dealing with Stephen's childhood—and opened with Stephen going to school (cf. JJ, 264). We may assume[7] that the Chapter I version of

---

6   The surviving 'University episode' fragment of eleven chapters—XV to XXV—was posthumously edited (erroneously as Chapters XV to XXVI) by Theodore Spencer in 1944 and subsequently augmented by the text of a few stray additional manuscript pages. (James Joyce, Stephen Hero. Edited from the Manuscript in the Harvard College Library by Theodore Spencer. A New Edition, incorporating the Additional Manuscript Pages in the Yale University Library and the Cornell University Library, ed. by John J. Slocum and Herbert Cahoon (New York: New Directions, 1963).) The James Joyce Archive, vol. [8], collects and reprints photographically the 'University episode' and the stray manuscript pages.
       The writing of Stephen Hero, its relation to A Portrait of the Artist as a Young Man and its posthumous publication are briefly surveyed—albeit still in accordance with the Stanislaus Joyce/Richard Ellmann view of the origins—in the Appendix to Hans Walter Gabler, 'The Seven Lost Years of A Portrait of the Artist as a Young Man', in Approaches to Joyce's 'Portrait'. Ten Essays, ed. by Thomas F. Staley and Bernard Benstock (Pittsburgh: University of Pittsburgh Press, 1976), pp. 53-56. An edition reworked from the ground, based on the doctoral dissertation of Claus Melchior, 'Stephen Hero. Textentstehung und Text. Eine Untersuchung der Kompositions- und Arbeitsweise des frühen James Joyce', PhD dissertation, München (Bamberg, 1988), has hitherto remained unpublished.

7   For what follows, see my in-depth analysis in 'The Seven Lost Years ...' [cf. note 5]; and 'The Christmas Dinner Scene, Parnell's Death, and the Genesis of A Portrait of the Artist as a Young Man', James Joyce Quarterly, 13 (1975-76), 27-38. The two essays were integrated into 'The Genesis of A Portrait of the Artist as a Young Man', in Critical Essays on James Joyce's A Portrait of the Artist as a Young Man, ed. by Philip Brady and James F. Carens (New York: G.K. Hall, 1998), pp. 83-112.

autumn 1907 included neither the overture of the novel as eventually published, nor the Christmas dinner scene (which at first apparently belonged with material taken from *Stephen Hero* to construct Chapter II of *A Portrait*). By 7 April 1908, the new novel had grown to three chapters, but was making no further progress. In early 1909, it was sections of a work he had become despondent of that Joyce gave a fellow writer to read. Ettore Schmitz, or Italo Svevo—he was, at the same time, Joyce's language pupil—in a letter of 8 February 1909 proffered supportive criticism of Chapters I-III, in versions prior to those known from the published book, plus a draft opening of Chapter IV. Specifically—if inference may be trusted—the Christmas dinner scene was still apparently in Chapter II, and the conclusion of Stephen's confession in Chapter III was yet unwritten. Schmitz's response encouraged Joyce to complete Chapter IV and begin Chapter V. Yet this precipitated an apparently more serious crisis. Sometime in 1911, Joyce threw the entire manuscript as it then stood—some 313 manuscript leaves—in the fire.[8] Instantly rescued by a family fire brigade, it apparently suffered no real harm and was kept tied up in an old sheet for some months before Joyce 'sorted [it] out and pieced [it] together as best [he] could'. (*Letters* I, 136) This involved developing and rounding off Chapter V, thoroughly revising Chapters I-III and shaping the novel as a whole into a stringent chiastic design. It was an effort of creation occupying Joyce for over two, if not an ample three years. On Easter Day 1913, he envisaged finishing the book by the end of the year, but completing it spilled over into 1914. The surviving fair

---

[8] It was not the *Stephen Hero* manuscript, therefore, as a persistent legend would have it, but an early *Portrait* manuscript that was thus given over to the flames, a fact which a careful reading of Joyce's letter to Harriet Shaw Weaver of 6 January 1920 confirms. *Letters of James Joyce*, vol. I, ed. by Stuart Gilbert (New York: Viking Press, 1957, ²1966), p. 136. [*Letters* I].The year 1911 was one of deep despondency for James Joyce. After intense proofreading of *Dubliners* in the summer of 1910, any hopes of seeing the collection published were dashed by letters from George Roberts both in June and December. Roberts refused to perfect the edition if 'Ivy Day in the Committee Room' was not revised—which Joyce would not do (see in more detail the 'Introduction' to the critical edition of *Dubliners* in the companion volume to this, pp. 11-15). No solution was discernible. It was the second radical setback in the effort to publish *Dubliners*. If this contributed to Joyce's act of despair of throwing the *Portrait* manuscript in the fire, as we assume it did, it would seem even more likely in retrospect that Joyce was shaken, rather than buoyed up, by *Dana*'s rejection of the 'A Portrait of the Artist' essay in 1904.

copy bears the date line 'Dublin 1904 | Trieste 1914' on its last page. Yet the date '1913' on the fair copy's title page indicates that Joyce's Easter Day confidence was substantially grounded. Chapter IV, together with the opening pages of Chapter V, survive from the manuscript thrown in the fire, while Chapters I-III and V in the fair copy postdate the crisis of 1911. Since Chapter I as we have it was written out later than Chapters II and III, and since, in turn, sections of the Chapter V manuscript appear to coincide with the fair copy of Chapter III through fol. 100, 'putting together' the extant final manuscript meant writing out Chapters I-III afresh after revision, incorporating Chapter IV and the beginning of Chapter V from the earlier manuscript, and completing Chapter V. The stages may have been something like V/III, II, I, followed by the insertion of the final version of the villanelle episode in Chapter V, and the writing of the end of Chapter III, as finishing touches. If this represents Joyce's work on the novel from 1912 to perhaps early 1914, it was undoubtedly in 1913, as the manuscript title page indicates, that the design, and much of the text, was essentially realised.

Leaving the manuscript behind in Trieste when he moved to Zurich in 1915, he retrieved it in 1919 and presented it to Harriet Shaw Weaver for Christmas (*Letters* I, 136). She disposed of the Joyce manuscripts she possessed towards the end of her life and, respecting Nora Joyce's objection to her intention of depositing the *Finnegans Wake* papers in Ireland, she presented instead the fair copy of *A Portrait of the Artist as a Young Man* to the National Library of Ireland in 1951.

The Serialisation

On 15 December 1913, Ezra Pound wrote to Joyce asking whether he had anything publishable that he could place for him in any of the British or American journals with which he had connections.[9] He had heard about the young Irish writer exiled in far-away Trieste through Joyce's fellow Irishman in London, W. B. Yeats. During those vital London years of his passion to discover the new writers and promote the new literature, Pound was specifically associated with *The Egoist* (formerly

---

9 *Pound/Joyce. The Letters of Ezra Pound to James Joyce, with Pound's Essays on Joyce.* Edited and with Commentary by Forrest Read (New York: New Directions, 1967), pp. 17f.

titled *The Freewoman* and *The New Freewoman*) under the editorship of Dora Marsden. With the concurrent prospect of Grant Richards finally publishing *Dubliners*, it was the new novel that Joyce wanted Pound and *The Egoist* to consider. To provide copy, he gave his autograph out to be typed, beginning with what was available of it towards the end of 1913, and was also first required. The typed first chapter arrived in London in mid-January. Ezra Pound responded enthusiastically on 19 January.[10] The second chapter, typed by a second typist, followed in late March 1914. *The Egoist* undertook the serialization and began to run *A Portrait of the Artist as a Young Man* in brief fortnightly instalments on, as it happened, 2 February 1914, Joyce's thirty-second birthday. The third-chapter typescript reached London on 21 July 1914, as the time approached when it would be needed as *Egoist* copy. The likeliest explanation for the staggered arrival of the chapters is that Joyce was spreading the typing costs. Chapters IV and V in typescript were sent to London only in November, and became available indeed only after a hiatus in the serialisation. This would seem to have been due to the wartime situation. Eventually mailing it not from Trieste, but from Venice, Joyce appears to have held back the Chapter IV-V typescript until he felt sufficiently reassured both that *The Egoist* would continue to appear—even as it had changed from fortnightly to monthly publication—and that it would be safe to dispatch the typescript.

A Portrait of the Artist as a Young Man appeared in instalments in *The Egoist* from 2 February 1914 to 1 September 1915. Owing to difficulties the printers made for fear of prosecution, *The Egoist* employed three printers in succession, and even so the text did not escape cuts from printer censorship. The first paragraph of Chapter III, a couple of sentences in the bird-girl conclusion to Chapter IV, and a brief dialogue exchange about farting plus the occurrence (twice) of the expression 'ballocks' in Chapter V were affected. James Joyce did not read proof on the *Egoist* text.[11] Nor, beyond Chapter II, did he receive the published text to read until sometimes many weeks or months after publication. (The wartime disturbances in communication, again, are the obvious

---

10   See *Pound/Joyce*, p. 24.
11   Except possibly on the second and third instalments; see Hans Walter Gabler, 'Towards a Critical Text of James Joyce's *A Portrait of the Artist as a Young Man*', *Studies in Bibliography*, 27 (1974), 1-53 (pp. 44 f.).

reason.) Nevertheless, he spotted the censorship cuts immediately, was able to provide the missing fourth-chapter sentences *verbatim* from memory and insisted on an entirely uncensored text for the book publication.

Towards the First Edition

In the spring of 1915, several months before the run of the *Portrait* instalments in *The Egoist* ended, Harriet Weaver, assisted by Ezra Pound, and soon by J. B. Pinker, the well-established literary agent who, in May 1915, added Joyce to his extensive list of authors, embarked upon a protracted search for a British publisher of the novel in book form. Grant Richards had the right of first refusal, contracted with the publishing of *Dubliners*, and declined. Martin Secker and, after long deliberation, Gerald Duckworth followed suit. Ezra Pound's attempts to interest John Lane—who in 1936 was to publish *Ulysses*—and the tentative approach that Viola Hunt made at Pound's instigation to T. Werner Laurie, were unsuccessful. Duckworth's rejection of January 1916 was based on the reader's report of Edward Garnett which documents how categorically *A Portrait*'s construction and style were beyond the expectations, and therefore the powers of perception, of a most esteemed literary reader of the time.[12] Nor did the book fare better with William Heinemann, who in mid-1916 was given it for consideration, even though Harriet Weaver had on 30 November 1915 already proposed founding The Egoist Ltd. expressly to publish *A Portrait of the Artist as a Young Man*. Yet, just as the established British publishers had refused to take on the novel, British printers now proved unwilling to touch it uncensored. (The recent legal proceedings against D. H. Lawrence's *The Rainbow* no doubt influenced their attitude.) The course that remained for Harriet Weaver was to look to the United States in the hope of arranging with an American partner to supply her with import sheets for a British edition. The promise of a satisfactory arrangement with John Marshall collapsed when Marshall absconded to Canada. It was with B. W. Huebsch of New York that a joint venture finally succeeded.

---

12 Garnett's report is quoted in Ellmann, *James Joyce*, pp. 403-4.

The Book Editions

B. W. Huebsch had become aware of James Joyce through Grant Richards, who throughout 1916 negotiated with him to publish *Dubliners* in the United States with sheets imported from England. (The edition was brought out in December 1916, only a few weeks before that of *A Portrait*.) He was alerted to *A Portrait* through E. Byrne Hackett, an Irish-American bookseller and small-scale publisher to whom, on Ezra Pound's recommendation, Harriet Weaver had sent a set of tearsheets from *The Egoist*. Hackett forwarded these to Huebsch, who on 16 June 1916 offered 'to print absolutely in accordance with the author's wishes, without deletion' (*Letters* I, 91). Providing him with copy to allow him to do so was now the trans-Atlantic challenge. The Hackett tearsheets, although provided with slips and marginal additions restoring the censored passages, were uncorrected. A fully markedup set of tearsheets was in the hands of John Marshall with corrections by Joyce himself in Chapters I and II, authorial corrections transferred into Chapters III and IV by Harriet Weaver from lists Joyce had sent her,[13] and Chapter V in the original typescript. All attempts failed to obtain them for Huebsch. On 6 September 1916 Harriet Weaver sent him a substitute copy with Chapters III and IV marked up according to Joyce's lists, but Chapters I, II and V corrected merely on the strength of her own recollection of Joyce's changes or, with respect to Chapter V, merely her unaided impressions. Huebsch wisely refused to start printing from this copy, awaiting rather the receipt of Chapters I, II and V in exemplars Harriet Weaver had concurrently sent to Joyce freshly to mark up. These she was able to forward to Huebsch in late September. They reached New York on 6 October, and on 17 October Huebsch confirmed that the book was in the hands of the printer. The printer's copy—set EC-A, according to Chester G. Anderson's sigla—is made up of Chapters I, II and V with James Joyce's autograph corrections plus some clarifications of these in Harriet Weaver's hand, and Chapters III and IV marked up in Harriet Weaver's hand alone from Joyce's lists.[14] On the typesetting for the book,

---

13 They are still extant and bound in with another set of *Egoist* tearsheets now in the British Library; see my 'Towards a Critical Text...', pp. 3-15.

14 This corrects Anderson's description of them as corrected entirely in Joyce's hand (Chester G. Anderson, 'The Text of James Joyce's *A Portrait of the Artist as a Young*

no proofreading other than Huebsch's house proofing was feasible. Joyce was pressing for publication in 1916; this was even stipulated in the publishing contract. On 29 December, a few copies were ready and bound to justify the date 1916 on the first edition title page. In January 1917, the edition was on the American market, and 768 sets of sheets (for the 750 ordered), printed as a separate issue by stop-press alteration of the title page, arrived in London to be bound and marketed by The Egoist Ltd.

Joyce found the first edition extensively in need of correction. By 10 April 1917, he had drawn up a handwritten list of 'nearly 400' changes, which he sent to Pinker to be typed and forwarded in ribbon copy and carbon by two successive posts to Huebsch in New York. Yet by the time they arrived, Huebsch had already printed 'a second edition from the first plates' unaltered. Harriet Weaver, who was also considering a second edition, refrained from extending her joint venture with Huebsch when she discovered that freshly imported sheets would not contain Joyce's changes. She obtained the carbon copy of the corrections, augmented its 364 entries by another seventeen items from a list of seventy corrections which she herself had prepared—the remaining fifty-three items on that list coincided with Joyce's own corrections—and used it to mark up an exemplar of the English first edition (American sheets) as printer's copy for the reset English second edition published under the imprint of The Egoist Ltd. in 1918. (Harriet Weaver later gave this copy to the Bodleian Library in Oxford, where it is now shelved.) The third English edition under the Egoist imprint published in 1921 was bibliographically another issue of the first American edition. It once more used sheets imported from the United States. Huebsch had, in reprinting for the third time, forgotten or chosen to disregard the ribbon copy of Joyce's 1917 corrections which he still held (and which, decades later, he gave to the Poetry Collection of the State University of New York in Buffalo, where they still survive).

In 1924, Jonathan Cape took over *A Portrait of the Artist as a Young Man* and published the 'fourth English edition', which, in strict bibliographical terms, was the book's third edition. With the proofing and revising of *Ulysses* fresh in his memory, Joyce appears to have proofread the Jonathan

---

Man', *Neuphilologische Mitteilungen*, 65 (1964), 160-200 (p. 188)) and confirms the inference drawn in my 'Towards a Critical Text ...', p. 19.

Cape *Portrait* more thoroughly and consistently than any other of his books after their first publication. None of the actual corrected proofs have been preserved, but he mentions reading proof on the Cape edition on two separate occasions in letters to Harriet Weaver in the summer of 1924, from Saint-Malo. On 11 July, he reports on work done before he left Paris, which involved resisting suggested censorial cuts—Sylvia Beach records her 'amazement at the printer's queries in the margins'[15]—and insisting on the removal of the 'perverted commas ... by the sergeant-at-arms' (*Letters* III, 99 f.). The letter of 11 July refers to an enclosure to demonstrate that Cape had complied on both counts—that is, agreed to print without cuts, and reset all dialogue—and thus suggests that Joyce received two sets of proof in Paris. On 16 August, he reports that he has sent off revises to Cape. Unless these were the second proofs which by inference he received in Paris, Joyce would thus have read three rounds of proof on the Cape edition. This marked the end of his attention to the text of *A Portrait of the Artist as a Young Man* in his lifetime.

This Edition

The present edition is a copy-text edition of *A Portrait of the Artist as a Young Man*. Its copy text is the text in James Joyce's fair-copy holograph, preserved in the original in the National Library of Ireland and photographically reprinted in the *James Joyce Archive*.[16] To establish the critical text and the apparatus, the surviving fragments of the typescript, the surviving *Egoist* galleys, the *Egoist* serialisation (1914-15), the first edition (B. W. Huebsch, 1916), the second edition (The Egoist Ltd.,

---

15   Sylvia Beach, *Shakespeare and Company* (London: Faber & Faber, 1960), p. 56.
16   James Joyce, *A Portrait of the Artist as a Young Man*, MS 920 and 921 in the holdings of the National Library of Ireland.
    James Joyce, *A Portrait of the Artist as a Young Man. A Facsimile of the Final Holograph Manuscript*. Prefaced and Arranged by Hans Walter Gabler. 2 vols. (New York & London: Garland Publishing, Inc., 1977) (= vols. [9] and [10] of the *James Joyce Archive*).
    The photo reprint in the *James Joyce Archive* provides a reliable reproduction of the textual record of the original manuscript. For the terminological distinction between textual, inscriptional and material record in originals and visual copy, see my essays 'On Textual Criticism and Editing: The Case of *Ulysses*' in *Palimpsest: Editorial Theory in the Humanities*, ed. by George Bornstein and Ralph Williams (Ann Arbor: University of Michigan Press, 1993), pp. 195-224; and 'What *Ulysses* Requires', *PBSA*, 87:2 (1993), 187-248.

1918), and the third edition (Jonathan Cape, 1924) have been collated against the fair copy; and the marked-up *Egoist* tearsheets, the surviving separate lists of corrections, Harriet Weaver's marked-up printer's copy for the 1918 British edition, and published and unpublished correspondence itemizing textual changes have been checked. From the textual materials so collated and assembled, the edited text has been constituted.[17] Apart from emending obvious slips of the pen and authorial copying errors, it maintains the wording, spelling and punctuation of the copy text. Yet onto this have been grafted: first, the author's revisions, few in number, effected successively in the typescript, the serialisation and the book editions of 1916, 1918 and 1924; second, the authorial, or authorially instigated, restyling of capitalization and compound formation without hyphens (i.e., compounds in one word or two words) achieved successively in the book editions; third, the styling of dialogue with opening flush-left dialogue dashes only, as realised by authorial direction in the Jonathan Cape edition of 1924. According to the general concept of copy-text editing, the text in this edition is thus a critically eclectic text.

The textual situation which obtains for *A Portrait of the Artist as a Young Man*—draft material preceding the fair copy has not been preserved, nor was the text extensively revised in its straight passage from fair copy to print—suggests a mode of critical editing substantially different from that devised for James Joyce's *Ulysses*.[18] The methodology of copy-text editing holds out the requisite technical procedures. It stipulates that, from the transmission, the text in one document—or 'copy'—be selected as the edition's base text. By conventionalised operations of critical editing, the base text, or copy text, is then transformed into the edited text. The principal rule of method is to follow the base text in spelling and punctuation, as well as in such related features as paragraphing, word division, capitalizing or italicizing. A critically edited text, however, is not a diplomatic text: it does not aim at being faithful to the base text in all its inscriptional or graphic peculiarities, such as slips of the pen,

---

17 Except for letters, all manuscript materials relevant to the constitution of the text have been photographically reprinted in *The James Joyce Archive*, vols. [7], [9] and [10].

18 James Joyce, *Ulysses. A Critical and Synoptic Edition*, prepared by Hans Walter Gabler with Wolfhard Steppe and Claus Melchior, 3 vols. (New York & London: Garland Publishing, Inc., 1984; ²1986).

misspellings or printing errors, nor in false starts (other than reporting them in the apparatus), spacings, lineation or pagination. Therefore, subsidiary rules regulate the altering of the (base or) copy text.

Altering the base text means emending it, and emendation in copy-text editing is of a double nature. In one respect, emendation removes the base text's imperfections and transmissional corruption. It corrects (or may correct) authorial misspellings, or restores words accidentally dropped from a manuscript copy; or corrects copying, typing or printer's errors, or undoes house styling and other effects of the text's fashioning by publishers' editors. In another respect, emendation replaces good and authentic readings of the base text by their respective authorial revisions—equally good and authentic, but superseding the base-text readings by authorial intervention and change—as found in authoritative document texts other than the base text. In other words, the copy-text-edited text—as against, say, a version-edited text—is not definable in relation to any one historical document (whereas the base text, or copy text, is of course so definable). It is, rather, an eclectic text, constituted by grafting authentic (succeeding) textual revisions onto the authentic (preceding) substratum of the copy text.

Copy-text editing thus telescopes a textual development into one text, the edited text. Under, and on account of, its method of procedure, such an eclectically edited text is never an historical, but is always an ideal text, a text as it never historically existed. (Indeed, though assumptions and methods of critical editing may vary, no critically edited text is a text as it ever historically existed.) To produce such an ideal text by textual scholarship and critical editing is commonly justified by the claim that, as edited, it fulfils the author's (final) intentions. But this means taking an ideological perspective on the procedural solution of a pragmatic task. From the outset, an editor faces the situation that an author's intentions may be considered fulfilled in a general way in each manifest historical documentation of the text—say, an accomplished draft, a fair copy, the printer's copy, the first edition, each authorially revised edition. The document texts provide the editor with an historical series of intentional moments. Copy-text editing as it has methodologically evolved is recognised as one way of solving the pragmatic task of reconciling these successive moments. It observes authorial intention and invokes it as a superior consideration in each instance of adjudicating authenticity in variant readings among the documented states of the text. Yet the legitimacy is moot of claiming final authorial intention for the resulting editorial product. At the most, an edited text may claim to represent a text of composite authenticity. This is a claim which the textual situation for *A Portrait of the Artist as a Young Man* permits.

In the present critical edition, the copy text provides spellings, (a dearth of) capitalization, and a pattern of punctuation—in the delicate and rhythmically aware balance of colons, semicolons and, above all, a light use of commas—that are James Joyce's rather than those of a typist or printer's compositor. Being a fair copy derived from drafts, it must be assumed to hold its share of authorial copying mistakes. Since the preceding drafts are no longer extant, these may be indiscernible. But those discernible are few, and as easy to spot as to repair. In the course of the early printing history, on which Joyce took direct or mediated influence, a few verbal revisions were introduced, moreover, which are clearly identifiable so as to be established, by emendation of the copy text, as valid readings for the edited text. Yet the early printing history also brought about verbal and non-verbal alterations—changes in substantives and accidentals—which Joyce in part positively embraced, in part perhaps approved, or which he sometimes may have acquiesced in and occasionally let pass in silent protest—or which he never noticed. It is the editor's critical task to survey these and to declare rules and procedures for their admission or rejection in establishing the edited text.

The largest contingent of textual variants editorially to contend with are some 371 substantive differences between the fair copy and the serialisation. Some are verbal changes, but the majority manifest themselves as absences of fair-copy words and phrases from the serialised text. The fair copy carries no direction for changes or cuts. Did the author cut and change in the largely lost typescript (he could not have done so in proof, since he did not proofread the serialisation), or are the absences typist's and/or compositor's errors of omission? The analytical studies of the question undertaken have put the onus on the typist, or typists.[19] Again and again, the figures of verbal repetition in the intricate rhetoric of the *Portrait* prose would seem to have caused

---

19   Anderson, 'The Text ...', pp.171-78; Gabler, 'Towards a Critical Text ...', pp. 31; 39-47.

the copyist to lose his place, and the arrangement of the text in the visual image of the fair copy pages appears often enough to have induced such eye-skip.

Once the typist has been identified as the main perpetrator of the 371 substantive changes between fair copy and serialisation, a very clear pattern emerges by which a small group of eighteen variants out of the total of 371 may be critically singled out as Joyce's revisions.[20] The present edition emends its copy text by these eighteen revisions, but upholds it for the remaining 353 instances where the serialisation, and all subsequent printings before Chester G. Anderson's edition of 1964, departed from it. In so doing, our edition asserts the authenticity of the text of *A Portrait of the Artist as a Young Man* as it stands in Joyce's holograph fair copy. Whether it thereby also fulfils the author's final intention is ultimately unanswerable. There is no getting away from the facts that a) the typescript passed under Joyce's eyes (although there is strong indication that he only attended to queries marked by a thin lead pencil—Stanislaus Joyce's?—and did not read the typed text, and hence did not catch the typist's omissions at this initial stage); b) Joyce carefully prepared the serialised text as printer's copy for the first American edition; c) he similarly attended to the first-edition text, aiding Harriet Weaver in preparing the printer's copy for the first English edition; and d) he read two or three rounds of proof on the Jonathan Cape typesetting of 1924. What is recoverable as authorial intention from these rounds of authorial attention to the text is only what becomes positively manifest as written-in authorial revision, or as external instruction (e.g., in directions or comments by letter): the large-scale restoring of, and thereby the overall desire to restore, the manuscript punctuation; the changing of the manuscript system of capitalisation and compound formation; the introduction of a few verbal changes; and finally the insistence, for the 1924 edition, on the dialogue marking by initial dashes instead of the 'perverted commas' which Jonathan Cape had set in first proof (*Letters* III, 99 f.)—and the placing of these dashes flush left with the margin. In all these respects of positive restoration and change, the edited text realises a textual authenticity backed by final authorial intention. It cannot, and does not, however, claim to do so in respect of the typist's omissions of fair-copy text. Here, on the strength of

---

20 See Gabler, 'Towards a Critical Text ...', pp. 31-35.

the manuscript, the edited text overrides the tradition of the text in pre-publication and published transmission as, between 1914 and 1924, it passed repeatedly under Joyce's eyes. In restoring the typist's omissions, this edition asserts the authenticity of the manuscript. The edited text is thus a critically eclectic text of composite authenticity.

On the textual surface, the edition here offered does not essentially differ from the edition advocated in 1974;[21] where minutely it does, the difference lies in that it adheres without exception to the rule of hypothesis by which the omissions of manuscript text from the typescript/*Egoist* text are due to the typist, and refrains from realising editorially the few instances of authorial cuts which, within a limited area of Chapter III, it seemed possible critically to isolate.[22] While the critical distinction remains an attractive possibility, the possible critical gain would not outweigh the real loss in editorial consistency. But even though this is the copy-text edition which, on the grounds of its textual documentation and pattern of transmission, *A Portrait of the Artist as a Young Man* requires, the thinking behind the methodological option has developed since I put forward my first notions of how to realise it.

Under the premises of critical eclecticism, and its formal concomitants of copy-text-editing procedures, to propose, as the result of scholarly editing, a text of composite authenticity amounts to a refocussing of the objective of the methodology. As indicated, the orthodox goal of copy-text editing has been a text fulfilling the author's final intentions. The shift in the editorial attitude and approach advocated is from an overriding orientation towards the author to an orientation dominantly towards the text. To be sure, common denominators remain. The edited text of composite authenticity does not neglect or deny the author: both final intention and composite authenticity are author-related concepts. And, on the other hand: the text of final intention as well as that of composite authenticity, since eclectically arrived at, are at bottom editorial constructs. Nevertheless, there are clear distinctions. In the endeavour to establish final authorial intention, the editor will engage primarily with the author and the ultimate authority with which the author is taken to endow the text. Under such premises, the text is seen as dependent on, and functionally as subordinate to,

---

21 Gabler, 'Towards a Critical Text ...', p. 53.
22 Gabler, 'Towards a Critical Text ...', pp. 36-38.

the author. In striving for an edited text of composite authenticity, by contrast, the editor engages primarily with the text in the cross-currents of its processes of composition, revision and transmission.[23] In the dialectics of writing and rewriting which characterise these processes, the author becomes as much a function of the text as the text of the author, and 'ultimate authority', if not indeed both notionally and practically unattainable, resides in the text. What the concept of the text of composite authenticity foregrounds is the aporia of all critical editing, namely that an edited text is always an editor's text. This is particularly true of an eclectically edited text, the conventional invocation of the author and (final) intentions notwithstanding: an author's text (rather than an editor's), as definable historically and in terms of compositional structure, can by definition not result from eclectic assembly. This is the second aporia that must be faced: theory would categorically rule out the construction of an eclectic text; yet in practical terms, a critically eclectic text established by the rules of copy-text editing is, under the given circumstances of documentation and transmission, the optimal solution of the pragmatic task of editing a work such as James Joyce's *A Portrait of the Artist as a Young Man*.

The text of this edition, while offered as a reading text broadly within the standards and conventions of modern professional printing and publishing, endeavours yet to maintain the character of a scholarly edited text in preserving essential features of irregularity in the authorial writing of the copy text. Word forms and word divisions, spellings, capitalisation and punctuation have been neither normalised nor modernised, nor have typographical matters such as abbreviations or ellipses been standardised. The emendations undertaken,[24] or the refusals to emend, are recorded in the apparatus, with a few specific exceptions. The absence or presence of full stops after 'Mr' and 'Mrs' is

---

23 Under the premises of such engagement, the edition of *Dubliners* (see the companion volume to this edition) does not, because it cannot, aim for a text of composite authenticity. Its edited text is oriented towards authorial writing and the history of the text. This follows from the different textual situation obtaining for *Dubliners*, and is a theoretical repositioning not in kind, but in degree, responding to the pragmatic givens of editorial practice.

24 It should be made quite clear that 'emendations' are to be understood as emendations of the copy text, and not in terms of changes in relation to the previous, unedited or edited, editions; emendations, often drawing on the transmission, may in fact result precisely in agreement with the text in earlier print.

not noted, nor are quotation marks (inverted [or, as Joyce called them, 'perverted'] commas) surrounding dialogue speech reported, except when joined with emended punctuation. Full stops lacking in the copy text at the end of paragraphs have been supplied silently. At the end of dialogue speech they have been silently supplied only where the copy-text original is wholly unmarked, or marked by a dash only. Joyce's intermediate dialogue dashes have been explicitly emended. Taken together, this means that Joyce's manuscript habits of marking off the segments of dialogue speech by dashes have neither been followed, nor fully recorded. The patterns and effect of the manuscript mode of setting out dialogue is illustrated, and may be studied, in the draft and fair-copy texts from autographs included in the section 'Manuscript Traces' to the critical edition of *Dubliners*, or of course directly in the *James Joyce Archive* photo reprint of the *Portrait* holograph. The convention adopted in this edition's main text, however, is that of flush left opening dialogue dashes only. It is the typographical solution answering to Joyce's own strong views on the marking of dialogue which, in print, and at his forceful instigation, was realised in the third edition of *A Portrait of the Artist as a Young Man* (London: Jonathan Cape, 1924) and has now become the common feature of the critically edited texts of *Dubliners*, *A Portrait* and *Ulysses*.

This critical edition introduces for each chapter a through line numbering independent of the pagination that is identical also in the simultaneously published Vintage edition. In the printing, end-of-line hyphenation occurs in two modes. The sign '=' marks a division for mere typographical reasons. Words so printed should always be cited as one undivided word. The regular hyphen indicates an authentic Joycean hyphen. For an understanding of the status, structure and function of the apparatus of this edition, the explications in the companion edition of *Dubliners* ('Introduction', pp. 24-32) may be profitably consulted.

The present edited text and that of Chester G. Anderson's Viking edition of 1964 do not drastically differ. Anderson was the first carefully to explore the Dublin holograph of *A Portrait*. Yet for his 1964 edition he was forced into textual compromises. These our edition eschews when merging into its edited text the words and punctuation of Joyce's fair copy with the changes in wording and restyling of capitalisation and compound formation of his later revisions for *A Portrait of the Artist as a Young Man*.

Seeing James Joyce's *Ulysses* into the Digital Age:

Forty Years of Steering an Edition Through Turbulences of Scholarship and Reception

The Edition

Foundations

A post-doctoral fellowship from the Harkness Foundation in New York enabled me, from the autumn of 1968 to early spring 1970, to learn the ropes of textual criticism and bibliography in Charlottesville, Virginia, the Anglo-American way. On its own terms, the discipline's name was pleonastic in those days: textual criticism was bibliography; bibliography was textual criticism. Textual criticism as a foundational discipline in the humanities had, over centuries, developed procedures to explore the transmissions of texts through and across documents. On the age-old assumption that transmission must inevitably disintegrate texts and produce error, different document texts were compared: they were collated. They would vary, sometimes less, sometimes more, in their readings. By patterns of error, the less disintegrative—less 'corrupt'— document text was singled out to provide the basis for a given edition.

In the twentieth century, bibliography brought further refinement to the identification of errors in transmission. Bibliography used to be understood as a set of techniques to explore the history of books as artifacts. It was now harnessed to analyse the typesetting and printing of the text contents of books. Still predicated on the concept of error, bibliographical analysis encouraged inferences about what types of errors the printing–house workmen were prone to make and, therefore, how reliably or unreliably they could be assumed to have transmitted specific readings in a specific document text. Where changes between one document text and the next could not be discredited as errors, they were critically decreed to be revisions attributable to redactors or authors themselves. The assessments informed the selection of the so-called 'copy text'. An edition text was established by correcting the copy-text by readings from other text instantiations; and in particular by grafting authors' revisions from later-than-copy-text editions onto a first-version text itself. Just how to proceed in modifying a copy text into an edited text was specifically governed, moreover, by a methodology under one overriding axiom: namely, by evidence or inference, in an edition text to fulfil the author's intention. The editions so established were 'critically eclectic editions'.[1]

Or so they were hailed within Anglo-American textual scholarship. From the vantage point of textual criticism and editing outside the Anglo-American province, they were seen, and rejected, as contaminated editions. It was held against them as unsound, in an edited text to mix readings from historically distinct document texts, let alone from distinct authorial versions. Rather, an edition text, while by definition edited, should still essentially represent one historically identifiable document text, purged only of irrefutable errors of transmission (scribal slips, typos, and such). In terms of nomenclature, and in contrast to 'critically eclectic editions', German textual criticism and editing yielded 'historical-critical editions', true to the historical moment of, say, a given document text's first publication, or its later revised edition—perhaps 'at the author's last hand' ('Ausgaben letzter Hand' as they were called in German).[2]

---

[1] I critique the methodology in some detail in 'Beyond Author-Centricity in Scholarly Editing', https://books.openbookpublishers.com/10.11647/obp.0120/ch8.html#_idTextAnchor023

[2] A representative collection of German essays on editorial theory translated into English may be found in *Contemporary German Editorial Theory*, ed. by Hans Walter Gabler, with George Bornstein and Gillian Borland (Ann Arbor: University of Michigan Press), 1995.

'Historical' was the buzzword for German textual criticism and editing from its emergence in the nineteenth century onward. The historical perspective on transmissions carried the germ of a genetic awareness. By about the middle of the twentieth century, manuscript editions—'Handschrifteneditionen'—began to establish themselves as a distinct sub-genre of scholarly editions. Interest developed in writer's workshop materials, and solutions were sought to capture from them, and editorially to present, texts in progress. These advances were as yet experimental and, to begin with, without a critical, let alone a theoretical, grasp of the implications of textual variation.

It fell to French *critique génétique* in the final decades of the twentieth century to establish a critical discourse and a framework of theory by which to engage with writing in its temporal dimension. The genetic approach to texts assumes *a priori* that it is in the nature of texts to be variant. The materialisation of text takes place in acts of writing. A text will, in the continuous progress of being written, respond to itself with variation. Its modifications commonly spring from the creative energy invested in the thought process of revisional writing. Hence, writing is dialogic, and variants are the written traces of the dialogue. The sustained interaction of composing and revising is the engine (as it were) that drives the process of text formation, and of transforming text further into variants of—or against—itself.

The writing traces in drafts and follow-up documents constitute the subject matter of genetic criticism.[3] Genetic criticism, in its turn, opens up the genetic dimension of textual criticism. From the traces and disposition of the writing in a manuscript may be elicited the sequences of writing, and behind them might become interpretable the thought processes that were the impulses for that writing itself. In terms of documents of origin, it has become the basic challenge of genetic editing to edit what the documents witness not merely as sequentially readable text, but comprehensively, with justice given to the spatial disposition of the writing and the diachronic depth of the text. In terms of sequences of transmission through documents, the challenge widens because editing, genetically conceived, aims at capturing not merely the result of variation, but its dynamic movement. Thus, genetic editing seeks to

---

3   *Genetic Criticism. Texts and Avant-Textes*, ed. by Jed Deppman, Daniel Ferrer, and Michael Groden (Philadelphia: University of Pennsylvania Press, 2004).

transform the theoretical tenets and critical stance of *critique génétique*—genetic criticism—into innovative editorial practice: that is, to edit texts in progress.

This has deeper consequences still, both in theory and in pragmatics. The analytical exercise of textual criticism is founded no longer on the concept of 'error'. Its fulcrum is the variant. Nonetheless, because transmissions have always, and will always, involve what goes by the age-old term of 'textual corruption', the identification and elimination of error admittedly remains a necessary text-critical and editorial task. Yet a wider view of the nature of transmissions recognises 'error' as a sub-class (undesirable, it is true) of variation that, comprehensively, carries the textual movement. Committed to enabling the experience of that movement, the editorial endeavour shifts its theoretical stance. Above all, it ceases to aim for the stable and closed text. As its attention is focused on the text in progress, its frame of perception becomes critical throughout. Critical in nature, genetically oriented textual criticism and genetic editing thus form a twin discipline focused on the intelligibility of textual variation rooted in the dynamic variability of language.

The renewed perspective must ultimately, too, lead to procedural consequences. To recognise the potential inherent in genetic criticism and genetically oriented textual criticism means to redefine and reconceive the medium in which the scholarly edition, and radically so the genetic scholarly edition, takes shape and takes place. This should no longer—and for the genetic edition it categorically cannot—be paper and the book. Material carriers were the traditional medium for preserving and presenting texts in their linearly sequenced two-dimensionality for reading. Accepting the conceptual challenge of the three-dimensionality of writing—of 'texting'—and the temporal (i.e., fourth) dimension inferable from its overwritings, logically necessitates embracing the digital medium for the scholarly edition. Only the digital medium is capable of registering, selecting, and visualising at will the multi-dimensionality of text and texts in progress, as well as the multiple cross-relations among the several correlated discourses (introductions, apparatuses, commentaries, multi-faceted auxiliary information, and adduction of thought) that a fully fledged scholarly edition comprises, and will in the future comprise.[4]

---

4   See, for instance, my essay 'Theorising the Digital Scholarly Edition', https://books.openbookpublishers.com/10.11647/obp.0120/ch6.html#_idTextAnchor018

Ulysses: Candidate for an Edition

Midway through the years of reconceptualising textual and editorial scholarship as we understand the twin discipline today, James Joyce's *Ulysses* reached a crossroads. On its course from an author's novel in his time for the contemporary reader to a canonised literary text, it sought confirmation of its heritage quality: it reached out to be edited. In the 1970s, concerns grew loud in Joyce circles about how unreliable Joyce's texts were. The debates ran high and there was much uncertainty about what could be done about the situation. At the International James Joyce Symposium in Dublin in 1973, for instance, it was proposed, in all seriousness, to collect suggestions for text corrections and emendations for *Ulysses* and to set up a committee to arbitrate what to accept or reject. I listened with amazement to this cheerful proclamation of dilettantism. Home in Germany again after my US initiation into bibliography and textual criticism, I had begun to acquaint myself also with German editorial scholarship. I began to familiarise myself with the preserved documents carrying the written traces of the origin and growth of the text for the first edition of *Ulysses* of 1922. The nature of the materials suggested that a combination of Anglo-American and German approaches might be suited to penetrating and offering solutions for the novel's textual problems. Would a scholarly edition of and for *Ulysses* succeed within such a wider methodological framework?

With the first edition of 1922, Joyce made *Ulysses* public as a work of literature. The pre-publication documents and the successive states of their texts, however, brought to light rich evidence of multiple and variegated text slippages on the path to publication. As the book it resulted in, the first edition was very much what Joyce intended—and urged that it be published on 2 February, his fortieth birthday. The printing house, Darantiere in Dijon, complied by entrusting the first two copies to the driver of the night train to Paris, to be handed to Joyce first thing in the morning. But from a text-critical perspective, serious doubts arose from the pre-publication documents that the book's text was in every nuance of wording and phrasing Joyce's text for *Ulysses*, the work. The publisher's apology on the title-page verso, re-worded and given its rhythmical flow, as the proofs reveal, by James Joyce himself, denies point-blank that the book presents us in every particular its author's text for *Ulysses*: 'The publisher asks the reader's indulgence for typographical errors unavoidable in the exceptional circumstances.'

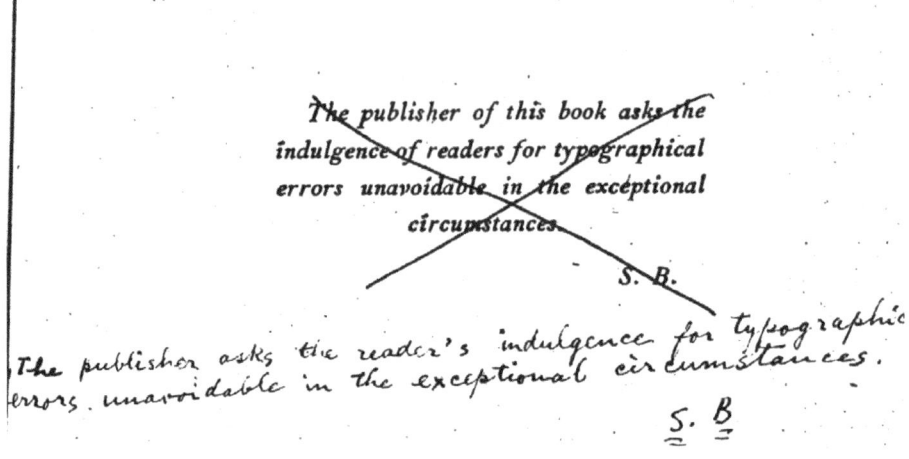

Fig. 5.1: *James Joyce Archive* 27, p. 305

Typographical errors? Surviving partial lists of amendments were drawn up by Joyce and assorted amanuenses over the years between 1922 and 1926, when the novel was typeset afresh and published in a second edition. These lists draw attention to a multitude of misprints that, though irritating and annoying, are by and large trivial, because they are commonly self-corrective. Yet in-depth textual scrutiny reveals that the phrase 'typographical errors' does not, by a long way, cover the range and diverse nature of the departures in the first edition's published text from the text James Joyce progressively wrote for *Ulysses*. Joyce's expressed awareness of textual blemishes in the first edition were the proverbial tip of the iceberg of a complex process of composition, revision and corruption in transmission through the pre-publication documents leading to the publication of *Ulysses* in its first-edition printing.

The Writing and the Documents

The writing of *Ulysses* in Joyce's own hand began with seminal note-taking and proceeded through successive first and intermediate drafts into final drafts and fair copy. Helpers, mostly amateur, prepared typescripts for the individual chapters (episodes) from either their final drafts or their fair copies. For about half the chapters, the fair-copy version in the Rosenbach manuscript is the direct ancestor of the typescript text; for the other half, the fair copy is the typescript's collateral sibling: that is, for these chapters, the fair-copy text and the typescript text radiate from a common source text in documents since lost. The collateral relationship of the document texts in fair copy and typescript for this group of episodes can be determined by critically analysing the text differences between these two document texts—a regular case of analytic investigation in the mode of textual bibliography.

The typescripts came commonly in triplicate as one top and two carbon copies. Joyce instantly overwrote them with changes and more text. From the overwritten typescripts, the text passed into print. First, in 1919 to 1920, one typescript exemplar provided copy for the publication in instalments of thirteen chapters (and the beginning of the fourteenth) in the Chicago magazine *The Little Review*. This typescript exemplar is no longer extant. Then, from mid-1921 to January 1922, another exemplar, now eked out to comprise the full run of the chapters, provided copy for the printer Darantiere in Dijon whom Sylvia Beach, a bookseller in Paris, had entrusted with manufacturing the book under her imprint—total lay woman though she was as a publisher undertaking such an enterprise. For Chapters 1 to 14, Darantiere's printer's-copy exemplar carried most, but not all, of the revisions made in the typescript exemplar used for the *Little Review* pre-publication. The *Little Review*'s printed text reveals that the journal's printer's copy must have contained a few changes unique to that (lost) typescript exemplar. Occasionally, too, revisions in the *Little Review* from its printer's copy were differently worded from corresponding entries in Darantiere's printer's copy; this exemplar of the typescript was, in addition, studded with further overwritings evidently entered before it was handed over for typesetting in 1921. The autograph changes to Chapters 15 to 18 in Darantiere's typescript exemplar are self-evidently first-time overwritings. Notably, however, these latter chapter units are intermittently mixed from (sometimes several) retypings. Where this is the case, the differences observable between the state of the text in the Rosenbach manuscript and the extant typed text, if not simply mistypings, are variants originating, as must be presumed, as overwritings on an earlier typing attempt discarded when retyped.

One would have thought, and Darantiere presumably thought, that his printer's copy, compositely comprising basic typing and autograph additions, constituted the author's considered final text. But this was not so in Joyce's view. Seeing his text as developed to the fair-copy/typescript stage then transposed into book print seems, on the contrary, to have acted as a stimulus to continued composition and revision. The proofs with their ample white space held out just too much temptation for further writing.

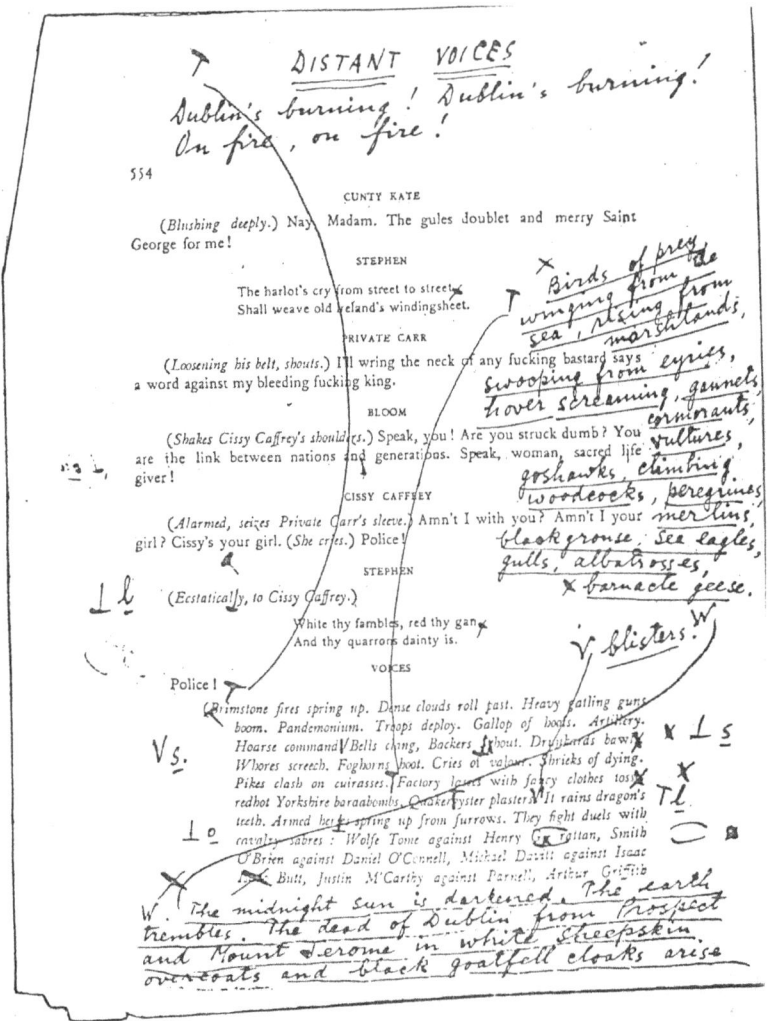

Fig. 5.2: *James Joyce Archive* 26, p. 304

Consequently, first the *placards*—i.e., 'galleys-in-page', meaning sheets on which eight typepages were lined up on one side only—and subsequently the successive sixteen-page gatherings were repeatedly sent back and returned, on occasion up to ten or twelve times, before they were approved for printing. Measuring the difference in sheer extension between the fair-copy (or near-fair-copy) manuscript of the eighteen *Ulysses* episodes and the book reveals an increase of text of about one third. What is essential to note is that not only is the holograph fair copy by definition Joyce's, but that all the overwriting in the typescripts and proofs are also in his hand. The entire text that James Joyce wrote for *Ulysses*, both as fair copy and thereafter as overwriting into the successive documents of the pre-publication transmission, exists thus literally, because materially, in autograph.

This document situation provides rich evidence of the processes of writing *Ulysses*. At its core, it shows two things: on the one hand, indeed, the multiple and variegated text slippages on the path to publication already mentioned; yet on the other hand, the creative and dialogic process of the writing itself. The identification of the text slippages serves the textual critic and editor in their efforts to bring into focus the authentic text for the book, at the point in time it was published, to represent *Ulysses*, the work. The material evidence for the text in its continuous process of variation, in contrast, supports the critic delving into the diachronic depths, into the text's development within the entire compass of the author's labour of composition and revision.

Considerations of Method and Procedure

It will be apparent how the full range of methods of textual criticism and editing initially sketched out in this essay should prove applicable to the path *Ulysses* took through its pre-publication documents toward publication in its first edition. Common copy-text editing practices, standard according to Anglo-American methodology, seem at best clumsy to handle the matter. Choosing, say, the fair-copy text as copy text would be thoroughly impractical. It would lead absurdly to treating all text variation and extension intervening between the fair copy and the first edition in a mode of emendation. Nor would the first-edition text be eligible as copy-text. To attend editorially to its 'typographical errors' as earmarked in the correction lists to the first edition would, of course, be easy, but it would be superficially corrective only. What, furthermore, would stand in the way of copy-text editing on the basis of the first edition are the first-edition divergences from the text as Joyce actually wrote it in the pre-publication documents. These divergences would need reversing by emending the copy text, but copy-text editing as a method offers no rule for handling even just the pragmatics of bringing pre-copy-text readings to bear on a copy text. The authentic Joycean readings for consideration as emendations to the first-edition text if used as copy text are spread over multiple documents; these documents all precede the first edition; and, still more problematically, they do so at an increasing reverse distance from the first edition. Pragmatics aside, copy-text editing as a fundamental mode and method of editing is founded on a concept of closure, of text as product, not as process. By definition it focuses exclusively on the final result of text writing. This would mean that an edition of *Ulysses* established on and from the first-edition text, while of course rightly accepting and confirming all Joycean text that successfully arrived intact in the first edition, would be systemically, and so quite radically, at a loss for how to make evident and analysable all progressive writing that preceded the first-edition text. On the very grounds of its preconceived method, such an edition would most likely elide, and keep silent about, the creative dynamics of the writing of *Ulysses*. Yet how could a scholarly edition in our age justify not making the genetic dimension of the text for *Ulysses* accessible to critical scrutiny?

Once the unfolding of the processuality of the text writing for *Ulysses* is perceived and accepted as an overriding demand on text-critical analysis and editorial skill of method and presentation, the fact that the evidence of the writing process is spread over multiple documents need not faze the editor. For me, it was the genetically oriented mindset of German textual scholarship and editing that helped me, initially, to deal with the situation. The solution was to build, from all the text, and all the text overlay across the real documents of the pre-publication transmission, a continuous text collocation as if inscribed on one imaginary manuscript. That text collocation was 'stratified': that is, it was genetically layered. In assembling the several document texts and their respective overlays to merge them into the heuristic construct of the one imaginary manuscript text, we differentiated the successive layers and overlays according to their document source. Each layer and overlay was 'earmarked': that is, it was given a unique markup tag indexing its provenance (pointing to the document witnessing it). The ruling distinction between 'layer' and 'overlay' is this: 'layer' = base text as inscribed on its document of original entry; 'overlay' = overwritings over the base text in the given document of entry. This implies an understanding that text carried forward identically through several successive documents is and remains, always, text of its document of first inscription. Its multiple identical copying through successive documents is seen as redundantly accidental. For the collocation of the continuous manuscript, its layering was distinguished and indexed through markup—just as would be the case with an author's real working manuscript multiply worked over. The layering from the several revision campaigns that went over such a manuscript would, in a digital transcription, be indicated through markup in just the same manner.[5]

Contiguously layered, the imaginary manuscript's text was, in essence, continuous, but it was as such a raw text, a heuristic construct. It was not yet an edited text. Yet it held a double potential for editing: it could be, and was, developed toward two separate targets. One target, yet by the edition's overall concept its secondary one, was indeed the customary 'end product' of scholarly editing: an established reading text,

---

5   The notion that 'text carried forward identically through several successive documents is and remains always the text of its document of first inscription' has important corollaries. It implies that what is text of a given document is only what is originally and uniquely written on it, not also what it repeats identically from its document predecessors. A given proof, for instance, is 'witness', in the traditional sense of the term in editorial scholarship, only to the autograph deletions, changes, and additions inscribed on it. The textual layer for which these deletions, changes, and additions are constitutive—that is to say, *become* constitutive—is materially in evidence in the typesetting of the proof following. In a conceptual sense, therefore, the fresh textual layer that the autograph interventions on their proof document of origin generate is constituted (hidden in the wings, so to speak) between their proof document of origin and the proof document on which they appear as integrated into the typesetting of that (follow-up) document. The theoretical significance of this distinction is the logical separation of document and text. In our cultural environment of writing and reading, texts and their carrier documents form a symbiosis—leaving oral transmission aside, we cannot pragmatically receive and experience texts other than through and from documents. Yet logically, text and document are distinct and separable entities. Otherwise, texts could not be materially transmitted through series of documents, nor could, for example, the imaginary continuous manuscript of *Ulysses* I posit be conceived of.

that is, its editor's proposition of a reliable text (as the term goes) for the titular work. The other and, in fact, primary target was the presentation of the development from fair copy to first edition of James Joyce's text for *Ulysses*. The raw-text assembly and markup of the continuous manuscript allowed us to generate a synopsis of the text development in and across the documents in which it was successively in evidence. It was this synoptic text presentation that was to constitute the edition's true core: an edition text both genetically fully stratified and critically established. Achieved, it was eventually laid out on the left-hand pages of the edition in book form. From this was to be derived—to be filtered out by what today would be called 'style-sheets'—what the edition proposes as its reading text. This runs parallel to the presentation of the edition text, and face to face with it, on the right-hand pages in *Ulysses. A Critical and Synoptic Edition* of 1984.[6]

Harnessing the Computer

The 1984 publication came as book in three volumes. Yet over the seven years it took me and my team to prepare and build the edition, we realised it from scratch with computer assistance. All original data representing Joyce's writing and text, as well as all auxiliary data of our own making and configuration were, over seven years, computer-inputted, computer-organised and multiply processed, and at the conclusion, digitally archived. The book volumes were generated entirely by computer typesetting from the processed data. From today's perspective, it seems a paradox to have worked on an edition entirely with computer assistance and then nonetheless to have published it in physical book form. However, considering the matter historically, to rely on computer assistance in scholarly editing was something thoroughly new in the late 1970s/early 1980s. A working environment other than transcriptions and notes on paper, and eventually the physical book as the output, was then unimaginable. No digital format was at the time deployable either to store or to access a product of scholarship of the complexity of an edition. This means that our edition was not, or could

---

6   James Joyce, *Ulysses. A Critical and Synoptic Edition*, prepared by Hans Walter Gabler with Wolfhard Steppe and Claus Melchior, 3 vols. (New York: Garland Publishing, 1984; ²1986).

not yet have become, what today we are on the way to conceiving of as a digital edition.

Harnessing the computer was something new and, more importantly, innovative. It was so, moreover, only accidentally because of the technical requirements of easing the text-critical and editorial work. Where it became essentially innovative was in multiply reconsidering the very object of the edition—its text and text elements—and equally so in re-thinking the trajectories and efficiency of editorial workflows. This amounted, at times, even to discarding age-old stages of editorial procedure altogether.

'Preparatory to anything else' (*U* 16, 1) came, encompassingly, the task of inputting the text to render it machine-readable. Digital scanning of typed or printed text was at the time not an option; scanning handwriting was absolutely out of the question. The way to go was to transcribe the text—essentially just as had been done in editorial work through the ages. To transcribe text into a machine-readable format was new, however. It meant to type it on an electric typewriter with a golf-ball writing head studded with OCR characters—characters as they were used in the banking business for capturing data from checks and the like by means of scanning devices specialised to read and digitally convert the typed script. The OCR golf-ball printed uppercase lettering only. Hence, in the transcription, letters intended as uppercase had to be individually tagged in order to remain uppercase when the digital conversion of the OCR transcript was converted into raw data for the edition.

But how then were our own mistypings in the course of the transcription to be detected? A traditional editorial workflow would, on completion of a transcription, have scheduled time for manual proofreading. Resorting to computer assistance, however, meant essentially leaving behind proofreading by hand and eye for good. We were extremely lucky to be able to use a system of text-processing routines, TUSTEP, developed in Tübingen, Germany in the 1970s and consolidated over the years since, and further refined by user requests, including ours. Quite simply: we would have been unable to realise the project without the TUSTEP toolkit. Thus, it was right from the outset that the TUSTEP collation routine, interlinked with an updating routine procedurally cog-wheeled into it, was deployed for proofreading and correcting the initial text input.

Our first raw-text input was the text of the first edition. As already discussed, this was not intended to serve as the edition's copy-text. However, and despite all its textual errors, it provided the most comprehensive reference base. It comprised all of Joyce's text that had 'made it' through to the first edition, and provided also the structure of the pagination and line-fall of the first edition as book. Against this base, the edition text could be assembled through the subsequent computer-aided workflow. Of course, the typed transcription could not be expected to be 'letter-perfect'. If, as noted, eye-and-hand collation was ruled out, a second full transcript was needed against which to machine-collate the first. Hence, we also typed and OCR-inputted the second edition of *Ulysses* as reset and published in 1926. This seeming redundancy of input paid off as the basis for machine-collation-supported proofreading. The TUSTEP collation identified every difference between the two inputs. So computer-assisted, human-intelligence proofing quite simply amounted to checking divergent readings against the original texts. Either their difference was genuine because the texts in the respective editions differed, or they differed due to faulty transcription in one input text or the other. In these instances, the transcription error was corrected— but not by hand. Instead, the amendments earmarked were fed as a set of correction instructions into the ensuing TUSTEP update routines to obtain corrected text files of both the first and the second *Ulysses* editions.

Collation—the comparison of two document texts for their identities and differences—has always been the opening move in textual criticism and editing. In the manuscript- and print-based environment of transmissions, it meant comparing by eye and hand texts inscribed in their carrier documents and compiling lists of their differences. No text transcription preceded such conventional first collations. In our computer-assisted work toward the *Ulysses* edition, however, the fact that transcription took first place in the workflow necessitated, as described, a preliminary round of automatic collation to verify our input. Only then could we proceed to successive collatings of the digital text records as the established representatives they now were of the material document texts. Thus, in our workflow, the mode of collation, which conventionally used to be the first phase of text-critical labour, came second. However, from our procedure we had already gained a significant spin-off. Storing our initial, verified transcriptions of the cornerstone document texts electronically meant securing them letter- and punctuation-perfect once and for all. Such spin-off repeated itself through all subsequent, collation-supported steps in the editorial workflow. It rendered ultimately redundant, too, the grand final proof-reading campaigns characteristic of editorial projects in print.

The Building of a Continuous Manuscript Text

To establish the edition comprehensively in the digital medium and environment, we progressively eked out our digital input of document texts, stored in separate files. Firstly, these comprised, together with the fair-copy text and the 1922 first-edition text, the *Ulysses* text materialised in the typescripts and the instalment texts from *The Little Review*. These, as will be explained shortly, were to be fused into the heuristic construct of an 'early-version' text. Secondly, over and above the text of the reset 1926 edition text that we had transcribed and input at the project's start, we stored digitally the texts from the 1932 Hamburg edition, the 1934 Random House (New York) edition, the 1936/37 private and public Bodley Head (London) editions, and the 1961 Random House (New York) edition. This latter sequence of text instantiations for *Ulysses* was intended for supplementary reference in the course of establishing the edition text and, at the conclusion of the project, to enable the collocation of the historical collation.

The advantages of computer assistance perhaps made themselves most significantly felt in realising the edition's conceptual centre: the building of a continuous text collocation as if inscribed on one imaginary manuscript. To this end, what we established first was the stepping-platform of an 'early-version' *Ulysses*. We constructed it as a heuristic counterpart to the *Little Review* serialisation by merging into one digital file the fair copy text and the typescript text as typed, together with its first overlay. We checked this merger against the *Little Review* pre-publication text in order to catch all first overlay in its (lost) printer's copy. The 'early-version' *Ulysses* already carried the markup for the phases of the text progression it covered. This construct became the point of departure from which we sought to encompass the subsequent text changes and accretions towards the first edition. Its formal counter-mooring was the computer-stored and verified first-edition text. This we cloned into a copy of itself, designated to become the digital basis of the continuous text collocation as if inscribed on one imaginary manuscript.

Computer-collating the early-version construct against this first-edition clone yielded as output every element of change and accretion beyond the early version. Predictably, the output revealed errors for correction in the first-edition printing against the early-version text. Where nothing else was called for than putting right something that, untouched by revision, should never have gone wrong, the respective list entries in the collation result were tagged for updating. The main cull of variation from the collation of the early-version construct against this first-edition clone was, of course, an accumulated assembly of all revision and augmentation elements as they extended from the second overlay to the typescript to the final overlay in the respective last proofs. What this accumulation lacked was a markup stratifying the writing progression. Besides, coming, as it did, from the text realisation in the first edition, it was infested, one might say, with typesetters' misreadings of Joyce's overlays, or their misplacing them, or overlooking them altogether in the documents. The errors needed to be eliminated and the markup provided.

It seemed to make little sense to touch up separately each individual revision and augmentation element as shown in the accumulated assembly delivered from the collation run. This would have been too error-prone a procedure; and the genetic marking-up of the elements—including a marked-up splicing-in of text deleted somewhere along Joyce's writing campaigns—would still require separate attention. What we did instead was to build a complete mirror text as a double, so to speak, to the revision and augmentation output from the computer collation of early-version text against the first-edition clone. To assemble the mirror text, we repeated, as it were, the typesetters' labours all over again. From the original documents[7] we transcribed Joyce's overlay

---

7   'From the original documents' meaning: from their high-quality reproductions in the facsimile of the Rosenbach manuscript and the photo-reproductions in the successive volumes of *The James Joyce Archive*, ed. by Michael Groden, *et al.*, 63 vols. (New York and London: Garland Publishing, 1977-79). Spread out as the originals are between (in the main) Philadelphia; Buffalo; Cambridge, Massachusetts; and Austin, Texas, we were fortunate to be able to work day-by-day from the reproductions. I had personally seen all originals before our project began, and I returned to them repeatedly for on-site inspection during the years of editing.

modifications—deletions, additions, deletions-and-replacements—into individual lists, double-checked our transcriptions textually with the help of suitable computer collation subroutines, and provided each listed group of entries (those, for instance, from the second typescript overlay, or from the placards, or, say, from the fifth proofs) wholesale with their respective level-defining markup. The individual lists were then pleated together. The composite transcription list thus comprised not only an authenticated text of all revisional change and accretion of the text for *Ulysses* between the printer's copy and the final proofs for the first-edition book. It held also, through its markup, all requisite information for that change and text increase as a genetic text progression. By design, moreover, the composite transcription list ran parallel, unit by unit, with the assembly of all revision and augmentation elements gained from the collation of the early-version construct against the base of the first-edition clone. These revision and augmentation elements, in their turn, although they were not marked up and were textually unreliable, here carried the precise first-edition page.line,word numbers of the collation base-text. As mentioned, an output element from a TUSTEP collation is (because of its reference specifications) re-deployable as an update instruction for the TUSTEP updating routine. The page.line,word numbering is the operative element of each update instruction. These operative elements alone could consequently be re-used: they would 'simply' need to be prefixed to the text elements required, namely those from the lists of our own re-transcription of the Joycean overlays in the documents, just as we wanted them for the continuous manuscript text. Thus, we removed from the output protocol of the collation the real first-edition text elements and left standing as pointers the page.line,word numberings only. To these we freshly attached the textual units as assembled, verified, and marked-up in our composite transcription list. This became the command list for the TUSTEP updating routine. It was eked out by the readings and reading configurations (for example, the mark-up) of the early-version text. Text and mark-up in conjunction were so grafted into the first-edition clone; added to the list of update commands, too, were the instructions, previously tagged, for the necessary corrections to the text rendering from the first edition. The update realised digitally the continuous text collocation as if inscribed on one imaginary manuscript. This was to form the raw foundation upon which subsequently we would build our critical edition text.[8]

What we had procedurally achieved, thanks to our encompassing deployment of the computer, was really quite a feat of abstraction. The assembling of the continuous text of an imaginary manuscript in one digital data file resulted from grafting that multiply marked-up text onto the matrix of the computer-stored transcription of the real first edition. That transcription was, in this operation, however, not embraced for its text, but for offering the 'empty form' of its reference structure, its stable page.line,word numbering. Paradoxically, one might say, we threw out from the digital transcription the real first-edition text and replaced it with the essential raw-text version of *Ulysses* as Joyce progressively wrote it through the pre-publication documents.

Critical Editing

The graft represented a continuous text as-if-transcribed from one imaginary manuscript. As collocated, it was born digitally, yet it was but a raw text assembly that still required conversion into the edition text. This was where editorial operations resembling copy-text editing began.

The continuous text collocation assumed the position of a base text to be subjected to critical editing. On the technical side, this can be taken literally. We installed the continuous text collocation as base text in a set of TUSTEP collation runs. Against it we collated, one by one, the successive published instantiations from our store of digital transcriptions. The individual collation protocols were fed into a visualisation module that fused them and printed the composite results from the several collations in parallel lines with the text agreements or differences arranged in vertical columns. In these 'editing scores', as we dubbed them, we assessed every variant in a later instantiation for its

---

8   Midway through the project, my team and I reported on it at a TUSTEP colloquium in Tübingen. For the minutes, see Hans Walter Gabler *et al.*, 'Computer-aided critical edition of *Ulysses*' (1979) at http://www.tustep.uni-tuebingen.de/prot/prot18e.html. This account details quirks of procedure I have not specified here. In relation to the present essay, it illustrates stages and formats of computer output with which we worked. As it so happens (considering the decades that have passed since we did the original work), these minutes give also the only illustration still digitally accessible of core stages of our editorial workflow.

acceptability as emendation to the base-text collocation of the continuous manuscript text. Emendations began at trivial levels. An overwriting in Joyce's hand may on a proof page appear as a sequence of words only. The typesetter spliced it in with punctuation marks into the previously set text. The punctuation in the first edition is thus a feature not of the text as Joyce wrote it, but of the text as transmitted. Deeming it critically acceptable or even necessary, we used it as emendation to our raw base text. Where the later instantiations of *Ulysses*, too, feature touch-ups that are critically justifiable as emendations to the continuous manuscript text, they generally cause no ripple (as it were) because they concur with the pre-1984 tradition of *Ulysses* in print. The case is different, and was in the early reception of the 1984 edition at times quite controversial, when the critical editing affirms the continuous manuscript text against the *Ulysses* instantiations in the publication history from the first edition in 1922 onward. Affirming the continuous manuscript text by critically accepting its readings against the publication history meant rejecting the *textus receptus* of *Ulysses* in print since its first publication. Critical editing always means either judgmentally departing from the chosen base text by amending and emending it, or affirming the base text by rejecting deviations from it documented in competing text instantiations collated. Under such premises, our endeavour was to establish the edition text as closely as possible in accordance with the text written and thus materially evident in and from the documents of composition and pre-publication revision. This resulted in a text from which all published texts, beginning with the first-edition text, were revealed to depart. The perspective was thoroughly unconventional and was, in early reception, as often as not re-accommodated to the conventional: *Ulysses. A Critical and Synoptic Edition* was mistakenly seen as amending and emending the first-edition text. But for our approach, it was not the first-edition text, but the collocated continuous manuscript text that was the base-text norm from which either critically to depart, or else critically to confirm.

Critically confirming the continuous manuscript text began again, in relative triviality, with capturing word forms or spellings that had not survived from Joyce's inscription into the first-edition text. For example, Joyce makes Bloom ruminate—if that is the word—on cheese: 'Cheese digests all but itself' and to add: 'Mity cheese' (*U* 8, 755). The adjective arrives in the first edition as 'Mighty'—with the pun orthographically lost. Joyce's spelling is 'mity', thus evoking cheese-mites. Sometimes the critical search for the text as written involved shifting whole passages correctly into position, as originally documented in the writing, from where by a typesetter's mistake they stood in the first edition.

By such archaeology of the writing process, even text lost in the pre-publication transition between documents was retrieved, most spectacularly so Stephen Dedalus's highly charged inward reflection during the 'Shakespeare debate' in the ninth episode, Scylla & Charybdis: 'Do you know what you are talking about? Love, yes. Word known to all men'. (U 9, 429–430) Because they are critically based, such retrievals naturally needed to be argued. In this particular instance, both interpretatively critical and strictly bibliographical reasoning was required. On the critical plane, an interpretable correspondence is relevant with the dialogue in the fifteenth chapter, the Circe, or nighttown, episode, between Stephen Dedalus, thoroughly drunk, and his dead mother, phantasmagorically re-arisen from her grave. At one juncture, the dialogue turns on the charged phrase. Stephen asks of his mother, '*eagerly*': 'Tell me the word, mother, if you know now. The word known to all men'. (U 15, 4192–3) Yet from this instance in the fifteenth episode, it is not sufficient to support by critical argument alone the restoration to the ninth episode of the lost manuscript passage—for perhaps the phrase is lacking in the first-edition text of the ninth episode not by error, but because it was deleted at a document stage not preserved. To minimise the likelihood of this option, therefore, the relationship between the fair copy and the typescript inscriptions for the text progression in question in the ninth episode needed to be bibliographically analysed.

The pattern of underlinings for italics, together with an assessment of the variation between the respective document texts in the fair copy and the typescript, helped the analysis. The fair copy narrates an interruption of Stephen's monologue about Shakespeare, fathers, and daughters by a murmur from Mr Best: '—The art of being a grandfather, Mr Best murmured.' Stephen speaks on audibly, but after a couple of sentences recedes into the stream-of-consciousness mode that embeds the self-dialogue in thought, 'Do you know what you are talking about? Love, yes. Word known to all men' and ends in a long quote in Latin. The quote in Latin is in the fair copy carefully underlined. The typescript, by contrast, lacks both the couple of sentences spoken by Stephen and the whole stream-of-consciousness passage, including not only the self-dialogue about 'love', but also the quote in Latin. Leading up to this lacuna in the typescript, we find (in seeming compensation?!) Mr Best's murmur extended by a quote in French: 'L'art d'être grandp . . .'. The quote in French is underlined in ink, and to all appearances underlined by Joyce himself.

Such underlinings in ink for emphasis occur regularly sprinkled over the typescript. Checking back, moreover, we find them correspondingly patterned in the fair copy, where they are positively Joyce's. It is this non-textual feature of underlining for emphasis that permits hypothesising what happened. The typist worked from a Joycean holograph. We assume that this was a lost final working draft and take this hypothesised document to have been the common source of both the fair copy and the typescript. It was characterised, we also assume, by the same features of inscription as the fair copy and the typescript; we infer this, in particular, from the congruence in underlinings in the fair copy and the typescript. The hypothesis then is this: the typist typed Mr Best's 'L'art d'être grandp . . .'; these words in French were, we presume, underlined in the final working manuscript; the typing then resumed after an underlining in the final working manuscript for words again in a foreign tongue (this time in Latin), but occurring two paragraphs later. The typist so inadvertently skipped, after Mr Best's murmur, the sentences Stephen audibly spoke and his silent reflections thereafter. The spoken sentences are necessary to carry forward his Shakespeare argument. The Latin quote is a beautiful narrative illustration of the convolutions Stephen gets into when giving associations of thought a free rein. It is untenable critically to argue that this double embedding had to fall by the wayside in order to eliminate from the author's valid text for *Ulysses* Stephen's silent self-dialogue, 'Do you know what you are talking about? Love, yes. Word known to all men.'

The bibliographical argument alone is equal to the case: the text lacuna in the typescript resulted in the heat of the typing from an eyeskip from one foreign-language underlining to the next. Where a critical argument is always potentially bidirectional—either of two readings could be 'intended'—a progression from correct to incorrect on the grounds of a material feature bibliographically evident can only be one-directional. In the present particular case one must also supportively adduce the strong critical argument that restoring Stephen's speech and his ensuing silent reflection restores an essential link in the run of his Shakespeare argument in the National Library. But it is the bibliographic assessment that provides the editor's lynch-pin—or you may say, buttresses his defence for critically retrieving the phrase as part of Stephen's inner reflection in the Scylla & Charybdis episode for the edition text of *Ulysses*.

The retrieval in this instance, be it nonetheless noted, is of text from a document, the fair copy, which is collateral to the typescript and thus not in the direct line of descent of the *Ulysses* text down to the first edition. The assumption must therefore also be that the fair copy replicates in identity text that was in the lost final working manuscript, in the first place, and thence made it, or rather, but for the typist's eyeskip, should have made it into the typescript. Moreover, while the editorial decision is both bibliographically supported and critically tenable, the example still captures in a nutshell that our edition text, as an edited text, establishes Joyce's text as critically assessed against its transmission in print. It remains simultaneously true that, as an edited text, it is, as always, the editor's text. An editor's edited text should not, for in truth it cannot, be given out to be the author's text, however close the editor's text might, and by-and-large in practice should, come to the author's text as documented.

Where, in our case, the edited text ends up as other than that in Joyce's writing, showed, alas, also in the errors we committed in response to the authorial inscription and thus incorporated in the edition text as published in the 1984 first impression of *Ulysses. A Critical and Synoptic Edition*. The instances were amazingly few where we had misread the autograph inscription. We adjusted and reported some half-dozen cases in the second impression of 1986. Somewhat spectacularly also, and mistakenly, the fifth chapter at first featured a 'Captain Culler', and the tenth had a cyclist by the name of 'H. Shrift' among the quartermile flat handicappers. These became again correctly 'Captain Buller' (*U* 5, 560) and 'H. Thrift' (*U* 10, 1259) in the 1993 reprint of the reading-text-only editions from Random House/Vintage. It was thanks to the vigilance of early users of the edition that we were able to eliminate these first-impression errors. As evidenced by these alerts, the edition was clearly fulfilling an edition's range of commitments right from the start; with the edition text it offered, it provided also the customary evidence record and tools of control to check its quality and performance.

The edition's evidence record, in conclusion, extended also to its incorporation of a traditional 'historical collation'. Once again, we set up a multiple collation procedure. Its base text this time was the edition's reading text as derived by 'style-sheet' extraction from the full edition text. The collated texts were the 1922 and 1926 first- and second-edition texts, and, in addition, the texts from the editions already mentioned, the 1932 Hamburg edition, the 1934 Random House (New York) edition, the 1936/37 private and public Bodley Head (London) editions, and the 1961 Random House (New York) edition. The collation protocols were merged and fused into one composite file. This passed through a judiciously submodified series of reformatting routines in the TUSTEP modular system to emerge in the end untouched by human hands in its substance, as a thoroughly conventional historical collation ready for printing.

The Impact

The Estate and the Estate's Advisers

The whirlpool activity during the edition's seven years of preparation was fueled by the reorientations of methods and media I have described. These were, in terms of conception and methodology, creative turbulences. This remained true regardless of the fact that, toward the end of the preparation phase, our concept and its textual outcomes met non-publicly with objections. From its beginnings, the edition project had operated with the good will of the James Joyce Estate. This good will had its origin in a brief but momentous exchange with Peter du Sautoy, trustee of the Estate, at an encounter in Paris. Peter du Sautoy was also, as it happened, a director of Faber & Faber publishers in London. At the International James Joyce Symposium in Paris in 1975, I had laid out my conception of a critical *Ulysses* edition. When we talked privately afterward, du Sautoy took the position that, 'As publishers, we receive texts from their authors and have the obligation to safeguard them as we received them'. My response was, 'I can accept this in principle. Yet in a case like that of *Ulysses* with its history of serious text corruption, manifest in the first edition and increasing further through its successive publications, you, as the James Joyce Estate, have a prior responsibility to the integrity of Joyce's text'. It was, I am happy to say, a counter-argument he fully accepted. With circumspection, at the same time, he appointed a triumvirate of advisers to the Estate to assess the editorial work and its outcome. The Estate wished to be guided by the triumvirate in understanding the scholarly scrutiny our endeavour lavished on *Ulysses*. Needless to say, the advisers to the Estate were also a significant support for me and my team in our work on the edition. They were, by name and standing, Richard Ellmann, the Joyce biographer; Clive Hart, an encyclopaedic Joyce critic and scholar with both great factual knowledge of things Joycean and editorial experience of his own; and Philip Gaskell, renowned book-historian and textual bibliographer of the British school. Peter du Sautoy, for the Estate, convened us repeatedly for critical scrutiny of progress made. The meetings set in after we had, in 1979, produced, and offered for discussion at the International James Joyce Symposium in Zurich that year, a prototype of the edition-to-come for the eighth chapter, the Lestrygonians episode. From our workshop in Munich, we brought to the meetings—or rather, circulated to the advisers beforehand—chapter printouts of both the edition text and the reading text as derived from the edition text, together of course with the respective apparatus listings. The live discussions of these materials—regularly attended, too, by Gavin Borden of Garland Press of New York, our prospective publisher—were fruitful and, in many an instance, seriously helpful in enabling us to affirm or reconsider editorial assessments. For well into the third year of consultations with the Estate's advisers, our exchanges were without controversy, which gave us the comforting impression that what we were doing not only found approval but was also well understood. Yet toward the end of the penultimate year our comfort was shattered. The advisers were discovering that the edition in the making did not conform to their expectations of an edited *Ulysses*. Apparently, it jarred increasingly with their traditional notions of 'the scholarly edition'. This put us in a quandary—and even the edition as such in jeopardy. The whole point of the edition was, after all, that it was to be innovative beyond conventional editions. It was a fundamental reversal of an edition's perspective on the text for a work to establish the edition text not from the first edition text and in observance of the author's intention, but instead from a genetic perspective according to the very evidence of the author's progressive writing in the successive pre-publication documents. Nor had it previously been heard of that the text of a first edition was defined as a departure from, and thus, by the nomenclature of textual scholarship, as the first corruption of the established edition text. But this was what formed the basis of, and followed from my, and our, approach to editing *Ulysses*. The Estate's advisers had, alas, been somewhat slow fully to take this in. But they now balked at it even to the extent of temporarily resigning their commission. The Estate's chief trustee was left alone to decide whether to follow their advice (implicit in the resignation) not to agree, on behalf of the Estate, to the publishing of the Critical and Synoptic Edition—which, by this time, was all but ready. I made it clear that the edition must not be seen as, or declared, the Estate's edition. As its scholarly editor, I laid claim to sole responsibility for it. At this sensitive juncture, I also received support and measured guidance from Michael Groden and A. Walton Litz at Princeton University.

Emotions subsiding, the advisers returned to the fold. It was not only the edition's (and, I suppose, my own) autonomous assertiveness, furthermore, which succeeded in bringing the edition before the public. What was essentially salvaged—all-important at the time when *Ulysses*, the work, was still in copyright—was that the edition was published with Estate consent. Nonetheless, it was unambiguously understood to be the edition prepared by Hans Walter Gabler with Wolfhard Steppe and Claus Melchior. The clear division of responsibility between the Estate and the editor rendered moot from the outset, too, all suspicion (variously voiced for a while within a few years of publication) that the edition, in the guise particularly of its reading text from which the first-edition text so notably diverged, had been established to favour the Estate's copyright interests.[9] Enterprisingly, in succession to his

---

9   The decade was the 1980s. It was a time when modernist writers' estates were seeing the end looming of the (then) fifty-year post-mortem copyright protection of their respective authors' works. The expectations, tenable or not, were that edited texts would create new copyrights. This was, to my knowledge, the wishful thinking, too, on the part of the James Joyce Estate. But the initiative to establish the Critical and Synoptic Edition of *Ulysses* did not come from the Estate, nor did they, or the

singularly pioneering sixty-three volumes of *The James Joyce Archive* out of Garland Press of New York from 1977 to 1979, Gavin Borden published the three-volume *Ulysses. A Critical and Synoptic Edition* in 1984. As the imaginative publisher he was, he infused into its formatting distinct ideas of his own. The facing-page arrangement of edition text and reading text, specifically, was his design solution. At the public launching of the edition at the International James Joyce Symposium held in Frankfurt in 1984, he and I jointly presented the symbolic first copy of the edition to Stephen James Joyce, James Joyce's grandson.

Initial Reception

Ulysses. A Critical and Synoptic Edition received highly positive and elated responses upon publication—even though for a time thereafter considerable streaks of adverse criticism came to overshadow the initial euphoria. The *New York Times* carried the news of the edition's publication on its front page with a good understanding of the edition's problematics and objectives.[10] As one of the journalists' pre-contacts via transatlantic telephone, I was impressed by their astute questions. Their German colleagues, by contrast, came nowhere near matching their sharp US colleagues in comprehension. Foremost among academic reviewers, Hugh Kenner, the eminent Modernism and Joyce critic, grasped the edition's central quality: the edition gave us not a new *Ulysses*, he emphasised, yet very much a text in which all blurring of textual detail from its descent through the pre-publication documents, exacerbated further during its decades of trade-driven transmission through printed editions, had been brought again into the clear focus of that text's first invention.[11] Jerome McGann, then and still today a

---

publishers, at any time take me into their service and pay, 'for hire', as the legal term would have been. The enterprise of the edition was solely my conception. It was comprehensively financed by German public grant money from the Deutsche Forschungsgemeinschaft. While always grateful for the James Joyce Estate's backing and moral support, I assumed and assume sole responsibility for the edition as an achievement of scholarship.

10 *The New York Times*, 7 June 1984, front page and continued on Page C19, Column 1. Hugh Kenner's essay 'The Computerised *Ulysses*' in *Harper's Magazine*, 1 April 1980, 89-95 may have helped the *Times* journalists to gain an advance understanding.

11 I believe I correctly remember Hugh Kenner on at least one occasion so characterising our edition—yet I regret to be unable to give a precise citation. On 13 July 1984, the

notable authority in the field of textual scholarship, was the earliest respondent to comprehend both concept and theory of the edition's genetic perspective on the writing and text of *Ulysses*.[12] A few years later, George Bornstein drew from the edition's genetic disposition a stringent interpretative discourse. For the benefit of Joyce criticism and literary criticism at large, he showed what insights into Joyce's art, and what critical appreciation of the work, could be drawn from the full edition text of the critical and synoptic *Ulysses* edition.[13]

Within two years of the publication of the three-volume edition, the commercial publishers with prior exclusive rights under copyright to *Ulysses* eagerly wished to realise the option held out to them in the contract for the Critical and Synoptic Edition (to which they were co-signees). For their general markets, they brought out the edition's reading text separately. Wholly subservient to educated cultural preconceptions, they advertised this as the 'definitive text'; soon, this catch-term was modified to the 'corrected text', and eventually to the 'Gabler text'. With the edition so named, the controversies that in the late 1980s broke out with the aim of sinking the edition were clearly seen to possess an advertising appeal.

As to the broadcasting of the buzzword 'definitive', this is an echo of the expectation to which scholarly editing has traditionally been held. It shows a total lack of awareness of a fundamental contradiction. A critical edition cannot, by definition, be definitive. Textual criticism requires 'the application of thought', as A. E. Housman over a century ago memorably phrased it,[14] and hence establishing an edition demands throughout the exercise of critical judgment. Reciprocally, reading and using an edition demands critical assessment. Ever since textual criticism and editing were academically established about two centuries ago, however, this twin discipline has also developed into a highly authoritarian branch of scholarship. Editors deferred to 'authority', that of texts and of authors,

---

Times Literary Supplement carried his review of the edition under the delightfully Kennerian title 'Leopold's bloom restored'.

12   Jerome J. McGann, '*Ulysses* as a Postmodern Text: The Gabler Edition', *Criticism*, 27 (1985), 283-305.

13   George Bornstein, 'Joyce and the Colonial Archive: Constructing Alterity in *Ulysses*', in *Material Modernism. The Politics of the Page* (Cambridge: Cambridge University Press, 2001), 118-39.

14   A. E. Housman, 'The Application of Thought to Textual Criticism', *Proceedings of the Classical Association*, 18 (1922 [August 1921]), 67-84.

and, in compensation, established for themselves and their editions the aura of being 'authoritative'. This led easily to the assumption that their edited texts were definitive. A dynamic critical dialogue with edited texts as 'texts' and as 'edited' was effectively subdued, if not outright smothered and cut off. Thus, the reading text for *Ulysses* as published by itself commercially was, by being labeled 'definitive', pushed into the corner of conventional expectations for editions. To skew the perspective further, the edition text on the three-volume edition's left-hand pages, moreover, was only dimly recognised, if at all, for its conception and critical potential. In the wake of the early death of its publisher, Gavin Borden, and the dissolution, in consequence, of the Garland Press, it went out of print and so withdrew, one might say, into hibernation. Yet currently it is re-awakening as a Digital Critical and Synoptic Edition.[15] The paradox of publishing a digitally assisted edition in book form is being overcome.

A Decade of Controversy

Tempests erupted over the edition in the late 1980s and early 1990s. Public opinion, initially enthusiastic, was for a time seriously swayed by publicity-seeking attacks. Their main spokesman was John Kidd, a young scholar affiliated with no academic institution, moved by a distinct Joyce craze, highly intelligent, and possessed with a collector's passion and knowledge about the material heritage of Joyce's texts in mainly their published forms. What he had no training in, let alone personal hands-on experience of, was textual criticism and editorial scholarship—nor did he have a genetic perspective on textuality. As the self-appointed adversary, for unfathomable reasons of his own, of *Ulysses. A Critical and Synoptic Edition*, he put fierce energy into pursuing the edition's self-documentation for its leads to and into the source documents. In principle, that is, he put these materials to uses that they were designed for. Yet what he clearly did not sufficiently fathom was how investigating the edition with these facilitating aids presupposed professional understanding of the editorial rationale and its pragmatics of procedure. What would have been required to critique

---

15   Ronan Crowley's and Joshua Schäuble's Digital Critical and Synoptic Edition has been under development since 2015/2016.

the edition justly was an independent pre-knowledge of existing systematics of scholarly editing, in particular those of the German and the Anglo-American schools. Aside from Kidd's insinuations about the incompetence of an editor, foreign (German) to boot, his materially massive attacks, viewed in sober retrospect, went essentially no further than stating that 'the edition does not conform to critical editing of Anglo-American conception' or 'the edition does not exemplify in pure consequence German genetic editing'. True assessments, for what they were worth, in both cases—yet largely unconnectable to the inundation of purported 'errors of execution' adduced, but never argued, in their support. The intellectual achievement that the edition claims for itself lies, by contrast, in the synergetic fusion of the systems that differ in some underlying principles, while agreeing in others, and so in their different ways result in coherent and valid scholarly editing. In our case, they do so in fusion together.[16]

Significantly, there was between, say, 1985 and 1995, and at places spread out between New York and Copenhagen, Miami, Monaco, and Dublin, a lively succession of Joyce meetings, and similarly of conferences

---

16 The first public onslaught of John Kidd's was launched in April 1985 with a *Washington Post* exclusive interview, accompanied by clandestine circulation of a conference paper to be delivered at the New York meeting of the Society for Textual Scholarship, where I was present to respond. Having had the pre-circulated paper 'clandestinely' leaked to me beforehand, my response was prepared and was, to the distinct consternation of the session moderator at the STS meeting, not civilly diplomatic. (*Studies in the Novel* named its volume 22, no. 2 [summer 1990] 'A special Issue on Editing *Ulysses*'. This included, from the 1985 STS meeting, John Kidd's paper, 'Errors of Execution in the 1984 *Ulysses*' [243-9] and my 'A Response to John Kidd's 'Errors of Execution in the 1984 *Ulysses*' [250-6].) In the meantime, and after the commercial reading-text-only edition had been published, Kidd found an editor of *The Papers of the Bibliographical Society of America* willing to undertake bringing the bulk of his indefatigable note-taking sufficiently into form for publication in these *Papers*. (See: John Kidd, 'An Inquiry into *Ulysses*: The Corrected Text', *Papers of the Bibliographical Society of America*, 82 (1988), 411-584. My response to this was Hans Walter Gabler, 'What Ulysses Requires', *Papers of the Bibliographical Society of America*, 87 (1993), 187-248.) After similar midwifery, the *New York Review of Books* had, in its characteristic vein of sensationalism, already carried Kidd's article 'The Scandal of *Ulysses*'. This was in June 1988. The piece was published in time for tall piles of copies of the issue to be set up outside the conference venue at the International James Joyce Symposium held around Bloomsday that year in Venice. It was somewhat ironic that, at this large gathering of Joyceans, the opponent did not turn up in person. But he had his spokesmen and spokeswomen at the event, with some of whom I had the opportunity to debate publicly. I suspect we tended to talk at cross-purposes, as well as over the heads of many in our audience.

on textual criticism, that incorporated discussions of our *Ulysses* edition. It has been said that very rarely had a scholarly edition received such attention in academia, as well as non-academically. It brought home to the discerning that there was such a thing as textual criticism and editing, that texts were not immutably given, and that the fact of life that texts in composition and transmission were variant was something essential that could be understood to matter. Yet in the short run, the attack, as it began to multiply and diversify, burgeoned into something popularly labeled 'the Joyce Wars'. This escalation was exacerbated by the circumstance that the attacks, personified in the original attacker, tended to be taken at face value. Nowhere was there a discernible, independent, and knowledgeable double-checking of the material of mass destruction heaped on the edition. The media broadcast the controversy worldwide, not necessarily with increased understanding of what, rationally, the whole dissent was about. Stephen James Joyce, the grandson who had in the late 1980s become the first member of the family to assume the trusteeship of the James Joyce Estate, felt helpless about it and pronounced on myself and John Kidd together Mercutio's curse from *Romeo and Juliet*: 'A plague on both your houses'. Doubtlessly, the controversies over the edition increased his distrust of, and aversion to, Joyce studies, particularly where they involved Joyce's texts themselves. Over the years, until the oeuvre came finally into the public domain on 1 January 2012, the James Joyce Estate was, by its extremely restrictive granting of permissions, the fiercest dis-enabler of Joyce studies involving original textual material. The regrettable 'Joyce Wars' label may, alas, have played a part in fossilising that mindset.

The US publisher, Random House/Vintage, was seriously unsettled by the negative press that broke out in the wake of their publishing in 1986 the reading text from the Critical and Synoptic Edition to replace outright their old *Ulysses* edition, with its US publishing history since 1934. They appointed a committee to investigate the integrity of their new edition, ours. As it turned out, the committee disbanded before ever getting down to business. The abortive attempt to have the new text adjudicated had one fundamentally welcome side-effect: in the early 1990s, Random House New York returned their pre-1986 edition to their list, without removing ours from it. In the UK, similar decisions were taken. The hardback publisher of the reading text from the Critical and Synoptic Edition was The Bodley Head (they have meanwhile become a division of Random House UK). They licensed Penguin UK to issue this in paperback. The license was returned in 1992. Instead, Penguin UK took it upon itself to publish The Bodley Head's pre-1986 text of Ulysses. While these moves no doubt at the time bowed to the dissent then rampant, they illustrated through Ulysses that works of literature may be represented publicly by competing editions variant from one another—something that the multitude of, say, Shakespeare editions regularly cohabiting on the market should have made us aware of long ago.

The fierce antagonisms against the edition in the late 1980s and through the early 1990s had as bottom lines furthermore, however, two noxious insinuations. One addressed unwary Joyce readers, students, and critics: 'Don't bother about this edition. It is a bad edition'. The other was aimed at textual scholars and editors: 'This is an edition unfit to be followed. It is both methodically unsound and replete with "errors of execution"'. Their dispersal can be dated to the meeting of the Society for Textual Scholarship in New York in 1995. With significant moves having taken place through the early 1990s to reorient and widen the professional horizon of Anglo-American editorial scholarship, it was a European society member, J. C. C. Mays, who at that meeting came to, as one might say, the final rescue. From his understanding gained from his own infusion of conceptions of German genetic editing into his editing of the poetry of Samuel Coleridge, he persuasively vindicated *Ulysses. A Critical and Synoptic Edition* to the gathered community of text-critical and editorial professionals.[17] Peter Shillingsburg, the voice of American textual scholarship at the meeting, did not gloss over the fact that give-and-take arguments between the Anglo-American and the German views and practices of textual criticism and editing formed an ongoing and at times controversial dialogue—one in which he was, has been, and indeed still is, a leading participant.[18] Speaking for James Joyce studies at the STS meeting in New York in 1995, it was Robert Spoo, erstwhile editor of *James Joyce Quarterly*, but since a professor of law and a highly

---

17 J. C. C. Mays, 'Gabler's *Ulysses* as a Field of Force', *TEXT*, 10 (1997), 1-13.
18 Peter L. Shillingsburg, *Textuality and Knowledge. Essays* (University Park, Pa.: Pennsylvania State University Press, 2017). Particularly pertinent is Essay 10, 'Scholarly Editing as a Cultural Enterprise', pp. 145-65.

regarded copyright expert, who analysed the reception deficits of Joyce scholarship and criticism toward the Critical and Synoptic Edition. Spoo also explained the somewhat defensive and aggressive helplessness of 'Joyce studies' in the wake of the edition.[19]

The Generation Shift

It was, I will admit, a source of quiet amusement to me to observe deeply read Joyceans balking at wordings in the critical reading text of *Ulysses* to which they were unaccustomed because they were so deeply familiar with the *Ulysses* they had always read, and, often over considerable stretches, memorised. I remember reflecting at the time that the edition we were presenting was really an edition for the next generation who would encounter the work directly in this edition. Laying open, as Robert Spoo did, how Joyceans were caught unprepared by what the edition offered, points to how the general public also found itself at a loss— and how the edition itself may from the outset have failed to make its objectives sufficiently clear and intelligible to its prospective and hoped-for users. Our edition did not adequately anticipate the disorientation arising from shocked first encounters of even knowledgeable readers with the 'otherness' of the edition and its edited text.

The edition did not, frankly, meet its readers and users where they were, back in the 1980s. It did not, alas, set out in plain language how and why the edition in its entire format, and most directly in the reading text in which it is first encountered, differs from the non-edited text for the novel alternatively available on the market. It assumes instead a pretty thorough prior understanding of the critical discipline of scholarly editing. My Afterword to the edition, as I conceived it at the time, is in tone and argument very much the editor addressing co-professionals in the trade. The Afterword speaks more about the edition's material basis and how this was dealt with, than about how the edition could be used. If we consider, in particular, that the edition would find its main audience among lay and professional users in the English-speaking world, the Afterword should have been more articulate and more explicit than it is about the genetic perspective the edition incorporates and its

---

19 Robert Spoo, '*Ulysses* and the Ten Years War: A Survey of Missed Opportunities', *TEXT*, 10 (1997), 107-18.

critical potential. The core of the edition is, after all, that it presents the processes of the text's development from its fair-copy to its first-edition instantiation. The Afterword would thus have done well to be very clear about what this means.

It is the edition's underlying conception that the text of the work *Ulysses* extends in time over the range of its material inscriptions. Hence, the edition offers the text of *Ulysses* in two guises: as a reading text, yes; but mainly as an edition text to be experienced diachronically, that is, in its temporal depth. To present text in its diachrony in an edition and so to present it as open in its manifold variation over time, is an editorial undertaking thoroughly unfamiliar to a cultural mindset in which texts are effectively synchronous and so essentially closed. In the Anglo-American environment, certainly, at the time the Critical and Synoptic Edition came out, there was no awareness either of perspectives on editing already well developed in Germany, or of genetic criticism as it was just emerging for instance in France as *critique génétique*.

Genetic criticism represents an approach to the material evidence for texts that does not take the material as vicarious, as one might say—that is, does not regard documents reductively as witnesses, to be exploited merely for the purpose of editing texts from them. Genetic criticism must not be mistaken, moreover, for a branch of scholarly editing. It is a method of literary criticism. It faces text, and the processes of its writing, on site, on the sheets of paper where it happens, or happened. The expanse on which the genetic critic works is the original papers or their print-facsimile, or digital-facsimile, reproductions.

The explorative processes of genetic criticism are analytic. They will, it is true, commonly involve manifold 'liftings-off' of the traces of writing from their material support: a copying-off, or transcribing, of all that is readable in the original papers, as well as somehow encoding what is otherwise discernible, such as positions (positioning of segments of writing above or below the main writing lines, or in the margin, or as overwriting with pencil over ink and such like), as well as doodles, coffee stains, and what have you. These procedures are commonly, too, preparatory steps toward editing. Yet for genetic criticism, they are properly auxiliary toward developing the genetic critic's interpretative argument. The similarities of initial operations led to mutual misunderstandings. For a long time, the German genetic editors never quite grasped that what the genetic critics were after were not editions, but critical interpretation. In the service of their own ends, the genetic critics did see, it is true, that somehow they needed to formalise their gathering of the ammunition for their critical argument and so made gestures toward organising it in a manner reminiscent of genetic editing. But their note-taking organisation of the material traces of writing and text must be understood as a mere stepping-stone toward critical interpretation of the intellectual and aesthetic essence of the processes of composition and revision.

By contrast, the genetic editors' representation and presentation of the materialised substance of writing and text was an end in itself. It constituted as such the core of the editorial endeavour, the edition. But just what this meant under changed theoretical conditions was not in itself much reflected. Millennial traditions of the craft of editing and its relation to criticism tended to go unquestioned. 'We, the editors, provide you with reliable texts; you, the critics, do something with them'. Yet neither genetic editors, nor critics traditionally trained, were as yet sufficiently competent 'to do something' with diachronically conceived edition texts. Behind the 'synopsising'—that is, the telescoping of the textual development of *Ulysses*, from fair copy to first edition, on the left-hand pages of *Ulysses. A Critical and Synoptic Edition* of 1984—lay, it is true, a considerable amount of genetically critical analysis. Yet what critical argument could be drawn from it never got articulated in critical prose. The edition, being an edition, left it to critics to develop this critical discussion from the synoptic presentation as editorially devised. It did this, however, at a time, four decades ago, when the genetic was not commonly yet a dimension of criticism. Since then, the situation has changed. Our fundamental notions of 'text' have shifted. In terms of theory, 'text' today is not conceived of as a closed and synchronous structure. It is open and extends in time. This implies that variance and variation are integral to it and not some mere external noise from its workshop environment.

Yet to realise and to deal with this, a commensurate medial access to 'text', so conceived, is required. The medial solution devised by German 'manuscript editors' and modified further into the left-hand pages of the *Ulysses* edition, however, was—if the truth be faced—fundamentally impossible. It is impossible to represent three- and four-dimensionality—the disposition of text-in-composition on paper, and its growth in time over perhaps whole sequences of documents—on a two-dimensional book page of an edition in print. 'Synopsis', it is true, is a high intellectual exercise, as well as a notable technical achievement of the Gutenberg era: think of 'seeing together' the Four Gospels in parallel columns on a facing-page book opening—and by analogy, 'seeing together' the states of a text development in editions by Hans Zeller of the poetry of Conrad Ferdinand Meyer—with those of *Ulysses* on the left-hand pages of our edition.[20] But synopsising text on paper pages fundamentally means levelling its diachrony into synchrony. However, nothing else was feasible until very, very recently. But now it is. The digital medium, as the originating site for modelling the genetic dimension of text, provides also the technical means for representing and presenting text as developing in time through dispositioning it into acts and spaces of writing in progress.

Reception and critique of *Ulysses. A Critical and Synoptic Edition* over close to four decades have on balance affirmed its success as a scholarly enterprise. The edition has moved scholarly editing in general innovatively forward. It has become apparent of late, furthermore, that its preparation forty years ago comprehensively with computer assistance laid the ground for the edition's full migration today into the digital medium. Our digital input and encoding of the *Ulysses* data was, back in the late 1970s and early 1980s, carefully prepared. This was at a time before even SGML, let alone XML as such, or XML differentiated for text encoding by means of XML-TEI, were recommended templates for marking-up text structures. From the early 1990s onward, our original data were first converted into an SGML format,[21] subsequently into XML-TEI P4, and most recently into XML-TEI P5 v 2 and 3, the TEI versions that incorporate diachronic encoding.[22] The advances that digitality has

---

20 See the web presentation of the Polyglot Bible: https://archive.org/details/ PolyglotBiblepolyglottenBibel 5 Volumes or Figures 15.25 and 15.29 in my essay 'Argument into Design: Editions as a Sub-Species of the Printed Book', https:// books.openbookpublishers.com/10.11647/obp.0120/ch15.html#_idTextAnchor051.

21 Even from the SGML format, an early attempt was already successful in displaying digitally the diachrony of the left-hand-page edition text in its individual layering, thanks to Tobias Rischer's astute deployment at the time of Peter Robinson's visualisation software, *Anastasia*.

22 Gregor Middell and Joshua Schäuble were successively at the controls of this crowning phase of conversion.

made since we first deployed the computer as our machine assistant has enabled turning the Critical and Synoptic Edition, published in its time in book form, into a Digital Critical and Synoptic Edition, usable and explorable, and so living dynamically, in the digital medium. The fresh realisation in Ronan Crowley's and Joshua Schäuble's Digital Critical and Synoptic Edition in progress, available at www.ulysses-online, has been under development since 2015–2016. With the (still) new wine of the novel's text edited with genetic awareness now properly maturing in this fresh bottle, I feel that James Joyce's *Ulysses* has successfully advanced into the digital age.

James Joyce's Text in Progress

James Joyce claimed he lacked imagination. His artistry craved supports and scaffolds: structures from which and into which to be textured. Joyce's conception of art reached out and back to the medieval. Setting up the illuminators of the *Book of Kells* as his artistic ancestors (*JJ*, 545),[1] he strove for the intricacy and significant complexity of their design in the text of his writing.

In, as well as towards, his compositional crafting, Joyce was as much a reader as a writer of texts. Jesuit-trained, he was thoroughly schooled in the reading skills which he early exercised with catholicity on textbooks and dictionaries, curricular and extra-curricular literature, or the canonical Book of Books. Through reading, he penetrated to the philosophical foundations of the act of reading. 'Signatures of all things I am here to read, seaspawn and seawrack, the nearing tide, that rusty boot' (*U* 3, 2-3).[2] Anticipating long in advance the conceptualisations of present-day text theory, he discovered the structural and semiotic analogies of language-encoded texts and experience-encoded reality; and, in a desire like Stephen Dedalus's to grasp the wholeness and harmony of things (their *integritas* and *consonantia*) for the sake of illumination (their 'radiance', or *claritas* (*P* V, 1347-1348)),[3] he taught himself to read streets and cities, landscapes, seashores or rivers, people, actions, events, dreams and memories, the randomness of everyday or the patterns (real or apparent) of history as texts in their own right.

---

1 Richard Ellmann, *James Joyce* (New York: Oxford University Press, ²1982), p. 545. (*JJ*)
2 James Joyce, *Ulysses. A Critical and Synoptic Edition*, prepared by Hans Walter Gabler with Wolfhard Steppe and Claus Melchior, 3 vols. (New York & London: Garland Publishing, Inc., 1984; ²1986).
3 James Joyce, *A Portrait of the Artist as a Young Man*, ed. by Hans Walter Gabler with Walter Hettche (New York and London: Garland Publishing, Inc., 1993; and New York: Vintage International, Vintage Books, 1993). [*P*]

Learning to read the world in this way was an act of intellectual self-liberation, and reading it in this way a new experience. Stephen Dedalus, exploiting Thomism for aesthetics and yet awaiting that new experience ('When we come to the phenomena of artistic conception, artistic gestation and artistic reproduction I require a new terminology and a new personal experience' (*P* V, 1271-1272)), mirrors James Joyce on the very brink of turning reading into writing. To circumscribe, and thus make readable, the wholeness of things means to unlock them, in a kind of deconstruction, out of their apparently amorphous contingencies. Such unlocking turns into a morphologising, or shaping, act. Through the constructive perception of things in their radiant wholeness, it makes them communicable, and thus writable. Hence springs a notion of writing as an act and process of transubstantiation ('In the virgin womb of the imagination the word was made flesh' (*P* V, 1543-1544)). The alternating pulse, and impulse, of deconstructive unlocking and constructive shaping as reading and writing is fundamental to Joyce's craft and art. As a governing principle, not only does it make available the external materials of literature and all manner of language-encoded pre-texts, of history, autobiography, and everyday experience so as to render them integrable into the text-in-writing, the work in progress; but inside the boundary lines, too, that separate Joyce's text from all the pre-texts it absorbs, that text itself may be seen to be propelled—and thus, progressively self-generated—by constant and continuous acts of reading and rereading.

Notes, sketches, drafts, fair-copies, typescripts, and proofs have survived for Joyce's entire *oeuvre,* albeit but fragmentarily for the early works, and with increasing comprehensiveness only from mid-*Ulysses* onwards. These workshop remains are sufficiently rich and varied to substantiate our general understanding of his mode of composition. One particularly illuminating instance of the complex interaction of the reading and the writing processes can be made out in the notes and drafts for *Exiles.* A surviving notebook contains trial fragments of dialogue and a number of passages of pragmatic, thematic, critical, and philosophic reflection on the play, its actions, its characters and their motivations, as well as on some of the audience responses envisaged;

material which is all but unique from Joyce's pen.[4] Beyond this material, there are three sections—interspersed among the rest, but clearly of a common nature that sets them off and links them to one another—which enact the reading and writing itself. The first carries two initialised openings sequentially dated, which also subdivide it into a reading and a writing phase: 'N.(B)—12 Nov. 1913' and 'N.(B) – 13 Nov. 1913'. The initials provide the signal justification for our decoding approach: Joyce's companion Nora and the fictional character Bertha stand to be read in terms of each other.

Under 12 November are listed three strings of notes which, except that they are grouped under subheads ('Garter:', 'Rat:' and 'Dagger:'), thoroughly resemble the seemingly disjunct listings that sprawlingly cover the *Ulysses Notesheets*, and endlessly fill the *Finnegans Wake Notebooks*. Here, the organising principle of the notes seems tolerably clear. They read Nora under aspects potentially to be written into the fictional character, role, and relationships of Bertha in the play. The first string of notes runs: 'Garter: precious, Prezioso, Bodkin, music, palegreen, bracelet, cream sweets, lily of the valley, convent garden (Galway), sea.'

Under 13 November follows a prose passage in four paragraphs. Progressively it incorporates these notes as jotted down the previous day, which shows it in part to be generated from them. In itself, it accomplishes the reading of Nora and Bertha in terms of each other in a mode of writing which from notes turns compositional and, as it unfolds, draws in an association of further pre-textual significations. It is a sufficiently unfamiliar piece of Joycean prose to need citation in full:

> Moon—Shelley's grave in Rome. He is rising from it: blond[.] She weeps for him. He has fought in vain for an ideal and died killed by the world. Yet he rises. Graveyard at Rahoon by moonlight where Bodkin's grave is. He lies in the grave. She sees his tomb (family vault) and weeps. The name is homely. Shelley's is strange and wild. He is dark, unrisen, killed by love and life, young. The earth holds him.

---

4   Reproduced in [vol. 11] *Exiles*: a facsimile of notes, manuscripts and galley proofs, prefaced and arranged by A. Walton Litz (1978) of *The James Joyce Archive* [*JJA*], 63 vols., ed. by Michael Groden, *et al.* (New York and London: Garland Publishing, Inc., 1978), pp. 1-61, and inaccurately appended to *E* (148-60).

> Bodkin died. Kearns died. In the convent they called her the mankiller. (Woman-killer was one of her names for me.) I live in soul and body.
>
> She is the earth, dark, formless, mother, made beautiful by the moonlit night, darkly conscious of her instincts. Shelley whom she held in her womb or grave rises: the part of Richard which neither love nor life can do away with: the part for which she loves him: the part she must try to kill, never be able to kill, and rejoice at her impotence. Her tears are of worship, Magdalen seeing the rearisen Lord in the garden where He had been laid in the tomb.
>
> Rome is the strange world and strange life to which Richard brings her. Rahoon her people. She weeps over Rahoon, too, over him whom her love has killed, the dark boy whom, as the earth, she embraces in death and disintegration. He is her buried life, her past. His attendant images are the trinkets and toys of girlhood (bracelet, cream sweets, palegreen lily of the valley, the convent garden). His symbols are music and the sea, liquid formless earth in which are buried the drowned soul and body. There are tears of commiseration. She is Magdalen who weeps remembering the loves she could not return.

Palpably, the passage originates in autobiographical memory, which yet in the writing at once acquires literary overtones in the romantic conjunction of 'moon', 'Shelley's grave' and 'Rome' to which that memory has been atomised. It is the moonlight radiance of this initial romantic image which carries the writing forward. Strikingly, it exploits a fluidity, even indeterminacy of personal pronouns which may remind one of the calculated pronoun indeterminacies of Penelope, the final episode of *Ulysses*. 'He is rising from (the grave): blond[.] She weeps for him.' In one sentence, a reading of Nora's presumed emotional response at the poet's graveside is projected into character behaviour and motivation for the Bertha of *Exiles:* Bertha appears superimposed upon Nora. In the progress of the passage, their composite figure becomes further overwritten by pre-texts of myth and the Bible. In a countermovement, Shelley is erased and successively overlaid by Bodkin, Kearns, I, and Richard. Was a character named Kearns envisaged as the counterpart in Bertha's memories of Michael Bodkin, the young man Nora had known as a girl, and whose early death and burial in Rahoon cemetery were the basis for the story of Michael Furey in 'The Dead', the final story of *Dubliners*? In the published play, Bertha is not given an Irish past, and hence does not weep over Rahoon in a rewriting of previous readings of Nora from within the

Joycean *oeuvre*. The absence of this dimension from the finished text would seem to represent the deliberate curtailment of a potential inherent in the compositional writing. As the death-and-resurrection imagery pervasive in the notebook passage suggests, it is the Roman exhilaration in life which, even from the poet's grave, raises the buried Irish past. An extant set of draft fragments for *Exiles* shows that the autobiographical pre-text of the Roman experience passed through further rewritings that were not in the end incorporated in the play.[5] With them, the structuring of Bertha as a text of receding experiential memories was abandoned.

The two related passages in the notebook are each similarly prefixed by strings of notes, in a single and a double list respectively. The first one is 'Blister—amber—silver—oranges—apples—sugarstick—hair—spongecake—ivy—roses—ribbon' and the second one 'Snow: frost, moon, pictures, holly and ivy, currant-cake, lemonade, Emily Lyons, piano, windowsill', followed by 'tears: ship, sunshine, garden, sadness, pinafore, buttoned boots, bread and butter, a big fire'. The written-out prose sections that in each case follow do not acquire the multiplicity of pre-text reference, nor do they move the pre-text 'Nora' as far towards the text 'Bertha', as does the 'N.(B.)' passage of 13 November. Yet they reveal with greater stringency the functional interrelation of a record of reading (the notes) with the compositional writing which that record generates. The writing allows us to infer that the notes, again, 'deconstruct' a biographical pre-text. At the same time, the writing clearly does not write these notes back into the text from which it derives; it cannot, for example, be read as a straight, let alone simple, retelling of the pre-text story. Instead, the notes represent concatenations of 'germs'—as Henry James would have called them—from which autonomous texts originate. The autonomy, and incipient originality, of these texts—the fact that they may properly be said to be generated from the notes—is measurable by the distance they move beyond narration. What discernible telling there is in the expansion of individual key-word notes into narrative becomes subordinated to, as it is immediately overlaid by, writerly reflection on the 'flow of ideas',

---

5 The fragments are reproduced in *JJA* [vol. 11], 64-85, and discussed in Robert M. Adams, 'Light on Joyce's *Exiles!* A new manuscript, a curious analogue, and some speculations', *Studies in Bibliography*, 17 (1964), 83-105.

on modes of memory, mental processes, emotions, psychological motivation and repression, or the overt or hidden significance of behaviour.

The process of transforming reading into writing is laid open here as a labour of interpretation holding a potential for artistic creation which at any moment may become actualised in 'original' prose. Such creative transubstantiation of the notes, it is true, occurs only intermittently in these passages which, after all, remain notebook entries. Yet consider, for instance, what happens to the concatenated note segment 'ivy—roses—ribbon' in the subsequent writing:

> Ivy and roses: she gathered ivy often when out in the evening with girls. Roses grew then. A sudden scarlet side in the memory which may be a dim suggestion of the roses of the body. The ivy and the roses carry on and up out of the idea of growth, through a creeping vegetable life into ardent perfumed flower life the symbol of mysteriously growing girlhood, her hair. Ribbon for her hair. Its fitting ornament for the eyes of others, and lastly for his eyes. Girlhood becomes virginity and puts on 'the snood that is the sign of maidenhood'. A proud and shy instinct turns her mind away from the loosening of her bound-up hair—however sweet or longed for or inevitable—and she embraces that which is hers alone and not hers and his also –

These eight sentences progress from a recall of a biographical given to the creation, via image and symbol, of the changing attitudes and moods of a young woman, who thereby—that is, by the constituent power of language—becomes imaginatively outlined as a fictional character. In the language itself, the transition is effected by a manner (or mannerism) of style that bears the hallmark of the James Joyce who wrote the fourth chapter of *A Portrait of the Artist as a Young Man*, *Giacomo Joyce*—or, indeed, the poems of *Chamber Music*. 'The snood that is the sign of maidenhood' comes from *Chamber Music*, xi. It parallels 'She weeps over Rahoon' in the preceding passage, the title of a poem which, though not published until 1927 in *Pomes Penyeach*, was written in 1913. The retextualisation of pre-text from the *oeuvre* is anything but an accident. On the contrary, it exemplifies one of the most significant, as well as one of the earliest and most persistent, among Joyce's authorial strategies.

Joyce tested his powers of structuring experience into language in the prose miniatures he wrote before 1904 and called 'epiphanies'.[6] While not the inventor of the genre, Joyce in adopting the epiphanic mode developed it and soon raised it to a significance within the evolving system of his aesthetics that has caused the idea of the epiphany to become largely associated with his name. Within the period of his main devotion to the form, a dialogue, or 'dramatic', type of epiphany appears to be followed by a set-piece-of-prose, or 'narrative', type; it is the latter type which resurfaces ten years later in the collection of prose miniatures entitled *Giacomo Joyce*. The dialogue epiphanies would seem to be strict records of observation and listening; the set-piece-of-prose epiphanies, by contrast, show increasing writerly concerns. If the dialogues are dominantly records of observational 'reading', the set-piece miniatures turn into writings of events, visions, or dreams.

When Joyce embarked upon his first novel, eventually to be published as *A Portrait of the Artist as a Young Man*, he used the epiphany texts as pre-texts from within his own *oeuvre*. The surviving epiphanies in holograph fair copy carry on their versos the vestiges of a sequential numbering. Uniform as it is, it gives no indication of representing the order of composition. Instead, evidently post-dating the fair-copying, it implies a rereading of the accumulated epiphany manuscripts, which resulted in a selection and serial linking of discrete items. Their serial contextualisation acquires narrative potential. Ordered into a sequence, the selected epiphanies form the substratum of a story to be generated from them. The barest structure of epiphanies turned by concatenation into narrative may be exemplified from a brief section in part two of *A Portrait*. A string of three epiphanies, each beginning 'He was sitting' (*P* II, 253; 275; 303), tells of Stephen's visits to relatives and conveys the thematic motif of the squalor and insincerity he encounters. By way of the rereading implied in the ordering of pre-written units of text, experiences with an ultimate origin in the author's life become brushstrokes in the emerging portrait of the artist as a young man.

---

6   Those that survive, in manuscript, are reproduced in *JJA* [vol. 7]: *A Portrait of the Artist as a Young Man. A Facsimile of Epiphanies, Notes, Manuscripts, and Typescripts*, prefaced and arranged by Hans Walter Gabler. Special note should be taken of the bilingual edition: *James Joyce: Epifanie (1900-1904). Rubrica (1909-1912)*, ed. by Giorgio Melchiori (Milan: Mondadori, 1982).

The author's life as a pre-text is, through intervening reading and writing processes, several times removed from the text of *A Portrait*. The pre-text from within the *oeuvre* which *A Portrait* most pervasively exploits is *Stephen Hero*, the novel planned to extend to sixty-three chapters, yet abandoned after the completion of twenty-five chapters on nine hundred and fourteen manuscript pages. The few planning notes that survive for *Stephen Hero* emphasise an organisation of autobiographic pre-text to render it available for the fictional narrative. Towards *A Portrait*, *Stephen Hero* in its turn served as a notebook and quarry for words and phrases, characters, situations and incidents. Yet the ways in which, after the abandonment of *Stephen Hero*, *A Portrait* proves itself not so much a revision as a genuine rewriting of the Stephen Daedalus novel may be properly gauged only by the extent and complexity of its un-locking and consequent rewriting of pre-texts other than either *Stephen Hero* or, ultimately, of the autobiographic experience.

In this respect, the writerly path from *Stephen Hero* to *A Portrait* is paved in *Dubliners*. The stories individually and as a co-ordinated collection show Joyce's developing concern with significant structures of form and matter in the writing, answering to a systematised reading of the pre-texts of Dublin: of her streets and citizens, of Irish history, politics and society, of works of literature, theological doctrine or biblical tales. Joyce criticism has read from, or read into, the *Dubliners* stories a rich array of intertextual reference, as well as incipient examples of that mode of auto-referentiality—one might term it the *oeuvre's* intratextuality—which is to become so prominent in Joyce's later work. If there is critical justification for claiming as pre-texts the biblical tale of Mary and Martha for 'The Sisters', of the Irish political situation for 'Ivy Day in the Committee Room', of the *Divine Comedy* for 'Grace', or of Dante or Homer for the macro-structure of the collection,[7] one may add that even the philosophy of Joyce's epiphany-centred aesthetics becomes

---

7   See Hugh Kenner, 'Signs on a white field', in *James Joyce: the Centennial Symposium*, ed. by Morris Beja, *et al.* (Urbana: University of Illinois Press, 1986), pp. 209-19; Matthew C. Hodgart, 'Ivy Day in the Committee Room', in *James Joyce's 'Dubliners': Critical Essays*, ed. by Clive Hart (London: Faber & Faber, 1969), pp. 115-21 (as one essay among many that make the political point); *Stanislaus Joyce: My Brother's Keeper*, ed. by Richard Ellmann (London: Faber & Faber, 1958), p. 225; Mary T. Reynolds, *Joyce and Dante* (Princeton: Princeton University Press, 1981), esp. p. 159; Brewster Ghiselin, 'The unity of Joyce's *Dubliners*', *Accent*, 16 (1956), 75-88, 193-213.

rewritten as narrative when the many-layered epiphanies of' 'The Dead' are made to occur on the night of the feast of the Epiphany—a fact of the story which, in its turn, is left to the reader epiphanically to discover.[8]

Moving beyond the trial experiment of *Dubliners*, it is *A Portrait* that first fully succeeds as a unified rewriting of intertwining pretexts. In the semiotics of *A Portrait*, the author's life as well as the Daedalean, Christian, and Irish myths, the martyrdom of Stephen Dedalus, St Stephen, Icarus, Parnell, and Christ, the sinner's descent into hell and the artist's flight heavenward are held in mutual tension. What guarantees the balanced co-existence and cross-referential significance of the pretexts is the tectonics of the writing, the novel's complex, intricate and firmly controlled structure. *A Portrait* marks an essential step in Joyce's art towards a dominance of structure and expressive form. Significantly, structure can be made out as a pre-writing as well as a post-writing concern. After interrupting *Stephen Hero* in the summer of 1905 with a view, presumably, to continuation, he utterly abandoned the early novel in 1907 from the artistic vantagepoint gained in the completion of *Dubliners*, and specifically 'The Dead'. Thereupon, the earliest indications of Joyce's intentions in reworking the autobiographical novel concern its structure. He now proposes to write the book in five long chapters, which, even before the fact, is very different from a sixty-three-chapter *Stephen Hero*. In the course of writing, *A Portrait* appears to have gone through progressive phases of structuring. It is quite clear, even from the scant surviving manuscript materials, that, in their ultimate refinement, the complexities realised in the five-chapter novel as released for publication are the results of revisions-in-composition, that is to say, of rereadings of the text as it evolved in the workshop. While the five-chapter sequence was determined before the writing began, the overall correlation and multi-patterned chiastic centring of the novel's parts was, in an important sense, achieved in retrospect. Similarly, it was by a single revision in the first chapter of the fair-copy manuscript—in other words, by a late response of the author, as reader, to his own written text—that a potential of suggestive parallels inherent in the writing was turned into an actual correspondence in the text. A revision in the manuscript instituted the day on which Wells shouldered

---

8   See for example Bernard Benstock, 'The Dead', in *James Joyce's 'Dubliners': Critical Essays*, ed. by Clive Hart (London: Faber & Faber, 1969), pp. 153-69.

Stephen into the square ditch at Clongowes as the seventy-seventh day before Christmas. In 1891, the year of Parnell's death, this was Thursday, 8 October. Parnell died on 6 October, and his body was brought to Ireland to be buried, arriving at dawn on Sunday, 11 October. This, in the fiction, is the morning Stephen, at the infirmary, revives from a fever. Parnell dies so that Stephen may live. The synchronisation of historical and fictional time was the precise result of one textual revision.[9]

It is prominently in a mode of rewriting within Joyce's own *oeuvre*, as well as on the level of concerns about structure that predate the actual writing, that the beginnings of *Ulysses* first manifest themselves. We may discover its earliest formation by evaluating the relation of *A Portrait* to *Stephen Hero*, and by analysing the process of rewriting and rethinking of written and unwritten *Stephen Hero* material in the light of Joyce's correspondence with his brother Stanislaus.[10] An early plan for *Stephen Hero*—one that seems to have been devised in conversation sometime in 1904, before Joyce's departure from Ireland—was to carry it forward to a tower episode.[11] *Stephen Hero* never reached that point. But the extant fair-copy of a Martello Tower fragment from the *Portrait* workshop, dating presumably from 1912 or 1913, is evidence that, at an intermediary stage of the rewriting, a tower scene was still conceived for *A Portrait*. Its ultimate exclusion provided the material for the opening of *Ulysses*.

No doubt the Martello Tower episode of *Ulysses* is different in execution and tone from whatever version of it would have entered *A Portrait*. Doherty's comment to Stephen in the fragment:

> 'Dedalus, we must retire to the tower, you and I. Our lives are precious ... We are the super-artists. *Dedalus and Doherty have left Ireland for the Omphalos'*—[12]

---

9   See the essay in this volume: 'The Genesis of *A Portrait of the Artist as a Young Man*', p. 110-111.
10 See Hans Walter Gabler, 'Preface' to *JJA* [vol. 8], 'A Portrait of the Artist as a Young Man': A Facsimile of the Manuscript Fragments of 'Stephen Hero', pp. vii-xii.
11 '[Cosgrave] says he would not like to be Gogarty when you come to the Tower episode', *Letters of James Joyce*, ed. by Richard Ellmann, vol. II (New York: Viking Press, 1966) (*Letters* II), p. 103.
12 *JJA* [vol. 8], *Portrait of the Artist as a Young Man*: a facsimile of epiphanies, notes, manuscripts and typescripts, prefaced and arranged by Hans Walter Gabler, 1219-22; cf. A. Walton Litz, *The Art of James Joyce* (Oxford: Oxford University Press, 1961), p. 133.

would seem to imply an intention of figuring the concept of exile which concludes *A Portrait* into a retreat to the tower, where the young aesthetes, seeking unfettered freedom in an abandonment to Nietzschean elitism,[13] isolate themselves from society; or, to preface Stephen's departure into an exile alone in the world by the attempt and failure of a retirement to the *omphalos*, the navel of friendship and art. The contextual ambience of *A Portrait* of course would hardly warrant the ironic view of an artistic revolt of the select in isolation which is implied from the outset in the Martello Tower setting of the opening of *Ulysses*. It is only as it enters Stephen's consciousness of himself in *Ulysses* that the ironic detachment from his Daedalean flight—so hard to define, within the confines of *A Portrait* alone, as a dimension of meaning of the tale told—becomes manifest.

By being made to part company with Mulligan and Haines and becoming a critical judge not only of others, but of himself, Stephen in *Ulysses* is rewritten as a character capable of action and reaction, one whom we accept as a self-searching Telemachus, within the fictional reality of his and Leopold Bloom's Dublin. Thus revised and refunctionalised in terms of the character realism as well as of the Odysseus myth of the new novel, he is made to look upon the Daedalean identification produced within the symbolic framework of the old one as a personal illusion. The authorial manner of the redefinition is significant for the new relation it provides between the narrative and the pre-text that is its governing myth. Whereas Stephen in *A Portrait* ardently aspires to Daedalean heights, neither Stephen nor Bloom in *Ulysses* possess any awareness of their mythical roles. These are communicated by means of narrative structures to the reader.

Stephen's recognition of himself as a foundered Icarus—'Lapwing you are. Lapwing be' (*U* 9, 954)—belongs to the library episode, or Hamlet chapter, Scylla & Charybdis, ninth of the eighteen episodes of *Ulysses*. This, it should be noticed, is a remarkably late point in *Ulysses* to refer back so outspokenly to *A Portrait*. We may assume that the chapter formed a section of the emerging novel's redefinition of Stephen before, by structural positioning, it entered into the functions of the Scylla & Charybdis adventure in the sequence of Odysseus'/Bloom's

---

13   See Wilhelm Füger, 'Joyce's *Portrait* and Nietzsche', *Arcadia*, 7 (1972), 231-59.

wanderings—where, even as it finally stands, it emphasises the rock and the whirlpool more than the wanderer. This assumption also helps to explain in part the divergences in the early structural plans for *Ulysses*. In May 1918, Joyce told Harriet Weaver that, of the book's three main parts, the Telemachia, the Odyssey, and the Nostos, the first consisted of three episodes.[14] Yet three years earlier, upon completing a first full draft of the Martello Tower episode, and with an initial outline of the whole probably quite freshly conceived, he had stated on a postcard written on Bloomsday 1915 to Stanislaus in awkward German that the Telemachia was to comprise four episodes.[15] The fourth can hardly have been any other than Stephen's Hamlet chapter, prepared for by theme and hour of the day in the Martello Tower opening.[16] Thus the indication is strong that both these chapters, finally placed as the first and the ninth, belong to the vestiges of *A Portrait* carried over into *Ulysses*. The Hamlet chapter notably revolves on a restatement of Stephen's aesthetic theories, and it is not inconceivable that, at some stage and in some form of pre-textual planning, it might have been designed for a position in part V of *A Portrait* analogous to that which is in fact held there by the 'Villanelle' section. As an episode located inside the National Library, it might have fitted between the part V movements which, by peripatetic conversations on themes divided between nationalism, literature, art, and aesthetics on the one hand, and religion on the other, lead up to the library steps, and away from them.

Together, the tower and library episodes show that the earliest writing for *Ulysses* from the autobiographical fountainhead originated in Joyce's endeavours—approximately between 1912 and 1914—to define a line of division between *A Portrait* and *Ulysses*. As for the matter of Dublin, *Ulysses* reaches back to *Dubliners*, and to a time of conception in 1906. As we know from letters to Stanislaus (*Letters* II 190), a story to be named 'Ulysses' was planned for *Dubliners*, though it never got beyond a title. Yet there is a strong indication that its nucleus may be recognised in the sequence of the concluding night-time events in *Ulysses* (i.e., the

---

14 *Letters of James Joyce*, ed. by Stuart Gilbert, vol. I (New York: Viking Press, 1957, ²1966) (*Letters* I), p. 113.
15 *Joyce: Selected Letters*, ed. by Richard Ellmann (New York: The Viking Press, 1975) (*SL*), p. 209.
16 Buck Mulligan raises Haines's expectations: at (*U* 1, 487): '—Wait till you hear him on Hamlet, Haines.'

brawl in Nighttown, and the rescue of Stephen by Bloom, who takes the injured and drunken young man back to his house in the early morning hours).[17] The emerging novel thereby possessed a point of departure, and a goal. A middle was provided by the simple act of foreshortening the Telemachia as first planned, and moving the library chapter into a central place as the Scylla & Charybdis episode of the Odyssean adventures. The redesigning took place before October 1916, when in a letter to Harriet Weaver (*Letters* II 387), Joyce declared that he had almost finished the first part—i.e., the Telemachia—and had written out part of the middle and end. He had thus moored the pillars over which he proceeded to span the treblearch construction of *Ulysses*.

It is only from this point onwards in Joyce's writing career that reports and surviving evidence directly testify to his working methods. Passing over the cryptic post-1905 marking-up of the *Stephen Hero* manuscript, interpretable as related, though only obliquely, to the composition of *A Portrait*, and leaving out of further consideration the notes for *Exiles* as being less of a compositional than of a critically reflective nature, it is with *Ulysses* that for the first time we begin to catch glimpses of the author in the workshop. Frank Budgen gives lively accounts of how his writer friend, wherever he went, gathered scrap matter to go into the 'glorious Swiss orange envelopes' for later use in the book; of how Joyce worked with words in the manner of a Byzantine mosaic artist; of how he encountered Joyce in search of the *mot juste*, as he (Budgen) presumed, but really seeking the 'perfect order of words in the sentence'.[18] What Budgen observed from the distance at which Joyce was careful to keep even him, and what he related with such evident sympathy, are labours and processes of writing essentially like those we have already

---

17 Richard Ellmann, in the Introduction to *Ulysses on the Liffey* (London: Faber & Faber, 1972), and in more detail in the Afterword to the old Penguin edition of *Ulysses* (Harmondsworth: Penguin Books, 1968), has been the foremost spokesman for the hypothesis that the Nighttown episode at its genetic core reflects the projected *Dubliners* story 'Ulysses'. Hugh Kenner, on the other hand, interprets the Calypso to Wandering Rocks sequence as the novel's expansion of a typical *Dubliners* story for which the title 'Ulysses' would have been appropriate (see Kenner, *Ulysses* (London: Allen & Unwin, 1980), p. 61).

18 Frank Budgen, *James Joyce and the Making of 'Ulysses', and Other Writings* (London: Oxford University Press, 1972); quotations on pp. 177 and 20. The comparison of Joyce to a Byzantine artist is Valery Larbaud's, from 'The *Ulysses* of James Joyce', *Criterion*, 1 (1922), 102.

analysed. A deeper understanding of Joyce's creative artistry may be derived from the draft manuscripts themselves that survive from the *Ulysses* workshop.

The seminal manuscripts for *Ulysses* that Joyce speaks of in his letters are lost: for example, the first completed draft of Telemachus, of which Stanislaus was told on Bloomsday 1915 (*SL*, 209), the draft materials of 'the beginning, middle and end' as achieved in 1915/16, or the 'nearly completed' Telemachia of October 1916 (*Letters* II, 387). The earliest extant *Ulysses* draft[19] is a version of Proteus (V.A.3 in the Buffalo Joyce collection). It is contained in a copybook which, by the evidence of its label, was purchased in Locarno. Dateable therefore to the autumn of 1917, which Joyce spent in Locarno finishing and fair-copying the Telemachia, the draft belongs to the final phase of work on the chapter.

Its derivation from lost draft antecedents is palaeographically indicated by the clean and fluent manner in which at least its opening is written out, before expansions, revisions, and second thoughts begin increasingly to overcrowd the pages and disturb the handwriting. Other extant draft manuscripts open similarly, notably Oxen of the Sun (V. A. 11) and Circe (V.A. 19). In drafts that have come down to us, whether pre-fair-copy or fair-copy, there is always some suggestion of a descent from pre-existing text. Cyclops manuscript V.A.8, for example, or the Nausikaa copybooks Buffalo V.A.10/Cornell 56, clearly first or early drafts, suggest particularly clearly a manner of composition by which Joyce thought out at length, and in minute detail, the structures and phrasings of whole narrative sections before committing them to paper. The look which even first extant drafts have of being derived emphasises the importance which the pre-writing processes had for Joyce's writing.

---

19 My phrase 'The earliest extant *Ulysses* draft' dates from the late 1980s. It should meanwhile read: 'One of a minority of early *Ulysses* drafts still extant, that is of drafts preceding the fair copy state preserved in the Rosenbach manuscript'. The acquisition of a significant cache of draft manuscript material from Joyce's workshop preserved, since safely stored away in the basement of the Paris house of Paul Léon, was acquired by the National Library of Ireland in 2002. This material has been repeatedly described and commented on, notably by Michael Groden, 'The National Library of Ireland's New Joyce Manuscripts: An Outline and Archive Comparisons', *Joyce Studies Annual*, 14 (2003), 5-17; or Luca Crispi, 'A *Ulysses* Manuscripts Workbook', *Genetic Joyce Studies*, 17 (2017) [Electronic Journal for the Study of James Joyce's Works in Progress], 34 pages, with comprehensive links to digital copy of the materials discussed.

To all appearances, his compositions were conceived and verbalised in the mind, as well as extensively, it seems, committed to memory, before being written out in drafts. These, consequently, immediately became carrier documents of transmission. Holding the texts available for re-reading and revision, Joyce's autograph manuscripts, whether sketches, drafts, or fair copies, were his secondary *loci* of writing.

Extended periods of intense work on sometimes multiple drafts were the rule of his workshop. 'It is impossible to say how much of the book is really written', Joyce remarked to Harriet Weaver in May 1918. Beyond Hades, which was being typed at the time, 'several other episodes have been drafted for the second time but that means nothing because although the third episode of the *Telemachia* has been a long time in the second draft I spent about 200 hours over it before I wrote it out finally' (*Letters* I, 113). 'The elements needed will fuse only after a prolonged existence together' (*Letters* I, 128). In August 1919 he told John Quinn that a chapter took him about four to five months to write (*Letters* II, 448). This was a fair statement at the time, and as an average it held true for all subsequent chapters except Circe, which required six months, and Eumaeus, which took only about six to eight weeks to complete from the earlier drafts. The work on Oxen of the Sun, for which the pre-fair-copy draft stages are documented, Joyce estimated at one thousand hours (*Letters* II, 465). His agonies over Circe found expression in statements on the number of drafts written that vary between six and nine.

There is interesting circumstantial evidence that a physical release of energy promoted the release of Joyce's creative energy. For all the innumerable hours spent in libraries, at tables and desks or on top of beds with his notes and drafts spread out around him, Joyce was a peripatetic writer. The account he gives of his state in September 1921 is as extraordinary as it seems significant. Incessant writing and revising of *Ulysses* had precipitated a nervous breakdown which Joyce counteracted by cutting his sedentary hours from a daily sixteen to six or eight and taking twelve to fourteen kilometre walks along the Seine instead (*Letters* I, 170). The result was not a slackening but, by all evidence, a concentration of the work on *Ulysses*: the final breakthrough towards the completion of Penelope and Ithaka (in that order) and the composition of the 'Metropolitan police' section for Cyclops and the 'Messianic scene' for Circe all date from September/October 1921.

In the light of Joyce's roamings along the Seine to give a final boost to the composition of *Ulysses*, the peripatetics of his artist *alter ego* Stephen Dedalus take on an added significance. In part V of *A Portrait*, Stephen Dedalus walks the streets of Dublin exercising traditional arts of memory, conscious as he is that the city's topography serves to recall his thoughts and emotions. (*P* V, 71-86) In *Ulysses*, he walks along Sandymount strand writing a text of himself—for this, precisely, is the function to which the author puts the narrative technique he employs to verbalise the Stephen of Proteus. If that text, though we may read it as Joyce's creation, never gets written down by Stephen himself, his roamings through much of the chapter also constitute the pre-draft peripatetics towards his own (plagiarised) poem which he eventually jots down on the strip torn from Deasy's letter. (*U* 3, 399-407)

Taking our cue from the creative situation thus mirrored in Proteus, we may attempt yet further to analyse the nature and procedures of Joyce's composition before he put pen to paper. From a survey of all extant manuscript materials for *Ulysses*—drafts and fair copies as well as revisions and additions to the chapters in typescript and proofs—the unwavering structural stability of most of the novel's episodes becomes strikingly noticeable. With the single exception of the Aeolus chapter, recast in proof by the introduction of segmenting cross-heads, no episode changes shape, but retains the structural outline it possesses in the fair copy, regardless of how extensive the subsequent additions and revisions to its verbal texture. Moreover, except in the cases of Cyclops and 'Circe (to which we shall return), that structural outline is by and large already characteristic of an episode's earliest extant drafts. Again, structure appears to have been a concern even in advance of the physical writing, and it is tempting to infer that, in the mental creative process, the structural design preceded the verbal texturing. In so doing, the design could serve as a 'house of memory' for organising the composition and situating all verbal detail as it accumulated. In the deployment of his creative artistry, Joyce thus cultivated a proleptic memory—as is indeed also manifestly indicated by the precision with which he is reported to have known where to place the materials collected in his orange envelopes, in notebooks and on notesheets for insertion into the typescripts and proofs.

That the structure provided by the myth and epic narrative of the *Odyssey* preceded the text of *Ulysses* as a whole is patently true. Ezra Pound saw the *Odyssey* as a scaffolding for *Ulysses*, yet felt that, as such, it was of little consequence for the reader, since, as the author's private building device, it had been effectively dispensed with in the accomplishment of the novel itself. T. S. Eliot, in his rival early critique, showed a greater sensitivity to the intertextual dynamism actuated by the Homeric reference,[20] and his response to the mythic interaction has been thoroughly ramified by the progressive critical exploration of the many additional pre-texts which dynamise *Ulysses* in 'retrospective arrangements'.

Proteus, again, proves instructive. To present-day criticism, it seems that the Homeric reference, far from being dispensable, best accounts for the chapter's fascinating elusiveness of style and character consciousness: on the levels of language and thought, the episode's effect is expressively Protean. At the same time, however, its structure, its design as a house of memory to hold a character consciousness verbalised in the language of an interior monologue, has also been felt to be largely elusive. Yet read on the level of its relationship to *Hamlet*, the episode appears to be retrospectively controlled by Stephen's parting gesture: 'He turned his face over a shoulder, rere regardant' (*U* 3, 503). It re-enacts Hamlet's farewell to Ophelia 'with his head over his shoulder turned', which she so heart-rendingly recounts in Act II, scene i of the play. Shattered to the depths by his encounter with his father's ghost, Hamlet, cutting all ties of kinship and severing the fetters of love that bind him to Ophelia, walks out on his past. Stephen, who has been visited by the ghost of his mother, severs all ties of friendship and, unsure of the love of woman, walks on to evening lands. If thus, in the structure of bodily movement, the episode constitutes an imaginative rewriting of a reported scene from *Hamlet*, it was ultimately in a pre-text from within the *oeuvre* that Joyce found a structure to contain both that movement and the Protean verbal texture. In *A Portrait*, Stephen's movement from childhood and adolescence to artistic self-sufficiency and exile is articulated in a structure of flying by the nets of 'nationality, language, religion'. In

---

20   Ezra Pound, 'Paris Letter: *Ulysses*', *Dial*, 72 (1922), 623-29; T.S. Eliot, '*Ulysses*, Order and Myth', in *Selected Prose of T.S. Eliot*, ed. by Frank Kermode (London: Faber & Faber, 1975), pp. 175-78.

Proteus, an analogous triad of nets is conceived for Stephen to desire to fly by.[21] These, now, are family relations (Aunt Sara and Uncle Richie), religion (the lures of priesthood visualised in the seclusion of Marsh's Library), and exile (Patrice and Kevin Egan imprisoned in their Parisian exile). A pattern derived from *A Portrait*, therefore, may be recognised to control the conclusion of the Telemachia in *Ulysses*. Yet in redeploying the pre-text of *A Portrait* to gain a design by which to organise the text of Proteus, it would seem that Joyce, too—rere regardant while moving onward—walked out on his own and Stephen's past as represented in *A Portrait of the Artist as a Young Man*. This is redoubled and deepened in Stephen Dedalus' parting from Buck Mulligan towards the end of episode nine, Scylla & Charybdis.

For *Ulysses*, Calypso and the emergence of Leopold Bloom constitutes, after the Telemachiad, a re-departure. It carries through to Lestrygonians and leads so to the novel's midpoint (in terms of chapter count) in Scylla & Charybdis. An auto-reflexivity of the novel itself—a redeployment of its own actualisation of the Homeric design and of its earlier episodes in pre-text functions for its later ones—sets in with programmatic intent in Wandering Rocks. Tenth of the book's episodes, it is the chapter by which, in a sense, *Ulysses* may even be said to come fully into its own. Wandering Rocks is a non-episode according to any Odyssean scheme, for it shapes an adventure Odysseus eschewed, choosing the path through Scylla & Charybdis instead. Not Bloom, therefore, nor of course Stephen, but *Ulysses* moves to the centre of the chapter's attention. Standing outside the plot structure of the myth, the episode functions like a pause in the action. Its relation to what precedes and what follows arises exclusively out of the text and design of the novel itself. What *Ulysses* realises in Wandering Rocks is a potential for alternative and variation held out in the *Odyssey*. At the same time, it frees itself, at a decisive juncture of its development, from structures of event and character prefigured for the episodes actualised in the epic. In artful ambivalence Wandering Rocks does, and does not, step outside the Odyssean frame of reference for *Ulysses*. What it lacks is a textual substratum in Homer's epic to refer to.

---

21 As I have argued in Hans Walter Gabler, 'Narrative rereadings: some remarks on "Proteus", "Circe" and "Penelope"', in *James Joyce 1: 'Scribble' 1: genèse des textes*, ed. by Claude Jacquet (Paris: Lettres Modernes, 1988), pp. 57-68.

But exactly such a textual reference base had meanwhile become available in the new *Odyssey* of *Ulysses*.

In extending his *oeuvre's* text by the episodes of the novel in progress, Joyce was effectively, and significantly, broadening the basis for the combinatory play of reading and writing within that text, so characteristic of his art. Even in the process of being written, the text proved increasingly capable of oscillating between text and pre-text functions, and it is in Sirens, the episode succeeding Wandering Rocks, that such oscillation becomes codified. Structurally, an 'antiphon' of short fragments introduces the chapter, which then unfolds from these sixty segments, as if generated from them in sequence, theme, tonality, and mood. In terms of the author's writing techniques, it appears that here, finally, a typical Joycean set of notes (such as those for *Exiles* considered earlier) enters the published writing, so as to render explicit a dynamic dependence of text upon pre-text. A look into the manuscripts further reveals a thorough reciprocity of the text and pre-text relationship. By the manuscript evidence, the antiphon was prefixed to the entire chapter when the latter was already extant in fair copy. In other words: it was placed to give the appearance of generative writing notes, and arranged to be read as a set of reading instructions, but was in fact itself generated, and condensed into a set of reading notes, from a comprehensive reading of the fully realised chapter. The material evidence of the manuscript, therefore—a critical consideration of which, at this point, thus proves absolutely indispensable—renders wholly transparent, as well as functional to the accomplished composition, the interdependence of text and pre-text, and points to the ultimate circularity of their relationship.

A deepened sense of the peculiar strengths of his creativity thus becomes recognisable in and behind Joyce's work around the time of the launching into the second half of *Ulysses*. It appears that he perceived with increasing clarity the principle of self-perpetuation of his *oeuvre's* text which he now at length carried into his ongoing writing. In response to Harriet Weaver's unease at what she felt was 'a weakening or diffusion of some sort' in Sirens, Joyce expressed strongly his sense of writing *Ulysses:* 'In the compass of one day to compress all these wanderings and clothe them in the form of this day is for me only possible by such variation which, I beg you to believe, is not capricious' (*Letters* I, 129). The artistic principle of textual variation or self-perpetuation engendered Joyce's conception of his art as work in progress. This term, it is true, was a coinage of later years for the successive publication of the segments of text which were finally to coalesce into *Finnegans Wake*. But the attitude to the artistic production which it implies begins to govern the writing of *Ulysses* from Wandering Rocks onwards.

Joyce's chapter drafts that survive generally bear witness to a process of composition guided and controlled by a conception of design anticipating the writing. A few fragmentary initial drafts, though, as for example to Cyclops (V.A.8) and Circe (V.A. 19), are exceptions to this rule. Here, it appears that Joyce committed a text to paper early enough in the compositional process to provide us with some evidence for the evolving of chapter structures. What is particularly notable is that these Cyclops and Circe drafts divide into discrete narrative units. Such a framing of sub-episodes yet to be unified in an overall chapter design is an anticipation of the standard procedure of composition for *Finnegans Wake*. In terms of the writing of *Ulysses*, the initial drafts for Cyclops reveal a struggle for a structure to contain and to sustain the opposition of the chapter styles of gigantism and realistic dialogue. Both the Cyclops and the Circe early fragments, moreover, are still indeterminate in their structural direction. The chapter designs later achieved at the fair-copy stage can in neither case be inferred from the initial drafts.

Complementary to the extant draft manuscripts are the compilations of note materials for the novel as a whole in copybooks widely separated by date: the Dublin/Trieste Alphabetical Notebook, begun around Christmas 1909, from which the material divides equally between *A Portrait* and *Ulysses*; the Zurich Notebook of 1918 (VIII.A.5), remarkable for its garnering of notes from Victor Berard's *Les Pheniciens et l'Odyssie*, W. H. Roscher's *Ausführliches Lexikon der griechischen und römischen Mythologie*, Thomas Otway's plays, and Aristotle's *Rhetoric*, which Joyce consulted in the Zentralbibliothek in Zurich; a companion Zurich notebook rediscovered among the copies of notebooks prepared by Mme Raphael for Joyce's *Finnegans Wake* use; and the Late Notes for typescripts and galleys of 1921/1922 (V.A.2).[22]

---

22 The entries from the Alphabetical Notebook are accessible in *The Workshop of Daedalus*, ed. by Robert Scholes and Richard M. Kain (Evanston: Northwestern University Press, 1965); notebooks VIII.A. 5 and V.A. 2 have been transcribed, edited and discussed by Phillip F. Herring, *Joyce's Notes and Early Drafts for 'Ulysses'*:

Analogous in terms of format, yet preceding the 'Late Notes' in the order of compilation, there is, most particularly, the series of *Ulysses Notesheets,* which received the earliest attention and, among workshop materials, have elicited the most detailed discussion in Joyce scholarship.[23] Neither *Notesheets* nor 'Late Notes' can be taken to represent Joyce's original jottings, executed, as Frank Budgen records, on whatever surface material happened to be at hand. Instead, as has often been shown, they contain a systematic arrangement of what became the additions in Joyce's handwriting to the documents that survive from typescript to final proofs for the 1922 book publication—though they by no means account for all revision and rewriting in evidence on those documents. For the original jottings, no doubt, the orange envelopes served as sorting receptacles, and only after such pre-sorting—probably by episode, and within episodes apparently sometimes by theme or motif—did Joyce proceed to compile the extant *Notesheets* and 'Late Notes' arrangements.

The notesheet format appears to have been first found useful for Cyclops, the last episode written in the autumn of 1919 in Zurich, and Nausikaa, succeeding in early 1920 in Trieste. If the reference to a 'recast of my notes (for Circe and Eumaeus)' in the first letter to Harriet Weaver from Paris in July 1920 (*Letters* I, 142) is again to notesheets, the format may have been induced by the need for light travelling back from Zurich to Trieste after the end of the war. At any rate, it seems clear that the surviving notesheets represent extracts from the bundles of slips in the orange envelopes and did not supersede them. For when Joyce departed anew from Trieste, this time to Paris, and by far outstayed the short weeks or months he had originally expected to spend there, specifically to write Circe and Eumaeus, one of his anxieties was to retrieve from Trieste 'an oil-cloth briefcase (total weight... estimated to be Kg 4.78), containing the written symbols of the languid lights which occasionally flashed across my soul'. 'Having urgent need of these notes in order

---

Selections from the Buffalo Collection (Charlottesville: University Press of Virginia, 1977); Danis Rose and John O'Hanlon's edited and annotated transcription of the Madame Raphael notebook VI.D. 7 (*VI.D.7: The Lost First Notebook*) turns out to be derived from a companion notebook to VIII.A.5.

23 Phillip F. Herring, *Joyce's 'Ulysses' Notesheets in the British Museum* (Charlottesville: University Press of Virginia, 1972). The Notesheets were first discussed by Litz in *The Art of James Joyce* (see note 12).

to complete my literary work entitled *Ulysses*', he implored Italo Svevo to obtain them for him from the flat of Stanislaus (*Letters* I, 154). He received them (*Letters* I, 161) and used them in the composition of Ithaka and Penelope as well as for the encompassingly great revisional expansions of the entire book in typescript and proofs.

Joyce's writing notes for Circe, we may be sure, were his garnerings from the fourteen episodes preceding the Nighttown chapter. It is common critical knowledge that Circe essentially depends on Joyce's comprehensive and detailed rereading of the pre-text of *Ulysses* itself up to this point. Yet, curiously, little critical thought has been given to the significance of the rewriting of that text into the text of Circe. Fundamentally, it conditions the chapter's mode of referentiality. Traditional notions of narrative referentiality are concerned with the empiric substratum of the fiction: fiction as written and read is assumed to refer to truth or probability in the real world of experience. Framed by such preconceptions, critics have struggled to define and distinguish strata of real action and of 'surreal' visions or hallucinations in Circe. Yet the implications of the rewriting of *Ulysses* in Circe are surely that the preceding narrative of Bloomsday is made to function as if it constituted not a fiction, but itself an order of empiric reality. This assumption allows us to perceive the episode's discrete narrative units as straightforward tales told, or dramatised. They lend new narrative surfaces to Leopold Bloom or Stephen Dedalus, whether as characters or as vehicles of consciousness, as well as to all other recurring personages, objects, events, and incidents that in Circe realise new narrative potential from their fictionally real existence in the pre-narrative of Bloomsday. The combinatory virtuosity of the tales unfolded from the Bloomsday pre-text is often breathtaking, yet assumes a surreal quality only if we insist on their ultimate referability to empiric reality alone. If, instead, we accept a raising of the pre-narrative that so obviously engenders the episodes of Circe to the level of absolute reality, or else—which is at least as intriguing—a 'lowering' of empiric reality to the state of relativity of fiction, we recognise the chapter's mode of referentiality as one that, rather than making the text conform to traditional notions of the rendering of reality in fiction, enlarges instead its field of reference so as properly to accommodate itself. Thus Circe succeeds in challenging and modifying traditionally received and theoretically articulated notions of the referentiality of fiction. Its method of procedure would appear as the systematic extension of the generative, or regenerative, compositional process that from its very origins governed Joyce's work in progress.

In Circe, Joyce may thus be seen to embrace the full consequences of his creative artistry: by no other pre-text than that from within his own *oeuvre* could he have rocked the foundations of traditional narrative. The challenge to narrative referentiality raised in Circe is, in the conclusion to the novel, paralleled by a challenge to the historicity of fictional time. Penelope, I suggest, is a final rewriting from a rereading of the pre-text of *Ulysses* itself. The episode is organised from within a central consciousness, and the structural element of the preceding narrative which it rereads is that hierarchically superior, and thus external, consciousness of the text sometimes known as the 'Arranger'. Having in varying degrees made its presence felt through seventeen episodes, that superior and external consciousness is conspicuously absent from Penelope. The Arranger's main function throughout these seventeen episodes has been to transform the *histoire* behind *Ulysses* into the *discours* of Bloomsday—but, aware of its function, we have as readers and critics throughout been as busily reversing its arrangement and transforming the '*discours*' back into '*histoire*', adjusting parallax, constructing biographies, mapping topographies, discovering untold episodes, and generally putting horses properly before carts. In Penelope, however, where the Arranger's functions are relinquished to a central consciousness internalised in the fictional character of Molly Bloom, we at last—amazingly and with amazement—give ourselves over to a flow of discourse characterised by that essential quality of *discours*, the dehistoricising of history, or dechronologising of time. As Molly thinks herself to sleep, we learn at last what it may mean to awake from the nightmare of history. In the rewriting of *Ulysses* in Penelope— constituting a text designed to allow the consciousness of Arranger, of Molly Bloom, and of the reader to intersect in a narrative mode so clearly pointing the way to *Finnegans Wake*—we are taught, if we wish finally to learn, how to read the novel, which in its author's terms means how imaginatively to rewrite in constant progress the pre-text of the Joycean *oeuvre*.

The achievement of *Ulysses* set the stage for Joyce's last work. It was slow in starting, as each of his previous works had been. Yet within a few years, he began to publish it in segments. During the sixteen years of its growth, he invariably referred to it as 'Work in Progress', withholding its final title—*Finnegans Wake*—until the moment of integral publication in 1939. Significantly, before entering into fresh reading and writing phases, he secured a basis from within his own *oeuvre* by reassembling workshop materials from all his existing texts in the so-called 'Scribbledehobble' notebook (Buffalo VI.A).[24] Beyond, the mass of *Finnegans Wake* notebooks holds overwhelming evidence of his wide reading of the most heterogeneous array of source materials as pre-texts for the writings of the final extension to his *oeuvre*'s text.

As Joyce's private material repositories, the notebooks are the mere preliminaries to all subsequent constitution of compositional text. The writing of *Finnegans Wake* itself from its pre-texts—whether or not encoded, successively, in related notebooks—passed through much the same stages as did that of *Ulysses*, albeit over an appreciably longer timespan; as it happens, Joyce's writing years from the beginnings on *Stephen Hero* to the conclusion of *Finnegans Wake* neatly divide in half with the publication of *Ulysses*. From the second half of his writing life, guided as it was by the notion of creative authorship as work in progress, such as it became now publicly declared in its title itself, we possess in abundance sketches and working drafts, fair copies, typescripts, segment publications and multi-revisional proofs that, even as they first emerge for sections and sub-sections that only eventually coalesce towards *Finnegans Wake*, relate in far more complex ways than anything to be observed in the organisation of the writing for *Ulysses*. For sheer quantity, as well as for organisational intricacy, the sixteen years it took Joyce to wind off 'Work in Progress' yielded a rich document legacy. Much more, however, the compositional and revisional testimony which the documents preserve appears unrivalled for its quality. But it is a qualitative testimony that has as yet only begun to be critically explored. To do genetic justice to Joyce's creative art and artistry in 'Work in Progress', Joyce scholarship is yet in process and progress to acquire a new critical outlook and a new corporate experience.

---

24 *James Joyce's Scribbledehobble: The Ur-Workbook for 'Finnegans Wake'*, ed. by Thomas E. Connolly (Evanston: Northwestern University Press, 1961).

The Rocky Road to *Ulysses*

To the memory of

Richard Ellmann (1918–1987)

and

Hugh Kenner (1923–2003)

—Ten years, [Mulligan] said, chewing and laughing. He is going to write something in ten years.

—Seems a long way off, Haines said, thoughtfully lifting his spoon. Still, I shouldn't wonder if he did after all.

(*Ulysses* 10, 1089-92)[1]

May Joyce, James Joyce's sister, remembered in a letter to her brother of 1 September 1916 that Jim would send all the younger brothers and sisters out of the room and, alone with his dying mother, would read to her from the novel he had just begun to write. May remembered because once or twice she managed to get overlooked, hiding under the sofa; and eventually Jim allowed her to stay for chapter after chapter.[2] This must have been in the summer of 1903. It cannot have been later, for their mother died that August. Nor is it likely to have been earlier, since that would have been before Joyce left for Paris in early December 1902; nor, presumably, did these readings take place during the two or

---

1 James Joyce, *Ulysses. A Critical and Synoptic Edition*, prepared by Hans Walter Gabler with Wolfhard Steppe and Claus Melchior, 3 vols. (New York: Garland Publishing, 1984; ²1986). The reading text from this edition is published in James Joyce, *Ulysses*, ed. by Hans Walter Gabler with Wolfhard Steppe and Claus Melchior (London: The Bodley Head; New York: Random House, 1986; ²1993).

2 *Letters of James Joyce*, vol. II, ed. by Richard Ellmann (New York: Viking, 1966), (*Letters* II), p. 383.

three weeks from late December 1902 to mid-January 1903 when Joyce, homesick, returned from Paris to spend Christmas in Dublin.

We believe we know what James Joyce's first attempts at writing were, in his late teens, before he left Ireland for Paris. They comprised juvenile and early poems, some journalistic efforts, two translations from the German of plays by Gerhart Hauptmann,[3] and a miscellany made up of brief dramatic and narrative scenes and vividly visual accounts of dreams. Joyce considered this miscellany of short, intense and often highly poetic miniatures, quite original, to constitute a genre of its own. He defined it in terms of medieval theological philosophy, calling these early pieces 'epiphanies'.[4] They do not all survive, but some of those that do were actually written on board ship between France and Ireland. In Paris, he began to study medicine, spent many hours reading non-medical books in libraries, and was altogether absorbed in the life of the city until called back by a telegram from his father. It reached him, let us assume, just as such a summons on a regular blue French telegram form reaches Stephen Dedalus in *Ulysses*: 'Nother dying. Come home. Father.' (*U* 3, 199) In Joyce's life, this occurred in April 1903. Until August, he lived in Dublin, sharing the pain of his mother's last four months. After her death, and a year of mourning, he left Ireland with Nora Barnacle on 8 October 1904, for what was to become a lifetime's exile.

Joyce's three and a half months or so in Paris in 1902 to 1903 seem to have been the gestation period for his first attempt at a longer narrative. If he did not actually begin writing his first novel there, he must have done so during the vigil, on his return. May Joyce, in her 1916 letter, congratulates her brother on the publication of *A Portrait of the Artist as a Young Man*, which came out as a book that year. Waiting to receive

---

3 Of these, the translation of 'Before Sunrise' survives in a carefully penned fair-copy manuscript. The translation of 'Michael Kramer' is lost, its last recorded whereabouts being among Mr Duffy's papers in his desk drawer in the *Dubliners* story 'A Painful Case'. Judging from 'Before Sunrise', the translations were hampered by Joyce's limited competence in German. Nonetheless, they are highly impressive in his own language: Joyce captures the atmosphere of the Silesian dialect of the original in such a way that he anticipates, and so effectively invents, the stage Anglo-Irish that Synge and O'Casey introduced a few years later at the Abbey Theatre under the aegis of W. B. Yeats and Lady Gregory.

4 To be precise: it is Stephen Daedalus in *Stephen Hero* who gives definitions and a discussion of the epiphany (cf. James Joyce, *Stephen Hero* (London: Jonathan Cape, [1944] 1969), pp. 216-18; and see further, below).

and read her copy, she expects to recognise in it the story she had heard the beginnings of under the sofa back in her childhood, though much changed. Doubtless, what Joyce had read to his mother were its opening chapters, freshly drafted. It was thus in the summer of 1903, as James Joyce's mother lay dying, that Stephen Daedalus/Dedalus was born into the life of his fictions, and of Joyce's, and ultimately our, imagination. Taking him first through an entire novel of his own, from which he made him depart into exile, Joyce then brought him back to open *Ulysses*. There we encounter him suffering from the trauma of having failed his mother on her death bed. Substituting an Irish ballad for a Christian prayer, Stephen sang the song of Fergus at his mother's bedside. James Joyce apparently solaced his mother with his own emerging fiction told in childhood scenes formed out of their close early relationship. And he, too, may in real life have sung the song of Fergus to his mother—and even have done so in a setting of his own.[5] That he would have read her what he had written and sung her what he had composed goes together. Under the emotional strain of seeing her suffer, his creativity budded doubly into literature and music.

The earliest traces that survive of the early Stephen Daedalus novel are notes dateable to late winter of 1904 at the back of a copybook. Prospectively sketching out the narrative from chapter VIII onwards, they suggest that its first seven chapters were by that time written. The grand plan, apparently, was for a book of sixty-three chapters, so a mere one-seventh was accomplished. Since, however, the '63' seems to have been meant to be numerologically related to the periods of life of a man, the seven chapters were the rounded first seventh of a ninefold division into units of seven, and evidently encompassed early childhood. It makes sense to assume that these were the chapters Joyce wrote during his mother's final illness and read to her before she died.

The effect of dating those seven lost opening chapters of the early Stephen Daedalus novel to the summer of 1903 is to shed new light on the text that constitutes the main entry in the copybook, and on its

---

5   The speculation is suggestive: cf. *The James Joyce Songbook*, ed. by Ruth Bauerle (New York: Garland, 1982), pp. 116-17. And the timing is right: Joyce's attempts at musical composition, of which mainly echoes and fragments have come down to us, plausibly tie in with his preparation for a singing career, on which he was seriously bent precisely during the last span of his mother's life and the ensuing year of mourning.

status in Joyce's writing life. The copybook contains the autograph fair copy (and it is a fair copy, despite traces of having been worked over) of the narrative essay 'A Portrait of the Artist'.[6] Reassessing its position allows us, among other things, to regard it as a milestone in the process of development that ultimately led to *Ulysses*. James Joyce's brother Stanislaus, asserting that the essay was written out of nowhere in a few days or a couple of weeks in January 1904, celebrated this essay—and prompted Richard Ellmann to do likewise—as a spontaneous overflow of genius. (In vindication of Stanislaus's assumptions, it should, however, be remembered that Joyce himself could well have left his brother in the dark as to where the essay sprang from, and how he came to write it.) Brilliant though it undoubtedly is, it went entirely over the heads of the editors of *Dana*, who declined to publish it—and we can easily sympathise with their point of view: without hindsight as to the directions into which Joyce's thoughts were taking, and the ways his writing was developing, we would find the essay's arcane (actually, early modernist) aesthetics, its symbolist imagery and its convoluted and hermetic argument obscure, much as *Dana*'s editors must have done.[7]

With no evidence to the contrary, we must accept Stanislaus's boast that it was he who invented the title 'Stephen Hero' for what his brother sat down to write when *Dana* rejected 'A Portrait of the Artist'. (Stanislaus also found the title 'Chamber Music' for James Joyce's first collection of poems intended for the public.) What we can no longer accept is Stanislaus's assertion that Joyce began writing *Stephen Hero* only after 'A Portrait of the Artist' was rejected,[8] and that the essay is

---

6   For a photo-offprint reproduction of the copy-book, see *The James Joyce Archive*, vol. 7, (New York and London: Garland, 1978), pp. 70-94; a transcription of the text only of 'A Portrait of the Artist' is incorporated in James Joyce, *Poems and Shorter Writings*, ed. by R. Ellmann, A. W. Litz and J. Whittier-Ferguson (London: Faber & Faber, 1991), pp. 211-18.

7   I gratefully acknowledge that it was John O'Hanlon who alerted me to May Joyce's letter of 1 September 1916 and began himself to consider its implications in private correspondence. Had the letter not been overlooked in all previous criticism and biography, we would long have lived with a different sense of Joyce's emerging creativity, and of the structural lines in his early oeuvre.

8   Though what Stanislaus heard James read, or was given to read, of the beginning of *Stephen Hero* after the *Dana* rejection of 'A Portrait of the Artist', may well have been the first he was allowed to know of the emerging narrative; only their sister May, it seems, was let in on Jim's secret writing experiments in the summer of 1903.

therefore the manifesto from which *Stephen Hero* first sprang. It is indeed a manifesto in the context of James Joyce's oeuvre as a whole. But the blueprint it provided was not for *Stephen Hero*; it was, in essential points, for *A Portrait of the Artist as a Young Man*. Yet its rejection by *Dana* made Joyce shy away from realising it, at least for the time being. Instead, he fell back on the Stephen Daedalus narrative—on *Stephen Hero*—which he had already begun, developing it further along the lines of that first beginning. This is indicated by the jottings and, in particular, the planning notes as they appear at the back of the 'A Portrait of the Artist' essay in the copybook. Returned by the editors of *Dana*, its spare blank pages were used for notes that bear no relation to chapters I to VII, but are earmarked for chapters VIII and after of *Stephen Hero*.

It is now possible to recognise that 'A Portrait of the Artist' was an effort to break the pattern set up by the seven first chapters as read out in the summer of 1903, an attempt to work out an alternative way of writing the novel Joyce wanted to write. In other words: the essay marks not a point of origin, but a point of crisis in the emergence, eventually, of *A Portrait of the Artist as a Young Man*. The incomprehension the essay met with, however, prevented the vision it expressed from being realised until after *Stephen Hero* had foundered a second time. By the summer of 1905, Joyce had reached the end of his tether with it. In exile in Pola and Trieste, he had persevered with it through twenty-five chapters, arriving at the threshold of the present moment within his blatantly autobiographic narrative.[9] Now his own life and that of his hero were zeroing in on one another, and it is no wonder he broke off; for, given the unabashed autobiography at its core, how could a novel conceivably be invented and carried forward from it to its hero's old age by chapter 63? The impasse was inescapable, as was the need to recast the narrative in symbolic forms—in other words: precisely the need that 'A Portrait of the Artist' had acknowledged could be staved off no longer. Yet it took Joyce a further two years, until the latter half of 1907, to work up the

---

9   The autobiographical element was quite obvious. The chapters were sent piecemeal from Trieste to Stanislaus in Dublin as they were written, and Stanislaus gave them to chosen friends to read, who then discussed just how Joyce might be expected to introduce them into his text, or to handle touchy situations, such as the notorious quarrel with Gogarty and Trench at the Martello Tower in Sandycove. This scene, though eagerly awaited by everyone in 1905, was not, in fact, composed until some time between 1912 and 1917; and it provided, in the end, the opening for *Ulysses*.

necessary momentum to rewrite his novel. The stories he accumulated in the interim and collected as *Dubliners* seem to have catalysed the Stephen Daedalus matter into a form expressive of its content; shifting it from autobiography to the deliberate artifice of an autonomous fiction.

In the progress of Joyce's oeuvre towards *Ulysses*, *Dubliners* is generically situated ahead of the Stephen Daedalus/Dedalus novel. This is so, in the first place, because the stories set the scene: they tell the city; but also, secondly, because they present themselves, both in their manuscripts and in print, as the writings of Stephen Daedalus. In 1904, *The Irish Homestead* (dubbed the 'pig's paper' by Joyce) published the early versions of 'The Sisters', 'Eveline' and 'After the Race' one by one between July and December under that name.

Since Joyce had begun to fictionalise his youthful autobiography through the *persona* of Stephen Daedalus, a thoroughly transparent version of himself, this appears at first sight no more than a private joke, aimed at his circle of Dublin friends who had been allowed to read the successive draft chapters for *Stephen Hero*. But he also signed the *Dubliners* stories in manuscript with Stephen's name, and continued to do so during the entire time he was writing *Stephen Hero* and *Dubliners* in parallel; it was only after mid-1905 that he changed over to signing his story manuscripts 'JAJ'. This persistence indicates how serious Joyce was in exploring the artistic identity that the pseudonym afforded. 'Old father, old artificer, stand me now and ever in good stead' (*P* V, 2791-92) is the invocation at the end of the final diary section of *A Portrait of the Artist as a Young Man*,[10] expressing the diarist's self-identification with Daedalus/Icarus; and Stephanos garlanded in a martyr's crown is accosted in mocking Greek in the latter half of *A Portrait*'s fourth chapter at the very moment when Stephen has decided to accept the martyrdom

---

10 The editions of *A Portrait of the Artist as a Young Man* and *Dubliners* used for this essay are: James Joyce, *A Portrait of the Artist as a Young Man* (Critical Edition), ed. by Hans Walter Gabler with Walter Hettche (New York and London: Garland Publishing, 1993); identical in text and line numbering with: James Joyce, *A Portrait of the Artist as a Young Man*, ed. by Hans Walter Gabler with Walter Hettche (New York: Vintage Books, 1993; London: Vintage Books, 2012, also as e-book); and: James Joyce, *Dubliners* (Critical Edition), ed. by Hans Walter Gabler with Walter Hettche (New York and London: Garland Publishing, 1993); identical in text and line numbering with: James Joyce, *Dubliners*, ed. by Hans Walter Gabler with Walter Hettche (New York: Vintage Books, 1993; London: Vintage Books, 2012, also as e-book). [*P*]

of art. Together, the martyr and the artificer offered role models that helped to construct the central character of the autobiographic novel, enabling Joyce also to devise a *persona* through whom he could identify his artistic self. It is as if, by inventing Stephen Daedalus, Joyce cut the key to unlock the portals to his own art and devised an agency and agent to transmute the contingencies of life into the meaningful structures and shapes of art. This agent allowed recognition, self-recognition, and reflection, and the laying open (or concealing) of the processes of transformation, as it also allowed aesthetic distancing, ironically refracting or radically subverting these processes. Signing his own work with his autobiographic hero's name indicates just how intensely James Joyce felt and embraced its potential. And thereafter to rename the focal character of *A Portrait of the Artist as a Young Man* 'Stephen Dedalus' (however seemingly slight the change), and to name himself James Joyce, that novel's author, signalled further a decisive advance in reflection and artistic distancing.

Once *Stephen Hero* had been put aside, the stories for *Dubliners* were written in swift succession, enabling Joyce to expand into an intense training period that developed his skills and crystallised the main strategies of his art. Narrative substance, plot and character needed to be sustained for the length of only one story at a time. Attention could be concentrated on significances, and on working them out in language. The stories' pervasive quality lies in their precision of language—an aspect in which Joyce took particular pride: 'I am uncommonly well pleased with these stories. There is a neat phrase of five words in *The Boarding-House*: find it!'[11] Precision in the narrative rendering of reality went hand in hand with the linguistic precision, resulting in a symbolic heightening of the realistic detail; one might term Joyce's manner of encapsulating significance in the realistically specific his symbolic realism. Father Flynn's breaking the chalice, for instance, in 'The Sisters', and his lying in state with the broken chalice on his breast; or his sisters' dispensing crackers and sherry (or: bread and wine) exemplify the strategy, as do the curtains of dusty cretonne in 'Eveline', the harp ('heedless that her coverings had fallen about her knees') in 'Two Gallants', Mary's singing of 'I dreamt that I dwelt in marble halls' in 'Clay', or the rusty bicycle

---

11   Letter to Stanislaus Joyce, 12 July 1905 (*Letters* II, p. 92), accompanying the dispatch of the manuscript.

pump in the garden of the deceased priest at the opening of 'Araby' (it lacks air, or pneuma, much like the 'rheumatic [pneumatic] wheels' in 'The Sisters'). Significant structuring and symbolic form, furthermore, become increasingly conscious devices, as when in 'Two Gallants' the futile circularity of the daily life of unemployed young men in Dublin is expressed by Lenehan idly circling through the Dublin streets while Corley is taking advantage of a slavey to induce her to steal from her employer a 'small gold-coin'; or when 'Grace' moves from the hell of a downstairs pub lavatory, via the purgatory of Kernan's lying convalescent in bed, to the paradise of Father Purdon's perverse sermon to 'business men and professional men' that sets up 'the worshippers of Mammon' as their example. This last structure, in particular, is devised to refer both to the orthodox Christian division of the realms of the dead, and to an intertext, Dante's *Divina Commedia*.

Writing against the foil of intertexts becomes central to Joyce's art of narrative; from *Dubliners*, via *A Portrait of the Artist as a Young Man* and *Ulysses*, to *Finnegans Wake*, it grows into a pervasive retelling of known stories. 'The Sisters', for example, the opening story in *Dubliners*, can be and has been successfully read against the foil of the Biblical narrative of Jesus visiting Mary, Martha and their resurrected brother Lazarus; and the full irony of the story that Frank tells in 'Eveline' unfolds only as one realises that the art of telling 'Eveline' depends on sustaining, alongside Eveline's explicit text, the hidden subtexts of both Frank's and the father's stories. *Ulysses*, as is well known, combines the homeomorph stories of Odysseus, Don Giovanni and Hamlet (to mention only the most significant), and in *Finnegans Wake* such homeomorphology becomes the all-encompassing principle of weaving the text, and of patterning the very language devised to voice its narratives.[12]

How this strategy of retelling stories becomes increasingly central to the progress of Joyce's art can be observed in stages from the final *Dubliners* tale, 'The Dead', via *A Portrait of the Artist as a Young Man*

---

12 Hugh Kenner has frequently guided Joyce readers to multi-level readings of Joyce's texts; see, for example, *A Colder Eye* (London: Penguin Books, 1983), esp. pp. 189-92; or *Joyce's Voices* (Berkeley and Los Angeles: University of California Press, 1978), pp. 80-81, and throughout. The notion of homeomorph narratives is developed in the first chapter of *The Pound Era* (Berkeley and Los Angeles: University of California Press, 1971).

to the inception of *Ulysses*.[13] The night of 'The Dead' is, specifically, Twelfth Night, by which the Christian feast of the Epiphany of the Lord overwrites the Saturnalia of the Roman calendar. And, as it happens, there already exists a well-known Latin text dating from early Christian times that provides a model for the cultural shock implied in that act of substitution. This text is the *Saturnalia* by Macrobius, in which a Christian, Evangelus, with two companions, breaks in on a convivial gathering of representative pre-Christian intellectuals. The story invokes, and gains significant structural parameters from, a traditional Varronian rule that defines and limits the number of guests at a feast: they should be no more than the number of the Muses (nine), and no less than the number of the Graces (three). In the ensuing argument between the host at the ongoing party of nine and the three new arrivals, they agree to suspend the rule so as to make room for twelve guests. Evangelus, however, urges on behalf of the (ungracious) trinity of gate-crashers a further juggling with the numerology so that the host (Christ-like) is simultaneously included and excluded in the count, thus suggesting the 12+1 constellation of the Christian Last Supper.

Deliberate references to Macrobius's *Saturnalia* can be seen in 'The Dead': the Miss Morkans are apostrophised as the three Graces of the Dublin musical world, and the rest of the female characters add up to nine, albeit not without some further juggling to accommodate Miss Ivors' early departure, perhaps made up for by The Lass of Aughrim's late appearance (and in a song only, so that she is at once absent and present), and/or Mary Jane Morkan's doing double duty as Grace and Muse—her model in Greek mythology, in this respect, would be Thalia, at once one of the Graces and the Muse of history. The (mock-)

---

13   In what follows, my account of the intertexts for 'The Dead', as well as for *A Portrait of the Artist as a Young Man*, derives from the 2003 Munich PhD dissertation by Dieter Fuchs, 'Menippos in Dublin. Studien zu James Joyce und zur Form der Menippea', published as *Joyce und Menippos. 'A Portrait of the Artist as an Old Dog'*. (*ZAA Monograph Series* 2) (Würzburg: Königshausen & Neumann, 2006). Fuchs sees Joyce's writing from 'The Dead' onward as an archaeology and a rediscovery of Menippean and symposiastic narrative ontologies in the Western tradition, harking back to antiquity and pre-Christian philosophical and literary modes that were buried during the Christian era. In the course of his analysis, he identifies intertexts from antiquity for 'The Dead' and *A Portrait of the Artist as a Young Man* that already have the type of functional relationship to these works that Homer's *Odyssey* has to *Ulysses*. These are important discoveries that I incorporate in my argument.

substitution of the symposiastic sum of 9+3 by the thirteen of the sacramental Christian meal is reflected in the precisely thirteen good-nights exchanged as the party breaks up. In the chatter of voices when everybody is saying her or his 'good-night' almost simultaneously, the moment is rendered with realistic precision. But, as set out on the page, it is also so conspicuous that we recognise its design in the vein of Joyce's symbolic realism.

The local effect of this symbolically realistic moment is thus coupled with the encompassing intertextual patterning, and the two reinforce each other. Both are Joycean strategies to invoke larger significances for a given narrative, and to universalise the stories being told. But the setting up of Macrobius's *Saturnalia* as a foil for 'The Dead' creates significations that are only apparent to the reader. None of the characters possesses, nor does any feature of everyday contemporary Dublin life betray the least consciousness that they relate to, and may be read in terms of, an underlying intertext. But for the reader recognising the connection, text and intertext appear knitted into a web of meanings whose ironies and subversions arise from the narrative and its submerged foil together. We are accustomed to recognising such intertextual interweaving in the case of *Ulysses*, but until now, the assumption has been that the construction of *Ulysses* against the intertext of Homer's *Odyssey* constituted a genuinely new departure for Joyce (despite a playful anticipation or two, such as the Biblical story of Mary, Martha and Lazarus suggested as a frame of reference for 'The Sisters'). Recognising that this structural principle is already firmly in place in 'The Dead' certainly increases our understanding of the complexities of signification in Joyce's texts, and of the continuities within the oeuvre.[14] Heading for *Ulysses*, these continuities are carried forward from *Dubliners*, and 'The Dead', through the Stephen Daedalus/Dedalus novel as rewritten into *A Portrait of the Artist as a Young Man*.

A Portrait of the Artist as a Young Man has traditionally been contrasted with *Ulysses* on the grounds that, while Stephen Dedalus in *A Portrait*

---

14 I reconceptualise the term 'intertext' of critical convention as 'perception text' in subsequent essays, as in '"He chronicled with patience": Early Joycean Progressions between Non-Fiction and Fiction' (2018). https://www.openbookpublishers.com/htmlreader/978-1-78374-363-6/ch2.xhtml#_idTextAnchor006, to suggest James Joyce's encompassing perception of reality and texts as transformable creatively afresh into text.

is only too conscious of his double identity as Daedalus and Icarus (as well as of a third identity as Stephen the martyr, which he extends to include Charles Stewart Parnell, and even grandiosely Jesus Christ), the Stephen Dedalus of *Ulysses* has no awareness that he is Telemachus, nor does Leopold Bloom know he is Odysseus, nor Molly Bloom that she is Penelope—and this applies to every other character, fleetingly cast into one or another Odyssean role or constellation; it even applies to Bloom's cigar that he smokes in Cyclops, which only the reader can relate to the spear with the glowing tip used by Odysseus to blind the Polyphemus; or to the waterways of Dublin that, for the reader, stand in for the four rivers of the underworld. While this distinction holds good, there is more to *A Portrait of the Artist as a Young Man*, in terms of intertextuality, than has hitherto met the eye. Indeed, Stephen Dedalus's eagerness to subscribe to the Daedalian identifications ought to have raised our suspicions— ought to have raised them when the text's complex ironies were first recognised half a century ago—that the demonstrative self-awareness with which he is endowed conceals something beyond,[15] something that we ought to have recognised over (as it were) his head. What it conceals is an intertext cunningly hiding beneath an identical name. The equation of identity that governs *A Portrait* might be formulated as: 'Dedalus : Daedalus = Metamorphoses : Metamorphoses'. The apparently identical terms 'Metamorphoses' in this equation actually refer to different texts: one is Ovid's *Metamorphoses*. The other is Apuleius's *The Golden Ass*, which since antiquity has also always been known by the alternative title, 'Metamorphoses'.

But, how do the Apuleian *Metamorphoses* differ from those of Ovid, with regard to the legend of Daedalus? Ovid, one might say, gives civilised Rome the civilised and acculturated aspect of the myth. He tells of the great craftsman and artist who, to fly from the realm of barbarian tyranny in Crete, ingeniously constructed wings for himself and his son. Yet fate was tragically against him: he lost his son over the sea. But precisely because of this tragic turn, Ovid's Daedalus stands assured of our respect and compassion. The noble tears he sheds for Icarus are vicariously ours, and the humane obsequies he observes for him are communal bonds of our culture and civilisation that the

---

15   The study from which above all the readings of Joyce's ironies emanated was Hugh Kenner, *Dublin's Joyce* (London: Chatto and Windus, 1955).

myth helps to establish. Daedalus, in supreme command of his skills and art, wings loftily through safe middle air towards an Apollonian apotheosis. Adopting Ovid's perspective on the Daedalian legend, we marginalise or repress the darker side of the myth. But it is this that the *Metamorphoses* of Apuleius remember. *The Golden Ass* does not allow us to forget that Daedalus aided and abetted lust and deceit, was subservient to Minos, the tyrant of Crete, and pandered to the bestial cravings of his queen Pasiphae. The Minotaurus is the offspring of Pasiphae's unnatural coupling with Taurus, the sacrificial bull, with whom she deceived Minos, but whom she equally deceived in her cow's disguise that Daedalus welded—or, in proper *A Portrait* parlance: forged—for her. The Minotaurus is thus the horrible incarnation of the Daedalian craftsmanship; and the labyrinth, built to hide away the monster, is the consummation in perversity of Daedalus's art, designed as it is to contain and conceal the scandal infesting that art to the very roots. The secrets that it harbours and the desires it serves are the Dionysian earthbound entanglements of the heavenward Daedalian flight.

Stephen Dedalus, however, is unconscious of the dark sides of the Daedalus myth. He is unaware that, if he can see himself as Icarus, he might equally link himself in imagination with Taurus and Minotaurus. His father, it is true —who 'had a hairy face' (*P* I, 6)—hands down to him, as if in a gesture of initiation, his veiled version of the family legend. As a toddler hearing the tale, Stephen does not connect the moocow—in other words Pasiphae, now translated, as it were, into a fairy-tale—either with Taurus, the sacrificial bull, or his own mother. Consequently, he remains ignorant—as the child remains ignorant of the sexuality of its parents—of how deeply the story implicates and compromises the father. There comes the moment, on the threshold to adolescence, when Stephen (Stephen Minotaurus, one might say) imagines himself a foster child (*P* II, 1359). Yet to test that truth, if truth it is, it never occurs to him to anagrammatise his father's given name: Simon = Minos. Nor does Stephen, as he grows in self-awareness and learns both intellectually and emotionally to project his aspirations to art onto the Ovidian Daedalus, ever find a text—other than the guilt-inducing Christian text of the fall of man into sin—through which to acknowledge the sensual and instinctual sides of his experience, and specifically those of his bodily cravings and sexual lusts, as integral to the human condition.

If these weavings of the Apuleian *Metamorphoses* into *A Portrait of the Artist as a Young Man* are so manifest and so significant, how is it that they have passed unnoticed for so long? The simplest explanation is that we have listened too uncritically to Stephen Dedalus, and with too insufficient an awareness to the text that tells his story, and to his author. Stephen, as he himself records, has been taught to construe the *Metamorphoses* according to Ovid (cf. *P* V, 188), and it is in this mode that he identifies with Daedalus (and Icarus). But if Stephen thoughtlessly adopted Ovid's Apollonian perspective as his own, then so, commonly, have we. And so we have failed to extend to Stephen's self-identification with Daedalus the general critical insight that, throughout, *A Portrait of Artist as a Young Man* ironically distances, as it narratively undercuts, its protagonist. Perhaps we should have known to know better. For James Joyce actually goes to the length of staging his own authorial self to announce that the tale the reader is about to encounter will turn the mind to the unknown—though he does so most cunningly, in words culled from Ovid. *A Portrait of the Artist as a Young Man* is unique among Joyce's works in carrying a motto: 'Et ignotas animum dimittit in artes'—'he turns the mind to unknown arts', the words Ovid uses of Daedalus at *Metamorphoses* VIII, 188. Prefaced as they are to the book about Stephen Dedalus, it might plausibly be assumed that they refer to its protagonist. But they may also refer to the book itself and express its author's sense of its artfulness. For what are these 'unknown arts'? And might they equally be 'dark', 'hidden', 'lowly'? since these are also lexically possible meanings for 'ignotus'.[16] Hidden in this motto may be reading instructions that open wider perspectives to our understanding.

Such perspectives are opened by James Joyce's archaeological explorations of modes of writing and thought from antiquity, modes that challenge those privileged by the traditions of Christianity, and what Christianity canonised from the Graeco-Roman literary and philosophical heritage. Thus in spelling out for himself what it would mean to leave the Church and become a writer, Joyce proceeded radically,

---

16 Dieter Fuchs, at this point, goes on to argue that Joyce is here actually hinting at the literary archaeology he is embarking upon, which in this case would be aimed specifically at unearthing the lowly genre of Menippean satire.

in the literal sense of the word, to unearth the roots of marginal or lowly texts from antiquity such as the *Saturnalia* of Macrobius and *The Golden Ass*, or *Metamorphoses*, of Apuleius. Yet he did not do so as an historian or ethnologist of literature, but as an aspiring writer endeavouring to anchor the heady intellectualisms of his day—Pater, Nietzsche, Wagner, Ibsen, Maeterlinck, Hauptmann —in a literary enterprise of his own, grounded upon prose narrative. The strategy he developed to shape that enterprise was to project contemporary everyday experience onto ancient texts and their frameworks of character and plot, theme, ethics and morality.[17] In 'The Dead', the main emphasis of the allusions to the *Saturnalia* of Macrobius would seem to be thematic and moral. The intertextual relationship helps to move Dublin's paralytic stasis between death and religion onto a more general level of perception and understanding. At the same time, although it is adequately signalled, the intertextuality here remains largely an ingenious game and virtuoso performance. In *A Portrait*, by contrast, the Apuleius foil functions at the level of character and is intensely personalised. In this respect, it explores what it may mean to offer a portrait of the artist *as a young man* in terms of that young man's ignorance and blindness to aspects of his own identity. Once we have recognised the relationship between the Daedalian texts, we are invited to reflect just how carefully Stephen Dedalus avoids searching for his identity among the darker sides of the Daedalus myth. It seems that we are meant to perceive this as a youthful failing in Stephen. To weld the two halves—the conscious and the unconscious—of the Daedalus myth together into a whole would mean arriving at the maturity of a comprehensive world view, and a full sense and understanding of the human condition, a sense that Stephen Dedalus knows how to phrase, though not yet how to live, at the end of his novel: 'I go to encounter [...] the reality of experience and to forge in the smithy of my soul the uncreated conscience of my race.' (P V, 2788-90) It would mean reaching a world view and an understanding unfettered by religion and the precepts and threats of the Church, yet

---

17 The device was one of considerable originality in literature at the onset of the twentieth century, even though, through parallel developments, it was to become an important element, generally, in the formalist ethos of European modernism in literature, music and pictorial art; in the case of James Joyce, it was also modelled on the typological patterning of exegesis and thought he had found in medieval theology.

still tied into the text of an encompassing myth. But, for all its wholeness, where the text structuring the human condition and its perception is fatefully grounded, as is the Daedalian myth, its implications would be tragic. Arguably, *A Portrait of the Artist as a Young Man* brings Joyce as close as he ever gets to the tragic mode.

James Joyce's remark, made in a conversation in later years, has often been quoted—that as he was writing *A Portrait*, he increasingly felt that the myth of Daedalus needed to be followed by the myth of Odysseus.[18] He was never apparently asked, nor did he explain, just what he meant by that remark, yet it fits perfectly into the present argument. In compass, the myth of Odysseus surpasses the myth of Daedalus. From the private and individualised applicability of the myth of Daedalus to the artist, Joyce progressed to the universal applicability of the myth of Odysseus—Odysseus being, in Joyce's declared opinion, the most complete man: son, father, husband, citizen; and he added, significantly: in all this, Odysseus outscores Jesus Christ. This rendered the *Odyssey* both anterior and superior to any possible intertext from the Christian tradition,[19] and so, in terms of the Joycean enterprise, the line of foil narratives from antiquity led consistently back from Macrobius's *Saturnalia* via Apuleius's *Metamorphoses* to Homer's *Odyssey*. But now Joyce also decisively adjusted his strategies. With *Ulysses*, he abandoned his earlier hermetic silence. From the invention of the title, before the book was actually begun,[20] to the later devising of schemata to 'explain' *Ulysses* to its first readers, Joyce no longer concealed that he had chosen the *Odyssey* as a foil for his novel. With the widening compass of the *Odyssey*, moreover, and with Odysseus/Leopold Bloom as the universal man, Joyce also changed his note to comic.[21] He generated *Ulysses* from,

---

18 Joseph Prescott, 'Conversations with James Joyce [by] Georges Borach', *College English*, 15 (1954), 325-27.
19 Though when it comes to Stephen Dedalus in *Ulysses*, Joyce does not spurn the younger tradition; but it is characteristic also that *Hamlet* is a key reference text for Stephen (who knows, moreover, that he is Hamlet), yet not for Bloom.
20 The title considerably predated the work we know under the name: 'Ulysses' was originally the title for a story projected but never written for *Dubliners*.
21 What is also important to note is that, as Kevin Barry emphasises, the occasional writings from James Joyce the journalist and public speaker during his Triestine years, 'are a part of a process by which Joyce transforms himself between 1907 and 1914 into a comic writer. [...] Thereafter he writes in that mode which his aesthetics since 1903 had recommended as the higher mode of art: the comic.' James Joyce, *Occasional, Critical, and Political Writing*, ed. by Kevin Barry (Oxford

and inscribed it within, the tradition of the great European comic narrative of Rabelais, Swift or Sterne.

* * *

In the summer of 1905, *Stephen Hero* had been put on hold. *Dubliners* was ready to leave Joyce's hands in 1906, and would have been published as a collection of fourteen stories, with 'Grace' as its conclusion. But the vicissitudes that persisted until 1914 began to make themselves felt. With Grant Richards of London having withdrawn from the publication, and prospects of finding another publisher highly uncertain, Joyce wrote 'The Dead' in 1906–07; it became the collection's fifteenth story, and its capstone. Integral to the collection as it is, 'The Dead' is at the same time so singular that it might equally claim to stand on its own within the oeuvre. It is commonly understood, moreover, that it was writing 'The Dead' that opened up the impasse that the Stephen Daedalus narrative had reached in 1905. With 'The Dead', as we have noted, Joyce significantly developed strategies of narrating his fictions against the foil of intertexts, or in other words, to tell his stories as tales retold. In taking up his novel again, Joyce radically reconceptualised it. No longer did he tell it of himself in the guise of Stephen Daedalus, that is, in a mode of veiled autobiographic mimeticism. Instead, he projected his narrative of Stephen Daedalus onto the myth of Daedalus, and to this end he made the central character—whom he now calls Stephen Dedalus—in turn project his consciousness onto the mythical Daedalus and Icarus (even though only partially so, as we have seen); as well as onto several other figures besides.

But abandoning the straight (auto-)biographical tale required inventing a new narrative structure. How was the novel to be shaped, and the Stephen Dedalus story matter to be rearranged and fitted to the mould of the myth? In structural terms, relating a story and relating a myth are different processes: a story, and particularly a biography, progresses in time, whereas a myth is essentially timeless; its relation

---

World's Classics) (Oxford: Oxford University Press, 2000); 'Introduction', p. xxii.— See also my essay 'James Joyce *Interpreneur*', https://books.openbookpublishers. com/10.11647/obp.0120/ch3.html#_idTextAnchor011; initially at: *Genetic Joyce Studies*, Issue 4 (Spring 2004) http://www.geneticjoycestudies.org/articles/GJS4/ GJS4_Gabler.

consequently does not depend on (though it may resort to) a temporal organisation of the narrative. Here lay a formidable challenge, and Joyce embraced it. A *Portrait of the Artist as a Young Man*, as we know, works polyphonically on the levels both of biographical story and significative myth. Yet it took Joyce close to seven years to accomplish such a composition, from 8 September 1907 to late 1913, or even into the year 1914 when, from his thirty-second birthday on 2 February onwards, *A Portrait of the Artist as a Young Man* began to appear in instalments in the London literary magazine *The Egoist*.

Through those years, Joyce was living in Trieste with his young family, and teaching English at the Berlitz school, and as a private tutor. He also lectured occasionally at an institution for adult education, and periodically contributed articles on Irish themes to the Trieste newspaper *Il Piccolo della Sera*. He led an intense social life and, among other activities, organised a group of investors to finance a cinema in Dublin (the Volta theatre, which failed). He fought heroically to see *Dubliners* published, which (together with the Volta project) involved trips to Dublin in 1909 and 1912 (his only returns to Ireland in his lifetime). In his efforts on behalf of *Dubliners*, he met with setback after setback. While in Dublin in 1909, he also suffered—while equally contributing to the invention of—an injury to his sense of his intimate relationship with Nora. Falling for slanderous allegations from false friends, he imagined that Nora had betrayed him with a mutual friend back in 1904 when they were first courting. The imaginary situation, and the real anguish and jealousy it caused, were to become source texts to be retold fictionally both in the play *Exiles*, and in *Ulysses*.

Yet while such facts and circumstances of Joyce's life are well known, and we assume their close connection with his writing, we actually know very little about the effect that his daily life, its calms and turbulences, had on Joyce's progress with *A Portrait*. What evidence there is suggests that he had drafted three chapters, though probably without an end to the third, by 7 April 1908, and that he worked a beginning for the fourth in the further course of that year, but then got stuck. Early in 1909, he talked to one of his private pupils about their mutual aspiration to authorship, and Joyce gave him the three-and-a-half-chapters to read. The pupil was Ettore Schmitz, better known in early European modernist literature by his pen name, Italo Svevo. Schmitz, in a letter of

8 February 1909, made some shrewd criticisms. His response appears to have encouraged Joyce to continue writing, completing the fourth chapter, and commencing the fifth.

But then the second major crisis in the book's development occurred, comparable most closely to the phase of doubt and searching that befell Joyce upon self-scrutiny of the first seven chapters drafted for *Stephen Hero*. His self-doubt then—intensified, we may presume, through his mother's death—found release in the narrative essay 'A Portrait of the Artist' of 1904. It was Joyce's first blueprint for *A Portrait of the Artist as a Young Man*, the novel he eventually commenced in 1907. It stalled in turn after two years, yet this impasse similarly resolved itself into new openings. The crisis hit when *A Portrait* had materialised to the length of a draft of four chapters, and the opening of the fifth; and it culminated in the legendary incident of the burning of the manuscript. It was some time in 1911 that Joyce apparently fell into despair over his novel, and over the circumstances under which he was constrained to write it. The despair was honest enough, no doubt, though, at the same time, self-dramatisingly heightened. Joyce threw the manuscript in the stove (in the kitchen or in the living-room, in those days before central heating). But the fire brigade of the women in the family was at hand (as Joyce had shrewdly calculated, we may surmise) to pull the chapter bundles back out of the flames at once; we have, from burns, received not a blot in his papers.[22] Nora and Eileen wrapped the precious draft in an old

---

22 Meaning not a blot in the loose-leaf lots for chapters four and five that survive from that *auto-da-fé*. How chapters one, two and three looked, once out of the flames, we do not know. They were subsequently revised and recopied. An account of the incident was given by Joyce himself in a letter accompanying the gift of the final fair-copy manuscript of *A Portrait* to Harriet Weaver in 1920 (see *Letters of James Joyce*, ed. by Stuart Gilbert, vol. I (New York: Viking Press, 1957, ²1966) (*Letters* I), p. 136) Since that manuscript is extant and is now housed, as Harriet Weaver's gift, at the National Library of Ireland, it has also been possible to deduce from it, together with the manuscript fragment of *Stephen Hero* in the possession of the Houghton Library at Harvard, what Joyce himself does not reveal, nor any eyewitness has recorded, about the 1911 crisis in the writing of *A Portrait of the Artist as a Young Man*. My own previous in-depth investigations of the genesis of *A Portrait of the Artist as a Young Man* have been 'The Seven Lost Years of *A Portrait of the Artist as a Young Man*', in *Approaches to Joyce's Portrait*, ed. by Bernard Benstock and Thomas F. Staley (Pittsburgh: University of Pittsburgh Press, 1976), pp. 25-60, and 'The Christmas Dinner Scene, Parnell's Death, and the Genesis of *A Portrait of the Artist as a Young Man*', *James Joyce Quarterly*, 13 (1976), 27-38; these two essays were republished together, with minor revisions, as 'The Genesis of *A Portrait of the Artist as a Young*

sheet, where Joyce let it rest for several months before mustering the courage to resume the novel.

Joyce was not one lightly to discard anything once written. Though as a novel, and in terms of its overall conception and structure, *A Portrait of the Artist as a Young Man* was an entirely fresh work, it nonetheless reprocessed characters and numerous incidents from *Stephen Hero*, and drew a great deal on its language.[23] How Joyce turned the earlier text into a quarry for the later one can be studied from the surviving *Stephen Hero* fragment. Spanning chapters 15 to 25, on 401 leaves from the *Stephen Hero* manuscript that extended to approximately 914 leaves as a whole, it corresponds to the fifth chapter of *A Portrait*. In its pages, a large number of expressions and phrases are tagged as composition notes, or for direct reuse. Two interlined notes, moreover, are phrased 'End of First Episode of V' and 'End of Second Episode of V'. What they indicate is Joyce's new ground plan for the novel, abandoning the division of *Stephen Hero* into short chapters, and constructing the long *A Portrait* chapters, five in all, as sub-divided into 'episodes'. It is likely that over the years from 1907 to 1911, chapters one to four of *A Portrait* were throughout composed in this manner. This cannot be positively demonstrated. The fourteen chapters of *Stephen Hero* corresponding to chapters one to four of *A Portrait* would have shown how the new novel was rewritten from its forebear. But their section of the *Stephen Hero* manuscript is lost. Yet the effects of the rewriting process are discernible. In its final form, it is chapter two of *A Portrait* that still shows most clearly the kind of progression by episodic sub-division that would have resulted, had chapter five been designed according to the pattern implied in the markings for 'Episode [...] IV' and 'Episode [...] V' in the extant *Stephen Hero* manuscript fragment.

As finally shaped, however, the chapter five of *A Portrait* was composed in four sections, or movements, and their structure was not biographic, but thematic. The chapter takes Stephen through encounters

---

Man', in *Critical Essays on James Joyce's A Portrait of the Artist as a Young Man*, ed. by Philip Brady and James F. Carens (New York: G. K. Hall, 1998), pp. 83-112. It is this version of 1998 that is included in the present collection.

23 The most thorough analysis of the *Stephen Hero* manuscript in itself, and in its relationship to *A Portrait of the Artist as a Young Man*, is Claus Melchior, '*Stephen Hero*. Textentstehung und Text. Eine Untersuchung der Kompositions- und Arbeitsweise des frühen James Joyce', PhD dissertation, München (Bamberg, 1988).

with the dean of studies, fellow students and friends, debating, one after another, the subjects that trouble and concern him and are in one way or another relevant to the decisions he is about to reach concerning his own future. These encounters occupy the chapter's first and third movements. Dominant among the themes of the first movement is Stephen's aesthetic theorizing; the third movement gravitates towards his rejection of home, country and religion, and his decision to fly—though, unlike Daedalus, he does not fly back home, but into exile. These first and third movements frame the second that, in a manner, gives us 'a portrait of the artist as a young man': it describes Stephen waking up one morning and composing a poem. The fifth chapter's fourth movement, which concludes the book, is written in the form of excerpts from Stephen Dedalus's diary. It is a coda to the chapter. At the same time, taken as a part of the book as a whole, we recognise it as the novel's closing frame, corresponding to the brief initial movement of chapter one where Stephen's father tells the story of the moocow, and Stephen himself speaks the magic spell (in the mode of oral poetry) to ward off the threat of eagles coming to pull out his eyes. This is the book's opening frame: the whole novel is actually held between this prelude and the coda. Looking more closely at the narrative, we discover that chapter one is the mirror image of chapter five. After the early-childhood prelude, three movements follow, of which the second and fourth treat of Stephen's sufferings and triumphs at Clongowes; these again frame a contrasting scene, that of the Dedalus family's Christmas dinner.

How this mirroring was devised can be inferred from relating the physical features of the *A Portrait* fair-copy manuscript to Italo Svevo's 1909 letter to James Joyce. As explained above, only the pages of chapter four and the opening of chapter five in the extant fair-copy manuscript physically formed part, originally, of the manuscript thrown in the fire and rescued in 1911. This means that chapters one to three as contained in the fair copy were entirely recopied, and thus doubtless thoroughly revised, after the burning incident. We cannot therefore know exactly what it was that Italo Svevo read. Yet it is unlikely to have been what we now have as the beginning of *A Portrait of the Artist Young Man*. Svevo declared the novel's opening to be 'devoid of importance and your rigid method of observation and description does not allow you to enrich a fact which is not rich by itself. You should write only about strong things' (*Letters* II, p. 227). This would scarcely be a fair assessment of the chapter in its final state. Beside the poetic richness of the page and a half of the prelude of early childhood, an outstanding element giving the chapter strength is its third movement, the Christmas dinner scene. But this did not form part of the opening chapter that Svevo read. The Christmas dinner scene was moved from Chapter 2 to chapter 1. Viewed thematically, Chapters 1 and 2 now led inexorably into the darkness of Dublin and, in terms of Stephen's Christian education, of sin. Correspondingly, chapter four reversed that movement, since it led Stephen out of the prison of a life-long commitment to the Church, and into a Daedalian flight towards art. That was how the whole novel became pivoted symmetrically on the third chapter, with its hell sermons as the chapter's and the book's dead centre.

The compositional achievement was momentous. By superimposing a spatial, and hence an atemporal, structure on a sequential and chronological one, the novel resolved the contradiction between telling a story and telling a myth. This also decisively raised the significance of the story matter. While Stephen Dedalus's early years, as they unrolled from childhood to university, provided merely a personal and individual series of events and emotions ('devoid of importance', as Italo Svevo saw it), the mid-centred mirroring pattern, into which the relating of that life was organised, proved capable of generalising the story and lending it a mythic quality and a universal appeal. In addition, the temporal arrest that the framing symmetries effected created the illusion of a portrait, as it were, painted and rhythmicised in language. This fulfilled a central tenet of the 1904 blueprint in the essay 'A Portrait of the Artist': 'to liberate from the personalised lumps of matter that which is their individuating rhythm, the first or formal relation of their parts';[24] and one might add that Joyce was thus himself already endeavouring to fuse the modes in Gotthold Ephraim Lessing's distinction of the spatial *Nebeneinander* of pictorial art and the temporal *Nacheinander* in the arts of literature and music that he later made Stephen Dedalus reflect upon in the opening paragraph of the Proteus episode of *Ulysses*.

* * *

---

24   Joyce, *Poems and Shorter Writings*, p. 211.

In converting chapters fifteen to twenty-five of *Stephen Hero*—its 'University episode', as he himself referred to it—into chapter five of *A Portrait of the Artist as a Young Man*, Joyce found a new shape for the chapter and, in consequence, realised the mid-centred, chiastic structure for the entire novel that we have described.[25] His search for a solution to the chapter's and the novel's structural problems took him through an intense trial period, to be dated probably to 1912, after the 1911 burning incident. In its new form, as we have seen, the chapter leads Stephen into exile not through a sequence of disjunct narrative episodes, but through a rapid series of encounters with other figures whose conversations progressively define for him who he is and what he wants, in a process that is ostensibly dramatic and naturalistic, while at another level it is one of inner clarification and self-definition. To find an analogy and possible model for this structure we might profitably turn from literature to another art form, that of opera. It was *Die Meistersinger von Nürnberg* that Joyce, in his mostly pro-Wagnerian moments (though apparently he also had anti-Wagnerian ones), declared his favourite Wagner opera. In the third act of *Die Meistersinger*, Hans Sachs, the protagonist, moves through conversations that similarly induce a series of self-recognitions: with David, his apprentice; with Walther Stolzing, the young aristocrat who, to win Eva Pogner, wins Sachs to help him renew the masters' art of poetry; with Beckmesser, in every way the antagonist and blocking character in the comedy; and with Eva, whom Sachs, the aging widower, renounces in favour of Walther, whom she loves. The pivot of this sequence, framed between David's exit and Beckmesser's entry, is the composition, the working-out and drafting, of Stolzing's 'Preislied'. It emerges, one stanza after another, and flowers as a specimen of the new art from the seedbed (as it were) of the old—not altogether unlike the way that the 'Villanelle' emerges, stanza upon stanza, from the memories and emotions in the self-recognition of Stephen Dedalus. For both Stolzing and Stephen, too, their poems flow from the inspiration of an early morning dream. The 'Villanelle' movement in *A Portrait* culminates in a full-text rendering of the new poem. The third act of *Meistersinger*, having plummeted once more to the prosaic ground of

---

25 Baroque altar-pieces are typically organised thus on a central axis of symmetry, as well as baroque musical compositions, such as Johann Sebastian Bach's motet 'Jesu meine Freude', BWV 227.

Hans Sachs's exchange with Beckmesser, takes wing afresh and rises from level to level of ecstasy, in its turn not unlike the 'Villanelle' movement in *A Portrait*, and soars finally to the height of the celebrated quintet, epitome of the new art in music of Richard Wagner himself. For whatever circumstantial evidence is worth: it may well be relevant that, in 1909 in Trieste, Joyce arranged a live performance of precisely that quintet from the third act, with—may we assume?—himself, superior tenor, in the part of Walther Stolzing, the artist as a young aristocrat.[26]

Joyce also, apparently, carried out experiments on chapter five of *A Portrait* that he eventually abandoned, or suspended. While still composing the chapter in episodes, he drafted part of a kitchen scene between Stephen and his mother, which has been preserved. This is an attempt at recasting a similar scene from *Stephen Hero* and shows, by implication, that the decision to eliminate Stephen's mother from the chapter was taken at a late stage. More significant, perhaps, for the fields of creative force in which the experiments with chapter five are situated is the reference, in the fragment, to a character named Doherty. This is a fictionalised Gogarty, and thus a prototype of Buck Mulligan known from the opening of *Ulysses*. Seven years earlier, we may remember, the Dublin friends of the Joyce brothers who were allowed to read the 'University episode' chapters of *Stephen Hero* were eagerly awaiting the writing-up of the Martello Tower incidents. In view of the reference to Doherty in the kitchen scene fragment, it is tempting to assume that Joyce, at the time when he drafted and fair-copied the fragment, still considered narrating those incidents and actually contemplated a Martello Tower ending for *A Portrait of the Artist as a Young Man*. Reconceiving chapter five in its four-movement shape, and ending with

---

26 For the Wagner and *Meistersinger* connections, see Timothy Martin, *Joyce and Wagner. A Study of Influence* (Cambridge: Cambridge University Press, 1991), p. 230, note 76 *et passim*. If my speculation holds water, *Die Meistersinger* thus makes more than a 'cameo appearance' (cf. p. 230, note 80) in Joyce's work. The link between the opera and the novel, once perceived, is suggestively reinforced through the distinct verbal and situational echoes. As Dieter Fuchs has pointed out to me in a private communication, Hans Sachs urges Walther Stolzing to put into a formal poem 'what [he] has versified, what [he] has dreamt' ('Was Ihr gedichtet, was Ihr geträumt'). What the text of *A Portrait* knows about Stephen Dedalus is that 'In a dream or vision he had known the ecstasy of seraphic life' (*P* V, 1535), and it is from this that he begins to compose his Villanelle, emulating the old masters of poetry and the intricate rules of their art.

Stephen's departure into exile, therefore also entailed holding over for later use the unachieved writing that had accumulated around Stephen. Among that material was the Martello Tower matter. It was ultimately moulded into the beginning of *Ulysses*.

Nor is this the only indication that the paths not taken for *A Portrait* became roads to, and inroads into, *Ulysses*. Within the four-movement structure of chapter five of *A Portrait*, as Joyce reconceptualised it after he abandoned the episodic form, one may also find structural pointers to a time scheme which, although not realised, is nonetheless of great interest. Stephen Dedalus, we note, leaves the family house and kitchen at the beginning of the chapter and at the end goes into exile. If we take it that the verbal skirmishes he goes through in the chapter's first movement are strung out over the course of a morning, he would arrive on the steps of the National Library around midday. The time then feels like mid-afternoon when he leaves again from those steps to resume his debates and his wanderings, and he finally parts from Cranly in the evening. It is with this parting, of course, that his exile symbolically begins. If the string of encounters through which Stephen talks himself free of Dublin were continued without interruption over the midday hours, so as to link the morning and the afternoon sequences, the outward movement from the family kitchen and into exile would be accomplished in one sweep in a single day. This would create a neat pattern enveloping *A Portrait*: the first year in chapter one, Stephen's first and only school year at Clongowes, would be balanced against his last day at university in chapter five, the day he takes flight from Dublin into exile.

The single-day plan for the last chapter, of which the submerged outline can thus be discerned, was not realised. But it, too, was put to use in the book that followed: *Ulysses* was constructed upon it.[27] The existence of the scheme, if transitory, is not simply a matter of speculation. *A Portrait* provides the topography for it, and *Ulysses* holds a clue to how it would have been filled out. Since the first movement of the fifth episode in *A Portrait* ends on the steps of the National Library with Stephen going in, and the third begins on the same steps as he

---

27 It would also become seminal in the wider modernist context: Virginia Woolf, for instance, adopted it for *Mrs Dalloway*, her novel begun in 1923 and published in 1925.

comes out, the library itself would be the logical setting for Stephen to continue talking. And it is precisely the place where he does talk, holding his audience and the reader captive, in the Scylla & Charybdis episode of *Ulysses*. That chapter was eventually placed half-way through *Ulysses* (half-way, that is, by count of the novel's eighteen episodes): it was completed in roughly the shape in which we have it on New Year's Eve, 1918. But during the first years of his thinking about *Ulysses*, Joyce mentioned in correspondence that he already had four Stephen Dedalus episodes to go into the new book—meaning, we can assume, the three opening episodes (Telemachus, Nestor, Proteus), plus Scylla & Charybdis. Moreover, as early as 1916, before even a single episode for *Ulysses* had attained any shape we might be able to trace, he told Ezra Pound that he could let him have a 'Hamlet' episode as an initial sample. It stands to reason that this episode—an early version of Scylla & Charybdis—belonged, with the Martello Tower opening, to materials from the *A Portrait* workshop that were reworked into *Ulysses*.

* * *

We have considered the intertextual depths of *A Portrait of the Artist as a Young Man* and noted the novel's double construction through its counterpointing of (auto-)biography and myth. But *A Portrait* also has a further structural dimension, which might be defined as its epicyclical movement. In an early adumbration of Vico's *ricorso* structure, on which *Finnegans Wake* would later be built, each *A Portrait* chapter culminates in a moment of heightened awareness and triumph for Stephen Dedalus, followed by a shattering of illusions in the following chapter.[28] Thus, at the end of chapter one, Stephen gains justice from the rector of Clongowes but then discovers in chapter two that Father Dolan and Simon Dedalus had enjoyed a good laugh at his expense. At the end of chapter two, he experiences sensual fulfilment with the prostitute girl but falls into remorse and anguish in chapter three. At the end of chapter three, 'the ciborium [...] [comes] to him', but the beginning of chapter four finds him dedicated to amending his life through tortuous

---

28 'Each chapter closes with a synthesis of triumph which the next destroys.' Thus, inimitably succinct, Hugh Kenner in *Dublin's Joyce*, p. 129. *See also* Sidney Feshbach, 'A Slow and Dark Birth: A Study of the Organization of *A Portrait of the Artist as a Young Man*', *James Joyce Quarterly*, 4 (1967), 289-300.

religious exercises. At the end of chapter four, the vision of the bird-girl symbolises his aspirations to art, but the elation it gives is thoroughly undercut by the squalor of the family kitchen at the opening of chapter five. Only Stephen's sense of soaring into exile at the novel's conclusion seemingly endures—except that the Stephen Dedalus of *Ulysses* coldly strips it of all romantic idealism: 'You flew. Whereto? Newhaven-Dieppe, steerage passenger. Seabedabbled, fallen, weltering. Lapwing you are. Lapwing be.' (*U* 9, 952-54)

In terms of their materials and construction, the epicycles of *A Portrait of the Artist as a Young Man* depend upon the Joycean epiphany. The term acquired several distinct, though related senses as Joyce invented it, reflected upon it, and put it to productive as well as significant use over a period from the earliest beginnings of his writing until his immersion in the world of the realities and styles of *Ulysses*. The epiphany thus constitutes a seminal form of expression of Joyce's art and a fundamental strategy of his craftsmanship.

In *Stephen Hero*, it is Stephen Daedalus who is made to invent the term and circumscribe the notion: 'By an epiphany he meant a sudden spiritual manifestation, whether in the vulgarity of speech or of gesture or in a memorable phase of the mind itself. He believed that it was for the man of letters to record these epiphanies with extreme care, seeing that they themselves are the most delicate and evanescent of moments.' To Cranly, he defines it in terms of aesthetics and epistemology:

> First we recognise that the object is *one* integral thing, then we recognise that it is an organised composite structure, a *thing* in fact: finally, when the relation of the parts is exquisite, when the parts are adjusted to the special point, we recognise that it is *that* thing which it is. Its soul, its whatness, leaps to us from the vestment of its appearance. The soul of the commonest object, the structure of which is so adjusted, seems to us radiant. The object achieves its epiphany.[29]

This definition covers perfectly the brief individual compositions—terse dramatic dialogues, sensitively rhetorical prose pieces and poetically heightened dream protocols—that James Joyce himself was wont to put to paper, even well before attempting to write narrative. His epiphanies were stirring pieces, and were inspired in the first place by the power of actual situations and overheard speech to move the intellect and

---

29 Joyce, *Stephen Hero*, pp. 216; 218.

emotions. Wrought in language, epiphanies recorded had the potential, furthermore, to induce a sudden insight into the essence of things, whether in the observer or the reader. Joyce thus came to conceive of the epiphany in terms of the medium of his art, and in terms both of the production and the reception of his writing. This double focus allowed the Joycean epiphany to develop from a brief and isolated individual composition and to become integrated into continuous flows of narrative. There it was used both to heighten given situations in the experience of the characters, and also to illuminate and structure moments of significance for the reader. In the development of Joyce's art, the narrative form thus came to absorb the epiphany. Notably, in consequence, the Stephen Dedalus of *A Portrait of the Artist as a Young Man* is made to reflect Joyce's changed perspective. Although he still implies the epiphanic concept in the aesthetics he develops to Lynch (cf. *P* V, 1082-469), he does not use the term 'epiphany'. The Stephen Dedalus of *Ulysses*, finally, no longer even seems to know his earlier namesake's aesthetic theory; instead, and with sarcastic self-irony, he remembers indulging in the practice of the epiphany: 'Remember your epiphanies written on green oval leaves, deeply deep, copies to be sent if you died to all the great libraries of the world, including Alexandria?' (*U* 3, 141-44)

As part of his workshop economy, Joyce evidently took a sober and practical view of his epiphanies. His surviving papers show that, in order to reuse them, he strung them together to provide a working grid for an extended narrative. A sheaf of epiphanies, each one fair-copied in his own hand, is numbered consecutively (though with many gaps in the sequence) on their otherwise blank versos.[30] This numbering does not seem to indicate the sequence in which the pieces were written, but appears intended for future use. Joyce's extant longer texts, *Stephen Hero*, *A Portrait of the Artist as a Young Man* and even particular passages in *Ulysses*, bear out this assumption.[31]

---

30 The surviving twenty-two epiphanies of the numbered sequence in Joyce's own hand are reproduced in photo-offprint in *The James Joyce Archive*, vol. 7, pp. 1-44; the text of the extant total of forty epiphanies (of which eighteen have been preserved only because Stanislaus Joyce copied them) are reprinted in Joyce, *Poems and Shorter Writings*, pp. 161-200.

31 I take a closer look, specifically at the integrative role of the epiphany in Joyce's early writing, in '"He chronicled with patience": Early Joycean Progressions

The step from the redeployment of existing epiphanies to the intensifying of the narrative to epiphanic heights was then perhaps not so difficult. But it was momentous. The epicyclical structure of *A Portrait* depends on an art of writing capable not only of imaginatively concentrating each chapter ending to produce the epiphanic effect, but also to express it as the experience of Stephen Dedalus. In this way, Joyce used epiphanic imaging to release the energies of language to induce insight, and equally to create the consciousness of his characters. The epiphanies were also aimed at the reader. In the case of *A Portrait*, the counter-epiphanies (as one might call them) at the beginning of each new chapter, employed to undercut each preceding end-of-chapter epiphany, fail to strike Stephen as moments of illumination. Although he registers them on a level of facts, they do not mean much to him, intellectually, or even, at a deeper level, emotionally. The disillusion they convey (the 'soul of the commonest object') is directed towards the reader, adjusting our empathy or our sense of distance. Most succinctly, perhaps, this is how the transition from chapter four to chapter five works. For Stephen, the bleak poverty of his home does not cancel out the bird-girl experience on Sandymount strand. He is not fazed by the stark realities that the reader is intended to perceive, and thus walks buoyantly straight out through the end of the novel, and into exile. It is only later that the Stephen Dedalus of *Ulysses* will see himself and the contingencies of his life with a sober sense of the real. Elevation and idealisation will no longer do. The epiphany, as a method of shaping the fiction and conveying the consciousness of its characters, has served its turn.

Nonetheless, Joyce did not relinquish the ingrained epiphanic habit of writing. Instead, he continued to prefabricate carefully phrased and narratively focused prose pieces that might, or would, eventually be fitted into larger compositional sequences. The most familiar example of this practice is the collection of segments of well-wrought prose known as *Giacomo Joyce*.[32] This is most likely to have been written and

---

between Non-Fiction and Fiction' (2018), https://www.openbookpublishers.com/htmlreader/978-1-78374-363-6/ch2.xhtml#_idTextAnchor006

32 The title for the collection derives from the name 'Giacomo Joyce' inscribed in a child's hand—eight-year-old Giorgio's, perhaps, or even six-year-old Lucia's?—on the inside cover of the notebook containing the segments fair-copied (around 1913) in James Joyce's own most calligraphic script.

compiled—perhaps while Joyce was working on *Exiles*—during a transitional period when the bulk of *A Portrait* had been completed, but the full-scale work on *Ulysses* had not yet begun. It reflects a fundamental habit of composition. The experimental exercises of 'Giacomo Joyce' are comparable, with hindsight, to the first-generation epiphanies of 1902–04, written between the poetry of his youth and his first attempt at longer narrative composition with the Stephen Daedalus/Dedalus novel. Looking forward to the interval between *Ulysses* and 'Work in Progress' (*Finnegans Wake*), we can see the same process at work in the longer and experimentally more variegated narratives of around 1923, which Joyce himself, in passing, thought should be collected under the title of 'Finn's Hotel'.

But what is arguably Joyce's most eloquent collection of purple passages has only recently been rediscovered. Just around the corner from Finn's Hotel— the real one in Leinster Street, Dublin, where Nora Barnacle was employed, and where the old name is still faintly visible in black on the red brick wall that faces west towards the grounds of Trinity College—just around the corner from the real Finn's Hotel, then, the National Library of Ireland now houses a newly acquired cache of *Ulysses* drafts. Among these is an early notebook assembly of segments of text, recognisably written in preparation for the third episode, Proteus. The seventeen passages, regularly separated by triple asterisks, bear witness beautifully to Joyce's persistent epiphanic mode of writing. Perfected, no doubt, from lost earlier drafts, these texts are carefully penned in a fair hand, though with a liberal sprinkling of revisions. Several groupings are discernible in the assembly, which does not as a whole, however, form a consistent narrative.[33] The Dublin notebook may be fruitfully compared with a manuscript subsequent to, though doubtless not contiguous with it that has long been known. This is the Proteus draft, assigned the signature V.A.3 in the Joyce collection at the University at Buffalo. Not only have the passages from the Dublin notebook been

---

33 The text of the Dublin notebook segments is available at http://catalogue.nli.ie/Record/vtls000357771/HierarchyTree#page/2/mode/1up. It is possible, however, to give an indication of their compass and sequence of assembly. The following is an index by line numbers of passages in the final text of the chapter to which they correspond: [1] (271-81); [2] (286-89); [3] (332-64); [4] (106-24); [5] (47-52); [6] (370-384); [7] (70-103); [8] (216-57); [9] (29-44); [10] (461-69); [11] (303-09); [12] (470-84); [13] (393; 488); [14] (393-98); [15] (312-30); [16] (406-19); [17] (209-15).

fitted into this manuscript, with only minor adjustments to their text; but during intervening phases of work (of which no evidence survives), the episode has also been given a continuous narrative line. Between them, the Dublin notebook and the Buffalo manuscript strongly suggest that, writing Proteus, Joyce found it easier to articulate sequences of thought for Stephen, and to devise particular situations on Sandymount strand, than to construct a narrative that would support them.[34] It is all the more fascinating, then, to be able to observe just how the structuring of this episode was eventually accomplished.

The progress towards Proteus from the Dublin notebook segments to the consecutive manuscript at Buffalo marks the moment when Joyce became fully aware that, in the process of writing, he could draw intertextually from his own earlier works just as much as from Bible stories, or the works of Macrobius, or Apuleius, or Homer, or Shakespeare. We have already noted that he quarried *Stephen Hero* for turns of phrase or narrative incidents to be used in *A Portrait*; and that, in *Stephen Hero*, as well as in *A Portrait*, he strung together epiphanies to generate narrative continuity. But what he was recycling there were largely raw materials, which he reworked into something new and different. *Stephen Hero* and *A Portrait* were not significantly linked through the probing of similarities and analogies in variation and contrast. On the contrary, *A Portrait* succeeds in thoroughly reworking the story of Stephen Dedalus precisely because its material is moulded to a structure radically different from that of *Stephen Hero*.

In the case of Proteus, however, Joyce's procedure was surprisingly different. The episode finds its form by invoking reminiscences of chapter five of *A Portrait*.[35] Each of these is itinerant. In chapter five of *A Portrait*, Stephen Dedalus, in what is essentially a single continuous movement, walks out of Dublin and into exile. In Proteus, returned from exile, he walks along Sandymount strand, his steps now firmly

---

34 Interestingly, the earliest surviving manuscript (Buffalo V.A.8) for Cyclops provides comparable evidence that the writing out of text passages—as sequences of dialogue in this case—preceded the overall structuring of the episode.

35 This is an idea I first put forward in 'Narrative Rereadings: some remarks on "Proteus", "Circe" and "Penelope"', in *James Joyce 1: 'Scribble' 1: genèse des textes*, ed. by Claude Jacquet (Paris: Lettres Modernes, 1988), pp. 57-68. With the material evidence of the Dublin notebook, it is now possible to make a much more incisive critical assessment of the compositional development of the Proteus chapter.

directed back towards Dublin. The significance of his purposeful, if protean, wandering through the episode is heightened by its contrast with *A Portrait*. Implicit within this contrast are Stephen's—and Joyce's—explorations of what Stephen's return to Dublin might mean. To this end, Joyce constructs Stephen's meandering consciousness upon or around his actual itinerary along Sandymount strand. In his reflections and memories, Stephen is much concerned, in the first half of the episode, with three subjects: family, religion, and exile. This triad of themes recalls his avowal from *A Portrait*: 'I will not serve that in which I no longer believe whether it call itself my home, my fatherland or my church' (*P* V, 2575-77), as well as 'the only arms of defence' he will allow himself to use: 'silence, exile and cunning' (2579). And we may also recall the rebellious impulse from which this sprang: 'When the soul of a man is born in this country there are nets flung at it to hold it back from flight. You talk to me of nationality, language, religion. I shall try to fly by those nets.' (1047-50)

Proteus proceeds, I suggest, through a consecutive narrative built on an analogous triad. Firstly, Stephen imagines a visit to aunt Sara's which he does not make; then, by way of recalling hours in Marsh's library, he reflects on the priestly routines of celebrating Mass; and thirdly, he embarks on memories of Paris, from where he has recently returned; memories that circle insistently around Patrice and Kevin Egan. These narrative exfoliations configure Stephen's new nets to fly by, and they are contrasted with the triad from *A Portrait* which they first recapitulate, but finally revise. By not making the visit to aunt Sara's, Stephen persists in evading the family net, just as by his sarcastic imagining of the priests at Mass he confirms his rejection of religion and the lure of priestly vows. Thus for a second time he successfully flies by two of the old nets, family and religion. But now, on returning to Dublin, he also realises that he has evaded a new net. Since *A Portrait*, he has experienced that the exile into which he fled from the snares laid for him in Ireland was in fact yet another net, cast out to entrap him. The narrative envisions the condition of exile, giving it significance through the figures of Patrice and Kevin Egan. They are Irish wild geese, banned from returning to their fatherland. Reflecting on their forlorn state—'They have forgotten Kevin Egan, not he them. Remembering thee, O Sion.' (*U* 3, 263-64)—Stephen recognises the threat to his being that his own yearning for exile had held.

Once Joyce had hit upon the idea of moving into the episode through this triad of themes evoked in Stephen's memories and reflections, the reorganising of the prose segments from the Dublin notebook must have followed with relative ease. Admittedly, there is no trace among these of the exposition of Stephen's epistemology with which Proteus now opens; but given Joyce's habits of composition, it is just as likely that this was written as the episode's capstone after he was sure of its overall structure. Otherwise the entire narrative body is already present in the shape of prefabricated building blocks. Linking together segments [9] (the two 'midwives'), [5] (the consubstantiality of Father and Son and the heresiarch in the watercloset), [7] (the imagined visit to uncle Richie and aunt Sara), [4] (Marsh's library and the priests at Mass), [17] ('Paris is waking rawly'),[36] and [8] (Kevin Egan) in a narrative flow brought the composition to the episode's midpoint.[37] The criss-cross movement [9]-[5]-[7]-[4]-[17]-[8] through the notebook confirms our assumption that the drafting of these segments predated the idea of how to stream them as a narrative.

With six of the notebook's seventeen entries used up in the first half of the episode, Joyce was then left with eleven segments from which to shape the second half. These, though again somewhat rearranged, are worked in largely as a sequence of immediate situations. For although the writing and the narrative remain complex because the entire episode is

---

36   This, in noticeably different ink, is the final entry in the notebook. As will be observed, it is a unit, reworked for *Ulysses*, from *Giacomo Joyce*: 'The lady goes apace, apace, apace [...]. Pure air on the upland road. Trieste is waking rawly: raw sunlight over its huddled browntiled roofs, testudoform; a multitude of prostrate bugs await a national deliverance. Belluomo rises from the bed of his wife's lover's wife: the busy housewife is astir, sloe-eyed, a saucer of acetic acid in her hand. [...] Pure air and silence on the upland road: and hoofs. A girl on horseback. Hedda! Hedda Gabler!' (James Joyce, *Giacomo Joyce*, ed. by Richard Ellmann (London: Faber & Faber, 1968), p. 8). See also my essay, 'Emergence of James Joyce's Dialogue Poetics' in the present volume, or in *Journal of Early Modern Studies*, 11 (2022), 229-52 (pp. 247-49).

37   The calculation is astonishingly accurate. In its final printed form, the episode runs to 505 lines; the Paris memories end with line 264. Subtracting from 505 lines the 28 lines of the chapter exposition leaves 477 lines, divisible into two halves of 238.5 lines. Letting the narrated chapter thus set in with the 'midwives' paragraph, we reach the proposed midpoint of the chapter after a stretch of 236 lines, leaving the second half-chapter no more than five lines longer.

being filtered through Stephen's consciousness, in the second half of the episode that consciousness simply takes the reader along Sandymount strand, registers what happens and what may be observed there, and draws in whatever past and present events the shore brings to mind as Stephen walks along it. He strides forth from the Martello Tower and towards Dublin, a pilgrim returning: 'My cockle hat and staff and hismy sandal shoon. Where? To evening lands.' (*U* 3, 487-88)

* * *

As we have noted, Joyce repeatedly held back his insistent urge to climax the 1903-to-1914 Stephen Daedalus/Dedalus novel project at the Martello Tower. He shaped the end of *A Portrait of the Artist as a Young Man* instead into a triumphant flight into exile. This permitted using the Martello Tower narrative freshly for *Ulysses*. In doing so, Joyce clandestinely (as it were) reversed the episode's vector. He opened the new novel not with Stephen Dedalus escaping into, but returning homeward from exile. The logic of the return as fresh departure is both stringent and significant. In any version of the earlier novel ending at the tower, it would have arrested Stephen on his flight inescapably still in Ireland. The new novel, by contrast, and to the echo in a Joyce reader's ear, perhaps, of 'O life! I go to encounter for the millionth time the reality of experience' (*P* V, 2788-89), brings him back from his Joyce-*alter-ego* exile reality in Paris. Plot-directed forward, he is now at the Tower in transit homewards to Dublin. Stephen is 'brought up' ('Come up, Kinch! Come up, you fearful jesuit!' [*U* 1, 08]) onto the tower platform within eyesight of 'the mailboat clearing the harbourmouth of Kingstown' (*U* 1, 83-84)—a boat maybe just arriving from France, refuge of the Irish wild geese captured there with no hope of a homeward return—the Egans, father and son, whom Stephen encountered in Paris, as we observed in the Proteus episode (*U* 3, 245-264).[38] The Martello Tower was once built to ward off the French threat. Stephen now feels it and its present inhabitants as a threat to himself. He casts off the nets of intimacy and

---

38 Stephen Dedalus, James Joyce's *alter ego* throughout, remembers in Scylla & Charybdis (*U* 9, 825-827) his return to Ireland, Kingstown pier, in answer to the telegraphic summons of his father: 'Nother dying. Come home. Father.' (*U* 3, 199) Kingstown harbour was also where Parnell's body was brought on 11 October 1891, a real event that Stephen dreams of in *Portrait* I, pp. 700-15.

cameraderie flung out by Mulligan and Haines and leaves the Tower. The home stretch to Dublin proves a rocky road still. To sustain him, he needs a job and so temporises at Deasy's school. As he leaves for the day – or for good? – Mr Deasy, the headmaster, waylays him: 'I just wanted to say ... Ireland, they say, has the honour of being the only country which never persecuted the jews. ... And do you know why? ...Because she never let them in.' While, to our anticipatory awareness, Bloom the Dublin Jew beckons from the horizon. Odysseus-Leopold Bloom will take over from Telemachus-Stephen Dedalus in episode four, and *Ulysses* will thus begin afresh in the midst of the city in Eccles street, within earshot of George's church, and with Leopold Bloom in dialogue with his cat preparing Molly Bloom's breakfast.

Yet before Bloom's entry, it is still Stephen Dedalus who traverses the Proteus chapter, third of the Telemachiad episodes. Now that he is a character in the upbeat to Joyce's new novel, he no longer identifies with Daedalus or Icarus, but with Hamlet.[39] By the end of the episode, he has adopted precisely the body pose and gesture with which Hamlet makes his final farewell to Ophelia: 'He turned his face over a shoulder, rere regardant.' (*U* 3, 503)[40] Patently, Stephen is unable to turn his eyes in the direction his feet are taking him. It is as if this was a fictionalised counterpart to Joyce's comment to Frank Budgen of about one year later that Stephen is 'a character that cannot be changed'. By contrast, Joyce himself is on the threshold of radical changes and is at this point palpably all eyes and pen for Leopold Bloom, whose fictional life and adventures are about to begin in the ensuing episode of *Ulysses*.[41]

The transition from episode three to episode four, though, with the novel's shift of protagonists from Stephen Dedalus to Leopold Bloom, was, as such, a revision of the earlier ground-plan by which the

---

39   Identifying with figures from myth, history, or literature—Daedalus/Icarus, Parnell, Hamlet—persists as a character trait of Stephen Dedalus, at the same time as he is quite oblivious of being Telemachus, in accordance with Joyce's new concept for *Ulysses*.

40   In a haunting scene brought vividly before our eyes in Shakespeare's play, even though Shakespeare does not stage it but has Ophelia describe it to her father. (William Shakespeare, *Hamlet*, II.i,87-100).

41   The time of writing is 1917; this is the year of the Buffalo Proteus draft V.A.3 and of the fair copy made of it. Its text will shortly, early in 1918, go directly into prepublication in the literary magazines *The Little Review*, New York, and *The Egoist*, London, and thence eventually into the novel's first edition, published in Paris in 1922.

Telemachiad extended to four chapters. There can be little doubt that Joyce prospectively considered, but then withdrew, allocating to the Telemachiad his second main Stephen-centred left-over from the *Portrait* workshop. This was his Hamlet chapter, grown no doubt out of his year or so of immersion in Shakespeare and Hamlet in 1912 and into 1913. Immediately upon re-working the saved-up end to *A Portrait of the Artist as a Young Man* into Telemachus, the opening episode for *Ulysses*, he composed in full a 'Hamlet chapter' and by 1916 offered it to Ezra Pound for publication in whole or in part as advance specimen of the new novel. (*Letters* I, 101) But once Nestor and Proteus were accomplished, the second and third chapters for the novel that were the first genuinely new episodes towards it, the rocks in the road to *Ulysses* had largely been cleared. Stephen Dedalus had served his first main turn in carrying the transition from *A Portrait of the Artist as a Young Man* to *Ulysses*. A fourth Stephen Dedalus episode at this juncture could be postponed. To stage Stephen finally as protagonist (and James Joyce *alter ego*) in *Ulysses*, and so (with Shakespearean support) to maximal narrative effect, could bide its time. First, Leopold Bloom now stood ready to take over with the novel's Odysseus narrative proper.

As he walks into Dublin, Stephen is also—though as later episodes will show, not irrevocably—striding out of Joyce's narrative. In leaving the Tower, the Dublin that Stephen walks towards is Bloom's domain— and that of James Joyce's sole authorship, freed of the Stephen Dedalus *alter ego* echo. '—Ten years [...] He is going to write something in ten years. [...] I shouldn't wonder if he did after all.' (*U* 10, 1090) And he did. Ten years after Joyce began to work on the Stephen Daedalus/Dedalus novel in 1903–04, *A Portrait of the Artist as a Young Man* started appearing in instalments in *The Egoist* in 1914—and on 2 February to boot, Joyce's thirty-second birthday. With his real-time hindsight, Joyce naturally had no difficulty in putting this prophecy into the mouths of Mulligan and Haines as in 1919 he wrote the tenth *Ulysses* episode, Wandering Rocks. But the writing and publication of *A Portrait* would not have meant much to them; instead, they would have been expecting to reappear, ten years ahead, in a fiction that included themselves. If only to gratify them, then, we should date the important material beginnings of *Ulysses* to around 1912. Joyce probably separated the Dedalus materials to go into *A Portrait* from those going into *Ulysses* during 1912-13. Ten years later—it falling out pretty much pat as Mulligan and Haines foresaw—the publication of *Ulysses* in 1922 revolutionised twentieth-century world literature. And the grid for Joyce 'to write something in ten years' permits yet further permutations. The time-span from 1903/04 to 1914, as said, takes us back to the onset and early development of Joyce's narrative writing, from *Stephen Hero* (begun in 1903) by way of 'A Portrait of the Artist', *Dubliners* and the rounding off of *A Portrait of the Artist as a Young Man* to at last seeing *Dubliners* published and *A Portrait* begun to be serialised. Interlaced into that ten-year span sets in the decade from 1907 to 1917, during which Joyce carried Stephen Dedalus through *A Portrait* and into the opening trio of the Telemachiad episodes of *Ulysses*—together even with a 1916 Hamlet chapter, lost, yet transitory to Scylla & Charybdis. With a one-year forward shift, still one further ten-year period may be delimited. *A Portrait* and its protagonist together were established 1907-1908 in a first-version text. It does not survive, since Italo Svevo's constructive comments in 1908 encouraged revising it. His intervention was to all appearances an important tributary to the evolution of Joyce's art through the ten years up to New Year's Eve 1918 when, in his fair-copy manuscript ending Scylla & Charybdis he declared the first half of *Ulysses* episodes done. The rocks in the road to *Ulysses* had been significant stepping stones throughout, and many a hurdle had had to be overcome. Its most persistent one was Stephen Dedalus. After close to twenty years, as Joyce ended the Proteus episode, and ultimately after the fanfares of Stephen's Hamlet performance of Scylla & Charybdis, he successfully laid by his *alter ego* symbiosis. This now freed him to cross his Daedalean ford of hurdles and engage with Leopold Bloom in the Odyssean adventures of *Ulysses*.

James Joyce's *Hamlet* Chapter

Chapter V in James Joyce's *A Portrait of the Artist as a Young Man* features a distinct discontinuity, a hiatus in the narrative unfolding of Stephen's departure from home in the morning and progress through Dublin to the day's, the chapter's, and the novel's end. To avoid running into his father, he slinks out of the family kitchen in the latish fore-noon, so that he arrives at University College in Newman House on Stephen's Green past 11AM. He has missed the English class wholly and is now also too late for French. With time to spare before physics at noon, he grasps opportunity by the forelock to teach the fire-lighting Dean of Studies the proper Anglo-English (or Lower Drumcondra) word 'tundish' for 'funnel'. After the 1PM end to the physics lecture, attended under *sotto-voce* buffoonery with fellow students, he converses at some length with Cranly, MacCann, Temple, MacAlister, and Davin, arguing over signing or not signing a resolution for universal peace, then engaging in a heated altercation over attitudes and opinions arising from their diverse personalities and values. Eventually Stephen walks on alone with Lynch, whom he exposes to his thoughts about proper versus improper and static versus kinetic art; about aesthetics, rhythm, and beauty; and about artistic apprehension—views, arguments, and bouts of theory largely inherited, while significantly modified, from *Stephen Hero*. Having refined, to his satisfaction, the artist God-like out of existence, Stephen arrives on the steps of the National Library going in ('Mind your hats goan in!' as *Finnegans Wake* admonishes, 8.9).[1] The time of day would be, let us say, going on for 3PM. Here follows the hiatus. Segmented off by Joyce's habitual triple asterisks, there ensues an early-morning scene of undetermined, non-determinable, date. Stephen wakes up from a wet dream and proceeds to compose line group upon line group

---

1 James Joyce, *Finnegans Wake* (London: Faber & Faber, 1939).

between phase after phase of emotionalised memory and reflection, a prosodically complex poem, by genre a villanelle. The finished poem is set out in full length on the final manuscript page of this segment of the narrative, followed again by the triple asterisks to mark the end of the hiatus—and there once more stands Stephen, now all alone, on the steps of the National Library going out. ('Mind your boots goan out', *FW* 10.22-3.) It is as if we were—or, indeed, we *are*—back on the fictional day on which Chapter V began. The time is specified as 'a late March evening' (though it is still light). Stephen passes on through Dublin in heady exchanges with Cranly until, through a curtain of final diary entries, he escapes into exile.

But what did Stephen do, what went on during those hours inside the National Library that we are never told, having been regaled with the artist as a young man's composition of a villanelle instead? Strictly speaking, according to certain orthodoxies of literary criticism, this is a question not to be asked. Yet under the control of genetic criticism, such enquiry is both allowed and fruitful. My contention is that what could have happened, by the author's experimental design, inside the National Library during two to three hours on the fictional day of Chapter V of *A Portrait of the Artist as a Young Man* was a performance ultimately achieved in *Ulysses*. As readers, we get it in real substance (as it were) in the 1PM to 2PM time-slot of another fictional day, the sixteenth of June 1904, in that novel's ninth episode, Scylla & Charybdis.

We know that the writing of *A Portrait of the Artist as a Young Man* hit its all-time low some time in 1911. Joyce threw the draft into the fire—though he made sure at the same time (apparently) that his life companion Nora, together with his sister Eileen, were near to save it from burning. As he told Harriet Weaver on 6 January 1920, the rescued pages were 'tied up in an old sheet where they remained for some months. I then sorted them out and pieced them together as best I could' (*Letters I*, 136).[2] So Joyce turned to the novel afresh, both to reshape what was written (which was already, substantially, Chapters I to IV) and to bring the whole to conclusion. In the manuscript with which he re-engaged, the novel's last chapter began with a torso of thirteen pages only. Chapter V remained, that is, essentially yet to be written. The

---

2   *Letters of James Joyce*, vol. I, ed. by Stuart Gilbert (New York: Viking Press, 1957, ^{2}1966) (*Letters* I).

source from whence the *Portrait* chapter was shaped still survives. This is the manuscript of what Joyce himself called the 'University episode' of *Stephen Hero*, the Chapters XV to XXVIII, which constitute the surviving fragment of that novel. At two points in this manuscript we find these working notes from the reshaping: 'End of First Episode of V', 'End of Second Episode of V'. They indicate that, in the reshaping, Joyce at first appears to have planned a serial sequence of narrative units for Chapter V, in progression somewhat akin, presumably, to *Portrait*'s dominantly episodic Chapter II. Chapter V as we have it, however, proceeds through what I have termed 'movements'. So structured, it is the mirror image of Chapter I.[3] Recognising this design and mirror correspondence between the last and the first chapter should prove relevant, at least collaterally, to an enquiry into what narrative content might have been considered to fill the hiatus in Chapter V between Stephen's arrival on, and his departure from, the steps of the National Library.

A couple of sketchings-out exist, presumably from the 1912-1913 phase of composition of *A Portrait*, that may have been intended for, but were never actually integrated into Chapter V as published. They survive among Harriet Weaver's papers in the British Library. A tower episode, though an apparent option, was in the event not used to conclude *A Portrait of the Artist as a Young Man*. Joyce designed instead a departure into exile for Stephen Dedalus and saved the Martello Tower episode to open *Ulysses*. The second example, at least as significant, of such a using-up of left-over *Portrait* writing, is Stephen Dedalus's Shakespeare performance in Scylla & Charybdis. So strongly has Irina Rasmussen argued in its favour in *Joyce Studies Annual 2019*[4] that, I would contend, this chapter may well be a core reason for Joyce's carrying over Stephen

---

3   Here, and implicitly or explicitly throughout this discussion, I build on my early immersion in the genesis of *A Portrait of the Artist as a Young Man*: 'The Genesis of *A Portrait of the Artist as a Young Man*', in *Critical Essays on James Joyce's 'A Portrait of the Artist as a Young Man'*, ed. by Philip Brady and James F. Carens (New York: G. K. Hall, 1998), pp. 83-112 [*second essay in the present collection*]. This essay is revised and integrated from 'The Seven Lost Years of *A Portrait of the Artist as a Young Man*', in *Approaches to Joyce's Portrait*, ed. by Bernard Benstock and Thomas F. Staley (Pittsburgh: University of Pittsburgh Press, 1976), pp. 25-60; and 'The Christmas Dinner Scene, Parnell's Death, and the Genesis of *A Portrait of the Artist as a Young Man*', *James Joyce Quarterly*, 13.1 (1975), 27-38.

4   Irina Rasmussen, 'Riffing on Shakespeare: James Joyce, Stephen Dedalus and the Avant-Garde Theory of Literary Creation', *Joyce Studies Annual 2019* (New York: Fordham University Press, 2019), pp. 33-73.

Dedalus at all and with the character incorporating his fictional *alter ego* again in *Ulysses*.

A significant clue that, for Joyce, a concern with Shakespeare and *Hamlet* goes back a long way, very possibly indeed to his time of writing *A Portrait of the Artist as a Young Man*, arises from his correspondence with Ezra Pound in the spring of 1917. Pound requested on 28 March: 'I want SOMETHING from you, even if it is only 500 words'. A couple of paragraphs later, he adds: 'From 500 to 3500 words is about the limit'.[5] Pound shows himself to be aware that Joyce is working on 'Odysseus' (*sic*). Joyce's answer by return on 9 April reads: 'As regards excerpts from *Ulysses*, the only thing I could send would be the Hamlet chapter, or part of it—which, however, would suffer by excision'. (*Letters I*, 101) *Ulysses*, it is true, features its Hamlet chapter eventually only as the ninth of it eighteen episodes. From the hindsight of the book as published in 1922, Joyce's offering 'the Hamlet chapter' to Pound as early as 1917 is thus astonishing. The Pound-Joyce correspondence in fact antedates the accomplishment for *Ulysses* of its second and third episodes, Nestor and Proteus, by some nine months.

Preparatory labour on the new novel began (we estimate) in 1914. It had thus been in progress for some three years, yet was apparently still very volatile in early 1917. Written testimony from the three early years of thinking and writing towards *Ulysses* does not survive, or at most indistinctly. Yet it is also true that Joyce had already in 1915, on a postcard (in German, and remarkably dated 16 June!) written to his brother Stanislaus, confined in Austrian wartime internment, that he had completed a first full draft of the Martello Tower episode.[6] Sustained drafting for *Ulysses* therefore began in Trieste. Within weeks after his postcard to Stanislaus, James Joyce and his family escaped to Zurich. Consecutive composition and fair-copying of the novel's eventual opening chapters, three in number—Telemachus, Nestor, Proteus—were yet some two years ahead. Whence could have sprung a fully blown 'Hamlet chapter' described as publishable in March/April 1917, and so elaborate even as perhaps to require excision? For a 'Hamlet chapter' to

---

5   *Pound/Joyce: The Letters of Ezra Pound to James Joyce*, ed. and with Commentary by Forrest Read (New York: New Directions, 1967), pp. 103-04.
6   *Joyce: Selected Letters*, ed. by Richard Ellmann (New York: The Viking Press, 1975), p. 209.

be conjured up out of a sorcerer's hat at this point in time would appear a doubtful proposition in terms of the *Ulysses* we know. Yet a 'Hamlet' unit that had been made ready early from vestiges of the *Portrait* workshop for the emerging new novel is thoroughly conceivable.

From James Joyce's postcard to Stanislaus we draw yet another intriguing piece of information. Outlining the design then envisaged for *Ulysses*, Joyce assigns four chapters to the opening Telemachiad. Taking this as his honest word from brother to brother, let us assume that these four episodes, by which the protagonist of *A Portrait of the Artist as a Young Man* is brought over into the new novel, fully circumscribe the conceptual and (in terms of preparatory writing) the textual 'Stephen Dedalus matter' to go into *Ulysses* from the *Portrait* workshop. Over and above Telemachus, Nestor, and Proteus, ultimately realised as the odyssey novel's Telemachiad, the episode to fill the fourth position for that opening according to the provisional design of June 1915 was most likely the 'Hamlet chapter'—testified by Joyce himself to exist fully blown in the spring of 1917.[7] For manifold compositional reasons, Joyce eventually moved that chapter—thoroughly revised and rewritten to become Scylla & Charybdis—into the central position of *Ulysses* by episode count. Concurring with Irina Rasmussen's assessment that this episode constitutes Joyce's modernist manifesto under the tenets of an avant-garde theory of literary creation, we realise that by relocation of 'the matter of Shakespeare' from an introductory to the central position in the novel's overall design by episode count, Joyce succeeded triumphantly in engaging his fictional *alter ego* Stephen Dedalus once more as his spokesperson in the fiction, now for expounding the artistic credo expressed through *Ulysses*.

However, we do not materially have the 'Hamlet chapter' that Joyce would have sent to Ezra Pound, had Pound taken him up on his offer. Even less do we have a 'Hamlet-chapter' instantiation as an

---

7   I already said as much in my essay 'James Joyce's text in progress' in *The Cambridge Companion to James Joyce*, ed. by Derek Attridge (Cambridge: Cambridge University Press, 1990), pp. 213-36 (p. 222); and incorporated, too, in this volume. Michael Groden drew the same conclusion independently in 'A Textual and Publishing History', in *A Companion to Joyce Studies*, ed. by Zack Bowen and James Carens (Westport, Conn., and London: Greenwood Press, 1984), pp. 71-128 (p. 93)— or Michael Groden and I may have exchanged views on the matter during his memorable four-week visit to our edition's working site in Munich during the month of July 1978.

unused leftover from the 1912-13 labours on Chapter V of *A Portrait of the Artist as a Young Man*. What we have in the way of a document text before Stephen's holding forth on Shakespeare in the National Library according to the fair copy of the ninth episode of *Ulysses* in the Rosenbach manuscript is a draft in three successive notebooks that form part of the Irish National Library's acquisition of Joyce manuscripts in 2002.[8] This draft comes very close to the fair-copy instantiation of 1918.[9] So clearly aggregated as a Scylla & Charybdis chapter as this draft is, it is ruled out as the document text of the 'Hamlet chapter' offered to Ezra Pound in 1917. This has simply not survived. Yet the pre-Rosenbach draft does allow an educated guess about its lost predecessor of 1916/1917. Through the first copy-book and until three-quarters down page sixteen in the second, the Shakespeare discussion runs on fluently, assured in its dialogue vitality. Revision and additional invention amounts largely to fine-tuning well-established text. This changes significantly from the entry of Buck Mulligan onwards. The draft manuscript's second half repeatedly features, in particular, extensive passages of first invention: the lavish 'Amen!' to 'Gloria in excelsis deo' passage on Buck Mulligan's entry itself (*cf. U* 9, 482-502);[10] the chanting of Shakespeare's Will (*cf. U* 9, 684-707); the ribald cast-list for the play 'Everyman His Own Wife' near the end (*cf. U* 9, 1167-1189). Such extensive fresh inventions tend to fill almost the entire left-hand pages of given openings—space that Joyce in composition habitually left blank precisely for extensions to the ongoing drafting. The conclusion, though speculative, seems significant: The 'Hamlet chapter' of 1916/1917 comprised essentially the core Shakespeare discussion. Its expansion to render the narrative fully functional for *Ulysses* is aptly heralded by the entry of Buck Mulligan in the pre-Rosenbach draft as preserved in its three copy-books.

This conclusion would likely be corroborated from yet another Shakespeare-related document in Joyce's hand that once existed but is

---

8   By NLI signature, the copy-books are MSS 36,639/08/A-C. See further, Luca Crispi, 'A First Foray into the National Library of Ireland's Joyce Manuscripts: Bloomsday 2011', *Genetic Joyce Studies*, 11 (Spring 2011). https://www.geneticjoycestudies.org/articles/GJS11/GJS11_Crispi#scylla

9   Cf. the transcription offered in Danis Rose and John O'Hanlon, *James Joyce Digital Archive*, http://www.jjda.ie/main/JJDA/U/ulex/k/k11d.htm.

10 James Joyce, *Ulysses. A Critical and Synoptic Edition*, prepared by Hans Walter Gabler with Wolfhard Steppe and Claus Melchior, 3 vols. (New York: Garland Publishing, 1984; ²1986).

also now lost. Last seen (apparently) in the La Hune exhibition in 1948 in Paris,[11] it belonged among the papers left behind when the Joyces fled to escape the German occupation of France at the onset of World War II. These papers were rescued by Paul Léon from Joyce's Paris flat and distributed for safe keeping among Joyce's, and Paul Léon's, acquaintances and friends. The dispersed materials were reassembled after the war and in 1948 exhibited at La Hune before going wholesale to the Poetry Collection in the SUNY Library in Buffalo—yet this one document never arrived there. We know it, or know of it, merely by description in the Slocum and Cahoon *Bibliography of James Joyce* (1953): 'Fragmentary conversations, which appear altered in the final version; on ten large unlined leaves, with a single exception written on one side only'.[12]

So described, the document and its content appear tentatively comparable to extant initial or intermediary Joycean working materials. To judge by the naming of its content—'fragmentary conversations' ['fragments de conversations']—it would have resembled the earlier of the two Buffalo drafts for Cyclops, Buffalo V.A.8. The indication of size as 'large leaves', in turn, recalls the intermediate Circe manuscript, acquired two decades ago by the National Library of Ireland, and quite pertinently as well, perhaps, the large-size note-sheets that Joyce assembled, apparently for the easier transport of written aids to further work, when, after the end of World War I, the move from Zurich back to Trieste was imminent. In one way or another, the appearance of the '10 large unlined leaves' represents, both in size and by nature and arrangement of contents, a preliminary-to-intermediate itemised disposition of a chapter prior to its being written out in narrative continuity. This lost episode outline, if written up in Zurich at some time after the Joyces arrived there at the end of June 1915, shows by its red-crayon marking that it was used for further texting for the episode. It could thus have served as the written pre-organisation for the narrative

---

11 Bernard Gheerbrant, *James Joyce. Sa Vie Son Oeuvre Son Rayonnement* [Exposition à Paris] Octobre-Novembre, 1949 (Paris: La Hune, 1949).
12 *A Bibliography of James Joyce: 1882-1941*, ed. by John C. Slocum and Herbert Cahoon (London: R. Hart-Davis, 1953), p. 140. No doubt, this description derives from the entry in French in the La Hune catalogue. It features one further detail: 'Nombreuses marques en crayon rouge.' ('Numerous markings in red crayon.') This indicates that the ten leaves were harvested in the writing of a succeeding document text.

elaboration of the 'Hamlet chapter' offered to Pound. This, however, is only one of three options for positioning it in a genetic stemma for Scylla & Charybdis. As an aid to drafting the chapter's eventual instantiation, it could alternatively have preceded the new NLI draft in three copy-books. Yet, though distinctly less likely, it could even have originated during the composition of *A Portrait*, Chapter V, as a planning sketch for composing a Shakespeare performance to fill the hiatus between Stephen's arrival on, and departure from, the library steps. Into whichever order the documents, lost or extant, of Joyce's 'Hamlet' progression should be configured, the roots of that progression in the gestation of Chapter V of *A Portrait of the Artist as a Young Man* is hauntingly recalled at the conclusion of the Scylla & Charybdis episode in *Ulysses*: 'The portico. | Here I watched the birds for augury.' (*U* 9, 1205-1206)

Composing the 'Hamlet chapter' was Joyce's first sustained writing campaign on *Ulysses* in Zurich—as has not, in so many words, been stated before; nor has it yet been made explicit what this signifies. That Joyce wrote a 'Hamlet chapter' in 1915-16 to such satisfaction to himself that he felt he could offer it to Ezra Pound as a pre-publication promise on the novel *Ulysses* in progress means that, through the years 1914 to 1917, he was not merely—not one-sidedly, as it were—occupied with plotting and peopling the new fiction and working up his knowledge of Homer and of *verismo*-historic analyses of the Odyssey of his own times (and eking out, besides, his considerable Latin with some less Greek[13]). His urge, at the same time, was to anchor the new venture into writing fiction in a rethought aesthetics and understanding of literary creation. We can be confident, even while confined to supporting this assessment from the latter-day Scylla & Charybdis, that the 'Hamlet chapter' of 1916 in essence began to articulate James Joyce's revised conception of his art to carry the literary fiction *Ulysses*.

Significantly, Joyce reached this new stance by a route paralleling that by which earlier his systematised notions and perceptions of literary art were infused into those of the Stephen Daedalus/Dedalus characters

---

13   Prominent among Joyce's contemporary sources for the Odyssey was, as is well known, Victor Bérard's *Les Phéniciens et l'Odyssée* (1902). As to Joyce's working up some Greek, see his Greek notes in the *James Joyce Archive*, ed. by Michael Groden, *et al.*, 63 vols. (New York and London: Garland Publishing, 1977-79), vol. [3], pp. 258-353—preceded in that volume from p. 136 onwards by his notes on English drama, Shakespeare, and *Hamlet*.

of his earlier prose. What Stephen sets forth, first in *Stephen Hero*, and then, partially re-thought and re-phrased, to Lynch in *A Portrait of the Artist as a Young Man*, derives (as we can verify still from Joyce's papers) from impressive collections of notes of theory that Joyce compiled and, more pertinently, from the range of essays and lectures Joyce wrote and gave during his Dublin years. On an analogous epistemological route, Joyce prepared to turn knowledge gained through systematic scholarly research into imaginative literary art in *Ulysses*—and to do so again through his trusted spokesman Stephen. He embarked on that fresh route in 1912, which brings us back to precisely the time of the frame construction for the narrative movement to go in between Stephen's arrival at, and departure from, the National Library in Chapter V of *Portrait*. There is no telling how far a Shakespeare-related drafting of the matter to be inserted into that frame ever got. It is at any rate not fanciful to believe that a Shakespeare performance by Stephen Dedalus was considered to be staged inside the library at that interstice of the *Portrait* narrative.

Support for the hypothesis may be drawn from circumstantial evidence grounded in material proof. Joyce, while bringing *A Portrait* to conclusion, was simultaneously deeply engaged with Shakespeare, the author, and *Hamlet*, the play, as well as indeed with Hamlet, the character, and Shakespeare, the man and his life. William H. Quillian has investigated, and published in transcription, the notes with which Joyce prepared for his 'twelve lectures on *Amleto di G. Shakespeare*, given from November 1912 through February 1913 in the Universita Populare in Trieste.[14] The coincidence with the period of finishing *A Portrait of the Artist as a Young Man* is perfect. For these lectures, Joyce's extensive and deep-searching notes have been preserved. The appendix to Quillian's essay transcribes them from the originals held in Cornell University Library. Given that there is, at his time of writing, no other text to link them to than Scylla & Charybdis, Quillian naturally relates them to that ninth episode of *Ulysses*, even though it was written as it survives in the Rosenbach fair-copy manuscript some five to six years after Joyce's note-taking for the Trieste lectures. What Quillian argues, at the same time, and makes fascinatingly apparent by letting the notes

---

14 William H. Quillian, 'Shakespeare in Trieste: Joyce's 1912 *Hamlet* lectures', *James Joyce Quarterly*, 12, nos. 1/2 (1974/1975), 7-63.

preparatory to the lectures speak for themselves, is Joyce's searching and intellectually alive range of enquiry, highly alert to Shakespeare's dramatic art and his life both in aesthetic and historic terms. As Quillian maintains, the Shakespeare/Hamlet lectures, preceded moreover by Joyce's Defoe and Blake lectures also at the Universita Populare in the spring of 1912, 'brought to a focus a period of aesthetic speculation' (7). Because James Joyce's lectures themselves have not been preserved, Quillian, of necessity, illustrates their presumed stance on aesthetics, as on historicity in the mode of *verismo*, from Stephen's rhetoric in 'Scylla & Charybdis'; yet he concludes, 'The notes which survive from Joyce's own *Hamlet* lectures suggest that his method was very close to Stephen's' (9).

But would this have been true or, indeed, could it have been achieved in a Shakespeare performance by Stephen Dedalus in *A Portrait of the Artist as a Young Man*? Having so far emphatically argued that Joyce had at least the transitional intention to let Stephen speak up for Shakespeare and Hamlet in Chapter V of *A Portrait*, I must now alter the perspective. In terms of the flow and structure of the narrative, it is irrefutably evident that Joyce made careful preparation for putting into compositional practice his idea of transforming his own public lectures on *Amleto di G. Shakespeare* into a performance given by Stephen Dedalus in *Portrait*. He built into Chapter V those narrative bridge-heads of Stephen first arriving on, and hours later leaving from, the steps of the National Library. Yet, on reflection, what havoc would a Shakespeare performance of Stephen's have wrought to the novel as a whole? How impossibly, at closest narrative distance, would the delivery of Stephen's Aristotelian and Thomistic aesthetics from *Stephen Hero* have clashed with the avant-garde understanding of art inspired by Shakespeare when articulated only pages later again through Stephen? Against the background of the whole *Portrait* novel, moreover, the Stephen Dedalus of *A Portrait of the Artist as a Young Man* was altogether simply too much still the artist as a young man. He was not yet conceived as mature enough a character and artist to stand up and hold his own against Shakespeare. Nor was Joyce, as author, yet sufficiently secure in the originality of his art to design with full assurance the fictional Stephen as his *alter ego* in maturity. This insight may also lie behind his remark to Frank Budgen in Zurich that Stephen Dedalus could not be changed. Not for nothing, either, as it would seem, did Joyce in *Ulysses* proceed to organise the fiction around the distinctly less autobiographical figure of Leopold Bloom. As for the narrative design of Chapter V of *A Portrait*: against the danger of destabilising the novel as a whole if he infused into it his matured aesthetics and grasp of his literary art gained through his Hamlet lectures, closing the gap between the National Library bridge-heads proved a merely pragmatic problem. Joyce inserted into the space prepared for a Shakespeare performance by Stephen Dedalus a narrative of his fictional artist-as-a-young-man's creation of a pre-*Portrait* villanelle poem of his, Joyce's, own authorship.

Once *A Portrait of the Artist as a Young Man* was out of his way and in the process of being published from 2 February 1914 to 1 September 1915 in instalments in *The Egoist* in London, Joyce turned his mind to two fresh tasks. One was the composition of his play *Exiles*. This he largely wrote in Trieste, though he took the manuscript with him to Zurich in June 1915 and there touched it up with final revisions. What he wrote in Trieste and what he inserted into the fair copy to replace previous pages (discarded and consequently no longer extant) is easily distinguishable in the manuscript because, simply, the Trieste and Zurich pages differ in size. The other task was both to conceptualise and to begin to write *Ulysses*. For the writing, the unused materials from the *Portrait* workshop paved his way. As his entry into the new novel, he penned, still in Trieste, a first draft of the Martello Tower episode and reported it done to his brother on 16 June 1915. The unfinished *Portrait* business that remained was to turn the 'Hamlet chapter' into an episode of *Ulysses*. This can be dated to 1916, assuredly if broadly, by Joyce's offering it to Pound in April 1917. The efforts between 1914 and 1917 of fleshing out the fresh enterprise of *Ulysses*, and stocking the new workshop accordingly, remain much harder to gauge. Richer materials, which bear witness that the overall design of *Ulysses* was a protracted and multi-directional business over these years, have only lately come to light through the 2002 acquisitions at the National Library of Ireland. From them, we are learning better to understand, in particular, the volatility of options arising from Joyce's intense immersion into 'the matter of Odysseus/Ulysses' during his first two years in Zurich, and to estimate better why the full composition of the two Telemachiad episodes without a *Portrait* pre-history, Nestor and Proteus, cannot be safely attested earlier than around the middle of 1917. The early copy-books now at the NLI may yet enable fresh discoveries about Joyce's pre-1918 work patterns—among them, for example, the one copy-book (NLI 36,639/07/A), which comprises not only note and pre-draft assemblies for the future episodes Proteus and Sirens—surprisingly enough together in the one copy-book—but also contains, interspersed in the Proteus section, jottings suggestive of the tentative planning of a 'Lacedemon chapter' for the Telemachiad, and thus the Stephen-Dedalus domain to which Sirens can never, of course, have been thought to belong.[15] A 'Lacedemon chapter' was never realised. The 'Hamlet chapter', as we have seen, was removed from the Telemachiad position first intended for it—as before it had already once been removed from the position into which it had meant to be embedded in *A Portrait of the Artist as a Young Man*. Transformed into Scylla & Charybdis, rock and whirlpool, it was anchored at mid-point of the Odyssean adventures of *Ulysses*. What this meant, as through Irina Rasmussen's essay we freshly understand, was nothing less than installing Stephen Dedalus maturely in *Ulysses* as the spokesperson for James Joyce's modernist manifesto of aesthetics and art, which is persuasive to us as Joyce's reading audience, if less so to Stephen's listeners on the fictional occasion in the National Library—and to many a Joyce critic since. So, narratively positioned in the episode's centre, Stephen Dedalus, the novel's Telemachus, in fact steals the show from the novel's Ulysses, Leopold Bloom. That Bloom at the episode's end slinks out between the rock-and-whirlpool placeholders, Stephen and Mulligan, is at most an arabesque compared to the emblematic image we derive from the episode as a whole of Stephen, tied to the mast of his vision of modernist aesthetics and art, steering his course between the rock of Plato and Aristotle and the whirlpool of St. Thomas and Ignatius Loyola, while himself all ears to the siren-song of Shakespeare.

A fact that tantalisingly beckons us toward further paths by which we might feel our way to Joyce, as he builds his art from associative

---

15 *See* Daniel Ferrer, 'An Unwritten Chapter of Ulysses? Joyce's Notes for a "Lacedemon" Episode', in *James Joyce: Whence, Whither and How: Studies in Honour of Carla Vaglio*, ed. by Giuseppina Cortese, Giuliana Ferreccio, M. Teresa Giaveri, Teresa Prudente (Alessandria: Edizioni dell'Orso, 2015), pp. 363-77, http://www.item.ens.fr/articles-en-ligne/an-unwritten-chapter-of-ulyssesjoyces-notes-for-a-lacedemon/, preceded by his essay 'What song the sirens sang . . . is no longer beyond all conjecture: A Preliminary Description of the New "Proteus" and "Sirens" Manuscripts', *James Joyce Quarterly*, 39-1 (2001), 53-68.

intuition, is that, for a long time, the episode directly following Scylla & Charybdis was to be Sirens. Next in line after Scylla & Charybdis for the novel's adventures-of-Odysseus sequence, Sirens was also the one episode towards which Joyce's thoughts already projected in that notebook (NLI 36,639/07/A) that he also used to sketch out ingredients for the narrative units destined to form the novel's Telemachiad opening. What he sketched between asterisks in the notebook turns up dispersed and integrated into the textual flow of the pre-Rosenbach draft manuscript for Proteus. Now, at the turn of 1918 to 1919, Joyce became very conscious that he had reached a half-way mark for the novel in progress. He under-wrote the Scylla & Charybdis fair copy with the autograph *finis*: 'End of First Part of "Ulysses"'. After considerable mulling over how to proceed, he bridged the mid-way hiatus with a structural *tour-de-force*. He intercalated before Sirens as the novel's tenth chapter a non-Homeric counter-episode, Wandering Rocks, with Dublin as protagonist, and, as its template in Greek myth, Jason's quest for the Golden Fleece on a sailing adventure analogous to that between Scylla & Charybdis which Odysseus chose on his route to Ithaca.[16]

As the novel, over its second nine-episode half, pursues its 'odyssey of style' (to use Karen Lawrence's felicitous title),[17] memory and memories of the author's, of the readers', of the text itself of itself play key roles, fulfil multiple functions, generate the narrative progression, and altogether propel *Ulysses* forward. Very soon, Joyce's first readers balked at the avant-garde course he was now steering. The experimental narrative structure of Wandering Rocks was at once outdone by the musical tone and sequentiality devised for Sirens. On reading Sirens in typescript, both Ezra Pound and Harriet Weaver voiced their unhappiness. Initially, this quite disturbed Joyce, yet upon taking a few deep breaths, he insisted to Harriet Weaver that he knew what he was doing: '[I]n the compass of one day to compress all [*Ulysses*'s] wanderings and clothe them in the form of this day is for me only possible by such variation which, I beg

---

16   The outcome warrants an essay of its own: 'Structures of Memory and Orientation: Steering a Course Through Wandering Rocks', in the present volume; and also in: *Text Genetics in Literary Modernism and Other Essays* (Cambridge: Open Book Publishers, 2018), pp. 81-110, https://www.openbookpublishers.com/htmlreader/978-1-78374-363-6/ch4.xhtml#_idTextAnchor014

17   Karen Lawrence, *The Odyssey of Style in 'Ulysses'* (Princeton: Princeton University Press, 1981).

you to believe, is not capricious'. (*Letters I*, 129) Under the over-arching modernist tenet of segmentation and refraction that Joyce here terms 'variation', *Ulysses* in its entirety progresses over seventeen episodes within an Aristotelian framework of narration from beginning through middle to end—past-present-future—to reach the large-period end of Ithaka. 'The *Ithaca* episode [. . .] is in reality the end as *Penelope* has no beginning, middle or end' (*Letters* I, 172). At its ultimate conclusion, *Ulysses* thus turns non-Aristotelian. Its final variation triumphantly breaks the fetters of conventional narrative order and expectation of sequentiality. Its end soliloquy, voiced through Molly Bloom, draws both the past and the future into one ever self-renewing present in the never-ceasing stream of her awareness verbalised and so projected through the mind and pen of her author.[18]

But not to lose touch with the *Portrait* roots of *Ulysses*: What was, perhaps, the most important and encompassing rescue from the *Portrait* phase of James Joyce's narrative art was, I suggest, the salvaging for *Ulysses* of the original structural ground-plan for *A Portrait*, Chapter V. When Joyce pulled back from letting Stephen hold forth on Shakespeare in the National Library in the third movement of that chapter, he also sacrificed the structural design by which Stephen would have proceeded from home into exile on a straight course and timeline from fore-noon to evening in one day. Yet the one-day structure was not abandoned. It was only momentarily shelved. Salvaged for re-use, it was turned into the momentous overall timeframe for *Ulysses*.

---

18 This shift in terms of even the novel's narrative mode I have set forth in German in 'Nachwort', in *James Joyce, Penelope. The Last Chapter of 'Ulysses'*, ed. by Harald Beck (Stuttgart: Philipp Reclam, 1989), pp. 175-89, http://epub.ub.uni-muenchen.de/5802/1/5802.pdf. From and beyond this grew the twelfth essay in this volume, 'Composing *Penelope* Towards the Condition of Music'.

From Hamlet to Scylla & Charybdis: Experience into Art

To the memory of
Michael Groden (1947–2021)

In 2002, the National Library of Ireland in Dublin acquired a draft of the ninth chapter of *Ulysses*. It had previously not been known to exist. Sometime in the 1930s, James Joyce had given it as a present to Paul Léon. The treasure-trove of such presents given and received apparently throughout the 1930s was unearthed in the 1990s in the basement of the Léons' home in Paris. It was to become, in the first years of the new millennium, the main division of the NLI's Joyce holdings.[1] The ninth-chapter draft is, to all appearances, the immediate ancestor, or ancestor once removed, of the fair copy of the episode in the Rosenbach manuscript housed in Philadelphia. Joyce's own working title for the chapter was Scylla & Charybdis. The episode remains universally identified as such, even though Joyce's working titles were not included as chapter headings in the book edition.

Does the NLI document represent the first and only origin of composition of this ninth chapter for *Ulysses*? By the core of its narrative content, we strongly suspect otherwise. What foremost carries the episode is its sustained argument about Hamlet and Shakespeare. Stephen Dedalus provocatively challenges his listeners, the librarians in

---

[1] Michael Groden, 'The National Library of Ireland's New Joyce Manuscripts: A Statement and Document Descriptions', *James Joyce Quarterly*, 39 (2001 [2003]), 29-51; also Michael Groden, *'Ulysses' in Focus: Genetic, Textual, and Personal Views* (Gainesville: University Press of Florida, 2010), pp. 14-31. Luca Crispi, 'A First Foray into the National Library of Ireland's Joyce Manuscripts: Bloomsday 2011', *Genetic Joyce Studies* 11 (Spring 2011), https://www.geneticjoycestudies.org/articles/GJS11/GJS11_Crispi.

the National Library—where the very draft now lives—with his notions about Shakespeare and Hamlet and the poetological implications of the creative relationship between autobiography and art. While the novel's main character is otherwise Leopold Bloom, the protagonist in this episode, as in the tripartite Telemachiad which opens *Ulysses*, is Stephen Dedalus. The dialogically patterned narrative by which he is developed in Scylla & Charybdis follows in direct line not only from the three initial episodes, Telemachus, Nestor, and Proteus. It reaches back, even beyond, to *A Portrait of the Artist as a Young Man*. Its Chapter V, in particular, is built on a sequence of encounters of Stephen in dialogue with fellow students in the chapter's first and third movements, and with himself in its second and fourth movements.[2] There are distinct indications that the Scylla & Charybdis episode of *Ulysses* had its earliest roots in the *Portrait* workshop. For this, there exists external evidence. The first such piece is that Joyce early on in his structural design planned the initial Telemachiad to comprise four episodes. The likeliest candidate for a fourth episode to go with the three Stephen Dedalus chapters—Telemachus, Nestor, and Proteus—would be the Stephen Dedalus chapter Scylla & Charybdis, ultimately ninth in *Ulysses*. The second external indication, substantially stronger than the transitory planning of the Telemachiad to run to four episodes, is Joyce's assertion in 1917 that what, from his new novel-in-progress, he could already offer Ezra Pound for advance publication was all or part of a Hamlet chapter.[3] What this means for our assessing early work on *Ulysses* is nothing less than that Joyce, in his initial advance toward the new novel, turned two sets of left-over materials from the *Portrait* workshop into chapter drafts for *Ulysses*. One opening gambit consisted of converting Joyce's Martello Tower materials into the *Ulysses* opening. These materials may be taken to have been originally intended as providing

---

2   Hans Walter Gabler, 'The Genesis of *A Portrait of the Artist as a Young Man*', in *Critical Essays on James Joyce's 'A Portrait of the Artist as a Young Man'*, ed. by Philip Brady and James F. Carens (New York: G. K. Hall, 1998), pp. 83-112; and in the present volume. Recently discussed and further substantiated in Luca Crispi, 'The Afterlives of Joyce's "Alphabetical Notebook" from *A Portrait* to *Ulysses* (1910-20)', *Genetic Joyce Studies* 20 (Spring 2020), https://www.geneticjoycestudies.org/articles/GJS20/GJS20_Crispi.

3   James Joyce to Ezra Pound, 9 April 1917, in *Letters of James Joyce*, vol. I, ed. by Stuart Gilbert (New York: Viking Press, 1957, ²1966) (*Letters* I), p. 101. I reiterate here the gist of my argument in the preceding essay, 'James Joyce's Hamlet Chapter'.

the climax of the 'University episode' of *Stephen Hero*, but the episode's end was not realised, and *Stephen Hero* was discontinued altogether.[4] Subsequently, there is evidence in James Joyce's correspondence with his brother Stanislaus that *A Portrait of the Artist as a Young Man* was once prospected to finish at the Martello Tower, but as realised, it ends on the hawk-like flight into exile instead. Joyce converted existing Martello Tower workshop materials into the opening episode for *Ulysses* in 1915, still in Trieste. Drafting the initial episode went hand in hand with elaborate planning for content and structure of the new novel. A postcard to Stanislaus survives, dated (remarkably) 16 June 1915, to confirm the initial accomplishment.[5] In late June 1915, James Joyce and his family, enemy aliens in Hungaro-Austrian Trieste during World War I, moved to Zurich.

In Zurich, Joyce continued multi-tasking as he assembled material and notes toward assorted further episodes for the new novel. He also carried out, in his early weeks or months in Zurich, final revision and rewriting of his play *Exiles*. The first sustained episode drafting for *Ulysses* he embarked upon was for what he defined as the 'Hamlet chapter'. In advance of all other writing for *Ulysses* in Zurich, this so swiftly satisfied him that he expressly offered it to Ezra Pound for (pre-)publication, in whole or in part.[6] Nothing came of the offer. Though it was Pound who had enquired about publishable material, he did not—for whatever reasons—then grasp the opportunity. After the novel's opening Tower episode (Telemachus) composed in Trieste, the Hamlet chapter was thus the second of the novel's episodes altogether to be achieved in draft— even though it ended up ninth in the eventual sequence of eighteen *Ulysses* episodes. The circumstantial evidence is compelling that it grew out of leftover Shakespeare and *Hamlet* notes and sketches brought, like the *Exiles* manuscript, from Trieste. These hypothesised materials one may safely associate with James Joyce's intense preparation for, and eventual delivery of, twelve lectures on *Amleto* in 1912–13 at Trieste's Universita Popolare. It so happens, moreover, that 1912–13 was also

---

[4] Stanislaus to James Joyce, 31 July 1905, in *Letters of James Joyce*, vol. II, ed. by Richard Ellmann (New York: Viking, 1966) (*Letters* II), p. 103.

[5] James to Stanislaus Joyce, postcard 16 June 1915, in *Joyce: Selected Letters*, ed. by Richard Ellmann (New York: The Viking Press, 1975), p. 209.

[6] James Joyce to Ezra Pound, 9 April 1917, *Letters* I, p. 101.

the period to which we must assign Joyce's similarly intense struggles toward achieving his novel *A Portrait of the Artist as a Young Man*. He had begun to write it in 1907. Early in 1909, he faltered somewhat over the transition from Chapter III to Chapter IV. He sought and found encouragement from a Triestine pupil and friend, the businessman and writer Ettore Schmitz, a literary author known under his Italianised name, Italo Svevo. This apparently helped Joyce to get through Chapter IV and compose and fair-copy a thirteen-page beginning to Chapter V. Yet at this point he was hit fully by writer's block. In despair, sometime in 1911, he threw the manuscript in the fire. His partner Nora and his sister Eileen were nearby to rescue the bundle of pages from the flames. When eventually (in 1920) presenting the novel's final fair copy to Harriet Weaver, he recounted that the manuscript had for a long time remained bundled up in old sheets, until eventually he had returned to work on it.[7]

All that we materially have in order to assess how *A Portrait* was ultimately achieved is the fair copy Joyce presented to Harriet Weaver and which she in turn gave to the National Library of Ireland. The novel's fifth chapter is structured predominantly as a sequence of dialogues with fellow students, friends, and antagonists, whom Stephen Dedalus encounters walking through Dublin in the course of the day. By the end of the first itinerary segment through the city, Stephen and Lynch reach the steps of the National Library and are about to go in. A second segment follows: Suspending Stephen's ambulatory progress, it narrates him outside the rest of the chapter's time-scheme on an unspecified morning waking up and, line group by line group, composing a villanelle poem. With this segment ended, Stephen reappears on the steps of the Library, going out. Resuming his walk through Dublin, now in dialogue only with Davin, he takes flight, at the novel's end, into exile.

What is materially remarkable about the fair-copy manuscript is that the villanelle segment is unquestionably an insert between the moments of Stephen entering and Stephen leaving the National Library. This renders it imaginable that these narrated moments of entry and exit are the residual pillars demarcating a manuscript space to be filled otherwise than by the artist as a young man's early-morning composition

---

7   James Joyce to Harriet Shaw Weaver, 6 January 1920, *Letters* I, p. 136.

of a villanelle poem. As it stands, it is true that this content matter is eminently suited to the novel. Yet—as I have argued before, though in less critical detail–it is alternatively conceivable that Stephen was, at some stage in the compositional deliberations for the fifth chapter of *A Portrait*, cast to carry his progress in dialogues through Dublin into the library, there to measure his wit with the librarians'. This leads to the question where the idea would have originated for this option speculatively antecedent to the villanelle movement. Biographically assessed, it would have sprung from those months, almost one year all told, of Joyce's Shakespeare study and Hamlet-Shakespeare delivery in 1912–13. This was simultaneously very closely the time during which he would also have grappled with the compositional impasse for Chapter V of his novel in progress. In his euphoria over the *Amleto* lectures, Joyce may well have fancied himself re-using them in his novel through his *alter ego* Stephen Dedalus. With more sober judgment, he desisted. There is absolutely no telling how much, if anything, he might already have written out toward use in the novel. But what is certain by all circumstantial evidence is that he brought materials from his intense Shakespeare year with him to Zurich. From our perspective, these materials may legitimately be termed 'residues' from the *Portrait* workshop. Clearly, they must have been maturely enough developed to sustain the full-scale drafting of the first wholly fresh episode for *Ulysses*. Alas, though: The 1916 manuscript version of the Hamlet chapter has not survived. But Joyce's assertion in 1916 that a 'Hamlet chapter' then existed allows us to posit that the draft for Scylla & Charybdis now in the NLI in its turn derives from that 'Hamlet chapter' of two years earlier. It is, in other words, the earliest material document extant from James Joyce's endeavours to write on Hamlet and Shakespeare.

One other document once materially existed. It is described in the Slocum and Cahoon Joyce bibliography: 'Fragmentary conversations, which appear altered in the final version; on 10 large unlined leaves [. . .]', to which the description in the catalogue for the La Hune exhibition of 1948, where these ten leaves were last seen, adds: 'Nombreuses marques en crayon rouge' ('Numerous markings in red crayon').[8] This indicates that, true to Joyce's working habits, the text on the '10 large [. . .] leaves'

---

8   John J. Slocum and Herbert Cahoon, *A Bibliography of James Joyce, 1882-1941* (New Haven: Yale University Press, 1953), p. 140. Bernard Gheerbrant, *James Joyce. Sa Vie*

was likely harvested from an earlier document. The markings in red suggest a working-over and transfer to a succeeding document. One hypothesis for the relative timing of the lost ten pages might be that they preceded the 1916 Hamlet. Or else, because they came to the 1948 La Hune exhibition from among James Joyce's papers abandoned in 1940 in his apartment in Paris—where they likely enough would have been filed in company with the NLI draft before this was given as a present to Paul Léon—they should preferably perhaps be thought of as intermediary between the 'Hamlet chapter' manuscript of 1916 and the 1918 Scylla & Charybdis draft now at the NLI.

The NLI draft proves dateable to 1918. Correspondence from the end of November 1918 survives between Joyce and Karl Bleibtreu, German journalist and player in the game of proposing 'alternative Shakespeares' that was current in scholarship and criticism around the turn of the nineteenth to the twentieth century.[9] Joyce's first letter of enquiry of 21 November states that '[i]n the book I am writing *Ulysses* there is an allusion to your interesting Shakespearean theory'. On 27 November, he becomes specific and sends a questionnaire with eight queries. The questions do not survive, only Bleibtreu's four pages of 28 November that pick up the queries by numbers. Details from Bleibtreu's answers register at base and second-overlay level of the NLI draft.[10] Facing the NLI draft as it presents itself richly overlaid with layers upon layers of revision, it seemed to me nonetheless that its most stable units at its basic first-inscription layer was the text of Stephen Dedalus's Hamlet-and-Shakespeare performance. Clearly, at the same time, the NLI draft is a document of composition for a *Ulysses* chapter. Yet on the hypothesis that at its first-inscription layer, if anywhere, one could still discern in this extant draft text original residues or close derivations from its lost antecedents, I computer-generated from the composite writing of the NLI draft a first-inscription rendering. To this end, I gratefully availed myself of Danis Rose and John O'Hanlon's online transcript of the

---

Son Oeuvre Son Rayonnement [Exposition à Paris] Octobre-Novembre, 1949 (Paris: La Hune, 1949).

9   Karl Bleibtreu and his Swiss wife lived in Zurich and, as transpires from the end of Bleibtreu's letter to James Joyce of 28 November 1918, the Joyce and Bleibtreu couples were on familiar terms.

10   See Danis Rose and John O'Hanlon, *James Joyce Digital Archive*, http://jjda.ie/main/JJDA/u/FF/ubiog/ulett.htm, scroll to items under the dates given.

manuscript.[11] I converted its private layer-coding from the ground up to XML-TEI-tagging, which allowed me automatically to distil the first-inscription rendering. Additionally, in a very few instances, I amended the Rose/O'Hanlon transcription readings.

What the first-inscription base confirms is that the draft text is a chapter state-of-text for *Ulysses*. Stephen's inner thought is rendered throughout in stream-of-consciousness, no longer in the *Erlebte Rede* mode of *A Portrait*. Haines or Mulligan, characters from the opening chapter of *Ulysses*, are referred to by the chapter's *dramatis personae* long before Mulligan enters in person at the episode's midpoint. Leopold Bloom, too—pure inhabitant of *Ulysses* that he is, and of course even less related to Shakespeare than Mulligan—naturally also needed to be brought slinking in. The draft reveals comprehensively that Joyce thoroughly met the challenge of turning his earlier Hamlet chapter, of whatever shape, into a *Ulysses* episode. Thus, the Shakespeare/Hamlet theme ends, in effect, with Stephen admitting that he does not believe his own theory. Beyond, it is Stephen's emotional parting from Buck Mulligan that closes the chapter—'Part. The moment is coming now.'— but now no longer to the flourish of birds to be watched from the steps of the National Library, as in *A Portrait*, but rather with two frail plumes of smoke from the chimneys wafting the episode to conclusion, a poignant echo of the Shakespeare theme in the quote from *Cymbeline*. The focus of this essay is essentially the Hamlet-Shakespeare strand in Scylla & Charybdis. By all indications, it preserves the core text inherited from the preceding lost versions of Joyce's grappling with what in 1916 he called his Hamlet chapter. My approach is genetically critical and bent on analysing Joyce's poetics underlying the argument and performance of Stephen Dedalus.

In the NLI draft for Scylla & Charybdis, after just over one page of Goethe to Milton to George Moore name-dropping between the librarians, John Eglinton leads from contemporary Irish poets to Shakespeare:

---

11   Danis Rose and John O'Hanlon, *James Joyce Digital Archive*, http://www.jjda.ie/main/JJDA/U/ulex/k/k11d.htm.

2.08| —Our young Irish bards, John Eglinton

2.09| said, have yet to create something

2.10| which the world will set beside Saxon

2.11| Shakespeare's *Hamlet*. The peatsmoke

2.12| is exhilarating, George Moore says.

2.13| We want men not wraiths and

2.14| spooks.[12]

'Stephen, seated between', as the narrative specifies nine manuscript lines earlier, takes a breath (as it were) to respond: '—What is a ghost? Stephen asked. Is it not' (NLI draft, 2.15)—but the gesture of composition to bring Stephen into the discussion at this point is struck out in mid-writing: ~~What is a ghost? Stephen asked. Is it not~~ What could have been his opening fanfare is immediately cancelled, yet its presence in the draft, if not in the resulting text, is at once a significant signal. On this first impulse to let Stephen speak, the words that flow from Joyce's pen spring from his own sense of Shakespeare's Hamlet, or rather, Joyce's sense of the characters as *dramatis personae* and of the real and theatrical relationship of the two Hamlets in *Hamlet*. The Prince's father already bears the name, and tradition has it that the actor on the Globe stage who took the part of the Prince's father was William Shakespeare. Hamlet, the father, is the play's ghost. Shakespeare, impersonating him, dons the dead king's ghostly self. His acting enables him to blend his real presence into the stage representation. This means (for Joyce) that Shakespeare, the stage father, senses from his stage son Hamlet the ghostly emanations of his own, Shakespeare's, son Hamnet who died in early boyhood. What evidence survives from James Joyce's lectures on *Amleto*—given in late 1912 and early 1913 in English(!) in Italian-speaking Austrian Trieste—indicates that the momentary first impulse to introduce Stephen Dedalus with 'What is a ghost?' into the Scylla & Charybdis action in the National Library episode in *Ulysses* re-presents— brings into renewed presence—his, James Joyce's, deeply ingrained

---

12 All text citations in this essay are from my draft *Basic Hamlet Proposition*, linkable through https://www.academia.edu/50815114/Basic_hamlet_proposition.

sense of the ghost, or two ghosts, as the conceptual and emotional core of Shakespeare's play.

This indicator, though fleeting and aborted, yet establishes a genetic line of Joyce's composition and text from the Scylla & Charybdis draft we have, back to Joyce's exploration of Shakespeare's work at large, and to his, Joyce's, 1912 period of preparation for the *Amleto* lectures in particular. By implication, too, this renders inevitable defining the lost 'Hamlet chapter' of 1916 as the missing link, both in terms of document and of text, between the Trieste lectures (which will never have existed as text in writing, since likely delivered orally from notes) and the NLI Scylla & Charybdis draft that has survived. What arises, moreover, over and above the chronology question of the genesis of Joyce's writing, is the super-imposition of fictional Stephen Dedalus over the real-life James Joyce—or of the real-life Joyce over the Stephen Dedalus he creates and inscribes into fiction. This doubling becomes manifest at once on our first encounter with the fictional character's seamlessly taking possession of its (his?) author's conception of the art of another author canonised in Western literary heritage. And this is only the beginning of the consummately tangled art that unfolds before us. In the immediate progression of the text, Joyce holds Stephen back a while longer 'seated between', and listening with increasing impatience, we assume, to Russell's pronouncements on art and aesthetics. 'All [such] questions are purely academic [. . .] For professors of the university. I mean if Hamlet is Shakespeare or James or Essex.' Stephen will, as the chapter's discussion in the library eventually takes its course, pick up on Russell's rejection of biographic positivism and construe it quite differently. What really, now, first drives him to abandon his role of silent observer is the spiritualist alternative to the biographical one that Russell proclaims: 'Art has to show us ideas, formless spiritual essences. The supreme question about a work of art is out of how deep a life does it spring. [. . .] The deepest poetry of Shelley, the words of *Hamlet*, bring our minds into contact with the eternal realities. The rest is speculation of schoolboys for schoolboys'. (NLI draft, 2.16-33) At this point, Stephen raises his voice for the first time in the chapter's unfolding dialogue pattern. He intercedes laconically and with fine irony to reject, in his turn, Russell's spiritualist stance. What Stephen sees, one might say, is the structural bond of a teacher-student relationship of these ancient Greek philosophers.

    2.34| —The schoolmen were schoolboys at

    2.35| first, Stephen said. Aristotle

    2.36| himself was Plato's prize

    2.37| schoolboy at first.

To which Eglinton remarks:

    2.38| —We hope he is so still, John

    2.39| Eglinton said maliciously. I can

    2.40| see him quite proud of it too.

As if in direct response, and insisting on Aristotle as his guarantor, Stephen interjects—yet not until a full twenty manuscript lines further on:

    3.16| —That model schoolboy, Stephen said,

    3.17| would no doubt find Hamlet's

    3.18| thoughts on the immortality

    3.19| of his soul as shallow as Plato's.

Enraged,

    3.20| John Eglinton said

    3.21| sharply:

    3.22| —I confess it makes my blood

    3.23| boil to hear anyone compare

    3.24| Plato and Aristotle.

Yet Stephen tops him and, as we know, but as the first readers of Scylla & Charybdis might be unaware of, narrows in on the discussion's central theme to come:

    3.25| —Which of the two would have

    3.26| banished the creator of *Hamlet*

3.27| from his commonwealth?,

3.28| Stephen asked.

The twenty-line distance is notable between Stephen's first and second utterances on Aristotle as Plato's schoolboy. Over a page break, a lengthy passage of Stephen's silent thought occupies a whole twelve of the twenty manuscript lines. This takes its cue from Russell's 'formless spiritual essences' and transforms them on the fly in terms of the mystery by Christian doctrine of 'Father, Son and Holy Breath'. In his associative stream of thought, Stephen is made fleetingly to translate the trinity of Hamlet (the father), Hamlet (the sons), and their emanation as ghosts—according to Joyce's sense of this Shakespearean threesome— into the trinity of Christian dogma. In continuation of what Stephen is made to associate in the passage, Joyce introduces for him, and rapidly spins further, humorously snide remarks on the spiritualist aspersions of the Theosophy rage of the late nineteenth/early twentieth century, specifically in Dublin and Ireland.

Spinning threads of conversation and inner thought that link and diverge around the chapter's yet-to-be-reached core theme proves to be the main mode of composition for the draft's first five pages. Indeed, this method sets a pattern for the NLI draft as a whole. In its progress, the narrative is scenically conceived. The librarians and library assistants speak and listen, come and go, are called out and re-enter, and their movements account for many a linking passage between the blocks of lines through which the Hamlet-Shakespeare discussion moves increasingly into the foreground until it becomes inescapably the chapter's focus. The text-in-progress, at the same time, is definitely recognisable as text for *Ulysses*. John Eglinton, for instance, tells Mr Best that Haines— newcomer to Joyce's narrative personnel in *Ulysses*—has been to the library to enquire about 'Hyde's lovesongs' (NLI draft, 3.32-9). The author is clearly in charge. He takes care to substantiate the pointer he planted in the novel's Martello Tower scene: '—That reminds me, Haines said, rising, that I have to visit your national library today' (*U* 1, 469). This remark in the opening chapter likely enough indicates that, from the beginning, there was an intention, somewhere and somehow, to carry the *Ulysses* narrative to and into the National Library. But by the time Joyce settled for the Scylla & Charybdis episode that he did draft, he seems to have had little use for Haines. As fast as he pops into the chapter—which he does twice, though each time by report only—he vanishes again, yet he does not escape Mulligan's taunt, in episode 10, for having missed Dedalus on *Hamlet* (*U* 10, 1058-9).

Eglinton's mention (at 3.32-9 in the draft we are discussing) that Haines has gone in search of Hyde's love songs is picked up by Russell, who in swift succession warns about the danger of love songs, the six-shilling novel, and music-hall songs. By such indirections we move toward France and Mr Best's assessment of 'the finest flower of corruption in Mallarmé' (NLI draft, 4.03-4.16). This is Best's cue for one of the chapter's exquisite touches, his evocation of '*Hamlet / ou / Le Distrait / pièce de Shakespeare*'.

4.38| He repeated to John

4.39| Eglinton's new frown:

4.40| —[. . .]

4.42| *Pièce de Shakespeare*, don't

5.01| you know. It's so French. The

5.02| French point of view. Hamlet or

5.03| —The absentminded beggar, Stephen

5.04| said.

5.05| —Yes, I suppose it would be, John

5.06| Eglinton laughed. Excellent people,

5.07| no doubt, but distressingly

5.08| shortsighted in some matters.

With his quip, Stephen scores a laugh over Best's and Eglinton's belittling the French. Also, with a virtuoso sleight-of-hand, he draws a contemporary allusion: according to Eric Partridge, the lexicographer, and commentators who draw on him, everyone around the turn of the nineteenth to the twentieth century would have been aware of Arthur Sullivan's song to the words of Rudyard Kipling's Boer War poem *The Absentminded Beggar*—the title had become a nickname for a soldier. In their uniforms, moreover, Boer War soldiers broke with every past military dress code: They wore khaki. That this association came to Joyce at this point in the writing of the library scene shows in his momentary fumbling about how to introduce the idea. He writes and strikes out three speech openings for Stephen:

5.09| —More than one Hamlet has put off

5.10| black for khaki, Stephen said.

5.11| —He changes his inky cloak for

5.12| khaki in act five, Stephen

5.13| said.

5.14| —A khaki Hamlet, why not? Stephen

5.15| said. He kills nine lives for his

5.16| father's one, Stephen said. A khaki

5.17| Hamlet, as Mr Balfour has it,

5.18| doesn't hesitate to shoot.

Thus, in deciding on how the contemporary absentminded-beggar allusion might be brought to fit into the matter of *Hamlet*, Joyce posits, but rejects on the spot, the idea that, in Act V of Shakespeare's play, Hamlet, having escaped his near-fatal extradition to England, returns to Denmark in khaki. Joyce settles on having Stephen exceed Shakespeare by making Hamlet responsible for nine deaths, not the eight, including his own, for which he may be held responsible in the play. Perhaps, reflecting Joyce's sense of Shakespeare the actor's encompassing empathy, Shakespeare's son Hamnet is felt to be the play's ninth casualty.

Scrutiny of the ground layer in the NLI Scylla & Charybdis draft through its first five pages thus shows how the Hamlet theme is being built up obliquely, and from multiple angles. With the flourish of a khaki Hamlet as absent-minded beggar imagined in the narrative's illusioned 1904 real-time present, the vision has become spooky enough to bring Stephen into full command of the conversation as he introduces his notion of the two ghosts in the trebled Hamlets of the play *Hamlet*. The moment has come for this topic, aborted at line 215 in the NLI draft, to be spoken, but before it is sounded by Stephen himself, to our considerable surprise, John Eglinton intuitively anticipates him:

5.21| —He insists that *Hamlet* is a

5.22| ghoststory, John Eglinton

5.23| said for Mr Best's behoof.

5.24| ~~I am thy father's spirit~~

5.25| ~~doomed for a certain term to walk the night~~

5.26| Like

5.27| the fat boy in Pickwick he

5.28| wants to make our flesh

5.29| creep.

Words uttered by Eglinton (unbeknownst to him) serve Stephen, who now, through three silent phrases, works up his full energy to speak:

5.30| Hear, hear, O hear!

5.31| My flesh hears, creeping,

5.32| hears.

5.33| *If thou didst ever* . . . .

5.34| —What is a ghost? Stephen said

5.35| with tingling energy.

Eglinton feels, indeed already knows, what is coming. He has apparently heard it all before. So to have Stephen's—or, as we know, James Joyce's—sense of the ghost, or two ghosts, announced through Eglinton before Stephen begins is, at bottom, a touch of Shakespearean dramaturgy. It makes us feel that we are drawn into an ongoing action that began before we came in. We are nudged into assuming that Stephen Dedalus must have held forth on Shakespeare and Hamlet already many a time to members of his present audience.

5.34| —What is a ghost? Stephen said
5.35| with tingling energy. One who has
5.36| faded into impalpability through
5.37| death, ~~or~~ through absence or and
5.38| through change of manners,
5.39| through that oblivion which
5.40| death and absence bring. Elizabethan
5.41| London lay as far from Stratford
5.42| as corrupt Paris lies from this city
5.43| in our day. Who is this ghost,
6.01| a sablesilvered man returning to the
6.02| world that has has forgotten him? Who
6.03| is King Hamlet?
6.04| John Eglinton shifted his
6.05| spare body, leaning back to hear.
6.06| Lifted him.
6.07| —It is this hour of the day, Stephen
6.08| said, begging with a swift glance
6.09| their hearing, in Shakespeare's London.
6.10| We are in his Globe theatre on the
6.11| bankside. The flag is up. The
6.12| bear Sackerson growls in the
6.13| bearpit hard by. Sailors who
6.14| sailed with Drake chew their
6.15| sausages and stand with the
6.16| groundlings. The play begins.

6.17| An actor enters, clad

6.18| in the cast-off mail of a buck

6.19| of the court, a wellset man

6.20| with a deep voice. It is the ghost,

6.21| King Hamlet. The actor is

6.22| Shakespeare. And Shakespeare

6.23| speaks his words, calling the

6.24| young man to whom he

6.25| speaks, by name

6.26| *Hamlet, I am thy father's spirit*

6.27| and bidding him to list. To his

6.28| son he speaks, to his son the

6.29| prince, young Hamlet, and

6.30| to his son Hamlet Shakespeare

6.31| who has died in Stratford that

6.32| his namesake may live

6.33| for ever.

6.34| Is it possible that that

6.35| actor, a ghost by absence, in the

6.36| vesture of the elder Hamlet,

6.37| a ghost by death, speaking his

6.38| own words to his own son,

6.39| (for had Hamlet Shakespeare

6.40| lived he would have been

6.41| then a young man of twenty)

7.01| is it possible that he did not draw

7.02| the logical conclusion of those premises.

7.03| I am the murdered father; you are

7.04| the dispossessed son: your mother is

7.05| the guilty queen.

Savouring this draft exposition of Stephen's oration to the librarians, what may strike us is how it diverges from what, richly embellished, we remember reading in *Ulysses*, the book (at *U* 9, 147-80). Yet we recognise distinctly here already the stringent argument. Rereading the published text in contrast to the draft, what we also rediscover is Stephen's later double framing, in silent reflection, of the dramaturgy of his delivery.

Local colour. Work in all you know. Make them accomplices. (*U* 9, 158)

Composition of place. Ignatius Loyola, make haste to help me! (*U* 9, 163)

By the tingling energy of his opening, it appears, Stephen has instantly made his listeners accomplices. The effect is underscored on the narrative level by a first touch of 'composition of place' as Eglinton relaxes to enjoy the performance. Lest we pass over this as just a marginal mention, Eglinton's composing himself bodily gains weight from Stephen's noting it: 'Lifted him.' To make Stephen comment thus is an authorial touch of composition. It is so written to impress upon us that he, Stephen, is rendered aware of what he must and will do now and through all text revisions to follow over the draft's multiple layers. Stephen will work in all he knows, and rhetorically fulfil, as well, Loyola's maxim of 'composition of place'. On these terms, even at the text's basic layer that I am singling out, he already commands a place, imaginatively composed (for him), of the theatre and its expectant audience, among whom, for all we (with Stephen) may know, were some of Drake's sausage-chewing sailors on furlough among the groundling regulars. In the ensuing draft expansion, Joyce further invents, and so has Stephen unfold, another 'composition of place' prefatory to that of the buzz in the theatre before the play begins. This gels into a veritable film scene of real-life Shakespeare leaving his home in Silver street and making his way across the river to the Globe Theatre, there to impersonate the ghost of Hamlet's father. But the NLI draft's successive revisions do extend to casting Stephen-in-performance as aware of himself as an orator trained in ancient rules of rhetoric. Unprepared-for in material traces of drafting, Stephen's self-encouragement to work in all he knows, and his prayer to Ignatius Loyola to help him, stand fair-copied, suddenly in place only in the chapter version finalised, beyond the draft, in the Rosenbach manuscript. These two silent phrases in the achieved chapter text, 'local colour' and 'composition of place' thus constitute revisions in meta-textual response to the composition of *Ulysses* in progress. In trajectory of thought and in articulation, they veritably fuse the author James Joyce and the fictional Stephen Dedalus. Author and character are made reciprocally to mirror each other in their awareness of the text creation for, and dramaturgic control over, the narrative. This is an aspect of the author-and-character relationship to which we shall have occasion to return.

Russell meets Stephen's climactic peroration with utter incomprehension. The moment repeats and cuts more deeply than the clash between Stephen and Russell some minutes earlier over the teacher/schoolboy relationship of Plato and Aristotle. If Russell at that point voiced a biographist counter-position, though soon allowing himself to slip into a spiritualist argument, he now much more forcefully denies Stephen's tenets—or rather, what he misunderstands Stephen's tenets to be:

7.06| —But this prying into the family secrets

7.07| of a man, Russell said impatiently,

7.08| is interesting only to the parish

7.09| clerk. I mean we have the plays.

7.10| I mean when we read the poetry

7.11| of *King Lear* what is it to us

7.12| how the poet lived? As for living,

7.13| Villiers de l'Isle said, our servants

7.14| can do that for us. This peeping

7.15| and prying into a the greenroom

7.16| gossip of the day, ~~whe~~ the poet's

7.17| drinking habits, the poet's

7.18| debts.

There is one sentence in Russell's harangue of commonplaces that Stephen would subscribe to: 'I mean we have the plays.' But Stephen would construe it utterly differently. What Stephen says at the climax of his speech is secured precisely in his awareness that 'we have the play'. Yet how he reads the play has nothing to do with 'prying into the family secrets of a man'. Joyce casts Stephen as the radically logical reader of the text Shakespeare created for him, Stephen, and for us to understand. The play text is, as Samuel Beckett would phrase it years later, not about something; it is the thing itself. The perspective Joyce establishes for Stephen made itself already felt in Stephen's earlier comment on the relationship between Plato and Aristotle. That Aristotle began as Plato's schoolboy, Stephen sees not as contingently fortuitous, but as a structured relationship rooted in, and through, culture and education.

The peroration Stephen gives now is decidedly more complex: 'speaking his own words to his own son [. . .] is it possible that he did not draw the logical conclusion of those premises. I am the murdered father; you are the dispossessed son: your mother is the guilty queen.' The key to the logic of this conclusion lies not in the imagined theatrical moment at the Globe, nor in the contingent biographies of Hamlet father and son in the play, nor in William Shakespeare and Hamnet, his son in real life. It lies in the phrase 'speaking his own words to his own son'. What establishes the triangular structure of murdered father, dispossessed son, and guilty queen from the past theatre performance, recreated in the spoken words of Stephen Dedalus, is at the core the text that William Shakespeare, the author, wrote and William Shakespeare, the actor, spoke, speaking his own words. Joyce construes the text of Shakespeare's play not as an entertaining narrative, historical or theatrical, but as a structured set of signifiers, redoubled as spoken language from performing and performed characters. Joyce literally (as one might say) observes Shakespeare living the text he, Shakespeare, created. Through Stephen Dedalus as reader and performer, in turn, Joyce renders the Shakespeare text meaningful to signify a morally fraught human and social relationship.

In an earlier essay, I scrutinised Joyce's fundamental mode of perception, reading, and writing and posited the Joycean 'perception text' as node and link in the progress of his original composition.[13] Behind the Scylla & Charybdis draft from his own Hamlet chapter is Shakespeare's play text. From it, the moment when the ghost of Hamlet's father appears in questionable shape to his son Hamlet becomes, as Joyce reads it, his perception text. This he transforms into his own writing scene, which he gives to Stephen Dedalus to perform to his audience of librarians. When we in turn read the Scylla & Charybdis narrative, we must be aware that what we read is Joyce's envisioning and reading of real-life Shakespeare performing the ghost of old Hamlet confronting young Hamlet, his son, whom in a double-take he, real-life Shakespeare, imagines as the ghost of his son Hamnet 'who would have been then a young man of twenty' had he lived. James Joyce achieves the writing of his scene on the assumption that the author, William Shakespeare, construed his text for the play, now Joyce's perception text, from roots of creativity and writerly sensitivity fundamentally akin to his own. What Joyce assumes, foregrounds, and lets Stephen define as the structure of the relationship between Hamlet, the father; Hamlet, the son; and the guilty queen are thus the characters and character relationships Shakespeare presumably derived, in turn, from his assumed perception text. Materially speaking, this would have been the Saxo Grammaticus chronicle (though neither Joyce nor Stephen draws attention to the fact). To understand Shakespeare's conversion of the chronicle account into his dramatic text for *Hamlet* the way Joyce assumes he did rests on what we must assume to be Joyce's prior assumption that Shakespeare's creative mind worked like his own: that it was natural for both authors to order their perceptions into perception texts, and from such source reading, through recognition of their sources' relational structuring of signifiers, to convert their perception texts into their own creative writing.

---

13   The essay came out in parallel: '"He chronicled with patience": Early Joycean Progressions between Non-Fiction and Fiction', in *Joyce's Non-Fiction Writings*, ed. by Katherine Ebury and James Alexander Fraser (Cham, Switzerland: Palgrave Macmillan, 2018), pp. 55-75. Identical, though with additional end paragraphs, is '"He chronicled with patience": Early Joycean Progressions between Non-Fiction and Fiction', in *Text Genetics in Literary Modernism and Other Essays* (Cambridge: Open Book Publishers, 2018), pp. 47-64, https://www.openbookpublishers.com/htmlreader/978-1-78374-363-6/ch2.xhtml#_idTextAnchor006.

From Hamlet to Scylla & Charybdis: Experience into Art   291

For James Joyce, clearly, the analogy worked. He read Shakespeare's play text—together with the circumstance, established in tradition, that William Shakespeare acted Hamlet the ghost—as his, James Joyce's, perception text. From it, he shaped his new original text for Stephen to deliver. Behind this rationalisation on Joyce's part lay Joyce's imagined construction of Shakespeare's text as imagined from Shakespeare's perception text, the constellation of characters and events in the chronicle source for Shakespeare's play. That Chinese-box regress from one (Joyce's) perception text to the other perception text behind it (Shakespeare's) did no more, however, than render irrefutable Stephen's contention (as John Eglinton announces it) 'that *Hamlet* is a ghoststory'. It would not have allowed developing the discussion in the National Library from its opening on *Hamlet* to its wider sweep embracing 'Shakespeare' and Shakespeare. We discern in the draft manuscript itself that Joyce realised the difficulty, and with a sleight of hand instantly resolved it:

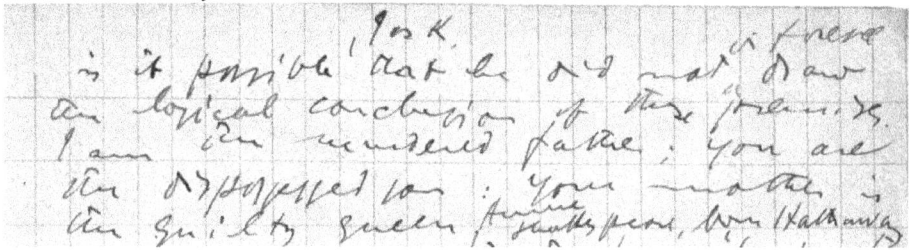

Fig. 9.1. Part of the NLI draft manuscript of the Scylla & Charybdis chapter.

The paragraph at first ends with the half-line 'the guilty queen.'—a line of three words closed with a full stop. The naming 'Anne | Shakespeare, born Hathaway' (without concluding full stop) is crowded into the line's remaining blank space later. While clearly, to judge from its positioning, this is a textual after-thought, it represents an addition made before the draft text had developed much further: it supplies explicitly the prior point of reference for the next sequence of Stephen's argument. After Russell's impatience about 'this prying into the family secrets', followed by Stephen's silent ruminations about having borrowed a pound from AE that he now argues himself into not paying back, Eglinton picks up the earlier thread. He easily follows Stephen's jump from the *dramatis persona* of the queen in *Hamlet* to Anne Shakespeare, born Hathaway in real life. Yet for Eglinton, the queen's guilt in the play does not by transposition attach also to Anne Shakespeare—or at least, the tradition of three centuries (as one might say) has erased it: 'Her ghost [. . .] has been laid for ever':

7.35| —Do you mean to fly in the face

7.36| of the tradition of three centuries?

7.37| John Eglinton asked. Her ghost at

7.38| least has been laid for ever. She

7.39| died, for literature I mean before

7.40| she was born.

8.01| —She died, Stephen retorted, sixtyseven years after

8.02| she was born.

Eglinton's attempt to counter Stephen is as irrelevant to Stephen's point as Russell's. Where Russell's argument expresses his misunderstanding of Stephen as contingently biographistic, Eglinton, in refuting Stephen, takes recourse in a canonised interpretative abstraction. Stephen's rejoinder to Eglinton, by contrast, lays the foundation for apperception and understanding in historical fact, irrefutable and irrespective of either biography fictionalised into narrative or drama, or a mythified latter-day reception of literature.

The 'She' that both Stephen and Eglinton talk about is no longer the guilty queen. She is Anne Shakespeare, born Hathaway. She will, as the chapter progresses, be a main subject developed through several sequences of Stephen's performance. Joyce, by his creative leap of introducing Anne Shakespeare/Hathaway where he does, shifts the focus of the Library discussion from *Hamlet* and Hamlet to real-life-Shakespeare and author-Shakespeare in conjunction. Fascinatingly, Joyce models this shift on what he has composed for Stephen Dedalus to deliver as William Shakespeare, the actor's, climactic equation of the guilty queen and Anne Shakespeare born Hathaway. The creative leap that Joyce has Shakespeare the actor make, in the play he authored, is to attribute to the actor, in his real-life identity Joyce imagined for him, a transformative extension to the 'logical conclusion' arising from the play's premises. This is tantamount to Joyce, in his turn, shifting the perception text he reads. It ceases to be William Shakespeare's play text for *Hamlet* and becomes instead what Joyce in his own person has assimilated from contemporary nineteenth-century scholarship and from all the plays of Shakespeare he has read (as opposed to those Stephen claims that he [Stephen? Joyce?] has not read). Joyce has thus assembled for himself a perception text from which to understand Shakespearean biography, historical circumstances of the Elizabethan age, and the dramatist's work—and to blend and write them into original parodistic text of his own. The first forceful signal of the matter-of-Shakespeare that Joyce construes for himself and creates as the text to be performed by Stephen Dedalus is Stephen's no-nonsense, historically precise rejoinder to John Eglinton: 'She died [. . .] sixtyseven years after she was born.' Stephen presents a concise overview of Anne Hathaway-Shakespeare's life, overtly biographical in nature:

8.01| —She died, Stephen retorted, sixtyseven years after

8.02| she was born. She saw him into and out

8.03| of the world. She suffered his first embraces,

8.04| she bore and bred his children and she

8.05| closed his eyes in death.

This is the opposite of a prying into family secrets. It anchors the life—Anne Hathaway's life—in reality, and it is the point in Stephen's explication of Shakespeare from which biography merges into art. Understanding Shakespeare's art becomes interwoven into life: the lived life of Anne Hathaway both with William and through his absences, and equally the lived life of William Shakespeare, his fellow men and female consorts in London, his brothers, his father, and the widening of Shakespeare's after-lives in the eyes and sensibilities of Frank Harris, Oscar Wilde, and Shakespeare scholars in Joyce's and the librarians' day.

As for the Hamlet chapter's anchoring Shakespeare in Anne Hathaway's life, her presence is all-encompassing. Anne 'saw him into and out of the world', suggesting that eight-year-old Anne assisted the midwife at Shakespeare's birth (and, perhaps, that Anne babysat for William well into her teens). Stephen's phrase spans the union of William Shakespeare and Anne Hathaway over Shakespeare's entire life. Their bonding is declared absolute. In union, William and Anne are perceived in a lifelong structured relationship. This carries and generates meaning, whereby in turn it becomes both narratable and performable to Stephen's eager listeners. In other words, Joyce's perception text, from the outset, springs from the lifetime bond uniting Anne Hathaway and William Shakespeare. From this core in turn is structured the performance text that Joyce generates for Stephen to speak in the National Library. Joyce's text for Stephen explores the implications of the structure of lifetime bonding into which, by Joyce's perception-text premise, Shakespeare was born. In this, radically and simply, the narrative and performance hinge on words Stephen speaks twice:

11.19| —There is no reconciliation, Stephen

11.20| said, unless there has been a

11.21| sundering.

13.15| —There is no reconciliation, Stephen

13.16| said, without a sundering.

The lifetime bonding draws dynamic energy from the ebb and flow of repulsion and attraction driven by the paired forces of sundering and reconciliation. Such energy metamorphoses contingency into meaningful order and ordered meaning. Stephen is made to explore this first through the phase of Anne and William's consummating their union in a cornfield—ryefield, we should say—and thence, soon afterward, through William's absconding to London. Stephen's librarian audience, intriguingly, offers explanations galore of contingency to rationalise that sundering, adducing even Socrates and his purported shrew of a wife, Xanthippe, in assumed parallel to William and Anne's (the parallel shrew's) separation. The curtest dismissal of meaning inherent in Shakespeare's choice to aim for Romeville—London—singing 'The girl I left behind me' is Eglinton's suggestion, based on hearsay, that Shakespeare may have made a mistake in marrying Anne. Once again, Stephen will allow no such rationalisation:

8.11| —Bosh! Stephen said rudely. A man of

8.12| genius makes no mistakes. His errors

8.13| are volitional and are the portals of

8.14| discovery.

In other words, while mistakes are contingent, 'errors' are 'volitional' and integral as signifiers into structuring a life—be it for the liver, be it for the life's reader. The union that structures William's and Anne's lives also harbours their separate living over many years—the unfaithfulness in Stratford of which the assembled librarians suspect Anne, and William's involvements in London—that even the sparse biographical data we have seem to point to. Again, Joyce through Stephen sees William's union with Anne and his promiscuity in London not as separate. Instead, he construes union and promiscuity to have their common root in William's original 'undoing'. It sealed his bond with Anne but kindled his promiscuity. This is thus declared a systemic consequence of their union.

15.19| [. . .] No wealth of words or

15.20| richness of experience will make ~~the~~

15.21| him who was overborne in a

15.22| cornfield, excuse me, a ryefield

15.23| a victor in his own eyes ever. No

15.24| later undoing will efface the

15.25| first. He may allow it to enflame

15.26| and darken his understanding

15.27| of himself. In youth he thinks

15.28| to put miles between himself

15.29| and it. No assumed dongiovannism

15.30| will save him. That goad of the

15.31| flesh will [. . .]

15.33| [darken] after a

15.34| moment of flame his own

15.35| understanding of himself.

The portals of discovery that volitional error unlocks, open up, not to triumph and self-aggrandisement, but to the insight that '[he] who was overborne in a cornfield, excuse me, a ryefield [will never be] a victor in his own eyes ever', but on the contrary be '[darkened] after a moment of flame [in] his own understanding of himself'. 'No assumed dongiovannism will save him.' Remarkable as this argument is in psychological terms, what is creatively seminal for the text-in-progress is that it intensifies the text's overall movement toward the linking of Shakespeare's life and his art in structured causality as Joyce construes the connection, and as Stephen is in process of presenting it. The life-as-source-of-art argument was already intensely discernible a couple of manuscript pages before, after Stephen's discussion of the 'middle period' of Shakespeare's *oeuvre*, the great tragedies. Joyce makes Stephen associate these plays with the life phases of Anne's and William's sundering. But 'the plays of Shakespeare's last years [. . .] breathe a different spirit'. Russell (this time) has caught on to Stephen's drift of reasoning. He instantly comments ('appeasingly'): 'The spirit of reconciliation'. Stephen thereupon continues:

13.23| Who and what is it that softens

13.24| for awhile the heart of a man,

13.25| of Pericles, shipwrecked in the

13.26| storms of a life's bitterness?

13.27| A baby girl. Marina [. . .] child of seastorm[.]

14.09| [. . .] That which was lost in

14.10| youth is reborn strangely in his wane

14.11| of life: his daughter's child. But

14.12| who will love the daughter if he

14.13| has not loved the mother?

14.14| [. . .] [W]ill he not see in her

14.15| recreated and with the memory of his

14.16| own youth added to her the images

14.17| which first awakened his love?

14.18| Do you know what you are

14.19| talking about? Love, yes. Amor vero

14.20| aliquid alicui bonum vult, unde a

14.21| et ea quae concupiscimus——

Joyce (through Stephen) constructs as reciprocal the resurgence in Shakespeare's art of Pericles's daughter Miranda in *Pericles*, the first of the late plays, and Shakespeare's experience of the birth of his grandchild. (In real life, the daughter who bore Shakespeare's first grandchild was Susanna, offspring of his and Anne's awakening to one another in the ryefield.) The reciprocity coalesces for Joyce through Stephen as the felt experience of a rebirth of love. The impulse to reconciliation after sundering, as Joyce reads his perception text and generates from it Stephen's delivery text, is absolutely rooted in the *a priori* assumption of the systemic interrelation of life and art. Joyce makes Stephen utter for his audience the rhetorical question, '[W]ill he not see in her recreated and with the memory of his own youth added to her the images which first awakened his love?' To deepen this moment, Joyce provides Stephen, and readers of the *Ulysses* narrative, with a pause of silent reflection: 'Do you know what you are talking about? Love, yes. Amor vero aliquid alicui bonum vult, unde et ea quae concupiscimus——'[14] The silent question 'Do you know what you are talking about?' and its answer may take a felt length of time to read, and to dwell on. In thought, the silent dialogue takes but a split-second to flit through Stephen's mind. As if in one breath, he speaks on in syntactical flow straight from the rhetorical question to his essential answer:

---

14 Stephen's silent reflection in English and Latin, be it noted, is already firmly in place at the draft's basic layer. Somewhat touched up, it reached the fair copy. But, together with spoken context, it got lost in transmission to the first edition. Its restoration on text-critical grounds in the critical and synoptic edition caused considerable critical turbulence. I have repeatedly explained the transmissional mishap at typescript level by which this passage and its preceding context failed to reach the 1922 edition and remained unacknowledged until 1984. The latest rehearsal of the problem may be found in 'Seeing James Joyce's *Ulysses* into the Digital Age', *Joyce Studies Annual 2018* (New York: Fordham University Press 2018), pp. 3-36 (pp. 19-22), and in this volume, essay 14, 'Love, yes. Word known to all men.'

14.22| —A man of genius above all whose own

14.23| image is to him, morally and

14.24| materially, the Handmaid of all

14.25| experience.

Insisting on the 'man of genius' as subject of his text, Joyce through Stephen triangulates the interdependence of life and art as a field of force among genius, self-image, and experience. The key to comprehending life and art in conjunction is the faculty of 'memory' transubstantiated into 'experience'. Through experience gained from memory, life and art in conjunction model, manifest, and express the self. It should not escape us as Joyce's readers that with the key word 'experience', the *Ulysses* text for Stephen picks up and carries forward Stephen's self-reflective words to Lynch in *A Portrait of the Artist as a Young Man*: 'When we come to the phenomenon of artistic conception, artistic gestation and artistic reproduction I require a new terminology and a new personal experience'. (*P* V, 1269-72) However far experience itself has carried Joyce since he put that sentence into Stephen's mouth, Stephen's tenets and reflections on Hamlet and Shakespeare in Scylla & Charybdis decidedly and repeatedly turn around 'the phenomenon of artistic conception, artistic gestation and artistic reproduction'. Thus, projecting forward from *A Portrait*, we should understand that it is essentially by his sense of himself, and out of his own self, that, in his Scylla & Charybdis chapter for *Ulysses*, Joyce claims to be shaping William Shakespeare. Morally and materially, Joyce models Shakespeare out of his own experience, and so essentially in his own image. The assertion of 'the man of genius', however, 'whose own image is for him the handmaid of all experience', is not as triumphant as it sounds when singled out as we have done. The train of thought devised for Stephen into which it falls carries on, as we have seen, from the near-apotheosis of reconciliation in his silent reflection, 'Do you know what you are talking about? Love, yes', to the deepened awareness of the 'darkening after a moment of flame [of] his own understanding of himself', which springs from the state of sundering. Remarkably, from here on over a stretch of twenty-nine manuscript lines from the bottom of page fifteen to page sixteen, line 26 in the NLI draft, we witness a text progression that had begun assertively but now grows less and less sure of itself:

15.30| [. . .] That goad of the

15.31| flesh will drive him into a

15.32| new passion—its darker

15.33| shadow—darkening after a

15.34| moment of flame his own

15.35| understanding of himself. A like

15.36| fate awaits him and both

15.37| rages like whirlpools

15.38| commingle. But the later

16.01| *rage* is a fever of the blood which

16.02| tortures but does not strike mortally

16.03| the soul. Under the apparent dialogue

16.04| and diatribe the speech is always

16.05| turned elsewhere, backward.

16.06| He returns, unsatisfied by ~~his~~ the creations

16.07| he has piled up between himself

16.08| and himself, to brood upon his

16.09| wound. Imogen the ravished is

16.10| Lucrece the undeflowered. There

16.11| are no mangods in our time. Shakespeare

16.12| passes towards eternity,

16.13| in undiminished personality,

16.14| unvisited by the eternal wisdom

16.15| ~~we heard about just now, unscathed by~~

16.16| untaught by the laws he

16.17| has exemplified. His beaver

16.18| is up a but he will not speak

16.19| or stay. A ghost, his words are

16.20| ~~for the night of mourning in~~

16.21| ~~which heard only in~~ For the night

16.22| ~~of despair, as~~ the wind around

16.23| Elsinore's rocks, ~~or~~ the sea's

16.24| voice, and only by him who is

16.25| |||*left blank*|||, the son

16.26| Consubstantial with the father

This stretch of speech drafted for Stephen to deliver is distinctly less assured than his preceding performance text has been, and it stumbles to an indecisive end. To read, in contrast, the published text corresponding to these twenty-nine manuscript lines—the draft comprises less than 200 words; U 9, 450-81 extends to approximately 430 words—shows how provisional Joyce must have felt the manuscript text to be, and how in response he rethought and significantly revised it. Shakespeare seems for a moment to escape Joyce altogether ('Shakespeare passes towards eternity') or to metamorphose back into the ghost whom William Shakespeare, the actor, impersonates ('His beaver is up'). This, in a fresh 'composition of place' over several syntactical fragments, conjures up 'Elsinore's rocks' and in the atmosphere of night and wind around them evokes a vision of 'the son / Consubstantial with the father'. We are back with Hamlet the father and Hamlet the son. It is the constellation in Shakespeare's play from which Stephen's performance started. The father-son constellation will once more recur toward the end of Stephen's performance, as we shall see. To express his sense of the unity of father and son, Stephen uses the strongest language he can command, the notion from Christian doctrine of their consubstantiality. Or should he be heard blaspheming? This is precisely the response Buck Mulligan chooses, eternal mocker in *Ulysses*. The consubstantiality of father and son is his cue, which he answers with his counter-blasphemous outcry 'Amen!'

We might even consider it a piece of self-irony on Joyce's part to let Mulligan enter just here. The NLI draft documents the *Ulysses* episode Scylla & Charybdis in the making. Occurring near the end of page sixteen of the manuscript, which extends to thirty-three pages, Mulligan's entry marks its midpoint. We assume that this draft draws on a parent 'Hamlet chapter' that Joyce in 1916 offered for pre-publication to Ezra Pound and preserves a significant residue from it. The Hamlet-Shakespeare matter indeed represents, I suggest, the core of that predecessor and provides the main narrative strand of the Scylla & Charybdis episode for *Ulysses*. This remains true for the Hamlet-Shakespeare passages yet to follow in the NLI draft's second half. Yet what the NLI manuscript materially also shows is that, by its midpoint reached, the substantial transformation of the lost 1916 *Hamlet* chapter into a *Ulysses* episode could and would be held back no longer.

Materially, from Buck Mulligan's entry on, the manuscript drastically changes its appearance. Starting right there in the bottom half of page sixteen, and onward over many of its subsequent leaves, it is heavily overcrowded with revisions and additions between the lines, in the right-hand-page left margins and on the facing left-hand versos of the pages preceding. To a large extent, all such revision and addition amplifies the situational matter arising from Buck Mulligan's fresh presence in the National library—although, it is true, changes in the Shakespeare matter are also involved. Thus, left-hand pages accommodate first draftings of such a set piece in the Shakespeare-Anne Hathaway context as the second-best bed dramulet, or the similarly stage-set appearance of William Shakespeare's brothers. These and a plethora of other changes and additions to the base-level run of writing in the draft, by such evidence in the penning itself, do not indicate that the texting was inherited from the 1916 *Hamlet*. They are more likely evidence of fresh invention in the NLI draft that parallels the revision and accretion of the matter of Mulligan through manuscript pages seventeen to thirty-three. This culminates in the episode's third playscript sequence, a list of characters, and even an opening dialogue exchange, for Mulligan's obscene invention of a play, 'Everyman His Own Wife'—of which only the list of characters, but not the attempt at dialogue, let alone the play, ever makes it into *Ulysses*.

Mulligan on arrival is welcomed to join the ongoing Shakespeare discussion, which he acknowledges facetiously enough: 'Shakespeare?' [. . .] '—To be sure, he said. The chap that writes like Synge.' Mr Best instantly tells him, too, that 'Haines was here [. . .]. He'll meet you after at the D.B.C.'—by which we learn for a second time in the chapter that Haines has come and gone again 'to buy the *Lovesongs of Connacht*'. The chapter's doubling of the information betrays, it feels, Joyce's concern to write a *Ulysses* episode beyond its predecessor, the 'Hamlet chapter' of 1916.

The matter-of-Shakespeare that we take to be the core sequence of the 1916 Hamlet does not end at the chapter hiatus of Mulligan's entry. It soon re-asserts itself with Eglinton's remark:

17.15| —Shakespeare's fellowcountrymen, John

17.16| Eglinton said, are rather tired of

17.17| our brilliancies of theorising.

One of these (Irish) theorisings, Oscar Wilde's 'picture of Mr W. H.', is cited as the most brilliant. On this the assembled librarians themselves have so much to say that Stephen can for a moment opt out of the Shakespeare discussion. To keep us aware of his presence, the narrative draws him in as he is mocked by Mulligan about the telegram he sent to 'Malachi Mulligan' and his drinking companions—among them Haines—at '[T]he Ship, Middle Abbey Street, Dublin'. Important for the chapter composition as a whole, Leopold Bloom's first appearance on the margin of the library scene is staged at this juncture, before the matter-of-Shakespeare resumes. Eventually, four draft pages on from Mulligan's entry, Eglinton's second attempt succeeds in bringing the library entertainment back on its original track:

20.18| —We want to hear more, John Eglinton

20.19| said. We are beginning to be interested

20.20| in Mrs W. Till now we had thought

20.21| of her, if at all, as a patient Griselda

20.22| or as Penelope stayathome.

Notably Eglinton identifies Ann as 'Mrs W.', that is, as Mrs William Shakespeare, the customary Victorian and post-Victorian form of written address for a married woman, so identified as an adjunct to her husband's household. In the book, this has been changed to 'Mrs. S.' To judge by the level and tone of this resumption of the earlier theme, Stephen's—that is, Joyce's—poetics behind his complex strands of argument in the first half of the episode-in-the-making have apparently thoroughly passed by John Eglinton and his fellow librarians. 'We are beginning to be interested in Mrs W.' instead betrays simple gossip curiosity. Stephen, no longer set on delivering a theoretical treatise, half plays along. In the end, as we know from the book text, he denies believing in his 'theory'—as his listeners call it—altogether; and indeed this is his exit strategy already in the NLI draft. Stephen also plays subversively at his listeners' level of interest. He sketches in gossipy terms Shakespeare's affluent living in London and regales them with Sir Walter Raleigh's rich apparel when he was arrested, and Queen Elizabeth I's under-linen that 'was as great as that of the queen of Sheba'. However, the sketch of Shakespeare as feudal dramatist, and of his private life in London consorting 'with Mary Fitton and lady Penelope Rich (I say nothing of the punks on the Bankside)' leads over to its counterpart question: 'What do you imagine poor Penelope was doing in Stratford?' Here Stephen subverts the gossip with his author's life-into-art logic. His rhetorical gambit—'Say that Shakespeare is the spurned lover in the sonnets. Once spurned twice spurned.'—re-establishes the interrelation of life and art, experience and creativity. The lines following distinguish the second spurner, Mary Fitton, from the first, Anne Hathaway:

21.11| [...] At least

21.12| one, the court wanton, spurned him

21.13| for a lord.

[...]

21.17| —For one younger and handsome.

21.18| Nor did she betray a vow.

The vow makes the essential difference. This, in Stephen's argument, pivots on the perception text itself, the fundamental situation that

Shakespeare the author composed for *Hamlet*, with Shakespeare the actor impersonating the ghost:

21.18| [. . .] For these

21.19| two offences are as raw in the ghost's

21.20| mind as is the carnal act

21.21| itself: the broken vow and

21.22| the dullbrained yokel on whom

21.23| her favour has descended.

Yet the words Stephen is here cast to speak do not morally condemn 'Penelope stayathome'. She in Stratford and William in London live in mutual sundering. Life, and from it experience, that earlier in Stephen's argument '[darkened] . . . his own understanding of himself' are correspondingly (if somewhat summarily) invoked in mitigation for Penelope—that is, for Anne who overbore William in a ryefield:

21.23| [. . .] Women

21.24| who seduce men younger

21.25| than themselves are, I daresay,

21.26| hot in the blood. And once a

21.27| seducer, twice a seducer.

The case is thus altered when the focus shifts to Joyce's poetics of life-into-art, delivered by Stephen, of Shakespeare's creative response in his art to life experience, and so to the creative capacity of the 'man of genius'. Stephen posits: 'Say that Shakespeare is the spurned lover in the sonnets', and with great urgency he challenges his listeners to grasp what he wishes to convey:

21.32|—The burden of proof is with you

21.33| and not with me, he said

21.34| frowning. If you deny that

21.35| in the third scene in *Hamlet*

21.36| he has branded her with

21.37| infamy explain why there is

21.38| no mention of her ~~for the~~

21.39| during the thirtyfour years

21.40| between the day he married

21.41| her and the day she buried

21.42| him.

One very practical reason for there being 'no mention' of Anne (or only one, as Stephen instantly corrects himself) is that, if Shakespeare's life is but scantily known, let alone documented, biographical data about Anne Hathaway is virtually non-existent. Stephen and his librarian listeners know this from the contemporary Shakespeare scholarship they keep referring to in the chapter's exchanges. Through the argument devised for Stephen, this indeterminate lacuna becomes, paradoxically, the very ground on which Joyce's poetics thrives: 'life *into* art *equals* experience *into* creativity'. No facts can falsify the assumptions and conclusions of this formula. Clutching, as the librarians all do, at the seemingly only known fact of documented intercourse between William and Anne, William's specific bequest of the second-best bed to her in his will, Stephen and the librarians (at Joyce's authorial behest) give free rein to speculations about the second-best bed, but offer nothing more than gossip. To objectify this mode in an adequate literary genre, their exchange resurges, as a play within the play in the novel's printed text. Further gossipy bantering ensues in the draft, covering Shakespeare as ruthless businessman, 'jobber and moneylender' 'who drew Shylock out of his own long pocket'—a playful, fresh instance of the life-into-art transformation that Stephen promotes. Might Shakespeare therefore be proven a jew, John Eglinton wants to know, whereas an opposite opinion (Irish to boot, favoured, as he instantly points out, by Stephen's 'dean of studies') claims him as a 'good Roman Catholic'. As for Anne, recipient of the second-best bed under whatever assumption: Stephen's own assessment of Shakespeare is of 'a man who holds so closely to what he calls his rights over what he calls his debts will hold tight also to what he calls his rights over her whom he calls his wife'. Stephen himself crowns this pronouncement with the well-known jingle: 'If others have their will [. . .] Ann hath a way.' Whether or not the bequest ('he omitted her name from the first draft' but 'was urged [. . .] to name her' in a codicil) betokens a reconciliation, Anne's survival in widowhood is the irrevocable seal on their final sundering.

24.37| [. . .] In

24.38| her age she takes up with lollard

24.39| preachers and hears about her

24.40| soul. Venus has turned bigot. It

24.41| is the agenbite of inwit, the

24.42| remorse of conscience: it is the

24.43| age of exhausted whoredom

24.44| groping for its god.

By this time, Stephen's and the librarians' anatomising of William and Anne appears roundly summed up in John Eglinton's digest:

25.04| [. . .] I should say that

25.05| only family poets have family lives. The author

25.06| of the Falstaff was not a family man. I feel

25.07| that the fat knight is his supreme

25.08| creation.

Stephen is given a brief interior monologue to call the bluff of Eglinton's 'denial of kindred'. Stephen recalls, and so we learn, that Eglinton has a father in Antrim who habitually visits him at the Library. Thereupon follows an astonishing narrative gambit of Joyce's in two parts. Its second part is another stretch of self-dialogue in Stephen's mind. We shall return to it because it is essential for understanding Joyce's poetics of art from life and experience in this chapter, and throughout *Ulysses*. The first part is a stretch of neutral narration to the reader: a simple, yet strange step in the narrative mechanics of the scene-in-progress. It brings in an attendant announcing to Eglinton that there is a gentleman outside to see him. 'Says he's your father.'—that is, precisely the man, if he is who he says he is, whom just before Eglinton has implicitly denied, but whom, and whose visits at the Library, Stephen has silently remembered. The gentleman himself is not brought onto the library scene, nor is the attendant seen or heard of again. The moment is irrelevant for the chapter's setting or plotting. Its one contextual function is to extend Stephen's awareness of family with the (for him) fraught significance of the 'father':

25.27| —A father is a necessary evil, Stephen said

25.28| battling with despair.

'Necessary' yet 'evil'—and the despair Stephen battles with arises, as we will see, from the self-dialogue just preceding it. Joyce, through Stephen's delivery, poses that the writing of *Hamlet* arose from Shakespeare's experience of the death of his father and that this freed Shakespeare in his creativity to reach absolute realms of pure art:

25.27| —A father is a necessary evil, Stephen said

25.28| battling with despair. He wrote the play

25.29| in the months following his father's

25.30| death.

[. . .]

25.43| [. . .] Fatherhood,

25.44| in the sense of conscious begetting,

25.45| is unknown to man: it is a

25.46| mystical estate, an apostolic

25.47| succession. When he wrote the

25.48| play he was not the father

25.49| of his own children merely, but

25.50| because no longer a son, he was

25.51| and felt himself the father

25.52| of all his race, the father

26.01| of his own grandfather, the father of his

26.02| unborn grandson who, by the same

26.03| token, never was born[.]

The position that Stephen has thus reached in his argument allows him over another five manuscript pages to unroll the panorama of 'family' that he posits Shakespeare transformed into his dramatic art. The range of family all-round provides, for the 'man of genius', experience so to be transubstantiated. Having discussed Anne in depth with the librarians, and having introduced and dismissed Shakespeare's father, Stephen now reaches out to Shakespeare's mother and his three brothers, Gilbert, Richard and Edmund. Responding to Eglinton's commonsense objection that the brothers' names were, after all, already in Shakespeare's sources, Stephen counters first with the question:

28.36| —Why did he take them in preference

28.37| to others?

and immediately follows up with his own trenchant rebuttal:

29.11| —Why? Stephen answered himself.

29.12| Because the theme of the false brother

29.13| is to Shakespeare, what the poor

29.14| are not, always with him.

It is a theme, therefore, to be metamorphosed into art: that is, the contingency of brothers in real life is a source of experience to be transfigured into theme through art, nourished on the creative gift and energy of genius.

Stephen's strategy to relate the contingency of family members in life and the construct of characters in dramatic art via the attribute—or is it the essence?—of names acquires stringency of its own in the final phase of his performance. Unsurprisingly, this thread in the discourse opens with the familiar quote from *Romeo and Juliet*:

26.46| —Names, John Eglinton said. What's

26.47| in a name?

27.01| —Much, Stephen said.

Within half a manuscript page Stephen's speech culminates for a second time in an apotheosis of Shakespeare he once earlier reached out for, if vaguely worded: 'Shakespeare passes towards eternity, in undiminished personality'. (NLI draft, 16.12-13) Stephen now focuses on the celestial representation of William Shakespeare's given name:

27.18| [. . .] A star, a daystar rose

27.19| at his birth. It shone by day

27.20| in the heavens over delta in

27.21| Cassiopeia, the *strange* constellation

27.22| which is the signature of his

27.23| name among the stars.

Equally unsurprisingly, this leaves the librarians puzzled:

27.28| —What is that, Mr Dedalus? the

27.29| quaker librarian asked. Was it a

27.30| celestial phenomenon really?

In spoken response, Stephen side-steps into Old Testament phrasing:

27.31| —A star by night, Stephen said.

27.32| The pillar of the cloud by day.

Yet in extension, James Joyce endows him with an unspoken, deep-searching self-definition:

27.33| Names. The fabulous artificer, a

27.34| hawklike man. You flew. What to find?

27.35| Paris. What did you find? Stephanos

27.36| Dedalos. Your crown where is it? Here.

27.37| Young men, christian association

27.38| hat. ~~Lapwing, you sit here. You sit~~

27.39| ~~with~~ Name yourself: Lapwing.

The two deletions of phrasing toward the end indicate how Stephen's giving himself the name 'Lapwing' is in the very writing being chiseled to best effect. Stephen is made to take recourse in the situation in *Hamlet* Act 5, Scene 2 when Osric, the detestable courtier (a 'base fly' in Hamlet's words), has just left, having delivered Claudius's challenge that Hamlet appear before the court to fight a duel with Laertes. Horatio comments, 'This lapwing runs away with the shell on his head' (*Hamlet* 5.2.178). Stephen adopts the name, picturing himself under it as a runaway akin to Osric, and like him in appearance even to the 'shell', or 'christian association hat' on his head (otherwise, as at NLI draft 10.11-12, his 'black hat' or 'casque'). Stephen's self-image as hatted, ground-creeping lapwing stands in strongest possible contrast to Shakespeare emblematised under 'delta in Cassiopeia [. . .] signature of his name among the stars'. At bottom, however, it is not Stephen Dedalus who is so set in opposition. It is James Joyce who reads himself in contrast to his perception text 'William Shakespeare'. This is inscribed undisguised into the silent monologue texted for Stephen.

27.33| Names. The fabulous artificer, a

27.34| hawklike man. You flew. What to find?

27.35| Paris. What did you find? Stephanos

27.36| Dedalos.

This is pure Joycean biography. It re-biographises the Stephen at the end of *A Portrait* into his author, and now, in retrospect, defines that novel's apostrophe, 'Welcome, O life! I go to encounter for the millionth time the reality of experience' (*P* V, 2788-9). Paris is the environment for encountering experience in the reality of life. What the silent reflection here in the NLI draft for Scylla & Charybdis specifies, with the greatest authenticity possible, is that in his months in Paris, James Joyce invented for himself the pseudonym 'Stephen D(a)edalus'. Between late 1902 and spring 1903, the then medical student James Aloisius Joyce lived in the French capital. These were intensely formative months. In self-projection into the future, the name he gave himself toward later renown as Irish author was, as the NLI draft declares in Joyce's handwriting and pseudo-Greek spelling, 'Stephanos Dedalos'. Joyce published the earliest *Dubliners* stories under this pseudonym and signed most, if not all, of his private correspondence, too, 'Stephen D(a)edalus'. It was not until around mid-1905 that he ceased so to name himself—coincidentally, as it happens, with breaking off and abandoning the writing project *Stephen Hero*. Over the time he asserted his identity with the self-created pseudonym, the name Stephen D(a)edalus constituted Joyce's repository to gather and articulate experience encountered in his life's realities. As a pivotal passage, the silent reflection written for Stephen Dedalus succinctly reveals Joyce's self-scrutiny. It allows us to grasp firmly the mutual identity of James Joyce and Stephen Dedalus in the present Scylla & Charybdis draft and the fully shaped chapter it progressively materialises into, as well as in all text extensions throughout the first half of *Ulysses* (Telemachus, Nestor, Proteus, and Scylla & Charybdis) that Joyce narrates through Stephen. If, in the course of this chapter, I have emphasised how Stephen Dedalus as fictional character functions to articulate and develop the underlying poetics governing James Joyce's experience of literary art in reception and in creation, it becomes increasingly evident from the moments of Stephen's silent thoughts in the NLI draft that it is Joyce himself who expresses himself directly. So revealed, Joyce may be seen and understood to express himself undisguisedly and in a near one-to-one symbiosis with Stephen Dedalus.

Some reflections narratively located in Stephen's mind clarify this essential identity of the author's and the narrated character's consciousness. One, trivial enough to be obvious, is the instance when the exchange with the librarians about brothers momentarily deviates silently into:

28.25| Where is your brother? In

28.26| the Apothecaries' hall.

This is a self-query of real-life Stephen Dedalus—that is, of James Joyce under the guise of his pseudonym. At the beginning of 1904, the year into which *Ulysses* is fictionalised, James Joyce's brother Stanislaus was, quite simply, a clerk in the Apothecaries' hall in Dublin—albeit that by 16 June, the fictional day of the Shakespeare discussion in the

National Library, he had quit the job.[15] For the moment of symbiosis or super-imposition where the fit of Joyce's trains of thought over those he composes as Stephen's is poignantly perfect, we return to the moment when Stephen recalls that John Eglinton has a father in Antrim who has a habit of visiting his son at the National Library. This stirs Stephen to reflect on his own situation:

25.19| And mine?

25.20| Hurrying to her squalid deathbed

25.21| from gay Paris on the quayside I touched

25.22| his hand. Fine, brown and shrunken. A

25.23| drunkard's hand. The voice, new

25.24| warmth, speaking new tones remembered.

25.25| The eyes that wish me well. But do they

25.26| know me?

This is Stephen facing an existence he feels is fatherless and solitary. It is, at the same time, authentically Joyce's deeply felt response to the moment when he returned from Paris at his father's bidding by a telegram telling him that his mother was dying. The curve of emotion in the text's movement is both wholly Stephen's and wholly James Joyce's. Just how intimately true it is, is reflected retrospectively in the one slight author's emendation at the end of the published text. The final pair of sentences in the draft: 'The eyes that wish me well. But do they know me?' are revised in the published *Ulysses* as 'The eyes that wish me well. But do not know me.' The change from query to statement, and consequently from question mark to full stop in the end punctuation, severs the assessment of the well-wishing eyes from the tentative anxiety of a James Joyce in Stephen Dedalus guise. It releases fictional Stephen Dedalus into autonomy as the character in the novel that he is—with a life-in-art and thus a narrated judgement of his own: 'But do not know me.' That final sentence pair, so precisely adjusted in the revision, is the

---

15 As may be gathered from Richard Ellmann, *James Joyce* (Oxford: Oxford University Press, ²1982), p. 144.

gesture by which James Joyce, the author, frees himself from the double identity in which he has (since Paris days) lived with Stephen Dedalus. Frank Budgen reports that Joyce admitted in conversation that Stephen 'has a shape that can't be changed'. Stephen, he said, 'no longer interests me to the same extent'.[16] Budgen specifies that Joyce made these remarks 'at about the time of the publication of the *Lestrygonians* episode'. Lestrygonians was, after the three episodes of the Telemachia, the fifth of the first sequence of Bloom chapters in *Ulysses*. The character of Joyce's shaping who was now constantly subject to change was Leopold Bloom. With Bloom, Joyce acquired, and through him expressed, 'a new personal experience'. He no longer creatively depended on Stephen Dedalus. Lestrygonians appeared in *The Little Review* in two instalments in September and October 1918. It was very much the time when Joyce braced himself for Scylla & Charybdis. Stephen may have 'no longer interest[ed him] to the same extent' because he had 'a shape that [couldn't] be changed', but clearly Joyce decided to work himself out of his erstwhile symbiosis with Stephen Dedalus by finally realising his plan of long standing. He fell back on his project, conceived and grown, I believe, already in the wake of his Triestine *Amleto* lectures, to let Stephen Dedalus *in loco auctoris* perform on Hamlet and Shakespeare in the National Library. Through to its conclusion, the Scylla & Charybdis chapter, from the NLI draft onwards where it is earliest documented, is progressively intensified as a chapter of sunderings. James Joyce strips off the fetters of the Stephen Dedalus role. The darker purpose of introducing at mid-chapter the mocker Buck Mulligan to scoff at Stephen's explication of Hamlet and Shakespeare to the librarians in the National Library proves by the chapter's end, once the bardolatrous entertainment is over, to stage Stephen parting company with him:

32.46| Part. The moment is coming

33.01| now.

33.02| My ~~soul~~ will, his will that fronts me,

33.03| seas are between.

---

16 Frank Budgen, *James Joyce and the Making of 'Ulysses' and Other Writings* (Oxford: Oxford University Press, 1972), p. 107.

Here once more—because we are in the Scylla & Charybdis chapter—Joyce still thinks and speaks through Stephen Dedalus. Yet at its most fundamental level, the moment turns into *Ulysses* narrative the inner parting of James Joyce from Oliver St. John Gogarty. Both of Joyce's sunderings, that from Stephen Dedalus and that from Buck Mulligan, do not preclude reconciliations of sorts. Stephen and Mulligan are granted reappearances in the nine-chapter sequence progressing through the second half of *Ulysses*, yet now purely as narrative characters among their fictional likes in the novel's web of recurrences, no longer as the real-life intellectual sparring partners: Mulligan, *alias* Oliver St. John Gogarty, and Stephen, *alter ego* of James Joyce, author of *Stephen Hero*, *A Portrait of the Artist as a Young Man*, and the first nine episodes of *Ulysses*. In the episodes that follow, Stephen Dedalus is liberated to booze with his cronies at the Maternity Hospital and at Burke's pub in Oxen of the Sun. He is narratively also set free for adoption by Leopold Bloom (and in wishful thinking, too, by his wife Molly) as their surrogate Hamnet for Rudy, the son they lost. Strongly under the influence of the novel's encompassing givens, Stephen moves through Circe, Eumeus, and Ithaka until, from Ithaka, and the Blooms' kitchen in 7 Eccles street, he 'passes towards eternity' in the manner he had imagined for William Shakespeare (at NLI draft 16.12-13). He does so 'in undiminished personality' as we engage with him as the creation in art, Stephen Dedalus, the pseudonymous *alter ego* experience of his real-life author, James Joyce. Life engenders experience that the man of genius metamorphoses into art. Below the *finis* stroke marking the end of the episode in the Rosenbach manuscript, Joyce implicitly reflects the experience that life with *Ulysses*-in-progress has opened and promises further to expand for him. Uniquely self-commenting the fair copy, he encrypts his own awareness of what, at mid-point by episode, his labours have accomplished. Joyce's coda to Scylla & Charybdis on the last leaf of the episode's fair copy states:

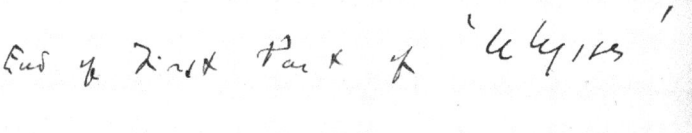

Fig. 9.2. Joyce's inscription at the end of the Rosenbach manuscript.

Emergence of James Joyce's Dialogue Poetics

To the memory of Wolfgang Clemen
who taught me Shakespeare

In the year 2022, we commemorated the publication of James Joyce's *Ulysses* one hundred years ago. On 2 February 1922, his fortieth birthday, Joyce held in his hands the first copy of the book towards and on which he had crafted his art, and developed himself, for twenty years and more. Our closest encounter with the emergence of that writing comes through the unfolding of its processes themselves. Focused on the genetics of literary texts, this essay endeavours to respond to the signals of creative awareness, experience, and pre-reading issuing into composition, such as they remain materially discernible in the authorial writing that survives. Our genetic pursuit sets in where Joyce's writing begins, with his epiphany vignettes. Our central interest is on his literary work in prose from *A Portrait of the Artist as a Young Man* to mid-*Ulysses*. This is a period of creativity in which self-reflection on his art, in terms of both poetics and technique, is at perhaps its most intense. At its centre in the mid-1910s is Joyce's encounter, from author to author, with William Shakespeare. It is the period through which he develops into a modernist writer.

Just upon reaching the age of eighteen, James Joyce on 20 January 1900 lectured to the Literary and Historical Society of University College Dublin from his essay 'Drama and Life'.[1] 'Drama' of the present and the prospective future is 'life', we understand, under a condition of literature. The crown witness is Shakespeare. 'Shakespeare was before all else a literary artist … [his] work … was literature in dialogue' (*Joyce:*

---

1   *James Joyce: Occasional, Critical, and Political Writings*, ed. by Kevin Barry (Oxford & New York: Oxford University Press, 2000), pp. 23-29.

Occasional, Critical, p. 23). The present essay builds upon the assumption that here lies the origin of Joyce's poetics as it grew and exfoliated, over close to two decades of writing, to reach Scylla & Charybdis, his Hamlet-and-Shakespeare chapter at the midpoint of *Ulysses*. 'Literature' is his chosen medium of art. 'Drama' is his narrative aspiration. 'Life' is the key to attaining it. He perceives—senses, observes, experiences, reads—life epiphanies throughout his day-to-day and night-to-night existence. Whether he senses, observes, experiences, reads: we posit reading-into-text as Joyce's core mode of perception, and of committing perception—perception text—into his prodigious memory. It is from his read and memory-stored perception texts that he creates and generates literary texts in and of his own writing. For these, he develops an increasingly refined poetics of drama narration, constitutive of narrative character and action in scene and dialogue. This narrative mode, too, deepens progressively to the protagonist's self-dialogue—scenically silent, audible only in the reading. Inviting, indeed demanding, reader perception and participation, the silent protagonist's self-dialogues in narrated scenes also establish the reader as participatory character dialogically within the literary artefact. It is under such premises that the following essay in its own mode of genetically critical analysis and argument reviews the emergence of Joyce's literary art.

I

James Joyce lived and thrived from 1904 to 1915 in Trieste. He was there liberated to the full to English as his language of literary creation.[2] As his language of public address, at the same time, he chose Italian. From 1907 onwards, and in the native language of his audiences and readers, he delivered lectures at the Università Popolare and wrote articles for the newspaper *Il Piccolo della Sera*. Significantly, the one theme that united his lectures and articles was Ireland and things Irish, historical and contemporary. He wished to convey to his fellow citizens in his chosen exile a perception and experience of his home country. In 1914, he planned a collection of his Triestine essays on the matter of Ireland for Italian

---

2 At somewhat greater length, I argued as much in 'James Joyce Interpreneur', *Genetic Joyce Studies* 4 (2004), https://www.geneticjoycestudies.org/articles/GJS4/GJS4_Gabler.

readers. The war broke out, the book was never published. It was to have borne the title *L'Irlanda alla sbarra* (Ireland at the Bar). The 1907 *Il Piccolo della Sera* article so named was to have opened it. 'Ireland at the Bar' sets out the case of an, in effect, colonialist British atrocity of condemning and hanging an accused native Irishman not guilty of the deed under sentence. In August 1882, a whole family by the name of (English) Joyce, (Gaelic) Seoighe, had been murdered in their home in Maamtrasna in Western Ireland. Brought to court with the perpetrators of the deed was also one Miles Joyce. He was related to both the murdered family and the gang rightly accused. Court procedures by which he could have been vindicated foundered catastrophically on the insuperable language barrier between the English judge and the Gaelic-only accused.

Opening the collection of Joyce's Triestine journalism, this narrative would have made its impact through its high levels of personal engagement. Joyce does not tell the story only from the de-personalised middle distance of the historian. He brings home a deep contemporary concern: the condition of Ireland under British rule, with its indigenous population in effect permanently muted through the absolute language barrier.[3] The narrative's strong personal undercurrent is likely due, too, to Joyce's felt knowledge that the Maamtrasna murders happened in his own lifetime. Admittedly, he was just six months old and cannot in any sense have had a memory of them. Yet not only would he have heard them talked about, but being who he was, he would also have read of them. Among his father's books was shelved the pamphlet account of 1884 by T. Harrington, M.P., *The Maamtrasna Massacre: Impeachment of the Trials*. This is how it reads:

> The third prisoner, Myles Joyce, was, before a quarter of an hour had elapsed, brought into the dock to stand his trial for complicity in the murder. The prisoner is older than either of the previous men who have been tried. He was dressed in older garments, but, unlike them, he did not appear to have the slightest knowledge of the language in which his trial is being conducted. He sits in the dock like them ... with his head leaning upon his arms, which he reels upon the bar of the dock. (1884, Appendix, p. 29)[4]

---

3   A recent account is Margaret Kelleher, *The Maamtrasna Murders: Language, Life and Death in Nineteenth-Century Ireland* (Dublin, University College Dublin Press, 2018).
4   The Appendix to Harrington's report is an abridged version of the text the *Freeman's Journal* published on 14 November 1882, in Timothy Harrington, M.P.,

This, by contrast, is what we read by James Joyce:

> The old man, as well as the other prisoners knew no English. The court was obliged to have recourse to the services of an interpreter. The cross-examination conducted with the help of this individual was sometimes tragic and sometimes comic. On one side there was the official interpreter and on the other the patriarch of the wretched tribe, who being little used to civil customs, seemed stupefied by all those judicial proceedings.
>
> The magistrate said: "Ask the accused whether he saw the woman on that morning."
>
> The question was repeated to him in Irish and the old man burst into complicated explanations gesturing, appealing to the other accused men & to heaven. Then worn out by the effort, he was silent again and the interpreter, addressing the magistrate, said:
>
> —He says that he did not, your worship.
>
> —Ask him whether he was close by that place at that time.
>
> The old man began again speaking and protesting; shouting, almost beside himself with the anguish of not understanding and of not making himself understood, weeping with anger and terror. And the interpreter, again drily:
>
> —He says no, your worship.
>
> At the end of the cross-examination the poor old man was found guilty and the case was sent forward to the Higher Court, which sentenced him to death. On the day of the execution of the sentence the square in front of the gaol was filled with people who on their knees were howling prayers in Irish for the repose of poor Miles Joyce's soul. Legend says that even the hangman could not make himself understood by the victim and that losing patience, he gave the miserable man's head a kick to thrust it into the noose.[5]

The Maamtrasna Massacre: Impeachment of the Trials (Dublin: Nation Office, 1884), https://archive.org/stream/maamtrasnamassac00harr/maamtrasnamassac00harr_djvu.txt.

5   The translation here given is not the one offered in *Joyce: Occasional, Critical, ...*, p. 145-47 [fn. 1] (which usefully appends, however, all of Joyce's Triestine articles in the Italian original; see *L'Irlanda alla sbarra* on pp. 217-19). *The James Joyce Archive*, ed. by Michael Groden, *et al.*, 63 vols. (New York & London: Garland Publishing Inc., 1977-1979), vol. 2, pp. 664-65, provides a sequence of translations into English from Joyce's Italian that may have been a communal effort of family and friends in Trieste in the mid-1910s. These survive, somewhat fragmented, from the archives of Stanislaus Joyce, meanwhile in the holdings of Cornell University Library. They are likely to have been prepared for an edition in English of Joyce's Triestine Italian articles that, like its Italian counterpart, was never realised. The translations were with some probability overseen, at least through select stretches, by Joyce himself. In their language and style, the Triestine translations feel distinctly closer to

This is Joycean narrative. At the same time, it is not Joycean invention. James Joyce did not invent freely. His artistry craved supports and scaffolds: structures from which and into which to be textured. Undoubtedly, his extraordinary powers of memory helped him at many a stile. But why, and most pertinently how, was memory activated into creative thinking and writing? Recourse could be taken in time-honoured traditions of memory systems that reach back even into antiquity:

> The rainladen trees of the avenue evoked in him, as always, memories of the girls and women in the plays of Gerhart Hauptmann: and the memory of their pale sorrows and the fragrance falling from the wet branches mingled in a mood of quiet joy. His morning walk across the city had begun: and he foreknew that as he passed the sloblands of Fairview he would think of the cloistral silverveined prose of Newman, that as he walked along the North Strand Road, glancing idly at the windows of the provision shops, he would recall the dark humour of Guido Cavalcanti and smile, that as he went by Baird's stonecutting works in Talbot Place the spirit of Ibsen would blow through him like a keen wind, a spirit of wayward boyish beauty, and that passing a grimy marine dealer's shop beyond the Liffey he would repeat the song by Ben Jonson which begins: *I was not wearier where I lay*.[6]

This accords with a Ciceronian memory template: text triggered from memory by recalling, in the imagination, given pre-defined nodes of an ambulatory circuit. In the case of Cicero, the rhetor would memorise a speech, ambling, say, through the rooms of a house. In performance, he would mentally pass again through that house, and in each room re-envisaged recall the memory-stored text allocated to this room, or that piece of furniture, for his next argument in the speech under delivery.[7] What Joyce describes for Stephen Dedalus is, we may be sure, modelled on his own practice. The memory marks in Dublin by which Stephen's morning walk leads, or might lead him, call up texts that he (Stephen *a.k.a.* the young student James Joyce) has read. The narrative

---

James Joyce's tone, rhythms and usage of English in the early 1910s than do later translations more readily accessible.
6   James Joyce, *A Portrait of the Artist as a Young Man: Authoritative Text Backgrounds and Contexts Criticism*, [P] ed. by Hans Walter Gabler, with Walter Hettche (New York & London: Garland Publishing Inc., 1993), V, 71-86.
7   A standard reference work for enquiring into memory systems is still Frances A. Yates, *The Art of Memory* (London: Routledge and Kegan Paul, 1966).

progress in the passage cited relies on atmospheric association. This is increasingly aggregated into textual echoes and culminates in a text quote from a poem by Ben Jonson. In other words, Joyce in the process of writing generates his composition from a bouquet of felt texts of perception—perception texts. Amalgamating the perception texts in all their fragrances results in a fresh, imaginatively scenic telling of Stephen Dedalus' late-morning ambulation through Dublin.

It is texts mentally or physically given, perception texts, that Joyce in composition transforms into text of his writing. His every experience, lived experience just as reading experience, was throughout, it appears, patterned in memory as text. To call up these perception texts therefore meant to read them. Creatively to do so meant to perceive and grasp their narratable core so as to transform it into autonomous narration. In the example of Joyce's telling *The Maamtrasna Massacre* in 'Ireland at the Bar', memory from experience and memory from reading coalesce. The emotional jolt when encountering the event in first reading the record of it can be felt through Joyce's text engendered from the record. While the past recounted by Tim Harrington as information to be read in print thus amounts to being the very perception text anterior to the text that Joyce shaped, it is unlikely that, writing *L'Irlanda alla sbarra* in 1907 in Trieste, he would actually have had Harrington's pamphlet at hand to re-read. He re-perceived from memory the text once read and the emotion experienced from it.

Through Joyce's creativity, then, Harrington's record was remoulded. But in so summarising, we hardly begin to discern what constitutes the quality and originality of the target text engendered from its perception text. In generating 'Ireland at the Bar' from its perception substrate, Joyce composed the narrative—specifically the opening as extracted above—scenically, both as a scene in dialogues among the characters in the court room and, in parallel, as a latent dialogue between the narration and the reader. Even in its guise as narrative, the passage thus becomes thoroughly dramatic. It exemplifies *in nuce* Joyce's notion of the 'esthetic image' that he has Stephen Dedalus offer to Lynch in *A Portrait* (V, 1464-1465): 'The esthetic image in the dramatic form is life purified in and projected from the human imagination'. There is hardly a more succinct definition, and indeed awareness, conceivable of Joyce's sense of the interrelationship between his perception texts and the target texts he turns them into. The concept of the 'esthetic image' that Joyce has Stephen define also deepens our understanding of the ever-quoted punch line that follows: 'The artist, like the God of creation, remains within or behind or beyond or above his handywork, invisible, refined out of existence, indifferent, paring his fingernails' (1467-1469). This proclamation is quintessentially dramatic and so in itself of the nature of an esthetic image. The perception texts from which it is generated, that give it power, and through which we fathom its depths, extend through western writing from Aristotle through medieval theology and philology up to literary renewals by Joyce's recent literary forebears, one Flaubert among them.

* * *

I proposed the term 'perception text' in an earlier investigation. A conference in York in 2012 explored the nature and range of Joyce's non-fictional writing. This theme offered a frame within which to discuss the relationship between perception texts and texts of James Joyce's fictional writing. On the premise that Joyce never invented independently when writing, I sought to show that what he wrote derived from—no: was kindled by—experience, emotion, knowledge and understanding perceived and read, and thence memory-stored in mental text mode for recycling into subsequent text composition. In his writing, Joyce relied on perception texts from which his own texts were creatively generated.

James Joyce's perception texts may be exogenous, as was the account of the Maamtrasna case at court. Equally, they may be texts of his own earlier writing. By common understanding, *Stephen Hero*, for example, is the genetic antecedent to *A Portrait of the Artist as a Young Man*. As drafted, *Stephen Hero* was hence the perception text for *A Portrait*. The surviving draft fragment as a matter of fact even preserves written traces of how it was reworked into the novel.[8] *Stephen Hero*, in its turn, sprang largely, we must assume, from Joyce's memory store of biographical and autobiographical perception. The writing aggregates the perception matter into a cumulated, and thereby at most proto-fictional, narrative. Hence I argued (and still do) that, in contrast to *A Portrait of the Artist*

---

8 See Claus Melchior, '*Stephen Hero*. Textentstehung und Text. Eine Untersuchung der Kompositions- und Arbeitsweise des frühen James Joyce', PhD dissertation, München (Bamberg, 1988).

as a Young Man, the fiction, the narrative *Stephen Hero* is basically still non-fictional.[9] As we are beginning to see, the 'perception text'-to-'text' correlation touches in essentials on James Joyce's creativity. It thus sheds light on his emergent poetics. What these are, and how he endeavours to write in accordance with them, Joyce seldom talks about, it is true, *in propria persona*. We must both intuit and analyse what he does and critically assess just how he shapes language and narrative into the design and articulation of his original writing.

* * *

Joyce's first endeavours to realise original writing in practice are the vignettes in language he himself labelled his 'epiphanies'. In the words of Stephen Daedalus of *Stephen Hero*, he defines the epiphany by its nature, which he decrees as a spiritual manifestation: 'By an epiphany he meant a sudden spiritual manifestation, whether in the vulgarity of speech or of gesture or in a memorable phase of the mind itself'.[10] Emphasising the effect a piece of writing must have so as to be recognised as an epiphany, Daedalus, for the benefit of his conversation partner and for ours, casts himself as an outside observer, an analyst and (as it were) a critic. He does not reveal the secrets of the workshop, does not lay open how an epiphany should be composed to attain that effect; that is: how, practically, to make it. What we initially have to go on, therefore, are the written outcomes of Joyce's epiphany writing, such as:

---

9   The York conference was held in 2012, the essays from it were published in 2018. My contribution came out in parallel: Hans Walter Gabler, '"He chronicled with patience": Early Joycean Progressions Between Non-Fiction and Fiction', in *Joyce's Non-Fiction Writings: 'Outside His Jurisfiction'*, ed. by Katherine Ebury and James Alexander Fraser (Cham: Palgrave Macmillan, 2018), pp. 55-75, comprises end paragraphs left out of the otherwise identical '"He chronicled with patience": Early Joycean Progressions Between Non-Fiction and Fiction', in *Text Genetics in Literary Modernism and Other Essays* (Cambridge: Open Book Publishers, 2018), pp. 47-64, https://www.openbookpublishers.com/htmlreader/978-1-78374-363-6/ch2.xhtml#_idTextAnchor006.

10 James Joyce, *Stephen Hero*, ed. by John J. Slocum and Herbert Cahoon (New York, New Directions, 1963), p. 211.

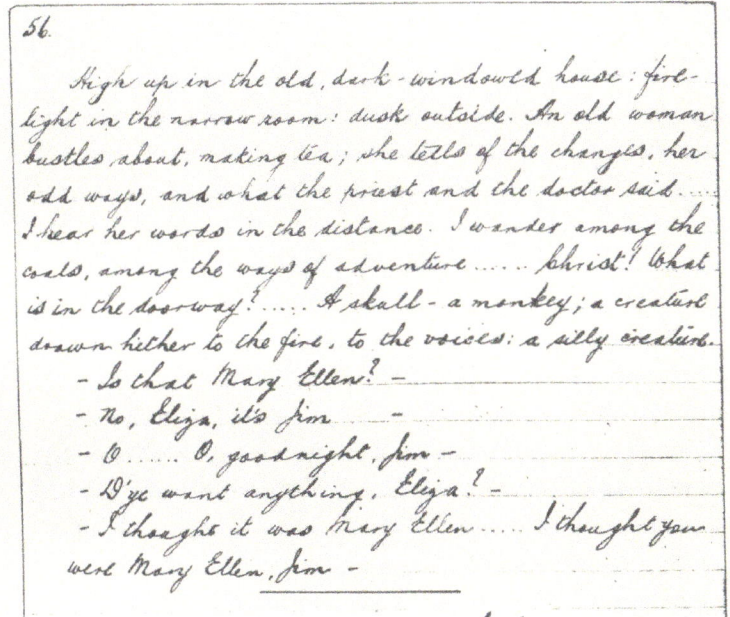

Fig. 10.1 'Epiphany 5' by the Joyce numbering.[11] *The James Joyce Archive*, Michael Groden et al., 1977-1979, vol. 7, p. 54.

High up in the old, dark-windowed house: firelight in the narrow room: dusk outside. An old woman bustles about, making tea; she tells of the changes, her odd ways, and what the priest and the doctor said. .... I hear her words in the distance. I wander among the coals, among the ways of adventure ...... Christ! What is in the doorway? .... A skull – a monkey; a creature drawn hither to the fire, to the voices: a silly creature.
—Is that Mary Ellen?—
—No, Eliza, it's Jim ...—
—D'ye want anything, Eliza?—
—I thought it was Mary Ellen ..... I thought you were Mary Ellen, Jim—[12]

This is unmistakably the texting of a situation remembered. At the same time, the altercations in spoken words betray a basic pre-organisation in text shape of the moment recalled. Joyce's notions of 'the esthetic image in the dramatic form' are a guide to appreciating how he worked the epiphany. The text vignette basically sets out a scene. This is played out

---

11   James Joyce, *Poems and Shorter Writings*, ed. by Richard Ellmann, A. Walton Litz, and John Wittier-Ferguson (London: Faber & Faber, 1991).
12   Epiphany no. 56 in Stanislaus Joyce's numbering; the handwriting is his.

between three characters: Eliza, an answering voice from a character of no name, and 'I'=Jim. It begins with a lengthy introduction wavering between narrative and stage direction and culminates in dialogue directly rendered, encapsuled in opening and closing dashes. What the record does not convey is what caused it to be written at all, nor what, in reading, we should make of it: 'what it means'.

James Joyce wrote poetry and composed epiphanies largely before venturing into extended prose. His epiphany phase lasted essentially until his sojourn in Paris from late 1902 to well into 1903. His epiphany vignettes began to serve as perception texts for narrative. Apparently his earliest writing of extended prose can be dated to 1903. In the spring a telegram called him back from Paris to the deathbed of his mother. Over the summer months, her son read to her his first attempts at the narrative that a few months later was, by a suggestion from brother Stanislaus, given the title *Stephen Hero*.[13] Neither do those attempts survive, nor does anything of the continuation until the 'University episode' as encompassed in the narrative's one extant fragment. Ample evidence of Joyce's re-use of epiphanies as perception texts pervades *Stephen Hero* as we have it, as well as *A Portrait of the Artist as a Young Man*, and even *Ulysses*.

The writing history of *A Portrait* is complicated. In the extant fair copy, Chapter II is materially the earliest. It dates, it appears, from a period of composition prior to that of the novel's first chapter as we have it, and of the chapters following. In its second segment, we re-encounter the Eliza epiphany: Eliza is now Ellen, the person mistakenly expected is Josephine, and Jim is of course Stephen. The vignette, revised as it is, comes second in a concatenation of scenes (ll. 253 to 356) that recognisably incorporates three epiphany adaptations. The integration of epiphany cores in this stretch of the Chapter II text bears witness to the determination to weld such erstwhile individual vignettes into the narrative. What this involves is revision of the identifiable perception texts to splice them into the continuous text flow, while at the same time lending the narrative a dramatically scenic quality.

---

13 Detailed by me on pp. xv-xvi in the Introduction to James Joyce, *A Portrait of the Artist as a Young Man*, ed. by John Paul Riquelme (New York: Norton, 2007). This edition adopts the reading text from James Joyce, *Ulysses. A Critical and Synoptic Edition*, prepared by Hans Walter Gabler with Wolfhard Steppe and Claus Melchior, 3 vols. (New York & London: Garland Publishing Inc., 1984; ²1986).

Most momentous in this respect is the integration into the *Portrait* fiction of the epiphany that in its vignette original reads thus:

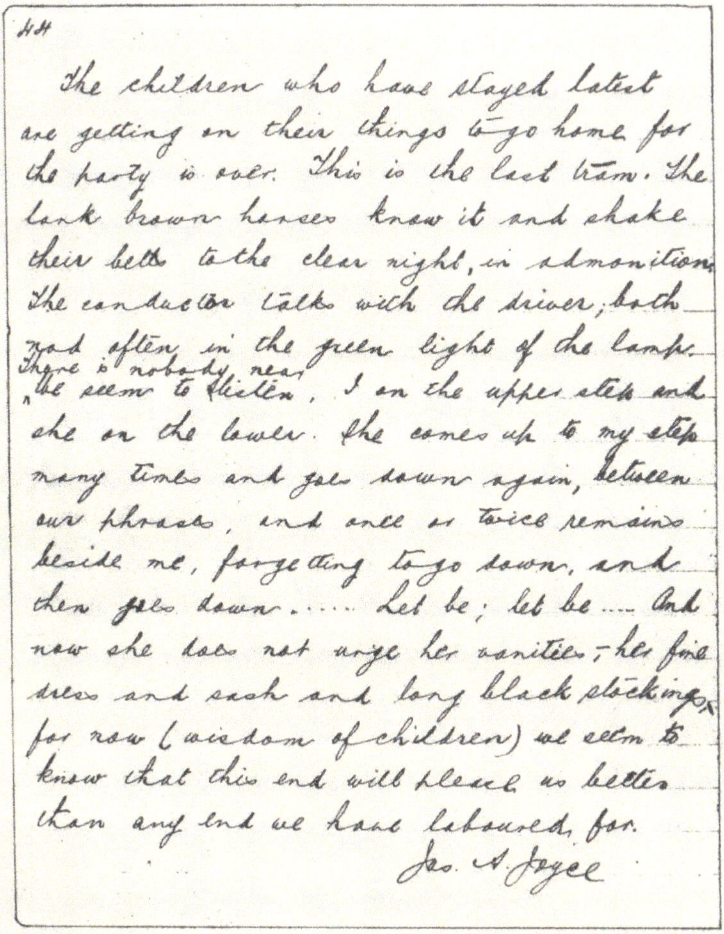

> [44]
>
> The children who have stayed latest are getting on their things to go home for the party is over. This is the last tram. The lank brown horses know it and shake their bells to the clear night, in admonition. The conductor talks with the driver; both nod often in the green light of the lamp. There is nobody near. We seem to listen, I on the upper step and she on the lower. She comes up to my step many times and goes down again, between our phrases, and once or twice remains beside me, forgetting to go down, and then goes down...... Let be; let be.... And now she does not urge her vanities — her fine dress and sash and long black stockings, for now (wisdom of children) we seem to know that this end will please us better than any end we have laboured for.
>
> Jas. A Joyce

Fig. 10.2 'Epiphany 3' by the Joyce numbering. *The James Joyce Archive*, Michael Groden *et al.*, 1977-1979, vol. 7, p. 64

In the fiction of *A Portrait*, its fresh instantiation is embedded in a continuous narrative culminating at this point in the re-use of the epiphany. The first sentence of the original record is extended into a full paragraph. Then follows the re-instantiation in the narrator's rendering (*Erlebte Rede*) from what was in this case a truly intimate perception text:

It was the last tram. The lank brown horses knew it and shook their bells to the clear night in admonition. The conductor talked with the driver, both nodding often in the green light of the lamp. On the empty seats of the tram were scattered a few coloured tickets. No sound of footsteps came up or down the road. No sound broke the peace of the night save when the lank brown horses rubbed their noses together and shook their bells.

They seemed to listen, he on the upper step and she on the lower. She came up to his step many times and went down to hers again between their phrases and once or twice stood close beside him for some moments on the upper step, forgetting to go down, and then went down. His heart danced upon her movements like a cork upon a tide. He heard what her eyes said to him from beneath their cowl and knew that in some dim past, whether in life or in revery, he had heard their tale before. He saw her urge her vanities, her fine dress and sash and long black stockings, and knew that he had yielded to them a thousand times. Yet a voice within him spoke above the noise of his dancing heart, asking him would he take her gift to which he had only to stretch out his hand. And he remembered the day when he and Eileen had stood looking into the hotel grounds, watching the waiters running up a trail of bunting on the flagstaff and the foxterrier scampering to and fro on the sunny lawn, and how, all of a sudden, she had broken out into a peal of laughter and had run down the sloping curve of the path. Now, as then, he stood listlessly in his place, seemingly a tranquil watcher of the scene before him.

—She too wants me to catch hold of her, he thought. That's why she came with me to the tram. I could easily catch hold of her when she comes up to my step: nobody is looking. I could hold her and kiss her.

But he did neither: and, when he was sitting alone in the deserted tram, he tore his ticket into shreds and stared gloomily at the corrugated footboard. (*P* II, 322-356)

This has become a thoroughly narrative text, while it has retained and in moments even intensified its scenic potential. Retained, too, is the dialogic quality we have begun to recognise as constitutive of the composition of original Joycean 'target' text from perception texts. Significantly, though, dialogue in the ordinary sense of exchanges in spoken words is absent. Exchanges between driver and conductor are reduced just to their nods. Response or the lack thereof between the boy and girl expresses itself, and is in the telling rendered, through gesture and in body language alone. Dialogue verbalised is cast as inaudible. Given exclusively to the boy, Stephen, it is altogether interior self-dialogue. It feels, one might say, like 'stream of consciousness' before the fact.

Over and above this, the singularity of this instance of a text of narrative fiction generated from its perception text lies in the reversal of the core insight of the event mirrored. The perception text's phrase: 'And now she does not urge her vanities' turns in the *Portrait* instantiation into its opposite: 'He saw her urge her vanities…'. Re-focussing the perception text's 'I' into the narrated 'he' permits in the fiction to reverse the characters' characters into their respective opposites: a coyly prude girl and an uncommunicative boy insecure in his vain superiority. In the service of Joyce's composition of narrative prose, the mode of perception text modified liberates at will the fictional realisation from the contingencies of the source perception.

What went by the wayside from the perception text in the present instance, however, was its epiphany nucleus, its 'sudden spiritual manifestation'. The phrase in the perception text that marks the moment is 'And now she does not urge her vanities', and the awareness drawn from it '(wisdom of children)' is confirmed in the third-person narration through the perception text's entire peroration. In contrast, the gain in characterisation—let us call it: realistic characterisation—achieved in re-composition meant a sacrifice of the original epiphanic moment. The loss was recognised and made up for in the narrative continuation. This allows us to witness the birth (as it were) of a perception text on the fly, instantly turned into narrative. The key phrase defining that moment is: 'And he *remembered* [my emphasis] the day when he and Eileen had stood looking into the hotel grounds …'. This conjures up a perception scene at once paralleled with the present experience on the steps of the tram: 'Now, as then, he stood listlessly in his place …'. Stephen is shown locked in his inertia. Alone he departs in the deserted tram and, tearing his ticket into shreds, 'stare[s] gloomily at the corrugated footboard'. This nadir of mood marks the climactic moment of the redoubled perception-through-memory scene. It kindles insight—yet not, within the fiction, Stephen's subjective insight, but instead objectively the sudden manifestation to the reader of the significance, the 'sudden spiritual manifestation', engendered through the transubstantiation of the 'It was the last tram' epiphany into the narrative fiction, now here in *A Portrait*, Chapter II, redoubled through the telling of a second perception remembered.

The effect achieved is momentous. It evidences how Joyce performed the task he appears to have set himself: to write prose in terms of the parameters of drama. Puzzled as we may long have been by, generally, no more than observing how pre-existing epiphanies were strewn out *literatim* or modified over Joyce's works from *Stephen Hero* to *Ulysses*, we gain from the present example a closer understanding of Joyce's early poetics. Evolving his prose writing practice, he deployed the epiphany template as a blueprint for narrative composition centred dramatically on character, dialogue and scene.

As character, the narrated 'he' of the fiction is, as shown, distinct from the perception text's 'I'. Whereas that 'I' is contingent on the epiphany's memory substratum, the novel's 'he'—its protagonist—is engendered from language in the original autonomy of fiction. In this autonomy established through the art of writing, 'he' has, like any and every narrated character, the potential for development, for being developed, through the fiction's narrated events and time.

* * *

The potential for text development is a main driving force of the creative process. In course of the emergence of a composition, it springs from impulses of revision. Re-visioning, seeing text written afresh and anew, relies essentially on the author's reading capacity. It kindles in turn the author's reimagining and recomposing text already written. The author's response on re-reading text in progress is hence properly a very first reader response to it. Reader response is thus an integral element of creativity in literary art. This is a dimension that Joyce recognised in his writing and re-writing—in his own creative response to texts of his that become for him fresh perception texts. He demonstrates such recognising and responding in Chapter V of *A Portrait of the Artist as a Young Man*, where, after ten years of the protagonist's life through the novel narrated, 'he' is made to anchor his memory once more in the conception text of the 'It was the last tram' epiphany:

> He had written verses for her again after ten years. Ten years before she had worn her shawl cowlwise about her head, sending sprays of her warm breath into the night air, tapping her foot upon the glassy road. It was the last tram; the lank brown horses knew it and shook their bells to the clear night in admonition. The conductor talked with the driver, both nodding often in the green light of the lamp. They stood on the steps of the tram, he on the upper, she on the lower. She came up to his step many times between their phrases and went down again and once or

> twice remained beside him forgetting to go down and then went down. Let be! Let be!
> Ten years from that wisdom of children to his folly. If he sent her the verses? They would be read out at breakfast amid the tapping of eggshells. Folly indeed! The brothers would laugh and try to wrest the page from each other with their strong hard fingers. The suave priest, her uncle, seated in his armchair, would hold the page at arm's length, read it smiling and approve of the literary form. (*P* V, 1706-1723)

This instantiation of the 'It was the last tram' epiphany may be said to have two perception texts. One is the seminal notation in Stanislaus Joyce's hand from James Joyce's early experimental days of writing vignettes in drama or prose notation. This version is re-instantiated here in much of its setting, in the noddings of conductor and driver, the ups and downs on the steps of the tram, the girl's 'remain[ing] beside him forgetting to go down and then [going] down'—a courtship dance apostrophised, as in the epiphany, as 'wisdom of children'. The other perception text for this passage from the novel's fifth chapter is, cannot help being, the instantiation in the second chapter. The double encounter in the one fiction with this text—the same and not the same—provides significant interpretational leverage; or, more specifically: the contrast between the instantiations in the second and in the fifth chapter demands, even as it activates, heightened reader participation. We note, for example, that an awareness on Stephen's part in Chapter II that 'she urges her vanities' is in Chapter V not repeated. Do we understand, therefore, that the narrator behind the second chapter's 'he' is unreliable; meaning: should we have read, should we read the observation as given in Chapter II as 'his' (Stephen's) 'mis-reading' of the girl? This is a serious option. It goes together with, even as it adds to the complexity and depth of interpretatively assessing, Stephen's insisting on his 'folly' then, ten years ago, and now.

Recognising and exploring correlations of perception texts and narrated text generated from them does not narrow interpretation. It opens the range of options for reader response to, and participation in, the text read. Looking at the two instantiations of the use in *A Portrait* of what was originally the 'It was the last tram' epiphany, we realise that they are in essence the author's, James Joyce's, arrangement into the narrative of perception texts, dissonant in their consonance, for the reader. In the Chapter II instantiation, it is the reader's task to perceive the youths on the steps of the tram as a coyly prude girl and an uncommunicative boy insecure in his vain superiority, as well as to measure the girl's perception against the neutral narrator's rendering. From the Chapter V instantiation, the reader is challenged to second-read the girl's perception of the passage in Chapter II, as well as to relate both instantiations, the past in Chapter II and the present in Chapter V, to Stephen's now-present memory recall of the parting on the steps of the tram ten years ago and to his self-awareness now, both as he articulates it and as the narrative conveys it. The perceptions and the likely enough manifold understandings generated from them in the reader are 'spiritual manifestations'—if we wish to uphold the high-falutin' Dedalus coinage—else, interpretative insights, or even just reading options. In all events, the text in its author arrangement offers challenges and gives incentives to active participatory reading. From the reading spring moments of each and any reader's experiencing the narrative read in the text through which it presents itself. The reader memory-stores such reading experiences to re-read from memory, whenever and wherever, under given recall stimuli.

* * *

As materially written down, Joyce's epiphanies record experience gained from observation, memory or dreams. We have seen that he turned to them for the perception and memory they stored, so as to develop from them new and original writing. The effect of their transfer was to infuse into his evolving narrative prose the principle of the dramatically heightened instance of perception. Albeit that the records of epiphanic moments as they happen to have been preserved are but incidental survivors from the workshop, they have yet paradigmatic significance. They help us to understand an essential dimension of Joyce's mode and nature of creative writing. Transferred and integrated into the run of Joyce's early narratives, his epiphany vignettes furthered essentially the development of his narrative art in practice as well as conceptually. His texts with increasing intensity invite, indeed necessitate, reader perception and participation. Joyce thus decisively extended the 'perception-text' to 'text' networking of his writing to encompass also the reading of that writing. His entire oeuvre will eventually imply the assumption, and the demand on the reader, that the text read enters, as read, into the reader's realms of experience. Through attaining the stance and the capacity to write and to narrate texts that the reader must always co-construct, Joyce establishes himself as a modernist writer.

II

The resumption of the 'It was the last tram' epiphany in Chapter V of *A Portrait* dovetails with Joyce's momentous re-encounter with Shakespeare. Focused on his in-depth exploration of *Hamlet*, it culminated in a series of twelve *Amleto* lectures, given in English, in late 1912 and into 1913 at the Università Popolare in Trieste—a grander appointment than his occasional earlier engagements at that institution, let alone his stints as a journalist in Trieste since 1907. The invitation now, a dozen years after lecturing on 'Drama and Life' to the Literary and Historical Society of University College Dublin, stimulated him to delve deeply into Shakespeare studies. From early spring through the summer and into the autumn of 1912 he did extensive research in preparation for his subject.[14] Through this immersion, he came to realise—not to put too fine a point on it—that Shakespeare wrote like him.

The perspective is not paradoxical, nor as aggrandising as it appears. Joyce had, in the process of his own writing over the dozen or so years since 'Drama and Life', experienced the force and responded to the creative stimulus of his erstwhile phrasing that Shakespeare's work was 'literature in dialogue'. The notion meanwhile answered very individually to his deep urge for innovation: to 'make it new' as Ezra Pound would summon the writers and artists of his generation to do—and as he soon did, not least under the strong impression that Joyce's *A Portrait of the Artist as a Young Man* made on him.

For Joyce, researching Shakespeare over those months from early summer to autumn 1912 meant intense immersion in the works and a most searching engagement with their author. The encounter and rapport were deeply felt from author to author. The scrutiny of *Hamlet* in particular was for Joyce, no doubt, foremost an explorative adventure under a fellow author's guiding question: 'How does he do it?' How does Shakespeare arrange, say, the situation in the play when the ghost of Hamlet's father demands of the son Hamlet to revenge the murder by which the father

---

14 William H. Quillian, 'Shakespeare in Trieste: Joyce's 1912 *Hamlet* lectures', *James Joyce Quarterly* 12, 1/2 (1974-1975), 7-63.

was killed? An anecdote that goes back to Shakespearean times served as pivot to the writer's, Joyce's, perception of how the writer, Shakespeare, construed the dramatic situation and correlated its significances. The anecdote has it that the actor who played the role of the ghost of Hamlet's father was also their leading playwright, as well as a main shareholder of the company—and the author of the play to be performed. The actor was William Shakespeare. On top of this, Joyce draws on William Shakespeare's personal tragedy. Shakespeare had a son by the name of Hamnet, or Hamlet, who died at the age of eleven years.

For the sake of argument, let us posit that Joyce read, and so construed as Shakespeare's, the author's and actor's, reading of the moment very much as he makes Stephen Dedalus set it out to his audience, the librarians in Dublin's National Library in the Scylla & Charybdis episode of *Ulysses*:

> The play begins.
> An actor enters, clad
> in the cast-off mail of a buck
> of the court, a wellset man
> with a deep voice. It is the ghost,
> King Hamlet. The actor is
> Shakespeare. And Shakespeare
> speaks his words, calling the
> young man to whom he
> speaks, by name
> *Hamlet, I am thy father's spirit*
> and bidding him list. To his
> son he speaks, to his son the
> prince, young Hamlet, and
> to his son Hamlet [sic] Shakespeare
> who has died in Stratford that
> his namesake may live
> for ever.[15]

To create the Russian-doll effect of Stephen Dedalus' speech to the librarians, James Joyce the author chooses his language carefully. 'Shakespeare speaks his words': that is, William Shakespeare speaks (Stephen says) the words he (Shakespeare) has written for the actor

---

15 This is a transcription strictly from Joyce's first extant penning of the Scylla & Charybdis episode of late 1918, in the copybook NLI8_A in the National Library of Ireland in Dublin, *The Joyce Papers 2002*, II.ii.1.a. Notebook, pre-numbering page [9] 7, https://catalogue.nli.ie/Collection/vtls000194606. Cf. *U* 9, 174-180.

(Shakespeare) to deliver in pronouncing what he (Shakespeare), impersonating the ghost of Hamlet's father, by his own (Shakespeare's) playscript has to utter. This is the performative situation that James Joyce sees in the configuration of Shakespeare's play at this scenic moment, and on which he, Joyce, consequently draws to configure the fiction's soliloquy for Stephen Dedalus. Texting that soliloquy, Joyce momentously transforms the perception text drawn from Shakespeare's play text. The intense emotional involvement of the play's characters, as well as of at least one of the actors: William Shakespeare, and the double-take on the son(s) Hamlet and Ham(n)et, are manifest only in Joyce's text for Stephen—yet they follow all from James Joyce's, the author's, guiding question in exposing himself to William Shakespeare, the pre-author: 'How does he do it?' James Joyce's answer through Stephen Dedalus is simply (as it were) that it is all a matter of logic:

>Is it possible that that
>actor, a ghost by absence, in the
>vesture of the elder Hamlet,
>a ghost by death, speaking his
>own words to his own son,
>(for had Hamlet [sic] Shakespeare
>lived he would have been
>then a young man of twenty)
>is it possible that he did not draw
>the logical conclusion of those premises.
>I am the murdered father; you are
>the dispossessed son: your mother is
>the guilty queen. (*Ibid.*)

Joyce construed into Stephen Dedalus' delivery of his, Stephen's, views on William Shakespeare, *Hamlet* and Hamlet/Hamnet, the text he, Joyce, read from the perception text as configured in Shakespeare's, the author's, arrangement of the character constellation and dialogue in *Hamlet*. An implication of Joyce's recognition that Shakespeare wrote like himself is likely to have been, too, an assumption that Shakespeare constituted his text and dialogue from, in turn, perception texts available to him. Shakespeare's main source for *Hamlet* was, as we know, the *Historica Danica* of Saxo Grammaticus. I will not here open an academic investigation of the text correlations between the play *Hamlet* and the source or sources within Shakespeare's material reach to assess whether Joyce was objectively correct in his assurance about Shakespeare's working methods and strategies, let alone the modes in which Shakespeare's creativity expressed itself. It is Joyce's imaginative leap that Shakespeare wrote like him which spurs on his, Joyce's, creativity. We do not need to validate Shakespeare through Joyce. But there is every reason to pay Joyce respect for validating by Shakespeare his early poetics and his endeavour to realise them through the early decades of his creative writing as literature in dialogue.

* * *

We noted above that Stephen and the girl in the 'It was the last tram' episode in Chapter II of *A Portrait* were not in spoken dialogue with each other, but that instead the narrative was texted as an intense silent self-dialogue of Stephen with himself. In the novel's mode of being, told through a third-person neutral voice, that dialogue is narrated, not acted. The narrative feels, as suggested, like stream of consciousness before the fact. Without mediation through a neutral voice, we encounter instead in the opening passage of the Proteus episode of *Ulysses* a self-dialogue of Stephen's in dramatic immediacy:

> Ineluctable modality of the visible: at least that if no more, thought through my eyes. Signatures of all things I am here to read, seaspawn and seawrack, the nearing tide, that rusty boot. Snotgreen, bluesilver, rust: coloured signs. Limits of the diaphane. But he adds: in bodies. Then he was aware of them bodies before of them coloured. How? By knocking his sconce against them, sure. Go easy. Bald he was and a millionaire, *maestro di color che sanno*. Limit of the diaphane in. Why in? Diaphane, adiaphane. If you can put your five fingers through it it is a gate, if not a door. Shut your eyes and see. (*U* 3, 1-9)

The use of the stream-of-consciousness technique for character narration sourced to the flow of awareness, observation and thought of the (given) protagonist is, as we know, the change of narrative stance of *Ulysses* over *A Portrait*. Stephen Dedalus is the protagonist of Telemachus, Nestor, and Proteus, the first three episodes of *Ulysses*, as he was throughout *A Portrait*. Once more he is given that role in Scylla & Charybdis, the ninth episode of *Ulysses* as published. Fascinatingly, there existed of that chapter a forerunner, a Hamlet chapter that Joyce announced to Ezra Pound in 1916 as written and sharable, and months later in 1917 offered him for publication in whole or in part (though it would suffer, Joyce said, were it published only in excerpts).[16] Pound, though it was he who had enquired about something publishable, did not take Joyce up on the Hamlet chapter offer.

What this means is that the first episodes that Joyce drafted for *Ulysses* were Telemachus and the Hamlet chapter that was to become Scylla & Charybdis. Telemachus and Hamlet in conjunction allow us to assess how Joyce, moving on from *A Portrait* to *Ulysses*, radicalised his declared poetics. In terms of narrative patterning, he broke through to his own original realisation of 'literature in dialogue'. He eliminated the third-person narrator. The foundations for the new modes of dialogue to which he advanced were laid in Telemachus and the Hamlet chapter. Their dialogic patterns were to govern *Ulysses* through its entire first half of nine episodes, with Scylla & Charybdis, finally datable to 1918, as the eventual capstone.

Telemachus represents the first phase in the process. From beginning to end, dialogue is the chapter's dominant propulsive force. Into its constant flow of the spoken word between Mulligan, Stephen, and later Haines (not to forget the milkwoman), it is true, are interspersed textual islands of Stephen's reflection, most memorable among them his vision of his mother after her death appearing to him in a dream (*U* 1, 102-110).[17] Yet Stephen's silent reflections and memories are relatively few and far between in the chapter. Overall, and in terms of narrative technique, Telemachus carries forward the mode that the first and third section of Chapter V of *A Portrait* progresses. These sections run an untrammelled course of spoken dialogue between Stephen and all his fellow students who cross his path through Dublin and whom, scene upon scene, he takes on in groups, or sequesters singly in discussions that he, soliloquising, dominates. Telemachus radicalises what those two *Portrait* sections began. It reduces to near-zero the mediation through a third-party narrator. It proceeds instead as a playscript in disguise. In narrating Telemachus on the pattern once already realised in Chapter V of *A Portrait of the Artist as a Young Man*, Joyce strove to emulate and to re-originalise the notion and

---

16   James Joyce to Ezra Pound, 9 April 1917, *Letters of James Joyce*, vol. I, ed. by Stuart Gilbert, (New York: The Viking Press, 1966 [1957]), p. 101.

17   Originally, it should be borne in mind, this was an epiphany, possibly the last one Joyce wrote. Now, in the incipient new fiction, it is redeployed according to the pattern of epiphany reuses in *A Portrait*.

practice of 'literature in dialogue'. The literature he achieves in such self-telling narrative possesses the performative quality of drama.

In his ensuing bid, in the Hamlet chapter to shape his literary practice to accord to his literature-in-dialogue poetics, Joyce focuses on the dramatic potential of soliloquy and rhetorical performance. For this, he needs just one protagonist performer—besides, of course, an audience. His performer is his trusted stand-by (and *alter ego*) Stephen Dedalus. Him he casts to lecture on Shakespeare and Hamlet to the librarians at his (Joyce's and Stephen's) regular haunt, Dublin's National Library.

*   *   *

The earliest material state in which Scylla & Charybdis exists is a draft from late 1918 in three copybooks.[18] It is the closest we get to the lost Hamlet of 1916. While it thus provides but mediate evidence, it yet permits detailed inference and fair deductions about the nature and timing, and pertinently about the state, of the 1916 text. The 1918 draft for Scylla & Charybdis runs sure-footed, on the whole, through its thirty-three copybook pages. There sprout throughout revisions and additions, accommodated between the lines and in the margins to the consecutive writing on the right-hand pages, as well as spread over the blank areas opposite on the left (i.e., the versos of the preceding pages). I stripped the many-layered draft text (with computer aid) to its basic level before accretion of all revisions and editions.[19] So assured is this core text of the draft that we may confidently posit that it represents the main substance of delivery from the lost 1916 Hamlet chapter. It renders evident a carefully worked progression, stage by stage, through Stephen's performance to his audience of librarians. The basic process design is dialogically scenic. Throughout, the librarians intercalate their responses, questions and queries that spur Stephen on in his lecturing. Yet at its core, this basic draft layer strings together the series of Stephen's soliloquies on the theme Hamlet; and beyond, on Shakespeare and on all the biographical circumstances Joyce read and structured as his perception texts to visualise and turn into narrative his sense of Shakespeare's art. For this, Joyce operated the rhetorical strategy of deduction through logic to steer his perception of Shakespeare's presumed perceptions into the text

---

18 Copybooks NLI8_A, _B and _C.
19 The link to my *Basic Hamlet Proposition* (2020) is: https://lmu-munich.academia.edu/HansWalterGabler/Drafts.

for Stephen's soliloquised performance in Scylla & Charybdis, erstwhile the Hamlet chapter. To get his perspective across, Joyce lets Russell, one of the librarians, pontificate in contrast:

> Art has to show us ideas, formless spiritual essences. The supreme question about a work of art is out of how deep a life does it spring.
> ....
> The rest is speculation of schoolboys for schoolboys.

To which Stephen retorts:

> —The schoolmen were schoolboys at first, Stephen said. Aristotle himself was Plato's prize schoolboy at first.

And the quips and bantering go on:

> —That model schoolboy, Stephen said, would ~~no doubt~~ find Hamlet's thoughts on the immortality of his soul as shallow as Plato's. John Eglinton said sharply:
> —I confess it makes my blood boil to hear anyone compare Plato and Aristotle.
> —Which of the two would have banished the creator of *Hamlet* from his commonwealth?, Stephen asked.[20]

This is strictly foreplay to Stephen's Shakespeare exegesis, which starts in earnest with the 'What is a ghost?' soliloquy already quoted, and from which Stephen's logical soliloquising against the librarians' scoffings takes its course. We have skipped, however, in the bantering sequence

---

20 See above, n. 15. Cf. *U* 9, 48-60—giving an example of considerable accretion of text from the basic layer of the 1918 draft, as here shown, to the text of *Ulysses*, first edition of 1922.

just given an important intercalation after 'Aristotle himself was Plato's prize schoolboy at first'.

> Formless spiritual essences. Father, Son and Holy Breath. I am the fire on the altar. I am the sacrificial butter. Masters of the Great white lodge. The Christ's bridesister, moisture of light, born of a virgin, repentant Sophia departed to the plane of buddhi. Mrs Cooper Oakley saw H.P.B's elemental. Fie! Fie! You naughtn't to look, missus, when a lady's a showing of her elemental.[21]

This is a full-blown 'stream of consciousness' silent self-dialogue of Stephen's. It picks up Russell's late nineteenth-century secularised conception of art and mock-rechristianises it. It is, at the same time, integral to the bantering sequence about Plato and Aristotle, schoolboys and schoolmen, and Hamlet and his creator in their commonwealth. We may take this sequence in all its elements as exemplary for the mode of realising literature in dialogue through the Hamlet chapter of 1916 to Scylla & Charybdis of late autumn 1918. What the draft's basic layer makes manifest is a mode for narrative in dialogue different from that realised for Telemachus. In contrast to Telemachus, the Hamlet chapter/ Scylla & Charybdis alternative has one actor protagonist, Stephen Dedalus. It realises the literature in dialogue stance through combining Stephen the orator with Stephen the silent reflecting thinker. His speech-runs, often extensive, are dialogic in themselves, both through their rhetoric and through always either provoking or parrying the librarians' responses. At this overt level, the episode acts out (as it were) a stage play theatrically, as an entertaining playlet titled, say, 'An Afternoon at Dublin's National Library'. Yet interwoven into the performable playlet is a dimension of literature in dialogue, that is, in drama mode, that the reader alone is given the privilege to discern and savour. This is the Stephen-only mental drama in silent self-dialogues.

---

21 See above, n. 15. Cf. *U* 9, 61-73.

* * *

The Scylla & Charybdis episode was finished in fair copy on New Year's Eve 1918. The text at this time gives ample evidence of Joyce's ease, after five Leopold Bloom chapters, of negotiating silent self-dialogue in an episode's overall flow. The extant draft for the chapter antedates the fair copy by only around two months. The cumulative accretion of revisions even during this brief timespan comprises a fair number of additions of self-dialogues of Stephen's—not to mention that such additions further increased throughout the typescript, two typescript revisions and several proofs towards the first-edition text. On the other hand, stripping the draft to its basic-layer text reveals that Stephen's silent self-dialogues, as an element of the episode's compositional design, are fully present already at the earliest material level of the chapter text that survives. The alternation of dialogic soliloquy and silent self-dialogues gives every appearance of being a basic pattern already of the earlier lost instantiation of the Hamlet chapter text, and so of Joyce's writing it in close succession to the drafting of the opening episode for *Ulysses*, Telemachus.

In his self-dialogues in Scylla & Charybdis, Stephen reflects threefold: on his ongoing overt performance; on his self-awareness and the changes it has undergone; or on moments of memory. What all three modes have in common in narrative terms is that the third-person neutral narrator as mediator of Stephen, the person narrated, has been replaced by Stephen in person as his own dialogic respondent in silent reflection. This suggests that Joyce's new-found-land of the silent self-dialogue in the stream of consciousness mode is his response, as text-dispositioning author, to his earlier narrative solution that we pinpointed above from the example of Stephen's self-dialogic silent rejection of the girl on the steps of the tram in the 'It was the last tram' sequence in *Portrait*, Chapter II. Joyce's own earlier writing mode has now become the perception text against which he pitches his present urge to find a new narrative solution for conveying Stephen in silent self-dialogue.

His reflections on his ongoing overt performance often take the form of unvoiced interjections:

>   —As we weave and unweave our bodies,
>   Stephen said, from day to day
>   so does the artist

> weave and unweave his image. And
> as the mole on my left shoulder is
> where it was when I was born
> though all my body has been
> woven of new stuff time after
> time so fro [sic] the ghost of unquiet
> father the image of the unliving
> son looks forth. At his age I
> shall see myself as I sit here
> today but by reflection from
> that which then I shall be.
> **Got round that neatly.**[22]

The final 'Got round that neatly.' is precisely such an unvoiced interjection after the intellectually demanding explication of weaving and unweaving in art as in body. The model of artistic creation that Stephen here sketches out we may even read, under our preoccupation in the present essay, as supporting that very model of generating original writing from perception and perception texts.

It is possible to dig yet deeper, though. Even just a single-line silent comment given to Stephen can reveal how far back into ultimately Joycean memory its ancestral line reaches. About one quarter into the base text of the 1918 draft, Stephen and the librarians begin to argue about how to judge the intimacy of William Shakespeare and Anne Hathaway, and how their relationship fared once Shakespeare left for London:

> Had the
> sensual poet who wrote Venus and Adonis,
> do you think, his eyes in his back that
> he chose in all Warwickshire the ugliest
> doxy to lie withal? He was chosen more
> than a chooser. The goddess who bends
> over the boy is a young, ripe and
> ardent woman who forces in a
> cornfield a lover, younger than
> herself.
> —Ryefield, Mr Best said.
> He murmured then with blond

---

22 See above, n. 15. Cf. *U* 9, 376-386 where the silent comment given in the draft has been altered.

> delight for all who would hear:
> Between the acres of the rye
> These pretty countryfolk would lie

Whereupon follows enigmatically Stephen's one-line silent interjection:

> Paris: a wellpleased pleaser.[23]

This is at the draft's base level one of as yet but few one-line interjections of silent thought into Stephen's overt oration. What such interjections have in common is that they are a dialogic response to the spoken text into which they are spliced. They sound so frequently as Joyce's self-dialogue with his text in progress, as self-comments on having managed turns of phrase or complex lines of argument successfully. Happily, he has his *alter ego* Stephen at hand in the fiction as spokesman for his own satisfaction with what he has artfully achieved. Through subsequent re-readings and re-workings of the chapter text, the Joycean self-dialogues in the guise of Stephen's silent thought accumulate. Among the chapter's intercalations of reflections in silent thought, the instance 'Paris: a wellpleased pleaser' has an intriguingly complex ancestry. Just how it is supposed to reflect on Stephen's sense of Shakespeare's predicament uttered in the preceding lines is difficult to pin down, in the first place. On second reflection, though, it might seem possible for the reader to link it back to the Proteus chapter:

> Paris rawly waking, crude sunlight on her lemon streets ... In Rodot's Yvonne and Madeleine newmake their tumbled beauties ... Faces of Paris men go by, their wellpleased pleasers, curled *conquistadores*. (*U* 3, 209-215)

But the connection is not easy to establish at the level of Stephen Dedalus, the fictional character. The paragraph of reference in Proteus is not one in the stream-of-consciousness narrative mode. Stephen Dedalus cannot, therefore, as the character in the fiction he is, be altogether plausibly assumed to remember having thought it. The memory, however elusive in *Ulysses*, is that of James Joyce. Its earliest source is to be found in a collection of prose vignettes Joyce assembled and calligraphed on loose sheets around 1914 in Trieste. We are back in those seminal Trieste years of Joyce's creativity from *A Portrait of the Artist as a Young Man* towards *Ulysses*. A child's hand (Giorgio's? Lucia's?)

---

23   See above, n. 15. Cf. *U* 9, 245-268.

wrote 'Giacomo Joyce' on the front of the notebook cover. This has since been taken as the collection's title. One vignette in the sequence reads:

> *The lady* goes *apace, apace, apace* .....Pure air on the upland road. Trieste is waking rawly: raw sunlight over its huddled browntiled roofs, testudoform; a multitude of prostrate bugs await a national deliverance. Belluomo rises from the bed of his wife's lover's wife: the busy housewife is astir, sloe-eyed, a saucer of acetic acid in her hand.....Pure air and silence on the upland road: and hoofs. A girl on horseback. Hedda! Hedda Gabler![24]

This is a vivid scene in the mode of Joyce's epiphanies of a decade earlier, and similarly composed out of an autobiographic impulse powerful enough to ignite a sudden spiritual manifestation—which we do not, however, have enough extra-textual knowledge to specify. The prose vignette, under the aegis of Joyce's writing economy, finds re-use. Within two to three years at most, since written from what we assume was a moment in Joyce's experience, it served him as perception text for a largely identical sketch, last in a series of seventeen brief prose vignettes divided off by asterisks in preparation for the Proteus chapter of *Ulysses*:[25]

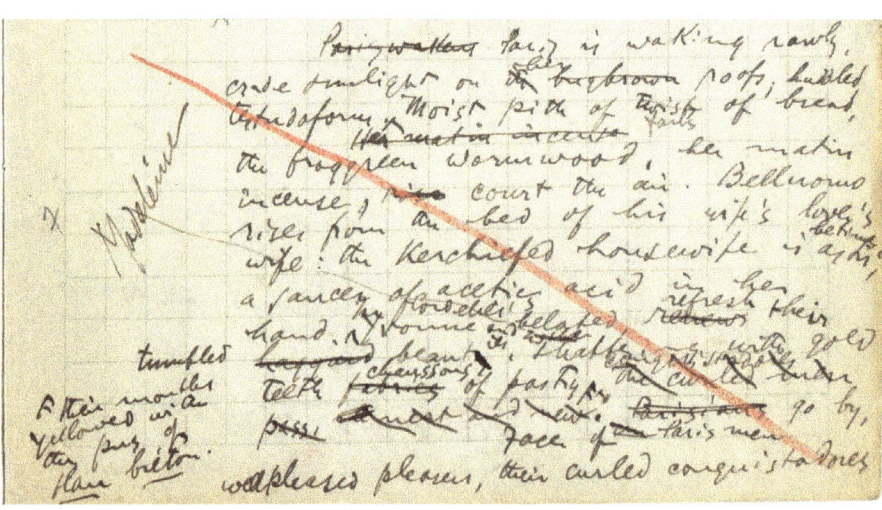

Fig. 10.3 National Library of Ireland, *The Joyce Papers 2002*, II.ii.1.a. Notebook, pre-numbering page [9] 7.

---

24 *Giacomo Joyce by James Joyce*, ed. by Richard Ellmann (London: Faber & Faber, 1968), p. 8. In the holograph original, I relish encountering my family name scripted in James Joyce's hand.

25 The full sequence of seventeen text vignettes between asterisks, of which this is the last, constitutes the first section of the notebook with earliest extant draft writing for Proteus and Sirens, http://catalogue.nli.ie/Record/vtls000357771#page/2/mode/1up.

The densely worked-over draft demonstrates what creative energy went into the re-perception of the perception text from *Giacomo Joyce*. The result of the authorial working-over of the draft sketch reads:

> Paris is waking rawly, crude sunlight on her roofs, huddled testudoform. Moist pith of farls of bread, the froggreen wormwood, her matin incense, court the air. Belluomo rises from the bed of his wife's lover's wife: the kerchiefed housewife is astir betimes, a saucer of acetic acid in her hand. In Cordelier's Yvonne and Madeleine belated, refresh their tumbled beauties, shattering with gold teeth chaussons of pastry, their mouths yellowed with the pus of flan bréton [*sic*].
>
> Faces of Paris men go by, wellpleased pleasers, their curled conquistadores

We get some sense of the surge of creativity, as well as emotion, that energized the enigmatic moment of silent reflection now in Proteus narrated as Stephen's.[26] The creative thought and emotion are in truth James Joyce's in his real-life authorial presence.

It is, then, once more James Joyce who, maybe two years after writing and working over the 'Paris is waking rawly' vignette, and approximately a year after integrating it into the episode text for Proteus, at the moment of composing the Scylla & Charybdis draft, responds again to a flash of memory. He writes it now as a spurt of silent reflection into Stephen's mind: 'Paris: a wellpleased pleaser'. Stephen Dedalus the fictional character is merely the author's vehicle for conveying his, the author's, James Joyce's, present and remembered thought and feeling. Or does he, on top of all that, reflect on his ongoing work of writing the present novel, halfway into it by episode count as he now is? Perceptive reading reception, in its full potential, extends to the perception of the creative dimensions of the text written. True enough, via its antecedent perception texts, the 'Paris: a wellpleased pleaser' phrase suggests a Trieste-to-Paris city trajectory. Yet, over and above that, as intercalated into Scylla & Charybdis, it may in addition reference Paris, infamous ravisher of Helen, causer of the Trojan war—and prize opponent thus of Odysseus.[27]

Through the Hamlet chapter draft, even at its basic level of inscription that we have isolated, the author in person moves insistently to the fore. While Stephen remains—of course—in the narrated foreground, James

---

26 For the state of the text published, cf. *U* 3, 209-215.
27 Daniel Ferrer: your suggestion (in private) helped me at this stile.

Joyce's simultaneous presence is more and more insistently felt within Stephen's impersonation. As the chapter proceeds, Stephen is cast to grow increasingly unsure in his self-estimation:

> The fabulous artificer, a
> hawklike man. You flew. What to find?
> Paris. What did you find? Stephanos
> Dedalos. Your crown where is it? Here.
> Young men, christian association
> hat. Lapwing ...
> Name yourself: Lapwing.[28]

To re-orient the self from memory grows painful. Stephen recognises his Daedalian flight as his Icarian fall, even though thereby he found Paris and his name (in the pseudo-Greek original). Yet, despondent, he feels reduced even to that ground-creeping bird by the image of which Horatio disparages King Claudius' messenger in the fifth act of *Hamlet*.[29] Still, outwardly the situation in the library remains contained. After an infinitesimal moment in time, Stephen smoothly continues in his overt delivery. Somewhat earlier he had suffered a stronger memory shock. An attendant entered with a message for Mr Best that Stephen for a moment thought was for him. He was caught off-guard and, with a sense of despair, felt defenceless against the influx of memory:

> —Sir, there's a gentleman outside
> to see you. **Me?** Says he's
> your father. **Enter Magee Mor: Japhet**
> **in search of a son**
> And mine?
> **Hurrying to her squalid deathbed**
> **from gay Paris on the quayside I touched**
> **his hand. Fine, brown and shrunken. A**
> **drunkard's hand. The voice, new**
> **warmth, speaking new tones remembered.**
> **The eyes that wish me well. But do they**
> **know me?**
> —A father is a necessary evil, Stephen said battling with despair.[30]

---

28 See above, n. 15. Cf. *U* 9, 952-954.
29 William Shakespeare, *Hamlet* 5.ii,178.
30 See above, n. 15. Cf. *U* 9, 819-28.

His initial reaction to the attendant's message is to divert a memory response. Stephen gasps silently '**Me?**' off-script of his performance, and into the text given him encroaches a sketchy notation on a non-personal level, strictly a stage direction ('**Enter Magee Mor: Japhet in search of a son**'), that is neither further realised nor deleted. The shock of the attendant's announcement that a man outside 'says he is your father' is however too strong to fend off: '**And mine?**'

The scene remembered is deeply fraught. In terms of the narrative and our academically critical parameters for assessing composition and guiding our reading of fiction, what we are given to read is fictional Stephen Dedalus in Scylla & Charybdis linked back to the fictional Stephen Dedalus in the Proteus chapter at the moment when he received that (mis-spelled) French telegram: 'Nother dying. Come home. Father.' (*U* 3, 199) By our critical conventions we would leave explication at that. Yet the author of *Ulysses* dramatically pulls down the fences of academic enclosure. He does so too when he makes Stephen Dedalus remember that he found the name Stephanos Dedalos in Paris. It is James Joyce as the man and author in person who, through the text he has written to be fictionally delivered or thought by Stephen Dedalus, communicates what he felt and thought at a key moment in his life directly to the reader. The situation conveyed in his words, through the narrative's protagonist, is his experience. Under the reading contract for fiction, it is recounted as thought and remembered by Stephen Dedalus. Yet what we read and experience is simultaneously not fictional. It is not to be re-experienced in reading merely as invented for the reality-effect of the narrated protagonist in a fictional never-never-land, on the occasion of the performance of a playlet at the National Library in Dublin on the fictional date of 16 June 1904. The experience is James Joyce's personal experience on a real day in March 1903 when, summoned by the telegram, he came home to Ireland and was met on the quayside (in Kingstown, now Dun Laoghaire) by his father, John Stanislaus Joyce.

The perception-text referent, then, for Telemachus, with Nestor and Proteus, and for the Hamlet chapter as it is progressing to become Scylla & Charybdis, is the man James Joyce. But just what, artistically and compositionally, does Joyce the author do to achieve this double perspective for the reader? Receptively reading the text in published print as *Ulysses*, the novel, the reader yet also receives through the text composed the unmediated communication—dramatically unmediated, it might be said—of the author's real-life experience and emotion behind the fiction. Joyce has already given us the template, I suggest, on which, in the Hamlet chapter Scylla & Charybdis he modelled the correlation-in-composition and relationship-in-performance of James Joyce and Stephen Dedalus. The logic of the scene as he, Joyce, perceives it when Hamlet encounters the ghost of his father, arises for him, as we noted, from the treble nature of that scene: the play as a whole was written by William Shakespeare. In performance, William Shakespeare the actor took the part of the ghost. The words he spoke as actor were the words written by him as the play's author. Taking this constellation seriously as Joyce's perception text for composing his Hamlet chapter Scylla & Charybdis, its interplay of Stephen Dedalus and his author becomes perfectly lucid. James Joyce is the chapter's text author. By strength of his pseudonym Stephanos Dedalos/Stephen Dedalus, he impersonates, he infuses himself into, the protagonist of the playlet in Dublin's National Library. The text that as actor he speaks is the text he wrote as author. Resurrecting that text in performing it through Stephen, his medium, Joyce is thus, in a manner, the ghost behind the text the reader reads. In that Joyce composed the episode text for Stephen at two levels, moreover, the overt and the silent, the situation is really fourfold in nature. The silent level Joyce short-circuited as his immediate line of communication from author to reader. On that circuit, Joyce is not the ghost behind the text. Not disguised or shielded by the mask of fiction, he communicates directly that he, the son—the felt Hamlet of the re-encounter—meets a ghost there on the quayside, his father in 'questionable shape': 'new warmth, new tones', and '[t]he eyes that wish me well. But do they know me?'. Instantly thereupon, though, Joyce the author has his *alter ego* resume the overt oration: '—A father is a necessary evil, Stephen said'. Yet, reading Joyce's message to us we sense his despair in real life at that moment in (photographically speaking) treble exposure, with Stephen's despair, too, and with Hamlet's. Joyce designs a poetics to compose like Shakespeare, since before him Shakespeare wrote like Joyce.

Structures of Memory and Orientation: Steering a Course Through Wandering Rocks

To the memory of Clive Hart

'End of First Part of "Ulysses" | New Year's Eve | 1918'. This was the note James Joyce appended to the last page of his fair-copy manuscript of the novel's ninth episode, Scylla & Charybdis. It affirms his accomplishment, as well as the assurance that *Ulysses* will go forward for another nine episodes. In early planning phases for the novel, Joyce had wavered between twenty-four and seventeen chapters, but at the time he reached mid-novel by chapter count, its extension to eighteen episodes stood firm. When declaring the end of the novel's first half, it is true, Joyce does not reveal how he intends to commence its second half. Reading along the surfaces of action and character movement, we feel nonetheless little surprised when, on leaving the National Library, the narrative takes us out into the throng of the city. The tenth chapter is universally recognised and celebrated as the novel's Dublin episode. In terms of the backdrop of *Ulysses* in Homer's *Odyssey*, however, we should by rights be intensely surprised that this chapter does not have a counterpart episode in Homer. By Joyce's workshop title, which we still universally use to identify the novel's chapters, it is the episode of the Wandering Rocks. With it, Joyce encompasses in *Ulysses* Circe's either/or suggestions to Odysseus concerning how, upon leaving her, he might continue sailing homeward. In Homer, Odysseus chooses to be rowed onward through the perilous narrows between Scylla & Charybdis, the rock and the whirlpool. He eschews Circe's alternative, the passage through the wandering rocks. Joyce, by contrast, steers *Ulysses* through both of Circe's routes. The legendary source for the novel's tenth episode is antiquity's epic of Jason's quest for the Golden Fleece. Joyce singles out its phase of greatest danger: the passage through the wandering or clashing rocks, the *symplegades*. Wandering Rocks in *Ulysses* has hitherto been explored almost exclusively as the book's Dublin chapter, with scarce attention to its workshop title. Closer regard to its singular design therefore seems warranted.

In form, the chapter stands out by its division into segments separated by triple asterisks. When written in early 1919, this tenth episode was the first *Ulysses* chapter to be in any way sub-segmented. The patterning of the seventh episode, Aeolus, using crossheads resembling newspaper headlines, happened later, in proof, while the novel's seventeenth episode, Ithaka, divided differently again into 'question-and-answer' units, was yet a long way from being written. In the surviving materials from Joyce's workshop, only one precedent exists for the division of narrative material by asterisks. This is a collection of 'purple passages', separated by triple asterisks, in a notebook preceding the composition in narrative continuity of the third episode, Proteus. The individuation of the passages in the notebook precedes the structuring proper of the Proteus chapter, into which the passages are subsequently found to have been dispersed, and from which the asterisk dividers disappeared in the process. In the case of Wandering Rocks, however, the analogous dividers have made it into the published text: they actually determine the episode structure.

Is it an abstract structure? Is it properly divisional, or are we encouraged to read continuously across the dividers, much as we presumably do with Aeolus—since in that chapter the crossheads, while they act as momentary jolts to smooth reading, can always be 'overread' in favour of the continuous narrative that remains discernible beneath them. The case is altered with Wandering Rocks insofar as each segment is a self-contained micronarrative. Does the segmentation as such derive, one might wonder, from an assembly of material for the chapter akin to the 'purple passages' preliminarily assembled for Proteus? It does not seem unwarranted to speculate that the aggregation of text for the chapter may have begun with the collection of more or less self-contained units; in their published form, they are still sufficiently detached from one another in narrative content—Clive Hart's just plea for the chapter's very special mode of unity notwithstanding.[1] It is through modes of correlation across its detached segments that the episode succeeds in being the novel's Dublin chapter and does not fall apart as an assembly of vignettes of Dublin citizens in their city surroundings. However individually independent the texts between asterisks may have been in their first writing, in the published text, and before it in the pages of the Rosenbach manuscript,[2] they structurally cohere, and the asterisks marking their division are integral to the structure.

Essential to that structure is their number, nineteen in all. The Rosenbach manuscript happens to give specific evidence that the number nineteen was on Joyce's mind at the time of writing. At the bottom of manuscript page 24 a passage lies concealed, since struck through, replaced by other text, and itself (further revised) repositioned elsewhere. As originally written, it reads: 'Two bonneted women trudged along London bridge road, one with a sanded umbrella, the other with a black bag in which nineteen cockles rattled.' The uneven total organises the sequence of segments symmetrically around the middle segment, the tenth. This is where Leopold Bloom sneak-previews and buys *Sweets of Sin* for Molly. What Joyce thus does in pivoting the Wandering Rocks chapter upon its tenth segment is, in miniature, what he had accomplished once before in structuring the entire novel *A Portrait of the Artist as a Young Man* symmetrically around its middle segment. Underneath this novel's division into five chapters lies a total of 19 segments, already characteristically divided by asterisks, too.[3]

That the manuscript of the Wandering Rocks chapter for *Ulysses* as we first have it is not wholly in Joyce's hand but, in approximately its final third, in the hand of Frank Budgen, is unique in the Rosenbach manuscript. Joyce himself, again in his own handwriting, authenticates

---

[1] Clive Hart, 'Wandering Rocks', in *James Joyce's* Ulysses. *Critical Essays*, ed. by Clive Hart and David Hayman (Berkeley–Los Angeles–London: University of California Press, 1974), pp. 181-216 (pp. 188-89).

[2] Pages 1 to 31 a holograph in James Joyce's hand, pages 32-48 written out by Frank Budgen at Joyce's dictation.

[3] This is discussed in detail in Hans Walter Gabler, 'The Genesis of *A Portrait of the Artist as a Young Man*' in the present volume; previously published in *Critical Essays on James Joyce's A Portrait of the Artist as a Young Man*, ed. by Philip Brady and James F. Carens (New York: G.K. Hall, 1998), pp. 83-112.

it on the last manuscript page: 'pp. 32-48 were written by my friend Francis Budgen at my dictation from notes during my illness Jan Feb 1919[.] James Joyce[.]' Joyce's illness was an acute worsening of his chronic eye troubles. What 'notes' would he have had to resort to that he felt incapable of himself rewriting in holograph beyond page 31, yet was capable of dictating at an equal level of fluency and literary stringency to Budgen for pages 32 onwards? The text does not in any significant way change in character between the pages in Joyce's hand and the subsequent lines penned by Frank Budgen, hence we cannot suppose that the source materials that stood behind the respective document sections changed when the hands changed. We cannot but assume that what Joyce called 'notes' for the Budgen stretch was simply the continuation of the kind of draft material from which he prepared his own fair copy through the preceding thirty-one pages. It seems natural enough to posit that the draft material in its entirety was already segmented throughout into units delimited by asterisks. However, the fair-copy inscription carries evidence of distinctly greater significance. Clive Hart, and Frank Budgen before him, have taught Joyce readers to pay attention to what Clive Hart calls the 'interpolations' throughout the chapter segments: stray snippets of text that seem displaced, since their narrative context is not integrated in the segment where they are found, but in one or more other among the nineteen segments in all. The interpolations have been noted, but have hitherto remained under-explored as to their function and effect in the episode. In particular, moreover, we have as yet no knowledge of when, genetically, they were interpolated into their respective positions in the chapter text.

The Rosenbach manuscript reveals that the interpolations were not an afterthought—that is, the fair-copy and dictation sections contain the interpolations, in their majority, already in place, even while, quite naturally, and according to Joyce's constantly accretive mode of composition, a few more were added both to the Rosenbach pages and in successive proofs. Taken together, the presence of interpolations at the fair-copy/dictation stage and their further increase go to prove that there is narrative method and functional purpose behind them. In other words, we may with confidence assume that Joyce's 'notes' were essentially the outcome of the creative thought he had already invested in the texting and structuring of the episode before it reached the Rosenbach manuscript stage, and that Joyce very well knew what, in particular, he wished to construct and achieve with those conspicuous text dislocations throughout the chapter. To put an initial thesis in a nutshell: they are, and were to Joyce, textual devices bracketing the chapter's segment divisions. They are innovative in the manner in which they create cohesion: in the spirit of modernism, they do so non-narratively. They make full claim upon the reader's alertness and memory. At a distinct further level of complexity, moreover, they constitute the textual markers by which the novel's chapter about Dublin turns simultaneously into its epic template, the mythic episode of Jason's navigation through the Wandering Rocks. In this sense, surely, the snippets in dislocation are wandering rocks. The reader's opportunity lies in commanding the passageways through the text like another Jason, and surviving the episode's quest.

To his own essay of 1974 on Wandering Rocks in *James Joyce's* Ulysses. *Critical Essays*, Clive Hart usefully attaches a list of the dislocations he names 'interpolations', extending to thirty-one items.[4] Hart's list constitutes a text specification, with commentary, on the interpolation patterning to which Frank Budgen already draws attention in his book, *James Joyce and the Making of* Ulysses.[5] Budgen simply assesses the interpolations as dislocations in terms of place and time in the reality of the episode's narrative Dublin environment. In contrast, Hart attempts (and is sometimes at a loss) to interpret why the interpolations should have been placed in just the context into which they are set. Neither Budgen nor Hart see or reason the interpolations as a compositional feature *sui generis*. They relate them firmly to time, place and personnel in Dublin as the chapter tells them, but do not provide narratological reflections on the structural and significative potential inherent in the episode's modes of construction. Only Budgen, in a few instances,

---

4   Clive Hart, 'Wandering Rocks'; the List is on pp. 203-14. Hart omits one early passage qualifying as an 'interpolation', overlooking, it seems, that Budgen before him had opened his account of the displacements with just this half-sentence: 'Father John Conmee stepped into the Dollymount tram on ‹Annesley› Newcomen bridge.' [The bridge name revised in Joyce's manuscript.]

5   First published London 1934. Clive Hart himself re-edited this early classic of Joyce studies in 1972: Frank Budgen, *James Joyce and the Making of 'Ulysses', and other writings*, with an introduction by Clive Hart (London: Oxford University Press, 1972, 1989); Budgen's discussion of the 'interpolations' extends over pages 126 to 129.

fleetingly invokes memory as the faculty with which to allay the puzzlement of the text dislocations. He hints thereby at the role to be played by the reader in comprehending the episode's multiple significances.

The interpolations are forward-directed as much as backward-directed elements in the text. Where their direction is backward, the links they establish are likely to be picked up with just a small effort of memory. Where they project forward, however, the linkings they aim at remain obscure, or may not be picked up at all on a first reading. But as soon as we engage in a second reading, we appreciate at once what stimulus springs from the forward-directed linkings. The recall established on a first reading turns into an anticipatory memory co-active in creating for the reader, during the re-reading process, the text that is yet to come. Such openness and perception in reading and re-reading gains exponential significance (so to speak) in this chapter that, in terms of Homer and Odysseus, tells a non-story. 'The episode's mythic template is an absence—a route not taken.' With the narrative he designs in Wandering Rocks, Joyce 'encourages the (re)reader to construct, through her reading and the memory of her reading', and so to imagine, with him, the route from among Circe's alternatives that Homer did not choose for Odysseus.[6] Thus, Wandering Rocks models the way the cultural skill of reading works and how written texts challenge that skill. The episode exercises for us and with us what it means, through active and engaged reading, to construct and experience worlds.

The interpolations found in the second to fourth chapter segments help to specify the technique and its effects. The mention in the second (Corny Kelleher) segment that 'Father John Conmee stepped into the Dollymount tram on Newcomen bridge' (213-14) becomes an interpolation proper, it is true, only at the sixth stage of proofing through its there visibly being separated as a paragraph. Yet, as the 'Father Conmee' element, it is in a 'Corny Kelleher' segment, and, synchronising sequences of events between the first and second episode segments as it does, it is essentially an interpolation already

---

6   'Such reading...for Odysseus.' These sentences render Lucy Barnes' insight into Joyce's creative imagining and forming of Wandering Rocks. The phrasings within quotation marks are *literatim* her words in the proof margins of this essay as she was attending to it as publisher's editor.

in the Rosenbach manuscript. The other interpolative half-sentence in the second segment, '[...]while a generous white arm from a window in Eccles street flung forth a coin' (222-23), signals the potential of interpolations to refer back not just to matter narrated in the current chapter, but to activate, too, reading memories of the preceding narrative of *Ulysses* as a whole. It allows one to consider in one's imagination why that arm should be white at all, that is: naked. The first interpolation in the fourth (Dedalus sisters) segment combines and tops the functions of those preceding: 'Father Conmee walked through Clongowes fields, his thinsocked ankles tickled by stubble.' (264-65) It is double-tiered. On the surface, it is merely a link back to the 'Father Conmee' segment. Yet at its core, it aims to activate powers of multiple discernment through reading memory. Not only must the mention in the episode's first segment that 'Father Conmee walked through Clongowes fields' (185-86) be recalled. It must also be remembered that he did so only in memory. Hence it must, or should, be recognised that the retrospective link is established, beyond the confines of *Ulysses*, to *A Portrait of the Artist as a Young Man*, to which the 'Clongowes fields' belong.

The first example of a forward-directed interpolation, by contrast, bursts into the one-legged sailor's jerking himself up Eccles street in the third segment: '^J. J. O'Molloy's white careworn face was told that Mr Lambert was in the warehouse with a visitor.^' (236-37) We are never anywhere in the episode (I believe) enlightened as to who tells J. J. O'Molloy where to find Ned Lambert. More than 200 lines on, in the eighth segment, he joins Lambert and a visitor—identified only by his visiting card as the reverend Hugh C. Love—in the vault of St Mary's Abbey. As the reverend is about to depart, the narrative is interrupted, enigmatically to a first-time reader, by another forward-directed interpolation: 'From a long face a beard and gaze hung on a chessboard.' (425) The reader's memory will, on a second perusal, construct this as an anticipatory projection across another eight segments to the sixteenth, where Buck Mulligan points out to Haines (the Englishman) John Howard Parnell 'our city marshal' (1049) with a partner over a chessboard in the DBC ('damn bad cakes') bakery.

Numbers of further interpolations which need not be cited individually are simply either backward- or forward-directed. Yet a few interestingly, too, fulfil additional functions. By capturing characters notoriously roaming through Dublin, some interpolations help to enrich the episode's telling the city: the H.E.L.Y'S sandwichmen, for instance (at 377-79), or Denis J. Maginni, professor of dancing &c (added in only at the fourth proof stage, twice: at 56-60 and 599-600); or Richie Goulding carrying the costbag of Goulding, Collis and Ward (at 470-75); or Denis Breen leading his wife over O'Connell bridge (at 778-80); or Cashel Boyle O'Connor Fitzmaurice Tisdall Farrell, a Dublin presence just by the mention of his name (at 919-20); or the two old women with umbrella and midwife's bag (originally at 752-54, but repositioned with revisions to 818-20); or even, in anticipation of the subsequent Sirens episode, 'Bronze by ‹auburn› gold, Miss ‹Douce's› Kennedy's head ʳ¹[with] byʰ Miss ‹Kennedy's› Douce's head, appeared above the crossblind of the Ormond hotel.' (962-63).[7] Here one observes, by the retouching of the colours and their reattribution between the Misses, how fluid the text for Sirens must still have been while Wandering Rocks was being written. Similarly, though eventually only at the first proof stage, and not strictly by way of an interpolation, even Gerty MacDowell has a flash appearance in the chapter (at 1206-07) among the crowd attending at the grand finale, the viceroyal cavalcade—regardless of the fact that her true hour in *Ulysses* is yet three episodes ahead.

There are, furthermore, a couple of interpolations at mid-chapter that are again likely enigmas to a first-time reader. The isolated mention in the ninth segment is puzzling that 'The gates of the drive opened wide to give egress to the viceregal cavalcade.' (515-16) It gives the first inkling of the matter on which the episode eventually closes. A companion piece two segments further on reinforces it: 'The viceregal cavalcade passed, greeted by obsequious policemen, out of Parkgate.' (709-10) Neatly framing the episode's symmetrical centre—its tenth, or Bloom, segment—and preparing for the narrative staging of the cavalcade at the episode's end, these two forward-directed interpolations halfway through the chapter assume a veritable expositional function. As Ithaka, the novel's penultimate episode, in due course will show, belated exposition is one more modernist wrinkle to Joyce's narrative art.[8]

---

7   The markings indicate changes in the manuscript.
8   Exposition in the penultimate chapter is, admittedly, not only a poetological idiosyncrasy. It also springs from the conditions of the book's production. See the end paragraphs in the section 'The Finish: "Penelope" and "Ithaca"' in 'Afterword'

In a singular category, finally, should be classed the two interpolations registering 'a skiff, a crumpled throwaway [...] Elijah is coming, [riding] lightly down the river.' In slightly variant wording, the skiff interpolation is entered twice in the manuscript margin, once against lines 294-98, and once against lines 752-54. Consecutively lined, the manuscript carries the narrative forward in Joyce's autograph. The two additions in the margin, by contrast, are in Frank Budgen's hand. They thus record Joyce's revisional response to the main-column text as already in place when test-read (no doubt) to Joyce by Budgen. The shift between main column and margin, redoubled to boot in the shift of hands between author and amanuensis, yields positive proof of Joyce's creative engagement in the episode's segment technique. Its challenge clearly grew on him in the progress of the chapter composition. The interpolation of the crumpled throwaway in Wandering Rocks involves, in the first instance, a reading memory reaching back into the eighth *Ulysses* episode, Lestrygonians (*U* 8, 57-58), where Bloom throws this crumpled paper into the river. Here, in the flow of Wandering Rocks at lines 294-98, the throwaway courses downriver, eastward—and so sails aimlessly in parallel to the cavalcade passing from west to east, first on the north, then on the south side of the Liffey. But when the throwaway is brought back at lines 752-54, the narrative focus changes. The skiff becomes the still centre of the moment. It seemingly no longer flows eastward down the river. Skiff and river become as if stationary. It is the North wall behind the throwaway on the Liffey that is now seen in motion as-if drifting westward.

> North wall and sir John Rogerson's quay, with hulls and
> anchorchains, sailing westward, sailed by a skiff, a crumpled
> throwaway,
> rocked on the ferrywash, Elijah is coming.

This translates into terms of Dublin topology Jason's challenge of focussing and gaining an always unfailing perspective onto the ever-changing aspect of the wandering rocks.

* * *

---

to James Joyce, *Ulysses. A Critical and Synoptic Edition*, prepared by Hans Walter Gabler with Wolfhard Steppe and Claus Melchior, 3 vols. (New York: Garland Publishing, 1984).

Having made our way as first-time readers through Wandering Rocks to the end of its eighteenth segment, and having laid the ground, with its interpolated text dislocations, for such special reading skills as this chapter requires, the nineteenth segment should be plain sailing. However, in speed, density and sheer artistry of language, the final segment overwhelms anew. Again and again, it would seem, it tests just how genuinely skilled we have become in playing along with its orientation game founded on reading memory.

To explore this contention, here is an abbreviated version of the first seventy lines or so of the episode's end segment:

> William Humble, earl of Dudley, and lady Dudley, accompanied by
> lieutenantcolonel Heseltine, drove out after luncheon from the viceregal
> lodge. [...]
>> The cavalcade passed out by the lower |1180|
>> gate of Phoenix park saluted
> by obsequious policemen and proceeded past Kingsbridge along the
> northern quays. The viceroy was most cordially greeted on his way through
> the metropolis. At Bloody bridge Mr Thomas Kernan beyond the river
> greeted him vainly from afar. [...]
> [...] In the porch of Four |1190|
> Courts Richie Goulding with the costbag of Goulding, Collis and Ward saw
> him with surprise. [...]
> From its sluice in Wood quay wall under Tom Devan's office Poddle river
> hung out in fealty a tongue of liquid sewage. [...]
> [...] On Ormond quay Mr Simon Dedalus, steering his
> way from the greenhouse for the |1200|
> subsheriff's office, stood still in midstreet
> and brought his hat low. His Excellency graciously returned Mr Dedalus'

greeting. From Cahill's corner the reverend Hugh C. Love, M. A., made

obeisance unperceived, [...]

[...]. On Grattan bridge Lenehan and M'Coy,
taking leave of each other, watched the |1205|
carriages go by. Passing by Roger

Greene's office and Dollard's big red printinghouse Gerty MacDowell,

carrying the Catesby's cork lino letters for her father who was laid up,

knew by the style it was the lord and lady lieutenant but she couldn't see

what Her Excellency had on

[...]Over against

Dame gate Tom Rochford and Nosey Flynn watched the approach of the

cavalcade. [...]

[...] A charming soubrette, great Marie |1220|
Kendall, with

dauby cheeks and lifted skirt smiled daubily from her poster upon William

Humble, earl of Dudley, and upon lieutenantcolonel H. G. Heseltine, and

also upon the honourable Gerald Ward A. D. C. From the window of the

D. B. C. Buck Mulligan gaily, and Haines gravely, gazed down on the

viceregal equipage over the shoulders of |1225|
eager guests, whose mass of forms

darkened the chessboard whereon John Howard Parnell looked intently. In

Fownes's street Dilly Dedalus, straining her sight upward from

Chardenal's first French primer, saw sunshades spanned and wheelspokes

spinning in the glare. [...]

[...]. Opposite Pigott's

music warerooms Mr Denis J Maginni, professor of dancing &c, gaily

>   apparelled, gravely walked, outpassed by a |1240|
>   viceroy and unobserved. By the
>   provost's wall came jauntily Blazes Boylan,
>   stepping in tan shoes and socks
>   with skyblue clocks to the refrain of *My*
>   *girl's a Yorkshire girl* [...]
>   [...]As they drove along Nassau street [...]
>   [...] [u]nseen brazen highland laddies
>   blared and drumthumped
>   after the cortège: |1250|
>
>> But though she's a factory lass
>> And wears no fancy clothes.
>> Baraabum.
>> Yet I've a sort of a
>> Yorkshire relish for |1255|
>> My little Yorkshire rose.
>> Baraabum.
>
>   (1176-
>   1257)

With a reading memory of the chapter's preceding segments, we understand that we are in Dublin and that the viceregal cavalcade of carriages and riders is proceeding from its north-westerly point of departure at Phoenix Park along the river, crossing at Grattan Bridge and moving further in a south-easterly direction down Dame Street and along Nassau Street outside the south wall of Trinity College. But just how well do we instantly identify all those people dropped into the text by not much more than their names and seemingly arbitrarily-sketched features, gestures, appurtenances and fragmentary actions? Does this relentless parataxis of listings and names aggregate into anything with a claim to be understood as narrative? In their sequence, the utterances and statements have a seminal narrative appeal. Yet they appear randomly collocated without a compellingly inherent relation. Singularly bare of explicit context, they fail to become a stringent narrative. Nonetheless, it is true, we feel urged to fall back on our reading experience to construct (as best we can) the chapter's end. From our efforts to understand it arises afresh an apprehension of the build of the episode.

This may be illustrated by one exemplary network of texts from the many that make up the chapter. Against the mention (1183-84) 'At Bloody bridge Mr Thomas Kernan beyond the river greeted him vainly from afar', we recall from the episode's twelfth segment:

> A cavalcade in easy trot along Pembroke quay passed, outriders leaping, leaping in their, in their saddles. Frockcoats. Cream sunshades.
> Mr Kernan hurried forward, blowing pursily.
> His Excellency! Too bad! Just missed that by a hair. Damn it! What a
> pity! (794-97)

In the nineteenth text segment, the mention of Mr Thomas Kernan is seemingly cryptic. Yet in substance it recalls—and, as we realise, mirrors from the opposite side of the river—the appearance of Mr Kernan within his own storyline earlier in the chapter. It is initiated in the eleventh segment with the mention that he is pleased at having booked an order (673). This human interest aspect is taken up at the opening of segment 12, which properly develops the storyline centred on Mr Kernan. He goes through in his mind once again the negotiations that led to the deal, remembers that he and his business partners made small-talk over the day's top headlines about the General Slocum catastrophe of yesterday in New York, and is aware that he was appreciated as much for his looks and dress as for his business acumen. Urged by his vanity as he walks, he preens himself 'before the sloping mirror of Peter Kennedy, hairdresser' (743) and a few lines later (755), 'Mr Kernan glanced in farewell at his image' to continue his perambulations. He mentally recalls names of people he knows, some of whom are our reading acquaintances, too: Ned Lambert, for instance, and this because he mistakes a person he sees for Ned Lambert's brother; or Ben Dollard, whose masterly rendition of the ballad 'At the siege of Ross did my father fall' he remembers from his reflections on moments of Irish history—such as the execution of Emmet, an association triggered by his, Kernan's, present itinerary, along which he identifies the actual place: 'Down there Emmet was hanged, drawn and quartered.' (764) His trying to remember by further association where Emmet was—or is said to have been—buried: 'in saint Michan's? Or no ... in Glasnevin' (769-70), in turn bringing Kernan back to this morning's burial: 'Dignam is there now. Went out in a puff. Well, well.' (771) In effect, it is because he enmeshes himself so thoroughly in reminiscences, associations, reflections and vanities that poor Mr Thomas Kernan misses what would have been his crowning satisfaction: greeting properly, and being greeted by, the lord lieutenant of Ireland whom, passing by on the other side of the river, he at Bloody bridge instead merely 'greeted … vainly from afar'.

This example shows how reading the chapter depends on internalising the models of reading configured throughout the episode by way of its methodically distributed interpolations and text dislocations. To read, or re-read, the episode from the vantage platform of its final segment demands skills of memory, association and freely jumping backwards over segment demarcations of the episode, as well as across chapter divisions. To make the connection from the nineteenth back to the twelfth segment, we must synchronise the segments and learn that progression in reading time does not equal progression in narrated time—an illusion we may perhaps be initially excused for having fallen for through the sequence of segments 1 to 18. But whatever regularity in their temporal sequence existed through segments 1 to 18, segment 19 does a repeat run through that time sequence. It does so equally through Dublin characters who have made appearances once or repeatedly in those earlier segments, as for instance Tom Rochford, Nosey Flynn, Simon Dedalus, Hugh C. Love, Lenehan, M'Coy, Blazes Boylan and more. Given as names in the end segment, they could be 'filled in' as Tom Kernan was filled in from segments eleven and twelve. Other names, however, cannot be so substantiated, or could not be from the chapter alone. One example is Tom Devan, by whose office in a building above Wood Quay wall the sluice is located from which 'Poddle river hung out in fealty a tongue of liquid sewage' (1196-97)—and who, as a person, is not a character in the Wandering Rocks, or *Ulysses*, narrative; but he is a man with an office in the Dublin of 1904, and it is true that his name turns up once more in the novel when Molly Bloom in the final chapter identifies him as the father of two sons, young men she is aware that Milly 'is well on for flirting with'. (*U* 18, 1023-24)

But if we must go back to segment 12 to read with contextual understanding the one snippet in the viceregal cavalcade segment about Mr Kernan, 'At Bloody bridge Mr Thomas Kernan beyond the river greeted him vainly from afar'—does this mean that there one is told the full context in a satisfying instance of narrative closure? Far from it. Instead, the segment sends the reader off on further adventures of contextualising. Shackleton's offices, Peter Kennedy the hairdresser, or 'John Mulligan, the manager of the Hibernian bank,' not to mention all the callings-up of buildings, streets or bridges by hardly more than their names, catapult us right out into extra-textual Dublin. For *Ulysses*, and our reading of it, extra-textual Dublin, to be sure, has a strong intra-textual counterpart. That is where, say, Ned Lambert, or Ben Dollard, and (sadly) Dignam belong. But it is not the local narrative, not Kernan in his inner-monologue roaming, nor the mediating narrative voice, that places them there. The contextualising reinforcement, whether in the extra-textual or the intra-textual direction, is wholly the reader's achievement. Challenges of contextualisation keep the reader on the alert and send him or her constantly beyond the moment of easy, since present, linear reading progression through the text. Formally speaking, this is supported by the fragmentation of textual continuity into short sub-segments, many of which are challenges again to contextualise beyond the segment under scrutiny into the episode as a whole, and further beyond into *Ulysses* in its entirety, or beyond *Ulysses* comprehensively into Joyce's oeuvre—which, be it emphasised, works not only retrospectively; it works prospectively too into *Finnegans Wake*—and, not to forget, it contextualises also the reader's experience of Dublin, as of the world throughout.

The significance of the segmenting technique—that is, its importance for constituting connections and thereby meanings of the narrative through reader participation—is underscored by the way the chapter comprehensively trains the reader to it and draws her into collusion with it. This works in the first instance through the interpolations and dislocations. One of their functions has been recognised as a synchronising of events in different areas of Dublin during (roughly) the hour from three to four allotted to Wandering Rocks on 16 June 1904. For the reader to grasp the synchronisation means having to jump between the segment divisions and thus to generate the necessary contextualisation. Its other main function therefore lies in ensuring constant reader alertness. Examples in the twelfth segment include lines 740-41:

—Hello, Simon, Father Cowley said. How are things?

—Hello, Bob, old man, Mr Dedalus answered, stopping.

a dialogue Tom Kernan cannot hear, since he is not *en route* at that moment on Ormond Quay Lower where it takes place. This circumstance is confirmed when segment 14 in lines 882-83 commences *literatim* with the same exchange, and localises it in front of Reddy and Daughter's antique dealers, or lines 778-80:

> Denis Breen with his tomes, weary of having waited an hour in John Henry Menton's office, led his wife over O'Connell bridge, bound for the
> office of Messrs Collis and Ward.

again a movement not within Tom Kernan's vision. Even less can, or does, he (at 752-54) see the passage of the throwaway skiff on the Liffey, whether focusing properly on the skiff sailing on the river eastward, or fixing on it before the North wall and Sir Rogerson's quay that hence apparently sail westward. These latter two intercalations at 778-80 and 752-54, even while picked up once more in segment 19, do not properly provide references that link within the Wandering Rocks episode at all. They constitute, as we are able to contextualise, continuations of the *Ulysses* narrative from a preceding chapter, the eighth episode, Lestrygonians.

Not that, in being trained, we as readers are not also being played with when we are tested about how alert we are to the game, and perhaps momentarily fooled. Thus (once more), just what further point does inserting the 'North wall and Sir Rogerson's quay ... sailing westward' intercalation make in this Tom Kernan segment? Might it be a warning to us not to lose focus in our reading? Only on the surface does the intercalation tell us of the change of perspective by which fixation on the throwaway makes the North wall and Sir Rogerson's quay seemingly sail westward. Surely the question we should on reflection move on to asking is: why is Tom Kernan's vision fixated? We would then understand that this intercalation (added late) is not just narratively re-refocusing-by-arresting the skiff in relation to its surroundings. The arrest in perception turns out to be Tom Kernan's: the intercalation reveals his state of mind. So fixed in anticipation is he on the passing-by of the viceregal cavalcade on the opposite side of the river, and before the backdrop of the North wall, that he misperceives the river-to-shore correlation. His optical illusion could be serious. It would be fatal were it Jason's in calculating the relative motions of the wandering rocks.

Furthermore, just how discerning and knowledgeable are we when, in following Kernan's associations apropos Emmet's execution, we read (lines 764-66):

> Down there Emmet was hanged, drawn and quartered. Greasy black rope. Dogs licking the blood off the street when the lord lieutenant's wife drove by in her noddy.

No, that was not Lady Dudley just come by, whom we know is this very moment cavalcading along Dame Street or thereabouts with her husband, lord lieutenant William Humble, earl of Dudley. In the historic account, the mention is of 'a woman who lived nearby'. It is Kernan who is made to upgrade her into the wife of the lord lieutenant in office back in 1803, insidiously so, to lure us into the trap and, by better contextualising, extricate us from it again.

Alerted to the need to cross the visible or felt divisions segmenting the material surface of the text, we become aware of the generative energy invested in the rigorous segmentation of the tales told and the consequent reduction of narrative plenitude. Yet this is but a seeming reduction. By making the narrative, and specifically understanding it, dependent on an alert cross-over reading between text segments, continuity of the tale is, on the reception side, created through the acts of reading themselves; while on the production side, the continuity and discontinuity of the narrative may be said to be construed and constructed in conjunction. With increasing immersion in the chapter, as must be emphasised, narrative plenitude is not reduced at all. On the contrary, the narrative method enables an aggregation of narrative content far richer than could be achieved through explicit straightforward telling of an hour's events in Dublin on 16 June 1904.

* * *

Not surprisingly, the chapter's main narrative substance in fictional terms is triple-centred, aggregating around Stephen Dedalus, Molly Bloom, and Leopold Bloom. Most circumstantially and comprehensively, it aggregates around Stephen. Not only are two segments (6 and 13) given largely to him, but his sisters at home feature in the chapter, in segment 3 boiling dirty clothes (not food) on the kitchen stove; his sister Dilly abroad in town waylays her father in segment 11 to wheedle housekeeping money from him, and she is (in segment 13) herself run into by her brother at a second-hand bookdealers' where, unsuccessful in selling a book or two (of Stephen's), she has become engrossed in a French primer instead. Their father Simon Dedalus figures not only with his friends—he and they are, as we know, recurring characters in *Ulysses* (which stimulates once more the jumping of chapter boundaries to establish the pertinent connections); here alone in *Ulysses* is Simon Dedalus encountered, too, in his strained relationship with his daughters, especially over money for the family, and this in turn, by the by, gives a pawnbroker and an auctioneer's lacquey walk-on roles in the episode.

All this belongs to what might be called the Joycean 'matter of Dedalus', and we realise that nowhere in *Ulysses* outside Wandering Rocks is that 'matter of Dedalus' so comprehensively laid out. Be it noted that even the very first segment of the episode belongs firmly to it. Stephen Dedalus was a pupil of Father Conmee's back in the Clongowes days of *A Portrait of the Artist as a Young Man*, as we know, although Father Conmee is not made to recall the fact. Without our knowledge of the connection, Conmee's dominance over the lengthy opening would make distinctly less sense in the episode and for the novel—or it would make sense only at the level of symbolism: Church in the episode's first segment against State in its last one, as has often been observed. The 'matter of Dedalus' brought to bear on Wandering Rocks is thus particularly rich—yet for us to activate it, we must jump segment barriers not only within Wandering Rocks or *Ulysses*. We must, from our reading memory of *A Portrait of the Artist as a Young Man*, too, generate comprehensive implications for the meaning of the narrative localised in Wandering Rocks.

The chapter is furthermore interwoven with 'the matter of Molly'. Molly, admittedly, makes her appearance in the chapter metonymically only, by merely an arm. But with it, she throws a coin out of the window to a onelegged sailor, himself in turn important enough to the chapter's web to be seen hobbling along on his crutch in three separate segments. Right at the chapter's opening, Father Conmee registers him as a British navy veteran. His missing leg therefore should be taken to stand in (an unhappy turn of phrase admittedly in this instance) for his admiral's (of a century or so earlier), Lord Nelson's missing arm—to be contrasted, in its turn, with Molly's very present arm. Nelson is dubbed the 'onehandled adulterer' in the seventh, the Aeolus episode, of *Ulysses*. In other words, 'the matter of Molly' is by, again, combinatory association of carefully distributed segmental snippets, to be grasped in terms of the theme of adultery—which should cause no surprise: for, after all, the Wandering Rocks hour from three to four culminates in the preparation for the adulterous tryst pending at 7 Eccles Street (set for four, though delayed eventually until four thirty). The preparations, private and intimate, are Molly's. The preparations, public, extrovert and very much promiscuity-tinged, are Blazes Boylan's, so that (again in a spread over chapter segments) we accompany him in turn on his walk through the city, stand by his side as he orders his fruit-basket present for Molly, watch him flirting hotly with the fruit-and-flowershop girl, and overhear his telephone call to his secretary, whom, set apart by a chapter segmentation, we also meet herself, bored and abandoned, at her typist's desk. In such ways, 'the matter of Molly', variously aggregated and distributed, plays beautifully into, and at same time emerges out of, the episode's game of segmentation.

It is debatable, perhaps, whether a 'matter of Bloom' can be established in the chapter on a scale similar to that of the 'matter of Dedalus' and 'matter of Molly'. But Bloom is present in the chapter, and the way he is present is related, on the one hand, to the chapter's establishing its themes, and on the other hand, it is importantly related to its technique of segmentation. Segment 10 is the episode's Bloom segment. It is a close-up of Bloom alone at the bookstall trading under-the-counter porn at Merchant's Arch. Selecting a book to bring home for Molly, as he does, we see and overhear Bloom, alas, perversely pandering to her erotic longings in his own way as we have seen, and anticipate seeing, Boylan doing in his. Through his sample reading of *The Sweets of Sin*, at the same time, Bloom is stimulated just as, towards the end of the preceding (ninth) segment, Lenehan relates having been aroused when sitting next to Molly's warmth once on a winter's-night carriage ride back from (aptly) Featherbed Mountain. In one sense, therefore, the Bloom segment together with the Lenehan passage closely preceding it extends the chapter's 'matter of Molly'. At the same time, though, segment 10 is the episode's one autonomously Bloomian stretch of narrative. As, numerically, the episode's mid-point, it runs counter to the technique's distributive, dispersive and associative effects with which I have hitherto been concerned. To this point, I shall shortly return.

If one may define the 'matter of Dedalus', or the 'matter of Molly', dispersed over the chapter by means of its construction by segments, one will also join in the general consensus that 'the matter of Dublin' pervades, indeed dominates, Wandering Rocks. Extrapolating from what we have observed of the generative power of the narration by segments, we have no difficulty in appreciating just how richly Dublin grows in our imagination by our participatory engagement with the text—as well as, it must be emphasised, from what real-life experience and knowledge one may possess of the city and its lore of history, legend and myth. Many have contended that this would be the episode to start from to realise Joyce's boast that, were Dublin to be destroyed, it could be rebuilt afresh from *Ulysses*. Perhaps. But if so reconstructed it could be as an imaginary city only, extrapolated precisely out of a generative engagement with the segmented, indeed fragmented nuclei for Dublin that the text of Wandering Rocks and of *Ulysses* gives.

Put simply: Dublin could from *Ulysses* be reconstructed only through acts of reading, not through any material reconstruction and reliving. This can be supported by the fascinatingly successful failure of the experiment of re-enacting Wandering Rocks onsite in Dublin on the occasion of the International James Joyce Symposium in 1982, the centenary year of Joyce's birth. With actors, large numbers of the populace, and even with the city itself, in a sense, participating, all dressed up for the occasion, and with the chapter's segments staged at their diverse locations and as precisely as possible to their inferred times within the Wandering Rocks hour, *Ulysses* could, through this mid-novel episode, be brought back to Dublin and become a real-life presence. Or so it was thought. Triumphant the idea was—and bathetic at the same time. The individual events were entertaining, but the chapter, one might say, fell completely apart. For it was impossible for any individual observer to read it whole, that is to say: to be in more than maybe two or three locations in time to witness what happened there. Connections to all other 'matter of Wandering Rocks' were completely severed. The experience of Clive Hart, for instance, eminent Joycean, was extreme.

Got up in clerical garb as Father Conmee, he walked from Mountjoy Square to Newcomen Bridge and there duly boarded a tram (turned into a bus in the meantime) to follow his prescribed itinerary from Mud Island, now Fairview Park, to Artane along streets that a hundred years earlier had been largely open fields. Returning to the Symposium gatherings later in the afternoon, he sadly had to admit that his exercise had been entirely solitary. Nobody was out there in Dublin's north-east watching his progress, that is: reading Clive Hart's Conmee itinerary in *Ulysses* terms. And even to begin with, when he started off from Mountjoy Square, no-one watching Stephen and Buck Mulligan leaving the National Library in Kildare Street shortly after 3pm could possibly at the same time be in Mountjoy Square for Father Conmee's encounter with Mrs Sheehy, or his little clerical intimacies with the schoolboys from Belvedere. Wandering Rocks, in other words, holds together not through any material or topographical localisation, but through acts of reading alone: reading the episode from its construction as a text. The unifying experience that arises from reading the chapter, moreover, is generated precisely (and paradoxically, one might say) from its narrative technique of dispersive segmentation.

* * *

Segmentation is a technique and an art of dispersing text and content into an 'open' narrative construction designed to stimulate acts of reading that will re-discourse and thereby recontextualise the text so dispositioned. At its surface, the text is centrifugal. Against its centrifugality is then set a reading energy that generates effects of understanding and insight. These can thus far surpass and hence be far more encompassing than any that a consecutive, narratively 'closed' text could achieve. Logically, therefore, it follows that, as counterweight to the surface centrifugality of a segmented text, the reading energy invested in it should be seen as a centripetal force. That this is no fanciful assumption may be demonstrated on the structural level of Joycean texts.

Experimenting with and deploying techniques of segmentation is a mode of literary composition not unique to James Joyce. On the contrary, writing and narrating in segments is a pervasive device of high modernism in literature (and as such has often been paralleled with, for instance, the fracturing of surfaces and colour in cubism).

Virginia Woolf, to name but one example, appears, in the process of writing her novel *Jacob's Room* in 1920, to have discovered for herself the core potential of text arrangement by segments. Her narrative was configured into stretches separated by void interstices for the reader imaginatively and co-constructively to enter into and thereby to join the narrated segments through co-constructive reading interpretation. For Joyce, segmenting and the segment itself were early preoccupations that grew firstly, it appears, out of structural concerns. His epiphanies, while initially discrete as individual compositions, soon offered themselves for concatenation, that is: for arrangement as nuclei from which to generate consecutive narratives. The numbering on the back of the leaves containing the epiphanies that survive in Joyce's hand bear witness to such an arrangement, and the composition of both *Stephen Hero* and *A Portrait of the Artist as a Young Man* confirms that such was the purpose of the numbering. A stretch of text in the second chapter of *A Portrait of the Artist as a Young Man* shows materially how Joyce built a narrative progression out of concatenating epiphanies. This is the sequence of Stephen's visits to relatives and to a children's party, on offer to the reader because Stephen is said to have 'chronicled with patience what he saw' (*P* II, 251). What Stephen saw is, as we realise, recorded in epiphany form: in their majority, the text passages in question happen still to survive as epiphanies. They are asyndetically arranged over some hundred lines in the *Portrait* text, and it is really from their interstices that the tension arises that holds them together—and holds the reader's attention.

Joyce planned *Stephen Hero* throughout in units, in groups of chapters, before he properly began to write it. He wanted to write it to the length of sixty-three chapters, or nine groups of seven chapters, schematised according to the ages of man. He accomplished four of these nine groups. Yet, filling in the pattern by 'reading' his own biography, life and age drifted seriously apart in the fourth group: the narrative's protagonist should have reached the age of twenty-eight at the end of it, but Stephen Daedalus is barely over twenty-one, just as James Joyce was in real life, when the fragment breaks off near the end of chapter 28 and, in terms of narrated action, on the verge of the 'Departure for Paris'. We may speculate that Joyce encountered not only the increasing impossibility of telling a literalised autobiography beyond the age and the experience of his real life, but also the problem of the concatenation of the narrative units incrementally progressing. The section from *Portrait* just discussed seems to indicate this factor as one imaginable reason for Joyce's abandoning the *Stephen Hero* project. *A Portrait of the Artist as a Young Man* as finished solves what we implicitly recognise as the structural impasse encountered with *Stephen Hero*, namely the serial, and thus the exclusively forward, movement of the narrative.

A Portrait, by contrast, is a novel in five chapters. As has been rightly argued, there is a relentless forward movement to them, of which one effect is to ironically distance Stephen: the position of awareness, even self-awareness, that Stephen reaches at the end of each chapter is regularly undercut and collapsed at the beginning of the subsequent one. At the same time, however, the novel's disposition in five chapters, an uneven number, centres it. *Portrait's* centre is chapter three, the chapter that turns on the retreat in honour of Saint Francis Xavier, at the core of which in turn stand Father Arnall's three hell sermons. Moreover: not only is *Portrait* thus divided into five chapters centred on the third chapter. Below the chapter level the novel's text as a whole is articulated, too, into nineteen segments divided by asterisks—the number, as we have noted, that recurs for Wandering Rocks. Their mid-segment ten is again precisely Father Arnall's hell sermon segment. It thus perversely constitutes the dead centre of *A Portrait of the Artist as a Young Man*.

Hence, it was in *A Portrait of the Artist as a Young Man* that Joyce discovered how to contain in chapters, and to pivot on a structural centre, a narrative progressing by serial segmentation. Within the *Portrait* segments, though, it is true, the narrative propels forward still in essential linearity. Nor does this narrative mode much change throughout the first half of *Ulysses*—up to New Year's Eve 1918, so to speak. Yet under the surface (as it were), it must have become ever clearer that reading and understanding *Ulysses*—and in fact writing and composing it, in the first place—depended on simultaneous forward and backward as well as crosswise reading, remembering and contextualising. Hence, Joyce devises a meta-narrative strategy for Wandering Rocks—the first out-and-out one, perhaps, of its kind, to be followed by his teaching of reading in terms of the perception of music in Sirens, or of foregrounding the dependence of world views on the deployment of style (Cyclops and Nausikaa), or indeed on the very epistemology built into language in its historically variable constructions of perspective (Oxen of the Sun). Through Wandering Rocks, the episode that disperses its narrative widely, and yet firmly anchors it on a central segment and character, we are taught how to read *Ulysses*, and Joyce's work as a whole, always crosswise—besides, of course, always in relation to the city of Dublin.

* * *

Yet why should it have been needful to explore free relational reading techniques just with the novel's tenth episode, Wandering Rocks? In terms of the novel's overall progression, the chapter marks the moment when *Ulysses* embarks on as yet unchartered courses across the depths and shallows of its adventurous second half, for which not just its author, but its readers, too, will stand in need of fresh navigational aids and tools. Was it, at their point of invention, Jason, the commander of the Argo, who proffered the template for orientation? His hope for survival lay in navigating those narrows between the rocks that were constantly moving. This required a sense of timing of the rocks' movements and a stereoscopic eyesight.

To all appearances, James Joyce derived the idea of how to deal with Jason's navigational problem, and the reader's problem of how to steer unscathed through Wandering Rocks and *Ulysses*, from Leopold Bloom. Of his ruminations, we read in the eighth episode, Lestrygonians, the following:

> After one. Timeball on the ballastoffice is down. Dunsink time. Fascinating little book that is of sir Robert Ball's. Parallax. I never exactly
> understood. [...]
> Par it's Greek: parallel,
> parallax. Met him pike hoses she called it till I told her about the transmigration. O rocks! (*U* 8, 109-13)

Here, constructed into Bloom's mind, is a link between parallax, the scientific term for an optical phenomenon conditioning and enabling stereoscopic sight (*stereopsis*), and a time-measuring device of which Bloom fumblingly tries to make sense. Never exactly having understood 'parallax' gives him—at the back of his mind, so to speak—the advantage of 'parallactically' correlating the stereoscopic and the stereo-temporal. For another four hundred lines of the chapter text he subliminally broods on the problem until he verbalises it again and understands that synchronising Greenwich time and Dunsink time is, in Dublin, performed by the falling time-ball at the ballast office. This, for him, exemplifies 'parallax'—which, having to his own satisfaction so understood it, he now wants defined by an expert:

> Now that I come to think of it that ball falls at Greenwich time. It's the clock is worked by an electric wire from Dunsink. Must go out there
> some first Saturday of the month. If I could get an introduction to professor
> Joly [...] man always
> feels complimented. [...]
> Not go in and blurt out what
> you know you're not to: what's parallax? [...] (*U* 8, 571-78)

What for the present argument is most amazing is that the first of the preceding quotes ends with Bloom's exasperated expletive 'O rocks!' over Molly's dexterity in playing hard words by ear. Could there be a creative undercurrent from it overflowing into Wandering Rocks? In exemplifying from the chapter's Tom Kernan narrative, the linking of segment 19 back to segment 12, I drew attention to the circumstance that Kernan's vain greeting of the viceroy from one side of the river in segment 12 was narratively registered from across the Liffey divide in segment 19: 'At Bloody bridge Mr Thomas Kernan beyond the river greeted him vainly from afar.' So mirrored and synchronised, the moment is doubly caught by Bloomian parallax. Once alerted, we find, retrospectively from segment 19, multiple such double anchorings with sightlines across and between them. Throughout the chapter, the structural game is often amusingly playful, too—as for instance in the case of the skiff, the crumpled throwaway, 'Elijah is coming.' At lines 294-98 it is floating regularly eastward down the river. At lines 752-54, by contrast, the text holds the river bank firmly in sight from the point of view of the throwaway rocked on the ferrywash. It fixes the North wall which, consequently, unmovable in its position as it is, appears to sail westward. The correlations build up to a principle of structure for the chapter. The interpolated dislocations of text with which we began this discussion equally realise the principle. Their function, as generally recognised, is prominently to synchronise narrative strands and events between the chapter segments. This in its turn means that Wandering Rocks deploys 'parallax' on the Lestrygonian terms of both space and time.[9] It turns Bloom's fuzzy notion of 'parallax' into an innovatively modernist mode of narrative.

* * *

With Wandering Rocks, then, we as readers are cast as Argonauts bent on safely passing through the *symplegades*. By Jason's ruse, as the rocks sway hither and thither, doves are sent out between them, both (stereoscopically) to focus and (stereo-temporally) to time their movement: witness the many tail feathers trapped, or wedged into the swaying rocks, or en-taled, that is: worked by the cunning author into the tales interpolatively configured in the main chapter segments. Every feathery sub-segment that 'really', according to time and personnel and topography, does not belong within the chapter segment in which we find it, playfully represents, I suggest, such a snipped-off tail/tale feather. Once we detect it and identify it for what it is and where it does connect, our orientation parallactically focusses and we are set and safe for the next stretch of navigation. This is part of the enjoyment of reading and, from our reading, co-constructing Wandering Rocks. Through its narrative matter, the chapter anchors us firmly in Dublin. Yet in structure and performance, it answers with high ingenuity to Joyce's working title for it: Wandering Rocks. The episode performs with us, through its challenges to our reading skill, an ultimately successful passage through its segments and wandering snippets of narrative. As through the passageway of the episode's rocks, swaying but ultimately all focusable in position and time, we enter into the novel's second half, we steer irrevocably out on its open seas to sail before the crosswinds of the unending rereading adventure that is *Ulysses*.

---

9   As Wikipedia meanwhile already knows, 'The word and concept feature prominently in James Joyce's 1922 novel, *Ulysses*', https://en.wikipedia.org/wiki/Parallax.

Composing *Penelope* Towards the Condition of Music

Imagination is memory. (James Joyce)

In *Ulysses*, published in February 1922, the concluding episode shows a clear design. It divides into eight segments—or 'sentences', as James Joyce himself named them: '*Penelope* is the clou of the book. The first sentence contains 2500 words. There are eight sentences in the episode.'[1] The chapter units that Joyce terms its sentences are marked off by white spacing and first-line indentation. Regardless of these typographical aids, however, the narrative flows both within the segments and across the segment divisions wholly unarticulated by apostrophes, commas, colons, semi-colons, question or exclamation marks. Most radically, they lack entirely divisions by full stops—or almost entirely. There is one full stop to end segment 4, and another to end segment 8. These are both graphically and structurally significant. They confer prospective significance, too, onto the full stop with which episode 17 ends. Joyce urged the Dijon printers to render that dot 'bien visible'. Being well visible, it does double duty. It both closes the seventeenth and initiates the eighteenth episode. The special emphasis on the dot gives it weight and a claim to being recognised as a conscious measure of composition. It both divides the adjoining chapters and bridges their divide. As the closing token it is, it ends the novel's 17 episodes in the Aristotelian narrative mode: beginning—middle—end (well-visibly dotted). Joyce himself expressed to Frank Budgen that '*Ithaca* [...] is in reality the end as Penelope has no beginning, middle or end.' (*Letters I*, 172) In fact, its non-beginning is underscored by the dot 'bien visible' that, directly

---

[1] *Letters of James Joyce*, ed. by Stuart Gilbert, vol. I (New York: Viking Press, 1957, ²1966) (*Letters* I), p. 170.

preceding, in closing episode 17 simultaneously serves as entry to episode 18. This janus quality of the well-visible dot is not accidental, as close attention to the history of composition of the pair of final *Ulysses* chapters reveals. The eighteenth episode was finished and type-set close to two months before the end of the seventeenth, 'in reality the end', was reached. This means that when the final dot of episode 17 was set in place and was emphatically required to be made well visible, it was quite literally position-pointing towards opening an already existing episode 18.

The final chapter, as the eight-segment textual body it is, is thus articulated by means of one opening, one middle, and one final dot, or full stop. They render discernible, and so make graphically circumscribable, the chapter's symbolic contours. To suggest his sense of the episode's structure visually, Joyce took recourse to the graphics of a horizontal '8'—∞—the mathematical symbol of infinity:

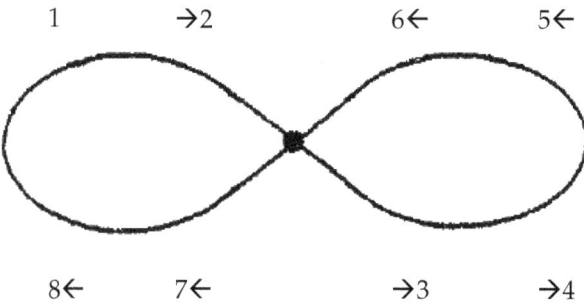

In Christian connotation, the number '8' symbolises renewal. After the six days of creation and the seventh Sabbath day that biblically together comprise the Old Testament Hebrew dispensation, Christ's resurrection on the eighth day initiates the Christian New Testament dispensation. Christ incarnate as Jesus of Nazareth is the son of his mother Mary. From her thus, in earthly terms, springs the renewal culminating and epitomised in the resurrection. By the ingenuity of ancient cabalistically trained numerologists, therefore, Mary's birthday already falls on an eighth day, a day of renewal, the eighth of September (in the ninth month of the year). Her birthday is in *Ulysses* given to Molly Bloom.

Thus by Joyce's design are superimposed in the textual body of the novel's final episode the symbols of infinity and renewal. Figuring the final chapter's eight segments arranged on the template of the ∞—as in the image above—we find segments one and two swinging on the first half-circle upper to the middle. Segments 3 and 4 continue on the second half-circle lower to the point of graphic return. Segments 5 and 6 swing back through the second half-circle upper and through the graphic midpoint into the first half-circle lower that fulfils segments 7 and 8, so as to reach the ∞'s end, which, springing from the seventeenth episode's end, was the eighteenth episode's beginning. Thus the episode's textual body is fully encompassed and set to renew itself ever and ever into infinity.

Joyce would not be Joyce, though, had the ∞ not also evoked in him playful recalls of the *Ulysses* text just written, or still in the making. He associates with the shape of the ∞, surely, also both the 'adipose anterior and posterior female hemispheres' that Bloom yearned after in the preceding episode (*U* 17, 2232),[2] and the breakfast eggs that, at the opening of the final episode, Molly imagines he asked for—'breakfast in bed with a couple of eggs' (*U* 18, 2)—when, on the point of dropping into sleep, he murmured something about 'roc's auk's egg.' (*U* 17, 2328-29)

* * *

The structure and the flow of the episode were intensely in the making in the summer and early autumn 1921. The earliest extant draft for the chapter survives in a notebook. This comprises a cover and twenty leaves (forty pages) of which the final one is blank. Joyce's inscribed text begins on the recto of the first leaf and overflows to the left onto the verso of the notebook cover, which thereby becomes serially the first manuscript page. Materially and visually, the episode's composition so extends over nineteen verso-recto openings (thirty-eight pages). Of these, the ten initial openings especially are densely inscribed on both the recto (or right-hand) and the opposite verso (or left-hand) pages.

Joyce commonly used notebooks for drafting, opening by opening. The way he proceeded was first to fill right-hand pages with main columns of run-on writing and (at the outset, at least) to leave the

---

2   James Joyce, *Ulysses. A Critical and Synoptic Edition*, prepared by Hans Walter Gabler with Wolfhard Steppe and Claus Melchior, 3 vols. (New York & London: Garland Publishing, Inc., 1984; ²1986).

opposite left-hand writing space blank. The inscription flow in the right-hand page columns is consecutive and basically linearly readable as text. True enough, it is frequently embellished already with interlinear changes and additions, as well as with changes and additions in the left and top and bottom margins. Such writing 'in surround' on the right-hand pages complicates, but does not render impossible, reading these right-hand pages consecutively as (provisional) text. The left-hand pages of each opening, by contrast, that is the versos of the respective preceding notebook leaves (or, in the case of the first opening of the Penelope notebook, the verso of the notebook cover), provide always open space that, if used, becomes progressively filled randomly with further writing-in-progress.

Writing on the left-hand pages is not organised in (potential) text flow. It is randomly scattered in 'islands', instead, in line or block or single-word units readable strictly within themselves. There is in this writing space no text continuity between the island units other than when indicated by the author's connecting links. Since, however, these units constitute revisions, mostly addition material to the composition run on the facing right-hand pages, the left-hand inscription islands are commonly, though not unfailingly, ear-marked with symbols connectively referred to from corresponding symbols in the right-hand-page text flow.

* * *

Joyce's to-and-fro itineraries of composition between the right-hand and left-hand side of the page openings are seriously challenging to unravel. In the Penelope notebook, the episode opening is laid out across facing page spaces: the verso of the notebook cover, page 0v (leaf zero-verso), and page 1r (the recto page of the first notebook leaf). This page-spread allows us to establish a template for tracing how the facing page spaces were successively filled. However chaotic the crowded result looks at first sight, the progress of composition can be made out. (Fig. 12.4 = page 1r, and Fig. 12.3 = page 0v, below, show each side of the initial opening visually.)

Joyce follows his habitual matrix and writes onto the right-hand blank page first the heading Penelope. In the present appearance of the page, it is true, this is no longer easily discernible. Written above that heading, and so in the upper margin, are now two lines, and below it three lines of addition text. Under the heading, hence, Joyce at first also left ample white space before positioning, indented, the opening text line:

'Yes because he never did a thing'

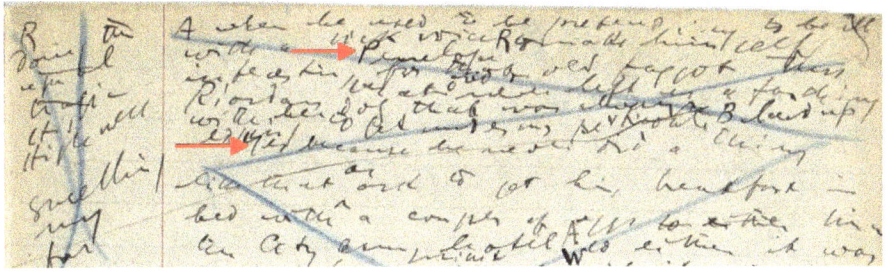

Fig. 12.1 Top of page 1r.

I set out here entire, line by line, the flow of the core inscription column on page 1r. Into it I have intercalated instant deletions |-...-| and additions |+...+| as they occur in-line or between lines; or, for marginal additions, |m+...+m|. I have moreover registered Joyce's linking symbols as they occur in the right-hand-page core column for extended changes/additions written and squeezed into the right-hand-page margins. (To follow visually the core inscription in the right-hand page with all its margin enrichments, consult Fig. 12.4 below.) Registered are also the linking symbols in the core column to the revisions and expansions that, in the further course of composition, were distributed diversely over the facing left-hand page space.

      Penelope
Yes because he never did a thing
like that |+as+| ask to get his breakfast in
bed with a couple of eggs |-so either-| since
the City Arms hotel ||>A[,]W<|| so either it was
one of those |+night+| women if it was
down there he was really and the
hotel story |+he made up+| a pack of lies |+to hide it+| ||>R<|| or
else it

> was some |-person-| |m+little bitch+m| he got in some-
> way or picked up somewhere ||>F<|| yes
> because the day Dignam died he
> was writing a letter and then he
> covered it |+up+| with the blottingpaper
> pretending to be thinking about
> business so very probably that was
> it to someone who |-thought-| |+thinks+| she
> had a softy |+in him+| because all men
> get a bit like that at his
> age especially getting on to
> forty so as to wheedle any
> money she can out of him
> |+no fool like an old fool+|
> and then kissing my bottom
> was to hide it ||>M<|| yes because
> he couldn't |m+possibly+m| do without it |-so-| |+that+|
> long |+so he must do it somewhere+| and the last time he
> came on my bottom was the
> night Boylan |-was squeezing my hand-|
> |+gave my hand a great squeeze+| singing the young
> May moon she's beaming
> love going along by the Tolka
> with the full moon because he|-'s-|
> has an idea about him and
> me in any case God knows
> he's a change in a way
> not to be always |+wearing the same old hat+| doing that
> frigging ||>A<|| |+find out things+| simply ruination

This renders an individual consciousness—female, unnamed—in a silent, highly aware flow of observation, reflection, memory. Her thoughts and articulated emotions, unspoken, yet all the more pertinently rendered for that in written narrative, circle around and focus on a 'he'—male, equally unnamed. The text mesmerises us readers into identifying the unnamed 'she' as Molly and the unnamed 'he' as Bloom. This is an equation far from safe, however: readers live with the episode's constant thrill of subversion of the 'he' reference: in the stream of 'her' consciousness, 'he' is whoever the man happens to be whom 'she' recalls and thinks of at the given narrative moment. This mental slight-of-hand begins to show already in this core inscription towards the end of page 1r where 'he' refers to Boylan. Off and on, the text does give personal names, it is true, but they are reserved for individuals (Dignam, Boylan), identified by 'her' in the whirlwind moments of 'her' reflection and memory.

* * *

Strikingly, the base draft opening, when stripped to its written-out core column, while it reads like last-episode *Ulysses* text, somehow does not (yet) quite feel like the 'Molly Bloom' chapter we remember from the finished book. By scrutinising Joyce's extensive and substantial changes in the right-hand page margins, eventually augmented significantly further by those randomly strewn over the opposite left-hand page, we may begin to get a feel for and understanding of Joyce's mode of revision, and altogether of his creative impulse towards how as text to realise his novel's final episode.

We may commence from the five-line addition in what was, to begin with, white space in the page's top margin. In the fully filled page, it near-obliterates the episode title just discernible as the third line of the crowded top-of-the-page inscription. We cannot be sure that the five-line addition (two lines above, and three lines below the episode title, as Fig. 12.1 shows) was, in the chapter opening's overall composition, in truth the first substantial text addition to the right-hand page core column of writing. But these five lines provide a start to our analysis and argument. This is how they read:

> [key symbol: ||>A<||]
> |u[pper]m[argin]+when he used to be pretending to be |-ill-|
> |+laid up+| with a sick voice |m+doing |-the usual tragic-| |+His Highness+|+m| to make himself
> interesting for that old faggot Mrs
> Riordan that |+died &+| never left us a farthing
> with her dog that was always
> edging to get under my petticoats
> |m+smelling my fur+m|+u[pper]m[argin]|

Obviously enough, the individual consciousness that, in the right-hand page text column, Joyce aims at narratively modelling in simulated thought, is in this extension at once being made associatively to sprout tentacles of diversification. The City Arms Hotel of the right-hand page core text—a *currente calamo* afterthought, in the first place, for which the deletion |-so either-| in the main column text provides the evidence—leads to Mrs Riordan, to 'his' making himself interesting to her and the attitude 'he' assumes for the purpose, and to the futility of 'his' subservience, since Mrs Riordan is remembered to have died and left not a farthing. Remaining alive in present consciousness is Mrs Riordan's dog only, titillatingly remembered for his under-petticoat indecency. Entertained (indeed: ourselves increasingly titillated) by the flowering acrobatics of memories brought into simultaneity in the present moment of the text and our reading, we find at the same time our own memories stimulated to recall moments from the novel's preceding seventeen episodes. At *U* 6, 378 Bloom recalled 'Where old Mrs Riordan died.' At 8, 847-49, it is by 'Old Mrs Riordan with the rumbling stomach's Skye terrier in the City Arms hotel. Molly fondling him in her lap. O, the big doggybowwowsywowsy!' that Bloom remembered a close version of the scenery 'she' in memory now, ten episodes later, also rehearses. We recall, too (should we ever have stopped to wonder), the question and response clarification in episode 17, lines 479 to 486, that established the triangulation of Stephen Dedalus, Leopold Bloom and Mrs Riordan. She is Stephen Dedalus's aunt Dante from *A Portrait of the Artist as a Young Man*. For her to be included in the *Ulysses* personnel, she has been made to have played a role in the life of the Blooms too. Significantly, we understand all this through activating our own reading memory of the novel. It is in response to the recall whirlwind of 'her' reflection and memory that the opening of the novel's last episode begins to unleash. In a manner, the memory patterns of the novel's personae and of its readers mirror each other.

* * *

Graphically, in the inscription outlay, the top of the first draft page for Penelope resembles the top of the page of the earliest extant draft for episode 9 (Scylla & Charybdis). Its first inscription reads:

> —And we have those priceless pages of Wilhelm Meister, the quaker
> librarian said, have we not? A great poet on a great brother
> poet. A soul confronted with a task beyond its
> powers, torn by conflicting doubts.

In multiple rounds of revision, this is over-written; the blank space above the original inception is here equally used, as this manuscript image shows:

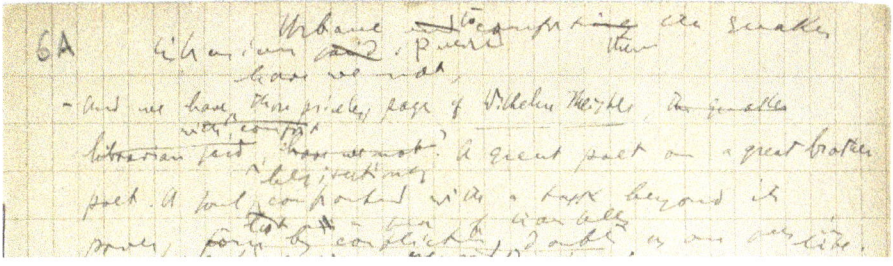

Fig. 12.2 Top of page 1r of Joyce's 1918 draft of *Ulysses*, episode 9.

Eventually, by the time the chapter reaches publication, episode 9 opens with only modest further modification from this draft as overwritten with revisions:

> Urbane, to comfort them, the quaker librarian purred:
> —And we have, have we not, those priceless pages of *Wilhelm Meister*. A great poet on a great brother poet. A hesitating soul taking arms against a sea of troubles, torn by conflicting doubts, as one sees in real life.

(*U* 9, 1-4)

Yet, although the draft openings of episode 9 and episode 18 thus look similar, they are strikingly contrasted in impulse. Episode 9 sets the scene in the National Library for Stephen Dedalus' Hamlet lecture. It does so by means of verbal fireworks that, right at the outset, define the audience he has to contend with. What the text strives to achieve and, through its revisions, intensifies is the impact of the moment, so as from it to build the forward drive of the episode action and its narrative rendering. The vector of the over-writing with revisions, focused as it is on the progression of the action in congruence with narrative time, is insistently centripetal.

For episode 18, the drive of composition is the entire opposite. What happens, as over and alongside the core column of the draft's first opening Joyce's whirlwind of revision and addition sets in, is (as said) a diversification of associations. How this operates, to what lengths and into what variegated convolutions it goes, grows increasingly evident already from our paradigm, the draft manuscript's opening. What even at a first close reading becomes evident is that, here, Joyce's ever injecting the stream of thought and association of the individual—female, unnamed—with additions, revisions, extensions, is multi-directional. The shaping of the 'she' in text, and so in the narrative's silent, highly aware flow of observation, reflection, memory, is centrifugal—and yet simultaneously centred on 'her' incessantly diversifying consciousness.

This notably manifests itself in the long addition in the lower-quarter and bottom margins of the right-hand page; it is in fact quite possible that the sequence near the bottom-left of the page was the first extended addition for integration into the core text column on the right-hand page, and thus chronologically preceded the diversifications that sprouted associatively from 'the City Arms hotel' in the early lines of the text column. The bottom-left notes were squeezed into the margin, coded with key symbol ||>M<||:

> not that I care who he does it with |m+or knew before that way but I'd like to find out+m| so long as I don't have |m+the two of+m| them under my nose all the time like that slut, that Mary, padding |+up+| her false bottom to excite him ||>P<|| and stealing my potatoes and oysters ||>A<|| for her aunt, if you please, common robbery, |+it takes me to find out things+| O yes her aunt was very fond of oysters I told her what I thought of her ||>H<||

Within this sweep of addition text we now see, as indicated in this transcription, the further key symbols: >P<, >A< and >H<. They point to additional flourishes of authorial add-ons to be found in the left-hand verso page space.

* * *

The left-hand verso page provides free space for writing to be integrated further into the core column on the right-hand page. To establish from the full range of writing notation, across the draft opening, a text in full composition—that is, a flow of writing consecutively readable as text—is, in material practice, to be achieved only by means of an eventual integrative copying of the dispersed elements of writing on the right-hand and left-hand pages together—in other words, through (fair-)copying. This is what an author commonly does: transfer writing from document to document in the progress of composition towards text, often enough through sequences of copies, each originally 'fair', but soon overlaid with further changes; even printing-house typesetters are (or used to be) known to be capable of typesetting directly from drafts into text for the printed book. Conceptually, indeed, and with an awareness of the material nature of documents of transmission, it is properly not what is initially drafted in writing that should be designated 'text'. Drafting, as the material manifestation of composition it is, does not yet in itself constitute text. 'Text', consecutively to be read linearly, results genuinely first in copying(s) of draft writing. This is what (fair-)copying authors or printing-house typesetters accomplish. Naturally (one might say), they privilege achieved text. In this, they work teleologically. Their *telos*, or goal, is 'the' text.

By contrast: the genetic critic, even the genetically aware editor, privileges elucidating the process and progress of writing. Hence, in analysing Joyce's earliest extant drafting of the episode that he heads Penelope, my concern is not foremost to focus on (the) text that results from the drafting. I wish to foreground the material presence and inscriptional appearance of writing that, in its arrangements and patterns, is not yet text fully achieved, but which allows us to trace the composition as process and production. For a first sampling of this graphic, and therefore visual, perspective on drafting, the left-hand page of the first notebook opening of episode 18 should suffice—though it boggles the mind somewhat at first sight, densely inscribed as it is with randomly strewn islands of writing:

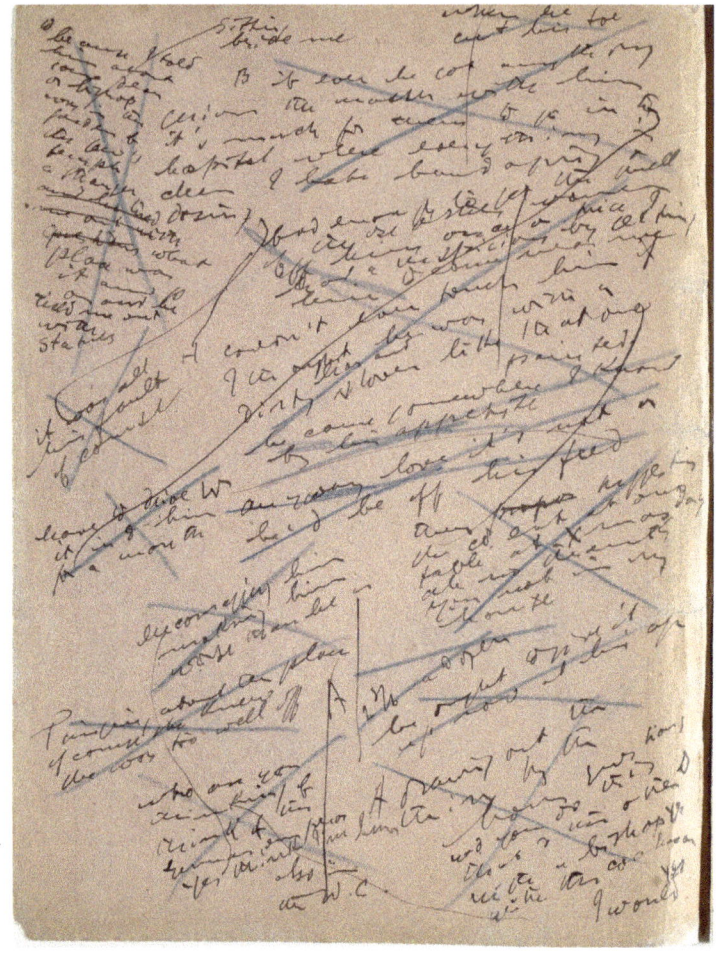

Fig. 12.3 Page 0v [note: the crossings-out in blue are the author's; he has, in copying, used each writing unit so deleted.]

From this left-hand page of randomly distributed writing islands, in conjunction with the relatively consecutive writing sequence on the opposite right-hand page, arises the challenge to retrace the paths of composition to and fro across the facing sides of the opening. The mosaic of individual units of writing on the left-hand-page, singly or in discrete combinations, craves to be related to the writing in existence in the core column on the right-hand page opposite, as well as its extensions in the right-hand margins. In other words, the call is to search out and follow the paths the fair-copying author trod in transforming his writing into text; or that a genetic critic, and maybe a genetic editor, is and will be obliged to retrace, in turn, to critically as well as editorially measure out the composition.

With the precedence of the inscription of the right-hand page established, its core column of writing together with its interlinear and marginal accretions provide an orientation grid towards successfully joining together the mosaic pieces. In support, what is given here, first, is the image of the right-hand page of the first NLI draft opening; and, following it, a rendering in full of the text that comprehensively results from all the acts of composition and writing discernible in their spread over the two pages 1r and 0v.

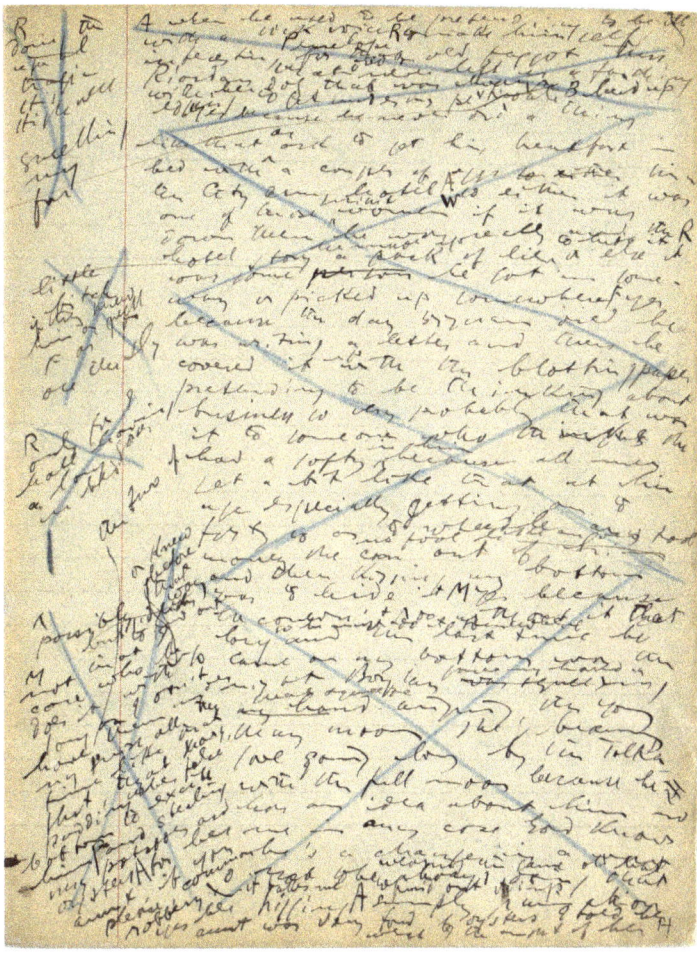

Fig. 12.4 Page 1r.

What follows is the text achieved in the course of the draft's multi-layered composition. This rendering I have purposefully broken up into its every constituent small or large unit, to elucidate the multiple writing acts distinguishable in the two manuscript pages. I have, though, left out all tagging (except for deletions) so as to ease, I believe, locating the puzzle pieces at their points of inscription on the two pages and joining them together into an achieved consecutive text for reading. The presentation in this irregular line-fall should help to trace back the bits of the puzzle to their appearance as writing events in the composition space of the facing-page opening:

      Penelope
Yes because he never did a thing like that
as
ask to get his breakfast in bed with a couple of eggs so either
since the City Arms hotel
when he used to be pretending to be
ill laid up
with a sick voice
doing the usual tragic His Highness
to make himself interesting for that old faggot Mrs Riordan that died &
never left us a farthing with her dog that was always
edging to get under my petticoats
smelling my fur
if ever he got anything serious the matter with him it's much
for them to go in to
hospital for a month
have to drive it in
where everything is clean I hate bandaging & dosing
when he cut his toe
it was all his fault of course
he came somewhere I know by his appetite
anyway love it's not or he'd be off his feed
so either it was one of those
night
women if it was down there he was really and the hotel story
he made up
a pack of lies
to hide it
only for I hate having a long goster in bed
or else it was some

person little bitch
he got in someway or picked up somewhere
on the sly
if they knew him as well as I do
yes because the day Dignam died he was writing a letter and then
he
covered it
up
with the blottingpaper pretending to be thinking about business so
very probably that was it to someone who
thought thinks
she had a softy
in him
because all men get a bit like that at his age especially getting on
to forty so as to wheedle any money she can out of him
no fool like an old fool
and then kissing my bottom was to hide it
not that I care who he does it with
or knew before that way but I'd like to find out
so long as I don't have
the two of
them under my nose all the time like that slut, that Mary, padding
up
her false bottom to excite him
singing about the place
also in the W.C.
of course she knew she was too well off
and stealing my potatoes and oysters
2/6 a dozen
for her aunt, if you please, common robbery,
it takes me to find out things
O yes her aunt was very fond of oysters I told her what I thought of
her
bad enough to get the smell of those {other}
painted
women off him once or twice I had a suspicion by getting him to
come
near me
I couldn't even touch him if I thought he was with a dirty
liar and
sloven like that one
then propos suggesting she cd eat at our table at Xmas day ah no
thank you not in my house

yes because he couldn't
possibly
do without it
so that long
so he must do it somewhere
and the last time he came on my bottom was the night Boylan
was squeezing my hand gave my hand a great squeeze
singing the young May moon she's beaming love going along by the
Tolka with the full moon because he's he has an idea about him and
me in any case God knows he's a change in a way not to be always
wearing the same old hat
doing that frigging
drawing out the thing by the hour questions wd you do this that &
the other
because I told him about some dean or bishop was
sitting beside me
in the garden of the jew's temple a stranger
and he tired me out with questions
what place was it and so on
and he tired me out with statues
with a bishop yes with the coalman yes I would who are you
thinking
of think of the German emperor yes think I'm him
encouraging him making him worse than he is he ought to give it
up now at his age
simply ruination

* * *

Assuming, for the sake of argument, that the column of consecutive text on page 1r, the right-hand page of the opening, was initially the whole first-page extent of the episode's beginning, it is amazing to see, after the working-over on this and its facing left-hand page, what the beginning has turned into. The difference is drastic in mere quantity. The flow of the core inscription column on page 1r (that is, Fig. 4 without its interlinear and marginal additions) extends to 263 words. The wordcount for the entire opening, the core column together with the writing events cumulated from the right-hand-page interlinings and margins plus the facing left-hand page, is 670 words: an increase of approximately 250 percent.[3]

---

3   The word count for the draft's opening stretch, to 'ruination', it should be mentioned, is close to 1500 words in the first-edition text of 2 February 1922—an increase over

But quantity is in truth not the issue. The significance of the text's extensive diversification lies in the transcendent quality of the creative process. What Joyce seeks and achieves is to induce a change in reading response from an objective to a subjective awareness of time. Felt through the narrative, this permeates our reading experience. Or, less abstractly: in terms of the draft's first opening, telling the beginning of 'her' silent roaming in language within the compass of the right-hand-page core inscription assumes a conventional reading reception. The time it takes to read the right-hand core column text feels roughly equivalent to the time it takes 'her' to pursue the ruminations told. As readers trained in the reciprocity convention of narrative to reading, we live through, in the right-hand page core column, a stretch of reading time as comprehension time commensurate with narrated character time. The extent and diversity of the character's mental associations do not (as yet) overstretch a customary character-to-narrative-to-reader correlation. Yet by means of the text expansion accomplished through the intense working-over across the two-page opening, time of narration-and-reading is made hopelessly to exceed the instant momentariness of the flashes of association and memory, or the jumps-to-conclusion about the present or the future, that so rapidly tumble through 'her' brain and emotions. What we see and have endeavoured to analyse from pages 0v and 1r carries forward throughout the first ten openings of the NLI Penelope draft, in particular. Joyce, seemingly crazily, continues to compose as we have seen him doing in the first opening. In floods of marginal and opposite-verso additions to the right-hand core-column text, he lavishly fills up and enriches the density and scope of 'her' memory recalls and emotional associations, her non-sequiturs, her projections into imagined futures.

He clearly knows, though, what he is doing. In their exuberant accumulation, the multitude of 'her' instant mental flashes bank up and arrest a sense of time passing, as by convention, with the time of reading. Rather, Joyce establishes the tumbles through 'her' mind as whirring equally through our minds and reading. We are force-fed her thinking, reflecting, remembering, associating, speculating, projecting 'in no time'. The constant clash that results, with the time the text craves in telling and reading, neutralises a character- and event-related

---

the first-draft's core column of more than 500 percent.

succession-in-time. It minimises, even erases thereby, the very sense of a passing of real time in 'her' past-present-future mental spontaneity. For 'her', everything that crosses her mind is simultaneously present. To experience this clash of temporalities in reading also suspends our sense of time passing.

But how can through narrative the spell be cast that 'she', the central consciousness, reflecting in simultaneity instant observations, feelings, memories, thereby inhabits an ongoing present subjectively apart from clock time? We know ourselves, though, that such experience may be had: it may take an infinitesimal moment, or extend over a length of clock time. If the latter, we may, when 'waking' from an absence in subjective presence only, exclaim: 'O, what I just thought and felt absorbed me so much, I forgot the time.' Joyce in fact makes 'her' fleetingly reflect, too, even such awareness: 'wait theres Georges church bells wait 3 quarters the hour 1 wait 2 oclock well thats a nice hour of the night for him to be coming home' (U 18, 1231-33). Closely considered, moreover, this explicit interjection of clock time reveals that 'her' thought and re-présenting reflection has indeed, up to this point, moved entirely within a subjective time capsule: 'he' is not returning home at the hour she apparently registers. He has, after all, been asleep beside her since he, she believes, ordered those eggs for breakfast. It is only now, at the time of night the clock strikes, that she becomes clock-time aware of when he did come home: 'that *was* a nice hour for him to be coming home' [my italics], in the first place.

* * *

The coming-to from an absence in subjective presence is of the nature of the experience of playing and hearing music. Music in progression establishes an autonomy of experience. "This is one of the magical things about music. It changes more than the atmosphere, it can change one's perception of existence, it can change the way you sense and feel, while you're listening to it."[4] Thus music in progression distinctly also establishes its autonomous time—while clock time of course

---

4 Sir George Benjamin, composer and conductor, was in May 2023 in Munich awarded this year's renowned Ernst von Siemens Musikpreis. John Hyman, Professor of the Philosophy of the Mind and Logic at University College, London, cited these words of Sir George's in his laudation. George Benjamin articulates the musician's

relentlessly passes. Yet, absorbed by and in the music, we disconnect from the dominance of clock time, even though 'afterwards' we remind ourselves, and throughout know subliminally anyhow, that the music we (as audience) heard or (as musicians) performed commenced an hour ago. The awareness of time so redoubled under the experience of music, moreover, engages the memory, in particular, in specific ways and modes of remembering. To experience, to feel and think within the flow of the music, requires that we are capable of présenting and re-présenting, together, moments with past moments of the flow of that experience. A work of music depends on one's remaining aware, and not forgetting, at any given moment of its passing in real time, what at any moment within the flow of its subjective past it intoned and configured. Experiencing music thus involves holding in mind and emotion its past-in-action and thereby continuously re-présenting it.[5] In this way, music establishes itself as total presence even though at the same time (!) it passes in time—in contrast to narrative that, even though progressing now, tends at the same time (!) always to be felt as 'safely' in the past. A composition in language, a narrative, may be interrupted at any time and picked up again five minutes, an hour, or a day or more later without loss of perception or understanding. A composition in music, by contrast, whether played or listened to, lives in performance and is essentially un-interruptible—interruption kills its lines of thought and emotion, its power of communication and its meaning in imagination.

This means, for *Ulysses*, no less than that James Joyce has, in concluding the novel with Penelope, invented yet a new and original narrative mode. *Ulysses* has, throughout its earlier course, challenged us with re-inventions of modes of narration. For episode 10, Joyce devised a narrated Dublin constructed on a grid of cross-linked simultaneities between characters and events at separate locations. The narrative of

---

      experience felt and lived that James Joyce, fellow musician, conveys through musicalising, by ever enriching, the flow in language of his Penelope composition.

5   Intriguingly, and in kinship with George Benjamin's utterance, Jerome McGann in a recent essay circumscribes the experience in a mode of what he, with Charles Bernstein, terms 'Close Listening': 'You listen and you think, "didn't I hear that before somewhere?" But the music keeps playing and while you are carried forwards, you are haunted backwards.' Jerome McGann, 'Breakthrough into Performance. A Touchstone Work of Late Modernist American Poetry', *PAJ: A Journal of Performance and Art*, Volume 44, Number 1, January 2022 (PAJ 130), 16-29, https://doi.org/10.1162/pajj_a_00594

episode 11 he based on principles of forms of music composition and rendering. Every subsequent chapter, from episode 12 to episode 17, constitutes, in whole or in part, a further fresh experiment with a narrative stance or stances. For episode 18—for Penelope, 'the clou of the book'— Joyce now invents a mode of narration to cast the suspension of time into real-time timelessness. The reading awareness this elicits generates a sensual experience of the very structure abstractly conceived for the episode. The suspension of time into timelessness, an illusion created through the mode of narrative deployed, answers in our acculturation to endlessness as (transcendental) eternity, or correspondingly to infinity (as secular eternity vectorialised through mathematics)—whose symbol is the figure ∞ on which Joyce expressly structured the episode.

Relating the timelessness of the narrative mode deployed to the infinity of the endlessly circumscribed ∞ is the objective correlative to the sensual experience of the suspension of real time in reading. This, in the realm of human responses, proves akin to the experience of music. In 'her' roaming in memory, thought, association, projection, everything is, since all-present, seemingly simultaneous. We read episode 18 as we hear music: we know and sense that it passes in time, yet it is to our perception 'at the same time' entirely an autonomous capsule in clock time, in itself an experience-as-if of an a-temporal presence. The final *Ulysses* episode is thus narrated wholly in the mode of music. The text composed through its many-layered extensions does not *tell* 'her'—it represents in that it *performs* 'her'.

Samuel Beckett a few years later found the perfect formula for Joyce's writing. His verdict on *Work in Progress*, Joyce's labour towards *Finnegans Wake*, is fully applicable, too, to the final episode of *Ulysses*. 'It is not written at all. It is not to be read—or rather it is not only to be read. It is to be looked at and listened to. His writing is not about something; it is that something itself.'[6] To look at it means to read its score, and to listen to it is to hear its music—thus, simultaneously looking and listening means to respond to the episode as performed in the temporal mode of music.

In overall terms of literary writing, the episode so realises, even as it performs, the re-configuration of narration (*diegesis*) into representation

---

6   Samuel Beckett, 'Dante... Bruno. Vico... Joyce', in *Our Exagmination Round his Factification for Incamination of Work in Progress* (London: Faber & Faber, 1929, p. 14.)

(*mimesis*). This means, for *Ulysses* as a whole: telling the novel in the time-honoured mode of teleologic and therein diegetic Aristotelian narration—'beginning – middle – end'—is brought to its close with episode 17. 'The *Ithaca* episode [...] is in reality the end as *Penelope* has no beginning, middle or end' as Joyce himself remarked to Harriet Weaver (*Letters* I, 172). As science distinguishes Euclidian and non-Euclidian mathematics, so does Joyce, ultimately in *Ulysses*, overreach Aristotelian with non-Aristotelian narration. Out of the final full stop 'bien visible' of episode 17 is triggered, in mimetic narration, 'her' time-capsuled past-present-future simultaneity under the condition of music.

Ulysses 1922 and the Golden Mean: Shaping His Text Into Book

James Joyce's *Ulysses* is a twentieth-century modernist novel published in book form on 2 February 1922. Produced from the printing-house of Maurice Darantiere in Dijon, France, the book is the product of high professional skill and workshop procedure. The house of Darantiere specialised in *deluxe* editions. Remarkably, in the early twentieth century, they still practiced typesetting by hand. The *Ulysses* printers-copy typescripts identify no less than twenty-six typesetters at work. Darantiere's practice, in evidence for *Ulysses*, too, was to set not in lengthy galleys to be cast off at a later stage into numbered pages, but to format the typesetting at once into page size, though with the pages as yet unnumbered. These unnumbered page-size text units were proof-printed consecutively in groups of eight, four over four, on one side of sheets named 'placards', to be submitted to the author for first proof-reading. Returned with autograph changes and additions in the margins, the changes from them were worked into the standing type and the placard texts were freshly adjusted into pages and now numbered. The numbered pages were bundled, sixteen by sixteen, into gatherings. The gatherings were, successively singly or in groups, multiply re-submitted to the author for proofing. In, at times, up to twelve rounds of proof-reading, each round carries a fresh set of author corrections and frequently significant text additions. Joyce wrote about one third of *Ulysses* in the process of proof-reading—indeed, the text originally submitted in typescript he augmented by about one third in proofs. This made high demands on the typesetters nimbly and correctly to shift stretches of text forward through the accumulating pages in and across gatherings. On last proofs that commonly carry the *'bon à tirer'* approval of James Joyce (author) and Sylvia Beach (publisher), the final control of the printing house is in evidence with its last touches to text and typography. Both in placard and in page, the Darantiere proofs are virtually all preserved. The final state of the text and the ultimately valid pagination beyond placards and page proofs shows first and only in the first-edition printing. The author, typists, printing-house workmen, and author again and again thus interacted over some nine months (midsummer 1921 to 1 February 1922) on transposing the *Ulysses* text composition, revision and augmentation into the artefact of the 2 February 1922 first-edition-*Ulysses* book.

The 1922 book is a product of the book trade. As that product, it accommodates the first text instantiation of James Joyce's novel, *Ulysses*. The two perspectives, book and text, need to be kept distinct. The book, as the product of the book trade, is singular. The text contained in the book bodies forth materially, as it so happens, the first public appearance of a text representing a work and is therefore, as is any first edition, popularly much revered. Yet it is but one instantiation in transmission of its author's text after all pre-publication exertions of composition and revision, and before the material text's subsequent passage through multi-faceted re-publication. As presented in the first edition—being therein in reality 'neither first nor last nor only nor alone in a series', as Leopold Bloom would have it (*U* 17, 2130)—it offers a text as contingent as is any, and are all, of its antecedents and successors. The relation of the book artefact and the first-edition text instantiation that it happens to carry deserves a closer look.

In this respect, James Joyce's *Ulysses* presents a very special case. Joyce did not 'just' provide the text content for the book entrusted to Darantiere for production. He also actively shaped the material body of that text content. For *Ulysses* in its first edition, Joyce saw the text extension of his writing inscribed as a text body into the first-edition book. This text body he arranged in a book-space-encompassing design articulated in proportions of culturally inherited significance. He thus gave the book's material content extension a singular structure. This extension structure of the text body coexists with, yet is still autonomously distinct from, the literary text composed as art in language. The text matter that instantiates the literary work *Ulysses* is thereby no longer solely to be seen, as by convention, technically contained between book covers. It becomes an element of the book, genuinely integrated in the book as cultural artefact. Text body and book are fused to mutually and jointly express the singularity of the first-edition *Ulysses*.

* * *

Books and the art and craft of book making look back on an autonomous history. How the art and craft impinge on text contained in, and presented and made public through books is of high cultural complexity. In book making history, the transmedialising of text into book has correspondingly strong traditions of aesthetic signification. Book aesthetics are established through numbers and proportion. What measurements should a book be given? How should its height and its width be proportioned to one another? How should the type-page height and width relate to that of the book? An ingrained tradition survives in the proportioning of book-size and type-page dimensions to the ratio of the golden mean. As has been asserted and demonstrated before,[1] the material stretch of pages in the first-edition-*Ulysses* book fulfils that ratio. This has, to this day, not been appreciated in its full significance as a fact, and even less as a dimension of Joyce's art, his intellectual and artistic range and achievement.

Of the novel-text's eighteen episodes, a first sequence of eleven episodes runs to 279 pages, the end of Sirens. Seven episodes still lie ahead. The eleven to seven ratio is correlatable in terms of Joyce's chapter ground-plan for *Ulysses*. The ratio of the number of chapters remaining to those already typeset works out as (18:11)=1.61.... This is the ratio of the golden mean (1,6180339887, an irrational number). For the text body of the book *Ulysses* in production, the ratio needs to be translated into page extensions. With the writing of the novel essentially realised in the autumn of 1921, it is clear that the text sequence of eleven episodes ending at page 279 closes the shorter stretch of text for the book in the making. The remaining seven episodes will constitute its longer stretch. They are, at most, in proof, in some parts not yet even fully written. But what can be calculated, on the strength of the '279' page count for the shorter stretch in the golden mean ratio, is that the book text yet ahead would need to fill 451 pages. The seven post-Sirens episodes, Cyclops

---

[1] Susan Sutliff Brown, 'The Geometry of Joyce's *Ulysses*: from Pythagoras to Poincare: Joyce's Use of Geometry for Structure, Metaphor, and Theme', PhD dissertation, University of South Florida (Tampa, FL, 1987).

through to Penelope, would constitute the text body's longer stretch and bring the page total for the book up to 730 pages. The 451 pages of the longer stretch would stand in a (451:279)=1.61...relation to the shorter stretch from Telemachus through to Sirens. In actual fact, the book text ends on page 732. While the ratio of the whole to the actual longer stretch (732:453) thereby still remains at 1.61..., that of the longer to the shorter stretch (now: 453:279), rises to 1.62...—an overreach yet to be attended to.

The material text of the 1922 edition as book content is hence manifestly laid out in ratios of the golden mean. Given the book-making art expended on the book, this goes essentially to strengthen the singular iconicity of the first-edition volume of *Ulysses*. I posit that this proportioning of the material text content was conceived and realised by James Joyce, the author, not by Maurice Darantiere and his printing house. The book they produced displays superior crafting, yet as an artefact it shows no distinct trace of implementing the book-making tradition of golden-mean dispositioning in its formats of book size, page size or type-page size. Darantiere, in fact, may even have been oblivious of—or have been left in the dark about—the golden mean aesthetic disposition of the material text content of the book he was producing. He certainly does not uphold the aesthetics of the first-edition text layout when re-setting *Ulysses* for the second edition of 1926. This circumstance plays further into the author's court the assumption that the proportioning of text extensions according to the golden mean in the 1922 *Ulysses* was indeed Joyce's. It was, for him, the ultimate authorial measure to frame specifically and exclusively the first-edition text instantiation into the singular iconicity of the first edition as book.

Joyce's decision to choose this shaping would have been taken with the control of the final proofs having gone into print, resulting in the page count for the printed book up to the end of Sirens. Printing at Darantiere's proceeded successively episode by episode, upon which the type was immediately broken up and distributed for re-use. Consequently, the page number '279' would stand firm. From here, a page count to the end of the text body in terms of the golden mean ratio was safely calculable. As for reaching it: a touch of familiarity with the progress of composition of *Ulysses* helps us to remember that astonishingly expansive late additions to Cyclops and Circe accrued while the book production was already in full swing. For Cyclops, the so-called 'Metropolitan Police' Section (*U* 12, 534-608) stands out, composed as a fresh narrative sequence close to three years after the chapter's original completion. Joyce correction-marked for Darantiere's workmen where to insert it in the Cyclops chapter. Sirens was, at the time, in the last rounds of page-proofing and Cyclops in third placards.[2] To all appearances, thus, the 'Metropolitan Police' section was a practical response to the need to fill pages towards ultimately reaching the page-number goal. For Circe, the print production, ultimately long drawn out until late January 1920, actually began on 20 October 1921—amazingly only a day after the final proofs for Cyclops were returned to Darantiere to go into print, and so with the 'Metropolitan Police' section incorporated. The first placard typesetting for Circe in its turn was done on that 20 October out of order of the chapter text for precisely the stretch of the 'Messianic Scene' addition. Joyce only subsequently, weeks later, instructed the typesetters where to insert the scene in the consecutive text of the Circe episode. Eventually, the 'Messianic Scene' in the 1922 first edition extends to eighteen pages (around sixteen pages in *U* 15, 1398-1958). In the first edition it begins a third down on page 453—a circumstance and a page number to which we shall return. Ithaka, finally, underwent an ultimate craze of augmentation to become the novel's second-longest chapter after Circe. Though the novel's penultimate episode, it was not only the last to be finalised in composition. It was also typeset and proofread under last-minute pressure throughout the very final weeks of readying *Ulysses* for publication. Its extensive late accretions to the novel's text body helped significantly to reach the page-count goal for the book.

At the end of the novel's thirteenth episode, Nausikaa, we find positive proof that Joyce himself engaged in the proportioning of the book's text body: this chapter, closing as it does the day-time half of *Ulysses*, ends on page 365. To set the novel-text's midpoint at '365' (i.e., half of '730') makes sense only if the text-extension end point is already pre-calculated from here—regardless of the fact that considerable

---

2   All detail of the advance in the printing process through placards and proofs is listed in tabular form on pages 1914-1915 in volume 3 of James Joyce, *A Critical and Synoptic Edition*, edited by Hans Walter Gabler with Wolfhard Steppe and Claus Melchior (New York, Garland Publishing, 1984; [2]1986). The tables permit follow-up research in volumes [12] to [27] of *The James Joyce Archive*, ed. by Michael Groden, *et al.*, 63 vols. (New York and London: Garland Publishing, 1977-79).

stretches of the novel-text's second half were not yet typeset, or printed, and the penultimate episode, Ithaka, was not yet even fully written. At the moment of production when Nausikaa was printed and the chapter type distributed, only the author can have known that the middle of the book was reached and, thus, which end-page-number was thence pre-calculated.

* * *

Joyce had something of a fetish for the numbers eleven and twenty-two. In the *Ulysses* fiction, Bloom's and Molly's son Rudy lives for just eleven days. Stephen, in the fiction, is twenty-two years old (which in the fiction's reality mirror-year 1904 was James Joyce's age). To top the making of the work, Joyce was determined to see *Ulysses* published on 2.2.22 (his fortieth birthday). In terms of the novel's overall web of significances, we may thus safely posit that it would have appeared to him a meaningful starting-point to bracket eleven episodes as one unit towards a comprehensive proportioning of the novel's text extensions according to the golden mean ratio. He was given firm ground to work from with the page count for the novel's first eleven chapters. The signposts in the body of the seven episodes to come, Cyclops to Penelope, are sufficiently discernible to authenticate the assumption that, between 27 October 1921 and the end of January 1922, Joyce actively reached out for page '730' to end the novel. His stretching the goal out finally to '732' is, as we shall see, the result of an increase of complexity through overlapping calculations.

It is possible to establish a timeline for the book's production from the end of Sirens onwards. The final page proofs for Sirens are dateable to 25-26 October. At this point, as mentioned, the page end '279' stood fixed. Cyclops, which followed, had two rounds of page proofs still to go: typesetting work and proof corrections on the chapter were completed on around 15 November. The succeeding episodes, Nausikaa and Oxen of the Sun, were in the works in parallel from the last week of October. The last proof date for Nausikaa is 23 November. The chapter ends, in proof as in book, on page '365', which marks, as already mentioned (albeit only virtually so far), the mid-point of *Ulysses*. The textual moment suggests that the mid-pointing is indeed intended.³ The novel's midpoint by content confirms the post-Sirens calculation by proportion. Doubling the page count from page 365, the end of Nausikaa, reaches out again to the novel's estimated end page 730. This confirms the numeric disposition we are assuming for the aesthetic contouring of the book's text body according to the ratio of the golden mean.

For the novel's second half by material content, a keen eye must have been kept on the progression of typesetting and accommodation of changes and accretions of text from the multiple revisions in page. Since work on the book-in-the-making often progressed on several of the remaining episodes concurrently, page numbering as it clocked up must have been important for orientation. Before work on Oxen of the Sun came to an end, the episode Penelope – the novel's final episode! – went into first placard proof as early as 17-18 October. The placard text was four times proof-revised, but understandably put on hold (on 24-26 November) until print production, and so pagination, of the intervening episodes could catch up with this final chapter. Typesetting in placards on Circe began on 20 October and was kept in placards until the first week of December, understandably again until setting and proofing Oxen of the Sun ended to give the correct pagination to begin Circe.

A sequence of paginated gatherings for Circe was sent to Joyce on 8 December for proof correction. Gathering 29, page 453 shows the beginning of the 'Messianic scene' in place. Through several subsequent further accretions, it eventually extended over eighteen pages to the first-edition page 470. What we cannot retrace from the surviving proofs in detail is how it was directed from the placard typesetting of 20 October to what, seven weeks later in the book, was to be its opening on page 453. Its insertion on this page does not fit with precision into a golden mean proportioning of 279 pages (the final page number of Sirens) + 451 pages (pre-calculated from the end of Sirens) = 730 pages. Page 453, on which the 'Messianic Scene' is inserted, is, however, precisely 279 pages distant from page number '732' on which the *Ulysses* first-edition text in fact ends. That is: if from the end of Sirens (page 279)

---

3   And numerologically so. John Kidd helped me at this stile. At a time before taking issue with *Ulysses. A Critical and Synoptic Edition*, he suggestively explored aspects of Joyce's awareness of and play with numbers in *Ulysses*. He drew specific, though isolated attention to the calculated mid-novel day-to-night transition.

the final page number '730' was to be attained by the golden mean ratio through another 451 pages to reach the novel's last page as prospectively pre-calculated, then mirroring the ratio from the novel's end page as eventually attained brings us (after subtraction of 279 from 732 pages) back, now, to real page 453.

The manifest back-calculating of the insertion of the 'Messianic Scene' into Circe by 279 pages from end page number '732' to page number '453' focuses essentially, if not with minute precision, that Joyce concurrently with the golden mean proportioning also mid-centred the text body of the first-edition *Ulysses*.[4] The 'Pprrpffrrppffff. Done.' end of Sirens on page 279 (*U* 11, 1293-1294), and the splicing-in at page 453 of '(Prolonged applause. [etc.])' (*U* 15, 1398) to open the 'Messianic Scene' apotheosis of Leopold Bloom, form a frame to the novel's midpoint that is equidistant from the novel-text's beginning and end. This in turn confirms that halving *Ulysses* at the transition from Nausikaa to Oxen of the Sun is a conscious and significant decision. The text body of *Ulysses* in the Darantiere first-edition book is both proportioned according to the golden mean ratio and mid-centred. At the same time: what has shifted since the original pre-calculation to an end-page-number 730 is that, as seen from the insertion of the 'Messianic Scene' at page 453 in Circe, the day-to-night centre pivot of the text body has shifted from page 365 (end of Nausikaa) to page 366 (opening of Oxen of the Sun). This is linked to an awareness that the mid-novel page numbers indicate days in the calendar year. A regular year has 365 days. Yet every fourth year is a leap-year with 366 days. The real calendar year 1904 in which *Ulysses* the fiction is anchored was such a leap year.[5]

* * *

---

[4] In its mid-point-pivoted chiastic design, *Ulysses* directly succeeds *A Portrait of the Artist as a Young Man*. See my argument, first laid out close to half a century ago, and since re-published in 'The Genesis of *A Portrait of the Artist as a Young Man*', in *Critical Essays on James Joyce's A Portrait of the Artist as a Young Man*, ed. by Philip Brady and James F. Carens (New York: G. K. Hall, 1998), pp. 83-112; and in the present volume.

[5] The second chapter in Susan Brown's brilliant and many-faceted dissertation (see above, footnote 1) analyses at length the 'crisis' the composition of Circe underwent. One in a range of outcomes from it was the slight warping of the book's page number calculation.

By 8 December, placard typesetting began, too, on Eumaeus and Ithaka. Through December and until 5 January, these episodes saw two placard proofreadings each. Casting-off into page for Circe had begun in December and been carried forward sufficiently in the first third of January for Eumaeus, in consequence, to go into a third round of proofing and correction, now in pagination for book printing, between 6 and 11 January. With Circe fully in page, the finishing of Eumaeus and Ithaka in page followed between 16 and 20 January. This was also when Darantiere once more picked up the placards of Penelope, left hanging since late November, and now paginated them in follow-up to Ithaka, to send them to Joyce (and Sylvia Beach) for final proofing.

The final-proof pagination for Ithaka ends in gathering 43 on a page '682'. Final proof for Penelope begins in the last stretch of that gathering through its pages 683 to 688, then runs on through gathering 44, pages 689 to 704. These final-proof pages 689 to 704 have a *bon à tirer* approval from Joyce and Sylvia Beach without a Penelope-specific date. The end-of-Ithaka and beginning-of-Penelope proofs came as a bulk consignment that was given the authorial *bon-à-tirer* on 25 January and was received in Dijon on 27 January. The remainder of Penelope, gathering 45 and two-and-a-half pages of gathering 46, bear James Joyce's/Sylvia Beach's *bon-à-tirer* with the date of 31 January 1922. This means, be it noted, that Joyce and Beach sent to Dijon the final corrected proofs of the final stretch of the final episode, and thus of the end of the book, just three days before the date Darantiere had committed himself to deliver the finished book to the author on his fortieth birthday—and did.[6]

The novel's end page in this final proof stage in gathering 45 carries the page number 723. Among the Darantiere page pulls preserved by Sylvia Beach there exists, beyond the corrected proofs ending the novel on page 723, yet a four-page final-final proof run, paginated 729 to 732. As against the final proofs' end page number, these four pages

---

6 James Joyce himself likely felt his fortieth birthday a mid-life marker. From Christian education, Psalm 90:10 resonates: 'The days of our years are threescore years and ten; and if by reason of strength they be fourscore years, yet is their strength labour and sorrow.' [Or, in Martin Luther's life-asserting translation into German: 'Unser Leben währet siebenzig Jahre, und wenn's hoch kommt, so sind's achtzig Jahre; und wenn's köstlich gewesen ist, so ist's Mühe und Arbeit gewesen'—as, author of this essay, I recall at the age of eighty-five.] The psalm's leeway of a decade allows Leopold Bloom too a mid-life age at thirty-eight—that his author had out-lived by two years when *Bloomysses* came out.

thus ultimately reach the end page number of the first edition of *Ulysses* as published. In other words: the regular final proofs for Penelope, and equally of course for Ithaka, had, upon being submitted, been fully corrected at Darantiere's. All Joyce's additions had been worked in, the page contents shifted forward accordingly and the pagination adjusted to its final sequence. The ultimate page numbering shows in the printed edition only. Ithaka ends in the final proof on page 682. In the first-edition book text, it ends seven pages further on, on page 689. Consequently, Penelope in the final proof begins on page 683 and ends on 723, halfway down the page. In the first-edition book text, it begins on page 690 and ends nine pages on, half-way down page 732.[7]

Our retrospective analysis shows that with the final-proof lengthening of Ithaka by seven pages, the pagination goal as pre-calculated after Sirens would have been perfectly hit. Unaltered, Penelope in its end-of-November typeset shape would have precisely attained the end of the first-edition book text on page 730. Yet, over and above the extensions already worked into the final Ithaka proofs, Joyce, at the very last moment of opportunity—and against Darantiere's urge to stop revising—wrote in yet a page-and-a-half's worth of additions into the final proofs of Penelope that he returned on 31 January. These additions successfully extended the length of the novel's text body to page 732: the final page number aimed for, traceably, since the insertion of the 'Messianic Scene' into Circe on book page 453. Conceivably, the unique survival among Sylvia Beach's papers of actual print pages for the book, a pull of the ultimate pages 729-732, neatly the second half of the book's last gathering, indicates that these pages were expressly requested from Paris when Joyce and Beach returned the addition-augmented final proofs. It suggests the purpose of the assumed request: Joyce wished to be absolutely sure that his last additions had brought the text forward

---

7   Bibliographically speaking, the last gathering in the set of the last Ithaka/Penelope page proofs from the printing house ends on its eighth and last leaf, paginated 723 (recto)/724 (verso). The Penelope episode, and *Ulysses*, thus ended at that point on a page 723; page 724 remained blank. Darantiere submitted these last page proofs to Joyce on 31 January 1922. By return, Joyce sent Darantiere revisions sufficient to expand the text to the goal of page 732 in the printed book. This required a fresh half-gathering of eight pages. The final pages in the first edition thus accommodate book pages 725-726-727-728[sown in the gutter]729-730-731-732. The surviving pages as preserved by (presumably) Sylvia Beach are hence the second half of the ultimate half-gathering as typeset at the book's end.

to end on page 732. They had. James Joyce saw his aim fulfilled of shaping the text extension of the book *Ulysses* in proportioned iconicity of aesthetic harmony and form.

* * *

'We are still learning to be James Joyce's contemporaries...' This stunning opening to Richard Ellmann's James Joyce biography of 1959/1982 has not lost its stringency. We have, over generations since the publication of *Ulysses* in its first-edition book, immersed ourselves in the text given us to share and endeavoured to learn how Joyce's mind and thought and reading, his emotion and writing was all in advance of his own times, to be attained and understood by us in ours. Over these one hundred years, there can be little doubt about it, we have made headway in, as Ellmann closes that opening, 'understand[ing] our interpreter'. In this, Ellmann's perspective points forward to our engagement with Joyce's creative achievement. Just how creative that achievement is in itself, as it richly feeds on Joyce's innate awareness and sense of his cultural and intellectual background in his time and his past (and ours), is still in need of exploration. The reception history in Joyce studies of his creative deployment of the golden mean ratio is a case in point. The present essay does not perform that exploration. It merely scratches a surface from which Joyce studies may feel encouraged to dig more and deeper, to better encompass contemporaneity with Joyce's sense, feeling and understanding of his, yet thereby ultimately also our, cultural past. Joyce, in his deep immersion in shaping language into text for a novel, lived, thought and worked concurrently on a significantly distinct level of composition by semantics and meaning of the structure of text matter, of numbers in their dimensions of meaning (that is, by their semantic potential known and practiced and honoured of old), and of the Pythagorean ratios, through millennia understood to order the world and creation, though meanwhile merely modulated into a favoured device of aesthetic proportioning.

An aura of James Joyce's presence in his time, present undiminished in ours, is integral to the powers from which his creativity sprang. It relies on patterns of living and thinking and feeling, on systems of thought and understanding of the past and their forms and modes of signification and expression in culture and epistemology since antiquity.

Pythagoras' monochord permitted proportioning its one string into lengths sounding tones and scales. Music thus became calculable in terms of mathematics. Proportional measuring was diversely, two- or three-dimensionally, applied for signification to surfaces or bodies. Among surface measurements, the *sectio aurea* or *sectio divina* (the golden mean) was especially revered over the millennia. From the Pythagorean monochord concept ultimately—in the full sense of the word: encompassingly—evolved the model of the nine spheres: concentrical to the earth, they sound the world order of divine creation in music. Joyce ensured in the first edition of *Ulysses* that the text which the volume materialised formed in itself a body as singular and unique as was the crafted book that contained it. The 1922 *Ulysses* became, throughout its materiality, a twice-ordered and proportioned creation, in and through itself to embody the cultural icon which we since recognise *Ulysses* 1922 to be. Which is only a beginning, we may take James Joyce's word for it: 'I've put in so many enigmas and puzzles that it will keep the professors busy for centuries [...] that's the only way of insuring one's immortality.'[8]

---

8   Quoted by Richard Ellmann in *James Joyce* (Oxford: Oxford University Press, ²1982), p. 521.

'Love, yes. Word known to all men.'

To the memory of
Kinga Thomas
Attentive first reader[1]

James Joyce wrote *Ulysses*—as the saying goes. The phrase—as far as it goes—is true. Yet it is a shortcut. It compresses a complex web of simultaneously sequential mental and scripted processes into one material result, a word in the past tense: he 'wrote' *Ulysses*. The fact that Joyce's (or any writer's, author's) processes of language composition interacted in thought and in draft to result in a material record preserved, is the pre-condition for text we possess in transmission. Material records of writing have, often enough it is true, come down to us only in descent through derivative removes from their authors' own first materialising their composition in written text. In the case of James Joyce, consecutive early writing—inscription on paper in his own hand or in the hands of scribes and typesetters—has very largely been preserved. Joyce's holograph/autograph writing itself frequently shows distinct traces of its pre-material ancestry, or offers at least the possibility of intuiting pre-material moments or processes of composition. What is more: the material records of Joyce's composition and writing frequently survive in series of states of descent, from authorial drafts and fair copies in

---

1   A student assistant in our editorial team forty years ago, Kinga Thomas pursued her stint to check the editing of Scylla & Charybdis. I had (clearly) given it but routine attention (two paragraphs to be restored? OK.). She read in depth and, excited, came to my office. She saw and felt the significance of our restoring the two paragraphs that had gone missing, and so of ascertaining as *Ulysses* text Stephen Dedalus's self-assurance that he knew what he was talking about. Kinga Thomas, still a student, died mountaineering.

Joyce's hand to typescripts and proofs, often multiply derivative one from the other, in transcript by others. Typescripts and proofs were always basically the work of typists and printers' compositors. Variation, by contrast—that is: text changes on top of surviving typescripts and proofs—were Joyce's, again in his own hand.

* * *

One third of the way into the ninth episode of *Ulysses*, Stephen Dedalus is in full swing performing his Hamlet lecture to his listeners, a circle of librarians in Dublin's national library. He draws from Shakespeare's last plays the names of their protagonists' daughters and recalls from *Pericles* how Marina, Pericles' daughter, searches out her father. A section of Stephen Dedalus' speech to the Dublin librarians in the episode as published runs as follows:[2]

> —Marina, Stephen said, a child of storm, Miranda, a wonder, Perdita, that which was lost. What was lost is given back to him: his daughter's child. *My dearest wife*, Pericles says, *was like this maid*. Will any man love the daughter if he has not loved the mother?
> —The art of being a grandfather, Mr Best gan murmur. *L'art d'être grandp.....*
> —His own image to a man with that queer thing genius is the standard of all experience, material and moral. Such an appeal will touch him. The images of other males of his blood will repel him. He will see in them grotesque attempts of nature to foretell or to repeat himself.

To prepare for a scholarly edition, one undertakes a search into the spread of all documented instantiations, often variant, of the text in transmission. When Joyce, accomplishing the novel one episode after another, felt he had sufficiently stabilised a given episode, he would write it out in fair copy.[3] In the fair-copy rendering of the passage that concerns us, the text reads as follows:

> —Marina, Stephen said, a child of storm, Miranda, a wonder, Perdita, that which was lost. What was lost is given back to him: his

---

[2] Or ran as follows from the first edition of *Ulysses* in 1922 onwards before a scholarly edition, the Critical and Synoptic Edition, was established in 1984. The episode and line reference for the critically edited text of 1984 is: (*U* 9, 421-435).

[3] The fair copy of Scylla & Charybdis survives in the Rosenbach manuscript, archived in the Rosenbach Museum in Philadelphia.

'Love, yes. Word known to all men.'   409

>daughter's child. *My dearest wife*, Pericles says, *was like this maid*. Will any man love the daughter if he has not loved the mother?
>—The art of being a grandfather, Mr Best murmured.
>—Will he not see reborn in her, with the memory of his own youth added, another image? Do you know what you are talking about? Love, yes. Word known to all men. *Amor vero aliquid alicui bonum vult unde et ea quae concupiscimus_*...
>—His own image to a man with that queer thing genius is the standard of all experience, material and moral. Such an appeal will touch him. The images of other males of his brood will repel him. He will see in them grotesque attempts of nature to foretell or to repeat himself.

As Stephen pauses briefly from his first rhetorical question: 'Will any man love the daughter if he has not loved the mother?', Mr Best mumbles: '—The art of being a grandfather, Mr Best murmured.' Thereafter, this fair-copy instantiation of the passage includes two paragraphs that are lacking in the novel's first edition as published (my first quote above). Unresponsive to Mr Best's interjection, Stephen climaxes his rhetorical questions with the second: '—Will he not see reborn in her, with the memory of his own youth added, another image?' This is the climax to Stephen's rhetorical questions. Apostrophising 'reborn', it refers specifically, too, to a core motif in Shakespeare's last plays. Above all: at this point Stephen pauses in his performance. He is moved to a self-querying silent reflection: 'Do you know what you are talking about? Love, yes. Word known to all men. *Amor vero aliquid alicui bonum vult unde et ea quae concupiscimus_*...' Only thereupon does he pick up again his performance to the librarians in the National Library.

The Critical and Synoptic Edition of *Ulysses* restores this pair of paragraphs. The restoration has been controversial in Joyce criticism for the past forty years. The bone of contention has been that, from within the second of the restored paragraphs, it renders available three sentences in English from which springs, in turn, a long, yet still only half-finished quote in Latin. The three sentences in English read: 'Do you know what you are talking about? Love, yes. Word known to all men.' They alone have drawn attention. That they do not resurface and so remain absent in the subsequent transmission was taken to indicate that they were consciously deleted. Little thought was given to the situation in full.

Two whole paragraphs, short but complete, are no longer present in the book *Ulysses*. Hence, we need to know and to understand on what grounds these two paragraphs got lost together, in the first place; and why they were editorially restored together again in the scholarly edition. Additionally, there arises within these two paragraphs of text a particular question, contextually complex, in the light of *Ulysses* as a whole. Does Stephen Dedalus here, or ever in the novel, himself articulate the '[w]ord known to all men'? This specific question, however, is not for the reader or critic to decide. Nor can the editor follow a mere hunch that either to leave it out, or else to restore it, results in the text as it should be.

In analysing, arguing, and decision-making, the editor follows principles of editorial procedure. The task is comprehensively to assess the textual situation, to recognise and adjudicate whether there is a problem to be solved—not with regard to the presence vs. absence of three sentences, but comprehensively to the flow of the narrative of the two paragraphs *in toto*, as a unit of writing and consistent argument— and to take editorial measures, or not, accordingly. With respect to the records in material transmission, there is, in the first instance, only one question to be answered: were the two paragraphs in revision deleted, or were they passed over by accident in the text's descent through copying from one document to the next? This one question, binary as it is, is independent of the content and meaning, in whole or in part, of the text contained in the variant in question.

Knowledge of Joyce's working practice needs at this stage to be adduced in terms of how an episode established for *Ulysses* was handed over to those responsible for its typing and eventual typesetting. In principle, the fair-copy text was meant without delay to go into typescript and thence into proof. Yet there were time gaps between finishing fair copies and passing on the text to prepare typescript copy for typesetting at the printing house. In these intermittent periods, Joyce would have further ideas about touching up the fair-copy text. How and where were they to be inserted in standing documents? In the early *Ulysses* episodes, he would tend to revise in the fair copy itself. Yet this impaired the clean appearance of the fair copy. For a succession of episodes from about episode five onwards, he therefore went back to the final document from which he had established the fair copy. This final working draft does not survive. But from rich collation, it has been analytically established that there existed a 'final working draft' document from which the fair copy (the Rosenbach manuscript) was written out, and to which he went back to enter revisions after finishing the fair copy. In our brief excerpt alone, we stumble over two instances. The phrasing 'Mr Best gan murmur. *L'art d'être grandp.....*' is a variant in the first edition beyond the text of the fair copy. The same goes for the change from 'his brood' to 'his blood' ['will repel him'] in the last paragraph of our passage. In terms of document analysis and collation, it is clear that the changes passed on into the typescript from the final working draft. Hence we safely conclude that the episode Scylla & Charybdis was typed not from the fair copy, but from the final working draft. The typescript in turn served as copy for the typesetting of the first edition. 'Mr Best gan murmur. *L'art d'être grandp.....*' and 'his blood' are therefore Joyce's revisions beyond the fair copy in the final working draft, and were so ultimately established, and italicised for Mr Best's French, in the published text.

One feature, however, can be assessed only by hypothesis, due to the material absence of the final working draft itself. In the fair copy (extant) in Joyce's hand, it is notable that words and phrases to be italicised are underlined throughout. No doubt Joyce himself so italicised the fair copy. There is thereupon, as said, a gap in the document descent. The final working draft—revised after the fair copy—is missing. The text reappears in the typed transcript from it. The typescript provides Mr Best's post-fair-copy mumble in revised wording '[...,] Mr Best gan murmur. *L'art d'être grandp.....*'. The pressure of Stephen's ongoing performance curtails Mr Best's interjection, doesn't leave room for him to finish his sentence even under his breath. Significantly, it is Stephen's climax that follows: '—Will he not see reborn in her, with the memory of his own youth added, another image?', which makes narrative sense of the cutting-in-half of Mr Best's murmur in French. But that climax is missing in the typescript, as is Stephen's silent reflection following upon it, before he resumes his performance to the librarians. The gap in the typescript text, and in *Ulysses* as first published, thus comprises two distinctly separate elements of Joyce's composition at this juncture: the climax of Stephen's argument about fathers and daughters in Shakespeare's late plays, and his silent reflection on whether he knows what he is talking about. Our hypothesis on which to ground the restoration of the sequence of paragraphs as Joyce composed them relies on a strictly formal feature of his writing in the fair copy, projected also onto the post-fair-copy revision in the final working draft. We confidently assume that Joyce underlined *'L'art d'être grandp.....'* in the revision he added to the final working draft. For this, we even have indirect evidence in the fact that the half-phrase was manifestly (albeit shakily, most likely by a scribal hand) underlined in pencil in the typescript. Notably, this half-phrase in French ends with four dots. We proceed then (according to the fair-copy text) through the two paragraphs that the fair copy features (but the documents from typescript to first-edition printing in 1922 do not). The second of these paragraphs in the fair copy ends in a long passage in Latin, which, again, we confidently assume was underlined for italics in the final working draft, just like Mr Best's interjection actually is in the typescript, and again peters out into four dots.

In this situation, the discipline of scholarly editing and the bibliographical evidence together guide us to the only consistent assessment and consequent solution. On account of the visual near-identity of the closing phrases of the paragraphs as styled in the final working draft, both underlined (as we hypothesise) for italics and ending in rows of dots, the typist fell victim to an eye-skip from the end of one paragraph to its counterpart, both ends being underlined for italics and running out into dots. This solution is neatly text-independent. No critical assessment is required based on reading, understanding, and interpreting the text and its meaning. The restoration of two paragraphs simply corrects a human error. In particular, the question never arises whether or not Joyce might have considered, or approved of, the removal of the three sentences that Stephen thinks in silence. Whether or not Joyce ever had second thoughts about them is simply unknown. 'Authorial authorisation' does not exist other than that inscribed in the second of the two paragraphs in Joyce's fair copy. To consider, let alone claim, authorial authority for the disappearance specifically of the three sentences within the second missing paragraph is, without authorial affirmation in word or writing, wholly speculative. Without such affirmation, editorial scholarship, on the foundation of the text's material transmission, upholds the integrity in composition of the two paragraphs in their entirety. In other words, editorial scholarship operates in situations like this not with reference to 'authority', whether authorial or legitimised otherwise, nor can—or does—it speculate on what the author might have intended. It proceeds from the material evidence of the text transmission. Responsible to it, and to professional competence, it establishes the critical scholarly edition. The three sentences within the two paragraphs that disappeared entirely between fair copy and typescript in Scylla & Charybdis belong in this segment of the materially transmitted text as Joyce wrote it. They belong in *Ulysses* as book (and in the material instantiation of the work *Ulysses* that the book represents, in its turn), and have thus, through critical editing, been restored to their place of composition in the novel's ninth episode.

* * *

With regard to Joyce's novel *Ulysses* as a whole, this brings up a text occurrence in the novel's fifteenth episode, Circe, that might seem inconsistent with Scylla & Charybdis as authentically restored. Stephen Dedalus encounters his dead mother and is drawn into anguished exchanges with her. In their course, he urges her: 'Tell me the word mother, if you know now. The word known to all men.' (*U* 15, 4192-93) Is Stephen—shaken by fear and thoroughly drunk as he is—hoping to learn from his mother now, dead though she is, what she never assured him of in her life? Or else: does the re-balancing of the text of *Ulysses*, by restoring two paragraphs in Scylla & Charybdis, establish also a restored basis for reading and interpreting Stephen's encounter with his mother in Circe? Stephen challenges her to speak at last, from beyond death, that word of which he, alive, is certain. In silently reflecting upon what he is holding forth about to his listeners in Scylla & Charybdis, he 'know[s] what [he is] talking about'. The subsequent progress of *Ulysses* gives no indication of his wavering from that certainty now. 'Now' is the key to Stephen's attitude to his mother, dead though she is, in Circe. In the first draft of the passage, his appeal at the onset reads: 'Tell me the word mother, if you know', yet it is above the line on the instant revised to: 'Tell me the word mother, if you know now.' Behind his appeal is not a sense that his mother died with a knowledge she had kept to herself in her lifetime. Rather, Stephen craves that she admits to having gained a knowledge now, beyond her death, that, for all her motherly care, she never grasped in life. Stephen on the contrary has, since the ninth episode of *Ulysses*, remained certain in thought and emotion of knowing the word known to all men. Which we as Joyce's readers, know, too, to be the ultimate word of affirmation, the last word of *Ulysses*: 'Yes.'

> and the night we missed the boat at Algeciras the watchman going about serene with his lamp and O that awful deepdown torrent O and the sea the sea crimson sometimes like fire and the glorious sunsets and the figtrees in the Alameda gardens yes and all the queer little streets and the pink and blue and yellow houses and the rosegardens and the jessamine and geraniums and cactuses and Gibraltar as a girl where I was a Flower of the mountain yes when I put the rose in my hair like the Andalusian girls used or shall I wear a red yes and how he kissed me under the Moorish wall and I thought well as well him as another and then I asked him with my eyes to ask again yes and then he asked me would I yes to say yes my mountain flower and first I put my arms around him yes and drew him down to me so he could feel my breasts all perfume yes and his heart was going like mad and yes I said yes I will Yes.
> Trieste-Zurich-Paris
> 1914-1921

'Do you know what you are talking about? Love, yes. Word known to all men.' Despite all accidents that befell the transmission in descent through its processes of pre-publication, careful attention to the text, scholarly, genetically critical, and editorial, has proved capable still of fine-tuning the novel *Ulysses* again to its core affirmation.

Appendix

James Joyce's 1916 version of his Hamlet chapter for *Ulysses* is lost.[4] His draft for developing it towards the novel's ninth episode, Scylla & Charybdis, is datable to October or even November 1918. The episode's fair copy was underwritten in autograph on New Year's Eve 1918. It is fascinating to observe how minutely within this brief timespan Joyce revised the context and text of Stephen Dedalus' silent reflection on his query to himself: 'Do you know what you are talking about?' Here in parallel lines is a synopsis of the versions. The text achieved is in bold print. The passages in regular font above give the passages and wordings antecedent to their bold-print versions.

---

4 See in more detail essay 08. James Joyce's *Hamlet* Chapter.

Synopsis

       the child of seastorm,   childish
—Marina, Stephen said, a child of storm, Miranda, a wonder,

Imogen, [left blank]
    Perdita, that which was lost.

That which was lost in youth is reborn strangely in his wane of life:
What was lost is given back to him: his daughter's child.

[not yet present   ]   But who will
My dearest wife, **Pericles says,** *was like this maid.* **Will any man love the daughter if he**

        I don't know.   [not yet present   ]
has not loved the mother?   —The art of being a grandfather,
Mr Best murmured.

But will   in her recreated and   added to her
—Will he not see reborn in her, with the memory of his own youth added,

the images which first awakened his love?
another image?

        [not yet present   ]

    Do you know what you are talking about? Love, yes. Word known to all men. *Amor vero aliquid alicui bonum vult unde et ea quae concupiscimus_...*

—A man of genius above all whose own image is to him, morally and materially, the Handmaid of all experience. He will be touched by that appeal as he will be infallibly repelled by images of other males of his brood in whom he will see grotesque attempts on the part of nature to foretell or repeat himself.

—His own image to a man with that queer thing genius is the standard of all experience, material and moral. Such an appeal will touch him. The images of other males of his brood will repel him. He will see in them grotesque attempts of nature to foretell or to repeat himself.

Ulysses 1984: To Edit and Read in Flow of Composition

An Envoy

On Bloomsday 16 June 2024, the Critical and Synoptic Edition of James Joyce's *Ulysses* of 1984 celebrates its fortieth anniversary. To mark the occasion is a pleasure, a stimulus, and a challenge. Through these four decades since its release, the edition has for me been history. I am today its reader, explorer, and critic. Yet at the same time it has remained an anchored commitment and responsibility.

What, from the privilege of this double perspective, is there for me to say? My support comes from *Ulysses*. From the essay fresh to this book, 'Composing *Penelope* Towards the Condition of Music', I turn with rekindled curiosity to the eleventh *Ulysses* episode, Sirens. How did Joyce there reach out for language and narration to resound through music? What resonant poetics did the attempt imply? To what depth prospectively in his art did Joyce reach in what he did not explicate when writing to Harriet Weaver to defend his composition of Sirens:

> I understand that you may begin to regard the various styles of the episodes with dismay [...] But in the compass of one day to compress all these wanderings and clothe them in the form of this day is for me only possible by such variation which, I beg you to believe, is not capricious.[1]

What, then, would it have been about the eleventh episode that worried Weaver, and Ezra Pound similarly with her: the two readers with whom alone Joyce shared the episode while (as we know) it was in transitory

---

1 *Letters of James Joyce*, ed. by Stuart Gilbert, vol. I (New York: Viking Press, 1957, ²1966), (*Letters* I), p. 129.

progress? Weaver and Pound read the episode at the stage it had reached by July 1919. They were unaware of any writing processes prior to that stage. Joyce, though—as today we also know—must, as he embarked on Sirens, have been acutely conscious that preparatory attempts to work out the episode had occupied him from close to the earliest stage in his writing towards *Ulysses*. Scholarship and criticism, in turn, learnt very late that first draftings of just these phases of work on the episode had survived. In 2002, eventually, they re-surfaced as part of an essential cache of early drafts from across the stages of progress of the whole novel, and were integrated in the holdings of the National Library of Ireland in Dublin.

* * *

The Critical and Synoptic Edition of *Ulysses* of 1984 stands in an oblique, if not indeed a contrasting relation to *Ulysses*, the First Edition, of 2 February 1922. Or, simply: the critical and synoptic edition does not edit the first edition. It synopsises, and so edits, the evidence that survives in material transmission of Joyce's composition and revision of, for, and towards his work *Ulysses*. Encompassing the range and span of this evidence means accounting for both its linear, synchronous and its temporal, diachronous dimensions. Bringing this evidence into communicable shape in tune with, essentially, the foundational traditions of editing has meant bringing the linear and the temporal text vectors synoptically together into one in-line progression on a scripted carrier—printed (back in 1984) in book, the medium of communication in analogue mode, as scripting has ever been since humans learned to message in writing. So to bring the linearly synchronous and temporally diachronous dimensions together has meant, simply, to correlate the text vectors by synoptically presenting their flow in progression on the printed page. Technically, back in 1984, nothing but print was practicable as medium to present and access the Critical and Synoptic Edition of *Ulysses*. Meanwhile, however, from the self-same digital storage that generated the edition in print, the Digital Critical and Synoptic Edition that Ronan Crowley and Joshua Schäuble have engineered is in development as their renewal enterprise. It enables access to the edition's core diachronic substance in successive digital display and sequential accessibility to its diachrony.[2]

The left-hand page of the Critical and Synoptic Edition of *Ulysses*, synoptically designed, constitutes the core of the 1984 edition. It is innovative in conception. It does not 'just' illustrate, as a side-line, the labour that writing went through so as eventually to reach its final accomplishment. It respects and presents, from all surviving material documentary evidence, the full creative investment in that accomplishment throughout the novel's composition and revision. It identifies fresh invention on the fly, or the author's creative response in revising text earlier penned. It acknowledges the writing achieved thus not just as product, but as process endured and accomplished in and over time. The Critical and Synoptic Edition of 1984 hence attends to *Ulysses* under its own double perspective. At its core in the left-hand page synopsis it renders the novel diachronically through the process of writing from the Rosenbach fair copy to the final proofs *towards* the first edition of 1922. The right-hand pages in parallel offer the text instantiation as product, an accomplishment striven for by author, printer and publisher of *Ulysses*—the book text, critically established, that renders Joyce's novel which over the past century has attained the rank of a work of world literature.

In this envoy, it is the synopsis of the process of writing *Ulysses* that I wish to single out in one extended example. In the presentation of the synopsis, we encounter Joyce as both the author and writer of the novel, and as his own first reader in response to, and in writing responding to, the novel's composition in progress. He lived with the work of art he strove to accomplish for close to ten years. When composition in 1921 was at long last tangibly drawing to a close, he wished, indeed he essentially decreed that *Ulysses* was to see publication on 2 February 1922, his fortieth birthday. So to set an end stood in contrast to Joyce's long endurance with the novel's individual episodes, Sirens prominently among them. He thought about and attended to it from the earliest phases of conceiving the novel. Sketches and stretches of early drafting date back to 1914/1915 beginnings. After the episode Wandering Rocks, newly conceived in early 1919, he positioned Sirens

---

2   Accessible at http://ulysses.online/index.html

eleventh in his scheme of episodes for *Ulysses*. It became Joyce's focus of composition in two phases. Following Wandering Rocks in 1919, he wrote Sirens and saw it pre-installed in *The Little Review*. Yet he gave it close and careful attention again two years later when, up until the end of October 1921, he readied it for *Ulysses* 1922. Framed within this larger picture of Joyce's work on the novel, what did it mean for him, and what at the same time did he conceal, when asserting to Weaver even back in mid-1919 that writing Sirens meant: 'in the compass of one day to compress all these wanderings and clothe them in the form of this day,' and to do this 'by such variation which, I beg you to believe, is not capricious' (*Letters* I, p. 129)? What he concealed he yet pointed to in marking out his mode of composition. 'Variation' encompasses the creative volatility and changeability in and of Joyce's art of writing. What he wished Weaver and Pound to sense and to experience was not 'just' the accomplished work of art, but equally its dynamics and progress in invention and composition. What Weaver and Pound could at most have sensed, though they did not, we are today in a position to explore from the material evidence of the processes of Joyce's writing. Such material has survived surprisingly richly from Joyce's years of work towards *Ulysses* as book in its first edition of 1922. This is why, even in an edition in book print that is linear and synchronous in mode, we can synopsise its successive temporalities and, in (as it were) diachronous reading, experience the flow and progress of composition as an essential vector of writing to constitute meaning in text.

* * *

I immersed myself in the the synoptic arrangement of the variation in the left-hand pages of the 1984 edition: in its display of the progress of composition of the *Ulysses* text that the Critical and Synoptic Edition makes available to us. The great advantage of the engagement this time: no longer was my focus on how to edit the text. What I could take in now was how the text, in and through the genetic editing, was shown to be composed and modified. How did this become explicit? Reading *Ulysses*, reading Sirens anew, and reading the episode through the sequence of its revisions, made the diachrony freshly perceptible and interpretable. From the stages of progress of invention and composition through the episode it became exhilaratingly evident how the novel strove for and reached the state, shape, and significantly modulated narrative mode upon which it culminated through the process of preparing the first-edition book publication of Joyce's *Ulysses*.

From the autograph fair copy of the writing of Sirens towards the first edition, I pick out the narration of the climactic stretch of Simon Dedalus's singing the finale of Flotow's aria *M'Appari*, 'When first I saw that form endearing':

> 725 First night I met her at Mat Dillon's in Roundtown. Yellow,
> 726 black lace she wore. Musical chairs. We two the last. Fate. Fate. After her.
> 727 Round and round. Slow. Quick. Round. We. All looked. Halt. She
> 728 sat. Yellow knees.
> 729 —Charmed my eye …
> 730 Then singing. Waiting she sang. I turned her music. Full voice of perfumes
> 731 of the lilactrees. Bosom I saw, both full, throat
> 732 warbling. When first I saw. She thanked me. Why did she me? Spanishy
> 733 eyes.
> 734 At me. Luring. Ah, alluring.
> 735 —Martha! Ah, Martha!
> 736 Quitting all languor he cried in grief, in cry of passion
> 737 to love to return with deepening and rising chords of harmony. In cry
> 738 of loneliness that she should know, must feel. For her he
> 739 waited. Where? Somewhere.
> 740 —Co-ome, thou lost one!
> 741 Co-ome, thou dear one!
> 742 Alone. One love. One hope. One comfort me. Martha, ∧chestnote, ∧
> 743 return!
> 744 —Come < ! > …!
> 745 It soared, a bird, it held its flight, a swift pure cry, soar silver orb it
> 746 leaped serene, speeding, sustained, to come, don't spin it out too long long
> 747 breath he breath long life, soaring high, high resplendent, crowned, aflame,
> 748 high in the effulgence ∧symbolistic∧, high, of the etherial bosom<.> high of the vast irradiation, high,

749 everywhere all soaring all around about the all, the
750 endlessnessnessness ....
751 —To me!
753 Consumed.
754 Come. Well sung. All clapped. She ought to. Come. To me, to him, to
755 her, you too, me, us.
756 —Bravo. Clapclap. Good man, Simon. Clappyclapclap. Encore!
757 Clapclipclap clap. Sound as a bell. Bravo, Simon! Clapclopclap. Encore,
758 enclap, said, cried, clapped all, Ben Dollard, Lydia Douce, George Lidwell,
759 Pat, Mina Kennedy, two gentlemen with two tankards, Cowley, first gent
760 with tank and bronze miss Douce and gold miss Mina.
761 Blazes Boylan's smart tan shoes creaked on the barfloor, said before.
762 Jingle by monuments of sir John Gray<.>, Horatio Nelson, onearmed ∧ handled∧ adulterer,
763 reverend father Theobald Mathew, jaunted, as said. Atrot,
764 in heat, heatseated. Cloche. Sonnez la. Cloche. Sonnez la. Slower the mare
765 went up the hill by the Rotunda, Rutland square. Too slow for Boylan,
766 Blazes Boylan, impatience Boylan, joggled the mare. (*U* 11, p. 592, p. 594)

Line 725 opens with one sentence recalling a past situation. The narrative is neutral and seemingly uninvolved. Yet quickly, through to line 728, the rendering modulates into fragments of memory. Line 729 climaxes in a first double presence: that of the narrative voice with that of the *M'Appari* aria in performance. The narrative voice's (Bloom's) memory of when '[f]irst I met her' becomes increasingly interwoven with the presence of Simon's singing. The doubling is upheld through fifteen lines, 730 to 744. The narrative is shaped as a progression simultaneously read by sight and heard by ear—it is seen and listened to, as if in performance. Through lines 745 to 750, the narrated, yet thereby intensely heard presence takes flight into music. This stretch of text fills in Simon Dedalus's singing the aria's climax as, musically speaking, the fermata (lines 744; 751): 'Come...! [...]—To me!' that Simon long sustains—from which, at the same time, the narrative judiciously distances itself: 'don't spin it out too long' (line 746). The narrative mediation—the narrative voice? Bloom? and/or, as both writer and listener in live presence together: Joyce?—takes account even of the singer's breathing rhythm: 'long breath he | breath long life' (lines 746–47). This, in turn, induces us to read in print while simultaneously hearing, like music, what the narrative conveys. The effect bears comparison with the intensification of cinematic action through film music.

The ensuing paragraph, lines 753 to 760, transforms in its turn the memory of the audience reaction to Simon Dedalus's performance into acoustic presence. The names of all present at Barney Kiernan's render that immediacy audible (as it were). In the final paragraph, even the fleeting visitor who has already left, Blazes Boylan, is in narrative imagination for a moment brought back. True to the episode's dimension of music, Boylan is re-présented through recall of a noise: 'Blazes Boylan's smart tan shoes creaked on the barfloor, said before' (line 761). That he flirted with the barmaids is acoustically recalled in verbal repetition of 'Cloche. Sonnez la. Cloche. Sonnez la.' Unfortunately, though, with 'Cloche. Sonnez la', Bloom slips back into the preoccupation that, between four and four thirty that *Ulysses* afternoon, he has been at great pains to silence. His last resort, however, in (half-)suppressing the image of Boylan's carriage ascending the hill by the Rotunda, Rutland square, heading for his *rendezvous* with Molly at 7 Eccles street, is to focus not on the impatient carriage passenger, but on 'Slower [...] joggled the mare' (lines 764–66).

* * *

The shape of the episode in composition at its fair-copy state is accomplished and ready for publication. For which, in principle, it was at that point destined. Within weeks, we must assume, upon completion of the fair copy, *The Little Review* signaled through Pound (Joyce's middleman in London, negotiating the pre-publication of *Ulysses*, episode by episode, with this monthly journal from Chicago) that it was ready to receive the novel's eleventh episode for its ongoing serialisation. What reached Chicago was not the holograph fair copy by which Joyce had satisfied himself that the episode was publishable. Through Pound, the episode reached Chicago in typescript. The typescript exemplar from which it was typeset has not survived. Collating the 1919 published instalments of the Sirens episode in *The Little Review* against the preceding holograph fair copy reveals that what reached the journal's publishers shows significant variation from the fair copy. Fortunately, the typed carbon that served as printer's copy for the 1922 first edition of *Ulysses* (printer: Maurice Darantiere in Dijon, publisher: Sylvia Beach in Paris) can serve as a check copy against the lost *Little Review* printer's copy in typescript. To all appearances, this carbon is of the 1919 typing, of which the *Little Review* printer's copy, lost, was the top copy. As it survives, the Darantiere/Beach exemplar features some revisions in Joyce's hand. These autograph changes and additions date patently from a renewed working-over for added revision in 1921. They do not cast in doubt that, at its typed level, this printer's copy for Darantiere, the carbon of a lost top copy, originated in 1919. Significantly, though, collating this carbon strictly against the holograph fair copy of 1919 and *The Little Review* shows that the *Little Review* serialisation of 1919 does not reproduce the fair copy text identically. *The Little Review* features revisions that must post-date the fair copy. We conclude, therefore: Joyce did, in 1919, within weeks after writing out the holograph fair copy, intensely work over a holograph document that preceded the fair copy. I have called this predecessor the [lost] 'final working manuscript'.[3] It was this [lost] 'final working manuscript' that he revised into the genetic state manifest both in the *Little Review* serialisation and in the carbon typescript that served as Darantiere's printer's copy for the first edition of *Ulysses*.

Thus my sample passage, genetically advanced at the initial post-fair-copy level in 1919, reads as follows [revision changes in red]:

> 725 First night when first I saw her at Mat Dillon's in Terenure. Yellow,
> 726 black lace she wore. Musical chairs. We two the last. Fate. After her. Fate.
> 727 Round and round slow. Quick round. We two. All looked. Halt.

---

3   See the passage 'The Continuous Manuscript Text' in the 'Afterword' to James Joyce, *Ulysses. A Critical and Synoptic Edition*, prepared by Hans Walter Gabler with Wolfhard Steppe and Claus Melchior, 3 vols. (New York and London: Garland Publishing, 1986), Volume 3, pp. 1895-96. 'If thought of as projected onto a single imaginary document, it will be perceived as a many-layered and highly complex text that carries the dynamics of an extended textual development within it.' (p. 1895).

Down she
728 sat. Lips laughing. Yellow knees.
729 —Charmed my eye ...
730 Singing. Waiting she sang. I turned her music. Full voice of perfume
731 of what perfume does your lilactrees. Bosom I saw, both full, throat
732 warbling. First I saw. She thanked me. Why did she me? Fate. Spanishy
733 eyes.
734 At me. Luring. Ah, alluring.
735 —Martha! Ah, Martha!
736 Quitting all languor Lionel cried in grief, in cry of passion
737 to love to return with deepening yet with rising chords of harmony. In cry
738 of lionel loneliness that she should know, must martha feel. For only her he
739 waited. Where? Somewhere.
740 —Co-ome, thou lost one!
741 Co-ome, thou dear one!
742 Alone. One love. One hope. One comfort me. Martha, chestnote,
743 return!
744 —Come ...!
745 It soared, a bird, it held its flight, a swift pure cry, soar silver orb it
746 leaped serene, speeding, sustained, to come, don't spin it out too long long
747 breath he breath long life, soaring high, high resplendent, aflame, crowned,
748 high in the effulgence symbolistic, high, of the etherial bosom, high, of the
749 high vast irradiation everywhere all soaring all around about the all, the
750 endlessnessnessness ....
751 —To me!
753 Consumed.
754 Come. Well sung. All clapped. She ought to. Come. To me, to him, to
755 her, you too, me, us.
756 —Bravo! Clapclap. Good man, Simon. Clappyclapclap. Encore!
757 Clapclipclap clap. Sound as a bell. Bravo, Simon! Clapclopclap. Encore,
758 enclap, said, cried, clapped all, Ben Dollard, Lydia Douce,

George Lidwell,
759 Pat, Mina Kennedy, two gentlemen with two tankards, Cowley, first gent
760 with tank and bronze miss Douce and gold miss Mina.
761 Blazes Boylan's smart tan shoes creaked on the barfloor, said before.
762 Jingle by monuments of sir John Gray, Horatio onehandled Nelson,
763 reverend father Theobald Mathew, jaunted, as said before just now. Atrot,
764 in heat, heatseated. Cloche. Sonnez la. Cloche. Sonnez la. Slower the mare
765 went up the hill by the Rotunda, Rutland square. Too slow for Boylan,
766 blazes Boylan, impatience Boylan, joggled the mare. (*U* 11, p. 592, p. 594)

There are two revisions straight away in line 725. The second chooses the alternative name 'Terenure' for 'Roundtown', where Bloom and Molly first met. The first revision is more momentous. Read (synoptically) against the reading it replaces, it secures resoundingly at the passage's outset the musical dimension of the episode. It double-focuses narrative from memory with the present moment of Simon Dedalus's singing. It narrates Bloom's remembering his first encounter with Molly to the words 'when first I saw [that form endearing]' that he hears Simon singing. Through slight shifts in phrase and sentence rhythms, furthermore, the intense memory of the first encounter is re-présented and enlivened in eye- and emotional contact. 'All looked' (line 727, fair-copy texting) finds resonance in 'Lips laughing' (line 728, phrase added in revision). Joyce's attention to this first-revised rendering was to be deepened two years later in the further texting for *Ulysses* towards the book publication.

Simon's sung phrase next: '—Charmed my eye ...' (line 29) as narrated, clearly again resonates the consonance of memory and the present moment of the musical performance. The remembered past and the heard presence fully interweave, and they do so at four levels, as lines 754–55 eventually confirm. 'To me, to him, to her, you too, me, us' (in fair-copy wording unchanged) marks severally the levels of Bloom's memory, the heard music, the singer Simon's awareness, and the awareness, too, of the community of both readers and listeners.

'Singing.': the (in revision) one-word assertion opening line 730 thus fully synchronises past and present singing. Three sentences thereafter, furthermore, this synchrony ties back into yet another memory loop. It calls upon the reader. She remembers from reading the novel's fifth episode, Lotus Eaters, the phrase now inserted as a snippet recalled from Martha Clifford's letter. The Sirens revision accordingly modulates the fair-copy reading 'Full voice of perfumes of lilactrees' into 'Full voice of perfume of what perfume does your lilactrees.' Grammatically truncated as it is, however, the revision suggests, significantly, just a flash of retrospective Bloom memory (forgetfulness is specific to the Lotus Eaters episode). It is but a fleeting mental reflex at the present narrative moment to signal Bloom's felt anticipation of what Simon is just on the point of singing. Bloom's auditive imagination, 'At me. Luring. Ah, alluring' (line 734) pre-vibrates the emotion in the next line (735) that Simon sings from the opera: '—Martha! Ah, Martha!' This outcry in its turn deepens Bloom's presence, now fully involved, in the ongoing singing performance—a deepening that will be yet further intensely responded to at the third level of revision of the printer's-copy text towards the first edition of *Ulysses*. Here, in the course of the revisions from the (lost) final working draft, Bloom (through the narrative) emotionally reaches out to identify with the character whom Simon's singing impersonates: Lionel (line 737); lionel and martha, in lower-case lettering, persist in Bloom's, the listener's, mind through the ensuing sentences: 'In cry of lionel loneliness that she should know, must martha feel. For only her he waited' (lines 737–39).

Thus with intense engagement, lines 725 to 739 in particular, from our sample, underwent significant creative revision, and this, we assume, within weeks upon completion of the holograph fair copy (the Rosenbach manuscript). The remainder of the passage, too, received changes. They were, in the main, style adjustments—with one exception. 'Horatio Nelson, onearmed ∧ handled∧ adulterer', according to the *currente calamo* sequence of changes of the holograph fair copy, in the final working-draft revision loses the mark of adulterer. The mention of which he does still prove worthy is distilled into what one might call a *portmanteau* phrase: 'Horatio onehandled Nelson.'

* * *

So far, then: lines 725 to 739 are evidence of Joyce's resonantly creative revision of the text instantiated in the holograph fair copy. To effect the changes this involved without compromising the appearance of his fair copy, Joyce went back to the episode instantiation from which he had derived it: namely, the [lost] final working manuscript. It was this he further revised to make the changes evident in the *Little Review* serialisation of the episode in 1919. They recur identically, as noted, also in the printer's copy deployed in 1921 towards the typesetting for the 1922 first edition *Ulysses*.

It was materially in the surviving carbon copy that Joyce in 1921 encountered afresh the text of Sirens in its state of post-fair-copy revision. His response was further attention. His fresh immersion in the text as it already existed from the writing phases of two years earlier, and which he now re-encountered in re-reading, rekindled his engagement in creative invention. The documents that survive from the workshop (to use the time-honoured concept) permit us to retrace from their surviving material record the progress and processes of invention, writing and revising through which Joyce rendered his art and artistry manifest. To specify his re-encounter with the Sirens episode in late summer to mid-autumn 1921, here in synopsis is the text of my chosen passage in progress from the [lost] final working manuscript (red) to autograph revision successively in the typed printer's copy (brown), the first proof level (green), and the third proof level (yellow):

> 725 First night when first I saw her at Mat Dillon's in Terenure. Yellow,
> 726 black lace she wore. Musical chairs. We two the last. Fate. After her. Fate.
> 727 Round and round slow. Quick round. We two. All looked. Halt. Down she
> 728 sat. All ousted looked. Lips laughing. Yellow knees.
> 729 —Charmed my eye ...
> 730 Singing. Waiting she sang. I turned her music. Full voice of perfume
> 731 of what perfume does your lilactrees. Bosom I saw, both full, throat
> 732 warbling. First I saw. She thanked me. Why did she me? Fate. Spanishy
> 733 eyes. Under a peartree alone patio this hour |+in old Madrid+|

one side in
734 shadow Dolores shedolores. At me. Luring. Ah, alluring.
735 —Martha! Ah, Martha!
736 Quitting all languor Lionel cried in grief, in cry of passion dominant
737 to love to return with deepening yet with rising chords of harmony. In cry
738 of lionel loneliness that she should know, must martha feel. For only her he
739 waited. Where? Here there try there here all try where. Somewhere.
740 —Co-ome, thou lost one!
741 Co-ome, thou dear one!
742 Alone. One love. One hope. One comfort me. Martha, chestnote,
743 return!
744 —Come ...!
745 It soared, a bird, it held its flight, a swift pure cry, soar silver orb it
746 leaped serene, speeding, sustained, to come, don't spin it out too long long
747 breath he breath long life, soaring high, high resplendent, aflame, crowned,
748 high in the effulgence symbolistic, high, of the etherial bosom, high, of the
749 high vast irradiation everywhere all soaring all around about the all, the
750 endlessnessnessness ....
751 —To me!
752 Siopold!
753 Consumed.
754 Come. Well sung. All clapped. She ought to. Come. To me, to him, to
755 her, you too, me, us.
756 —Bravo! Clapclap. Good man, Simon. Clappyclapclap. Encore!
757 Clapclipclap clap. Sound as a bell. Bravo, Simon! Clapclopclap. Encore,
758 enclap, said, cried, clapped all, Ben Dollard, Lydia Douce, George Lidwell,
759 Pat, Mina Kennedy, two gentlemen with two tankards, Cowley, first gent
760 with tank and bronze miss Douce and gold miss Mina.
761 Blazes Boylan's smart tan shoes creaked on the barfloor, said before.

> 762 Jingle by monuments of sir John Gray, Horatio onehandled
> Nelson,
> 763 reverend father Theobald Mathew, jaunted, as said before just
> now. Atrot,
> 764 in heat, heatseated. Cloche. Sonnez la. Cloche. Sonnez la. Slower
> the mare
> 765 went up the hill by the Rotunda, Rutland square. Too slow for
> Boylan,
> 766 blazes Boylan, impatience Boylan, joggled the mare. (*U* 11, p.
> 592, p. 594)

Within this passage, Joyce, in revising the 1921 typed printer's copy, adds just one phrase in line 728: 'All ousted looked.' Three words. They balance the two that, from the post-fair-copy revision of 1919, follow them. The added phrase rounds the effect. Only the two phrases together—'All ousted looked. Lips laughing'—achieve what the 1919 revision beckoned towards. They establish now, in conjunction, the mutuality of awareness between Molly and her audience.

The addition at page-proof level one, by contrast, draws in context and knowledge that, strictly, the reader does not yet have at the point of progress the fiction *Ulysses* has reached with Sirens, its eleventh episode. The addition (in lines 733-34): 'Under a peartree alone patio this hour |+in old Madrid+| one side in shadow Dolores shedolores' establishes a text extension that, in one respect, through its *currente calamo* addition 'in old Madrid', alludes to Molly's youth in Gibraltar. But this, in the novel's overall design, gains—will gain—its fullest narrative specificity only in the novel's final episodes. In another respect, the addition's 'one side in shadow' element alludes to authorial self-dialogue in the margin of a pre-fair-copy draft for Nausikaa (two episodes further on from Sirens) that was never scribbled as *Ulysses* text. In that extra-textual (private) note, Joyce reminds himself that he still needs to decide on which side of her face Molly prefers to let admirers gaze.[4] Untypically, thus, the additions to lines 733-34 do not intensify the narrator's bond with Simon Dedalus singing *M'Appari*. They are instead, one might say, nudges from the text as to how, using what convoluted associations, *Ulysses* offers itself to be read. Or else, from the 'workshop' point of view, they are

---

4 Traced for me by Daniel Ferrer in the margin of the second draft for Sirens: 'Molly likes left (?) side of her face best' (Buffalo V.A.5.15; *JJA* 13:47).

fragments of what happens to come to the writer-as-author's mind from recall, when revising, of earlier details of composition. In the contexts of *Ulysses* beyond Sirens, the 'peartree ... patio ... in old Madrid one side in shadow Dolores shedolores' associations to Molly do not lack charm. At the same time, though, they somehow lose touch with the passage as it otherwise synchronises Bloom's past in memory with his raptured presence at hearing Simon's aria performance. Such associative text enrichment can at times be in danger of falling flat. A third-proof level revision in line 739 baffles outright. 'Where? Somewhere' becomes: 'Where? Here there try there here all try where. Somewhere.' It seems, alas, to add wording to little effect other than bafflement. But then again: is this bafflement perhaps precisely the message, now insisted on, that we should read from the revision?

In strong and exhilarating contrast, the fusion of the narrator's bond with the singer climaxes in the two revisions to the third page-proof level at lines 736 and 752. With the extension of line 736 by just one word: '[Lionel cried in grief, in cry of passion] dominant', the narration signals hearing Simon's performance not just as and through narrated text but, in the scale relation of the aria's music, in its sounding the dominant (the fifth note in the scale) audibly. This opens the narrator's (Bloom's) ear in imagination—and with it, the reader's ear correspondingly—to hearing the music sung in pitch.

This is an important instance in the course of this music-focused episode conveying a moment of and in music itself. It prepares for setting the summit of revisions at line 752, with the paragraph cry in one word: 'Siopold!' Fusing the singer's name, Simon, and the listener's, Leopold, this outcry, newly added, is sandwiched between the fermata end (line 751): '—To me!' and the narration's laconic: 'Consumed' (now line 753). The full accomplishment in text of the rendering of Simon Dedalus's performance of Flotow's aria *M'Appari* is now, at the third level of revisions in proof, composed as a simple three-line conclusion to the aria's performance:

> 751 —To me!
> 752 Siopold!
> 753 Consumed. (*U* 11, 594)

* * *

To edit a work of literary art in the progress of its composition in time constitutes a fundamentally fresh approach to the cultural heritage we possess of the transmission of texts. Standard practice has been oriented towards the author as the absolute lode-star of such transmission. But to define and, moreover, to classify texts by the criterion that they are 'authorised': willed, decreed, and authenticated by their authors, is a strictly historically conditioned concept. It established itself increasingly since, and largely as an effect of, the invention of book printing. It culminated through the age of reason, beyond which, in the era of the 'original genius', the author won near-absolute dominance over text. It is from his—less pervasively her—genius that the work of art in language now springs—was understood to have sprung. True enough: the author creates the work. Yet (s)he so conceives it and forms it from language. Language is dialogically processual by nature. In shaping language into text, the creator of art from language is correspondingly challenged to live up to, and creatively respond to, the inherent dialogism as well as the diachronicity, the progress in time, of transubstantiating language through invention and composition into literary art. Our author-centric traditions of reading and scholarly editing have presented the work of literary art as an authorised, definite, definitive, and, through its book publication, synchronously laid out, a wholly finished product. What has fallen by the wayside, in seeing the work as product alone, is the recognition and exploration in the written record of the creativity in progress through all processes of shaping language into literature: of turning language into text, of evolving it through imagining, writing, rethinking, revising and, in variation again and again, insistently rematerialising the material text record.

Joyce lived with *Ulysses* for some eight years, from his beginnings in 1914 textually conceiving and writing the novel to when he saw it published in its first edition in 1922. Every texted note, every draft, every copy in fair hand, every autograph change and addition in typescripts and proofs testify to spans and moments of attention in imagination, to thought and reflection, to trial attempts at texting, writing, and rewriting; to re-reading text earlier penned and maybe reconsidering, changing, deleting, expanding or outright replacing it. Every such moment, to which its author's papers materially bear witness, testifies also to living moments in the years of composition for *Ulysses*. Presenting the creative art lavished on *Ulysses* in synoptic mode has enabled me to support endeavours to read what Joyce achieved over the time during which he created the novel. My centre of attention in this has been throughout the process and progress, the life, of the writing and the text. So to characterise the work, forty years after we released *Ulysses. A Critical and Synoptic Edition* in Frankfurt and Munich in 1984, is an invitation *to whom it may concern* to rise above the shoulders of my team and myself and take over.

Acknowledgments

Acknowledging the support of my work on James Joyce's early prose and *Ulysses* for half a century demands that I recall from the outset the tutelage in textual criticism and bibliography received in preparation thereof from Fredson Bowers in Charlottesville, Virginia, thanks to a postdoctoral fellowship 1968-1970 given me from the Harkness Foundation New York. From this arose the major grant I was honoured with from the Deutsche Forschungsgemeinschaft, to realise from 1978 to 1984 the Critical and Synoptic Edition of James Joyce's *Ulysses*. To have achieved this edition, my gratitude goes to the entire team who joined our partnership in the project, with Wolfhard Steppe and Claus Melchior, to round it off, assuming co-editorship of it. Its innovative dimension of deploying digital procedures from the ground up was made possible thanks to Wilhelm Ott, Kuno Schälkle and their data-processing team in Tübingen. To realise independent scholarship on the transmission still in copyright required permission to publish. Peter du Sautoy, head at Faber & Faber, publishers entrusted with the business of the James Joyce Estate, appointed Richard Ellmann, Clive Hart and Philip Gaskell to advise him on the procedures that our labours in Munich independently took. My thanks today must reach out to all four, alas, posthumously. As must my thanks to Hugh Kenner, earliest respondent since 1981 to the *Ulysses* edition in progress. The edition's presence in public as from 1984 passed through a period of fierce attack, focused not least on its editor. It is therefore, indeed, also with much personal gratitude that I acknowledge the reassessment of the edition performed by the three spokesmen at the STS conference in New York in 1995: J.C.C. Mays, Peter Shillingsburg and Robert Spoo.

My immersion in the art of James Joyce gathered renewed momentum through Irina Rasmussen's 'Riffing on Shakespeare' essay in the *Joyce Studies Annual* of 2019, aiming for 'the Avant-Garde Theory of Literary

Criticism'. I am grateful for the fresh impetus this gave me to explore the genetically critical potential of Joyce's writing. Core respondent in this throughout the recent years has been Roger Lüdeke of Düsseldorf University, with whom a good student-teacher relationship of old stimulates intellectual combat in ripened friendship. Svenja Weidinger's friendship, held in its turn from university days, has very practically, that is, substantially, helped render my writing fit to read. Warmest thanks to her for focussing this assembly of essays. Lucy Barnes' astute and sensitive copy-editing at Open Book Publishers I highly and gratefully admire.

Throughout, it has been my outstanding fortune to remain active in thought and work, beyond routine service years, on grounds of continued co-active relations with those younger than myself. The fountain in academia from which this strength wells has been the interdisciplinary postgraduate course work on 'Textual Criticism as Foundation and Method of the Historical Disciplines'. I had the privilege to direct this graduate college for six years around the turn of the millennium. Walter Hettche originally suggested submitting an application. We gained the support. Our interdisciplinary spread of colleagues became the guiding core of the teacher-student teams through three successive culls of graduates working towards their PhD graduation. The teamwork they performed enriched immeasurably my subsequent post-retirement years. What I have learned and remain deeply grateful for is what the team and team spirit of the *Graduiertenkolleg* taught me.

Bibliography

Primary Sources

Joyce, James, *A Portrait of the Artist as a Young Man* (Critical Edition), ed. by Hans Walter Gabler with Walter Hettche (New York and London: Garland Publishing, 1993).

Joyce, James, *A Portrait of the Artist as a Young Man*, ed. by John Paul Riquelme (New York: Norton, 2007).

Joyce, James, *A Portrait of the Artist as a Young Man*, ed. by Hans Walter Gabler with Walter Hettche (New York: Vintage Books, 1993; London: Vintage Books, 2012).

Joyce, James, *A Portrait of the Artist as a Young Man*, MS 920 and 921, National Library of Ireland.

Joyce, James, *A Portrait of the Artist as a Young Man: Authoritative Text Backgrounds and Contexts Criticism* (Critical Edition), ed. by Hans Walter Gabler, with Walter Hettche (New York and London: Garland Publishing, 1993).

Joyce, James, *A Portrait of the Artist as a Young Man. A Facsimile of Epiphanies, Notes, Manuscripts, and Typescripts*. Prefaced and Arranged by Hans Walter Gabler (New York and London: Garland Publishing, 1978).

Joyce, James, *A Portrait of the Artist as a Young Man. A Facsimile of the Final Holograph Manuscript*. Prefaced and Arranged by Hans Walter Gabler. 2 vols. (New York & London: Garland Publishing, 1977).

Joyce, James, *A Portrait of the Artist as a Young Man: Text, Criticism, and Notes*, ed. by Chester G. Anderson and A. Walton Litz (New York: Viking Press, 1968).

Joyce, James, *Dubliners* (Critical Edition), ed. by Hans Walter Gabler with Walter Hettche (New York and London: Garland Publishing, 1993).

Joyce, James, *Dubliners*, ed. by Hans Walter Gabler with Walter Hettche (New York: Vintage Books, 1993; London: Vintage Books, 2012).

Joyce, James, *Finnegans Wake* (London: Faber & Faber, 1939).

Joyce, James, *Giacomo Joyce*, ed. by Richard Ellmann (London: Faber & Faber, 1968).

Joyce, James, *Giacomo Joyce*, ed. by Richard Ellmann (London: Faber, 1968).

Joyce, James, *James Joyce Digital Archive*, ed. by Danis Rose and John O'Hanlon http://www.jjda.ie/main/JJDA/U/ulex/k/k11d.htm

Joyce, James, *James Joyce: Epifanie (1900-1904). Rubrica (1909-1912)*, ed. by Giorgio Melchiori (Milan: Mondadori, 1982).

Joyce, James, *James Joyce's Scribbledehobble: The Ur-Workbook for 'Finnegans Wake'*, ed. by Thomas E. Connolly (Evanston: Northwestern University Press, 1961).

Joyce, James, *Joyce: Selected Letters*, ed. by Richard Ellmann (New York: The Viking Press, 1975).

Joyce, James, *Joyce's 'Ulysses' Notesheets in the British Museum*, ed. by Phillip F. Herring (Charlottesville: University Press of Virginia, 1972).

Joyce, James, *Joyce's first extant penning of the Scylla & Charybdis episode of late 1918*, in the copybook NLI8_A in the National Library of Ireland in Dublin, The Joyce Papers 2002, II.ii.1.a. Notebook, pre-numbering page [9] 7, https://catalogue.nli.ie/Collection/vtls000194606

Joyce, James, *Joyce's Notes and Early Drafts for 'Ulysses': Selections from the Buffalo Collection*, ed. by Phillip F. Herring (Charlottesville: University Press of Virginia, 1977).

Joyce, James, *Letters of James Joyce*, ed. by Richard Ellmann (New York: Viking Press, 1966), II and III.

Joyce, James, *Letters of James Joyce*, ed. by Stuart Gilbert (New York: Viking Press, 1957; 1966), I.

Joyce, James, *Occasional, Critical, and Political Writing*, ed. by Kevin Barry (Oxford World's Classics) (Oxford: Oxford University Press, 2000), https://doi.org/10.1093/owc/9780199553969.001.0001

Joyce, James, *Poems and Shorter Writings*, ed. by Richard Ellmann, A. Walton Litz, and John Wittier-Ferguson (London: Faber & Faber, 1991).

Joyce, James, *Stephen Hero*, ed. by John J. Slocum and Herbert Cahoon (New York, New Directions, 1963).

Joyce, James, *Stephen Hero* (London: Jonathan Cape, [1944] 1969).

Joyce, James, *Stephen Hero. Edited from the Manuscript in the Harvard College Library by Theodore Spencer. A New Edition, incorporating the Additional Manuscript Pages in the Yale University Library and the Cornell University Library*, ed. by John J. Slocum and Herbert Cahoon (New York: New Directions, 1944; 1963).

Joyce, James, *The James Joyce Archive*, ed. by Michael Groden, *et al.*, 63 vols. (New York and London: Garland Publishing, 1977-79).

Joyce, James, *The James Joyce Songbook*, ed. by Ruth Bauerle (New York: Garland, 1982).

Joyce, James, *Ulysses* (Harmondsworth: Penguin Books, 1968).

Joyce, James, *Ulysses*, ed. by Hugh Kenner (London: Allen & Unwin, 1980).

Joyce, James, *Ulysses. A Critical and Synoptic Edition*, prepared by Hans Walter Gabler with Wolfhard Steppe and Claus Melchior. 3 vols. (New York & London: Garland Publishing, 1984; 1986).

Joyce, James, *Ulysses*, ed. by Hans Walter Gabler with Wolfhard Steppe and Claus Melchior (London: The Bodley Head; New York: Random House, 1986; 1993).

Secondary Sources

Adams, Robert M., 'Light on Joyce's *Exiles!* A new manuscript, a curious analogue, and some speculations', *Studies in Bibliography*, 17 (1964), 83-105.

Anderson, Chester G., '*A Portrait* . . . Critically Edited . . .', unpubl. Ph.D. dissertation, Faculty of Philosophy (Columbia University, 1962).

Anderson, Chester G., 'The Text of James Joyce's *A Portrait of the Artist as a Young Man*', *Neuphilologische Mitteilungen*, 65 (1964), 160-200.

Bach, Johann Sebastian, 'Jesu meine Freude', BWV 227.

Barry, Kevin, ed., *James Joyce: Occasional, Critical, and Political Writings* (Oxford & New York: Oxford University Press, 2000), https://doi.org/10.1093/owc/9780199553969.001.0001

Beach, Sylvia, *Shakespeare and Company* (London: Faber & Faber, 1960).

Beckett, Samuel, 'Dante... Bruno. Vico... Joyce', in *Our Exagmination Round his Factification for Incamination of Work in Progress* (London: Faber & Faber, 1929).

Benstock, Bernard, 'The Dead', in *James Joyce's 'Dubliners': Critical Essays*, ed. by Clive Hart, (London: Faber, 1969), pp. 153-69.

Bornstein, George and Williams, Ralph, eds., 'On Textual Criticism and Editing: The Case of *Ulysses*' in *Palimpsest: Editorial Theory in the Humanities* (Ann Arbor: University of Michigan Press, 1993).

Bornstein, George, *Material Modernism. The Politics of the Page* (Cambridge: Cambridge University Press, 2001).

Brady, Phillip and Carens, James F., eds., *Critical Essays on James Joyce's A Portrait of the Artist as a Young Man* (New York: G.K. Hall, 1998).

Budgen, Frank, *James Joyce and the Making of 'Ulysses', and Other Writings* (London: Oxford University Press, 1972).

Crispi, Luca, 'A First Foray into the National Library of Ireland's Joyce Manuscripts: Bloomsday 2011', *Genetic Joyce Studies*, 11 (Spring 2011), https://www.geneticjoycestudies.org/articles/GJS11/GJS11_Crispi#scylla

Crispi, Luca, 'A *Ulysses* Manuscripts Workbook', *Genetic Joyce Studies*, 17 (2017) [Electronic Journal for the Study of James Joyce's Works in Progress].

Crispi, Luca, 'The Afterlives of Joyce's "Alphabetical Notebook" from *A Portrait* to *Ulysses* (1910-20)', *Genetic Joyce Studies* 20 (Spring 2020), https://www.geneticjoycestudies.org/articles/GJS20/GJS20_Crispi

Deppman, Jed, Ferrer, Daniel and Groden, Michael, eds., *Genetic Criticism. Texts and Avant-Textes* (Philadelphia: University of Pennsylvania Press, 2004).

Eliot, T.S., '*Ulysses*, Order and Myth', in *Selected Prose of T.S. Eliot*, ed. by Frank Kermode (London: Faber & Faber, 1975), pp. 175-78.

Ellmann, Richard, *James Joyce* (Oxford: Oxford University Press, 1982).

Ferrer, Daniel, 'An Unwritten Chapter of Ulysses? Joyce's Notes for a "Lacedemon" Episode', in *James Joyce: Whence, Whither and How: Studies in Honour of Carla Vaglio*, ed. by Giuseppina Cortese, Giuliana Ferreccio, M. Teresa Giaveri, Teresa Prudente (Alessandria: Edizioni dell'Orso, 2015), pp. 363-77, http://www.item.ens.fr/articles-en-ligne/an-unwritten-chapter-of-ulyssesjoyces-notes-for-a-lacedemon/

Ferrer, Daniel, 'What song the sirens sang . . . is no longer beyond all conjecture: A Preliminary Description of the New "Proteus" and "Sirens" Manuscripts', *James Joyce Quarterly*, 39-1 (2001), 53-68, https://doi.org/10.1353/jjq.2012.0104

Feshbach, Sidney, 'A Slow and Dark Birth: A Study of the Organization of *A Portrait of the Artist as a Young Man*', *James Joyce Quarterly*, 4 (1967), 289-300.

Firth, John, 'Harriet Weaver's Letters to James Joyce 1915-1920', *Studies in Bibliography*, 20 (1967), 151-188.

Fuchs, Dieter, 2003 Munich PhD dissertation by, 'Menippos in Dublin. Studien zu James Joyce und zur Form der Menippea', published as *Joyce und Menippos. 'A Portrait of the Artist as an Old Dog'*. (*ZAA Monograph Series* 2) (Würzburg: Königshausen & Neumann, 2006).

Füger, Wilhelm, 'Joyce's *Portrait* and Nietzsche', *Arcadia*, 7 (1972), 231-59.

Gabler, Hans Walter, 'Zur Textgeschichte und Textkritik des *Portrait*', in *James Joyces "Portrait": Das Jugendbildnis im Lichte neuerer deutscher Forschung*, ed. by Wilhelm Füger (Munich: Goldmann, 1972), pp. 20-38.

Gabler, Hans Walter, 'Towards a Critical Text of James Joyce's *A Portrait of the Artist as a Young Man*', *Studies in Bibliography*, 27 (1974), 1-53.

Gabler, Hans Walter, 'The Christmas Dinner Scene, Parnell's Death, and the Genesis of *A Portrait of the Artist as a Young Man*', *James Joyce Quarterly*, 13 (1975-76), 27-38.

Gabler, Hans Walter, 'The Seven Lost Years of *A Portrait of the Artist as a Young Man*', in *Approaches to Joyce's Portrait*, ed. by Bernard Benstock and Thomas F. Staley (Pittsburgh: University of Pittsburgh Press, 1976), pp. 25-60.

Gabler, Hans Walter, et al., 'Computer-aided critical edition of *Ulysses*' (1979), http://www.tustep.uni-tuebingen.de/prot/prot18e.html

Gabler, Hans Walter, 'Narrative rereadings: some remarks on "Proteus", "Circe" and "Penelope"', in *James Joyce 1*: 'Scribble' 1: *genèse des textes*, ed. by Claude Jacquet (Paris: Lettres Modernes, 1988), pp. 57-68.

Gabler, Hans Walter, 'Nachwort', in *James Joyce, Penelope. The Last Chapter of 'Ulysses'*, ed. by Harald Beck (Stuttgart: Philipp Reclam, 1989), pp. 175-89.

Gabler, Hans Walter, 'James Joyce's text in progress' in *The Cambridge Companion to James Joyce*, ed. by Derek Attridge (Cambridge: Cambridge University Press, 1990), pp. 213-36.

Gabler, Hans Walter, 'What Ulysses Requires', *Papers of the Bibliographical Society of America*, 87 (1993), 187-248.

Gabler, Hans Walter, 'The Genesis of *A Portrait of the Artist as a Young Man*', in *Critical Essays on James Joyce's A Portrait of the Artist as a Young Man*, ed. by Philip Brady and James F. Carens (New York: G. K. Hall, 1998), pp. 83-112.

Gabler, Hans Walter, 'Introduction' in *James Joyce, A Portrait of the Artist as a Young Man*, ed. by John Paul Riquelme (New York: Norton, 2007).

Gabler, Hans Walter, 'Seeing James Joyce's *Ulysses* into the Digital Age', *Joyce Studies Annual 2018* (New York: Fordham University Press 2018), pp. 3-36, https://doi.org/10.2307/j.ctv941w0x.4

Gabler, Hans Walter, *Text Genetics in Literary Modernism and Other Essays* (Cambridge: Open Book Publishers, 2018), https://doi.org/10.11647/OBP.0120

Gabler, Hans Walter, 'Emergence of James Joyce's Dialogue Poetics', *Journal of Early Modern Studies*, 11 (2022), 229-52.

Gabler, Hans Walter, with Bornstein, George and Borland, Gillian, eds., *Contemporary German Editorial Theory* (Ann Arbor: University of Michigan Press, 1995).

Gheerbrant, Bernard, *James Joyce. Sa Vie Son Oeuvre Son Rayonnement* [Exposition à Paris] Octobre-Novembre, 1949 (Paris: La Hune, 1949).

Ghiselin, Brewster, 'The unity of Joyce's *Dubliners*', *Accent*, 16 (1956), 75-88, 193-213.

Goldman, Arnold, 'Stephen Dedalus's Dream of Parnell', *James Joyce Quarterly*, 6 (Spring 1969), 262-64.

Greg, W. W., 'The Rationale of Copy-Text', *Studies in Bibliography*, 3 (1950-51), 19-36.

Groden, Michael, 'A Textual and Publishing History', in *A Companion to Joyce Studies*, ed. by Zack Bowen and James Carens (Westport, Conn., and London: Greenwood Press, 1984), pp. 71-128.

Groden, Michael, 'The National Library of Ireland's New Joyce Manuscripts: An Outline and Archive Comparisons', *Joyce Studies Annual*, 14 (2003), 5-17, https://doi.org/10.1353/joy.2004.0006

Groden, Michael, *Focus: Genetic, Textual, and Personal Views* (Gainesville: University Press of Florida, 2010).

Harrington, Timothy, M.P., *The Maamtrasna Massacre: Impeachment of the Trials* (Dublin: Nation Office, 1884), https://archive.org/stream/maamtrasnamassac00harr/maamtrasnamassac00harr_ djvu.txt.

Hart, Clive, '"Wandering Rocks", in *James Joyce's* Ulysses', in *Critical Essays*, ed. by Clive Hart and David Hayman (Berkeley–Los Angeles–London: University of California Press, 1974), pp. 181-216.

Hodgart, Matthew C., 'Ivy Day in the Committee Room', in *James Joyce's 'Dubliners': Critical Essays*, ed. by Clive Hart (London: Faber, 1969), pp. 115-21.

Housman, A. E., 'The Application of Thought to Textual Criticism', *Proceedings of the Classical Association*, 18 (1922 [August 1921]), 67-84.

Joyce, Stanislaus, *Stanislaus Joyce: My Brother's Keeper*, ed. by Richard Ellmann (London: Faber, 1958)

Joyce, Stanislaus, *The Complete Dublin Diary*, ed. by George H. Healey (Ithaca: Cornell UP, 1971).

Kelleher, Margaret, *The Maamtrasna Murders: Language, Life and Death in Nineteenth-Century Ireland* (Dublin, University College Dublin Press, 2018).

Kenner, Hugh, *Dublin's Joyce* (London: Chatto and Windus, 1955).

Kenner, Hugh, *The Pound Era* (Berkeley and Los Angeles: University of California Press, 1971).

Kenner, Hugh, *Joyce's Voices* (Berkeley and Los Angeles: University of California Press, 1978).

Kenner, Hugh, 'The Computerised *Ulysses*' in *Harper's Magazine*, 1 April 1980, 89-95.

Kenner, Hugh, *A Colder Eye* (London: Penguin Books, 1983).

Kenner, Hugh, 'Leopold's Bloom Restored', *The Times Literary Supplement*, 13 July 1984.

Kenner, Hugh, 'Signs on a White Field', in *James Joyce: the Centennial Symposium*, ed. by Morris Beja, *et al.* (Urbana: University of Illinois Press, 1986), pp. 209-19.

Kidd, John, 'An Inquiry into *Ulysses*: The Corrected Text', *Papers of the Bibliographical Society of America*, 82 (1988), 411-584.

Kidd, John, 'The Scandal of Ulysses', *New York Review of Books*, 30 June 1988, 32-39.

Larbaud, Valery, 'The *Ulysses* of James Joyce', *Criterion*, 1 (1922), 102.

Lawrence, Karen, *The Odyssey of Style in 'Ulysses'* (Princeton: Princeton University Press, 1981).

Lidderdale, Jane and Nicholson, Mary, *Dear Miss Weaver. Harriet Shaw Weaver 1876-1961* (New York: The Viking Press, 1970).

Litz, A. Walton, *The Art of James Joyce* (London: Oxford University Press, 1964).

Martin, Timothy, *Joyce and Wagner. A Study of Influence* (Cambridge: Cambridge University Press, 1991).

Mays, J. C. C., 'Gabler's *Ulysses* as a Field of Force', *TEXT*, 10 (1997), 1-13.

McGann, Jerome J., '*Ulysses* as a Postmodern Text: The Gabler Edition', *Criticism*, 27 (1985), 283-305.

McGann, Jerome, 'Breakthrough into Performance. A Touchstone Work of Late Modernist American Poetry', *PAJ: A Journal of Performance and Art*, 44:1 (January 2022), 16-29, https://doi.org/10.1162/pajj_a_00594

Melchior, Claus, '*Stephen Hero*. Textentstehung und Text. Eine Untersuchung der Kompositions- und Arbeitsweise des frühen James Joyce', PhD dissertation, München (Bamberg, 1988).

Norman, H. F., Letter to James Joyce of 23 July 1904, now at Cornell.

Pound, Ezra, 'Paris Letter: *Ulysses*', *Dial*, 72 (1922), 623-29.

Pound, Ezra, *Pound/Joyce. The Letters of Ezra Pound to James Joyce, with Pound's Essays on Joyce*, ed. by Forrest Read (New York: New Directions, 1967).

Pound, Ezra, *The Selected Letters of Ezra Pound 1907-1941*, ed. by D. D. Paige (London: Faber & Faber, [1950] 1971).

Prescott, Joseph, 'Conversations with James Joyce [by] Georges Borach', *College English*, 15 (1954), 325-27.

Quillian, William H., 'Shakespeare in Trieste: Joyce's 1912 *Hamlet* lectures', *James Joyce Quarterly*, 12:1/2 (1974/1975), 7-63.

Rasmussen, Irina, 'Riffing on Shakespeare: James Joyce, Stephen Dedalus and the Avant-Garde Theory of Literary Creation', *Joyce Studies Annual 2019* (New York: Fordham University Press, 2019), pp. 33-73.

Reynolds, Mary T., *Joyce and Dante* (Princeton: Princeton University Press, 1981).

Scholes, Robert and Kain, Richard M., eds., *The Workshop of Daedalus* (Evanston: Northwestern University Press, 1965).

Scholes, Robert E., 'Grant Richards to James Joyce', *Studies in Bibliography*, 16 (1963), 139-60.

Scholes, Robert E., 'Some Observations on the text of *Dubliners: "The Dead"*', *Studies in Bibliography*, 15 (1962), 191-205.

Scholes, Robert E., 'Further Observations on the text of *Dubliners*', *Studies in Bibliography*, 17 (1964), 107-22.

Shillingsburg, Peter L., *Textuality and Knowledge. Essays* (University Park, Pa.: Pennsylvania State University Press, 2017), https://doi.org/10.1515/9780271079950

Slocum, John J. and Cahoon, Herbert, *A Bibliography of James Joyce, 1882-1941* (New Haven: Yale University Press, 1953).

Spoo, Robert, '*Ulysses* and the Ten Years War: A Survey of Missed Opportunities', *TEXT*, 10 (1997), 107-18.

Staley, Thomas F. and Benstock, Bernard, eds., *Approaches to Joyce's 'Portrait'. Ten Essays* (Pittsburgh: University of Pittsburgh Press, 1976).

Sullivan, Kevin, *Joyce among the Jesuits* (New York: Columbia University Press, 1958).

Sutliff Brown, Susan, 'The Geometry of Joyce's *Ulysses*: from Pythagoras to Poincare: Joyce's Use of Geometry for Structure, Metaphor, and Theme', PhD dissertation, University of South Florida (Tampa, FL, 1987).

Yates, Frances A., *The Art of Memory* (London: Routledge and Kegan Paul, 1966).

Index

Anderson, Chester G. 13, 27–28, 31–33, 44, 47, 51, 64–65, 67, 86–87, 150, 156, 159
'A Portrait of the Artist' 66, 71, 96, 143–144, 224–225, 238, 241, 256
A Portrait of the Artist as a Young Man 1–6, 11–16, 19–22, 26–29, 32, 34–36, 38, 40–41, 43, 52–54, 57, 61, 65–69, 71–74, 76–84, 86–87, 89–94, 96–107, 118, 120, 124, 128–129, 140, 143–153, 155–159, 202–209, 212–214, 216, 222, 225–228, 230–235, 237–251, 253, 255–262, 264–268, 270, 272–275, 277, 298, 310, 314–315, 320–321, 324–325, 327–329, 331, 334–335, 339, 341, 349, 353, 364, 368–369, 380
Apuleius 231–235, 250
Aristotelian 7, 266, 270, 373, 393
Aristotle 216, 268, 280–281, 288–289, 321, 337–338

Ballantyne, Hanson and Co. 21, 23–24, 39, 43
Beach, Sylvia 67, 152, 167, 395, 403–404, 424
Beckett, Samuel 7, 289, 392
Bleibtreu, Karl 276
Bloomsday 3, 208, 210, 218–219, 417
Bodleian Library 12, 36, 151
Borden, Gavin 184, 186, 188
Bornstein, George 187
Bowers, Fredson 1
Budgen, Frank 209, 217, 254, 266, 313, 349–351, 355, 373

Cape, Jonathan 11, 33, 36, 65, 67–68, 140, 151–153, 156, 159

Casey, John 95–96, 98–99, 101–102
Chamber Music 114, 118, 202, 224
chiastic design 2, 93–94, 146, 205, 242
Christmas dinner scene 2, 48, 80–81, 86, 93–105, 107, 146–147, 206, 216, 222, 240–241
Cicero 319
Clongowes 48, 59, 79, 93–96, 98–99, 101–105, 206, 240, 244–245, 353, 364
critique génétique 2, 163–164, 193
Crowley, Ronan 196, 418
Curran, Constantine 111, 114

Daedalus (mythical figure) 226, 231–236, 240, 254
Dana 71, 143–144, 224–225
Dante Alighieri 95–96, 99–101, 204, 228, 380
Darantiere printers 8, 165, 167–168, 395–396, 398–399, 402–404, 424
Davitt, Michael 101
Dubliners 3, 20, 71, 81–82, 109, 111, 113–119, 121–126, 128–130, 132–133, 135, 138, 140–141, 144–145, 148–150, 159, 200, 204–205, 208, 226–228, 230, 236–237, 256, 311
  'A Curious History' 123–124
  'After the Race' 112, 114–116, 126, 130, 135, 144, 226
  'A Little Cloud' 115–116, 124, 127, 130
  'A Mother' 114, 122, 124, 127–128, 130
  'An Encounter' 113–114, 121, 124, 127, 130
  'A Painful Case' 113–114, 116, 122, 124, 126–128, 130
  'Araby' 114, 130, 228

'Counterparts' 113–116, 127, 131, 135, 138
'Eveline' 112, 114–115, 126, 130, 135, 144, 226–228
'Grace' 114–117, 122, 124, 127–128, 130, 204, 228, 236
'Ivy Day in the Committee Room' 113–114, 119, 122, 124, 126–130, 138, 204
'The Boarding House' 113–115, 126–127
'The Clay' 112–114, 117, 130, 227
'The Dead' 81–82, 111, 117–118, 122, 125, 127–128, 130–132, 135–139, 145, 200, 205, 228–230, 234, 236
'The Sisters' 110–111, 114, 116, 124, 126–127, 130, 144, 204, 226–228, 230
'Two Gallants' 115, 126–127, 130, 227–228
Duckworth, Gerald 149
du Sautoy, Peter 183–184

Edward VII 119–120, 122
Eglinton, John 277–278, 280–282, 284–285, 287, 291–294, 302–303, 305–308, 312, 337
Egoist, The 12–22, 24–25, 27–28, 30–32, 36, 38–39, 41–44, 50, 54–55, 59–61, 63–65, 124, 147–153, 157, 237, 255, 267
Eliot, T. S. 213
Ellmann, Richard 63–64, 68, 144, 184, 221, 224, 405
Exiles 198, 200–201, 209, 215, 237, 249, 267, 273

Faber & Faber 183
Falconer, John 121
Finnegans Wake 75, 120, 147, 199, 216, 219–220, 228, 245, 249, 257, 361, 392
Füger, Wilhelm 1–2

Garnett, Edward 149
Gaskell, Philip 184
Giacomo Joyce 202–203, 248–249, 342–343
Gogarty, Oliver St. John (Doherty) 5, 83–86, 91–93, 206, 243, 314
Golden Fleece 7, 269, 348

Golden Mean 8, 395
Greg, W. W. 41
Groden, Mike 185, 271, 323, 325

Hackett, E. Byrne 27–28, 32, 150
Hamlet 4–6, 91–92, 207–208, 213, 228, 245, 254–257, 260–262, 264–268, 271–273, 275–287, 289–293, 298, 300–302, 304, 307, 310, 313, 316, 331–339, 343–346, 381, 408, 414
Harrington, Tim 317, 320
Hart, Clive 184, 347, 349–351, 366–367
Heinemann, William 26, 29, 114, 149
Homer 204, 213–214, 230, 235, 250, 264, 269, 347, 352
Hone, Joseph Maunsel 118, 121
Housman, A. E. 187
Huebsch, B. W. 12–13, 26–32, 34–35, 126, 130, 149–152

James Joyce Estate 183–185, 190
Jason 6–7, 269, 348, 351, 355, 363, 370, 372
Johnson & Co. 36, 39, 43
Joyce, Giorgio 113, 121, 145, 341
Joyce, Nora 104, 109, 112–113, 117, 119–121, 144, 147, 199–201, 222, 237–238, 249, 258, 274
Joyce, Stanislaus 79, 81, 96, 106, 112–118, 131, 143–144, 156, 206, 208, 210, 218, 224, 260–261, 273, 311, 324, 329, 345
Joyce Wars 3, 190

Kenner, Hugh 2, 79, 186, 221
Kidd, John 188–190

Lane, John 149
Laurie, T. Werner 149
Lawrence, D. H. 149
Léon, Paul 263, 271, 276
Lessing, Gotthold Ephraim 241
Lidderdale, Jane 27, 36
Little Review, The 167, 175, 313, 420, 423–424, 428
Litz, A. Walton 83, 185
Long, John 117, 123
Loyola, Ignatius 268, 287–288

Macrobius 229–230, 234–235, 250
Marsden, Dorothy 36, 54–55, 148
Marshall, John 26–31, 149–150
Mathews, Elkin 118, 123
Maunsel and Co. 118, 120–121, 123–124, 126–131, 133
Mays, J. C. C. 191
McGann, Jerome 186
Melchior, Claus 185

New York Times 186

Odysseus 207, 209, 214, 228, 231, 235, 254–256, 260, 267–269, 343, 347, 352
Ovid 231–233

Parnell, Charles Stewart 95, 100–105, 205–206, 231, 353, 357
Partridge & Cooper 38–39, 43
Pinker, James B. 12, 15, 20–25, 29, 33–35, 149, 151
Plato 268, 280–281, 288–289, 337–338
Pound, Ezra 5, 12, 20–23, 26, 63, 74, 124–125, 147–150, 213, 245, 255, 260–262, 264, 267, 269, 272–273, 301, 331, 334–335, 417–418, 420, 423

Quillian, William H. 265–266
Quinn, John 211

Rasmussen, Irina 4, 259, 261, 268
Richards, Grant 20–22, 24, 114–117, 120–121, 123–130, 148–150, 236
Robert Johnson & Co. 36
Roberts, George 118–119, 121–123
Rome 116–117, 199–200, 231
Rosenbach manuscript 167, 262, 265, 269, 271, 288, 314, 349–351, 353, 411, 419, 427
Russell, George (AE) 109–110, 279, 281–282, 288–289, 291–292, 296, 337–338

Saint-Malo 67–68, 152
Schäuble, Joshua 196, 418
Schmitz, Ettore (Italo Svevo) 73, 76–80, 106, 146, 218, 237, 240–241, 256, 274
Scholes, Robert 123, 132, 140
Secker, Martin 23–25, 123, 149

Shakespeare, Anne 291–297, 301, 303–306, 308, 340
Shakespeare, Hamnet 278, 283, 289–290, 314, 332–333
Shakespeare, William 2, 5–6, 8, 92, 180–182, 191, 250, 255, 259–262, 264–268, 270–273, 275–279, 281–287, 289–311, 313–316, 331–334, 336–337, 340–341, 346, 408–409, 411
Shillingsburg, Peter 191
Slocum Collection 13, 31
Southport 33, 35–36, 39, 65
Spoo, Robert 191–192
Stephen Hero 6, 71, 73, 76–77, 79, 82–85, 89–90, 93, 96–100, 102, 106, 109, 111, 113, 143–146, 204–206, 209, 220, 224–227, 236, 238–239, 242–243, 246–247, 250, 256–257, 259, 265–266, 273, 311, 314, 321–322, 324, 328, 368–369
Steppe, Wolfhard 185
Sullivan, Kevin 97, 282
Switzerland 19, 64

Thomas, Kinga 407

Ulysses. A Critical and Synoptic Edition 3, 7, 9, 172, 179, 182, 185–186, 188, 190–191, 194–195, 409, 418–419
Ulysses. A Digital Critical and Synoptic Edition 188, 196, 418

Venice 148
Viking Press 11, 132–133, 140, 159
villanelle 4, 6, 86, 88–89, 92–94, 107, 147, 208, 242–243, 258, 267, 274–275
Vintage Press 159, 182, 190

Wagner, Richard 234, 242–243
Weaver, Harriet Shaw 11–16, 19–40, 65, 67–68, 72, 147, 149–153, 156, 208–209, 211, 215, 217, 258–259, 269, 274, 393, 417–418, 420
Wilde, Oscar 293, 302
Woolf, Virginia 368
World War I 263, 273
World War II 263

Yeats, W. B. 109, 147, 452

About the Team

Alessandra Tosi was the managing editor for this book.

Lucy Barnes copy-edited and indexed this book.

The Alt-text was created by Anja Pritchard.

Jeevanjot Kaur Nagpal designed the cover. The cover was produced in InDesign using the Fontin font.

Cameron Craig typeset the book in InDesign and produced the paperback and hardback editions. The text font is Tex Gyre Pagella and the heading font is Californian FB.

Cameron also produced the PDF, XML and HTML editions. Jeremy Bowman produced the EPUB edition.

The conversion was performed with open-source software and other tools freely available on our GitHub page at https://github.com/OpenBookPublishers.

This book has been anonymously peer-reviewed by experts in their field. We thank them for their invaluable help.

This book need not end here...

Share

All our books — including the one you have just read — are free to access online so that students, researchers and members of the public who can't afford a printed edition will have access to the same ideas. This title will be accessed online by hundreds of readers each month across the globe: why not share the link so that someone you know is one of them?

This book and additional content is available at:
https://doi.org/10.11647/OBP.0325

Donate

Open Book Publishers is an award-winning, scholar-led, not-for-profit press making knowledge freely available one book at a time. We don't charge authors to publish with us: instead, our work is supported by our library members and by donations from people who believe that research shouldn't be locked behind paywalls.

Why not join them in freeing knowledge by supporting us:
https://www.openbookpublishers.com/support-us

Follow @OpenBookPublish

Read more at the Open Book Publishers BLOG

You may also be interested in:

Text Genetics in Literary Modernism and Other Essays
Hans Walter Gabler

https://doi.org/10.11647/obp.0120

Digital Scholarly Editing
Theories and Practices
Edited by Matthew James Driscoll and Elena Pierazzo

https://doi.org/10.11647/obp.0095

Yeats's Legacies
Yeats Annual No. 21
Edited by Warwick Gould

https://doi.org/10.11647/obp.0135

www.ingramcontent.com/pod-product-compliance
Lightning Source LLC
Chambersburg PA
CBHW062025290426
44108CB00025B/2783